Records

of the

First Reformed Church

of

Baltimore

M A R Y L A N D

1768–1899

HERITAGE BOOKS
2020

HERITAGE BOOKS
AN IMPRINT OF HERITAGE BOOKS, INC.

Books, CDs, and more—Worldwide

For our listing of thousands of titles see our website
at
www.HeritageBooks.com

Published 2020 by
HERITAGE BOOKS, INC.
Publishing Division
5810 Ruatan Street
Berwyn Heights, Md. 20740

Originally published in 1995

All rights reserved. No part of this book may be reproduced or transmitted in any form or by any means, electronic or mechanical, including photocopying, recording or by any information storage and retrieval system without written permission from the author, except for the inclusion of brief quotations in a review.

International Standard Book Numbers
Paperbound: 978-1-58549-316-6
Clothbound: 978-0-7884-9297-6

INTRODUCTION

First Reformed

The building originally occupied by the First Reformed Church was built before 1760 and stood on the east side of North Charles Street near Saratoga. The congregation moved to a new building in 1788. This was located at the northwest intersection of Baltimore and Fremont Streets. The congregation relocated again in 1796, moving to a building on Second (now Water) Street. This lot was purchased in 1772 during a period of great dissension within the congregation, and the deed was worded so that the property on Second Street would remain in the possession of those who adhered to the Church Order of the Palatinate and to the Pennsylvania coetus.[1]

After the Civil War, a new sanctuary was dedicated in 1867, at Calvert and Read Streets. In 1918 the congregations of First Reformed, and St. Stephen's Reformed Church (which had been organized in 1892) united and located at Guilford Avenue and 23rd Street. In 1928 the present building, at 6915 York Road, was begun. Delays were caused by the Depression and by World War II; and it was not completed until 1951. In 1934 the Reformed Church in the United States and the Evangelical Synod of North America merged, and in 1957 the combined body merged again, with the Congregational-Christian Church to form the United Church of Christ.[2]

The earliest records are in the Philip Schaff Library of the Lancaster Theological Seminary. The German entries were translated by Mrs. E. Duke of Lancaster. The births, deaths and marriages for the years 1768 through 1899 were published intermittently in the *Maryland Genealogical Society Bulletin* from volume 15 (1) (Feb. 1974) through volume 33 (2) (Spring 1992). It is these records that are being reprinted here.

The pastors of the First Reformed Church were for the years through 1800: Jacob Lischy, c.1753-1765; Christopher Faber, 1768-1771; Benedict Swope, c.1770; Emmerich Wallauer, 1772-1776; Charles Boehme, 1779-1783; Nicholas Pomp, 1783-1789; and George Troldenier, 1791-1800; John B. Dreyer, 1802-1806; Christian L. Becker, D. C., 1806-1818; Albert Helfenstein, 1819-1835; Elias Heiner, D. D.,

1836-1863; E. R. Eschbach, D. D., 1864-1874; and Joel R. Rossiter, D. D., 1875-1918.[3]

Robert W. Barnes

NOTES

1. *Pastors and People: Volume I: Pastors and Congregations.* By Charles H. Glatfelter. Breinigsville: The Pennsylvania German Society, 1980. Glatfelter cites Baltimore County Land Records AL#E, fol. 164.

2. "Introduction: Vital Records of the First and St. Stephen's United Church of Christ of Baltimore, Maryland," by Henry R. Kelly, *Maryland Genealogical Society Bulletin,* 15 (1) 32-33.

3. The list of Pastors from 1800 to 1918 was taken from the *Maryland Genealogical Society Bulletin,* 24 (4) 268.

FIRST REFORMED CHURCH OF BALTIMORE
VITAL RECORDS
OF THE FIRST & ST. STEPHENS UNITED CHURCH OF CHRIST
OF BALTIMORE, MARYLAND

Introduction by Henry R. Kelly

We are privileged to start printing the earliest records of the First Reformed Church of Baltimore, which church through several mergers is now the First & St. Stephens United Church of Christ located at 6915 York Road in Baltimore County. This congregation is the second oldest of Baltimore. Details of its early history are recorded in the 200th anniversary booklet printed in 1950, a copy of which is in the Maryland Historical Society library.

The precise date of origin is not know although a property transfer dated 1752 is in the church archives. The early records of the first Lutheran congregation in Baltimore state "up to the year 1758 both Lutheran and German Reformed worshiped together and great friendship and harmony prevailed". [1]

The church is now in its sixth edifice. The first wood structure was built 1757/8 on North Charles Street nearly opposite the present St. Pauls Episcopal church, the oldest Baltimore congregation. The first written record dated January 25, 1769 states the first minister was "John Christian Faber, born Mosback on the Neckar, in the Pfaltz in Europe". [2]

In 1770 a division in the church resulted in the organization of the Second Reformed church which called Rev. Philip Otterbein, later the founder of the United Brethern denomination, who however retained his Reformed church credentials until his death.

In 1787 the second edifice at the northwest corner of Baltimore and Front Streets was occupied. In 1797 the third edifice on Second Street between South and Gay Streets, known as "The Old Town Clock church" was dedicated. In 1818 the first preaching in English began, and thus it will be noted, the earliest records are in German script, requiring a large effort to transcribe and make available for this first public printing. Fortunately this work was undertaken by Mrs. E. Duke of Lancaster, Pennsylvania, where the records are located in the Philip Schaff Library of the Lancaster Theological Seminary. We are greatly indebted to her.

In 1850 the centennial of the church was celebrated. The fourth church structure was dedicated in 1867 at Calvert & Read Streets. In 1918 the First Reformed church and St. Stephens Reformed church, which was organized in 1892 and located at Guilford Ave. & 23rd St., were united and in 1928 the present edifice on York Road was started. The depression postponed completion until 1951 of this, the sixth edifice. In 1934 the merger

FIRST REFORMED CHURCH OF BALTIMORE

of the Reformed Church in the United States with the Evangalical Synod of North America occurred and in 1957 this combined body merged again with the Congregational-Christian Church to become the United Church of Christ.

The vital records start in 1768. Earlier records are presumed lost. Certain early member names however are know. A record of Weinbert Tschudi dating to 1710 and a record of Jacob Mohler dating from 1745 will be included. In the records of the church it is stated: "In the year 1756 or 1757 the congregation purchased a lot on which to erect a church and appointed a committee to oversee it, consisting of Andrew Steiger, Valentine Loersh, Frederich Meyer, Jacob Kuhboard, John Soller, and Conrad Smith".[3] In 1785 the memb listed were - Michael Diffendorffer, Henrich Lorch, Andreas Steiger, Konrad Schmidt, Andreas Greuzet, Philipp Crusius, Jakob Coberts, Nicholas Tschudy, Johann Hull, Peter Herr, Johann Dorgenberg, Frederich and Jakob Meyer, Daniel and Peter Diffenderffer.[4]

NOTES

[1] Dieter Cunz, *The Maryland Germans, A History* (Princeton, 1948), p. 97; Col. J. Thomas Scharf, *The Chronicles of Baltimore* (Baltimore, 1874), p. 40.

[2] *Ibid.*, p. 41.

[3] Cunz, *Maryland Germans*, p. 98.

[4] *Ibid.*, p 183.

BAPTISMAL AND BIRTH RECORDS

Transcribed by

Mrs. E. Duke, Lancaster, Pa.

The Baptismal and Birth Records gives the name of the child; baptismal date; birth date; parents names; and Godparents name. If any of these items were omitted from the original list they are indicated by *.

1768

GASCHA, MARGARETHA; Sept. 11; Aug. 29; Peter and Barbara; Jacob and Margaretha Majer

SEGESTER, JOHN PETER; Dec. 24; Dec. 20; Martin and Margaretha; Peter & Catharina Stribeck

1769

BERNED, BARBARA; Sept. 1; July 10; Andreas and Elisabeth; Matthias and Barbara Zimmermann

SEGESTER, JOHANNES; Dec. 29; Dec. 15; Martin and Margaretha Johann & Margaretha Bader

1770

ZIMMERMANN, JOHANNES; Jan. 19; Jan. 15; Mathias and Barbara; Johannes Gische (?) and Elisabetha Berned (in)

MAJER, JOHANNES and PHILLIP JACOB (Twins); Jan. 27; * ; Balthasar and Barbara; Johannes Sto- - -(page defect) and wife Friedrich Majer and wife

MÜLLER, JOHANNES; Febr. *; Dec. 28, 1769; Nicolaus and Eva; Johannes Ziegler and his wife

MAJER, JACOB; Febr. 25; Febr. 12; Jacob and Anna Margaretha; The father & a widow from Yorktown

RAHM, JACOB; May 24; Apr. 17; Jacob and Ursula, he is the schoolteacher of the Reformed Church; Winbert and Elisabeth Tschudj.

SCHLEGEL, ANNA MARIA; June 3; April 21; Heinrich and Elisabetha; John & Anna Maria Schlegel

REB, * ; July 5; June 16; Adam & Catharina

FABER, JOHANN WILHELM; July 1; June 13; Johann Christoph and Margaretha, he is the minister of the Reformed German Community; John Theobald Faber (also a minister in Penna.)

WOLFF, WILHELM; July 29; July 21; Michael and Salome; Wilhelm & Barbara Claus

MESENHEIMER, GEORG PETER; July 29; June 16; Georg and Cath.; Peter & Maria Trumbo

NEIS, CHRISTOPH; July 29; Dec. 14, 1969; Christoph and Christina; Friderich & Catharina Majer

KAUB, ELISABETHA; Aug. 19; June 1; Wilhelm and Barbara; Mathias & Elisabetha Brechtly

HAUSER, JOHANNES; Oct. 21; Sept. 29; Jacob and Margaretha; Johannes and Helena Grersetsch

WEISS, SARA: Nov. 25: Oct 6; Johannes and Barbara; John Feil & Margaretha Keen

DEGEN, ANNA CATHARINA; Dec. 23; Nov. 22; Georg and Catharina; Friedrich & Catharina Majer

1771

MÜLLER, CARL HENRICH; Jan. 27; Jan. 9; Carl and Maria Magdalena; Rudolph & Anna Maria Reis

TREIL, JOHANNES; March 4; Febr. 7; Johannes and Anna Maria; Johannes Augustus & Barbara Weiss

MOHLERS, WEINBERTUS; March 31; Febr. 17; Jacob and Elisabetha; parents

SPEK, MAGDALENA; April 1; March 1; Johannes and Catharina; Michael & Magdalena Rohrbach

REBOLD, JOSUA; April 27; March 19; Jacob and Sara; Josua and Sara Mitschel

ZIMMERMANN, ANDREAS; May 5; Dec. 27, 1770; Mathias and Barbara; Andreas .. Elisabetha Conrad, widow

REIS, JOHANNES; May 20; April 9; Ulrich and Anna Maria; Martin and Marg. Segester

DEVIS, MATHIAS; June 27; Dec. 14; Benjamin and Anna Maria; Mathias and Anna Maria Reitter

DOERR, ANNA MARGARETHA; Aug. 5; Jan. 6; Henrich and Catharina: Anna Maria Schmid

RAHM, CATHARINA; Aug. 25; July i; Jacob and Ursula; Friderich Majer & Ursula Huken

NOLL, WILHELM; Sept. 14; Aug. 11; Michael and Elisabeth; Wilhelm and Christina Noll

1770

KIENER, JOHANNES; Sept. 22; Aug. 7; Anna Margaretha and Peter; Peter Georg Kiborz and Catharina Kiener

1775

BÖHM, ANNA ELISABETHA; Sept. 22; Aug. 11; Phillip and Catharina; Carlus Heiss

1777

WEBER, ELISABETH; Nov.1; * ; Daniel and Charlotta; Phillip and Elisabeth Cruhsius

WEBER, DANIEL; Nov. 1; 10 Febr. 1772; Daniel and Charlotta; Phillip and Elisabeth Cruhsius

WEBER, LUDWIG; Nov. 1; 25 Dec. 1774; Daniel and Charlotta; Ludwig Seibel and his wife

WEBER, CHARLOTTA; Nov. 1; 29 March 1783; Daniel and Charlotta; Daniel Weber and his wife

1778

TSCHUDY, JACOB; Sept. 25; July 30; Nicolaus and Barbara; parents

1779

WOLFF, JOHANNES; Aug. 1; May 8; Michael and Salome; Wilhelm & Catharina Levely

PENSEL, CATHARINA; Aug. 29; Aug. 5; Johannes and Dorothea; Catharina Schneider

DEVIS, NANCY; Sept. 8; May * ; William and Barbara; Johannes Schlotz & Cath. Corrin (widow)

RAYLY, PETER; Aug. 29; * ; Georg and Juliana; Peter & Anna Maria Lid

BOEHME, SUSANNA; Sept. 15; Sept. 8; Carl Ludwig and Catharina (he is the minister at present time); parents

CUNZELMANN, SUSANNA; Oct. 2; May 18; Joh. and Maria; *

PANNEBEDER, MARIA; Oct. 3; Aug. 29 1777; Peter and Margretha; parents

PANNEBEDER, SARAH; Oct. 3; Sept. 12 1779; Peter and Margretha; Sarah Schrobb

SCHMIDT, * ; Oct. 12; Nov. 11 1778; Uland and Catharina; parents

SRAD, JOH. NICOLAUS; Nov. 21; Oct. 22; Wilhelm and Maria Eva; Nicolaus and Barbara Schudi

LÖBLE, WILHELM; Nov. 27; Nov. 22; Wilhelm and Barbara; father and Salome Wolf

SCHMID, JOHANN PHILLIP; Nov. 30; Dec. 26; Johannes and Anna; Phillip Crusius & Charlotta Weber

STONA, ELISABETH; Dec. 30; Nov. 20; Elisabeth Tamkin father:

Tomas Stona; Elisabeth Crousius

1780

WEYSSMANN, SAMUEL; Jan. 10; Jan. 5; Samuel and Maria; Nikolaus and Catharina Mueller

LOHRA, MARIA CATHARINA; Jan. 9; Sept. 7, 1779; Johannes and Christina; Grandparents: Henrich & Maria Catharina Lohra

FRANCISCUS, JOHANNES; Jan. 23; Dec. 16, 1779; Georg and Margretha; John & Dorothea Leobold

WEDMAN, PHILLIP DAVID; Febr. 15; May 1, 1776; Lorentz and Elisabetha; Parents

WEDMAN, SUSANNA ELISABETHA; Febr. 15; Oct. 20, 1779; Lorentz and Elisabetha; Phillip & Elisabetha Crousius

BENDER, MARIA ELISABETHA; Apr. 18; Nov. 26, 1779; Gottfried and Margretha; Daniel and Barbara Bender

MASERI, MARIA; Apr. 23; Febr. 24; Jacob and Catharina; Parents

WÜD, MARIA; June 1; July 25, 1779; Jacob and Elisabetha; Nicolaus & Barbara Schudy

BAYER, GEORG PHILLIP; June 1; * ; Georg and Catharina; Philipp Cruhsius & Regina Rahm (widow)

LOOS, URSULA; July 17; July 12; Johann Arnold and Barbara; Grandparents: Jacob & Ursula Zud (or Hud)

PENCEL, JOHANNES; July 28; July 13; Johannes and Maria Dorothea; Johannes Schneider

GRENCHETT, MARIA; Oct. 15; * ; Andreas and * ; Wilhelm and Barbara Löble

REDIG, ANNA MARIA; Oct. 15; Oct. 14; Christian and Maria; Etschberger(in)

WAGER, ANNA MARIA; Oct. 15; July 24; Phillip and Hanna; Maria Weg(in)

WIRTENBERGER, JOHANNES; Oct. 15; Oct. 12; Ludwig and Barbara; Johannes Schleif

RETTER, ELISABETH; Oct. 28; June 22; Henrich and Christina; Elisabeth Zeiser

PETER, ANNA ELISABETH; Nov. 12; Oct. 30; Daniel and Margretha; Johannes and Anna Zund (or Hund)

SCHMIDT, ELISABETH; Dec. 15; Nov. 11; Rouland and Catharina; Peter Trombauer and Maria Magdalena Breket

DIEFENDÖRFTER, NICOLAUS HENRICH; Dec. 24; * ; Michael and Dorothea; Friedrich Meyer and his wife

BOURFORD, SAHRA; *; * ; Georg and Paley; John Merdel and his wife Sahra

GROB, * ; Dec. 30; * ; the father is Grob; *

1781 *

SEGERHINDIN, JOHANN GEORG; Febr. 4; Febr. 2; Martin and Margaritha; Johannes and Maria Cathy Stohler

BAMBERGER, JOHANNES; Febr. 10; Febr. 5; Arnold and Elisabeth; Johannes and Dorothea Leopold

REISS, JOHANN JACOB; March 17; Jan. 5; Ulrich and Maria Magdalena; Jacob Welsch and Catharina Borns

SCELZ, JOHANNES; April 19; Apr. 13; Robert and Maria; Joh. Geiger

SCHMID, JOH. PETER; April 15; Apr. 3; Peter and Anna Maria; parents

FIRST REFORMED CHURCH OF BALTIMORE
BAPTISMAL AND BIRTH RECORDS
FIRST & ST. STEPHENS UNITED CHURCH OF CHRIST

Dates of Baptism / Birth		Name	Parents	Godparents
1781				
April 15	Febr. 15	Anna Margretha	Nicolaus and Anna Elisabetha Boos	Nicolaus & Anna Margretha Boos
April 15	Febr. 20	Anna Maria	Conrad and Catharina Rayli	Johannes & Anna Maria Delger
May 17	Febr. 26	Joh. Georg	Joseph and Elizabeth Devison	Nicolaus & Catharina Muller
May 21	Febr. 19	Emanuel	Martin and Magdalena Schudy	Grandparents Winberth & Elisabeth Shudy
June 3	Jan. 18	Ursula	Jacob and Eilsabeth Wüd (Wud)	Nicolaus and Barbara Schudi
June 12	Apr. 15	Johannes	Adam and Anna Maria Rohrbach	Johannes Rehter and Catharina Dorr (in)
June 1	March 30	Anna Elisabetha	Friederich and Elisabeth Mabs	Anna Elisabetha Rauben Hauer (in)
July 13	Dec. 10, 1780	Catharina	Daniel and Lonihe Diefendörfer	parents
June 27	May 21	Johannes	Samuel and Anna Maria Hensmann	Johannes & Anna Bok
Nov. 5	Oct. 11	Joh. Georg	Georg and Margretha Franciscus	Joh. & Anna Catharina Stohler
Dec. 10	Dec. 10	Anna Maria	Joh. and Christina Lohra	Grandparents: Henrich & Catharina Lohra
Dec. 16	Nov. 26	Anna Regina	Joh. and Anna Stund	W. Carl and Regina Leopold
1782				
Jan. 21	Dec. 29, 1781	Jacob	Georg and Feronica Kühbortz	The father
Febr. 3	Dec. 1, 1781	Ruland	Wilhelm and Maria Magdalena Bruchs	Grandparents: Ruland & Anna Maria Schmidt
Febr. 24	Jan. 24	Catherina	Wolfgang and Maria Etschberger	Abraham & Catherina Frantz
April 1	March 12	Elisabeth	Christian and Catherina Muma	Andreas and Maria Granchet
April 1	April 11, 1781	Margretha	Christoph Henrich and Anna Elisabetha Augustin	Parents

FIRST REFORMED CHURCH OF BALTIMORE

Dates of Baptism / Birth		Name of the Child	Parents	Godparents
1782				
April 17	Dec. 9, 1781	Anna	Richard and Catharina Kusk	parents
May 29	Sept. 22, 1781	Jacob	Johannes and Catharina Woss	parents
June 27	—	Salomon	Elisabeth .... named as father: Salomon Rutters	Jacob & Elisabeth Hud
June 27	May 19	Christof Michael	... Flötzer	Michael Kubertz or Kübortz and his wife
June 9	Nov. 28, 1781	Anna	Daniel and Catharina Weibel	Nicolaus and Barbara Schudy
May 9	April 29	Carl Friederich	Michael and Dorothea Diefendorfer	Friederich Mayer sen. & Dorothea Sob (in) from Lancaster
June 17	Apr. 3, 1767	Conrad)		
"	July 22, 1768	Magdalena)	Peter and Elisabeth Welm	—
"	Aug. 7, 1770	Catharina)		
"	Aug. 25, 1772	Elisabeth)		
June 17	Mar. 13, 1780	Feronica	Michael and Maria Sbeitz	—
—	May 23	Elisabeth	Johannes and Catharina Wostmann	Phillip and Maria Müller
July 28	Febr. 17, 1781	Franciscus	Frantz Martin and Elisabeth Holler or Zoller	parents
Oct. 17	—	—	Father: Adam Gantz	—
Oct. 13	March 17	Jacob	Ludwig and Barbara Würtenberger	—
Oct. 27	March 17	Johann Arnold	Michael and Catharina Measondin	Johann Arnold & Barbara Loos
Oct. 28	March 17	Anna Catharina	Peter and Catharina Stribek	Johannes and Catharina Stohler
Nov. 17	Nov. 2	Johann David	David and Sahra Muma	Johann Conrad Schmoll & Margretha Horner
Nov. 17	Sept. 17, 1781	John	James and Elisabeth Slon	parents
Nov. 17	Aug. 24	Daniel	Daniel and Elisabeth Peter	Peter and Conjunda Weigand

FIRST REFORMED CHURCH OF BALTIMORE

Dates of Baptism / Birth		Name of the child	Parents	Godparents
1782				
Dec. 26	Nov. 21	Catharina	Johann Christian and Maria Rettig	parents
Dec. 28	–	Franciscus Georg	The father of these two children is: –	–
Dec. 29	Dec. 15	Georg	Georg and Anna Maria Rotfrod or Rothrod	Jacob Rathrob and his wife Barbara
1783				
Jan 6.	Jan. 3	Johannes	Friederich and Dorothea Hoss	Johannes and Catharina Woss
Febr. 2	Nov. 20, 1782	Maria	Jean and Elisabeth Jvens	William and Maria Jvens
Febr. 16	Dec. 14, 1782	Catharina	Christian and Christina Dalliger	Conrad and Catharina Reyly
Febr.23	Febr. 2	Independens Friederich	mother: Hanna Wool, father not named	Friederich Güldener Barbara Weber (in)
Febr. 24	Jan. 30	Hermann	Johannes and Catharina Schröder	Hermann Lorsbach & Anna Regina Leopold (in)
Mar. 9 " "	Oct. 16, 1773 Febr. 8, 1776 Nov. 16, 1782	David) Wilhelm) Georg)	Hermann and Judith Stützer	parents
Mar. 10	Mar. 4	Salome	Samuel and Anna Maria Wäussmann	Johannes and Salome Lohl
1783				
Sept. 15	Sept. 8	Cathrina	Georg and Margaretha Franciscus	Cathrina Stohlin
Sept. 17	Febr. 10	Johannes	Johannes and Christina Lohra	Henrich Lohra
Oct. 4	Sept. 17	Sara	Peter and Anna Maria Schmeck	Sara Sauther (in) Joh. Willy Heydy
Oct. 12	Jan. 23	Elisabeth	Wilhelm and Magdalene McCallos	Daniel Weibel and his wife
Nov. 10 Nov. 10	May 28, 1781 July 16, 1783	Joseph Amy	Thomas and Amy Noll	Johann Henrich and his wife
Nov. 10	Sept. 11	Georg	Johann and Sofia Henrich	Georg Klass & Hanna Whi
Nov. 10	Nov. 10	Sarah	Balzer and Elenora Schâtzer	Henrich Mayer

FIRST REFORMED CHURCH OF BALTIMORE

Dates of Baptism / Birth		Name of the child	Parents	Godparents
1783				
—	Nov. 11	Henrich	Peter and Anna Maria Lid	Henrich Kreudel
Dec. 25	Oct. 9	Herta Barbara	Wilhelm and Herta Speil	Nicolaus Schüdy
Dec. 26	May 16	Wilhelmina Elisabeth	Nicolaus and Christina Morg (or Marg or Morf)	Willy Crecsius
1784				
Jan. 11	Dec. 12, 1783	Anna Maria	Christian and Anna Maria Rettig	Francis Marbel
Jan. 18	July 14, 1783	Barbara	Adam and Barbara Forny	—
Jan. 18	Aug. 13, 1783	Anna-Catharina	Johannes and Elisabeth Forny	—
Jan. 18	Oct. 11, 1783	Cathrina	Jacob and Regina Reder	Michael Reder
Mar. 1	May 15, 1783	Susanna Henrietha	Christof Henrich and Anna Elisabeth Augustin	—
Mar. 28	Jan. 26	Joh. Georg	Anton and Cathrina Petri	Johann Michael Gentil-Majer & Susanna Maria Miller
Apr. 12	Nov. 27, 1783	Elisabeth	Adam and Cathrina Booss	Johannes Eberhard & Anna Maria Hall (in)
Apr. 9	Febr. 26	Elisabeth	Johannes and Christina Lora	Henrich Düchart & Elisabeth Dotter
Mar. 7	Febr. 2	Joh. Jacob	Michael and Salome Wolf	—
Apr. 22	Febr. 25	Sophia Dorothea	Georg Henrich and Maria Cathr. Bleichroth	Johannes Lypold
May 16	April 6	Jacob	Adam and Christina Grund	Jacob Schmid & Elisabeth Mayer
June 6	April 29	Johannes	Johannes and Cathrina Hofl	—
May 31	May 11	Wilhelm	Christian and Cathrina Minna (Muna)	Wilhelm Löwely & his wife
July 13	June 30	Cathrina	Samuel and Anna Maria Heinzman	Cathrina Miller
Aug. 16	Febr. 12	Johannes	Herman and Cathrina Krilig or Kriliy	—
Aug. 21	Aug. 1	Cathrina	Christoph and Juliana Hill	Cathrina Grund

12 FIRST REFORMED CHURCH OF BALTIMORE

Dates of Baptismal / Birth		Name of the child	Parents	Godparents
1784				
Nov. 1 (house of Willy Böhm)				
	Sept. 1, 1783	Cathrina	Jacob and Mary Knigt	
	June 22, 1784	Thomas	Thomas and Mary Meek	
	Oct. 22, 1783	Georg	,,	
	Mar. 18, 1782	Nathaniel	John and Sarah Harris	
	Aug. 15, 1784	Sarah	,,	
	19 years old	Sarah	Joseph and Mary MacCallester	
8 years	Oct. 4, 1784	John	,,	
5 years old	Sept. 26, 1784	Loyd	,,	
	9 years old	Margareth	Abraham and Martha Schmid	
	7 years old	William	,,	
	5 years old	Elisabeth	,,	
1784				
Nov 14	Oct. 11	Suhsannah	Lorentz and Magdalena Stütz	Johanna (?) Meegheimer
Nov. 21	Oct 23	Johannes	Martin and Sarah Minna	
Nov. 2	Aug. 1	Sophia	Jacob and Elisabeth Heig (Hug?)	
Nov. 24	Oct. 24	Wilhelm	John and Elisabeth Cavans	
Dec. 6	Aug. 14	Cathrina	Nicolaus and Elisabeth Boss	
Dec. 17	Dec. 1	Joseph	Georg and Anna Maria Rotfrod or Rothrod	
Dec. 19	Nov 28	Ester	Lewis and Mary Pascault	John Schley and Elisabeth Thomson
Dec. 19	Dec. 18	Joseph	John and Elisabeth Heiner	John Keller
1785				
—	Aug. 11, 1782	Margareth	Henrich and Barbara Wolf	
Jan. 2	Oct. 13, 1784	Cathrina		Theobald Krämer
Jan. 13	Dec. 12, 1784	Michael	Jacob and Barbara Hofman	John Schwingel
Jan. 18	Nov. 11, 1784	Wilhelm	Wilhelm and Magdalena Brüder	
Jan. 17	Sept. 19	Anna Maria	Henrich and Anna Maria Georg	
Jan. 23	Dec. 18	Johannes	Thomas Warren and Anna Maria Warren	Johannes Brutzel and his wife

FIRST REFORMED CHURCH OF BALTIMORE

Dates of Baptismal / Birth		Name of the child	Parents	Godparents
1784				
July 20	July 15	Magdalena	Johannes and Magdalena Keller	—
Aug. 22	July 14	Margareth	Michael and Christina Kühner	—
Aug. 22	July 24	Johannes	Peter and Cathrina Striebel	Johannes Holzenberger
Sept. 12	Aug. 9	Johannes	Wolfgand and Maria Hirschberger	Johannes Schriyad & his wife
Sept. 20	Aug. 16	Elisabeth	Christoph and Barbara Henig	—
Sept. 26	July 14	Francis	Maga and Janet Anna Larue	—
Oct. 4	Sept. 29	Joh. Georg	Abraham and Cathrina Frantz	Jacob Harthman & his wife
Oct. 7	Sept. 3	Margareth	Gottfried and Anna Barbara Zumwald	—
Oct. 10	July 28	Wilhelm	Wilhelm Gross and Margareth Stovertawn	M. Hiess and his wife
Oct. 17	Sept. 7	Benedict	Benedict and Margareth Schwob	—
Oct. 17	Oct. 2	Susanna	Christian and Susanna Kühner	—
Oct. 16	Oct. 14	Sara	Peter and Anna Maria Schmid	Maria Sara Schneider

The following children have all been baptized on
Nov. 1 in the house of Willy Böhm, 8 miles from here:

	Dec. 25, 1780	Joh. Willy	Joh. Willy and Maria Böhm	—
	June 24, 1783	Wilhelm	Andreas and Elisabeth Bernet	
	May 12, 1783	Elisabeth	Andreas and Appolona Veit	
	Dec. 24, 1783	Elias	Georg and Sara Böhm	
	Oct. 23, 1782	Sara	Johannes and Margareth Minna	
	July 30, 1784	Maria Cathrina	Johannes and Cathrin Minna	

14   FIRST REFORMED CHURCH OF BALTIMORE

Dates of Baptismal / Birth		Name of the child	Parents	Godparents
1785				
Jan 23.	Jan. 18	Joh. Georg	Thomas and Cathrina König	
Febr. 6	Dec. 27, 1784	Joh. Adam	Adam and Anna Maria Frey	Gottfried Frey & his wife
Febr. 5	July 5, 1784	Jacob	Johannes and Cathrina Ebert	Jacob Hildebrand and his wife
Febr. 13	Febr. 4	Maria Cathrina	Martin and Maria Cathrina Weissbach	Christoph Reven and his wife
Febr. 27	July 29, 1783	Sara	Conrad and Anna Barbara Gamper	Conrad Ohrendorf and his wife
May 27	Oct. 7, 1783	Vallentin	Vallentin and Anna Maria Nelhy	Conrad Ohrendorf and his wife
Mar. 28	Jan. 28	Cathrina	Willy and Magdalena Ebhert	
Mar. 17	Febr. 22	Joh. Michael	Willy and Elisabeth Zumwald	
Febr. 16	Febr. 2	Carl Friedrich	Friederich and Cathrina Eyra	Carl Schoarf and his wife
Mar. 6	Febr. 14	Jacob	Ludwig and Maria Bayer	Jacob Hildebrand and his wife
Apr. 3	Mar. 19	Carolus Andreas	Andreas and Cathrina Lichtholt	Andreas Bobert and Maria Reitenauer
Apr. 24	Mar. 22	Maria Magd.	Nicolaus and Maria Magd. Steuck (?)	Theobald Faust
May 9	May 4	Susanna	Johannes and Margareth Bader	Martin Segensser
May 12	April 28	Willy	Willy and Cathrina Gardener	Willy Crusius and his wife
May 15	Nov. 8, 1783	Thomas	Elias and Margareth König	
July 9	Febr. 16	Susanna	David and Barbara Allspach	
May 15	Febr. 4	Friedrich	Frantz and Barbara Allspach	Friedrich Reiss and his wife
July 17	Oct. 26, 1784	Magdalena	William and Magdalena MacCalla	Martin Weissbach and his wife
July 21	July 6	Cathrina	Tobias and Rosina Wolf	Cathrina Wolf (in)
July 24	Jan. 4	Mary	Diedrich and Margareth Berger	
July 24	March 19	Mary	George Böhm and Sara Böhm	Christoph Henig
July 24	April 26	Georg	Georg and Jana Buch	

FIRST REFORMED CHURCH OF BALTIMORE

Dates of Baptismal / Birth		Name of the child	Parents	Godparents
1785 July 22	July 15	Peter	Phillip and Barbara Henig	Peter Hahn
Aug. 11	June 27	Anna Cathrina	Wilhelm an Meyl Cathrina Kraft	
Aug. 11	June 15	Anna Maria	John and Cathrina Hiesch	
Aug. 11	July 10, 1784	Juliana	John and Anna Maria Berbay	
Sept. 22	Febr. 26	Margareth	Freidrich and Elisabeth Caunselman	
Sept. 23	Aug. 10	Johannes	Jacob and Magdalena Theiss	
Aug. 21	Dec. 26	Jacob	Vallentin and Anna Maria Diev	Georg Weidener
Aug. 21	June 30	Elisabeth	Matheiss and Ida Brochel or Boochel	
Sept. 26	Sept. 15, 1784	Rebecka	Joh. Theis and Anna Maria Jesaias	
Sept. 27	Sept. 15	Joh. Georg	Joh. Georg and Cathrina Bachman	
Oct. 15?	Sept. 19	Anna	Adreas and Susanna Lutz	Anna Schmid
Oct. 15	May 17	Sara	David Minna sen. and Maria Barbara	Sara Minna
—	Sept. 22	Joh. Georg	Wilhelm and Herta Bauer	Joh. Georg Reyly and his wife
Nov. 6	Aug. 24	Elisabeth	Johannes and Christina Bauer	Ferdinand Lorentz and his wife
Dec. 26	Nov. 15	Johannes	Lorentz and Elisabeth Hardman	John Cooper
Nov. 24	June 30	Johannes	Ulrich and Maria Magdalena Reiss	
Dec. 26	Dec. 18	Susanna	Christoph and Juliana Hill	Susanna . . .
Dec. 26	Aug. 26	Cathrina	Adam and Elisabeth Gladener	

FIRST REFORMED CHURCH OF BALTIMORE

Dates of Baptismal / Birth		Name of the child	Parents	Witnesses
1786				
Jan. 1	Mar. 22, 1785	Peter	Jacob and Margareth Stethjor	Adam Grund and his wife
Jan. 8	Dec. 6, 1785	Jacob	Jacob and Anna Maria Zimmerman	Jacob Schmid
Jan. 15	Jan. 12	Maria Elisabeth	Johannes and Margareth Sander	
Jan. 7	Jan. 9	Michael	Martin and Margareth Segentzer	Michael Küfner
Jan. 22	Dec. 31, 1785	Christophe	Johannes and Anna Maria Schmid	Christoph Ditmar and his wife
Febr. 12	Jan. 16	Maria Cathrina	Friedrich and Cathrina Eyra	Christoph Kiener and his wife
May 11	March 27	Johannes	Daniel and Charlotte Weber	Johannes Schmid and his wife
June 5	April 23	Mary	Jacob and Margareth Schaffer	
—	Febr.	Wilhelm	Vallentin and Magdalena Gettelmora	
June 8	End of April, 1780	Georg	"	
June 8	Apr. 20, 1780	Wilhelm	David and Barbara Minna	
June 25	May 24	Jacob	Michael and Dorothea Diefendörfer	Jacob Mayer
June 20	June 17	Jacob	Wilhelm and Magdalena Etschberger	Jacob Kraiss
July 27	April 13	Abraham	Henrich and Magdalena Kuntz	
Aug. 20	Dec. 24, 1785	David	Peter and Catharina Byt or Begt	David Allspach
July 22	June 15	Maria Magdalena	John and Cathrina Holl	
Aug. 13	July 31	Michael	Michael and Salome Wolf	
Sept. 2	Whitsunday	James	Alexander and Cathrina Adams	
Sept. 3	July 27	Susanna	Christian and Cathrina Minna	Andreas Lutz

FIRST REFORMED CHURCH OF BALTIMORE

BAPTISMAL AND BIRTH RECORDS
FIRST & ST. STEPHENS UNITED CHURCH OF CHRIST
(FORMERLY FIRST REFORMED CHURCH OF BALTIMORE)

Dates of Baptism	Birth	Child	Parents	Godparents
1786				
Sept. 24	Juni 24	Henrich	Jacob and Anna Maria Peter	Henrich Moor
Oct. 3	April 25	Jacob	Herman and Cathrina Greulich	
Sept. 24	Sept. 2	Elisabeth	Samuel and Anna Maria Heinsman	Samuel Diefendörfer
Sept. 17	July 24	Cathrina	Wolfgang and Maria Etschberger	Abraham Frantz
Sept. 17	Aug. 24	Jacob	Jacob and Anna Maria Schmid	Caspar Stück
Oct. 8	Sept. 24	Johannes	Christoph and Barbara Ditmar	Johannes Schmid
Oct. 29	Sept. 24	Cathrina	Johannes and Cathrina Hofman (from Friedrichtown)	Henrich Schröder
Oct. 29	Sept. 11	Daniel	Phillip Gardener (mother?)	Daniel Peter
Nov. 5	Oct. 5	Johann Georg and Samuel	Michael and Christina Kühner	Martin Segensser and Samuel Diefendörfer
Nov. 5	Oct. 13	Christina Sophia	Henrich Weidener and Maria W.	Daniel Kriener
Oct. 22	Oct. 5	Joh. Carl	Jacob and Maria Barbara Henig	Carl Schwartz
Oct. 15	Sept. 2	Carl	Jacob and Anna Bernhard	Carl Schwartz
Nov. 4	Nov. 4	Cathrina	Ludwig and Maria Bayer	Cathrina Hildebrand
Nov. 26	Oct. 24	Georg	Thomas and Maria Warren	
Dec. 24	Nov. 8	Cathrina	Christian and Anna Maria Rettig	Ludwig Wirtenberger
Dec. 17	Nov. 17	Joh. Jacob	Martin and Maria Cath. Weissbach	Jacob Eberhard
Dec. 17	-	Cathrina	Willy and Susanna Pheil (from New York)	Cathrina Gessler (in)
Dec. 25	Oct. 14	Elisabeth	John and Elisabeth Eavans	

FIRST REFORMED CHURCH OF BALTIMORE

Dates of Baptism	Birth	Child	Parents	Godparents
1787				
Jan. 24	Jan. 20	Phillip	Georg and Anna Maria Rothrod	
Dec. 9, 1786	Dec. 9, 1786	Anna Maria	Johannes and Cathrina Schley	Francis Marbel
Febr. 18	Dec. 14, 1786	Henrich	Daniel and Catherina Rinmann	
Febr. 18	Jan. 26	David	David and Sarah Minna	Ludwig Herring
Sept. 17, 1786	Sept. 2, 1786	Susanna	Henrich and Elisabeth Dichart	
April 8	March 8	Lina	Georg and Cathrina Schäfer	Baltzer Schäfer
April 28	May 6, 1786	John	Benjamin and Susanna MacKinsey	
May 14	Nov. 4, 1786	Georg	Georg Boem and Sarah B.	
May 28	Dec. 20, 1786	Joh. Georg	Vallentin and Anna Maria Nelson	
June 29	Aug. 5, 1786	Johannes	Johannes and Catherina Ewald	Conrad Schug (or Schieg)
June 16	May 26	Margareth	Johannes and Cathrina Drotzebach	Margareth Gober
June 24	May 20	Barbara	Jacob and Catherina Kerner	Barbara Welsch
July 3	April 24	Charlotta	Johannes and Magdalena Keller	Anna Gootfried
July 3	June 20	Johannes	Johannes and Susanna Mann	
July 22	Aug. 9, 1786	Joseph	Christoph and Barbara Hennig	
July 22	Febr. 11	Elisabeth	Jacob and Mary Stitger	Peter Hayfal (or Haifel)
Aug. 12	July 23	Charlotta Magdalena	Friedrich Eyen mother: ?	Carl Schwartz
Aug. 19	March 10	Maria Margareth	Vallentin and Maria Drissler	Maria Marg. Drissler
Aug. 21	June 20	Priscilla	Georg and Joan Buch	

FIRST REFORMED CHURCH OF BALTIMORE 19

Dates of Baptism	Birth	Child	Parents	Godparents
1787				
Aug. 26	Aug. 20	William	Joseph and Elisabeth Davis	
Oct. 5	June 23	David	David and Barbara Allspach	
-	Jan. 29	Rachel	John and Mary Veween	
Dec. 9	Dec. 4	Daniel	Daniel and Anna Maria Rettig	
1788				
Febr. 24	Jan. 24	Anna Maria	Christoph and Barbara Ditmar	Maria Dotter and M. Crusius
March 30	March 15	Anna Maria	Martin and Anna Maria Fletscher	
March 30	Aug. 28, 1787	Elisabeth	Willy and Magdalena Ebbert	
March 16	Jan. 25	Elisabeth	Michael and Dorothea Diefendorfer	Daniel Diefendorfer
April 6	March 15	Cathrina	Daniel and Elisabeth Peter	M. Luthner (or Lethner)
April 30	July 28, 1787	Johannes	Johannes and Christina Roder	
May 12	March 9	Anna Maria	Daniel and Cathrina Rinmann	Daniel Peter
May 18	April 1	Jacob	Johannes and Cathrina Holl	
-	March 10	Ester	Martin and Margareth Stegensser	Elisabeth Küner
June 15	April 8	Henrich Dietrich	Dietrich Ratien	Henrich Willmans Nicolaus Konradt Herman Dehlers
June 15	Febr. 3	Johannes	Abraham and Cathrina Franz	Wolfgang Etschberger
June 22	July 10, 1787	Joh. Henrich	Willy Jacob and Cathrina Hartmann	-
June 25	July 19, 1782	Elisabeth	Alexander and Cathrina Almer or Alaner	-
June 25	Aug. 27, 1787	Mary	"	

Dates of Baptism	Birth	Child	Parents	Godparents
1788				
July 10	April 30, 1785	Diane	Johannes and Maria Schorr	
Aug. 3	Febr. 16	Joh. Jacob	Phillip and Cathrina Gardner	Jacob Lamm
Aug. 30	Aug. 15	Thomas	Joseph and Elisabeth Sewchon	John Nillen
Sept. 5	Aug. 13	Elisabeth	Georg and Cathrina Schäfer	Elisabeth Diefendörfer
Sept. 28	March 9	Conrad	Peter and Elisabeth Beckier	
Sept. 28	14 years old	Salome	Ebersin -	Jacob Hůrd
Oct. 5	Aug. 24	John	John and Elisabeth Evans	Jacob Hartmann
Oct. 12	Sept. 25	Samuel	Samuel and Margareth Porter	Carl .... Christian Heyer
Oct. 12	Sept. 11	Elenora	Peter and Anna Maria Herr	David Maschberger
Nov. 2	Oct. 25	Carl Hermann	Carl Herm. and Maria Weidner	
Nov. 23	Sept. 16	Anna Maria	Lewis and Mary Passoult	
Nov. 26	Nov. 17	Sara	Christian and Sussanna Kühner	
Oct. 16	Oct. 16	Johann Georg	Johannes and Cathrina Drotzebach	Conrad Schmoll
Dec. 12	7 weeks old next Monday	Johann Carl	Johannes and Maria E. Scherer	Carl Boorer Juliana Mary Dewalt
Dec. 12	Oct. 8	Juliana Appolonia	Friedrich and Cath. Juliana Kiner	
Sept. 6	Aug. 2	Nanzy	Johannes and Serowol Pfister	John Hegady
1789				
March 2	Febr. 7	Jacob	Christian and Magdalena Rattig	Jacob Lindor
March 26	March 20	Jacob	Georg and Maria Rothrod	

FIRST REFORMED CHURCH OF BALTIMORE

Dates of Baptism /	Birth	Child	Parents	Godparents
1789				
March 15	Febr. 20	Daniel	Balsar Schäfer and his wife	Daniel Kurz Luth. Pastor wife of Georg Schäfer
April 5	March 4	Gottlob Samuel	Friedrich and Cathrina Eyen	Carl Gottlob Schwarz
April 8	Aug. 26, 1788	Cathrina Margareth	Conrad and Elisabeth Schuy or Schieg	
April 12	Dec. 20, 1787	Henrich	Christian and Cathrina Müller	Wolfgang Etschberger
April 12	March 14	Cathrina	Samuel and Elisabeth Mischer	Georg Leithner and his wife
April 12	Febr. 18	William	Davy and Elisabeth Burck	
April 13	Febr. 18	Sophia	Johannes and Cathrina Schley	Anna Maria Mann
May 3	Febr. 9	Johannes	Ludwig and Hanna Kobold	Willy Molls
May 9	Jan. 3	Fanny	William Hattington	
May 9	July 4, 1782	Hannah	Alexander and Sandy Madewell	
May 11	March 25	Leggin	Henrich and Margareth Liston	
May 11	April 2	Wally	William and Elisabeth Haneod	
May 25	May 19, 1766	Abraham Minner	-	-
June 1	April 8	Maria Barbara	Martin and Cathrina Weissbach	Jacob Lehman
May 31	Jan. 14	Elisabeth	Michael and Christina Kuner	Gottfried Kahl
June 2	Jan. 14	Juliana	David and Barbara Minna	Anna Bernhard
June 24	March 25	Jacob	Lorenz and Elisabeth Heidman	Christian Dolder
June 21	March 13	Cathrina	Jacob and Susanna Schally	grandparents

FIRST REFORMED CHURCH OF BALTIMORE

Dates of Baptism /	Birth	Child	Parents	Godparents
1789				
July 19	March 7	Joh. Henrich	John and Cathrina Ewald	Joh. Porner
July 19	March 28	Georg	Jacob and Anna Maria Schmid	Johann Herman
July 12	Nov. 13, 1788	Peter	Georg and Frohna Degen	Peter Sauerwein
May 11	March 15	John Henrich	Joh. Wilhelm and Cath. Kraft	
Aug. 23	July 8	Cathrina Mary	Theobald and Maria Cath. Haiss	Wilhelm Holz
Aug. 31	June 20	Johannes	Wolfgang and Maria Etschberger	
Oct. 27	Sept. 30	Joh. Anton	Joh. Adam and Margaretha Arnold	
Oct. 12	July 21	Georg	Conrad and Magdalena Bayerle	Willy Fraud
Oct. 12	March 25, 1786	Johannes	Georg and Maria Cath. Lossman	
Sept. 13	July 16	Cathrina	Phillip and Cathrina Gardener	Johannes Bauer
Oct. 22	Sept. 24	Elisabeth	Johannes and Christina Hörner	Henrich Binder
Nov. 8	Aug. 17	Louisa	Peter and Louisa Bender	Leonhard Höhrman
Nov. 25	July 6	Abraham	David and Sara Muma	Conrad Schmoll
Nov. 25	Oct. 10, 1783	Joh. Georg	Johannes and Dorothea Bintzel	
Nov. 25	Aug. 30, 1788	Samuel	Johannes and Dorothea Bintzel	
1790				
July 4	June 11	Johan Michael	Johan Michael and Dorothea Dieffendörfer	parents
July 5	June 2	John Georg	John and Magdalena Cassel	Georg Deker
July 5	June 24	Catherina	Johannes and Maria Hasselbach	Carl Schwarz and Cathar. Hillesin
July 5	June 2	Maria	Peter and Maria Herr	Albert and Maria Sigand
Nov. 14	Oct. 6	Peter	Ludwig and Anna Kobold	Peter and Anna Maria Herr
Nov. 15	June 1	Anna Margreta	Johannes and Anna Schunk	Phillip Meyer and Anna Margreta Paulus

FIRST REFORMED CHURCH OF BALTIMORE 23

Dates of Birth	Baptism	Child	Parents	Godparents
1790				
Nov. 15	May 27	Anna Elisabeth	Daniel and Elisabeth Peters	Philip and Elisabeth Crusius
Nov. 15	Dec. 22	Wilhelm	Thomas and Maria Waren	parents
Nov. 16	Oct. 17	Heinrich	Jacob and Anna Bernhardt	Henrich and Elisabeth Burkhardt
Nov. 20	Oct. 17	Maria	Jacob Schmidt and Maria	Andreas and Maria Steiger
Nov. 21	July 1	Maria Cathrina	Johannes and Maria Cathr. Holl	
Nov. 21	Oct. 21	Maria Elisabeth	Johannes and Elisabeth Scherer	
1791				
July 24	Aug. 21	Catharina	Michael Dieffendörfer and Dorothea	Peter and Catharina Dieffendörfer
Oct. 3	Nov. 6	Johann Daniel	Jacob Schally and Susanna	parents
Oct. 11	Nov. 8	Catharina	Phillip and Nette Repdoger	parents
Sept. 24	Nov. 9	George	George and Maria Elisabeth Driess	parents
1780	Oct. 16	Abraham	Nikolaus and Elisabeth Le Fevre	parents
Oct. 26	Nov. 27	Johannes	Johann and Magdalena Edwards	Johann and Magdalena Hasselbach
Nov. 10	Nov. 27	Maria Magdalena	Johann and Magdalena Hasselbach	Carl Gottlob and Anna Magdalena Schwartz
March 6	4th Advent	Anna Emilia	Jacob and Margaretha Stetcher	parents
1792				
Oct. 24, 1791	Jan. 2	Martin	Martin and Maria Catharina Weisbach	Martin and Margaret Bauer
Nov. 20, 1790	Jan. 6	Johann	Christian and Catharina Mumma	Michael and Dorothea Dieffendörfer
Nov. 14, 1791	Jan. 8	Margaretha	Christian and Nancy Laudemann	Polly Bulhauss and James Bernards
Dec. 29, 1791	Jan. 8	Anna Magdalena	Frederich and Cathrina Eyen	Carl Gottlob Schwartz and Anna Magdalena Schwartz
Nov. 22, 1791	Jan. 10	Phillip Henrich	Christoph and Barbara Detmar	Philipp and Magdalena Schmidt
Nov. 3, 1791	Jan. 22	Maria Magdalena	Friderich and Juliana Cathrina Keim	Friderich and Maria Magdalena Kent

FIRST REFORMED CHURCH OF BALTIMORE

Dates of Birth	Baptism	Child	Parents	Godparents
1792				
March 5	March 17	Peter	Peter and Anna Maria Herr	parents
Febr. 16	March 12	Henrich	Jacob and Nancy Zeit	parents
Jan. 5	March 25	Susanna	George and Veronica Degen	Friderich and Elisabeth Boehmer
Jan. 9	March 27	Elisabeth	Johannes and Catharina Derzebach	Johannes and Magdalena Flax
Oct. 29, 1791	March 31	Anna Barbara	Johannes and Maria Elisabeth Forney	Barbara Forney
April 4		Juliana	Juliana Wagner (father not known)	-
Febr. 23	April 8	Johann Henrich	Jacob and Barbara Hegener	Johann Henrich and Juliana Keny (?)
Sept. 3, 1791	April 8	Johannes	Henrich and Barbara Emig	Johannes and M. Magdalena Schmidt
March 3, 1784	April 15	Maria Magdalena	Johannes and Anna Maria Stein	Leonhardt and Anna Maria Fuhrmann
Febr. 4	April 22	Salome	Phillip and Magdalena Kammer	Christian Eirdeler and Salome Kammer
April 8	April 22	Margaretha	David and Elisabeth Bad	Margaretha Kammer
March 3	April 29	Elisabeth	Lorentz and Catharina Pausmann	Johannes and Maria Pausmann
April 5, 1789	April 29	Catharina	Alexander and Catharina Adams	Lorentz and Catharina Pausmann
Jan. 16, 1791	June 20	Jacob	Georg and Catharina Kressmann	Conrad Ohrendorf
May 26	June 24	Johann Friderich	Phillip and Catharina Sieber	George Geltzer
May 20	June 24	Lydia	Johann and Magdalena Cassel or Cashel	parents
June 28, 1787	July 15	Sara	Johann and Magdalena Stemder or Stemler	Master (?) Ernst and his wife
Dec. 26, 1790	July 15	Margaretha		
Febr. 13	July 26	Elisabeth	Samuel and Maria Himmelreich (both from Phila.)	Daniel and Elisabeth Peters

FIRST REFORMED CHURCH OF BALTIMORE

Dates of Birth / Baptism		Child	Parents	Godparents
1792				
Jan. 15	Aug. 12	Anna Maria	Adam and Rebecca Mutter	Daniel Hoffmann and Sally Stammer
Jan. 12	Sept. 8	Anna	Martin and Barbara Tschudi	parents
March 3, 1791	Sept. 16	Anna	Abraham Frantz and his wife	parents
Aug. 14	Sept. 16	Katharina	Johann Frans and his wife	parents
Sept. 16	Oct. 5	Susanna	Georg and Elisabeth Frohlenier	parents
Oct. 19 died	Oct. 20 Oct. 22	Elisabeth	George Zohork or Zolrok and his wife Anna Maria	parents
Oct. 13	Nov. 25	Jacob	Henrich and Margaretha Scheithauer	Jacob and Elisabeth Simon
Nov. 2	Nov. 30	Elisabeth	Peter and Anna Maria Wyant	Georg and Elisabeth Frohlenier
Sept. 17	Dec. 16	Elisabeth	Phillip and Margaretha Cronmiller	parents
Nov. 10	Dec. 26	Sophia Juliana	Henrich and Elisabeth Blerhrodt	Johannes and Sophie Block
	Oct. 21	Daniel	Michael and Dorothea Dieffendoerfer	Daniel and Elisabeth Dieffendorfer
1793				
Jan. 13, 1792	March 30	Maria Elisabetha	Friederich and Catharina Krämer	Maria Magdalena Scherer
Febr. 12 1792	April 14	Elisabeth	Johannes and Catharina Koh	parents
Dec. 18 1792	Febr. 10	George	Jacob Hoffmann and his wife	parents
Febr. 18	April 21	Jacob	Theobald and Catharina Fautz	Jacob and Juliana Simon
Sept. 5 1792	May 26	Johann Phillip	Wilhelm and Catharina Krass	parents

FIRST REFORMED CHURCH OF BALTIMORE

Dates of Birth / Baptism		Child	Parents	Witnesses
1793				
March 6	May 26	Peter	Johannes and Maria Elisabeth Scherer	Peter Herr
March 18	April 26	Johann George Hartmann	Ludwig and Hanna Kobold	Hartmann Elkert and his wife
Nov. 11 1792	May 20	Jacob	Johannes and Anna Schunck	parents
Sept. 5 1792	May 20	Christian	Christian and Catharina Mumma	parents
April 20	June 16	Andreas	Johann Jacob and Anna Puhrmann	Andreas Herrmann and his wife
May 14	June 23	Samuel	David and Sara Mumma	Johannes Schunck and his wife
Jan. 25	June 23	Sara	Abraham and Catharina Frantz	parents
Jan. 16		Friderich	Samuel and Anna Maria Heintzmann	parents
Jan. 26	June 28	Maria Magdalena	George Ziesch (?) and Lille	Johannes Derzebach
Oct. 13 1792	July 7	George	George and Anna Elisabeth Beltz	parents
June 17	Aug. 14	Susanna	Jacob Bernhardt and his wife	Elisabeth Pomp
July 11	Sept. 22	Phillipine	Johann and Magdalena Stemler	parents
Sept. 3	?	Elisabeth	Johannes and Catharina Germann	father
1794				
July 19 1792	Jan. 20	Caspar Wilhelm	H. von Carnup	father

Dates of Birth / Baptism		Child	Parents	Witnesses
1794				
Nov. 27 1793		Johann Phillip and Dorothea Sophia	Johannes and Maria Pausmann	parents Sophie Jung
Jan. 29	March 12	Catharina	Johann and Maria Phillipina Britten	mother
Jan. 20 1793	March 30	George	Christian and Anna Lauhemann	George and Maria Cath. Ziesh
May 3 1793		Daniel	Johannes and Maria Juliana Schweitzer	Daniel and Elisabeth Dieffendoerfer
March 1	April 13	Joseph	Lorentz and Catharina Pausmann	parents
March 14	April 19	Jacob	Georg and Susanna Decker	Friderich and Anna Maria Decker
Febr. 8	June 15	Johann Joseph	Christian and Susanna Kuhner	parents
May 11	July 4	Johann Wilhelm	Wilhelm and Cathrina Kraft	parents
June 29	July 24	Salome	Johannes and Maria Cashel	parents
July 25	Aug. 24	Jacob	Peter and Anna Maria Herr	parents
July 25	Aug. 24	Friderich		Friderich Brendel and his wife
July 26	Aug. 24	Henrich	Phillip and Maria Kammer	Henrich Hoffmann and Tabitha Hooker
June 28	Aug. 24	Elisabeth	Mathias and Maria Barbara Miller	parents
July 15	Aug. 17	Catharina Margaretha	Johannes Ewald and Catharina	Leonhard and Anna Maria Suhrmann
Sept. 17	Sept. 21	Peter	Daniel and Catharina Schneider	parents
-	Sept. 23	Maria Salome	Friderich and Catharina Eyen	Daniel and Maria Salome Spiesser
Sept. 4	Oct. 3	Johanna Maria	Stephen and Rosina Claus	parents

FIRST REFORMED CHURCH OF BALTIMORE

Dates of Birth	Baptism	Child	Parents	Witnesses
1794				
Oct. 7	Oct. 22	Anna Barbara	Christian and Anna Maria Joppert or Juppert	Barbara Fornier(n)
Sept. 18	Nov. 6	Wilhelm	Georg and Catharina Kressmann	? and Catharina Ohrendorf
Oct. 6	Nov. 9	Philipp	Phillip and Catharina Maria Sieber	parents
Oct. 4	-	Nicolaus	Michael and Dorothea Dieffendoerfer	Nicolaus Tschudy and the mother of the child
1795				
Dec. 26 1794	-	Conrad	Conrad and Susanna Hugh	Barbara Los and children Joh: Jacob and Ursula Los
Sept. 1	-	David	Martin Tschudy and his wife	parents
Jan. 30	March 22	Anna Magdalena	Theobald and Catharina Faut	Carl and Anna Magdalena Schwartz
March 13	April 26	Johannes	Jacob Hoffmann and his wife	parents
May 31	June 21	Joseph Matthias	George Buch and his wife	Johannes Derzebach and his wife
Oct. 6	July 8	Samuel	Samuel and Margaretha Kunike	Catharina Charles
April 15	Aug. 12	Henrich	Abraham and Catharina Frantz	Jacob Hartmann and his wife
March 16	Aug. 29	Anna Maria	Johannes and Anna Schunck	Elisabeth Trohlenien or Troklenien
Aug. 15 1794	Aug. 29	Henrich	Lorentz and Elisabeth Heckmann	Phil. Detmor and his wife

Dates of Birth / Baptism	Child	Parents	Witnesses
1795 Jan. 1 Aug. 30	George	Christian Mumma and his wife	parents
April 20 1792 Aug. 30	Anna Maria)	)	Nicolaus and Barbara Tschudy (also Foster-parents)
Febr. 10 1794 Aug. 30	Kath.)	) Jacob and Sarah Mohler) (both died rather) early)	
July 23 1795 Aug. 30	Jacob)	)	David Mohler Peter Mohler
Aug. 25 -	Catharina	Jacob and Christina Cronmiller	Phillip Cronmiller and his wife
May 2 Sept. 13	Daniel Dieffendoerfer	Jacob and Anna Maria Klein	parents
Aug. 13	Jacob	Robert and Catharina Crush	Mstr.? Hildebrand and his wife
Dec. 20 1794 Oct. 4	Charlotte Christine	Cornelius and Elisabeth Heissen	Elisabeth Fischer Gustaf (?) Crusius
June 16	Henrich	Henrich and Elisabeth Blechrodt	Henrich and Anna Barbara Weihmann
Jan. 20 1793	Susanna	Andreas and Elisabeth Lobstein	Henrich Blechrodt
Aug. 23	Adam	Michael and Elisabeth Peters	parents
Sept. 20	Joh. Christian	Christian and Anna Lautemann	
Aug. 12 1787 last Sunday in Oct.	Wilhelm)	)	Adam Riess
July 1792 "	Johann Jacob)	) Daniel and Magdalena) Zapf	Jacob Riess and his wife
Febr. 20 1795 "	Daniel)	)	Daniel Banger
Sept. 23 Nov. 22	Francisus	Johannes Hoh and his wife	parents

FIRST REFORMED CHURCH OF BALTIMORE

Dates of Birth / Baptism	Child	Parents	Witnesses
1795			
Febr. 21	Jacob	David and Sara Mumma	parents
April 12	Johannes	Caspar and Marie Kaiser	parents
September 21	Anna Cathar.	Henrich and Elisabeth Emig	Mr. Pieters
July 2	Joh. George	John and Margaretha Bend	Jacob and Anna Maria Jantz
1796			
Nov. 2 1795	Johann Henrich	Henrich and Anna Maria Speck	Johannes and Maria Kerr
March 11	Barbara	Joh. and Maria Magd. Keller	Georg and Elisabeth Niepert
March 9	Juliana Margaretha	Henrich and Margaretha Scheithauer	Jacob Simon
March 23 April 3	Rosina Josepha and Petronella	Stephen and Rosina Claus	father "
Febr. 6 April 3	Maria Magdalena	Richard and Eva Greta Crawford	Christian and Maria Magd. Schmidt
Febr. 15 April 10	Susanna Henrietta	Henrich and Charlotte Hupfelder	Rosina Hupfelder & Henrich Duckhardt
March 11 April 16	Adam	Johannes Fornen and his wife	Father and Barbara Fornen
March 26 April 10	Joh. Georg	Mr. Bahnert or Zahnert and his wife	Louis Denner and his wife
June 22 1795	Christian	Christian Kuhner and his wife	parents
Jan. 31	Jacob	Wilhelm and Catharina Kraft	parents
Nov. 23 1795	Elisabeth	Michael and Catharina Schmal	Elisabeth Schmidt
Jan. 26	Wilhelm	Jacob and Catharina Bosch	parents

Date Birth / Baptism		child	parents	witnesses
1796				
May 28		Sally	George and Susanna Decker	father
May 20		Anna Maria	Lorentz Pausmann and his wife	parents
March 27	Aug. 2	Catharina	Friderich Eiselin and his wife (nee Kohl)	Anna Maria Heintzmann
Jan. 21	July 31	Catharina	Johannes and Magdalena Germann	parents
June 4	Aug. 4	Juliana Catharina	Johannes and Maria Elisabeth Scherer	parents
March 26		Elisabeth	Joh. Etschberger and his wife	Christian Funckert & the mother of the child
Jan. 26		Wilhelm	Lorentz Steitz and his wife	Mr. Peters/ stepfather and his wife
Aug. 24	Sept. 10	Sarah	Phillip and Margaretha Cronmiller	parents
Febr. 5	Oct. 2	Anna Maria	Wilhelm and Rahel Fortney	parents
Aug. 24	Oct. 4	Sarah	Martin and Anna Maria Flotzer	Anna Maria Decker
Sept. 8	Oct. 9	Johann George	Peter and Anna Maria Weyand	father and Anna Maria Steeg (grandmother of the child)
Sept. 26	Oct. 9	Anna Juliana Dorothea	Henrich and Gesina Stoffelmann	Juliana Charlotte Porper and Anna Zwisler
April 30	Oct. 16	Joh. Jacob	Jacob and Maria Pantz	Salomo and Veronica Hein

FIRST REFORMED CHURCH OF BALTIMORE

Date Birth	Baptism	child	parents	witnesses
1796				
Oct. 17	Oct. 19 (died after Baptism)	Joh. George Valentin	Nicolaus Emig and his wife	Valentin Lemmer and his wife
Aug. 25		David	Christian and Susanna Kuhner	parents
Aug. 10		Karl Friederich	Karl Friderich and Maria Zoller	parents
Oct. 4		Karl	Jacob and Else Riesh	Catharina Riesh
Oct. 25		Baltzer	Johannes and Cath. Ewald	Widow Forney
Dec. 4		Augustus	Peter and Maria Herr	parents
Dec. 3		Anna Catharina	Friderich Eulert and his wife	Anna Catharina Eulert
1797				
Jan. 16	Jan. 22	Elisabeth	Johann and Margaretha Bend	parents
Jan. 13		Catharina	Christian and Barbara Zell	parents
Febr. 17	March 19	Theobald	Theobald and Catharina Faut	father and Elisabeth Krahin
Febr. 12	March 19	Anna Marie	Henrich and Elisabeth Emig	parents
Dec. 18	April 14	Phillip Jacob	Phillip and Marie Kammer	parents
Apr. 8	Apr. 20	Susanna	Joh. and Catharina Derzenbach	Thomas and Anna Maria Hickson or Hirkson
Apr. 8	Apr. 13	Jacob	Samuel and Maria Heintzmann	mother
May 31	June 18	Juliana	Michael and Dorothea Dieffendoerfer	Daniel and Elisabeth Dieffendoerfer
April 21	June 19	Johanna Margaretha	Johannes Hase and his wife	Johanna Margaretha Repp or Kepp

FIRST REFORMED CHURCH OF BALTIMORE

Date Birth / Baptism	child	parents	witnesses
1797			
June 2 July 9	Carl Schwarz	George Hasselbach and his wife Barbara	Carl and Anna Magdalena Schwarz
July 4	Maria Louise	Johannes Arnold and Susanna Schmidts	Maria Louise Woodtraver
May 24 July 24	Henrich	Henrich and Margaretha Friburger	parents
1783 July 24	Johannes)	Jacob and Margareth Mueller	
1792 July 24	Catharina)		
1796 3 weeks before Christmas July 24	Adam	Jacob Mueller and his second wife Maria	parents
April 10,1794 July 28	Johann)		
Aug. 28 1795 July 28	Elisa)	Johann and Magdalena Hashelbach	Carl and Anna Magdalena Schwarz
May 5 July 28	Anna)		
April 15 July 29 1795	Maria)	Wolfgang Etschberger and his wife	parents
June 26 July 29	Wilhelm)		
Aug. 7	Anna Gertraud	Daniel and Maria Sabina Elis. von Bremen	Friederich Eulert and his wife
Aug. 5	Anna Maria	Johann Bribben and his wife	Johannes and Anna Maria Neipert
Aug. 3 Oct. 1	Elisabeth	Jacob and Anna Maria Klein	father
Oct. 3	Christian	Franz and Louise Woodtraver	Christian Kauderer & Anna M. Weber
Nov. 5	Margaretha Adelheid	**Peter and Rebecca Benzen**	parents
Nov. 21	Margaretha	Friderich and Sophia Detmor	Christoph and Margaretha Detmor
Oct. 4 1788	William)		parents
Febr. 28 1791	Elisabeth)		father and Elisabeth,
Febr. 13 1793	Catharina)	Peter and Catharina Dieffendoerfer	Dan. Dieffendoerfer's wife
Jan. 22 1795	Maria)		parents
March 23 1797	Anna Margaretha)		

FIRST REFORMED CHURCH OF BALTIMORE

Date Birth / Baptism	child	parents	witnesses
1798			
Dec. 24 1797	Christine	Hieronimus and Maria Elisabeth Schneider	Joh. and Christine Schmidt
Dec. 21 1797	Conrad	Jacob Feit and his wife, nee Henecker	Conrad and Eva Hennecker
Dec. 16	Elisabeth	Andreas and Eva Herrmann	Leonhard Fuhrmann and his wife
Jan. 11	Johannes Valentin	Nikolaus Emig and his wife	Johannes and Catharina Werle
Feb. 19	Rebecca	Phillip and Margaretha Cronmiller	parents
Jan. 10	Elisabeth	Richard Crawford and his wife	Johannes Derzebach and Elisabeth Sommer
March 3	Wilhelm	Johannes and Dorothea Lange	Peter Hahn
March 13	Maria Barbara	Henrich and Sarah Jung (Henrich Jung died after 6 months of marriage of yellow fever)	paternal grandparents
Oct. 12 1797	Johannes	Phillip and Cath. Margar. Sieber	parents
Oct. 5 1797	Maria Catharina	Christian and Susanna Kühner	parents
April 6	Johannes	Johannes and Sarah Lingenfelder	father and Anna Maria Zimmermann
Sept. 4 1797	Sarah	David and Sarah Mumma	Ludwig Heering and the mother of the child
June 12	Joh. Jacob and Phillipine	Andreas and Agnese Roehre	Joh. Jacob and Phillipine Lehmann
May 22	Johannes	Michael and Elisabeth Peters	parents
March 4	Johannes	Wilhelm Kraft and his wife	parents
June 14	Eliza	Lorenz Pausmann (dead) and his wife	Johannes and Margaretha Küpp

FIRST REFORMED CHURCH OF BALTIMORE

Date Birth/ Baptism	child	parents	witnesses
1798			
Dec. 13 1797	Elisabeth	Wilhelm and Rachel Portney	Dan. and Elisabeth Dieffendoerfer
May 24	Henrich	Christian and Anna Catharina Zell	parents
Aug. 5	Johannes	Jacob and Margaretha Decker	parents
May 31	Samuel	Cath. Bosch (father dead)	mother
Sept. 6	Lydia	George and Susanna Decker	Johannes and Magdalena Cashel
Aug. 29	George	Joh. Hen. and Elisabeth Emig	Christian and Elisabeth Capito
March 11	Johannes	Martin and Barbara Hoens	parents
Aug. 12	Elisabeth	Henrich and Maria Keilholz	parents
?	Johannes	..Emrich and Elisabeth (J. Muellers daughter/ dead)	maternal grandparents
Aug. 29	Anna Maria	Anna Maria Schaum (father unknown)	Maria Mueller (2nd wife of Jac. Mueller)
Oct. 12	Henric Nicolaus	Lueder and Eva Albers	Michael and Dorothea Dieffendoerfer
Oct. 7	Johann George	Martin and Anna Catharina Weisbach	Johannes Weisbach
Oct. 25	Henrich	Johannes Zahnert and his wife	Henrich and Anna Catharina Barles
Oct. 10	George Daniel	Ludwig Michael and his wife	parents
Aug. 2	Wilhelm	George and Maria Elisabeth Belz	Wilhelm Rischstein
Nov. 15	Jacob	Jacob and Magdalena Jung	parents
Nov. 16	Sophia Catharina	Karl Friederich and Maria Zollers	Johanna Maria Leonhard (wife of F. Leonhard)

Date Birth / Baptism	child	parents	witnesses
1798			
Nov. 4	Magdalena	Theob. and Catharina Paut	Joh. and Margaretha Keilholz
Oct. 27 1797	Henrietta	Christian and Catharina Stäuber	Cath. Rischstein and Cath. Halz (?)
1799			
Dec. 28 1798	Frantz Henrich Wilhelm	Tabitha Birgenham	mother
Dec. 23 1798	Maria Catharina	George and Elisabeth Hase	Phillip German and his wife
April 5 1798	David	Jacob Hagener (dead) and his wife	Nicolaus Emig and his wife, nee Eirich
Sept. 16 1798	Baltzer	Elisabeth Emig	Amos Dickinson and Peggy Emig
Feb. 17	Eleisa	John and Elisabeth Grant	parents
Jan. 31	Jacob	Jacob and Cath. Simon	Jacob Simon sen.
Aug. 19 1798	Elisabeth	...Kiernan (Baptist) and Catharina, nee Müller	mother
Sept. 1798	Maria Catharina	Johann Arnold and Susanna Schmidt	Johann Jost Becker Conrad Brenschitt Catharina Haff and Anna Maria Gertraud Capito
Jan. 2 1798	Barbara	Martin and Barbara Tschudy	parents
Jan. 3	Mathildis	Johannes and Maria Elisabeth Scherer	parents
Febr. 3	Susanna	Jacob and Maria Muller	parents
Nov. 17 1798	Louisa	Jacob and Anna Maria Klein	parents
Dec. 30 1798	Charlotte	Phillip and Marie Kammer	Charlotte Hoffmann

FIRST REFORMED CHURCH OF BALTIMORE

Date Birth/ Baptism	child	parents	witnesses
1799			
Jan. 28	Susanna	Jacob Hoffman and his wife	parents
Oct. 17 1798	Anna	Bernhard and Anna Zell	parents
May 11	Friederich Meyer	Peter and Catharina Dieffendoerfer	parents
Aug. 31 1798	Anna Catharina	Christian Mumma and his wife	parents
June 8	Adam	Adam and Sophia Müller	parents
June 30	Friederich	Friederich and Salome Eiselin	parents
July 30	Johann George	Dietrich George and Adelheid Elisabeth Geisler	father of the child & Friderica Geisler
June 16 1798 Oct. 2 1799	Joseph) Samuel)	Johannes and Anna Schunck	Elisabeth Fischer
April 2	Anna	Wilhelm and Anna Christ	
June 30	Jacob	Johannes and Catharina Ewald	Jacob Brenzen and his wife, nee: Forney
Sept. 15	George	Henrich and Margaretha Friburger	parents
Oct. 19	Anna Maria	Nicolaus and Maria Haack	Anna Maria Kimmelmeier
Sept. 6	Wilhelm	Peter and Anna Maria Herr	parents
Oct. 29	Peter	Johannes Hase and his wife	Peter and Hedwig Passbinder
Oct. 19	Johann Jacob	Jacob and Phillipine Lehmann	Johann Keilholz
Oct. 13	Johann	Johann and Christina Schmidt	George Kauder and Catharina Schneider

FIRST REFORMED CHURCH OF BALTIMORE

Date Birth/ Baptism	child	parents	witnesses
1799			
Sept. 27	Johann	Johannes Hasselbach and his wife, nee: Collodin	parents
Sept. 17	Joh. Engelhard	Wilhelm and Susanna Riem	Engelhard Riem and Marg. Weber
Nov. 24	Samuel	Samuel and Rebecca Ortelberger	father and fathers mother: Maria Elis. Ortelberger from Phila.
1800			
Dec. 31 1799	George Wilhelm	Wilhelm and Elisabeth Heckmann	George and Maria Elisabeth Belz
March 19 1799	Anna Barbara	Johann and Elisabeth Forney	Jacob and Anna Maria Brenzen
Sept. 29 1799	Maria Elisabeth	Nicolaus and Charlotte Forney	Johann and Elisabeth Forney
April 17 1799	Elisabeth	Johann and Sara Jun	Thomas and Peggy Heislung
Jan. 1	Simon	Johann Wilhelm Etschberger and his wife	Jeanne Robertson
Nov. 5 1799	Nicolaus	Wilhelm Kraft and his wife	parents
May 5 1798	Wilhelm August	Henrich and Marie Speck	Nancy Sinsenich
Jan. 30	Marie Cath.	Henrich Jac. and Else Riesh	Daniel Riesh and Marie Wilson
Dec. 22 1797	Christian	"	William Fields)
Nov. 3 1799	Henrich	Joh. and Anna Lautemann	Roberts Thomason)
Sept. 24 1799	Leonhard	Hieronymus Schneider and his wife	Leonhard Bange and Catharina Kifstein
Dec. 24 1799	Anna Margaretha	Mr. Kieman and Ketty, nee: Muller (Kiernan or Kieman)	mother

FIRST REFORMED CHURCH OF BALTIMORE

Date Birth / Baptism		child	parents	witnesses
1800				
Apr. 15 1799		Jacob	Johannes and Magdalena Cashel	parents
Febr. 24		Johann George	David and Sarah Mumma	Ludwig and Elisabeth Heering
April 22		Catharina Elisabeth	Johannes and Catharina Bämpfler	Gabriel Mörchen and Cath. Mullerin
April 3 1797 March 2		Anna) Catharina)	Joh. and Barbara Lehmann	mother and Henrich Stelmes (?)
April 18		Johanna Margaretha	Henrich and Charlotte Kupfelder	-
May 7		Sophia	George and Elisabeth Kauden	George Nauben and Sophia Feigin
June 26		Lydia	Phillip and Margaretha Cronmiller	parents
July 8		Ludwig	Lüder and Eva Albers	Mich. and Dorothea Dieffendoerfer
July 1		Theobald	Theob. and Catharina Faut	parents
Sept. 20	Dec. 1800	Nicolaus Philip	Nicolaus and Sophi Hacke	Philip German and his wife
1801				
Jan. 8	July 25 or 26	Theresia Dorothea	Peter Benson and Rebecca, nee: Herklotz	-
	July 26	Arnold	Schmitz	Johann Friederich Ebbecke Johann Stremmel Anna Fortine Carrol
1802				
Oct. 19 1801	July 1	Alexander	Georg Watel and Anna Margaretha, nee: Weber	mother
-	July 1	Anna Elisabeth	Johann Kraft Achenbach and Anna Elisabeth, nee: Weber	Christina Schmidt

FIRST REFORMED CHURCH OF BALTIMORE

Date Birth/	Baptism	child	parents	witnesses
1802				
1802	July 1	Friederich	Christian Krömer and Elisabeth, nee: Winkert	Friederich Krömer
June 14	July 4	Jacob	Christian Bald and Catharina, nee: Zahnin	Jacob Ticl and Anna Elisabeth, nee: Kauderin
July 26 1801	July 4	Anna Barbara	Johann Ewald and Catharina Margaretha, nee: Pingel	Anna Barbara Fornisen
April 11	July 18	Henrich	Johann Georg Hasselbach and Barbara, nee: Kaletin	parents
Oct. 24 1801	July 18	Wilhelm	Friederich Morgenthal and Maria Catharina, nee: Rudolph	Jacob Paupel
May 26	July 18	Georg Bernhard	Ludwig Schneider and Christina, nee: Kitz	Bernhard Weber
Nov. 29 1801	July 25	Nicolaus	Johann Forney and Sarah nee: Boyes	Johann and Elisabeth Forney
April 19	July 23	Christina	Hieronimus Schneider and Elisabeth, nee: Riston	Johann George Bange & Christina Riston
Feb. 26	July 25	Anna	Abraham Richter and Katharina nee: Uter	mother
May 15	July 4	Juliane	Hieronimus Zesch and Anna Maria nee: Simon	Jacob Simon
July 11	July 25	Wilhelmina	Johann Georg Riston and Katharina nee: Patt	Georg Franz Bange & Georg Ludwig Stremmel
Dec. 24 1801	Aug. 1	Georg	Peter and Katharina Diffendoerfer	parents
Jan. 3 1801	Aug. 7	Eva Margaretha	Friedrich Eislin and Salome nee: Mangold	parents
June 20	Aug. 29	Gottfried	Johannes Zuellich and Wilhelmine nee: Bonton	parents
Jan. 22	Aug. 29	Amelia	Elisabeth Braun (father not known)	grandparents: Joh. Henrich Braun and Maria Elis. nee: Weibel

FIRST REFORMED CHURCH OF BALTIMORE

Date Birth/	Baptism	child	parents	witnesses
1802				
Sept. 11 1801	Aug. 29	Henrich Wilhelm	Anna Maria Braun (father not known)	grandparents: Joh. Henrich Braun and Maria Elis. nee: Weibel
July 24 102	Aug. 29	Mathilde Elisabeth	Eva Barbara Albers nee: Diffendorfer (father died Aug. 15)	Michael Diffendorfer and Dorothea nee: Job (grandparents)
July 30	Sept. 1	Richard	Richard Ratien and Wilhelmina nee: Hertz	parents
Aug. 25	Sept. 2	Anna Margaretha	Johannes Friburger (the mother, Rahel Friburger nee: Mathaes, died Sept. 1)	Henrich and Margaretha Friburger
Aug. 30	Sept. 19	Wilhelmina Carolina	Peter Caspar Schmellenberg and Christina nee: Herminghaus	Cath. Wilhelmina Kall, Anna Florentina Kall, Carl Theodor Fuhrmann, Abraham Knapp
Jan. 22	Oct. 3	Jacobus	James Carnigham and Katharina nee: Miller	Peter Diffendorfer
Aug. 11	Oct. 10	David	David Simon and Elisabeth nee Krömer	Henrich and Margaretha Scheithauer
June 16	Oct. 22	Johannes	Joseph Kapp and Anna Maria nee: Fischbach	mother
July 17	Nov. 7	Georg Friedrich	Helfrich Thomae and Rosina Henrietta Dorothea nee: Hupfeld	Georg Repold
July 13	Nov. 7	Charlotta Rosina	Heinrich Hupfeld and Katharina, nee: Schneider	Rosina Henrietta Dorothea Thomae
Sept. 27	Nov. 21	Georg Franz	Leonhard Bange and Katharina, nee: Schneider	Georg Franz Bange
Oct. 12	Dec. 5	Susanna	Henrich and Elisabeth Emich	Nicolaus Emich

FIRST REFORMED CHURCH OF BALTIMORE

Date Birth	Baptism	child	parents	witnesses
1802				
Sept. 22	Dec. 8	Sophie	Adam Miller and Sophie nee: Henrich	Johann Miller
Nov. 10	Dec. 8	Isaak	Johannes and Regina Henrich	Isaak and Sophie Henrich
1802	Dec. 8	Henrich	Johannes Howard and Anna, nee: Henrich	Johannes Henrich
Dec. 2	Dec. 13	Johannes	Friedrich Detma and Elisabeth, nee: Suter	Johann and Katharina Keilholz
June 19	Dec. 27	Maria	Henrich Steenhuis and Margaretha, nee: Richter	parents
1803				
Oct. 8 1802	Jan. 2	Elisabeth	Friedrich Warner and Sarah, nee: Tany	parents
Jan. 2	Jan. 23	Daniel Conrad	Georg Diederich Geissler and Adelheit Elisabeth nee: Wunnenberg	parents
Dec. 23 1802	Jan. 23	Sophia Katharina	Peter Benson and Rebecca nee: Herklotz	Sophie Hoburg
Dec. 29	Jan. 30	Helena Carolina	Peter Schmachtenberg and Wilhelmina, nee: Weck	Carolina Weck, Helena Schauf. Peter Jung and Carl Fuhrmann
-	-	-	Jacob Derr junior	
Jan. 27 1802	Feb. 24	Peter	Jacob Jung and Magdalena nee: Zahn	Peter Jung and Johanna Katharina Trugs
Jan. 31	March 3	Johannes Henrich	Wilhelm Kiem and Susanna nee: Schertel	parents
June 4 1802	March 3	Henrich	Johannes Leibrand and Maria, nee: Speck	mother
Dec. 24 1802	April 10	Joseph	Christian Mumma and Katharina, nee: Wuaadt	parents
April 3 1802	April 10	Sophia	Daniel Schroeder and Elisabeth, nee: Leil	parents

FIRST REFORMED CHURCH OF BALTIMORE

Date Birth/	Baptism	child	parents	witnesses
1803				
Oct. 12 1800	April 11 1803	Elise	Johann Lengenfelder and Anna, nee: Wechsler	Maria Huck
Jan. 12 1803	April 11	Wilhelm	"	Abraham Knupp
1803	June 5	Jacob	Georg Geisler and Friderike, nee: Immessen	Christoph Trippel and Adelheid Elisabeth Geisler
March 12	June 12	Johann Georg	Johann Georg Watel and Margaretha, nee: Weber	Johann Matthaes and Katharina Riston
April 14	June 12	a son	mother	Henrich Braun and Wilhelm Weber
Nov. 25 1797	June 21	Heinrich	Wilhelm Dittman and Elisabeth, nee: Decker	parents
Aug. 15 1802	June 21	Katharina	Wilhelm Dittman and Elisabeth, nee: Decker	Katharina Reile
June 7 1803	June 26	James	Nicolaus Elgert and Maria nee: Heilmann	Johannes Elgert
Jan. 18	June 26	Elisabeth	Jeremias Terrelton and Katharina, nee: Heilmann	parents
Dec. 8 1802	June 17	Elisabeth	Johannes Zahner and Elisabeth nee: Hahn	parents
July 5 1803	July 17	Jacob	Bernhard Zoelle and Anna nee: Waker	parents
July 5 1803	July 17	Susanna	"	parents
Aug. 26 1802	Aug. 3	Carl Schwab	Christian Keener and Susanna, nee: Schwab	parents
Aug. 30 1802	Aug. 6	Johannes	Johannes Benfer and Katharina, nee: Strackbein	Johannes Hornrichhauser and Christina Schmidten
Nov. 8 1802	Aug. 6	Friedrich	Johann Peter Friederich Focke and Metta, nee: Stock	parents

Date Birth/	Baptism	child	parents	witnesses
1803				
-	-		Valentin Sander	
Aug. 7 1803	Aug. 25	Eduard	Andreas Jacob von Hemessen and Katharina, nee: Geyser (mother died Aug. 7)	Justus Ludwig Heinrich Hoppe and Joh. Andreas Christian Schneemann
Dec. 15 1802	Sept. 1	Maria	Johannes Scherer and Elisabeth, nee: Bernhard	parents
Aug. 4	Sept. 4	Anna Charlotta	Wilhelm Pobel or Tobel and Helena, nee: Marsilius or Marfilius	Anna Charlotta Marsilius
April 10	Sept. 18	Elisabeth	Phillip Kammer and Maria nee: Hoffmann	Elisabeth Hillmann
Aug. 9	Sept. 25	Johannes	Wilhelm Christ and Anna nee: Schunck	Johannes and Anna Schunck
Aug. 2	Sept. 25	David	Johannes Mumma and Elisabeth, nee: Adam	Ludwig Herring
Dec. 29 1802	Oct. 2	Hermann Wilhelm	Nicolaus Haacke and Sophia, nee: Richter	parents
Aug. 1	Oct. 11	Maria Katharina	Wilhelm Kraft and Kathrina, nee: Nicodemus	parents
July 20	Oct. 30	Elisabeth	Johannes Pantz and Katharina, nee: Pantz	Margaretha Pantz
Oct. 18	Nov. 13	Henrich	Peter Diffenderfer and Katharina, nee: Mayer	parents
Oct. 13	Nov. 15	Johann Andreas	Carl Heinrich Zoller and Johanna Maria, nee: Weidner	parents
Nov. 1	Nov. 23	Elias	Robert Bean and Elisabeth nee: Immessen	Friederich Brauer and Wilhelmina Kohlenberg
Oct. 13	Nov. 27	Peter	Nicolaus Emich and Elisabeth, nee: Elrich	Peter and Rebecca Benson
Jan. 23	April 3	Benjamin	mother: Anna Gertraud Brach	Benjamin Brach

FIRST REFORMED CHURCH OF BALTIMORE 45

Date Birth/	Baptism	child	parents	witnesses
1803				
Nov. 9	Nov. 19	Johann Ludwig	Ludwig Schneider and Christina, nee: Kitz	Johann Peter Claussen
?	Jan. 23	Rahel	Robert and Rebecca Carl	Ludwig Schneider
1804				
Sept. 30 1803	Jan. 15	Anna Katharina Elisabeth	Wilhelm Adolf Schaper and Anna Engel, nee Rother	Anna Katharina Elisabeth Lautn
Aug. 4 1803	Jan. 29	Carl Friedrich	Henrich Arnold Wilms and Anna Elisabeth, nee: Grammer	parents
Dec. 9 1803	March 11	Henrich	Hartman Elliot and Elisabeth, nee Proldeniez	parents
Jan. 1	April 2	Anna Katha-	Johann Kraft Achenbach and Anna Elisabeth, nee: Weber	Anna Katharina Krömer and Christian Gehlbach
Feb. 28	April 8	Samuel	Henrich Friburger and Margaretha, nee: Miller	parents
Aug. 28 1802	April 15	Samuel	Jacob and Jenny Cronmiller	Philipp Cronmiller and Margaretha, nee: Meier
March 10 1804	April 15	Thomas	Philipp Cronmiller and Margaretha, nee: Meier	parents
March 23 1804	April 22	Johann Georg	Johann Georg Weber and Eva Margaretha, nee: Braun	Henrich Braun and Maria Elis., nee Weibel
Nov. 3 1803	May 13	Nicolaus	Peter Benkert and Hanna nee: Dillen	Nicolaus and Maria Eva Dillen
March 23 1804	May 20	Katharina	Henrich and Katharina Lutz	Katharina Thomae
March 22 1804	April 29	Georg Peter	James Carnigham and Katharina, nee: Miller	Peter Diffenderfer
May 15 1804	May 29	Friedrich	Friedrich Detma and Elisabeth, nee: Suter	Friedrich Gebhard and Katharina
Jan. 16 1804	Feb. 20	Anna Barbara	James Tomson and Sophia nee: Dreher	Anna Barbara Göhring

FIRST REFORMED CHURCH OF BALTIMORE

Date Birth/	Baptism	child	parents	witnesses
1804				
April 29	June 24	Johannes	Jacob Simon and Katharina, nee: Wagner	Hieronimus and Maria Lesch
June 14	July 7	Anna Susanna	Peter Schmachtenberg and Wilhelmina, nee: Weck	Arnold Schmitz and Susanna, nee: Roy
April 16	July 7	Susanna	Jacob Hoffman and Barbara, nee: Schwengel	parents
Feb. 29	July 31	Salome	Friedrich Eislin and Salome, nee: Mangold	mother
July 16	Aug. 5	Andreas	Jacob Gensberg and Katharina, nee: Rees	Andreas Röhrich
March 23	Sept. 26	Maria Elisabeth	mother: Maria Elisabeth Münnich	mother
Aug. 7 1804	Sept. 27	Georg Henrich	Herman Neymeier and Katharina Elis., nee Karpenter	parents
Feb.? 1796	Sept. 23	Magdalena	Philip Beizel and Anna Gertraud, nee: Pippel	Katharina Stremmel
Feb. ? 1798	Sept. 23	Johannes	"	Kraft Achenbach
Aug. 30	Sept. 23	Peter	Philip Beizel and Anna Gertraud, nee: Pippel	Kraft Achenbach
Sept. 2	Sept. 23	Theodor Conrad	Conrad Schulz and Elisabeth, nee: Albrecht	Theodor Conrad Propstin and Maria Magd. Ehrenberg
Aug. 18	Oct. 4	Anna Sophia	Johann Valentin Sander and Maria Sophia, nee Piege	Elisabeth Kauderer and Johannes Stierle
Sept. 19	Oct. 7	Johann Jacob	Johann Jacob Krall and Maria, nee Stoerckel	Johannes Jade
July 28 1801	Oct. 20	Hiob	Samuel Alberger and Rebecca, nee: Garrison	parents
Sept. 15 1803	Oct. 20	Adam	Peter and Eva Haan	parents

FIRST REFORMED CHURCH OF BALTIMORE

Date Birth/	Baptism	child	parents	witnesses
1804				
April 9 1803	Oct. 20	Franz	mother: Maria Funk	mother
Aug. 27 1803	Oct. 20	Maria Margaretha	mother: Friderike Pulsgrove	mother
Aug. 17 1804	Oct. 29	Johannes	Johannes Leibrand and Maria, nee: Speck	Christina Maris
Oct. 21	Nov. 20	Elisabeth Anna	Peter Benson and Rebecca nee: Herklotz	Elisabeth Emich and Anna Hoburg
Oct. 14	Dec. 9	Johann Peter	Johannes Hees and Anna Maria, nee: Netz	Johann Peter Netz and Maria Elisabeth Köhlinger
Sept. 1	Dec. 23	Katharina	Friedrich Werner and Sarah, nee: Tany	parents
addition to the year 1804				
?	?	Susanna	Arnold Schmitz and Susanna, nee: Roy	Christine Karthaus, Dav. Friederich and Friederich Stremmel
1805				
Dec. 31 1804	Jan. 20	Johann	Georg Richstein and Anna Katharina, nee: Pattin	Johann Richstein
Dec. 7 1804	Jan. 27	Johanna Maria	Leonhard Bange and Katharina nee: Schneidern	Friedrich Lehnhard and Johanna Maria nee: Ortin and Johann Georg Bange
Sept. 12 1804	Jan. 27	Heinrich Hielfreich or Helfreich	Henrich Kupfeld and Charlotta Christina Phillipina, nee: Becker	Helfrich Thomae and mother
Oct. 18 1804	Feb. 6	Michael Lucas	Phillip Kammer and Maria nee: Hoffmann	parents
Nov. 27 1804	Feb. 12	Dorothea Sophia	Georg Reiter and Dorothea nee: Koch	Sophia Koch

FIRST REFORMED CHURCH OF BALTIMORE

Date Birth	Baptism	child	parents	witnesses
1805				
Feb. 12	Feb. 25	Simon Carl	Ludwig Schneider and Christiane, nee: Kitz	Simon Carl Volck
Dec. 21 1804	Feb. 25	Margaretha	Peter Franck and Elisabeth nee: Wahl	Margaretha Muck
Feb. 15	April 7	Wilhelm	Caroline Weck	mother
April 2	April 21	Dorothea Louisa	Georg Diederich Geisler and Adelheid Elisabeth, nee: Wunnenberg	Dorothea Kohlhausen
March 27	May 5	Elisabeth	Abraham Forney and Maria nee: Cordes	Leonhard Fuhrmann and Anna Maria
Jan. 1	May 25	Elisabeth	Wilhelm Kraft and Kathrina nee: Nicodemus	Elisabeth Geissendoerfff
April 4	May 30	Anna	Absalom Christfield and Anna Maria, nee: Schley	parents
April 10	June 5	Johann	Johann Wilhelm Weber and Anna nee: Hoeckmann	Johann Schauf.
June 3	June 10	Joseph	Phillip Cronmiller and Margaretha	parents
Oct. 26 1803	June 16	Johann	Eduard Hasson and Esther, nee: Schesroy	Johann Kohler
Sept. 1 1804	June 16	Elisabeth	Johann and Anna Sellers	Jacob and Regina Schweitzer
June 1	June 20	Johann Friederich	Friederich Peige and Anna, nee: Church	Johann Valentin Sander
Dec. 25 1804	June 23	Peter	Johann Hasselbach and Barbara, nee: Kolledin	parents
Nov. 2 1804	June 29	Carl	Henrich Meyer and Elisabeth, nee: Zelle	parents
Oct. 12 1804	June 30	Anna	Abraham Jung and Peggi Abrahams	Maria Hoffmann

FIRST REFORMED CHURCH OF BALTIMORE

Date Birth / Baptism	child	parents	witnesses
1805			
April 26 June 30 1805	Johann	James Carnigham and Katharina, nee: Miller	Peter Diffenderffer
May 13 July 14	Peter	Arnold Schmitz and Susanna, nee: Roy	
April 3 Aug. 15	Johann Jacob	Georg Waddel and Margaretha, nee Weber	Johann Hublitz and Elisabeth Britton
March 1 Aug. 24	Charlotte	Johann Fryburger and Nancy, nee: Yoice	parents
Aug. 13 Aug. 30	Maria Margaretha	Friedrich Detma and Elisabeth	Margaretha Detmore and Johann Schoeneberger
June 1 Sept. 8	Wilhelm	Georg Moore and Maria Margaretha, nee: Bancks	Johannes and Maria Margaretha Riet
Sept. 12 Oct. 9	Johannes Augustus	Peter Diffenderffer and Katharina, nee Mayer	parents
Oct. 13 Oct. 16	Anna Margaretha	Johann West and Elisabeth, nee: Wolf	Anna Margaretha Wolf
Sept. 15 Oct. 27	Sarah	Johannes Homrighaus and Polly, nee: Porck	parents
Oct. 11 Nov. 10	Anna Katharina	David Simon and Katharina, nee: Krömer	Johann Krömer and Anna Katharina Krömer
Sept. 22 Nov. 10	Anna Maria	Hermann Neymeier and Catharina nee Carpenter	parents
May 17 Nov. 12	Elisabeth	Phillipina Elisabeth Maurer (father unknown)	mother
Oct. 30 Dec. 1	Elisabeth	Georg Geisler and Friederike, nee: Immessen	Georg Diederich Geisler and Adelheid Elisabeth, nee: Wunnenberg
Oct. 19 Dec. 1	Lucia Sophia	Nicolaus Haake and Sophia, nee Richtern	parents
Oct. 30 Dec. 8	Johann Georg	Jacob Forney and Ewis, nee: Train	Johann Schauf and Maria Magdalena nee: Hoy

FIRST REFORMED CHURCH OF BALTIMORE

Date Birth	Baptism	child	parents	witnesses
1805				
Oct. 9	Dec. 8	Sarah	Johann Forney and Sarah, nee: Boys	Johann and Elisabeth Forney
Nov. 17	Dec. 15	Johann Wilhelm	Wilhelm Fobel and Helena nee: Marfilius	Johann Schmidt and Katharina Wilhelmina Knüpp
July 17	Dec. 25	Johann	Leopold Donsee and Friederike Sophie, nee Richstein	Johann Richstein and Katharine

FIRST REFORMED CHURCH OF BALTIMORE

MARRIAGE RECORDS OF THE

FIRST & ST. STEPHENS UNITED CHURCH OF CHRIST

(FORMERLY THE FIRST REFORMED CHURCH OF BALTIMORE)

Date		Names
Aug. 1	1773	Nicolaus Tschudy and Barbara Bürrer
		Both from Switzerland
Nov. 18	1769	Josua Herdester and Isabella Williams
		Both English
Dec. 26	1769	John Conrad Flori and Anna Maria Segesterin
Dec. 26	1769	Jacob Huck and Elisabetha Huckin
Jan. 1	1770	Benjamin Davis and Maria Ritterin
Jan. 8	1770	Georg Degen (widower) and Catharina Leehrin (single)
Jan. 9	1770	Ernst Carl Schlegel with Anna Margaretha Peifferin
July 28	1779	Nicolaus Müller and Catharina Magenheimerin
		(Pastor: Carl Ludwig Boehme)

1783	
Oct. 3	Henrich Schwartz and Barbara Schmidt
Oct. 9	Vallentin Pfissler with Mary Keam
	Both from Baltimore county
Oct. 14	John Bachley and Mary Ristor
Nov. 20	Christoph Sedlimeyer (or Sertimeyer) and Eva Schmidt
Nov. 28	Christian Diel and Hanna Steits
Dec. 22	Joseph Martin and Elisabeth Foy
Dec. 25	Lorentz Steids and Maria Heilman
Dec. 29	Johann Andreas Obhold with Elisabeth Odenbach

1784	
Jan. 2	Richard Wittle with Miss Elisabeth Burlam (or Burland)
Jan. 8	Philip Zomwald and Elisabeth Krebs
Jan. 8	Lewis Pauseault with Mary Shligh
Febr. 22	Friedrich Eyen and Cathrina Bosser
Febr. 23	Georg Jung and Elisabeth Eberhardin
Febr. 27	Jacob Hofmann and Barbara Schwingel
March 2nd	Tobias Wolf and Susanna Ulrich
April 8	Thomas Warren and Mary Cahn
May 4	John Brewitt with Mary Swop
May 7	John Cimgin with Mary King
May 25	Abraham Shinemann with (J) Uliana Schultz
June 3	Johannes Hasselbach with Maria Breidenharth
June 4	William Morris with Neemi Cannon
June 17	James Mc. Calle with Betzie Berny
June 24	Andreas Lichthold with Cathrina Steiger
June 29	William Powil with Susannah Carter
July 11	Wilhelm Bauer with Eva Reely
July 18	Caspar Iserlo with Mary Wily
Aug. 8	Jacob Knab with Cathrina Penoon
Sept. 7	Edmond Ford with Cathrina Bond
Sept. 21	William Grafft with Cathrina Mock
Sept. 21	Henrich Duchart with Elisabeth Dotter
Sept. 30	Thomas Mackelfresh with Martha Phelfis (or Phelps)
Oct. 10	Lucas Mac Mas with Cathrina

Date	Names
1784	
Oct. 15	Daniel Sullivan with Mary Gray
Oct. 19	Georg Sneider with Christiane Lora
Nov. 2	John Swarz with Mary Elisabeth Sholl
Nov. 14	John Major with Barbara Meyer
Nov. 15	Henry Mayer with Cathrina Gardiner
Nov. 25	Andreas Lutz with Susanna Muma
Dec. 2	Johannes Baier with Christina Becker
Dec. 16	Friedrich Brill with Elisabeth Riehm
Dec. 21	Jacob Danner (or Dauner) with Christina Brand
1785	
Jan. 18	John Sligh with Maria Elisabeth Carpeton
Jan. 22	Conrad Schug with Elisabeth Haller
Jan. 23	Ludwig Bayer with Polly Hildebrand
Febr. 16	Phillip Gorthener with Catharina Gütebach
Febr. 17	Peter Boss with Cathrina Allspach
June 30	Daniel Rieman with Cathrina Peter
July 20	Thomas Clerkson with Elisabeth Tompanks
July 31	Thomas Brown with Mary Betz
Aug. 23	Phillip Herman with Barbara Freymiller
Aug. 21	Vallentin Geltzer with Anna Lena
July 26	Lucas Mac Mas with Cathrina Schmid
Sept. 12	Paul Edwards with Sarah Travolet
Sept. 28	Henrich Rigor with Barbara Lora
Nov. 8	John Smidt with Sarah Gardiner
1786	
Jan. 3	John Shliy with Cathrina Balhrauer
Jan. 13	Aaron Hays with Elisabeth Brown
Jan. 22	Georg Wormer with Mary ...
Jan. 26	Charles Barbini with Mary Harthmann
March 29	John Ritter with M. Shreyer
April 18	John Doyl with Sara Grästan
May 30	Ephraim Smith with Beddy Schmid
June 1	William James Holmes and Ann. Wells
June 4	Allbrecht Henrich and Maria Margareth Sandonckin
June 5	Michael Reichart and Anna Margareth Kiess
June 10	Johsua Ford and Sarah Cole
July 10	Johannes Outhenrieth with Susanna Freiburger (widow)
Aug. 25	James Fritz Patrick with Lucy (?) Yeats
Sept. 5	Bazel John Dorsey with Polly Hanes
Sept. 6	Samuel Groason with Mary Lokerd
Dec. 4	Elyah Flemming with Cathrina Taylor
Dec. 21	Peter Diefendörfer with Cathrina Mayer
Dec. 26, 1786	Nicolaus Booss with Anna Maria Renner
1787	
Jan. 7	James Helmes with Betzie Striebeck
Jan. 16	Caspar Stück with Margareth Schall
Febr. 8	James Dorsey with Rachel Chapman
May 14	Jacob Davis with Mary MCallister
May 16	Georg Jung (?) with Maria Renner
June 16	Eduard Steele with Cloe Purvianna
June 19	John Evald with Cathrina Bingel
June 26	William Frigal with Margareth Meyer
Oct. 4	Phillip Hrutscha with Maria Steits

FIRST REFORMED CHURCH OF BALTIMORE

THE FOLLOWING TWO FAMILY RECORDS ARE IN THE CHURCH BOOK

I, Weinbert Tschudi, was born and baptized Aug. 3, 1710. My parents were Weinbert Tschudi, schoolmaster of Franckendorf (?), the mother is Anna Reingerin. Witnesses are Herr Hanses Rudolf Huber, town clerk, and Herr Emanuel Meier, both from Lichstadt, godmother was Anna Müllerin from Riechen.

1736, April 30 I got married to Miss Elisabet Rorerin from Riechen. Her parents were Martin Rorer and Anna Jantzin. She was born

1716, February 16. Witnesses at the baptism were Fritz Bassler, Elisabeth Göbel and Maria Binderin, all from Riechen. God blessed us with a daughter

1737 February 17 and she was named Anna. Witnesses were Leonhart Reinger and Mrs. Elisabet Frei from Franckendorf and Miss Mohlerin from Riechen,

a son

1739 November 22, he was named Weinbert. Witnesses were Eberhart Minier and Hanss Rorer and Mrs. Egerin, all from Riechen.

1739 December 9 he passed away and has lived in this world only 17 days.

1740 December 11 a son was born and named Martin. Godparents were Claus Boni and Martin Rorer and Miss Elisabet Junt all from Franckendorf.

1743 March 17 we received another daughter, she was named Elisabet. Witnesses were Hans Jacob Reinger and Miss Elisabet Zalock (Zalode?) and Elisabet Weib, all from Frankendorf.

1748 March 21 a daughter was born and named Anna Maria. Godparents are Martin Schmid and Ursula Rorerin and Anna Maria Peter, all from Riechen.

1748 April 5 she left us again. She had spent only 15 days in this world and was buried in Richau, (Riechen).

1754 June 29 a son was born and baptized July 28 and named Weinbert. Witnesses were Nikolaus Dill and Johann Michel and Barbra Gridy, all from the Kanna Waga, Pennsylvania.

1756 March 10 another son was born but he did not live till the dawn of the day. He died at the big Kanna Waga.

1752 December 26 I arrived in Pennsylvania with my wife and 3 children and lived at the Kanna Waga (Canawaga) 5 years, at York 2 1/2 years and moved then to Baltimore April 1, 1762.

JACOB MOHLER

1745 Was born into this world April 5. His parents were Ludwig Mohler and Anna Huntzigerin, presently living at the small "Pfristwig."

1768 April 4 he married Miss (virgin) Elisabet Tschudy and with God's Blessing in

1769 January 27 a son was born to us, baptized February 10. He was named Jacob, witnesses were his parents.

FIRST REFORMED CHURCH OF BALTIMORE

1771 February 24 another son was born to us and was baptized on March 31. He was named Weinbert. Witnesses at the Baptism were his parents.

1773 April 7 another son was born, baptized on April 25 and named Peter. Witnesses were his parents.

1773 September 12 Jacob Mohler died.

MARRIAGE RECORDS CONTINUED

Date	Names
1787	
Sept. 12	Hoper Gosnell with Susannah Spicer
Oct. 27	Peter Herr with Maria Gerwin
Nov. 27	Henrich Freudenberger with Sara Bondony
1788	
Jan. 6	Johannes Hess (?) with Maria Margareth M. Maurer
Jan. 29	Peter Verderok with Cathrina Wegener
March 2	David Burk with Elizabeth Murphy
March 9	Jacob Wilderman with Elisabeth Kiegerin (or Kiegerni)
March 25	Henrich Copens with Margaretha Wilderman
April 13	Friedrich Keim with Cathrina Sal. Kleisen
April 17	Wilhelm Kraft with Cathrina Nicodemus
May 1	Anthony Klein with Elisabeth Lowney
May 22	Luis Kobolt with Hanna Bahm
July 7	Johannes Freya (er) with Cathrina Schwartz
July 27	Johannes Speck with Anna Maria Mayer
Aug. 3	Jacob Schally with Susanna Horner
Sept. 7	Johannes Kastel (or Kasstel or Rassel) with Magdalena Deckerin
Sept. 11	Joseph M Clasky with Alse Jewel
Nov. 9	Georg Friedrich Dick with Maria Vallentin
Dec. 15	Hugh Long with Margareth Muslin
Dec. 28	Andreas Drabert (or Drebert) with Cathrina Feger
1789	
Jan. 16	Harthman Ehliart (or Ebhart) with Elisabeth Bernet (or Bornet)
Jan. 19	James Gornely (or Gormly?) with Jeminiah Berkly
Jan. 19	William Macinsky with Rebecka Feldner
March 1	Velten Krieger with Sandy Miller
March 1	Anton Cradel with Anna Maria Wagener
April 2	Luck Wages with Patience Phillips
April 9	Georg Forrester with Casandra Gardner
April 19	Gerrard Hopkins with Elisabeth Luer (or Luci?)
April 30	Josuah Gray with Rebecca Drane
May 22	John Giessler with Rebecca Bustlin (or Bustin)
May 26	Samuel Adams with Agnes Thomson
June 28	Christoph Duck with Charlotte Jugel
June 30	Lewis Calfus with Eve Weller
July 21	John Hurthly with Elisabeth Eavans
July 23	Nathan Joice with Hannah Bahsage
July 26	Jacob Hildebrand with Cathrine Pomz

Date	Names
1789	
Aug. 2	Samuel Robinson with Anna Holmes
October 27	Josuah Chilcoat with Rebecca Arnold
October 27	Lorentz Bausmann with Cathrina Kiz (P)
1790 no entry	
1791	
Oct. 30	Phillip Cronmiller with Margaretha Meyer
Nov. 27	Johann Carl Lohr with Cathrina Elisabeth Weston
1792	
Jan. 10	Johann Wisebach with Rahel When
May 3	Francis Dewis with Sarah Grin(or Goin)(or Zoin?)
Jan. 17	Christian Drebert with Maria Forney
Aug. 16	George Decker with Susanna Forney
Sept. 9	John Garmann with Catharina Caspel (or Chashel?)
1793	
April 2nd	Georg Schwingel and Maria Hausholder
May 26	Stephen Claus and Rosina Roland
Aug. 13	Johannes Meyer and Elisabeth Speilern
Oct. 22	Cornelius Heissen and Elisabeth Weber
Nov. 23	Jacob Lehmann and Philipine Meyer
Nov. 24	Johannes Schenkel and Margaretha Reichter (or Richter)
1. Advent	Philip Dinjes (?) and Susanna Korten
1794	
Feb. 6	Jacob Weikmann and Esther Penkert
March 30	Samuel Bitch and Sarah Wilson
June 28	Johannes Leibrandt and Mary Speck
Feb. 12	Jacob Hay and Elisabeth Schally
Aug. 4	Michael Mein and Catharina Stopps (or Nopps?)
Aug. 8	Joseph Gonyard (or Gougard?) and Susanna Gaurig
Aug. 2	John Schally (or Schallig) and Eva Meier (s)
Aug. 31	Elias Scherer and Elisabeth Hargood
Oct. 7	James Kelly and Rachel Rore
Oct. 13	Joseph Lepresh and Elizabeth Gregler
Dec. 14	Jacob Bender and Catharina Stein
Dec. 27	Caspar de Carnap and Elisabeth Richardson
1795	
Feb. 1	Conrad Renzel and Marie Holms
Feb. 1	Johannes Bantz and Catharina Kunz
April 13	Nicolaus Emich and Elisabeth Eirich
June 2	Richard Beayor (or Beagor?) and Elisabeth Fullhardt
June 2	John Bargett and Bäsche Night
June 7	Samuel Saar (or Saur?) and Elizabeth Lamuth
July 2	Conrad Muller and Nancy Robinson
Dec. 20	John Pennel and Peggy Schmok

Date	Names
1795	
Nov. 28	Joseph Brittingham and Catharina Rockes
1796	
Jan. 14	John Burkitt and Sarah Knabs
April 14	Theobald Faut and Catharina Schumack
May 22	Daniel Muller and Margaretha Collodin
June 30	Daniel von Bremen and M. Sabina Elis. Bielerin
July 14	Johann George Hasselbach and Barbara Collodin
Sept. 25	Jacob Deverbach (or Beverbach) and Cath. Horn
Nov. 24	Julius (or Josias(?) Green and Mary Mouck (or Monk?)
December	Friderich Detmor and Sophia Hardis
1797	
July 10	Stephen Spencer and Ali Rener
July 28	Samuel Longly and Catharina Rusk
Aug. 13	James Morrison and Elisabeth Heisson
Oct. 24	Adam Muller and Sophia Henry
Dec. 26	Phillip Finders and Sara Lenhard
1798	
Jan. 6	Lueder Albers and Eva Dieffendoerfer
Feb. 6	Thomas Heisling and Peggy Randall
Feb. 11	George Diedrich Geisler and Elisabeth Wonneberg
Oct. 29	Ludwig Schaefer and Rosina Valentine
March 31	John Grant and Elisabeth Leaver
1799	
Jan. 13	Nicolaus Haack and Sophia Louisa Richterin
Feb. 11	Phillip Ehrenberg and Magdalena German
April 9	Johannes Reichard and Anna Maria Kühner
April 15	Jacob Daer and Maria Scherer
Oct. 31	Johannes Ort and Catharina Klein
Nov. 17	George Kauder and Elisabeth Kellerin
Nov. 17	Christian Gronau and Peggy Kammer
Nov. 19	Henrich Helmesh (or Helmess) and Catharina Schwelk
Dec. 14	John Gray and Minta Foermann
Dec. 22	Johann George But and Catharina Kaiserin
1800	
Jan. 3	Dominic Bader and Marie Rabbow
Jan. 26	Johann Bämfler and Catharina Straakbein (or Maakbein?)
April 22	Johann Blot and Rosina Class
June 2	George Duft and Wilhelmine Hinckels
June 24	Johannes Stierle (or Mierle) and Peggy Berg
July 20	Wilhelm Faubel and Lene Morfilius
1801	

1802	
July 5	Carl Hintze, wid. and Henrietta Habliston, nee: Machaux
July 14	Friederich Warner and Sarah Tany
Oct. 17	Matthias Ort and Katharina Miller
Nov. 14	Abraham Knüpp and Katharina Wilhelmina Kall
Nov. 25	Hartmann Ellger and Elisabeth, wid. Troldenier

FIRST REFORMED CHURCH OF BALTIMORE

Date	Names
1802	
Dec. 8	Friederich Feyer and Nancy Church
1803	
Jan. 16	Peter Wyant and Maria Maul
April 23	Ferdinand Brach and Louis Oler
May 19	Phillipp Beitel and Maria Katharina Weisbach
June 12	Friedrich Stremmel and Elisabeth Capito
June 12	Johann Westz and Elisabeth Wolf
July 3	Nicolaus Pfeiffer and Barbara Deal
July 18	Isaak Henrich and Maria Polluch
Aug. 14	Georg Weaver and Eva Margaretha Brown
Oct. 21	Henrich Hachenbracht and Louise Lauterjung
Nov. 13	Henrich Bodensick and Sophia Berckmann
Nov. 20	Salomon Gottlieb Albers and Elisa Kipp
Dec. 14	Johann Abraham Junge and Rebecca Abrahams
1804	
April 2	Johann Abraham Wolferz and Maria Juliana Reigel
May 13	Johann Freeburger and Nancy, wid. Fennell, nee: Yoice
May 24	Carl Hagemann and Martha Cocheran
June 1	Hermann Neymeyer and Katharina Carpenter
July 11	Wilhelm Weber and Nancy Hickmann
Oct. 28	Johann Bentzel and Louise Keyser
Nov. 1	Henrich Hill and Polly Cling
1805	
June 12	Georg Mannes Lauber and Anna Maria, nee: Heye or Heyl
July 16	Johann P. Spies and Margaretha Tschudi

FIRST REFORMED CHURCH OF BALTIMORE

DEATH RECORDS

FIRST & ST. STEPHENS UNITED CHURCH OF CHRIST

(Formerly the First Reformed Church of Baltimore)

(Continued from Volume 16, Number 2)

Dates of Funeral	/ Death	Name	Relatives	Age
1770				
Jan. 28	Jan. 26	Barbara	wife of Balthasar Mayer	30 years, 5 months, 13 d.
Jan. 28		Jacob Dritter	single	not known
1771				
Aug. 22		Elizabetha	daughter of Jacob and Margaretha Mayer	5 years, 7 month, 15 days
1779				
July 28		Georg Washington Mayer	son of Jacob Mayer	1 year, 2 months, 4 d
1780				
June 24		widow Elkins		36 years, 6 month, 3 days
1780				
Aug. 18		Michael Schreiber		36 years, 4 month, 21 days
Nov. 5		Margaretha	wife of Daniel Peters	19 years, 4 month, 16 days
Dec.		Wille Clares (?) (or Claric)		about 61 years old
Dec.			daughter of Steitzer (?)	3 years
1781				
April 24		Susanna Madenheimerin		16 years, 3 month, 12 days
1782				
July 11		Elisabet	daughter of Martin Tschudy	9 years, 5 month, 2 days

FIRST REFORMED CHURCH OF BALTIMORE

Dates of Funeral / Death	Name	Relatives	Age
1782			
July 11	Nicolaus Müller		56 years, 2 month, 4 days
1785			
Jan. 6	a stranger single		
March	child of John Brooks		
March 5	Andreas Grayhit		
March 12	an elderly (by Fähr) woman		
March 12	child of the Riegt(en) or Riess		
March 11	Jacob Madern in Reisterstown		
April 3	2 children of Mr. Bleichroth		
April 11	Maria Catherina Lorain		
May 5	Peter Schmidt		
April 30	child of Adam Forney		
May 14	Magdalena child of Christian Stack (?)		
June 17	Michael Morgenstern		
July 22	child of Wolfgang Etschberger		
July 23	child of Lorentz Stietz(en)		
Aug. 25	son of Emanuel Martin Tschudy		
Sept. 8	Rudolph Brodbeck		
Oct. 12	Elisabeth Hofstätter		
Oct. 14	child of Jacob Peters		
Oct. 25	child of Daniel Diefendorfer		
Nov. 3	son of the widow Dörr(in)		
1786			
Jan. 2	child of N. Bosh(en)		1 month
Jan. 11	mother of Ephraim Skyster		85 years

Dates of Funeral / Death		Name	Relatives	Age
1786				
Jan. 15		son of M. Ohrendorf		22 years
Jan. 17		child of Wolfgang Etschberger		1 1/2 years
Jan. 24		child of Sander		9 days
Febr. 19		Henrich Booss		36 years
Jan. 8		child of Andreas Lutz		8 month, 18 days
Aug. 6		Weinbert Tschudy		76 years
Aug. 16		child of Andreas Wolf		13 years
Aug. 18		child of Löwoly		
Aug. 21		child of Oberman		
Aug. 26		Louisa Diefendörfer		30 years, 9 month
Sept. 3		child of Friedrich Byen		1 1/2 years old
Sept. 25		Anna Margareth Booss(in)		65 years
Sept. 29		John Bengel		32 years, 9 month
		+ 2 other children		
Nov. 8		Friedrich Mayer		67 years
1787				
Jan. 14		child of Job Dewis		
Jan. 18		son of Adam Ries		24 years
March 5		Christoph Riem		55 years
March 9		child of Michael Diefendorfer		9 month
May 16		Lena, child of Georg Schuster		a few month
July 21	July 21	child of Christoph Zill		
July 28	July 28	child of Michael Kühner		
Aug. 21		child of Wilhelm Etschberger		
Aug. 23		child of Michael Kühner		
Aug. 28		child of Christoph Dietmar		

Dates of Funeral / Death		Name	Relatives	Age
1787				
Sept. 11		child of Schop		
Sept. 11		Elisabeth Mohler		
Oct. 3	Oct. 2	Jacob Meyers		
1788				
Febr. 9		Catharina Speck	wife of John Speck	
Febr. 29		Child of Christian Rettig		
March 9		Carl Seobold		
Aug. 30		Johannes Wien		
Sept. 26		Johannes Speck		
Oct. 8		wife of David Weber		
Oct. 3		child of Abraham Frantz		
Oct. 14		widow Bingel		
Dec. 26		child of Christian Kühner		
1789				
Jan. 4		Christian Rettig		
Jan. 24		wife of Josua Gottry		
June 22		Michael Steitz		60 years old
June 24		Abraham Muma		23 years old
end of May		child of Daniel Rohman or Rehman		
Aug. 6		child of Samuel Porter		
Aug. 11		child of Sander		
Aug. 24		child of Christoph Detmar		
Oct. 24	Oct. 22	Henrich Fried (?)		
Nov. 11	Nov. 11	girl of Abraham Frantz		
1790	?	(no records)		

FIRST REFORMED CHURCH OF BALTIMORE

Dates of Funeral / Death	Name	Relatives	Age
1791			
Oct. 14	David Mumma		64 years old
Nov. 4	Anna Elisabeth	daughter of Daniel and Elisabeth Peters	1 year, 4 month, a few days
Nov. 6	Charlotte	daughter of Martha Lehmann (widow)	1 year, 3 weeks
Nov. 11 Oct. 27 (Mem. Service)	Maria Clara Hardich nee Wyants	wife of Jacob Hardich	37 years
Nov. 31 Nov. 30	George Franciscus	the oldest member of the community	99 years (?)
1792			
Jan. 1	Anna Emilia	daughter of Jacob Stetcher	10 month
Mem. Service Feb. 26	Adam Forney		53 years
March 9 March 7	Jacob Kuborz or Kabors		74 years
March 17 March 15	Maria Sophia Bentzel		39 years, 7 month
Mem. Service May 20 May 9	Phillip Crusius		66 years and 9 month
June 20 June 19	Johannes Weber		68 years and 9 month
June 22	Elisabeth	daughter of Johannes and Margaretha Bader	3 years
Mem. Service Aug. 19 Aug. 11	Andreas Kuhner		31 years, 1 month
Sept. 26	David Eli, child		4 years
Sept. 30		daughter of Adam Muller	7 month
Oct. 1 Sept. 30	George Friderich Bochmeg or Bochmer		
Dec. 27 Dec. 26	Abraham Theddier	(a stranger from Switzerland)	66 or 6?

FIRST REFORMED CHURCH OF BALTIMORE

Dates of Funeral / Death	Name	Relatives	Age.
1793			
	Anna Maria Schneider		75 years old
Mem. Service April 14 / April 5	Margaretha	daughter of David and Sara Muma	11 years, 11 month and 5 days
April 19 / April 17	Maria Elisabeth Degen		66 years
		son of Christian Kuhner	
		son of Michael Dieffendorffer	
August	Mrs. Ingenohl		63 years
Sept.		child of Mr. Frantz	
Sept.		son of Mr. Kraft or Kress	
Sept.		son of Jacob Schally	
Sept. in Philad. / Sept. 11	Jacob Tschudy		19 years, 6 weeks
Sept.		son of Nicolaus Tschudy	
Oct.	Louise Opp	wife of Frantz Opp (just arrived from Germany)	30 years
	Mrs. Damuth or Lamuth		30 years
	Jacob Klerer	(just arrived from Germany)	22 years old
		child of Mr. Pausmann	
	Mrs. Kuborz		73 years
	Johannes Mohler		79 years old
1794			
Jan. 2 / Jan. 1	Carl Schiel		66 years
Jan. 12 / Jan. 11	Anna Magdalena	daughter of Friedrich Egens	2 years
Apr. 11	Anna Elisabeth Geiger	(from Fräussheim/Pfalz= Germany)	33 years

64 FIRST REFORMED CHURCH OF BALTIMORE

Dates of Funeral	/ Death	Name	Relatives	Age
1794				
died Wednesday before Easter		Daniel Kahn	(from Seebach/Kanton Zurich = Switzerland)	63 years, 6 month
	May 19	Susanna Trokhnier	(born Sept. 16 1793	
	May 25	child of Mr. Ewald		about 2 years
died at Esterday		Ludwig Baier	(from Marburg = Germany)	about 41 years
died at 2nd. Whitsun Day		George Schwarz	(from Friedrichstown)	14 years, 11 month
	June 18	Mr. Lauhemann		about 74 years old
		daughter of Mr. Holl		ca. 4 years old
	July 20	Barbara Deems	Fosterchild of Nicolaus and Barbara Erhardt (?)	17 years, 10 month and 22 days
	July 27	George Lauheman		33 years, 7 month, 1 day
	July 31	Catharina German nee...Cashel (?)		23 years, 6 month
	Sept. 3	George Hiesh		26 years
	Sept. 3	George Buch		2 years, a few month
	Sept. 8	Catharina	daughter of P. Cronmiller	
	Sept. 10	Wilhelm	son of Wilhelm Field	2 years, 2 month, 14 days
	Sept. 13	Catharina Bantz, nee Franciscus		ca. 25/26 years old
	Sept. 22	Elisabeth	daughter of P. Cronmiller	2 years, 1 week
Sept. 28	Sept. 27	Michael Steeg	aus Yorcktown	ca. 26 years old
	Sept. 28	Peter Deis	(a stranger from the Pfalz)	
	Sept. 28	Peter	son of Daniel and Catharina Schneider	1 year, 11 days

FIRST REFORMED CHURCH OF BALTIMORE

Dates of Funeral / Death	Name	Relatives	Age
1794			
Sept. 29	Mrs. Schmidt (from the Point)		42 years, 8 month
Sept. 30	Clemens Ingenohl		61 years
from the ship ? Phoenix:			
1) a boy, age 14			
2) the brother and brother-in-law of Captain Becker			
Oct. 21	Elisabeth	daughter of Joh. Lehman	4 years old
Oct. 22	Mrs. Rothruck		
Oct. 27 Mem. Service	daughter of Friedrich Eyen		2 years
Nov. 9 / Nov. 2	Susanna Schroeder, nee: Schwarz (from Friedrichst)		28 years old, 7 month
Nov. 9	Sara Böhmer, daughter of the widow Böhmer		6 years, 7 month
Oct. 23	Anna Maria,	daughter of Andreas and Eva Hermann	1 year, 10 month
	Anna Ottila Schuppar		86 year, 8 month
	child of Mr. Blechrodt		2 year
1795			
Jan. 12	Sophia	daughter of Balzer Benzel	6 year old
Feb. 2	Friderich	son of Mr. Herr	
Febr.	Adam	son of Job. Forney	
Febr. 22	Johannes Stemler		48 years, few m.
March 11	Jacob Mohler		26 years
March 31	Elisabeth	daughter of Mr. Zahnert	4 years
May 18 / May 17	Johann Priederich	son of George Geissler	1 year, 7 month
May 18	Sophia	daughter of Johannes Schley	6 years, 3 month

Dates of Funeral	Death	Name	Relatives	Age
1795				
June 9	June 8	Margaretha Röser or Köser		36 years, 9 month
July 29	July 28	Friderich	son of Samuel Heintzmann	2 years, 6 month
	Aug. 8	Johannes	son of Alex Adams	15 years, 6 month
Aug. 11	Aug. 10	Johannes Nikolaus	son of Wilh. Speck	15 years, 10 month
Aug. 26	Aug. 25	Jacob	son of P. Herr	1 year, 1 month 3 days
Aug. 18	Aug. 7	Sarah Mohler		27 years
Sept. 11	Sept. 10	Anna Barbara	daughter of Mr. Forney	3 years, 11 month
Sept. 17	Sept. 16	Phillip Herschu or Herschn		31 years, 10 month a few days
Oct. 4	Oct. 3	Maria Elisabeth Capito		46 years, a few weeks
	Oct. 8?	Christian	son of Christian and Catharina Muma	3 years, a few weeks
		Lorenz Heckmann		about 45 years old
at Christmas		George	son of Mr. Derzebach	1 year, 6 month
at Christmas		Christian Drebert		34 years
1796				
	March	George Geltzer		about 39 years old
		Elisabeth Lingenfelder		67 years, 6 month
			child of Mr. Jell	
			child of Mr. Kaiser	1 year, 2 month
	June 18		son of Michael Dieffendorfer	1 year, 8 month
	July 14	Michael Kuhner		35 years, 9 month

FIRST REFORMED CHURCH OF BALTIMORE

Dates of Funeral	/ Death	Name	Relatives	Age
1796				
			son of Lingenfeld	5 years
	Aug. 4	Daniel Peters		40 years
	Aug. 13	Carl Ries		22 years
Aug. 24	Aug. 23	Juliana Simon		60 years
Aug. 4	Aug. 3	Martin Becker		55 years
Sept. 7	Sept. 7	Friderich Henck	(from the Grafschaft Witgenstein)	23 years
Sept. 24	Sept. 23	Wilhelm Berg		ca. 40 years
Sept. 28	Sept. 27	Mrs. Bulhaus		48 years
Sept. 28	Sept. 27	George	son of Mr. Hagener	2 years, 8 month & 8 weeks
			child of Jacob Miller	11 month
Oct. 26	Oct. 24	Johann Joseph	son of Christian Kuhner	ca. 2 years old
Nov. 12	Nov. 11	Elisabeth	daughter of Adam Muller	11 years old
	Dec.	Henrich	son of Mr. Blechrodt	18 month
1797				
Jan. 12	Jan. 11	Laurenz Steitz		38 years
Jan. 25	Jan. 23	Amalia Elisabet	widow of Dan. Peter	41 years
March 9	March 8	Rebecca	wife of Adam Muller	34 years
June 20	June 19	Anna Marg.	daughter of Bernhardt Zell	1 year, 5 month
June 25	June 24	Margaretha	Joh. German	1 year, 3 days
July 1	June 30	Anna Kern		24 years
July 29	July 28	William	son of Mr. Kayser	3 month
July 30	July 29	Catharina	daughter of Christian Zell	3 month
Aug. 2	Aug. 1	Johannes Stein	(from Behrstein in Isenburg)	65 years

FIRST REFORMED CHURCH OF BALTIMORE

Dates of Funeral	Death	Name	Relatives	Age
1797				
Aug. 9	Aug. 7	Johannes German	(from Steinbecken)	35 years
Aug. 10	Aug. 9	Carl Friderich	son of Doct. Zeller	1 year
Aug. 26	Aug. 25	Johann Christian	son of Christian Lautemann	2 years
Aug.	Aug. 25	Anna Gertraud	daughter of Dan. von Bremen	3 weeks
Sept.18	Sept.17	Anna Maria Bosh		62yrs,3weeks, 6 days
Sept.20	Sept.18	Matheus Redett		21yrs,7mos.,
Sept.26	Sept.26	Lorenz Pausmann		32 years
Sept.28	Sept.28	Johannes Zeller		46 years
Sept.26	Sept.26	Hen. Jung		24 years
Oct. 3	Oct. 2	Jacob	son of Sam. Heintzmann	6 months
Oct. 7	Oct. 7	George Burk		
Oct. 10	Oct. 9	Joh. Bosh		39 years
1798				
Jan. 13	Jan. 12	Anna Margaretha	Wife of Joh Gottf.Ulrich	48yrs,13 days
Mar. 26	Mar. 25	Christian	son of Franz & Louise Woodtraver	

FIRST REFORMED CHURCH OF BALTIMORE

Dates of Funeral	Death	Name	Relatives	Age
Apr. 22	Apr. 21	Barbara Dusius		54 years
Jun. 12	Jun. 10	Sarah from Dublin, Ireland	Wife of Joh. Pfeifer	37 years (Roman Cath.)
Jun. 17	Jun. 16	Theobald	son of Theob. Faut	1 yr, 4mos.
Jul. 10	Jul. 9	Maria Louisa	Joh. Arnold Schmidt	1 yr., 5 days
Jul. 25	Jul. 24	Maria Barbara	daughter of Hen. Jung	4mos, 1week, a few days
Jul. 30	Jul. 29	Margaretha Adelheid	daughter of Joh. Benzen & Rebecca	30yrs, 9mos.
Aug. 9	Aug. 8	Dorothea Hoffmann	Wife of Mich. Hoffmann	75 yrs, 4mos.
Aug. 15	Aug. 14	Michael Hottmann		81 yrs, 3mos.
Aug. 16	Aug. 15	George	son of Christ. Muma	3 yrs, 8mos.
Aug. 25	Aug. 24	Gesina	Wife of Hen. Stoffelman (from Bremen)	45 years
Aug. 27	Aug. 26	Melchior Kiener	(from Saarbrücken)	78yrs, 1 month, 1 day
Sept. 18	Sept. 17	P. Pfeifer		ca. 50 years
Sept. 19	Sept. 18	.....Ort	son of Matheus Ort	ca. 14yrs. old
Oct. 9	Oct. 8	Cath. Derzebach	Wife of Joh. Derzebach	

FIRST REFORMED CHURCH OF BALTIMORE

Dates of Funeral	Death	Name	Relatives	Age
Nov. 29	Nov. 29	Maria Magdalena Fantz	Wife of Jacob	20yrs, 6 weeks
Dec. 2	Dec. 1	Jacob Hagener		29yrs, a few weeks
Dec. 10	Dec. 9	Reinhardt Spanhoff	(from Langenwarten in Oldenb.) -Germany-	33 years, 3 month, 13 days

1799

Dates of Funeral	Death	Name	Relatives	Age
Jan. 18	Jan. 17	George Daniel Michael	son of Ludwig	3 month, 1 week
Jan. 20	Jan. 19	Anna Cathar. Ort	Wife of Mattheus Ort (from Waldcappel)	51 years old
Apr. 17	Apr. 16	Stephen Claus	(from Riswyck)	41 yrs, a few weeks
May 22	May 21	Barbara	daughter of Martin Tschudy	1yr, 4mos, 3 weeks
Mem. Service Jun. 2	Mar. 10 in Jamaica	Adam Schally		21yrs., 3mos., 11 days
June 2	June 1	Dorothea West	(otherwise Peters or Aldermush)	70 years
July 11	July 10	Elisabeth	daughter of Jacob Schneck	1 yr., 1 month
July 23	July 22	Michael Schomak	stepson of Theob. Faut	5 yrs., 6 month
Aug. 1	July 31	Maria Cathar. Riehm		58 years

FIRST REFORMED CHURCH OF BALTIMORE

Dates of Funeral	Death	Name	Relatives	Age
Aug. 5	Aug. 6	Elisa	daughter of the late Lorenz Pausmann and Catharina Pausmann	1 year, 1month 3 wks, 1 day
Sept. 3	Sept. 2	David	son of the widow Hagener	1 year, 5month
Sept. 22	Sept. 22	George Haase		37 years
Sept. 23	Sept. 22	Margaretha	daughter of Frid. & Sophia Detmor	1 yr, 10 month
Sept. 24	Sept. 23	Wilhelm	son of Jacob Beltz	1 yr., 6month
Oct. 8	Oct. 7	Christoph Detmor		48 years
Mem. Service Oct. 13	June at Campeche	Michael German		19 years
	Oct. 11	Samuel	youngest son of Joh. Schunk	9 days
	Oct. 28	Anna Maria	daughter of Nic. Hack	9 days
Nov. 7	Nov. 5	Maria	daughter of the widow Leuthold	11yrs, 5 weeks
Dec. 10	Dec. 9	Barbara Zahnert	Wife of Joh. Zahnert	33 years
Dec. 27	Dec. 25	Mrs. Zwisler		29 years

Dates of Funeral	Death	Name	Relatives	Age
1800				
Jan. 18	Jan. 16	Catharina Derr (widow)		63 years
Jan. 29	Jan. 27	Salome Degen (had been Kammer)		60 yrs., a few month
Jan. 31	Jan. 29	Henrich Speck		47 years
July 12	July 11	Theobald	son of Theob. Faut	11 days
Aug. 12	Aug. 11	Peter	son of Joh. Hase	9 month

FIRST REFORMED CHURCH OF BALTIMORE

CRITIQUE OF THE VITAL RECORDS OF THE
FIRST & ST. STEPHENS UNITED CHURCH OF CHRIST
(Formerly the Old First Reformed Church of Baltimore)
by
Henry R. Kelly

This critique deals with two major areas of concern. First is a comparison of two transcriptions made of these old German script church records. In the Maryland Historical Society Library there are two beautifully done handwritten books, the work of an unknown transcriber in 1899. A clue exists to this person as he, or she, transcribed the Church Rules in English opposite the German and signed it G.H.L. (clearly E.H.L. in the 2nd volume). We have published the work of Mrs. Duke done in 1974/75. There are differences in the two transcriptions due to the poor handwriting in the original books. A page from 1797 is reproduced to show the difficulty.

Due to the inconsistency, a recheck of the old church books was made. This recheck resulted not only in the changes which follow, but also a finding that the 1899 E.H.L. transcription contains a very large number of errors. We believe many other published German script church records could stand a similar triple check. We recommend the transcription made by Mrs. Duke, including the following changes to the birth records published. There are no changes to the marriage and death records since the triple check occurred before publishing. All future records of this church when published will have had the triple check. Many of the changes consist of additions or other possible spellings of the surname. The method of locating the change is to refer to the date of baptism from beginning to 11 Oct. 1791, and to date of birth from there on.

19 Jan 1770	Godparent Johannes FISHER, (not Gische?)
27 Jan 1770	Birthdate is Jan 21 for twins of Balthasar Majer.
19 Aug 1770	Surname is KAUS, not KAUB.
27 Jun 1771	Complete birthdate of Mathias Devis is December 14, 1769.
22 Sep 1770	The year is 1771, not 1770 for Johannes Kiener.
1 Aug 1779	Add to surname LEVELY possible LEVEDY?
12 Oct 1779	Change Uland to Roland Schmidt.

74 FIRST REFORMED CHURCH OF BALTIMORE

geb. d. 9 ten Oct.	Jacob Krieg u. Eve	Catharina Kiest
gab. d. 25 Oct.	Johannes Ewald u. Catharina	Mittelm Forney
us tus geb. d. 1 Dec.	Peter Herr u. Maria	eltern
Catharina nbg. d. 3 ten Dec.	Fridrich Culert u. S. Ehestein	Anna Catharina Culert

1797.

sabeth geb. d. 16 Jan: getf. d. 22.	Johann Bend u. Margaretha	eltern
harina geb. d. 13 Febr:	Christian Zell u. Barbara	eltern
eobald gab. d. 17 Sept: getf. d. 19 ten Marz	Theobald Faut u. Catharina	Uiber u. Elisabeth krahin
na Marie geb. d. 12 Sonn: getf. d. 19 ten Marz	Henrich Smig u. Elisabeth	eltern
ep Jacob geb. d. 18 Dec. ud: get. d. 14 Ap:	Phillip Kammer u. Marie	eltern
anna geb. d. Ap: getf. d. 13 ten	Joh: Leergbauch u. Catharina	Thomas Hirksen u. anna
geb. d. 8 Apr: bap. 13 ten Quot:	Samuel Heinkmann u. anna Maria	Mutter
na gab. d. 21 May bap. d. 18 Hundun:	Michael Diffendorfer u. Dorothea	Daniel Diffendorfer u. Elisabeth
nna Margaretha d. 21 April get. d. 1 ten Jun:	Johannes Hare u. J. Ehestein	Johanna Margaretha Hepp

30 Nov 1779	Change bp. date to 30 Dec 1779 and change SCHMID to SCHUECK.
30 Dec 1779	Change STONA to STONART, mother is Elisabeth TAMKIN (or TOMIN)
23 Apr 1780	Change surname from MASERI to MADERI.
19 Apr 1781	Surname SCELZ or SCETZ.
13 Jul 1781	Change wife from Lonine to Louise Diefendorfer.
16 Dec 1781	Surname STUND or HUND.
17 Jun 1782	Surname WELM or HELM.
17 Jun 1781	Change surname WOSTMANN to HOFFMAN.
13 Oct 1782	Change birthday of Jacob Wertenberger from Mar 17 to Sept 3.
6 Jan 1783	Surname HOSS or WOSS.
10 Mar 1783	Surname WAUSSMAN or HAUSSMANN.
10 Nov 1783	Change surname of Balzer from SCHATZER to SCHAFER.
25 Dec 1783	Change child Herta Barbara to Eva Barbara, and mother to Eva SPEIL or SPED.
26 Dec 1783	Change Wilhelma Elizabeth to Phillipina Elizabeth.
21 Mar 1784	b. Feb 12 Sophia to Michael Diffendorfer and Dorothea. Godparents Geo. Friedrich Mayer and wife
16 Aug 1784	Surname KRILER or KEILIG.
22 Aug 1784	Add birthdate July 24, 1783 to Johannes Striebel.
12 Sep 1784	Change surname from HIRSCHBERGER to ETSCHBERGER.
14 Nov 1784	Surname STUTZ or STEITZ.
24 Nov 1784	Change surname CAVANS to EAVANS.
2 Jan 1785	Surname Henrich WOLF or WELSH.
23 Jan 1785	Add Dec 18, 1784 as birth of Johannes WARREN.
27 May 1785	Change birthyear from 1783 to 1784 for for Vallentia Nelhy.
28 Mar 1785	Change Willy to Phillip EEBART.
12 May 1785	Change Willy to Phillip GARDENER or GRODENER.
24 Jul 1785	Change birth from Jan 4 to Jan 9 for Mary BERGER.
22 Jul 1785	Surname Phillip HENIG or EMIG.
11 Aug 1785	Surname John HIESCH or HUSCH.
26 Dec 1785	Surname Lorentz HARDMAN or HECKMAN.
20 Aug 1786	Surname Peter BYT or BEGT or BEST.
18 Feb 1787	Change surname Daniel RINMANN to RIEMANN.
17 Sep 1787	Surname Henrich DICHART or DINHART.

FIRST REFORMED CHURCH OF BALTIMORE

24 Jun 1787 Surname Jacob KERNER or KREMER.
12 May 1788 Change surname Daniel RINMANN to RIEMANN.
15 Jun 1788 Surname Dietrich RATIEN or RUTIEN.
25 Jun 1788 Change surname Alexander ALMER to ADAMS.
10 Jul 1788 Surname Johannes SCHORR or SCHAVER, daughter Diane or Anna.
30 Aug 1788 Change surname Joseph SEWCHEN to DEVISON.
23 Nov 1788 Surname Lewis PASSOULT or PAUSEAULT.
12 Dec 1788 Surname Frederick KINER or KRAM.
6 Sep 1788 Change surname Johannes PFISTER to MEISTER.
2 Mar 1789 Change witness Jacob LINDOR to DIEDER.
12 Apr 1789 Change surname Christian MULLER to MINNA.
3 May 1789 Change witness from Willy to Phillip Molls.
11 May 1789 Change surname William HANCOD to HANCOCK.
12 Oct 1789 Surname Georg LOSSMAN or LORSMAN.
22 Oct 1789 Change witness Henrich BINDER to BRUDER.
Add two items in 1790
   Birth May 6 Elizabeth to David and Sarah MUNNA.
   Birth Aug 22 Henrich to Theobald FAUT and Catherine, witness Henrich Kiefer, Magdalena Meyer
15 Nov 1790 Change Anna Margreta to Maria SCHUNK.
11 Oct 1791 Nette or Nelle Repdoger.
14 Aug 1792 Change surname Johann FRANS to IVANS or EVANS.
16 Sep 1792 Surname George FROHLENIER or TROHLENIER (also as witness Nov. 2).
13 Oct 1792 Child Elisabeth (not George) BELTZ.
2 Jul 1795 Witness Jacob JANTZ or FANTZ.
11 Mar 1796 Surname Johannes FORNEN or FORNEY, also witness Barbara.
26 Mar 1796 Change witness Louis DENNER to BENNER.
5 Feb 1796 Surname Wilhelm FORTNEY or FORNEY.
8 Sep 1796 Change witness Anna Maria to Catharine STEEG.
17 Apr 1799 Parents are Johann and Sara FORNEY not JUN.
22 Dec 1797 Christian was son of Joh and Anna LAUTEMANN, not RIESCH.
24 Dec 1799 Ketty is possibly Betty KIEMAN.
7 May 1800 Witness Georg NAUBEN is NAUBER.
13 Jul 1802 Wife of Henrich Hupfield should be Charlotta Christina Philippina, nee BECKER.
30 Sep 1803 Witness Anna LAUTEN, not LAUTN.
11 Mar 1804 Elisabeth Elliot is nee TROLDENIER, not PROLDENIER.

In the years 1802-1803 there is a cross entered after names of children who died, namely-

1802 Alexander Watel, Friedrich Krömer, Wilhelm
    Mogenthal.
1803 Sophia Benson, Johannes Kiem, Katherina Dittman,
    James Elgert, Jacob Zahner, Susanna Zolle,
    Eduard von Hemessen.
The second area of concern is that of the various surname spellings of the same individual.

A witness to the very first baptism was Jacob Majer. There were four other Majers. Friedrich Majer was also spelled Meyer and Mayer, and he died Mayer.
Jacob died Meyers. The best spelling is MAYER.

One name really caused trouble- Martin Segessers in 1768, Martin Segester in 1769 and 1771, Martin Segerhindin in 1781, Martin Segensser in 1785, Martin Segentzer in 1786, Martin Stegensfer in 1788. Anna Maria Segesterin was married in 1769. Which spelling really continued is unknown.

Another example of two spellings is Johannes Derzebach in 1792, 1793, and 1795, but in 1787 and 1788 his name is spelled Drotzebach. Derzebach continued.

Samuel Heintzmann in 1793, 1795, 1797 is spelled Heinsman in 1786, Samuel Hensmann in 1781 and 1784.

The church prominent Muma family has a short name but spelled four ways. David Muma in 1782, 1789, 1790 but David Minna in 1787, 1793 and David Munna in 1789. Christian Muma in 1782, Christian Mumma in 1792, Christian Minna in 1784, 1786, 1789, and Christian Muna in 1784. By 1798 all the death records were MUMA.

Freidrich Eyen must have been spoken oddly for the two spellings to exist. In 1784 as Eyen he married Cathrina Bosser (which name is spelled three ways also). In 1785, 1786 he is Friedrich Eyra. In 1787, 1789, 1792 he is Friedrich Eyen.

There are many others-

Allspach- Alpachtner
Berned- Bernet
Cassel- Cashel
Crusius- Creseius- Cruhsius
Detmor- Detmar- Ditmar- Dietmar
Eavans- Evans

Ebbert-Ebhart
Fautz- Faut
Forny- Forney
Franz- Frantz
Grayhit- Granchet- Grenchett
Kiborz- Küborz- Kübortz
Leopold- Leobold- Lypold
Laudemann- Lauhemann- Lauteman
Pauseault- Pascault- Passoult
Rayli- Rayly- Reyly
Redig- Rettig- Rattig
Tschudy- Schudy- Tschudi
Wüd- Hud- Zud
Zumwald- Zomwald

This is not a complete listing. The few examples shown above do show the importance, especially in old German and Dutch records, of the phonetic possibilities. The Cendex Division of the Genealogic Company of Austin, Texas has computerized certain early 1820, 1830, 1840 State census records in this fashion. Researchers in early German church records must try to do the same the hard way. However, it is worth the effort.

FIRST REFORMED CHURCH OF BALTIMORE

BAPTISMAL AND BIRTH RECORDS
FIRST & ST. STEPHENS UNITED CHURCH OF CHRIST
(Formerly First Reformed Church of Baltimore)

Date of Baptism	Name of the Child	Parents	Witnesses	Date of Birth
1806				
Jan. 19	Conrad Herman	Jacob Simon & Katharina, nee Wagner	Conrad Herman & Elise	Dec. 19, 1805
Jan. 26	Elisabeth	Nicolaus Elgert & Maria nee Heylmann	parents	Oct. 27, 1805
Jan. 31	Elisabeth	Johann Benzel & Louise nee Keyser	mother	Oct. 31, 1805
Jan. 31	Carl Wilhelm	Johann Peter Friederich Focke & Metta nee Stock	Carl Wilh. Ferd. Focke	Jan. 21, 1805
Feb. 23	Johann Wilhelm	Jacob Derr & Maria nee Scherer	Philipp Beitel & Maria Katharina	Nov. 2, 1805
Mar. 2	Anna Mathilda	Henrich Arnold Wilms & Anna Elisabeth, nee Grammer	parents	Aug. 11, 1805
Mar. 9	Daniel	Johann Knodt & Elisab. nee Schroeder	parents	Feb. 22, 1806
Mar. 29	Wilhelm Adolph	Wilhelm Adolph Scharper & Anna Henriette, nee Rohter	parents	Mar. 20, 1806

FIRST REFORMED CHURCH OF BALTIMORE

Date of Baptism	Name of the Child	Parents	Witnesses	Date of Birth
Apr. 10	Anna Elisabeth	Johann Benfer & Kath. nee Strackbein	Anna Elisabeth Potten	Mar. 19, 1806
Apr. 26	Elisabella	Johann Georg Doft & Wilhelmina, nee Henkels	parents	Mar. 4, 1806

The Following Children Were Baptized by Pastor Dr. Christian Ludwig Becker

1806

Date of Baptism	Name of the Child	Parents	Witnesses	Date of Birth
July 8	Catherina Louise	Georg Reiter & Dorothea Catharina	parents	Mar. 13, 1806
July 20	Anna Maria	Kraft Achenbach & Anna Elisabeth, nee Weberin	Maria Lesch	Mar. 24, 1806
July 24	Jacob	Johann Schmid & Christina, nee Kengerin	Friederich Feil & Helena Tobel	Dec. 23, 1805
July 27	Columbia Louis	Benedict Louis & Elisabeth nee Adkinson	mother & Maria Adkinson	June 2, (died 8, 1806
Aug. 15	Anna Maria	Johann Zellich & Susanna nee Burdongin (or Bundongin)	parents	Mar. 2
Aug. 17	Wilhelm	Heinrich Friburger & Margaretha nee Miller	parents	Apr. 27

FIRST REFORMED CHURCH OF BALTIMORE

Date of Baptism	Name of the Child	Parents	Witnesses	Date of Birth
Aug. 24	Elisabeth	Caspar Zodr & Barbara nee Filingin or Filiarsin	Johann Schmid & his wife	July 24
Aug. 28	Friederich Ernst Becker	Dr. Carl Hintze & Henrietta nee Machaux	Dr. Christian Ludewig Becker & Adelheid	Mar. 13 1803
Aug. 31	Johanna Louisa	Johan Conrad Barthauer & Anna Regina nee Ludi	Johanna Wilkin	Aug. 13
Sept. 7	Maria	Jacob Hendelick or Headelick & Elisabeth nee Frey	Johann Frey	Aug. 10
Sept. 14	Jacob	Heinrich Keilholtz & Maria	Friederich Busads or Buhads child Dorothea	Feb. 11
Sept. 27	Elisabeth	Jacob Miller & Maria nee Bodin	parents	July 27
Oct. 19	Heinrich	Jacob Krall & Maria	parents	Oct. 2
Nov. 23	Metta Henrietta	H. or K. Waesche and his wife	father and Mich. Repold	Sept. 26
Dec. 15	Samuel	Johann Leibrand and Maria nee Speck	parents	Oct. 25
Dec. 17	Louisa	Johan Spies & Margaretha nee Tschudy	Mr. Tschudy and his wife	Jan. 20, 1806

FIRST REFORMED CHURCH OF BALTIMORE

Date of Baptism	Name of the Child	Parents	Witnesses	Date of Birth
Dec. 25	Maria	Leopold Donsee and Sophia	Johann Richstein & Catharina	Sept. 22
Dec. 25	Johannes	Christian Krämer & Marta	Johan Krämer & Elisabeth Miller	Nov. 16
Dec. 28	Catharina	Christian Krämer and Maria	dto.	Apr. 1, 1803

1807

Date of Baptism	Name of the Child	Parents	Witnesses	Date of Birth
Jan. 1	Heinrich Christoph	Mr. von Kapf and Henrietta Esther	Heinrich Didier and Christoph von Kapf	July 8, 1806
Jan. 25	Wilhelm	Georg Weber & Margaretha nee Braun	James Reber & Maria Braun	Dec. 17, 1806
Feb. 22	Juliana	Henrich Emig & Elisabeth nee Fantz	Ludwig Wampler & Johanna	Jan. 13
Mar. 8	Maria	Abraham Le Feber & Elisabeth	Elisabeth Le Feber (grandmother)	Feb. 6, 1806
Mar. 17	Sarah	Friederich Warner & Sarah nee Tang. (or Jung?)	parents	Feb. 23
Apr. 3	Anna Elisabeth	Carl Folck & Margaretha	Ludewig Deqmeier & Miss Anspach	Jan. 28

Date of Baptism	Name of the Child	Parents	Witnesses	Date of Birth
April 5	Catharina	Georg Rich-stein & Catharina	Johan Schmid and Catharina Udi	March 18
April 22	Jacob	Johan Binsel & Louisa	mother	March 22
May 18	Johan Adam Heinrich	Adam Süsrab & Catharina	father himself and Catharina Hostedterin	Dec. 31, 1806
May 18	Johan Jefferson	Georg Wordel and Margareta	Johan Hublitz/ & Anna Elisabeth Achenbach	Dec. 31 1806
May 20	Sabina	Peter Schmachtenberg & Wilhelmine	Diderich Wolf/ Ludewig Schneider Carolina Setter Johanna Catharina Weck Heinrich Beckli and Maria Beckli	March 19
May 24	David	Johan Wilhelm Weber & Nancy	Adam Reili &/ Susanna	Jan. 13
May 24	Elisabeth	Peter Peuckert (Penckert) & Anna	Anna Catharina Weisambel	Aug. 27, 1806
June 5	David	Heinrich Hachenbracht & Louisa nee Lautering or Lautesung	grandmother of the child	Oct. 12, 1806
June 9	Maria	Johan Ard & Catharina	parents	Oct. 14, 1805
Nov. 9	Nancy	Johan Ard & Catharina	parents	Oct. 14, 1799
June 21	Anna Elisabeth	Johan Homrich-Shausen & Batty	parents	May 16, 1807

FIRST REFORMED CHURCH OF BALTIMORE

Date of Baptism	Name of the Child	Parents	Witnesses	Date of Birth
July 10	Charlotta	Valentin Sanders & Sophia	San-parents	April 12
July 24	Jacob	Friedrich Ditmar and Elisabeth	Ludewig Schneider and Anna Hermann	April 12
July 27	Anthony	Anthony Hindel & Catharina nee Forney	Johan Forney and Elisabeth	January 2
July 30	Catharina	Absalom Chrisbin & Anna Maria	Catharina Keier	January 17
July 30	at the same time Absalom Chrisbin was baptised			
Aug. 4	James	Andreas Schneider & Christina	father	4/7/1805
Aug. 4	Heinrich	Jacob Wirkinge & Elisabeth	mother	August 23
Aug. 4	Maria Catharina Philippina	Heinrich Neukirch & Catharina	David Post Catharina Clenau	April 7
Aug. 4	Maria Margaretha	Johann Adam Schmid and Jenny	Elisabeth Miller	July 24
Aug. 4	Anna Catharina	Georg Schaller & Franziska nee Honey	Jacob Bossert or Boshert and Anna Catharina Keilholtz	June 27
Aug. 30	Anna Maria	Johann Corel and Maria	mother	July 10

FIRST REFORMED CHURCH OF BALTIMORE 85

Date of Baptism	Name of the Child	Parents	Witnesses	Date of Birth
Sept. 6	Susanna	Herman Neu-meier & Catharina nee Karber	parents	July 21
Sept. 13	Margaretha	Philip Cronmuller & Margaretha	parents	Aug. 13
Oct. 11	Wilhelm Philip	Philip German jun. & Elisabeth Nee Kurtz (or Kuntz)	Philip German sen. and wife	Aug. 22
Oct. 12	Johan Heinrich	Johan Forné jun. & Sarah	Johan Forné sen. & wife	Sept. 24
Oct. 25	Ludewig	Herman Schneider & Margaretha	Heinrich Wilson	Sept. 28
Oct. 25	Juliana	Jacob Hofman & his wife	Heinrich Locher & his wife	Aug. 29
Oct. 29	Johannes	Johan Fige & Nancy	Valentin Sanders & wife	Oct. 22
Nov. 5	Heinrich	Jacob Lange & Elisabeth	parents	Sept. 27
Dec. 6	Mariana	Thomas Bolman & Barbara	Adam Gottlie Ruab & Magdalena	Nov. 4
Dec. 9	Sophia	Friedrich W. Meier & Salome	Adelheid Beckerin	June 2
Dec. 13	Georg Wilhelm	Jacob & Philippina	Georg Gabriel Merige & Rebecca Andre	Oct. 22
Dec. 26	Christina	Thomas Bonnet (or Bonnes) and Anna	Michael German	Jan. 20

FIRST REFORMED CHURCH OF BALTIMORE

Date of baptism	Name of child	Parents	Witnesses	Date of Birth
1808				
Jan. 17	Salome	James Thomson and Sofia	Salome Eichelerin	July 27, 1807
Jan. 31	Barbara	Leonhard Zügler & Louisa nee Bencker	Barbara Züglerin	Oct. 8, 1805
Jan. 31	Adelheit	Nicolaus Hacke & Sophia	Adelheit Becker & Mr. Kern	Jan. 10
Jan. 31	Joseph	James Carnigham & Catharina	Peter Diefendörfer	Aug. 20, 1807
Jan. 31	Ludwig Georg	Carl Schroeter & his wife	Ferdinand Ludewig Lender, Georg Schroeter & Elisabeth Blot	Nov. 11, 1806
Feb. 15	Ludwig Wilhelm	Ludewig Schneider & Christina nee Kiffeck (Kilsch?)	parents	Mar. 29 1807
March 13	Tobias	Johannes Benfer and Catharina	parents	Jan. 1, 1808
March 14	Andreas Friederich	Georg Reiter & Dorothea Catharina	Andreas Koch & Friederich Reiter	Feb. 11
March 27	Mariana	Johan Georg Brenecher or Brenesser & Margaretha	parents	Nov. 22
March 30	Susanna	Nicolaus Elgert & Maria	parents	Feb. 25
April 10	Elisabeth	Georg Skar or Skär & Magdalena	Elisabeth	March 18

FIRST REFORMED CHURCH OF BALTIMORE 87

Date of baptism	Name of child	Parents	Witnesses	Date of Birth
April 17	Jacobina Catharina Charlotta	Georg <u>Sprung</u> & Johanna Christina	Jacob Dorschheimer & Catharina Miller	Feb. 15
April 18	Wilhelm	Jacob <u>Simon</u> & Catharina	Johan Allenbach & Elisabeth Miller	Jan. 3
April 18	Carolina	David <u>Simon</u> & his wife	Mr. Krämer & his wife	Jan. 16
April 18	Johan Diederich	Diederich <u>Geisler</u> & Elisabeth	Capitain Johan Duncker & Johanna Weber	April 3
April 24	Johan Daniel	Nikolaus <u>Ger</u>-rman & Rebecca nee Garterbeck	parents	April 5
April 24	Elisabeth	Leopold Dorser or <u>Donser</u> Donsee & Sophia	Johann Richtstein & his wife	Dec. 8, 1807?
May 1	Johannes	Johann <u>Fre</u>-burger & Nancy	parents	July 31, 1807
May 8	Johann	Johann <u>Mumma</u> & Elisabeth	Conrad Reily & his wife	Dec. 21, 1805
May 8	Margaretha	"	Adam Reily & his wife	Feb. 2
May 8	Sarah	Jacob <u>Wetter</u>-stein & Elisabeth	Michael Mumma	Jan. 3
May 29	Maria	Mr. Laudeman & his wife	Nancy Thepert	Aug. 24, 1792
May 29	Friederich	"	John Pendel	Jan. 24, 1795
May 29	Jacob	"	Philip German	Feb. 23, 1797

FIRST REFORMED CHURCH OF BALTIMORE

Date of baptism	Name of child	Parents	Witnesses	Date of Birth
May 29	Edward	Mr. Laudeman & his wife	Thomas Scheppert	Aug. 14, 1800
May 29	Sophia	"	Veronica Frost	Dec. 14, 1807
May 29	James William	"	James Gibson	Jan. 15, 1805
May 29	Wilhelm	Stephanus Grof or Graf & his wife	parents	Feb. 11, 1808
May 29	Maria Magdalena & Elisabeth (twins)	Johan West and Elis.	Mr. Emig & Maria Magdalena & Rettpheli Scha	April 6, 1808
May 29	Wilhelm	The accused father Mr. Eckel & the mother Catharina Simmering	mother	March 23, 1807
May 31	Carl Gerhard	Georg Walther Hood & Susanna nee Gibs	parents	May 8
June 5	Johannes	Johan Ewald & Catharina	Heinrich Bollman & Anna Catharina	Feb. 16
June 5	Wilhelm	Heinrich Pösicke & Magdalena	mother	May 14
June 7	Christina	Caspar Zodi & Barbara	Johann Renners & Christina	April 5
June 13	Sarah	Daniel Schmid & Elisabeth	Barbara Render	May 12
June 14	Anna Henrietta	Friedrich Focke & his wife nee Stockin of Barmen	Madame Bolbin	May 24

FIRST REFORMED CHURCH OF BALTIMORE

Date of baptism	Name of child	Parents	Witnesses	Date of Birth
July 14	Daniel	Johan Schmid & Christina	Daniel Fobel & Catharina Richtstein	April 1
July 17	Johan Christian	Johan Conrad Berthauer & Johanna Regina	Johann Christian Erb & Lucia Dorothea	May 13
Aug. 7	Christian	Friederich Detmor & Elisabeth	Christina	July 31
Aug. 14	Elisabeth	Wilhelm Tobel & Helena	Johan Heil & Elisabeth	May 23
Sept. 14	Anna Maria	Nicolaus Keifel (or Keidel) & Anna Maria	Anna Maria Gaul of Philadelphia	Jan. 13, 1806
Sept. 14	Catherina Margaretha	"	Catharina Mecki of Philadelphia	May 30
Sept. 25	Rosina	Heinrich Friburger & Margaretha	parents	Jan. 21
Oct. 2	Johann Friderich	Benjamin Bausman & Elisabeth	Johan Bausman & his wife	Feb. 11
Oct. 10	Wilhelm Philip	Mr. Bader & his wife	Philip German & his wife	Sept. 21
Oct. 13	Friderich Wilhelm	Georg Dickhut & Johanna	Friederich Lepard & Elisabeth	July 1
Oct. 23	Wilhelm Presler	Georg Fischer & his wife	Jacob Frey & his wife	Sept. 19
Nov. 7	Salome	John Patman & Elisabeth	Salome Currau	Aug. 14

FIRST REFORMED CHURCH OF BALTIMORE
BAPTISMAL AND BIRTH RECORDS
FIRST & ST. STEPHENS UNITED CHURCH OF CHRIST
(Formerly First Reformed Church of Baltimore)

Date of baptism	Name of child	Parents	Witnesses	Date of Birth
Nov. 13	Elisabeth	Heinrich Arnold Wilmsen & Anna Elisabeth	parents	Feb. 8
Nov. 20	Anna Maria Elisabeth	Conrad Bergman & Elisabeth	Friederich Jansen & Anna Maria	Oct. 11
Nov. 27	Johan	Heinrich Becker & Catharina	parents	Nov. 7, 1807
Nov. 27	Maria	Johan Krämer & Elisabeth	William Kep & Maria Elisabeth Krämer	Oct. 19
Dec. 1	Johan Georg	Valentin Sanders & Sophia	Johan Georg Sauter & Margaretha	Oct. 24
Dec. 25	Johan Georg	Valentin Lutz & Catharina nee Wolf	Peter BEcker & Elisabeth	Nov. 14
Dec. 25	Heinrich	Adam Susrab (Susnab) & Catharina	Abraham Sibler (Sitler?) and Catharina	Oct. 24
July 7	Carl	Johan Diefendorfer & his wife	father	July 7 (died July 7, 1808)

1809

Jan. 8	Maria Susanna	Johan Georg Bange & Elisabeth	parents	Oct. 19, 1808
Jan. 8	Maria	Heinrich Keilholtz & Maria	Heinrich Working & Elisabeth	Feb. 24
Jan. 16	Sophia	Kraft Achenbach & Anna Elisabeth nee Weberin	Margaretha Wardel	Oct. 30, 1808

FIRST REFORMED CHURCH OF BALTIMORE

Date of baptism	Name of child	Parents	Witnesses	Date of Birth
Jan. 29	Elisabeth Wilhelmina	Johan Hublitz & Elisabeth nee Patt	Miss Meerfield & Sebastian Saltzer & Johan Wilhelm Hommerichshausen	Dec. 23, 1808
Jan. 30	Mariana	Georg Lucas & Carolina nee Hostedter	Maria Elisabeth Say	Oct. 17, 1808
March 1	Johannes	Heinrich Emig & Elisabeth	Johan Rothrock & Catharina Robbes	Jan. 11, 1809(?)
March 2 Died Mar. 2	Georg	Johan Leybrand & Maria	parents	Feb. 25
March 5	David	Jacob Lerroiw & Carolina	Theobald Faust & Margaretha	Feb. 10
March 23	Johann Heinrich	Peter Becker & Elisabeth nee Wolf	Valentin Lay	March 15
April 7	Mariana	Andreas Hitt & Sarah	Frantz Ridesel & Magdalena	Feb. 16
April 23	Wilhelm Heinrich	Mr. Reit, or Reil & his wife	Maria Leybrand	Feb. 4
May 11	Louisa	Peter Feige (or Feice) & Catharina	Maria Magdalena	March 1
May 16	Jenny	Georg Keller & Elisabeth nee Schweitzer	Philip Schweitzer	Sept. 8, 1808
May 21	Maria Elisabeth	Christian Krämer & Martha	Friedrich Krämer & Maria Winckert	March 12
May 21	Lidiana	Philip Cronmüller & his wife	parents	April 22

FIRST REFORMED CHURCH OF BALTIMORE

Date of baptism	Name of child	Parents	Witnesses	Date of Birth
May 22	Cornelius Wilhelm	Nicolaus Constantin Lacher or Lashir & Catharina Corneliche	parents	March 11
June 18	Johan Friederich	Carl Folck & Margaretha	Johan Friederich Arspach & Constantina	May 2
Jan. 25 or June	Appolinia	Jacob Wild & Margaretha	Johan Schmid & his wife	Feb. 24, 1806
Jan. 25 or June	Margaretha	Jacob Wild & Margaretha	Christian Cosman & his wife	Jan. 1 1809
July 3	Conrad	Jacob Lange or Large & his wife	parents	March 26
July 16	Johanna Maria	H. von Kapf & Henrietta Esther	Miss von Kapf	Nov. 4, 1808
July 18	Johan Georg	Johan Georg Richtstein & Catharina	father & Christina Richtstein	July 10
July 19	Maria	Adrian Christian Trotz & Helena Johanna nee Boter	parents	May 8, 1805
July 19	Adrian Christian	"	parents	Dec. 1, 1807
Aug. 20	Catharina	Herman Neumeier & Catharina nee Carpenter	parents	July 10, 1809
Aug. 21	Johannes	Johan Homrigshausen & Maria	parents	May 9

FIRST REFORMED CHURCH OF BALTIMORE

Date of Baptism	Name of child	Parents	Witnesses	Date of Birth
Aug. 27	Wilhelm	Wilhelm Rothe & Catharina	Wilhelm Holman	July 29
Sept. 5	Maria	Johan Weller & Nancy	parents	May 16
1808 by a Meth. Preacher	Samuel	Jacob Kraus & Rachel	parents	Oct. 13, 1806
Sept. 6	Maria	"	"	Jan. 20, 1808
Sept. 6	Elisabeth	"	"	Sept. 1 1809
Sept. 13	Margaretha	James Thomson & Sophia	Margaretha Codwald	Aug. 14
Sept. 17	Carolina	Jacob Lehman & Philippina	Dethart Töpken & Carolina	July 19, 1809
Sept. 20	Johann	Adam Schmid and Jenny	Maria Elisabeth van der Heide	Sept. 16, 1808
Sept. 24	Nicolaus	Nicolaus Emig & Elisabeth	parents	July 18, 1809
Sept. 25	Catharina Sophia	Johan Christoph Kelner & Anna Louisa	Sophia Margarathe Schraderin & Catharina Elisabeth	Aug. 24, 1809
Sept. 28	Johannes	Johan Zeller or Zoller & Susanna	Maria Zeller or Zoller	Mar. 1 1808
Sept. 28	Anna Maria	"	"	Aug. 22 1809
Sept. 29	Anna Maria	Friederich Werner & Sally	mother	Sept. 22
Oct. 15	Georg Wilhelm	Johan West & Elisabeht	parents	Aug. 8

FIRST REFORMED CHURCH OF BALTIMORE

Date of Baptism	Name of child	Parents	Witnesses	Date of Birth
Oct. 22	Johann Georg	Johan Kregler (or Krylor) & Barbara	Johann Marris & Catharina Schrenk	Oct. 12
Oct. 8	Johan Konrad Heinrich	Henrich Neukirch & Catharina	Johan Konrad Barthaufer & Johanna Regina	Sept. 28
Nov. 13	Carolina	Michael Kringerling (or Wengeling) & Christina	parents	Sept. 20
Nov. 26	Charlotta	Johan MecDonnel & Catharina nee Müller	Catharina Müller	July 12
Dec. 11	Joseph	Andreas Treppert & Catharina or Streppert	Rosina Bertrant substituting for her father Joseph Bertrant	Oct. 12
Dec. 13	Christian	Christian Zingling (died) & Johanna nee Weber	mother	Nov. 1
Dec. 24	Wilhelm	Wilhelm Warke or Wacke & Elisabeth	Johann Krämer & Elisabeth	May 22
Dec. 24	Maria Elisabeth	Beniamin Baurman & Elisabeth	Johan Baurman & his wife	June 7
Dec. 26	Christian Georg Eduart	Dr. Carl Friederich Zoller & Maria	Mr. Heidebach & Mr. Zwissler and his wife	Oct. 24

1810

Jan. 7	Catharina	Heinrich Becker & Catharina	parents	Dec. 10, 1809

FIRST REFORMED CHURCH OF BALTIMORE

Date of Baptism	Name of child	Parents	Witnesses	Date of Birth
Jan. 9	Catharina	Friedrich Detmar & Elisabeth	Johan Friederich Gebhard & Catharina	Nov. 22, 1809
Jan. 10	Georg	Georg Sprung & Johanna Christina	Georg Hase & Catharina Richtstein	Jan. 8
Jan. 15 (died)	Georg	Gotfried Feige & Juliana	parents	Oct. 28, 1809
Jan. 27	Georg Friederich (dead)	Georg Reiter & Dorothea Catharina	Friederich Reiter	Jan. 3, 1810
Jan. 30	Carolina	Georg Lucker & Carolina	parents & Michael Hostedter	Jan. 15
Feb. 12	Wilhelm (illegitimate)	Carl Schneider & Elisabeth, nee Simmering	mother	Jan. 25, 1807
Feb. 12	Christiana Jacobina	Wilhelm Samuel Rütgers & Anna Catharina	Jacob Zwisler & Christina Catharina	Jan. 31, 1810
Feb. 18	Heinrich Peter	Jacob Horden & Elisabeth nee Diefendörfer	Peter Diefendörfer & Catharina	Sept. 8, 1809
Feb. 18	Susanna Sophia	Peter Diefendörfer & Catharina nee Mayer	parents	Sept. 18, 1809
Feb. 28	Johannes Georg	Johannes Turf & Cath. nee Riedbühl	parents	Dec. 23, 1809
March 7	Christiana Adelheit	Nicolaus Hacke & Sophia	Dr. Christian C. Büler or Bacher & Adelheit	Feb. 16

FIRST REFORMED CHURCH OF BALTIMORE

Date of Baptism	Name of child	Parents	Witnesses	Date of Birth
March 13	Johan Heinrich	Johan Zanst & Maria	Wilhelm Scheierly & his wife	Aug. 30, 1808
March 26	Friederich	Johan Spies & Margaretha	Friederich Hammer & Sophia Hammer	July 26, 1809
April 12	Johan Adam	Johan Adam Anspach & Maria Catharina nee Reinhard	Elisabeth Reinhard	Jan. 9, 1810
April 17	Elisabeth	Peter Weygart & Maria nee Maul	Christian Capito & Elisabeth	March 2, 1810
April 22	Barbara	Jacob Forney & Eva	Johannes Schaaf & Maria Magdalena	Dec. 10, 1809
May 2	Georg Heinrich	Georg Spleich & Anna Catharina	Catharina König	April 27
May 13	Johan Jacob Gottlieb	Valentin Lutz & Catharina	Johan Jacob Zellich & his wife	March 16
March 13	Mariana	Johan Feyl (Feye) & Nancy	parents	March 3
March 13	Catharina	Johan Schmal & Louisa	Johan Kla & his wife	Feb. 18
May 24	Anna Maria	Jacob Eigenbrod & Catharina	parents	April 25, 1809
June 3	Elisabeth Margaretha	Stephanus Graf & his wife	parents	Aug. 17, 1809
June 10	Amelia Handy	Johan Diefendörfer & his wife	parents	April 23

FIRST REFORMED CHURCH OF BALTIMORE

Date of Baptism	Name of child	Parents	Witnesses	Date of Birth
June 11	Mariana	David Simon & Catharina	Wilhelm Miller & Mariana Tschinkers	Dec. 25 1809
June 15	Rebecca Louise	Diederich Rottermund & Wilhelmine	Rebecca Althaus & Helena Schaf	March 4
June 15 died June 25	Helena Carolina	Jacob Ritter & Anna	Mr. Schaf & Helena	March 31
June 17	Johannes	Peter Benckert & Johanna	Johan Seler & his wife	May 5
June 17	Heinrich	Anthony Stimpel & Margaretha	Michael Locher	July 3 1809
June 17	Henrietta	Jacob Hofman & his wife	parents	Feb. 1
June 24	Johannes	Johannes Alsfeld & Elisabeth	Johannes Meils (Keils)?	May 8
July 1	Elisabeth	Georg Bange & Elisabeth	Frantz Bange & Michael Schneider	May 8
July 1	Margaretha	Mr. Waddle & Margaretha	Johan Schmid & Rebecca Wild	Apr. 21
July 5	Samuel	Johan Ilgenfrontz & Margaretha or Ilgenfritz	mother	Oct. 22 1804
July 5	Rebecca	dto.	mother	Jan. 2 1807
July 5 Died July 6	Waschington	dto.	Mich. German	Sept. 4 1809

FIRST REFORMED CHURCH OF BALTIMORE

Date of Baptism	Name of child	Parents	Witnesses	Date of Birth
July 5	Salome	Heinrich Schultz & Catharina	Friedrich Kraft & Margareth	April 20
July 15	Wilhelm	Ludwig Schneider & Christina	parents	Jan. 6 1809,
July 22	Johan Heinrich Christoph	Johan Conrad Barthausen & Johanna Regina	Heinrich Christoph Wilke & Johan Heinrich Reacke	June 8
July 30	Heinrich Justus	Friederich Focke & his wife nee Stockin (of Barmen)	Justus Heinrich Hoppe	June 14
Aug. 12	Johan Georg	Thomas Bollman & his Wife	Mr. Schnaufer	June 14
Aug. 12 died Aug. 12	Samuel	Abraham Sittler & his wife	parents	July 6
Aug. 13	Anna Elisabeth	Johan Schmid & his wife	parents	June 28
Aug. 13	Wilhelm	Georg Kauterer & Anna Elisabeth	parents	Jan. 19
Aug. 16	Elisa	James Phibs & Anna Phibs	mother	June 7
Aug. 25	Johannes Steg	Jacob Bare & Elisabeth nee Geiger	parents	July 28
Aug. 27	Abraham	Conrad Rhode & Kraul	parents	Feb. 2

FIRST REFORMED CHURCH OF BALTIMORE

Date of Baptism	Name of child	Parents	Witnesses	Date of Birth
Sept. 12	Johannes	Abraham Lang & Maria	Mr. Kohler & his wife	Sept. 13 1807
Sept. 12	Hemes Thomas	dto.	dto.	July 10 1809
Sept. 23	Casiana	Christian Gelbach & Sally	Robert Sture (or Skure) & his wife Eva	July 28
Sept. 30	Louisa	Friederich Shurtz (or Shuutz & Catharina	parents	Feb. 6
Oct. 7	Jacob	Johan Fuselbach & Barbara	mother & Jacob Ziegler	June 1
Oct. 27	Maria Elisabeth	Georg Weber & Eva Margaretha	Maria Elisabeth Braunin	Jan. 9 1809
Oct. 28	Johannes	Johan Jacob Honderlich & Elisabeth	Johann Beck & Appollonia	Apr. 27
Nov. 9 Died Nov. 11	Elisabeth	Daniel Fobel & Susanna nee Robertson	Mr. Fobel & Elisabeth Williart	Nov. 6
Nov. 11	Elisabeth	Johan Kramer & Elisabeth	Friederich Kramer & his wife	Oct. 14
Dec. 9	Friedrich Jacob Wilhelm	Conrad Birgman & Elisabeth	Friederich James & Anna Maria	Oct. 22
Dec. 10	Georg	Nicolaus Elgert & Maria	parents	Dec. 1

FIRST REFORMED CHURCH OF BALTIMORE

Date of Baptism	Name of child	Parents	Witnesses	Date of Birth
Dec. 22	Elisabeth	Frantz Riedensel(?) & Magdalena	Elisabeth Schlusselberger	Oct. 5

1811

Date of Baptism	Name of child	Parents	Witnesses	Date of Birth
Jan. 7	Johan Georg	Georg Reiter & Dorothea Catharina	Mr. Schnaufer	Dec. 12 1810
Feb. 10	Sarah	Johan Mumma & Elis.	Mich. Mumma	Aug. 5 1810
Feb. 17	Johan Phillip	Philip Cronmuller & his wife	parents	Dec. 20 1810
Feb. 21	Margaretha	Johan Dornin Maria Magdalena	Margaretha Marzin & Georg Herrguth	Nov. 4 1809
Feb. 28	Wilhelm	Franciscus Bange & Catharina nee Zahner	parents	Nov. 1 1810
Mar. 12	Harriet	Heinrich Watts & Margaretha	Heinrich Watts & Margaretha	Feb. 19
Mar. 20	Wilhelm	Chrisbin & his wife	Mich. Sleiin	Nov. 26 1810
Mar. 31	Johan	Nicolaus Undeutsch & Metta	Johan Steinfort & Mich. Richtstein	Oct. 23 1810
Apr. 3	Georg	Georg Keller & Elisabeth	parents	Apr. 2 1810

FIRST REFORMED CHURCH OF BALTIMORE

Date of Baptism	Name of child	Parents	Witnesses	Date of Birth
Apr. 14	Georg	John Edler & Anna Maria	Georg Richtstein	Sept. 14 1810
Apr. 15	Catharina	James le Rou & his wife	Theobald Faust & his wife	Jan. 30 1811
Apr. 28	Anna	Johan Meier & Catharina	Anna Eiler	Jan. 9 1809
May 5	Johannes	Georg Rotemeier & Maria	parents	Mar. 29 1811
May 5	Johannes	Nicolaus Fortine & Anna Martha	Johan Heinrich Borman & his wife	Feb. 10 1810
May 26	Carolina	Heinrich Keilholtz & Maria	parents	Nov. 19 1810
May 24	Georg	Friedrich Ditmar & Elisabeth	parents	Mar. 31
May 30	Heinrich	Johan Leybrand & Maria	Heinrich Speck & his wife	Dec. 14 1810
May 2	Anna	Philip Schurck & his wife	Mr. Schurck & Doroth. Mackeltay	Mar. 26 1811
June 2	Anna	Wilhelm Weber & his wife	mother	Feb. 13 1809
June 3	Jacob Valentin	Michael Hofman & his wife	Jacob Hofman & his wife	Mar. 8

FIRST REFORMED CHURCH OF BALTIMORE

Date of Baptism	Name of child	Parents	Witnesses	Date of Birth
June 3	Heinrich	W. Fobel & his wife	Heinrich Morfiliner & wife	Oct. 8 1810
June 3	Rebecca	Nicolaus Keidel & his wife	Michael Fobel	June 3 1810
June 10	Wilhelm Heinrich	Ludewig Reiter & Johanna	parents themselves subst. for Wilhelm Reiter & Heinrich Little?	April 13
June 16	Wilhelm Cutherish	Wilhelm Bauer & Eva	John Stillit & Catharina Reitz or Reily	March 18
June 23	Louisa	Heinrich Becker & Catharina	Philip Muth & Louisa Becker	Jan. 4
June 30	Roxana Louisa	Mr. Karl & Elisabeth	father & Louisa Jacobi	March. 2
June 30	Jacob	Mr. Friburger & his wife	parents	April 15
July 9	Johan	Heinrich Daube & Maria Juliana	parents	Oct. 14 1810
July 14	Anna Margaretha	Herman Neumeier & his wife	parents	June 2
July 16	Heinrich Wilhelm	Heinrich Arnold Wilmsen & Anna Elis.	parents	Aug. 17 1810
July 21	Mariana	Peter Becker & Elisabeth	Maria Wolf	April 14

FIRST REFORMED CHURCH OF BALTIMORE

Date of Baptism	Name of Child	Parents	Witnesses	Date of Birth
July 21	Anna Maria Catharina	William Kemp & Maria Elisabeth	Anna Cath. Keilholtz & Mr. Albrecht	Jan. 11
July 26	Heinrich	Friederich Konig (?) & Elis. nee Getier	Parents	July 11
Aug. 4	Friederich August	Heinrich Rentze & Wilhelmina nee Weber	Friederich August Calenstein & Justina (or Culenstein)	June 11
Aug. 11	Philip	Philip Emig & Elisabeth	Elisabeth Emig	Feb. 19
Aug. 11	Samuel	Heinrich Emig & Elisabeth	Father	June 10 1810
Aug. 11	Elisabeth	Johan Worli & Catharina	Johan Farr	Aug. 8 1810

1812 (it is registered 1811, but that can hardly be possible considering the birth dates)

Mar. 29	Georg Wilhelm	Johan Homrichshaus & Maria	Parents	Oct. 5 1811
Apr. 9	Mariana	Gotfried Feige (or Feigl) & Julia	Valentin Sanders	Dec. 19 1811
Apr. 20	Amilia Jane & Emily Julie	Peter Diefendorfer & his wife	Mich. Diefendorfer, his wife & Mich. Diefendorfer & Daniel's wife	Mar. 26 1812

FIRST REFORMED CHURCH OF BALTIMORE

Date of Baptism	Name of Child	Parents	Witnesses	Date of Birth
May 18	Jacob	Georg Babler & Christina nee Seltzer	Jacob Seltzer & his wife	Apr. 6 1812
May 24	Catharina Susanna	Stephanus Grof & his wife	Parents	Oct. 11 1811
May 25	Susanna	Eduart Wise and Sophia	Grandmother	Mar. 17 1809
May 25	Maria	Eduart Wise and Sophia	Mother	June 5 1811
May 31	Nicolaus	Valentin Lug & Catharina	Nicolaus Schmid & his wife	Apr. 24
June 9	Michael Nicolaus	Johan Diefendorfer	Mother & Nicolaus Jub (Job?)	Apr. 22
June 10	Charlotta Henrietta	Georg Heinrich Otto & Wilhelmina nee Hepfeld	Mr. Domi & Michael Domi	Dec. 29 1811
June 14	Margaratha Catharina	Caspar Zode and wife	Marg. Cath. Zode and Catharina Schreiber	Jan. 8 1812
July 10	Friederich	Friederich Werner & Sara	Parents	Jan. 23
July 14	Jacob	Friederich Detmor & Elisabeth	Parents	July 5 1812

FIRST REFORMED CHURCH OF BALTIMORE

Date of Baptism	Name of Child	Parents	Witnesses	Date of Birth
July 21	Heinrich	Wilhelm Weber & Anna	Mich. Heckman	Jan. 9 1812
July 26	Hetti Henrietta	H. von Kapf and his wife	Parents	Mar. 27 1810
July 26	Johan Bernhard	H. von Kapf and his wife	Parents	Sept. 20 1811
Aug. 2	Carl Alexander	Georg Sprang and Christiana	Carl Wering & Maria Gantz	May 26 1812
Aug. 30	Friederich	David Simon & Catharina	Friederich Kramer & his wife	Mar. 25 1812
Sep. 1	Anna Maria	Carl Volck & Anna Margaretha	Parents	June 26 1812
Sep. 3	Johann	Nikolaus Mathaus (Mathews?) & his wife	Johan Mathaus & his wife	Oct. 2 1811
Sep. 14	Eduart	Joseph Grain and his wife	Parents	Oct. 2 1810
Sep. 14	Georg Washington	Joseph Grain and his wife	Parents	Aug. 20 1811
Sep. 14	Johanna	Samual Mumma & his wife	Mother	Aug. 14 1811
Sep. 20	Elisabeth	Jacob Caspari & Harriet	John Christian Rau Elisabeth	Aug. 1 1812
Oct. 9	Anna Maria	Daniel Gruber & his wife	Maria Kummer (Kramer?) & Heinrich Frey	Mar. 14 1812

FIRST REFORMED CHURCH OF BALTIMORE

Date of Baptism	Name of Child	Parents	Witnesses	Date of Birth
Oct. 15	David Heinrich	Diederich Rottermund & Wilhelmina	David Friederichs & his wife	Sep. 25 1812
Oct. 25	Johannes	Kraft Achenbach & Anna Louisa	Johann Zode and his wife	Aug. 8 1812
Oct. 29	Adelheid Ludovica Maria	James Zwisler Christina	Dr. Ch. L. Buler & Adelheit Becker & Mr. Ganderman (Gunderman?)	Mar. 25 1812
Nov. 1	Catharina	Thomas Ward & Anna Maria	Elisabeth Derr	Sep. 12 1812
Nov. 1	Catharina Maria	John Schmal & Louisa	Catharina Schmal & Maria Zinzerer	Aug. 22 1812
Nov. 26	Sophia	Johan Schmid & Christina	Valentin Sanders & his wife & Sophia Kauder	Sep. 7 1812
Aug. 26	Elisabeth	James Thomson & Sophia	Friederich Koch & his wife	May 12 1811
Aug. 27	David	Michael Kemperling & Christina	Parents	Mar. 10 1811
Sept. 1	Johan Christian	Jacob Lehman & Philippina	Christian Lehman & Margaretha	Mar. 25 1811
Sept. 1	Nelson Adam	Tobias Thomson & Hatti	Mother	Mar. 31 1810

FIRST REFORMED CHURCH OF BALTIMORE

Date of Baptism	Name of child	Parents	Witnesses	Date of Birth
Sep. 8	Anna Maria	Johan Wilhelm & his wife	Parents	May 2 1810
Sep. 28	Sophia Dorothea	Beniamin Bausmann & his wife	Johan Bausman & his wife	Mar. 30 1811
Sep. 10	Elisabeth	Mec. Danner & his wife	Mich. Miller	Jan. 1 1811
Sep. 22	Johan Ludewig	Jacob Seltzer & Maria nee Kreider	Johan Ludewig Seltzer & Miss Seltzer	Sep. 7 1811
Sep. 29	Louisa Catharina	Johan Schmal & Louisa	Wilhelm Rode & Catharina	July 10 1811
Oct. 1	Robert	Robert Faige & Sarah	Mother	July 1 1811
Oct. 6	Johan Thomas & Margareth (twins)	Thomas Bollman & his wife	Johan Michael Ruden Stein for the boy & Margaretha Ruden Stein for the girl	Aug. 30 1811
Oct. 8.	Barbara	Thomas Schmid & Catharina	Michael Lauch	Jan. 22 1811
Oct. 10	Georg Heinrich	William Hall & Maria	Heinrich Habliston & Henrietta Hintze	Aug. 31 1811
Oct. 20	Friederich	Georg Keller & Elisabeth	Parents	July 17 1811
Oct. 27	Johan Heinrich	Georg Weber & Eva Margaretha	Michael Braun	July 30 1811

FIRST REFORMED CHURCH OF BALTIMORE

Date of Baptism	Name of child	Parents	Witnesses	Date of Birth
Oct. 27	Elisabeth (died)	Adam Susrab (or Susnab) & Catharina	Michael Braun	Oct. 20 1811
Oct. 28	Johanna Catharina	Jacob Meky & Maria	Johan Reuter	Mar. 31 1811
Nov. 24	Sophia	Anthony Stimpel & Margaretha	Parents	June 11 1811
Nov. 29	Weily	Caspar Heinrich Peters & Rudy	Johan Schmid & his wife	Nov. 12 1812
Nov. 29	Margaretha	Friederich Wasche & his wife	Parents	Feb. 27 1811
Dec. 22	Sophia	Johan Feige & Nancy	Valentin Sanders & his wife	Oct. 31 1811
1812				
Jan. 1	Carl Ludewig	Johan Spies & Margaretha	Parents	Nov. 3 1811
Jan. 7	Johan David	Josua Lucas & Carolina nee Hostadter	David Trumbo & Henrietta	Dec. 29 1811
Jan. 19	Anna Catharina	Wilhelm Wucke & his wife	Mr. Kramer & his wife	Oct. 11 1811
Feb. 1	Susanna	James Renholtz & his wife	Mother & Adam Schally	Mar. 20 1804
Feb. 1	Catharina Elisabeth	dto.	dto.	Feb. 27 1808

FIRST REFORMED CHURCH OF BALTIMORE

Date of Baptism	Name of child	Parents	Witnesses	Date of Birth
Feb. 5	Jacob	Johan Fush & Catharina	Parents	Nov. 5 1811
Feb. 16	Wilhelm	Mr. Richstein & Frau	Wilhelm Fobel & Mich. Schneider	Dec. 16 1811
Mar. 3	Johan Georg	Georg Schleich & Catharina	John Durian & Maria	Jan. 15 1812
Dec. 27	Wilhelm	John Kepler & Barbara	Mother	Nov. 11 1812
Dec. 27	Carolina	Gregorius Andol & the mother Maria Wright	Carolina Luker	Dec. 3 1812
Dec. 27	Johan Jacob	Jacob Wolf & Elisabeth	John West and his wife	Jan. 11 1812

1813

Date of Baptism	Name of child	Parents	Witnesses	Date of Birth
Jan. 8	Susanna Mathilda	Jacob Wild & his wife	Susanna Monli	Apr. 2 1811
Jan. 20	Ludewig Friederich	Wilhelm Ludewig Reiter & his wife	Parents	Dec. 16 1812
Jan. 24	Elisabeth	Johan Miller & Elisabeth	Wilhelm Miller jun. & Anna Christin	Dec. 23 1812
Feb. 7	Emilia Carolina	Heinrich Berckhaus & Anna	Mother	Feb. 5 1812

FIRST REFORMED CHURCH OF BALTIMORE

Date of Baptism	Name of child	Parents	Witnesses	Date of Birth
Feb. 14	Wilhelmina Henrietta	Georg Reiter & Dorothea Catharina	Heinrich Koch & the mother	Jan. 15
Apr. 12	Margaretha (died April 14th 1913)	Abraham Krup & Margaretha	Parents	Mar. 21
Apr. 18	Johannes	Georg Vogelman & Catharina	Catharina Ewald	Feb. 13
Apr. 25	Sophia	Christian Gelbach & Sarah	Parents	Dec. 14 1812
Apr. 25	Jacob	Hanrich Ewald & Catharina	Georg Vogelman & Catharina	Oct. 16 1812
May 2	Anna Maria	Georg Rodemeier & Maria	Parents	Feb. 8
May 2	Susanna	Michael Hofman & his wife	Parents	Dec. 25 1812
May 2	Abellina	Beniamin Sanders & Maria	Mother	Apr. 22
May 2	Elisabeth	dto.	Mother	about 2 yrs. old
May 4	Christina	Michael Kemperling & Christina	Parents	Dec. 25 1812
May 10	Johannes	Wilhelm Fobel & his wife		Jan. 14

FIRST REFORMED CHURCH OF BALTIMORE

Date of Baptism	Name of child	Parents	Witnesses	Date of Birth
May 30	Margarethe Reid	Charles James & Elisabeth	Elisabeth Ried for Margarethe Ried	Apr. 20 1812
June 6	Catharina	Mr. Eckert & Catharina	Mich. Seltzer	almost 6 yrs. old
June 6	Clara	Wilhelm Flachskamp & Margaretha	Parents	May 15
June 17	James Henrich	Georg Keller & Elisabeth	James Dreiter (Doliker)	Feb. 29
June 20	Margaretha	Johan Fush & his wife	Mother	Jan. 10
June 20	Margaretha	Frantz Riedecke & Magdalena	Sarah Schmid	July 2 1812
June 24	Anna Catharina (died July 8, 1813)	Johan Felix Durst & Fanny	Parents	June 10
June 27	Maria Catharina	Adam Susrab & his wife	Adam Susrab, Sr. and Agnese	May 6
Aug. 1	Juliana	Herman Neumeier & Catharina	Parents	June 6
Aug. 2	Margaretha	John Trieburger (Frieburger?) & his wife	Margarethe Trieburger?	Feb. 1 1809
Aug. 2	James	Johan Frieburger & Nancy	Parents	Mar. 15 1813

FIRST REFORMED CHURCH OF BALTIMORE

Date of Baptism	Name of child	Parents	Witnesses	Date of Birth
Aug. 5	Hans Jacob	Mr. Heudorfer & his wife	Mr. Hassler and Miss Seltzer	Feb. 3 1813
Aug. 5	Johan	John Ebert & Margaretha	Sally Schmid	Aug. 5 1813
Aug. 15	Conrad	Conrad Bergman & his wife	Mr. Johnson	July 31
Aug. 22	Jacob	Peter Panckert & Johanna	Leonard Selger & his wife	May 15
Sep. 5	Wilhelm	William Kamp & his wife	John Kramer & his wife	Feb. 14
Sep. 5	Henrietta	Friederich Pass(?) Philippina	Mother	Feb. 5 1812
Sep. 20	David	John Jordan & Wilhelmina	David Friederichs & his wife	Sep. 5
Sep. 13	David	Mr. Keilholtz & his wife	Father himself & Regina Gauss	June 9 1813
Sep. 22	Friederich	Nikolaus Mattheus and his wife	Mother	Sep. 11
Sep. 25	George Washington (died Sept. 26)	Beniamin Bausman & his wife	John Bausman and his wife	Sep. 18
Sep. 26	Georg	Nikolaus Fortine & Anna Martha	Parents & Maria Hoffman	Sep. 18 1813
Sep. 27	Rosina	John Karl & his wife	Mother	Aug. 8 1813

FIRST REFORMED CHURCH OF BALTIMORE

Date of Baptism	Name of child	Parents	Witnesses	Date of Birth
Oct. 3	Rosina	Peter Becker & Elisabeth	Parents	July 18 1813
Oct. 18	Susanna	Mr. Thomson & his wife	Susanna Woodworth	July 4 1813
Oct. 24	Sophia	Johan Conrad Berghauer & his wife	Sophia Sanders	Aug. 29
Oct. 27	Georg Andreas	Mr. Schafer & his wife	Parents	Sep. 4
Nov. 14	Henrietta	Johan Kramer & his wife	Maria Kramer & Jacob Vantz	Jan. 2
Nov. 22	Maria	Georg Kerr & Magdalena	Michael Derr	June 19
Nov. 24	Elisabeth Maria	Lehman Haps & Catharina	Michael Kohler	Jan. 4
Nov. 28	Wilhelmina Elisabeth	Friederich Waesche & his wife	Father & Wilhelmina Ratien	Jan. 16
Nov. 30	David Rittenhaus	Mr. Voigd & his wife	Mother	May 31 1804
Nov. 30	Georg Washington	Mr. Voigd & his wife	Mother	Nov. 11 1806
Dec. 1	Wilhelm	Friederich Detmor & Elisabeth	Wilhelm Eberwein & Catharina	Nov. 20
Dec. 23	Christiana	Josua Lucas Carolina nee Hostedter	Mich. Hochstedter	Dec. 14

FIRST REFORMED CHURCH OF BALTIMORE

Date of Baptism	Name of child	Parents	Witnesses	Date of Birth
1814				
Jan. 2	Johan Wilhelm	Johan MacDonnel & Catharina	John Miller & Elisabeth & Wilhelm Miller	Oct. 15 1812
Jan. 9	Carl Friederich	Simon Becker & his wife, nee Hammer	Carl Hammer & Friederich Hammer	Oct. 22 1813
Jan. 23	Maria Elisabeth	mother: Sophia Braun father: Esaias Barlet	Mr. Kalckbronner & Maria	Jan. 6 1814
Jan. 23	Anna Maria Charlotta	Jacob Seltzer & Anna Maria	Maria Seltzer	Jan. 12
Jan. 23	Sarah	Mr. Emig & his wife	Peter Weigand & his wife	Dec. 3 1813
Jan. 23	Maria	Georg Emig & Elisabeth	Barbara Emig	Nov. 18 1813
Jan. 23	Jacob	John Pen & Margaretha	Mother	Apr. 18 1813
Jan. 23	Johan	John Pen & Margaretha	Mother	Mar. 31 1809
Feb. 16	Sophia	Jacob Lange & Elisabeth	Parents	Jan. 9 1814
Feb. 19	Anna Maria	Daniel Fobel & Anna	William Fobel & Anna Bock	Sep. 17 1812
Feb. 22	Georg Washington	John Wilhelm & his wife	Parents	Mar. 21 1813
Feb. 24	Allen	Daniel Graber & Nancy	Allen Daellen	Oct. 9 1813

FIRST REFORMED CHURCH OF BALTIMORE

Date of Baptism	Name of child	Parents	Witnesses	Date of Birth
Mar. 6	Eduart Laurentz	Henrich Orth & his wife	Parents	Jan. 4 1813
Mar. 13	Henrietta	Henrich Diel & Elisabeth	Christoph von Hollen & Henrietta	Dec. 7 1813
Mar. 14	Susanna	Abraham Krup & his wife	Parents	Mar. 7
Mar. 21	Lewis	John Kelly & Charlotta	Jakob Yaus (or Gaus) & Catharina	Aug. 26 1813
Mar. 22	Carolina Dorothea	Georg Mercil (or Merril) & Maria	Dorothea Schel	Nov. 11 1812
Mar. 22	Rebecca Catharina	Georg Mercil (or Oracell) & Maria	Mother	May 5 1813
Mar. 24	Johan Jacob	Georg Weber & Margaretha	Maria Elisabeth Braun	Dec. 18 1813
Apr. 6	Sophia	Absalom Chrisbin & his wife	Mich? Laier	Feb. 4 1814
Apr. 3	Elisabeth	Georg Richtstein & Catharina	Elisabeth Wild	Feb. 24 1814
Apr. 3	Carolina Wilhelmina	Nicolaus Hacke & Sophia	Heinrich Wilhelm Alers & Carolina Poppin	Dec. 22 1813
Apr. 17	Michel Philip	Friederich German & Anna	Philip German & his wife	Mar. 18 1814

FIRST REFORMED CHURCH OF BALTIMORE

Date of Baptism	Name of child	Parents	Witnesses	Date of Birth
Apr. 26	James Hackeus?	John Feige & Nancy	Parents	Oct. 17 1813
May 8	Milton Job	Philip Reigert & Sophia nee Diefendorfer	Nicolaus Job & Mich. Diefendorfer	Apr. 4 1814
May 18	Charles Rogers	John Diefendorfer & his wife	Parents	Apr. 7 1814
May 30	Carl	Valentin Luz(?) & Catharina	Dr. Carl Hintze & Henrietta	Apr. 2
June 5	Johan Beniamin	Johan Schmal & Louisa	Beniamin Kohlstadt & Elisabeth	Apr. 14
June 19	Johan	Abraham Biddel & Elisabeth	Richard Biddel & Eva Maria	Jan. 8
July 5	Juliana	Jacob Bare & his wife	Parents	May 25 1813
July 10	Maria Johanna	Johan Levon & Carolina	Friederich Brauer & Maria Faust	June 6
July 10	Veronica	Felix Durst & Veronica	Parents	May 15
July 10	Anna Catharina	Michael Hofman & his wife	Henrich Cocher & his wife	May 1
July 13	Georg	Georg Schleig & Catharina	Georg Konig	April 12

FIRST REFORMED CHURCH OF BALTIMORE

Date of Baptism	Name of child	Parents	Witnesses	Date of Birth
July 26	Jacob	Jacob Banckert & Maria	Parents	Dec. 23 1813
Aug. 4	Wilhelm Friederich	Herman Bremerman & Amalie	Wilhelm Brand	May 27
Oct. 17	Julia Elisabeth	Friederich Focke & his wife	Julia Frese	Aug. 8
Oct. 18	Fanny	Friederich Warner & his wife	Parents	Mar. 16
Dec. 26	Isabella	Georg Sprung & Christina	Mr. Orth	Oct. 25
Dec. 28	Ludewig Bernhard	Heinrich Maier & Elisabeth	Parents	Feb. 13 1808
Dec. 28	Otilia	"	"	Nov. 9 1809
Dec. 28	Albert	"	"	Feb. 11 1812
Dec. 28	Heinrich	"	"	Apr. 11
Dec. 28	Georg	Georg Babler & Christina	Michael Seltzer	Sep. 16

1815

Date of Baptism	Name of child	Parents	Witnesses	Date of Birth
Jan. 1	Georg	Mr. Reiter & his wife	Parents	Dec. 20 1814
Jan. 4	Johan Gregorius	Gregorius Hadke(?) & his wife	Johan Heinrich Wolf	Nov. 15 1814

FIRST REFORMED CHURCH OF BALTIMORE

Date of Baptism	Name of child	Parents	Witnesses	Date of Birth
Jan. 7	Nicolaus Jacob	Nicolaus Lehman & Elisabeth	Jacob Lehman & his wife	Dec. 27 1814
Jan. 7	Elisabeth	Georg Ricks & his wife	Parents	July 7 1814
Jan. 12	Anna Maria	Louisa Hachenbach (Hasenbeg?)	Maria Elisabeth Jordan	Dec. 11 1803
Mar. 27	Dorothea	Mr. Shafer & his wife	Dorothea Shrad	Feb. 12
Apr. 13	Maria Elisabeth	Wilson Yous	Mich. Dornbusch Joseph Wand & Mich. Richard	Feb. 7 1813
May 7	Georg Carl	Georg Rotemeier & his wife	Georg Stein	Feb. 9
May 28	Sarah Anna	Georg Grob & Margaretha	Sarah Eichler	Jan. 3 1814
June 4	Carl	Henrich Frieburger & his wife	Father	June 15 1814
June 5	Josephus Jacobus	Mr. Caspari & his wife	Parents	Aug. 1 1814
June 6	Georg	Georg Fogelman & Catharina	Parents	Feb. 25
June 15	Anna Maria	Martin Gruber & Elisabeth	Jacob Gruber & his wife	May 7 1815
June 28	Sarah (died June 30)	John Kepler & his wife	Mother	May 26

FIRST REFORMED CHURCH OF BALTIMORE

Date of Baptism	Name of child	Parents	Witnesses	Date of Birth
July 16	Heinrich	Elisabeth Wygant father presumably Heinrich Walter	Mother	Aug. 28 1814
July 16	Jacob Forney	Stephanus Groff & his wife	Parents	Apr. 2
July 16	Carl	Mr. Keilholtz & his wife	Leopold Donsca & his wife	Nov. 8 1814
July 30	Maria	Jacob Boyer & Margaretha	Mich. Boyer	June 19
Aug. 3	Johan David	Johan David Graber & his wife	Parents	June 17
Aug. 3	Margaretha (died Aug. 4)	Wilhelm Flachskamp & Maria	Mich. Hoffman	July 21
Aug. 8	William Henrich	David Peters and Sarah	Mother	Oct. 7 1814
Sep. 24	Jacob	Mr. Putzhard & his wife	John Richstein & his wife	July 3
Oct. 17	Emilie (died)	H. von Kapf and his wife	Mich. Dedier	Sep. 19
Oct. 17	Wilhelm	Nicolaus Matthaus & his wife	Parents	Oct. 7
Oct. 25	Maria Anna	Richard Luis (or Suis) & his wife	Phillipina Britton	Sep. 17

FIRST REFORMED CHURCH OF BALTIMORE

Date of Baptism	Name of child	Parents	Witnesses	Date of Birth
Oct. 29	Georg	Christian Spies & Nancy	Georg Spies	Oct. 29
Nov. 12	Wilhelmina Elisabeth	Herman Bremerman & Amalie	Elisabeth Corrolving	Aug. 23
Nov. 13	Juliana	James Mekim & his wife	Mother	July 8 1814
Nov. 19	John Beniamin	Johan Kraut & Elisabeth	Beniamin Gottlieb Wals & Christiophina Rosina	Sep. 8
Nov. 26	Anna Maria	John Jordan & his wife	Mr. Friederichs & his wife	Oct. 30
Dec. 10	Anna Christina	Herman Neumeier & his wife	Parents	Aug. 1
Dec. 24	Wilhelm Friederich	Wilhelm Kamp & his wife	Friederich Kramer, Sen. & his wife	Apr. 15
Dec. 24	Mariana Elisabeth	Friederich Kramer, Jr. & Maria	Robert Parkersen & Elisabeth	Jan. 24 1814
Dec. 25	Abraham	Peter Banckert & his wife	Nikolaus Dill	Nov. 6
1816				
Jan. 1	Valentin	Valentin Luz & his wife	Parents	Nov. 2 1810
Jan. 14	Michael	Michael Kemperling & his wife	Parents	Nov. 10 1815

FIRST REFORMED CHURCH OF BALTIMORE

Date of Baptism	Name of child	Parents	Witnesses	Date of Birth
Jan. 14	Anna Maria	Henrich Frey & Elisabeth	Parents	May 17 1811
Jan. 14	Lusiana Henrietta	" "	"	Feb. 6 1813
Jan. 14	Rebecca Sophia	" "	"	Feb. 24 1815
Jan. 14	Ferdinand	Carl Fuhrman & Margaretha	Cardo Bald Martin Metti & Catharina Stuver	Oct. 2 1815
Jan. 21	Elisabeth	Mr. Schmal & Louisa	Elisabeth Kochin	Dec. 11 1815
Jan. 26	Jacob & Magdalena (twins)	Jacob Dobler & Magdalena	Parents	Jan. 26
Feb. 6	Johannes	John West & his wife	Parents	Dec. 28 1815
Feb. 17	Johannes	Thomas Ward & Anna Maria	Mich. Derr	Jan. 4
Mar. 4	Jacob	Jacob Rotter & Johanna	Michael Rottermeier	Feb. 5
Mar. 10	Catharina Justina	Felix Durst & Veronica	Christoph Miller & Justina	Feb. 11
Mar. 14	Thomas Kean (died Mar.14,1816)	John Mellack & his wife	Parents	Sep. 25 1815
Mar. 17	Heinrich Fenelon	Philip Reigart (or Roigart) & Sophia	John Diefendorfer & Eva Albers	Feb. 10

FIRST REFORMED CHURCH OF BALTIMORE

Date of Baptism	Name of child	Parents	Witnesses	Date of Birth
Mar. 17	Rebecca	Nicolaus Hacke & Sophia	Mother	Nov. 28 1815
Mar. 31	Christina	Jacob Seltzer & his wife	Christina Badler	Mar. 28
Apr. 7	Elisabeth	Christian Gelbach & his wife	Parents	Nov. 13 1815
Apr. 10	Wilhelm	Georg Schleig & his wife	Parents	Jan. 31
Apr. 13	Mariana	Adam Susrab & his wife	Beniamin Siller & Catharina	Apr. 11
Apr. 28	Maria Catharina	Johan Miller & Elisabeth	Wilehlm Miller & Maria Catharina	July 27 1815
May 23	Thomas	Georg Lucas & his wife	Mich. Andree	Mar. 13
June 1	Franciscus	Frantz Riedesel(?) & Maria	Mother	Feb. 7 1814
June 2	Louisa	Georg Kaf & his wife	Grandmother	Nov. 10 1815
June 3	Catharina	Peter Becker & his wife	Valentin Luz & Catharina	Mar. 2
June 12	Johannes	Daniel Fobel & his wife	Mr. Bock & his wife	May 28 1814
June 16	Johan Georg Lochman	Michael Hoffman & his wife	Parents	Dec. 17 1815

FIRST REFORMED CHURCH OF BALTIMORE

Date of Baptism	Name of child	Parents	Witnesses	Date of Birth
July 6	Margaretha	Peter Stein & Sophia	Margaretha Zode	Jan. 17
July 13	Johannes	Jacob Lange & Sarah	Parents	Jan. 27
July 14	Uronia	Eduart Louis & his wife	Mich. Britton	Mar. 25
July 25	David Friederich	Mr. Reiter & his wife	Parents	May 28
July 26	Anna Elisabeth	Nicolaus Mattheus & his wife	Mother	July 5
July 29	Heinrich	Heinrich Graf & Catharina	Parents	Apr. 21
Aug. 21	Wilhelm	Michel Hoffman & his wife	Parents	May 25
Sep. 1	Johan Francis	William Biels & his wife	Mother	June 29
Sep. 9	Louisa	David Batterson & his wife	Parents	May 16
Sep. 9	Maria	Georg Batterson & his wife	Maria Peters	June 12
Sep. 11	Mariana	Christian Hiants(?) & Maria	Mich. Gruber	Feb. 24
Sep. 21	Susanna	Georg Fogelman & Catharina	Parents	July 24

FIRST REFORMED CHURCH OF BALTIMORE

Date of Baptism	Name of child	Parents	Witnesses	Date of Birth
Sep. 24	Mariana	Eduard Rodin & Jane	Mother	Jan. 31
Sep. 27	Maria	Jacob Magi & his wife	Mother	Oct. 10 1816
Oct. 13	Margaretha	John Neit & Catharina	Mother	Apr. 15 1815
Oct. 13	Jacob Thomas & Wilhelm Alexander (twins)	"	"	Aug. 18
Nov. 5	Johan	Carl Volck & his wife	Johan Eckert & his wife	Sep. 10 1815
Nov. 16	Elisabeth Margaretha	Joseph Dreier & Catharina	Friederich Busch & Mich. Schmal	Apr. 25
Nov. 21	Thomas	Thomas Schmid & his wife	Parents	May 1
Nov. 21	Margaretha	Thomas Schmid & his wife	Parents	Mar. 6 1813
Dec. 4	William	Mr. Yous & his wife	Mother	Jan. 2
Dec. 9	Johan	Johan Kramer, jr. & his wife	Grandmother of the child	Apr. 15 1815
Dec. 9	Georg	"	"	Oct. 7
Dec. 24	William	Hart van Neukirch & his wife	Mother	May 31 1814
Dec. 24	Maria	"	"	Aug. 14

FIRST REFORMED CHURCH OF BALTIMORE

Date of Baptism	Name of child	Parents	Witnesses	Date of Birth
1818				
Jan. 4	Adeline	Johan Wilhelm & his wife	Parents	Aug. 11 1815
Jan. 4	Eleonora	"	"	Nov. 6 1817
Jan. 15	Jacob	Ludewig Schneider & Christian	Parents	Sep. 18 1810
Jan. 15	Elisabeth	"	"	Feb. 22 1814
Jan. 15	Jacob	"	"	Sep. 12 1816
Jan. 15	Jacob	John Selber & his wife	Mother	July 11 1805
Feb. 1	Georg Alexander	Peter Wilhelm & his wife	Georg Rodemeier & his wife	Nov. 14 1817
Feb. 1	Henrietta	Jacob Schunck or Schurek & his wife	Mich. Schunck	Jan. 5
Feb. 12	Anna Margaretha	Abraham Kaup & his wife	Parents	Feb. 2
Feb. 12	Carl	Georg Keller & his wife	Parents	Jan. 1
Feb. 13	Jacob Alexander	Johan Berger & his wife	Mother	June 18 1817

FIRST REFORMED CHURCH OF BALTIMORE

Date of Baptism	Name of child	Parents	Witnesses	Date of Birth
Feb. 22	Johan Ulrich	Felix Durst & Vrene	Mathias Blatner & Vrena Blatner & the father of the child	Nov. 21 1817
Mar. 8	Sophia Christiana	Philip Reigert & Sophia	Catharina Diefendorfer	Jan. 25
Mar. 9	Mariana (died March 10)	Mr. Duhurst & his wife	Mich. Weber	Mar. 3
Mar. 15	Tobias Wolf	Valentin Lutz & Catharina	Mich. Wolf	Apr. 6 1817
Apr. 30	Wilhelm	Jacob Suter & Maria	Parents	Mar. 17
May 3	Anna Elisabeth	Ludewig Seltzer & his wife	Anna Elisabeth Nippert	Feb. 28
May 11	Wilhelm Hermann	Johan Miller & Elisabeth	Johan Herrman & Maria	Nov. 19 1817
May 11	Ernst	Georg Schleig & his wife	Ernst Schleig & his wife	Jan. 10
May 14	Johan Henrich	Daniel Graber & Anna	August Teglmeyer, Johan Friederich Benseman & Justina Maria Muller	Nov. 7 1817
May 27	James	John Nosher & his wife	Mother	Sep. 26 1815

FIRST REFORMED CHURCH OF BALTIMORE

Date of Baptism	Name of child	Parents	Witnesses	Date of Birth
May 27	Eduart	John Nosher & his wife	Mother	Sep. 7 1817
July 13	John Peter	Peter Becker & his wife	Parents	Apr. 6
July 26	Johanna Amalia Maria	Henry Bersh & Maria	Parents	June 29
Aug. 2	David	Peter Bankert & Anna	Parents	Apr. 14
Aug. 2	Anthony Henry	Herman Bremerman & Amelia	Anthony Shofer & Anna	June 16
Aug. 7	Henry Williams	Michael Kimberly & Christina	Mother	Dec. 23 1817
Aug. 15	William	David Simon & Katherine	Maria Kemp	Mar. 16
Aug. 15	Katharine Elisabeth	William Kemp & Maria	Katherine Simon	Aug. 11 1817
Aug. 17	Anna Maria	John Smith & Christina	Henrich Simonich & Elisabeth Kouderer	Mar. 2
Aug. 17	Henrich	George Kouderer & & Elisabeth	John Smith & Katharine Richtstein	Jan. 1 1815
Sep. 28	Wilhelm Henrich	Michael Hoffman & Marya	Parents	Aug. 1818
Sep. 28	Marya Elisabeth	Erasimus Uhler & Catharina	Parents	—

FIRST REFORMED CHURCH OF BALTIMORE

Date of Baptism	Name of child	Parents	Witnesses	Date of Birth
Dec. 20	Susanna Maxill Barbara	John Jerimer? Myers & Susanna	Parents	Nov. 4 1817
Dec. 20	Mary Ann Maxell	Rich. Dieffenderffer & Charlotte	Parents	Nov. 1
Dec. 20	Ann Elisabeth	"	"	Nov. 1
Dec. 20	Sophia Barbara	Jacob Bier & Susanna	Catharina Bier	Jan. 28

The following children were baptized by Albert Helfenstein, after he begun his ministry on April 4, 1819:

1819

1819	Luisa	Robert Lawson & Sarah	Parents	Feb. 12
May 19	Joh. Britton	Michael Schweitzer & Sophia	Maria Sophia Britton (Grandmother)	May 15
May 20	Susanna Dorothea	Wilhelm Ludwig Reiter & Susanna	Susanna Littel	Apr. 4
May 23	Caleb	John Wehr & Elisabeth	Parents	Nov. 10 1818
May 23	July Ann	George Rodemayer & Mary	Parents	Jan. 22

FIRST REFORMED CHURCH OF BALTIMORE

Date of Baptism	Name of child	Parents	Witnesses	Date of Birth
June 6	Eliza Ann	Jacob Winkelhausen & Henrietta	Henry Dukeheart & Mary Ann	Apr. 14
July 1	Heinrich Hoffman	John Retgreve & Elizabeth	Polly Hoffman	May 2
-	Luisa	Fredrick Sinsner & Luisa	Parents	May 19
July 6	Robert	Georg Patterson & Elisabeth	Mary Peters	Mar. 13
July 11	William French	Carter A. Hall	Parents	June 21
July 21	Mary Jain	Jacob Ritter & Hanna	Mena Schmidt	June 23
July 27	Emmeline Mathilda	Philip Reigart & Sophia	Parents	June 16
Aug. 3	Maria	Adam Sussnop & Cath.	Eliz. Ditmore	July 21
Aug. 15	Louis William	Nicolaus Lehman & Margaretha	Louis Pascault & Mary	Mar. 8
Aug. 20	Georg	Georg Ernst & Maria	Parents	Jan. 28
Oct. 18	Heinrich	Heinrich Kersch & Maria	Parents	Aug. 4

FIRST REFORMED CHURCH OF BALTIMORE

Date of Baptism	Name of child	Parents	Witnesses	Date of Birth
Nov. 6	Sybilla	Leonhard Wampler or Wamssler & Maria	Parents	Mar. 15
Nov. 6	Henrietta	Hermann Neumayer & Catharina	Parents	Mar. 15 1817
Nov. 22	Edward	Gustavus Anderson & Nancy	Joh. Gillard	Nov. 15
Dec. 2	Susanna Decker			
Dec. 2	Sarah Gross(?)	(both are adults)		
Dec. 26	Johan Jacob	Jacob Gruber & Anna Maria	Jacob Gruber & Anna Maria	Feb. 7

1820

Date of Baptism	Name of child	Parents	Witnesses	Date of Birth
Jan. 1	Michael	Michael Hoffman & his wife	Parents	—
Feb. 18	July Ann	Nicholaus Haike & Sophia	Mother	July 5 1819
Feb. 27	Ann Elizabeth	Fielding van Horn & Catharine	Parents	—
Mar. 4	Jacob	Conrad Bergman & Elizabeth	Parents	Nov. 4 1819
Mar. 5	Anna Maria	Jacob Boyer & Margaretha	Parents	Feb. 16
Mar. 5	Sarah Ann	John Kuner(s) & Margaret or Keener	Parents	Sep. 4 1819

FIRST REFORMED CHURCH OF BALTIMORE

Date of Baptism	Name of child	Parents	Witnesses	Date of Birth
Mar. 19	Sophia Amalia	Anthony Schaeffer & Maria	Sophia Maria Bremerman	Feb. 17 1819
Apr. 4	Jacob	Jacob Braun & Mary	Jacob Braun, Cath. Misler	Nov. 4 1819
Apr. 4	Johan Heinrich	Jacob Braun & Mary	Johan Heinrich Braun & Maria Elis.	Feb. 29
Apr. 17	Elizabeth Ann	William Root & Sarah	Elizabeth Mumma	Mar. 10 1819
Apr. 17	Elizabeth	John Mumma & Elizabeth	Elizabeth Mumma	Sep. 5 1819
Apr. 17	William Henry	Joseph Jost & Ann	Mrs. Chrish	March
— /	Margaret	Georg Ruhstein (Richstein?) & Cath.	Christopher von Hollen & Amalia	July 10 1819
May 21	John George	Jacob Lehman & Ketura	Jacob Lehman & Philippina	Mar. 26
May 22	John Frederick Christopher	Bernhard John von Kap & Hetty Henriette	Parents	Apr. 25
May 23	Elisabeth	Felix Durst(?) & Frena	Parents	Feb. 11
June 12	Irma Cath.	Abraham Knugg & Margaretha	Parents	May 31
June 24	Susanna Catharina	Henry Groff & Catharina	Parents	June 11

FIRST REFORMED CHURCH OF BALTIMORE

Date of Baptism	Name of child	Parents	Witnesses	Date of Birth
June 24	Mary	Nicholas Elliot & Elisabeth	Parents	Dec. 7 1819
July 26	Joseph	Henry Neukirch & Catharina	Father	July 24
July 30	John Jackson	Christian Gelbach & Cath.	Parents	June 12
Aug. 9	Herman	Herman Neumayer & Cath.	Parents	Dec. 30
Aug. 31	Rebecca Frederica	Fredrick Focke & Aletta	Justus Hoppe	May 25 1818
Aug. 31	Edward Lewis	"	"	Aug. 12
Oct. 27	Mary or Mary Ann	Edward Lewis & Ann Maria	Maria Philippa Britton	June 30
Nov. 27	William	Henry Bersh & Mary	Parents	Oct. 22
Dec. 5	Francis George	Francis Gatechaier & Mary	Mother	Aug. 7
Dec. 5	Rebecca Marbaret	John Etchberger & Aley	Mother	Oct. 25
Dec. 7	Henry	George Rodenmayer & Mary	Parents	Sep. 24
Dec. 8	Nicolaus	Nicolaus Mathias & Elisabeth	Mother	Feb. 4

FIRST REFORMED CHURCH OF BALTIMORE 133

Date of Baptism	Name of child	Parents	Witnesses	Date of Birth
1816				
June 23	Otilia Margaretha	Conrad Bergman & his wife	Nicolaus Lehman Mich. Dufeld & Adelheid Becker	Feb. 29
July 29	Johan Robert	Mr. Waddel & Margaretha	Johan Jost Zude(Zode?) & Elisabeth Schmid	Apr. 22
Aug. 9	Heinrich	Johan Berger & Maria	Anna Bernhard	Aug. 6 1815
Aug. 11	Maria & Juliana (twins)	John Schmid and his wife	Friederich Kramer sen. & Mich. Richstein	Aug. 7 1815
Aug. 13	Mariana	Jacob Humel & his wife	Mother	Mar. 1
Aug. 16	Johannes (died Aug. 20)	Jacob Comfort & Juliana	Father	Aug. 3
Aug. 20	David	Jacob Krauss & Elisabeth	Mother	Dec. 29 1815
Aug. 22	Wilhelm Heinrich	Fuling Onehorn & Catharina	Mother	Aug. 24 1814
Aug. 22	Anna Catharina (died Aug. 24)	"	Mother	July 10
Aug. 23	Sarah Anna & Nancy (twins)	George Keller & his wife	Parents	May 29 1815

FIRST REFORMED CHURCH OF BALTIMORE

Date of Baptism	Name of child	Parents	Witnesses	Date of Birth
Sep. 8	Wilhelm	Mathies Sinclair & Elisabeth	Parents	Apr. 7 1813
Sep. 8	Elisabeth	Mathies Sinclair & Elisabeth	Parents	May 15
Sep. 30	Johan Robert	Johan Diefendorfer & his wife	Parents	Aug. 14
Oct. 3	Charlotta	Georg Babler & Christina	Charlotta Bentz	Sep. 22
Oct. 10	Johan Friederich	Friederich Focke & his wife	Johan Friederich Frese & Rebecca	Aug. 19
Oct. 12	Friederich	Christian Kramer & Margaretha	Friederich Kramer & his wife	June 8 1815
Oct. 12	Jacob	David Simon & his wife	Friederich Kramer & his wife	July 2
Oct. 27	Elisabeth	Philip Schunck & Sophia	Philip German & Margaretha Marry (Murry?)	Aug. 30
Nov. 11	Susanna Rebecca	Wilhelm Fobel & his wife	Cecilia Stautz	July 10 1815
Dec. 15	Heinrich Ludewig	Jacob Boyer & Margaretha	Parents	Dec. 4
Dec. 22	Georg	Johan Kepler & Barbara	Parents	Aug. 4

FIRST REFORMED CHURCH OF BALTIMORE

Date of Baptism	Name of child	Parents	Witnesses	Date of Birth
Dec. 22	Anna Maria	Martin Weisbach & Esther	Parents	Feb. 4

1817

Date of Baptism	Name of child	Parents	Witnesses	Date of Birth
Jan. 1	Anna Elisabeth	Georg Breneisen & Margaretha	Parents	July 6 1811
Jan. 1	Bernhard	"	"	Apr. 26 1813
Jan. 1	Jacob Morris	"	"	Jan. 19 1815
Jan. 1	Hyronimus	"	"	Oct. 29 1816
Jan. 1	Wilhelm Tell	Peter Spies & his wife	Parents	May 4 1816
Jan. 26	Agnes	Georg Grob & Margaretha	Parents	May 14 1816
Jan. 30	Anna Maria	Georg Weber & his wife	Jacob Braun & Maria	Sep. 14 1816
Feb. 17	Elisabeth Dilly Wilson (Black children)	Martin Hamilton & his wife	Parents	Apr. 19 1816
Feb. 21	Anna Maria	Ludwig Seltzer & his wife	Mich. Seltzer	Feb. 7
Feb. 26	Adline	Henrich Welshofer & Maria	Mother	Apr. 4 1812
Feb. 26	Elisabeth	"	"	Dec. 4 1814

FIRST REFORMED CHURCH OF BALTIMORE

Date of Baptism	Name of child	Parents	Witnesses	Date of Birth
Feb. 26	Wilhelm Henrich	Henrich Welshofer & Maria	Mother	Sep. 18 1816
Mar. 16	Louisa	Johan Schmal & his wife	Parents	Jan. 8
Mar. 20	Jacob	Carl Fuhrman & Margaretha	Maria Friederichs	Mar. 2 1812
Mar. 25	Georg Friederich	Friderich Krieg(?) & Elisabeth	Georg Eberhard & Magdalena Grun	Jan. 10
Mar. 27	Johan	Mr. Gatschler & his wife	Mother	Apr. 1815
Apr. 1	Johan Jacob	Martin Gruber & his wife	Jacob Stick & Elisabeth Gruber	Feb. 26
Apr. 4	Christoph Gerhard	Christoph Keller & Anna Louisa		Mar. 5 1812
Apr. 13	Wilhelm Andreas	Georg Rodemeier & his wife	Parents	Nov. 30 1816
Apr. 13	Anna Sophia	Herman Bremerman & his wife	Mr. Gunderman & Sophia Depen	Feb. 9
Apr. 27	Henrietta & Philippina (twins)	Dr. Dellet & his wife	Johanna Wilcke & Carolina Jordan	June 3 1816
May 4	Anna Catharina	Peter Weigand & Mariana	Parents	Dec. 26 1816

FIRST REFORMED CHURCH OF BALTIMORE

Date of Baptism	Name of child	Parents	Witnesses	Date of Birth
May 4	Christian	Nikolaus Lehman & Margaretha	Christian Lehman	Jan. 22
May 4	Mariana	George Reck & Maria	Parents	Aug. 19 1816
May 6	August	Georg Keller & Elisabeth	Parents	Apr. 26
May 26	1) Jacob Hardy	Mr. Benniwel & his wife	Parents	−
	2) Leydi Schally			−
	3) James Baly			−
	4) Schally Kelim			−
	5) Elisabeth Burr			−
May 1	Friederica	Mr. Jordan & his wife	David Friederichs & his wife	Mar. 26
June 4	Susanna	Mr. Kohler & his wife	Parents	3 yrs. & 6 mos. old
June 4	Carolina Sophia	Mr. Kohler & his wife	Parents	Mar. 14
June 16	Andreas	Andreas Uhl Catharina	Mother	June 28 1816
June 19	Jacob	Jacob Seltzer & his wife	Father	June 12
June 29	Catharina Elisabeth	Ludewig Schroder & Maria	Parents	Aug. 31 1816
June 29	Mariana	Georg Richtstein & his wife	Maria Patterson	Apr. 9

FIRST REFORMED CHURCH OF BALTIMORE

MARRIAGE RECORDS OF THE
FIRST & ST. STEPHENS UNITED CHURCH OF CHRIST
(Formerly the First Reformed Church of Baltimore)

Date:	Names:	Address:
1806		
Feb. 6	Johann Metstruff to Anna Kromer	
Apr. 13	Adam Sisnop to Catherine Brown	
July 27	Georg Henry to Elisabeth Dick	of Baltimore County
Aug. 5	Abraham Sitter to Cornelia Wech (or Wechz)	of Baltimore
Aug. 16	Friderich Wilhelm Meyer to Salome Miller	of Baltimore County
Aug. 17	Heinrich Allisen to Catharina Benson	
Sept. 23	Georg Coock to Rebecca Schrein	of Baltimore
Oct. 12	Johan Hablitz (or Hublitz) to Elisabeth Pott	
Oct. 26	Jacob Lange to Anna Elizabeth Britten	
Dec. 30	John Foy to Anna Hawking	of Baltimore County
1807		
Feb. 8	Johan Heinrich Becker to Anna Catharina Welsch	of Baltimore County
March 23	Herrman Schneider to Rebecca Fletscher	of Baltimore County
May 18	Michel Warnecke to Beta Hormans	
May 21	Wilhelm Rothe to Anna Catharina Osterlohr	
May 24	Georg Walther Hood to Susanna Gibbs	
May 26	Jacob Wilt to Margaretha Clim (or Cline)	
June 11	Friderich Hammer to Margaretha Augustin	of Baltimore
June 14	Jacob Ritter to Anna Weck	
Aug. 31	Georg Wien to Mary Schmith	
Sept. 3	Georg Jacob to Sarah Anna Reiser	of Baltimore
Oct. 6	Andreas Hildebrandt to Catherina Caplern	
Oct. 13	Georg Koller to Elisabeth Schweitzer	of Baltimore
Oct. 26	Abraham Busch to widow Catharina Haber	
Oct. 29	Friederich Fige to Juliana Murray	of Baltimore

FIRST REFORMED CHURCH OF BALTIMORE

Dec. 15	Johan Kramer to Elisabeth Beilefeld	of Baltimore
Dec. 17	Nicolaus Fortune to Anna Burman (or Borman)	of Baltimore
Dec. 20	Georg Stoll to Maria Warner	of Baltimore

1808

Jan. 12	Conrad Birgman to Elisabeth Uyssnel (?)	of Baltimore
Jan. 14	Valentin Lutz to Catherina Wolf	of Baltimore
Mar. 13	Peter Becker to Elizabeth Wolf	of Baltimore
Feb. 9	Andreas Hitt to Sarah Meiers	of Baltimore
May 22	Georg Bange to Elisabeth Brungart	of Baltimore
Aug. 30	William Gough to Rachel Parks	of Baltimore
Oct. 25	Rev. Wilhelm Dechant to Rebecca Andree (?)	
Nov. 16	Johan Schweitzer to Elisabeth Miller	of Baltimore
Nov. 29	Christian Harpt to Latheysy Ensly	of Baltimore
Dec. 1	Christian Zingling to Johanna Weber	of Baltimore
Dec. 1	Michel Kemperling to Christina Nicholas	of Baltimore
Dec. 6	Gerhart Topken to the widow Johanna Pauli	
Dec. 28	Diederich Rotermund	of Bremen
	to the widow Wilhemina Schmachtenbergs (or Schmachtenberger)	of Baltimore

1809

Jan. 11	Friederich Wisotzky to Elisabeth Schmids	of Baltimore
Mar. 23	John Dunning to Maria Magdalena Stock	of Baltimore
Mar. 23	Anthony Stimpel to Margaretha Locher	of Baltimore
Apr. 16	Heinrich Ewerwein to Sarah Baxter	of Baltimore
May 22	Georg Spleich to Catharina Konig	of Baltimore
July 9	Michael Domini to Maria Braun	of Baltimore
July 16	John Alsfelt to Elisabeth Thiels	of Baltimore

July 23	Johan Schmal to Louisa Rossmeier (?)	of Baltimore
July 25	Salomon Benjamin to Catharina Lexee (?)	of Baltimore
July 30	Georg Capito to Irene Blatin	of Baltimore
Aug. 10	Fransiscus Bange to Catharina Zahner	of Baltimore
Sept. 1	Friederich Coack to Elisabeth Scharding or Schanding	of Baltimore
Sept. 18	Thomas Newman to Catharina Towsans	of Baltimore
Sept. 20	Erasmus Johnson to Anna Margaretha Huth	of Baltimore
Oct. 28	Heinrich Griffer to Anna Maria Geiser	of Baltimore County
Nov. 16	John Dohm to Elisabeth Hartman	of Baltimore
Dec. 21	Johan Jost Zadi to Margaretha Hildebrand	

1810

Mar. 29	Wilhems de (von) Clot to Catharina Spies	
Apr. 18	Justus Willer (n) to Maria Elisabeth Korrelvink	of Baltimore County
May 22	Nicolaas Matthews to Elisabeth Miller	of Baltimore
May 29	Johannes Berger to Maria Freyer	of Baltimore
June 8	Nicolaus Nickolson to Catherina Swears	of Baltimore
June 14	John Eilert to Catharina Haley or Kaley	of Baltimore
July 2	Ludewig Reiter to Johanna Little	of Baltimore
July 8	Franciscus Ridesel to Magdalena Yannaway	of Baltimore
Sept. 4	Jacob Selser to Marie Creider	of Baltimore
Sept. 20	Heinrich Rentze to Wilhelmina Weber	of the city
Sept. 25	Johan Christian Hildebrand to Rebecca Logus	of Baltimore
Nov. 25	Georg Breuning to Julian Barcker, widow	

1811

Jan. 29	Adam Dunbecker to Elizabeth Seumering	of Baltimore County

FIRST REFORMED CHURCH OF BALTIMORE

Jan. 30	Johan Eckert to Elisabeth Rhoad	of Baltimore County
Jan. 30	Johan Youston to Wilhelmina Loudergoung (or Louderoung)	of Baltimore County
Feb. 19	Franciscus von Durnbury to Marie Kreiter	of Baltimore County
Mar. 5	Georg Fogelman to Catherina Ewald	of Baltimore County
Apr. 22	Heinrich Welshofer to Maria Herr	of Baltimore County
Apr. 22	Jacob Caspari to Harriat Lepner	of Baltimore County
May 12	Mathias Kisler to Christina Lester	of Baltimore County
June 10	Abraham Ingles to Charity Prawbaugh	of Baltimore County
June 18	Georg King to Susanna Earing	of Baltimore County
July 4	Georg Babler to Christina Seltzer	of Baltimore County
Sept. 26	Johan Ellen to Anna Maria Braunin	of Baltimore
Sept. 29	John Knop	of Virginia
	to Maria Zoller (?)	of Baltimore
Nov. 28	Georg Sauer to Helena Metzger	of Yorck County

1812

Feb. 11	Andreas Uhl to Catherina Banckert	of Baltimore
Feb. 13	John Nicolaus Miller to Elizabeth Christin	of Baltimore
June 16	William Fachskorn to Margaretha Craig	of Baltimore
June 25	Abraham Knup to widow Margaretha Laronetto	of Baltimore
July 21	Cuerdo de Balke to Maria Defare (or Defano)	of Baltimore
Aug. 2	Georg Sprung to Christiana Hasin	of Baltimore
Sept. 24	Johan Felix Durst to Fanny Blatner	of Baltimore
Oct. 11	Daniel Graeber (or Gruler) to Nancy Frey	dto.
Nov. 26	Christopher Schiller to Rebecca Buschen	dto.
Dec. 6	Nicolaus Lehman to Elisabeth Gibsen	dto.

FIRST REFORMED CHURCH OF BALTIMORE

1813
- Feb. 3 — Heinrich Weaver to Dorothea Macelroy — of Baltimore
- Apr. 9 — Friederich Pien to Philippina Maurer — dto.
- Apr. 18 — Henrich Deal to widow Elisabeth Pien — dto.
- May 13 — Philip Reigard to Sophia Diefendorfer — dto.
- July 5/Aug. — Christian Kahn to Maria Myers — of Baltimore County
- July 11 — Thomas May to Anna Huler — dto.
- Aug. 1 — Herman Bremerman to Amalia Beerman nee Schafer
- Sept. 7 — John Metzger to Elisabeth Gelli — of Yorck County
- Nov. 16 — Charles Fuhrman to Margaretha Devinny — of Baltimore
- Dec. 26 — Richard Bell to Maria Rhady — of Baltimore

1814
- Jan. 6 — John Margret to Anna Dob, widow — of Baltimore
- Feb. 10 — John Smith to Rebecca MecNalten (or MacNallen) — dto. County
- Mar. 1 — Mr. Wekson (or Wison) (jun.?) to Sally Burgin — of Baltimore
- May 30 — Charles Hiesh to Catharina Haley — of Baltimore County
- June 30 — Daniel Kann to Catharina Schally — of Baltimore County
- Sept. 23 — Wilhelm Flachskamp to Maria Hoffman — of Baltimore
- Nov. 8 — John Radcliffe to Sarah Beach — of Baltimore County
- Nov. 10 — George Schminoke or Schmiroke to Anna Tschudy — of Baltimore

1815
- Jan. 1 — Georg Miller to Margaretha Croney — of Baltimore
- Jan. 12 — John Jordan to Maria Elisabeth Afterheide nee Minkin — of Baltimore
- May 23 — John Fuss to Susanna Rigby — of Baltimore
- June 6 — Henrich Poppe to Maria Diefenberger — of Baltimore
- June 22 — Jacob Hummel to Maria Leybrand — dto.
- July 18 — Jacob Crausse to Elisabeth Getier — dto.

FIRST REFORMED CHURCH OF BALTIMORE

Aug. 3		Christian Hahn to Elisabeth Desper	of Baltimore County
Sept. 26		Henry Miller to Catherina Meyer	of Baltimore
Nov. 9		Abraham Danner to Maria Schelly	of York County
Nov. 12		Ludewig Schroder to the widow Maria Reily	of Baltimore County
1816			
Feb. 1		Georg Wien to Elisabeth Heil	of Baltimore County
Feb. 15		Cardo Bolk to Carolina Storer	of Baltimore
Apr. 23		J. Arends Blanck to Friedericke Hanecke (Hancke)	of Baltimore County
May 3		Francis Lowrig to Mary Hoffhind (?)	of Baltimore County
May 6		Christian Hiants to Mary Gruber	of Baltimore County
June 6		Joseph Dreier to the widow Catharina Rhode	of Baltimore
Sept. 26		Friederich Getz to Maria Haber	of Baltimore County
Sept. 30		Earl Simmon or Simmor to Magdalen Hintz (or Hentz)	of Baltimore County
Oct. 1		Nicolaus Lehman to Margaretha Gibbs	of Baltimore County
Nov. 8		Johan Schneider to Hannah Merfield	of Baltimore County
Nov. 10		Jacob Braun to Maria Anna Whisel	of Baltimore County
Dec. 1		Peter Stein to Sophia Lauzatteln (?) (just arrived from Germany)	
Dec. 9		Henrich Hafekost to Johanna Levi	of Baltimore County
1817			
Mar. 20		Jacob Klerie to Catharina Headinger	of Baltimore County
May 29		Anthony Keifel to Sophia Kauder	of Baltimore County
June 22		Johan Casper Hofman to Elisabeth Deller	dto.
June 30		Peter Johan Gerard (or Gerass) to Maria M. Hagerman	dto.
July 3		Jacob Gruber to Anna Gruber	of Baltimore
July 16		Georg Geisler to Dorothea Kohlhauss	of Baltimore County

July 24	Heinrich Bersch to the widow Maria Hofman	of Baltimore County
Aug. 4	John Schaub to Elisabeth Bauer	dto.
Sept. 14	Michael Schweitzer to Sophia Britton	of Baltimore
Nov. 5	Friderich Foye to Elisabeth Anspach	of Baltimore County

1818

Jan. 5	Heinrich Tilge to the widow Helena Herz	of Baltimore County
Jan. 15	Jacob Jung to the widow	dto.
Jan. 22	Friederich Christian Schmid to the widow Wilhelmina Rottermund	dto.
Feb. 19	Rev. Jacob Geiger to Catharina Seltzer	dto.
Apr. 9	Rev. Daniel Kiefer to Elisabeth Sturm	dto.
May 3	John Michel to Margareth Achenbach	dto.
May 19	Georg Weidemeier to Carolina Gerlach	dto.
June 6	John C. Cockey to Maria Hoopert	dto.

1819

July 6	Thomas Murphy and Dorothy Etchberger	both from Baltimore
July 20	Johann Baptiste Parisot and Eliza Wilhelmina Betefuhr	both near Baltimore
July 23	Lewis Brewer to Catherine Neppard	both of Baltimore
Aug. 19	Thomas Dukheart to Mary Matthews	both of Baltimore
Oct. 19	Basel Fisher to Barbara Ewald	both of Baltimore
Oct. 20	Jacob Crever jr. of Carlisle, Pa. to Miss Margaret Decker of Baltimore County	
Nov. 18	William Dugan to Catharine Steiver	both of Baltimore
Dec. 2	Jonathan Sittlemyer to Elisabeth Wyant	both of Baltimore
Dec. 11	John Kuntz to Mary Prignon	both of Baltimore

1820

Feb. 10	Johan Kirchner to Chatarina Dreier(s)	both of Baltimore

Feb. 16	Carl Donis to Wilhelmina Petri	both near Baltimore
Feb. 23	William Hurst to Rebecca Tarnex (or Tarner)	both of Baltimore
Feb. 28	Isaac D. Johns to Susanna S. Laudenslager	both of Baltimore
Feb. 22	Neils Carlsons to Sophia Hanson	both of Baltimore
Mar. 30	George Eiler to Cathrine Smith	both of " County
May 10	Jacob Reed to Elizabeth Rendel	both of Baltimore
Oct. 15	Johan Miller to Jane Degroft	both of Baltimore

1821

Jan. 19	William A. Kipp to Catharine Kinsell	both of Baltimore
Mar. 18	Benjamin Bucknall to Mary Todd	both of Baltimore
Apr. 12	John P.W. Amelung to Ann Snyder	both of Baltimore
Apr. 15	Fredrick Ege to Sarah Smith	the former of Baltimore, the latter of B. County
May 3	Isaac Pettet to Elizabeth Mather	both of B.
June 28	Johan Bistor to Susanna Steiwers	both from Baltimore
July 3	Valentine Hoffman to Mary Brunner	of Philadelphia of Baltimore
July 12	Georg Heidelbach to Louisa Focke (or Focka)	both of Baltimore
Aug. 30	William Shier (or Slicer) to Margaret Witterfield	both of Baltimore
Sept. 18	Frederick Weidemayer to Elizabeth Smith	both of Baltimore
Oct. 12	Reese Williams to Ellen Davis	both of " County(?)
Oct. 12	Martin Tschudy to Elizabeth Price	both of Baltimore(?)
Oct. 19	Henry Worley to Margaret Cook	both of Baltimore(?)
Oct. 29	Reese Williams to Ellen Davis	both of Baltimore(?)
Nov. 15	Andrew Frauchi to Mrs. Eliza Ball (or Bull)	both of Baltimore
Nov. 22	William Wall to Miss Harriot Yoner	both of Baltimore
Dec. 20	Joshua Humphreys to Mary Ann Bell	both of Baltimore
Dec. 20	Henry Hook to Sarah Weaver	both of B.
Dec. 25	Dr. John Baltzel to Ruth Ridgely	the former of Fredricktown the latter of Baltimore

FIRST REFORMED CHURCH OF BALTIMORE

1822

Jan. 6	George Thomas to Mary Dunek	both of Baltimore	
Jan. 26	Philip Augustus Sandoz to Mary Ann Bargnet	of Philadelphia of Baltimore	
Feb. 28	Georg Mereica mit Catharina Mininger	both of Baltimore	
Apr. 28	Fredrick Trice to Mary Schafer	both of Baltimore	
May 21	Charles Fr. Wasmus to Ephemia Pein	of Gettysburg, Pa. of Baltimore	
May 27	Valentine Lutz to Christina Hedrich	both of Baltimore County	
June 2	John a Shimp (or Schimp) to Catharine Glesner	both of Baltimore	
July 2	William Adams to Catherine Schaeffer	both of Baltimore	
July 2	Mark Thurall to Cathrine James	both of Baltimore	
July 5	Henry Irwin to Isabella Martin	both of York County	
July 25	George L. Rous to Henriette Mary Schaeffer	both of Baltimore	
Aug. 20	Luke Kierster or Kiersted to Catherine S. Myer	both of Baltimore	
Aug. 27	Friedrich Hammenmann to Margaretha Rely	procl. by pastor Schneider in Otterbein's Church	
Aug. 29	John R. Hagen (or Guyen) to Ann Merryman	of Baltimore County of Baltimore	
Aug. 10	Joseph W. Entler to Miss Sarah Hopkins	both of Baltimore	
Aug. 12	Johan Christopher Helmton to Eliza Garrison	dto.	
Sept. 15	Charles Morgan to Mary B. Griffith	dto.	
Sept. 20	Richard Hartly to Susanna Mills	dto.	

1823

Feb. 5	George Bennett to Miss Elizabeth Burke	dto.	
Mar. 6	Henry Conn jr. to Catherine Wilhelm	dto.	
Mar. 9	Henry Keyser to Mary Crow	dto.	
Apr. 10	Federal Ereckson to Henriatta Magroth	dto.	
May 22	John Diffenderffer to Miss Cane	dto.	
May 22	Doctor Harper to Miss Norton	dto.	
June 5	Thomas W. Asken to Susan Amey	dto.	

June 5	John C. Chamberlain to Luisa Ann Knipp	both of Baltimore
June 17	Thomas Mannd to Metta Walsch	dto.
July 3	Robert Stirling to Ann Sutton	both of Balto. County
July 17	John Scheneman to Cathrine Lehman	the former of the city, the latter of the vicinity
July 24	Herman Jordan to Maria Elizabeth Sanders (or Sauders)	both of Baltimore
July 30	Benedict Martin to Mary Ann Meiner	both of Baltimore County
July 31	William Rassell (or Rasoell or Russell) to Mary Foble(?)	dto.
Aug. 18	John Weaver to Elizabeth Omera	both of Baltimore
Sept. 11	John M. Johannes to Caroline Lehman	dto.
Oct. 13	David H. White to Ann L. Laudenslager	dto.
Oct. 28	Aratus Alexander McGibbon to Mary Ruth Lee Edes	dto.
Nov. 27	Martin G. Schade to Eliza Allberger	both of Baltimore

1824

Jan. 1	George Mumma to Susan Ledley	both of Baltimore
Jan. 23	William Reinwahl to Louisa Rhode	dto.
Feb. 26	John Bodley to Mary T. Richards	dto.
July 11	Edmund Thomas to Hannah Jervis	dto.
Aug. 12	Alonzo Lilly to Mary Ann Entler	dto.
Aug. 26	William Mumma to Ann Appold	dto.
Aug. 26	John Campbell to Mary Ann Grant	dto.
Oct. 31	John Shreck to Mary Ann Kelly	dto.
Nov. 12	John Lewis to Jane Cunningham	dto.
Nov. 14	Samuel Hart to Arianna Truesman	dto.
Nov. 28	Samuel Montagne to Mary Thomas	dto.
Dec. 9	Wilmer P. Wood to Sarah Beall	dto.

1825

Jan. 20	Abel Spenser to Charlotte Price	dto.
Mar. 13	Isaac Baker to Charlotte Fruberger (or Freiberger)	dto.
Mar. 19	William Carruthers to Mary Worth	dto.
Mar. 29	Jacob Roberts to Ann Caffree	dto.
May 19	John B. Frey to Sarah Ann Bouis (or Bonis)	dto.

June 13	William W. More to Lacinda (or Lucinda) Ann Deposs	both of Baltimore
June 30	Fredrick Charles Henry Rodewald to Eliza Margaret von Kapp	dto.
July 10	John Glassner to Ellen Giddleman	dto.
Aug. 25	Joseph High to Mary Smith	dto.
Oct. 6	John Fruberger (or Freeberger or Freiberger) to Elizabeth Cooper	dto.
Dec. 8	Nicolas Schroeder to Sophia Langken	dto.
Dec. 11	Dennis Murphy to Clementina Thomson	

1826

Mar. 21	Martin Thomas to Margaret Jones	both of Baltimore
Apr. 20	Thomas Burnham to Susan Johns	dto.
Apr. 20	Peter Ealer to Elizabeth Ramsey	dto.
Apr. 20	John Steinman to Ellen Henkle	dto.
Apr. 27	Joseph Stout to Ann B. Stewart	dto.
July 18	Danford D. Jones to Catharine McDonald	dto.
Aug. 31	Hynson Hammilton Cole to Eveline Milleman	dto.
Sept. 9	Joseph Bond to Cath. Ring	dto.
Oct. 14	James H. Gale to Martha Gale	dto.
Oct. 14	Augustus Mathiot to Mary Hodges	dto.
Oct. 19	John Newball to Christiana Stevins	dto.
Dec. 14	Jacob Bayer (or Boyer) to Sarah Stafford	dto.

1827

Jan. 1	James Hanna to Lucretia Knott	dto.
Jan. 4	Ely Arquit to Mary Stafford	dto.
Mar. 8	David Pierce to Isabella Duley	dto.
Apr. 3	John Weaver to Catherine Healy	dto.
Apr. 10	George Nelson to Clarissa H. Penniman	dto.
May 13	Mathias N. Forney (Baltimore) to Amanda Nace of Hanover, Pa.	
May 17	Jacob Racher to Priscilla Weaver	dto.
May 31	Luther K. Swormstead to Henrietta Michael	dto.
May 31	Edward Habbard to Elizabeth Cleaven	dto.
Aug. 16	Francis Galbga to Ann McDonald	dto.

July 22	Fielding Hogner to Elizabeth Weaver	both of Baltimore
Sept. 2	John Shanaman to Hanna Wilks	dto.
Sept. 2	Jacob Schaeffer to Agnes Jane Shedel	dto.
Sept. 13	Daniel Shotts to Mary Hutchins	dto.
Oct. 21	Thomas Brakin to Margaret Royers (or Rogers)	dto.
Dec. 8	Henry Antonio to Maria Madison	dto.

1828

Jan. 8	John Gloninger to Mary Ringold	both of Baltimore
Jan. 15	James Armstrong to Mary Ann Glenn	dto.
March 6	Philip Thaeter to Elizabeth Neumayer	dto.
March 13	Thomas Lee Sim Binns to Mary Ann Cummins	dto.
March 30	Henry Casey to Barbara Ann Turner	dto.
April 29	Anthony Bonn to Eliza Ann Ring	dto.
Sept. 2	Josiah Baily to Susannah Neumayer	dto.
Sept. 14	David Sparr to Elizabeth Towble (or Fowble)	the former of Chamberstown, the latter of Baltimore
Sept. 21	John Krapf to Cathrine Niedham	both of Baltimore
Nov. 9	Henry Amy to Mary Banks	dto.
Dec. 18	Fielding Vanhorn to Mrs. Electa Walton	dto.

1829

Feb. 3	Richard G. Ridgely to Eliza Clarke	both of Baltimore
Feb. 5	John Saurin to Cinthia Howard	dto.
April 2	Jacob Smith to Henrietta Snyder	dto.
May 14	William S. Zimmerman to Caroline Hinckh (or Hincke or Hinckle)	dto.
May 18	George Levering to Eliza Miller	dto.
May 19	Aaron Hoffman to Mary Ann Smith	dto.
June 30	James Shaw to Susan H. Hilton	dto.
July 9	Adolphus Mellier to Priscilla Hindle	dto.
Aug. 30	William Yost to Eliza Henrietta Eichelberger	dto.
Sept. 3	Banjamin Saunders to Ellen Knott	dto.

Sept. 5	Joshua Cockey to Mary Cockey	both of Balto. County
1830		
Feb. 11	James D. Fisher (soldier at the Fort to Susan Hagon (or Hagan)	
Feb. 25	Henry Edwards to Margaret Grant	both of Baltimore
Feb. 28	John Chambers to Charlotte McDonald	dto.
March 25	Thomas J. Wentworth to Ann Lawrence	both of the Fort
April 4	William E. Durham to Sophia Crisfield	both of Baltimore
May 4	William Wattington to Sophie Laudeman	dto.
May 9	John George Teblemann to Mrs. Eliza Geisler	dto.
June 22	Thomas Weeden (?) to Mary Magdalena Etchberger	dto.
June 26	Alexander Hemphill to Rachael Aul	dto.
June 27	Henry Baker to Elizabeth Holland	dto.
July 24	Robert Baird to Eliz. J. P. Right	both of Virginia Balto. County
July 27	George Gelbach to Ann Lamb	both of Baltimore
Aug. 2	Thomas Robinson to Harriet Betson	dto.
Oct. 18	John Peterson to Johanna E. Smith	dto.
Dec. 9	Frederick Auchy to Margaret Garrett	dto.
Dec. 26	Peter Campbell to Sarah Fresh	dto.
1831		
March 20	Wm. Henry Starr to Ann Dashiels	dto.
March 23	Wm. Brushweeler to Elizabeth Ryne	dto.
March 26	Samuel B. (T.) Atwell to Mary Brown Spener (or Spence)	both of Virginia
April 3	Frederick Stine to Susannah Merchant	both of Baltimore
April 12	Elenezar N. Allen to Mrs. Mary C. Neill	dto.
	John M. Slater to Mary S. Cook	dto.
May 17	Robert Campbell to Ann Fanestock	dto.

May 18	John B. Magruder of Virginia to Esther H. Von Kapff of Baltimore	
May 22	David Victor to Hester E. Terry	both of Baltimore
June 2	Peter Brookhart to Lydia Wilson	both of Baltimore County
June 2	Joseph Wilson of Philadelphia to Sophia Smith of Baltimore	
June 26	John Manson to Sarah Etchberger	both of Baltimore
July 2	Thomas Carroll to Margaret Bell	dto.
July 10	Samuel McDonald to Harriot Griffith	dto.
Aug. 9	Alexander Sumwald to Catharine Emily Foss	dto.
Aug. 22	John B. Mathiot to Elizabeth Maybury	dto.
Sept. 4	Joseph O. Broon to Elizabeth A. Long	dto.
Sept. 18	Frederich Beutzel (or Beutzel?) to Rebecca Bear	dto.
Sept. 20	Jacob Whitmore of Chambersburg, Pa. to Mary Ann Diffenderffer of Baltimore	
Sept. 29	Henry S. Philips to Mary A. Sinclair	dto.
Dec. 9	John Fruburger (Freeburger) Jr. to Elizabeth Cath. McDonald	dto.
Dec. 12	John Kettlewell to Ann Levinia Graff	dto.
Dec. 27	Thomas Brambly to Mary Ehrman	both of Baltimore County

1832

Jan. 4	George W. Powell to Susanna Hoffmann	both of Baltimore
Feb.	Alexander Yeo to Mary Metz	dto.
Feb. 12	John Dohm to Jane B. Langford	dto.
Feb.	Duncan Creagh to Margaret Simmons	dto.
March 22	Jacob Stephen Smith to Widow Jane Freeman	dto.
April 17	Davis Brakin to Jane Jackson	dto.
Sept. 2	John Mathews to Priscilla Campbell	dto.

Sept. 6	David Wipperd (or Wippert) to Margaret Hussong	both of Baltimore
Sept. 27	Henry Long to Mary Dram or Drane	dto.
Oct. 11	Bernard Amand Courtois (or Courtous) to Sophia Maria Posey	of Baltimore of Virginia ?
Nov. 29	Otis Spear to Catherine Grove (?)	both of Baltimore
Dec. 1	Henry Weaver to Margaret Giddier	dto.
Dec. 17	William B. Smith to Louisa Presbury	dto.
Dec. 25	Isaac M. Chesborough to Mary Allen	dto.
Dec. 26	Elias Richtler to Margaret Rider	dto.

1833

Jan. 22	John Lewis Herring to Margaret Ann Zisby (or Lusby)	both of Baltimore
Feb. 3	William Kaylor to Mary Christiana Kerner	dto.
Feb. 7	Henry Mosts to Mary Jacobs	dto.
Feb. 14	Jonathan Parker to Jane Washington	dto.
Feb. 20	George Elliott to Catherine Baker	dto.
March 14	Edward Dallwick to Eliza Ann Frigger	dto.
March 20	Diedrich Motz to Mary Jane Von Kapff	dto.
April 18	John Rodemayer to Rebecca Entler	dto.
April 21	Nicholas Elliott to Elizabeth Alford	dto.
May 2	Henry Oliver Diffenderffer to Mary B. Smith	dto.
June 2	Herman Wilhelm Nikolai to Sophia Eleonora Schlacken	
June 2	Henry Henke to Rebecca Kakebart	
June 4	Frederick Cook to Sarah Henry	dto.
June 11	William P. Riebsam to Caroline Lowrie or Zowrie	both of Pennsylvania
June 27	Christopher Beartcheer to Susanna Swayer (or Swager?)	both of Baltimore
Nov. 5	Jeremiah Dietrich Herald to Mary Ann Mayer (or Magee)	dto.

1834

Jan. 20	Fredrick Ernst Wuelken to Dorothea Elizabeth Kreuser	both of Baltimore

FIRST REFORMED CHURCH OF BALTIMORE 153

Feb. 13	Alexander McCoy to Sabre Cox (?)	both of Baltimore
Feb. 20	Ezekiel Dairs to Mary Ann Phillips	dto.
March 17	John Grant to Rachel Vize	dto.
June 24	Daniel Baker to Masillon Ohio to Rebecca Fobler (or Foble)	dto.
July 17	Josiah Fuller to Sarah Ann Evans	dto.
July 24	Charles Davis to Elizabeth Miller	dto.
Aug. 5	Benjamin Gore to Temperence Ensor	both of Baltimore County
Aug. 16	George Edwards to Columbia Slaughter	Baltimore
Sept. 7	Gerhardt Henry Bever (or Rever) to Lena Tegeler	
Sept. 23	Peter Forder to Amelia Marshall	both of Baltimore County
Oct. 19	Israel York to Elizabeth Niles	both of Baltimore
Nov. 2	John Rae to Anna Maria Elizabeth Oderwalt	dto.
Nov. 2	John Henry W. Jatho to Eliza J. Price	
Nov. 27	Samuel J. Skinner to Harriot J. Mariam	dto.
Dec. 11	John Friederich Kaufner to Elisabeth Hickman or Hietzman	both of Baltimore County
Dec. 23	John Bond to Martha Ann Mays	dto.
1835		
Feb. 17	Henry Groverman to Amelia Hamly Diffenderffer	Baltimore
March 17	Henry Wolfe to Eliza Rollins	both of Baltimore
March 22	William Jones to Mary Labrognor	dto.
April 21	Nathaniel Yearly to Eliza Kelly	dto.
June 16	John S. Slade to Catharin Ann Mellen	both of Philadelphia
June 16	John B. Smith to Hannah Scarf	both of Baltimore

June 21	Charles S. Moran to Elizabeth Ann Etchberger	
July 5	James A. Dumbolton to Ann L. Dempsey	dto.
July 13	John Bolgiano to Hanna Ault	dto.
Sept. 10	George Fisher to Ann Maria Rodemayer	dto.
1836	*(Marriages by E. Heinert)*	
Jan. 23	John Parley to Elen Morrison	dto.
Feb. 23	Jacob Yelt to Elizabeth Stanford	dto.
March 24	Charles A. Oberteuffert (or Obertéuffers) to Mary L. Pennington	dto.
April 7	John R. Pedrick to Sarah Ann Grubb (?)	of Philadelphia of Baltimore
May 1	Eber F. Cook to Euphrasia (or Euphrania) Frances Mann	both of Baltimore
June 19	Henry N. Lock to Elizabeth Dumphrey or Pumphrey ?	dto.
July 19	Colbey Knapp M.D. to Catharine Shoffner	dto.
Sept. 4	Henry L. Bichley to Eliza Ann M. Cann (?) or (McCann)	dto.
Sept. 11	Thomas Bentley to Catherine Dykes	dto.
Oct. 2	George S. Pumphrey to Mary Ann Dykes	dto.
Oct. 6	Joseph Roman Jr. to Rebecca T. West	both of Baltimore County
Oct. 11	Thomas Lambert to Martha Hall	both of Baltimore
Oct. 20	Elias Magers to Mary McCreden	dto.
Nov. 16	John Henry Baken to Maria Seesnop	dto.
Nov. 17	Montgomery H. Bailey to Rosina Schaper or Schapey	dto.
1837		
Feb. 7	Wm. Glover to Marinda Noble	dto.
March 22	James Griffis to Sarah Ann Failes	dto.
April 24	Elijah Hurley to Sarah Lankford (or Lankfores)	both of Eastern Shore
June 30	John C. Collins to Ann P. Cummines	both of Baltimore

FIRST REFORMED CHURCH OF BALTIMORE   155

Aug. 10	William L. Morgan to Mary Harris	both of Baltimore County
Aug. 22	Alfred Haddaway to Mary Martin	both of Baltimore
Aug. 27	William S. Wonderly of Philadelphia to Miss Eleanor P. Cummins of Baltimore	
Aug. 30	Edward Shriver Esq. of Frederick to Lydia Stevenson	
Sept. 12	Richard Whitney to Agnes Grubb	both of Baltimore
Sept. 14	John S. Ward of Anne Arundel County to Susanna Wood of Baltimore	
Oct. 17	Elisha P. Ritenour to Margaret R. Rupley	both of Baltimore
Nov. 2	George C. Rodenmayer to Martha Ann Cook	dto.
Nov. 16	Levering (?) Jones to Elizabeth J. Hoserman	dto.
Nov. 21	James F. Harvey to Deborah Debeets	dto.
Dec. 11	James L. Thomas to Mary Light	dto.
Dec. 23	Ellis S. Chesbrough of Lexington, Ky. to Elizabeth Ann Freyer of Baltimore	

1838

Mar. 12	John P. Hopewell to Martha Jane Haslane (or Haslam)	of Pittsburg of Baltimore
Mar. 15	John Allen to Mary Edwards	both of Baltimore
Mar. 22	Ambroose Le Burn to Jane William	both of Baltimore
Aug. 23	Williams W. Parsons to Jennett Bussel	dto.
Sept. 9	John Thomas Hoffman to Christianna Cole	dto.
Sept. 18	John H. McManns to Ann Rowen	dto.
Oct. 7	John W. Holland to Ann Maria Crulle	dto.
Oct. 9	Charles Rogers Diffenderffer to Marlina Ann Neff (or Keft)	dto.
Oct. 11	John U. Durst to Susanna Henry	dto.
Nov. 1	John A. W. Walter to Sarah A. Southcomb	dto.
Dec. 6	Nicholas Hoffman to Miss Whitney	dto.
Dec. 26	Thomas W. Starr to Emily Hughes	dto.

FIRST REFORMED CHURCH OF BALTIMORE

1839

Jan. 10	Joseph F. Rahner (or Pahmer) to Ann Maria Freeberger (?)	both of Baltimore
Jan. 24	Alexander C. Cook to Emily Jane Carroll	dto.
Feb. 12	Henry Richmond to Mary Ann Seesnop	dto.
Mar. 28	Charles D. Shell to Cornelia Ann Beatty	both of New Market, Fred. County, Md.
Apr. 25	Alonzo Miller to Sarah Ann Keener	both of Baltimore
May 30	Goldsborough S. Griffith to Elizabeth Durst	dto.
June 6	Christian K. Thomas of Frederick County to Eviline Virginia Buckey of Baltimore	
June 20	Cornelius Green to Mary Ann Loury	dto.
July 27	Leon Heffele to Josephine Snifel	
Aug. 1	John Gable to Louisa M. Penniman	dto.
Aug. 15	Thomas Penington to Eurydice Mann	dto.
Sept. 8	Rev. Henry Scheib to Lisette D. Eisenbraut	dto.
Sept. 10	James Stiner to Mathilda A. Stouffer	dto.
Nov. 7	William Seip to Amanda Jane Cloud	dto.
Nov. 21	Thomas Dukart Sultzer to Elanora R.C. Cook	dto.
Dec. 5	David Adams to Elizabeth E. Tayler	both of Baltimore
Dec. 19	Alfred Friend to Ann Eliz. Diffenderffer	dto.

1840

Jan. 16	Henry Dickel to Ann Barbara Smith	dto.
Feb. 7	Martin Lewis to Rebecca S. Freyer	dto.
Feb. 12	Rev. Wm. H. Colliflower to Ann E. Fischer	dto.
Mar. 5	Thos. F. Wright to Mathilda Ann Shepperd	dto.
Apr. 9	Mr. Shugh to Miss Franklin	both of Carroll County
Apr. 14	Charles Heiner to Alice Rogan	both of Baltimore
May 28	Alexander M. Manning to Susah Fisher	dto.
June 23	Robert Allison to Elizabeth Davis	dto.

FIRST REFORMED CHURCH OF BALTIMORE

Date	Marriage	Residence
Sept. 29	Alexander B. Chirverl to Susan R. King	both of Baltimore
Nov. 12	Thomas B. Edwards to Sarah West	dto.
Nov. 19	John Henry Baker to Sarah Jones	dto.
Dec. 1	Samuel Parsons to Margaret Shaffner	dto.
Dec. 3	David Risther to Elizabeth Hogner	dto.
Dec. 11	Andrew Wigart to Mary Richmond	dto.

1841

Date	Marriage	Residence
Jan. 6	Christian Weishampel to Edith Scott Stansbury	both of Baltimore
Jan. 21	Richard B. Thompson to Adansla A. Muage or Mudge	" "
Feb. 7	George Laig to Elizabeth Schaffer	" "
Feb. 7	Henry Shuck to Catharine Plowman	" "
Feb. 17	John B. Charron to Rebeca Ann Courtois	" "
Mar. 18	John B. Mathist or Mathiot to Adaline Glasgow	" "
Apr. 5	Charles P. Brurien to Eliza Hoffman	" "
Apr. 15	Augustus D. Clemens to Henrietta M. Bryden	" "
May 13	Thomas Jefferson Wolfe to Harriet Beard	" "
May 25	Thomas L. Jones to Margaretta Richstein	" "
July 2	Jesse Woodcock to Elizabeth Davis	" "
July 11	George W. Bandel to Mary Reed	" "
Aug. 26	George W. Kirk to Balinda P. Amos	both of Harford Co.
Aug. 26	Edward G. Starr to Cecelia A. James	both of Baltimore
Sept. 14	Admiral Rupley to Appolona Rider	" "
Sept. 16	William Bersch to Susanna Rountree	" "
Nov. 3	Jacob D. Sheble to Rosina Baley	
Nov. 16	Henry Rhods to Mathilda E. Diffenderffer	" "
Dec. 2	Francis L. Hilberg to Sarah C. Abbes	" "

FIRST REFORMED CHURCH OF BALTIMORE

1842

Feb. 3	Robert P. Cunnins to Josephine A. Keys	both of Baltimore
March 8	Henry A. Keerl to Eliza A. Crook	" "
April 11	Joseph Harris to Mary Ann McLean	" "
April 12	Philip Reigart to Catharine Diffenderffer	" "
April 27	Washington Galt to Mary P. Derry (or S. Perry)	" "
May 10	Wm. S. Reese to Emeline M. Reigart	" "
July 6	Thaddeus Warner to Cath. O'Donnell	" "
Aug. 25	Mathias Shaffner to Ann Maria Cook (english)	" "
Sept. 8	Wm. L. Gray to Levinia Spicer	" "
Nov. 3	John Cunningham to Georgianna Geisler	" "
Dec. 11	John G. Eckman to Julia Ann Cunningham	" "
Dec. 6	David A. Peters to Sarah Jane Allen	" "
Dec. 22	Jacob F. Decker to Julia Ann Herring	" "

1843

Jan. 5	Capt. John E. Allen to Cornelia Marshall	both of Baltimore
Feb. 21	Wm. H. Martin to Ann Maria Thomas	" "
April 27	Wm. Thomas to Margaret Lehman	" "
May 11	Emerson J. Case to Margaret Ann Spangler	" of York, Pa.
May 23	Richard F. Maynard to Eliza M. Horton	" of Baltimore
May 30	Elijah G. Mc Cauley to Sarah Jane Eliz. Kneeland	" "
May 31	William Holland to Orilla M. Jennings	" "
June 6	Nicholas D. Hauer to Anne C. Myer	
June 6	Sylvanis or Sylvanus Bloodgood to Helen Bain	" "
June 6	Robert E. Aiken to Harriet E. Aiken	" "
June 14	William Smith to Catharine Gray	" "

July 4	Ephraigm Price to Eliza R. Pickett	both of Baltimore
July 20	William McClain to Susan Crawford	" "
Aug. 13	George Muth to Mary Ann White	" "
Aug. 27	Gabriel Herbert to Rachel E. White	" "
Sept. 18	William M. Brant to Barbara Bower	" "
Nov. 6	James Reesides to ....?	" "
Nov. 9	Aug. C. H. Beoheme to Juliet E. Dorsey	" "
Nov. 26	John Vance to Agnes M. Bowden	" "
Dec. 14	Samuel Price to M. Parsons	" "
Dec. 24	Charles E. Hughes to Catherine Howell	" "

1844
March 18	Robert Tenrinson (or Tennison) to Mary Stewart	" "
April 24	George D. Smith to Jane R. B. Windows	" "
May 2	Justus Keefer to Elizabeth Penn	" "
May 9	Jacob M. Buckey to Harriet E. Buckey	" "
May 22	Henry Storm to Cath. M. Lightner	" "
May 23	Adam Seltzer to Margaret Cooper	" "
June 20	Wm. Joseph to Mary Ann Andsens or Andrews	" "
?	Linard	" "
July 7	Daniel Stibbens to Helen Lagart (?)	" "
Sept. 11	Georg W. Herring to Rosena M. Diffenderffer	" "
Dec.	Richard R. Holland to Elexenia Holland	" "

1845
Feb. 9	Richard Bettee to Susan Pool	both of Baltimore
Feb. 11	Henry Schoper to Rachael Barrett	" "
Feb. 12	Charles M. Hagelin to Mary Jannings	" "
Feb. 25	Emanuel Joseph to Sarah Hack	" "
March 2	Nicholas Matthews jr. to Mary A. Kelley	" "
March 5	John Clark to Jane Slemmer	" "
March 10	Jus. or Jno. G. Johannas to Mary B. Waters	" "

FIRST REFORMED CHURCH OF BALTIMORE

March 13	Wm. H. Miller to Susanna M. Smithson	both of Baltimore
July 21	Wm. J. Hamilton to Julia Lankford	" "
Sept. 18	William Geo. Storch to Martha Abbes	" "
Oct. 2	John Jacob Faubel to Julia Leakin	" "
Oct. 2	Philip C. Uhlhorn to Mary Elizabeth Siemers	" "
Oct. 7	Dixon Crawford to Weathy E. Tilghman	" "
Oct. 9	Edward C. Conoway to Frances Eleston	" "
Nov. 5	Francis Buck to Lucretia Jane Cochen or Cochm	" "
Nov. 12	Lewis Lehman to Lucy Durham	" "
Nov. 18	Henry Bersch to Elizabeth A. Miller	" "
Nov. 30	Thomas E. Bartling to Virginia Smith	" "
Dec. 2	Thomas Elliott to Ellengder Jane Harrington	" "
Dec. 10	Edwin Hamilton to Susan Green	" "
Dec. 17	George W. Stansburg to Elizabeth A. Linthicum	" "
Dec. 17	Charles Diffenderffer jun. to Elizabeth A. Mc.Connell	" "
Dec. 23	Collen K. Warren to Margaret M. Hopkins	" "
Dec. 23	Samuel D. Johnston to Susanna M. Barbara Myer	" "

1846

Jan. 20	Christian Rosenbrock to Anna J. Haasen	both of Baltimore
Jan. 29	James A. Hurtt to Ann Elizabeth Abbes	" "
Feb. 12	Francis B. Loney to Anne E. Keller	" "
March 11	Frederick Spence to Caroline Watts	" "
March 12	William Hoffman to Anna L. Broaders	" "
April 4	George W. Hadley to Johanna Rurke or Rurhe	" "
April 15	Richard Plowman to Susanna Mumma	" "

April 27	Louis A. Bixler to Ellen M. Duhurst	both of Baltimore
May 21	William Randall to Sarah Elizabeth Hewell	" "
July 8	John Shelley to Elizabeth Linard	" "
Aug. 16	Charles E. Hickman to Juliet Shaffner	" "
Aug. 27	Daniel Mitten to Elizabeth Crouse	" of Carroll County
Sept. 15	Godfrey S. Miller to Marianna Sperry	of Winchester, Va. of Baltimore
Sept. 21	Joshua Howard to Margell or Mary M. Thomas	both of Baltimore
Sept. 30	Thaddeus Mabee to Mary Stevens	" "
Oct. 10	Marcellus League or Leagner to Julia Dougherty	" "
Nov. 12	Thomas Duncan to Ann M. Green	" "
Nov. 19	John Dobbin to Mary A. Tweedell	" "
Dec. 1	John Henry Sirich to Caroline A. Miller	
Dec. 15	James W. Gorman to Marella B. Jennings	" "
Dec. 17	Ross J. Pennington to Sarah Mumma	" "
Dec. 18	Alfred Hoss to Francina Powder	" "
Dec. 19	Davis Evans to Mary J. Lazareth	" of Penn.
Dec. 23	John H. Thompson to Mary Ann Pettitt	" of Baltimore

1847

Jan. 7	Wm. Stoddard to Emily V. Mc. Colm	both of Baltimore
Jan. 21	Henry Spilman to Laura Ann Campbell	" "
Feb. 10	Calhoun M. Deringer to Martha A. Bladen	
Feb. 25	Richard Manning to Meranda Everhart	" of Carroll Co.
March 1	Nicholas Foxcroft to Sarah Eliz. Mc. Gingan	" of Baltimore
March 4	Wm. H. Dixon to Heziah Gray	"both coloured of Baltimore"
March 7	David Hays to Frances A. Wolf	both of Baltimore
March 18	John Thompson to Ann M. Dunn	" "
April 20	Washington Barger to Mary M. League	" "
May 4	John Eigeon to Margaret Seltzer	" "

June 8	William H. Robsen to Maria Louise Bool	both of Baltimore
July 22	George Franck to Elizabeth Ann Rodenmayer	" "
July 25	Benjamin Reynolds to Christiana Miller	" "
Aug. 24	Alexander Forsyth to Martha Crawford	" "
Sept. 15	John E. Nimmo to Isabella Mongan	" "
Sept. 19	Lewis Alns to Susan Clift	" "
Sept. 21	Carton Masen (or Mason) to Elizabeth Jane	"both coloured"
Sept. 23.	James L. Cromer to Elizabeth Simpsen or Simpson	both of Baltimore
Oct. 28	George Duling to Lydia Gipson	"both coloured"
Nov. 4	James U. Dellahay to Josephine E. Meeks	both of Baltimore
Nov. 8	Joseph O. Dugan to Mary C. Dix	" "
Nov. 10	John H. Keener to Susan M. Holmes	" "
Nov. 15	Andrew H. Seeman to Margaret Smully ("Smully was her maiden name/Gard the name of her first husband. In Taking out license the name Smully instead of Gard was given. E.H.")	" "
Nov. 18	Wm. J. Pindall to Henriatta Piersen	"Coloured"
Nov. 25	John W. Dougherty to Priscilla Ann Jessop	both of Baltimore
Nov. 26	Gustavus Robinson to Eliza Beard	" "
Dec. 6	Alexander E. Worley to Mary Ann Rider	" "
Dec. 9	James A. Hilbert to Mary Jane Hill	" "
Dec. 13	John H. Shoemaker to Georgianna Munson	" "
Dec. 16	James H. Butcher to Catharine Frum	" "
Dec. 23	James J. (or T.) Stocker to Josephine E. Smith	" "

1848

Jan. 20	Jacob W. Miller to Sophia Busch	both of Baltimore
Jan. 27	Jacob M. Cooper to Mary J. Robins	" "

Feb. 16	Benjamin F. Cameron to Sarah Frum	both of Baltimore	
March 16	Albert Holland to Harriet Beard	"	"
March 23	George H. Naugen to Ann E. Woodden	"	"
April 11	William J. Tilghman to Ann Maria Jones	"	"
April 27	Philip J. (or F.) Thomas to Josephine L. Cook	"	"
May 9	Leven Canter to Rebecca B. Stevens	"	"
May 30	Hugh Hamilton to Sarah Arnold	"	"
May 31	Samuel M. Harris to Gulielma M. Mott	"	"
June 4	William Clark to Catharine M. Ford	"	"
July 27	George A. Schaeffer to Angeline Howard	"	"
July 27	Francis J. Mitchell to Melvina E. May	"	"
Sept. 14	William DeBeet to Mary Ann Keys	"	"
Sept. 14	David G. Garrison to Elizabeth Ann Onion	"	"
Sept. 21	George Patrick to Eleanor E. Ferrell	"	"
Sept. 21	Solomon S. Dillehunt to Cath. H. Cromer	"	"
Oct. 7	Robert May to Elizabeth Mc.Allister	"	"
Oct. 24	Wm. J.H. Onion to Elizabeth M. Garrettsen	"	"
Oct. 29	James R. Flemming to Elizabeth Patton	"	"
Nov. 14	Daniel S. Griffin to Eliza Shaffner	"	"
Nov. 22	Wm. G. Geckler to Frances A. Young	"	"
Dec. 21	Lloyd M. Miller to Eleanora Galloway	"	"

1849

Jan. 4	James C. Stevensen to Lonesa Waite	both of Baltimore	
Jan. 11	Thomas J. Chubb to Sarah P. Montrop	"	"
Jan. 15	John Bond to Fanny Brackenbridge	"	"

164 FIRST REFORMED CHURCH OF BALTIMORE

Feb. 21	John K. Hudgins to Sarah J. Cumings	both of Baltimore	
Feb. 15	Thomas Linville to Elizabeth Edwards	"	"
March 13	Washington Ruddach to Mary Cliffe	"	"
March 28	James Keys to Emily E. Keithley	"	"
April 5	John W. Boyer to Fanny B. Stansburg	"	"
April 8	John W. Winn to Welthy Ann Peregoy	"	"
April 15	George Wilson to Maria A. Simpson	"	"
May 10	Francisco Joseph to Eliz. H. Watts	"	"
July 5	John F. Cook to Angeline Cattrider	"	"
July 12	Robert Elliot to Rebecca Joseph	"	"
July 17	Samuel Taneyhill (?) to Ann Eliza Flemming	"	"
July 17	James H. Valiant to Elizabeth Pollock	"	"
Sept. 4	Patrick Roley to Elizabeth Hagg	"	"
Oct. 1	George Thomas Silvester to Ann Jane Saville	"	"
Nov. 29	Richard Armiger to Henrietta Baker	"	"
Dec. 20	Georg W. Spies to Frances Matthews	"	"
Dec. 20	James Dale to Margaret Chalt	"	"

1850

Jan. 20	Henry Spamer to Rosanna Ross	"	"
Jan. 27	Robert A. Clarke to Catherine Ann Miller	"	"
March 14	William Peffer to Susanna Edwards	"	"
March 31	Jeremiah T. Beebe to Ann Eliza Sutherland	"	"
April 4	Samuel J. (or F.) Gould to Margaret Ann Geddis	"	"
May 7	John Cruit to Anna A. Milroy	"	"
June 13	John J. Wise to Sarah C. Wise	"	"
June 19	John Steadman to Margaret Lawler	"	"

FIRST REFORMED CHURCH OF BALTIMORE

July 2	Joshua H. Parker to Emily V. McDowell	both of Baltimore	
July 7	John W. Kirby to Caroline Nicolai	"	"
July 23	John P. Jones to Julia A. Ackland	"	"
July 25	Henry Bookman to Eleanor Otter	"	"
Sept. 5	Augustus G. Mathiot to Rachel Ann Thompson	"	"
Sept. 5	Henry Heritage to Louisa M. Ehrman	"	"
Sept. 8	Robert Henderson to Margaret Dixon	"	"
Sept. 18	Christian Musselman to Kezia Wooden		
Oct. 10	Jackson Lewis to Catharine Chase	"	"
Oct. 31	George Wolff to Araminta Myer	"	"
Nov. 6	Robert W. Keyworth to Annie Andersen	"	"
Nov. 21	Wm. A. Baker to Mary Aspril	"	"
Nov. 21	Daniel Sheute to Mary E. Stoddard	"	"
Dec. 14	Peter Duncan to Isabella Duncan	"	"
Dec. 23	James M. Cochran to Elizabeth A. Moreland	"	"

1851

Jan. 2	John Lanohan to Catharine Brett	both of Baltimore	
Feb. 10	James Godfrey to Margaret Henry	"	"
March 6	Joshua S. Harrington to Eliza Busch	"	"
March 11	George P. Weller to Mary Wise	"	"
March 18	James Joseph to Mary Ann Humphreys	"	"
March 27	Thomas C. Price to Mary C. Scott	"	"
March 27	John McPherson to Sarah Jane Lyons	"	"
April 2	Charles Farrall to Mary Lane	"	"
April 15	John Steele to Elizabeth Linville	"	"
May 14	Arnold Jensfield to Mary Jane Bayly	"	"

FIRST REFORMED CHURCH OF BALTIMORE

May 29	Michael L. Berkheimer to Mary C. Holbrook	both of Baltimore	
June 28	James J. Stevens to Ellen D.B. Harris	"	"
Aug. 7	George A. Hoyle to Eliza Jane Luttz	"	"
Aug. 10	James L. Mills to Eliza Jane Taylor	"	"
Aug. 12	John J. Shappard to Isabella G. Barett	"	"
Aug. 26	Casper W. Younger to Maria Ann White	"	"
Aug. 31	Samuel Linton to Mathilda Ballauf	"	"
Sept. 2	John Immohard (or Nomohan) ? to Mary Ann Griffin	"	"
Sept. 5	William Guy to Sarah Ann R. Guy	"	"
Sept. 29	Wm. H. Randle to Lydia Rinby	"	"
Sept. 30	Greenberry A. Phumfrey to Mary A. Hemmick	"	"
Oct. 1	Wm. H. Quincy to Elizabeth Jane Sissen (or Jissen)	"	"
Oct. 2	Wm. P. Francis to Mary Julie Mathiot	"	"
Oct. 16	John L. Barrett to Elizabeth A. Blanchord	"	"
Nov. 11	William Hart to Mary C. Miller	"	"
Nov. 18	John Joseph to Mary Jane Wilson	"	"
Nov. 19	Wm. H. Wilson to Hannah Ann Dorsey	"	"
Nov. 20	John Coleman to Martha A. Wagner	"	"
Dec. 2	J. William Messersmith to Sarah F. (C.) Barron	both of Baltimore	
Dec. 11	John Enos Silva to Elizabeth Taylor	"	"
Dec. 21	Joseph Evans to Margaret Ann Claridge	"	"
Dec. 28	Theodor (?) W. White to Maria Mitchel	"	"

FIRST REFORMED CHURCH OF BALTIMORE

DATE	NAMES	
1852		
Jan 15	Elias Maggs to Mary R.F. Russell	by license
Jan 19	John Riley to Margaretta Tulby	"
Feb 26	Joseph B. Berger to Amy Riley	"
March 18	James Hopkins to Sarah Ryan	"
April 1	Lewis B. Helvestiner to Eliz. Ann Boden	"
April 21	William Blood to Eliza Moore	"
May 4	Casper R. Brown to Eliza. Seabrook	"
May 12	Wm. B. Phippin to Louisa Lewis	"
May 23	James H. Vance to Mary F. Watts	"
May 24	Robert E.R.Childs to Mary Ann Hughes	"
June 2	Ray S. Clarke to Susan Gerdner	"
July 19	Arthur Thomas Johnsen to Ann V. Collins	"
July 20	John H. Miller to Mary E. Wier	"
July 25	James M. Hart to Mary A. Warren	"
Sept 4	Wm. Hutcheson to Sarah Eliz. Merryman	"
Sept 16	Ephraim B. Daily to Julia A. Herring	"
Oct 14	Ed. G. Rencus to Ethalinda E. Harrison	"
Oct 19	Zeakiah Larmen to Laura F. Horten	"
Nov 16	Lycurgus (?) E. Savage to Amelia D.C.Yager	"
Nov 15	Jacob W. Honck to Susan F. Porter	"
Nov 24	Gotthelf T.R.Roessler to Mary Ann Koethen	"
Nov 25	William Caulk to Mary E. Warwing	"
Nov 30	J. Christian Kraft to Charlotte Diffendorffer	"
Dec 5	John H. Schultz to Mary Ann Davis	"
July 19	Georg W. Spence to Mary Ann Kelley	"

FIRST REFORMED CHURCH OF BALTIMORE

DATE	NAMES	
1853		
Jan 6	Henry G. Freeburger to Lydia Hoffnagle	by license
Jan 26	Leander Leut or Levt to Jemina R. Bell	"
Feb 24	Wm. C. Baker to Susanne Wagner	"
Feb 24	Benjamin Kidd to Mary Dewling	"
March 3	James D. Johnsen to Mary Ann Seeltzer	"
March 10	Samuel Mainly to Elizabeth Ayres	"
March 15	James Hamilton to Ann Maria Boyer	"
April 15	James Wilson Smith to Isabella Godfrey	"
April 19	Phil. Henry Muller to Mary Cath. Davis	"
April 25	Charles Emmons to Rosa Trenton	"
April 28	Robert Sim to Martha Thompson	"
May 1	Henry von Hoxar to Elizabeth Dinsmore	"
May 5	William L. Willis to Frances A. Finlay	"
May 12	James Cameron to Julia Mabee	"
May 26	James Hall to Sarah J. Quincey	"
June 2	David H. Macauly to Elizabeth Richardson	"
June 16	Perry C. Orem or Crem to Cath. M. Sheeler	"
June 23	S. Kimmel to Mary Lizzie Lambert	"
June 27	John H. Meckings to Emaline J. Wilby	"
July 16	Daniel D. Vaughn to Ann M. Carr	"
July 28	Wm. H. Martin to Barbara Shuck	"
July 31	Richard Montagno to Cath. Thomas	"
Aug 16	Simon D. Martinette to Philena F. Fussell	"
Aug 21	Erastus Brant to Mary A. Miller	"
Aug 23	Horatio D. Hewitt to Maria Louesa Gade	"
Sept 1	David Ardin to Sarah Stewart	"
Oct 12	Peter F. Kennedy to Caroline P. Burnett	"
Oct 13	Wm. Foster to Mary Ann Rountree	"
Nov 11	John M. Gregor to Ann Irwin	"

FIRST REFORMED CHURCH OF BALTIMORE

DATE	NAMES	
Dec 15	Samuel L. Thomas to Caroline Simpson	by license
Dec 18	Geo. Bukoffsky to Mary M. Hubbard	"
Dec 27	James J. Karre to Mary A. E. Silvester	"
Dec 27	Robert C. Beard to Ann E. Copes	"
Sept 13	Jerry Dowy to Margaret McNamara	"

1854

Jan 19	Charles Wilson to Mary Ann Godfrey	"
Feb 14	Geo. J. Bennet to Agnes M. DeBeet	"
Feb 23	Wm. Morrow to Susan Campbell	"
Feb 23	Henry Marker to Ellen Geaty	"
March 7	Felix V. Durst to Cordelia F. Lecompte	"
March 9	Daniel Makinson to Caroline Johannes	"
April 26	Josiah Davis to Martha Hoyt	"
May 3	Wm. H. Edwards to Anna M. King	"
June 20	John H. Goula to Mary F. Reveer	"
July 10	Thomas Webber to Eliza German	"
Aug 2	Ira C. Lyon to Martha R. Myer	"
Aug 7	John J. Heagy to Harriet Smith	"
Aug 8	Henry Dilling to Rachael A. Metzdorff	"
Aug 25	John Godfrey to Nancy Frien	"
Sept 20	John Richardson to Susan Hurst	"
Sept 21	John Staylong to Kate Sutts	"
Sept 24	Daniel W. Lowe to Isabel Jackle	"
Nov 7	Thomas Crawford to Mary Gourley	"
Nov 9	John Lehrs to Sarah H. McAroy	"
Nov 14	Purnell Newman to Amanda Troxel	"
Dec 12	Wm. H. Morehead to Lizzie A. Quincy	"
Dec 14	John Ryan to Susan J. Keeney	"
Dec 14	Henry Miller to Mary Tartell	"

FIRST REFORMED CHURCH OF BALTIMORE

DATE	NAMES	
1855		
Jan 2	James Ackland to Mary C. Kersey	by license
Feb 15	James Huey to Rachael Ebaugh	"
March 22	John Pomp to Mary A. Watlington	"
May 14	John H. Suter to Mary Jane Kidd	"
May 24	John Colton to Elizabeth J. Caldwell	"
May 31	James..Kenny to Ann M. Fardwell	"
June 12	James W. Arnett to Rose A. Cameron	"
June 7	James E. Cohn to Margaret Ellis	"
June 28	Alexander H. Hymnes to Sarah A. Sturgen	"
July 4	Andrew J. Hubbard to Dorthey E. Murphy	"
July 5	Geo. M.N. Carr to Maria D. Carsoll or Carwel	"
Sept 3	Joseph C. Wheeler to Sophia B. Medinger	"
Sept 5	John F. Sommerlock to Anna Wilkins	"
Sept 13	James N. Brian to Evaline Roache	"
Sept 18	Warren Welch to Mary A. Durst	"
Sept 18	Basil Mullnix to Menerva Gaither	"
Sept 25	Alfred Buck to Amelia-Indiana Goverman	"
Oct 13	Geo. C. Boniface to Margaret Hafferning	"
Oct 18	Octavian L. Mathiot to Ann Maria Nalls	"
Oct 25	Johnson Godfrey to Fannie Gabe	"
Nov 1	Richard Grey to Anne P. Hunt	"
Nov 27	William D. McCord to Charlotte L. Larr	"
Dec 5	Charles McCafferty to Margaret Everwine	"
Dec 18	John Reed to Kitty Ann Ebaugh	"
Dec 19	Frederick Colton to Jennet Carr	"
Dec 20	Charles F. Lockner to Rebecca Jones	"

FIRST REFORMED CHURCH OF BALTIMORE

DATE	NAMES	
1856		
Jan 7	George Gale to Susan Matilda Mathiot	by license
Jan 15	Thomas Hardester to Josephine Zimmerman	"
Feb 11	R.B.Merideth to M.A.V. Harris	"
Feb 22	Samuel Sutten to Mary A.A. Graham	"
March 11	Samuel J. Jennings to Cath. V. Kerner	"
March 23	Peter F. Kennedy to Caroline P. Burnett	"
April 10	David Haper to Louisa Lynn	"
April 14	Patrick Moffat to Ann Daley	"
May 8	James Taylor to Bridget Brannan	"
May 26	Charles Fahey to Mary Ann Linken	"
June 5	J. Taylor Starr to Jane Roberts	"
July 2	Charles F. Seebode to Anna Jane French	"
Sept 1,	Jacob J. Harman to Susan Fogleman	"
Sept 17	Charles Geiger to Clara Barched	"
Oct 2	Henry C. Jones to Mary E. Fisher	"
Oct 9	Jno. C. Orrloff to Cath. Ann James	"
Oct 13	Alfred Bennett to Sarah Murray	"
Oct 16	William che Manns to Ellanorah Evatt	"
Oct 30	Wm. F. Ast to Rosa Lambert	"
Nov 19	William Frost to Ann Rebecca Owings	"
Dec 6	Joshua Demmitt to Martha Nunlee	"
Dec 9	Armstead R. Hobbs to Caroline D. Gatchell	"
Dec 25	Henry C. Clautices to Magdalena C. Burnham	"
Dec 30	Edwin Henry Crouse to Sarah Cornelia Ensor	"
1857		
Jan 7	William Richstein to Elenora Kerner	"
Jan 7	Geo. W. Martenel to Marja Ann Conway	"
Feb 9	Edward Gilligan to Fanny Rogers	"
March 5	John Bairley to Mary E. James	"

172   FIRST REFORMED CHURCH OF BALTIMORE

DATE	NAMES	
1857		
March 19	Thomas E. Bryan to Bennetta Earlonghed	by license
May 26	Joseph B. Kerr to Mrs. Virginia Young	"
June 1	William Murray to Emely Jane Williams	"
July 30	Leonard W. Gray to Mary C. Ryan	"
1858		
Jan 6	James Yeats to Ethlan A. Grant	"
Jan 26	Thomas Emmett to Isabel Cooney	"
March 22	Benjamin L. Odell to Antoinetta H. Williams	"
July 1	Augustus Plowman to Ethelenda F. Mase	"
Oct 7	John Bestolay to Mary Fage	"
Nov 2	William Biddinger to Elizabeth Seltzer	"
Nov 24	James Menzies to Mary Cath. Caples	"
1859		
Jan 16	James M. Maloney to Ann A. Buchley	(Dr. Anspach)
Feb 24	James E. Deffres to Margaret R. Haines	"
March 17	Joseph Tayler to Alice A. Owens	"
March 30	James P. Milnor to Virginia B. Stephens	"
April 20	Daniel J. Albaugh to Mary F. Link	"
May 9	William Pinly to Elleanora Jennings	"
May 24	Jesse A. D. Kaufman to Emma V. Lindsey	"
Oct 4	Benjamin C. Cissel to Mary Eichelberger	"
Nov 30	Beal D. Riddler to Isabella Hume	"
1860		
March 6	Alfred Friend to Ellen D. Quincy	"
April 10	Rev. F. A. Anspach, D.D. to Susan M. Gole	"
July 8	Conrad Hipner to Rosetta B. Thamerd	"
July 9	John Hammel to Ann Maria Brensfield	"
July 26	George A. Houck to Emma R. Foyer	"

FIRST REFORMED CHURCH OF BALTIMORE

DATE	NAMES	
1860		
Oct 4	John Kernan to Emma S. Klockgether	by license
Oct 15	Henry G. Frederick to Caroline Weisinger	"
Nov 1	George Colt to Mary Kelly	"
1861		
Jan 23	Benjamin F. Lemmon to Danie E. Davis	"
Feb 7	Laban W. Carter to Ellen E. Burke	"
May 30	John E. Folk to Caroline A. Baker	"
Dec 2	Duncan H. DeBeet to Emma Keys	"
Dec 24	Joseph Guy to Mrs. Ann Gounly	"

FIRST REFORMED CHURCH OF BALTIMORE

PASTORS

Rev. John Christian Faber, 1768-1771
Rev. George Wallauer, 1772-1777
Rev. Charles L. Boehme, 1779-1782
Rev. Nicholas Pomp, 1783-1789
Rev. George Troldenier, 1791-1800
Rev. John H. Dreyer, 1802-1806
Rev. Christian L. Becker, D.C., 1806-1818
Rev. Albert Helfenstein, 1819-1835
Rev. Elias Heiner, D.D., 1836-1863
Rev. E. R. Eschbach, D.D., 1864-1874
Rev. Joel R. Rossiter, D.D., 1875-1918

Date of Birth	Date of Baptism	Name	Parents	Sponsors
Dec 16 1820	Jan 28 1821	Isaac	William Newton and Cathrine Newton	parents
April 30 1817	Jan 31 1821	Ann Barbara	Christian Keller and Ann Mary	parents
Oct 30 1818	"	Mary Margaretta	"	"
March 24 1820	"	William Tell	"	"
Sept 24 1820	Feb 21 1821	Elizabeth	John Redgrave & Eliza	Henry Hoffman and Mary
Jan 28 1821	Feb 26 by Dr. Kurts	Christian Albert	Albert Helfenstein and Mary	parents
Feb 5 1821	March 1st	Edward	Charles Diffenderfer and Ann	parents
June 18 1816	March 23 1821	Jacob	George Frans Redsil and Magdalena	parents
June 12 1820	March 23 1821	Daniel	"	"
Feb 11 1821	March 25 1821	Edward	Edward Gosbury & Elizabeth	Eliza Levingston
Feb 18 1821	March 25 1821	Gesche Margaret	Henry Fred. Holz and Martina	Elizabeth Gosbury

FIRST REFORMED CHURCH OF BALTIMORE

DATE OF BIRTH	DATE OF BAPTISM	NAME	PARENTS	SPONSORS
July 21 1848	Nov 3	Mary Frances	Geo. & Lucinda Sutter	
Aug 16 1849	Nov 17	John Haas	Geo. L. & M.A. Fisher	
March 4 1847	Nov 22	Sarah Ann	Wm. & Sarah E. Randall	
April 3 1849	Nov 22	Lewis Hewell	"	
July 13 1849	Nov 27	Francis Edward	F. & P. R. Uhl	parents
Dec 20 1848	Nov 29	Laura Virginia	H. & M. J. Tycon	mother
April 13 1849	Nov 29	Louesa Catherine	A. & S. J. Kauderer	parents
Jan 5 1848	Nov 29 1849	Margaret Jane	John & Barbara Kauderer	parents
Sept 2 1849	Nov 29 1849	Charles Zwingle	G. H. & B. Dickel	parents
Nov 5 1849	Dec 26 1849	Ida	John & ... Gade	parents
July 12 1827	Sept 11 1849	Mary	A. & Elizabeth Stevens	on profession
Nov 6 1829	"	Lucinda Baptist	"	"
May 18 1833	"	Virginia Baptist	"	"
Nov 3 1834	"	Josephine Elizabeth	"	"
March 1 1840	"	Thomas Murphy	"	parents
Dec 27 1841	"	Christopher Columbus	"	parents
July 22 1838	"	Matilda	"	parents
Feb 10 1828	"	Rebecca B.	"	parents
Aug 24 1848	Sept 11	Elexenia	Thadeus & Mary Mabee	parents
Dec 6 1847	Sept 11	Delvene	"	parents
Feb 11 1849	Sept 11	Ida Elexenia	Leven & Rebecca B. Canter	parents
Nov 29 1839	Sept 23	Alfred Hall	Edwin S. & Susanna Tarr	
Dec 12 1842	Sept 23	Edwin Sturges	"	

FIRST REFORMED CHURCH OF BALTIMORE

DATE OF BIRTH	DATE OF BAPTISM	NAME	PARENTS	SPONSORS
Feb 1 1846	May 14	Mary Louesa	Nicholas & Cath. Merryman	parents
March 18 1848	May 14	Wesley Martin	"	parents
April 1 1849	May 29	Sidney Norris [Morris?] [twins]	Adam & Margaret Seltzer	parents
April 1 1849	May 29	Adam Heck	"	parents
Jan 21 1849	June 11	Geo. Conrad	Jacob & Eliz. L. Yiesley	parents
Jan 2 1849	July 21	Charles Magnus	Charles M. & Mary Hagelin	parents
June 4	July 27	Wm. Kingsbury	Wm. K. & Marinda Gardner	mother
Feb 2 1849	July 28	Francis Lewis	F.L. & Sarah C. Hilberg	mother
May 19 1848	July 28 1849	Martha Cath.	Wm. G. & Martha Storch	parents
June 3 1849	July 28	Louesa	Thomas & Sarah Edwards	parents
June 13 1849	Sept 5	Laura Rebecca Seesnop	Henry & Mary Ann Richmond	parents
Nov 27 1848	Sept 9	Archibald John	A. H. & Sarah T. Robertson	parents
June 23 1848	July 6	Margaret	Alexander & Martha Forsyth	mother
Nov 30 1847	July 23	John Sebastian	Thomas D. & Elnora Sultzer	parents
July 3 1848	July 23	Margaret Elizabeth	Benj. & Christiane Reynolds	parents
Jan 30 1843	July 24	Elizabeth Virginia	Wm. S. & Elenora P. Wonderly	mother
Jan 30 1843	July 24	John Virginnus	"	mother
Dec 15 1847	July 24	Elenora Cummings	"	mother
March 28 1846	July 24 1848	Wm. Cummings	Jacob S. & Lydia M. Rogers	parents
Sept 16 1847	July 24 1848	Anna Pickhaver	"	parents
Sept 16 1847	July 24 1848	Mary Gordon	"	parents
Oct 8 1847	July 28 1848	Wm. Henry	Samuel & Rachel Harris	parents
Aug 24 1839	July 30	Emma Rachael	E.S. & Jane Freyer	parents
May 16 1842	July 30	Jane Olive	"	parents
April 14 1844	July 30	Elijah Samuel	Elijah S. & Jane Freyer	parents

FIRST REFORMED CHURCH OF BALTIMORE

DATE OF BIRTH	DATE OF BAPTISM	NAME	PARENTS	SPONSORS
Aug 4 1847	July 30	Henry Eugene	Elijah S. & Jane Freyer	parents
March 8 1848	July 30	Eugenia	Elias & Mary Heiner	parents
Aug 19 1848	Sept 19	Eliza Patterson	Geo. & Elizabeth Gurley	mother
May 12 1848	Sept 20	Simeon James	David & Frances Ann Hays	parents
Oct 11 1847	Sept 25	Susanna	Thomas & Ann Maria Duncan	parents
March 31 1848	Sept 25	James Smith	Wm. & Cornelia Duncan	parents
Jan 29 1842	Sept 30	Rebecca Ann	Geo. & Elizabeth Gray	parents
April 12 1844	Sept 30	Laura Virginia	"	parents
Feb 25 1846	Sept 30	Mary Elizabeth	"	parents
March 28 1848	Sept 30	Charles Wesley	"	parents
Feb 8 1847	Oct 1	Georgianna Ida	Washington & M. M. Barger	parents
Sept 1848	Oct 7	Richard Owen	R.F. & Eliza Maynard	parents

1848

DATE OF BIRTH	DATE OF BAPTISM	NAME	PARENTS	SPONSORS
Aug 21 1847	Jan 5	Justus Frisby	Felix J. & Clara Strawinski	parents
Sept 5 1847	Jan 5	George	James & Clara Crawford	mothers
July 18 1847	Jan 21	Frederick Broaders	Wm. & Anna L. Hoffman	mother
Jan 9 1848	Jan 25	Martha Jane Seesnop	Henry & Mary Ann Richmond	mother
Nov 8 1847	Jan 25	Isaac Henry	John H. & Mary Ann Thompson	mother
Sept 7 1847	Jan 26	Wm. John Worth	Wm. H. & Ann Maria Martin	parents
July 2 1847	Jan 26	Alice Euphenia	Wm. D. & Elizabeth Dorsey	mother
Oct 4 1847	Jan 30	Francis Thomas	Wm. & Leah Rodemayer	parents
Nov 2 1847	Feb 6	John	Wm. & Susan McLean	parents
Sept 10 1847	Feb 16	Mary Louesa	Daniel D. & Maria Lambart [Lonebart ?]	parents
May 27 1847	Feb 16	Mary Cath.	Wm. W. & Mary Ann Meades	mother
Jan 11 1849	Sept 23 1849	Ida Estella Diffenderffer	Edwin S. & Susanna Tarr	
March 29 1849	Sept 23	Charles Courtney	Mr. & Susanna Williams	
Jan 4 1849	Sept 23	Mary Ella	John E. & Cornelia Allen	
Feb 5 1849	Sept 23	John Francis	.... Gibben	

FIRST REFORMED CHURCH OF BALTIMORE

DATE OF BIRTH	DATE OF BAPTISM	NAME	PARENTS	SPONSORS
Feb 21 1846	March 14 1848	John Walter	Richard & Susan Battee	mother
Sept 28 1847	March 14 1848	Richard	"	mother
Jan 26 1848	March 29 1848	Marion	Robert & Jane Ann Grant	mother
Feb 11 1848	March 29 1848	John E.	John E. & Cornelia Allen	mother
March 4 1840	May 5 1848	Benjamin Franklin	John & Elizabeth Freberger	mother
Oct 27 1843	May 5 1848	Mary Elizabeth	"	mother
...	May 1 1848	James Wesley	John & Mary A. Dobbin	parents
May 15 1847	May 14 1848	Allen	John M. & Caroline Johannes	parents
Sept 15 1847	May 14	John Martin	John G. & Mary P. Johannes	parents
March 5 1846	May 15	William Henry	Henry & Rachel Schaper	parents
Jan 30 1848	July 3	Anna Maria	Conrad & Mary Ann Long	mother
May 27 1847	July 5	Ann	Wm. & Mary Jane Joseph	mother
Nov 22 1845	May 11	Josephine Mason	Joseph & Ellen Warner	parents
Feb 11 1838	May 12	Priscilla	David & Julia Mumma	parents
July 1 1841	May 12	Julia	"	parents
May 1 1843	May 12	Margaret	"	parents
Jan 27 1846	May 12	John Jacob	"	parents
Oct 9 1846	May 31	Georgianna	Thomas & Rebecca Kelly	mother
April 13 1847	June 5	Catherine Elizabeth	Charles M. & Mary Hagelin	parents
Dec 15 1845	June 5	Mary Louesa	Robert & Susan Jennings	mother
April 22 1847	June 7	Emerson	Marcellus & Julia League	parents
July 30 1846	June 16	James Edwards	John & Mary Allen	mother
Oct 27 1845	June 20	Jacob	John & Barbara Kauderer	parents
Jan 19 1846	June 20	John William	G. Henry & Barbara Dickle	parents
?	Sept 23	William	Charles & Elizabeth A. Diffenderfer	
Nov 24 1847	Oct 7	Esther Anna	R. A. & Esther Remare	
Jan 26 1849	Oct 7	Edward Payson	Charles & Henrietta Suter	

FIRST REFORMED CHURCH OF BALTIMORE

DATE OF BIRTH	DATE OF BAPTISM	NAME	PARENTS	SPONSORS
June 12 1847	June 30	Sherburn Langdon	Sherburn L. & Laurendia Moore	parents
Jan 1 1843	July 26	Clinton Wright	James & Adeline Lauderman	mother
Feb 4 1847	Sept 10	Edward Diffenderffer	Geo. W. & R.M. Herring	parents
Jan 30 1847	Sept 10	Mary	Charles & Eliz. M. Diffenderffer	parents
July 2 1847	Oct 4	Thomas	John & Lucinda Coburn	-
Aug 11 1847	Oct 13	Charles Jacob	Charles & Julia Hickman	mother
June 6 1847	Oct 13	George Washington	Emoson & Cath. Hickman	mother
Sept 8 1846	Oct 31	Mary Ann	Henry & Eliz. Ann Bersch	parents
?	Nov 21	Louis	Jacob F. & Julia Ann Decker	parents
Sept 11 1847	Nov 25	Elenora Virginia	Henry & Catharine Shuck	parents
April 13 1847	Nov 25	Sarah Jane	Richard & Susanna Plowman	parents
Oct 26 1847	Nov 30	Sophia Reigart	Wm. S. & Emeline M. Reese	parents
	1847			
?	Jan 31	Mary Helen	Geo. W. & ... Ziegler	parents
July 17 1846	Feb 17	Martha Isabella Julia	Francis L. & Sarah C. Hilberg	mother
Nov 22 1846	Feb 17	Antonetta Milcha	Wm. G & Martha Storch	parents
Oct 31 1846	Feb 17	John Henry	Henry & Catharine Betcher	mother
Feb 20 1845	March 7	William Henry Augustus	William J. & Julia Hamilton	parents
Feb 14 1847	March 25	Francis	Noah & Martha Donaldson	mother
March 6 1843	March 29	Alfred Diffenderffer	Alfred & Ann Eliz. Friend	parents
May 1 1845	April 14	Samuel Sands	Samuel S. & Susan Mills	mother
May 21 1846	April 14	Kate Elizabeth	William & Orilla M. Holland	mother
Sept 9 1846	April 15	Sarah Ann	Charles & Henrietta Suter	parents
Jan 19 1846	April 15	Mary Augusta	Washington A. & Eliz. H. Page	parents
July 29 1838	April 16	Mary Frances	Jacob & Margaret Miller	parents

FIRST REFORMED CHURCH OF BALTIMORE

DATE OF BIRTH	DATE OF BAPTISM	NAME	PARENTS	SPONSORS
Nov 11 1840	April 16	William Byers	Jacob & Margaret Miller	parents
Jan 31 1843	April 16	Amanda Jane	"	parents
Oct 1 1844	April 16	Ann Elizabeth	"	parents
May 22 1846	April 21	William Lawrence	Christian & Elizabeth Rash	parents
May 2 1845	April 23	Sarah Catherine	Thomas & Cath. Edwards	parents
Jan 8 1847	April 24	Caroline	Christian & Ama. J. Rosenbrock	parents
Oct 28 1844	April 26	William Clagget	Thos. H. & Mary C. Binnix	parents
April 18 1847	May 2	Ada Romanus	P. Roman & Mary C. Steck	parents
April 17 1847	May 6	Michael Diffenderffer	Henry & Amelia H. Groverman	parents
Feb 9 1844	July 13 1846	Frances	"	parents
Aug 9 1845	July 15 1846	Henry	"	parents
Dec 14 1839	May 11	Mary Jane	Joseph & Ellen Warner	parents
Dec 10 1843	Sept 21	Christian George	C.G. & Eliza Peters	parents
Aug 13 1845	Sept 21	David Alexander	"	parents
April 17 1845	Sept 28	William	Wm. & Mary J. Joseph	parents
Oct 28 1842	Sept 28 1845	John Frederick	Thomas D. & Elenora Sultzer	parents
Aug 29 1845	Sept 28	Mary Frances	"	parents
	1846			
Sept 14 1844	May 1846	Margaret	William & Susan McLean	parents
Jan 5 1846	?	Susanna	"	-
Sept 8 1842	June 1 1846	Harriet Krider	Philip & Harriet Schroeder	parents
Sept 6 1844	June 1 1846	Philip Korkhaus	P. & H. Schroeder	parents
Feb 15 1846	June 1 1846	Charles Frederick	"	parents
Feb 25 1837	July 16 1846	Edward John	James S. & Louesa Wilson	mother
May 27 1839	July 16 1846	Theodore Jarrett	"	mother
Feb 12 1845	July 16 1846	Elvira	"	mother

FIRST REFORMED CHURCH OF BALTIMORE

DATE OF BIRTH	DATE OF BAPTISM	NAME	PARENTS	SPONSORS
Jan 20 1846	July 16 1846	Sarah Rebecca	Samuel J. & Elenora Handy	parents
?	July 12 1846	Edwin Larr [Tarr]	John E. & Cornelia Allen	mother
Dec 7 1845	July 6 1846	Jacob	Conrad & Mary Ann Long	mother
Nov 25 1845	Aug 30 1846	Georgianna	Geo. F. & Mary Ann Fisher	mother
April 14 1846	Sept 20 1846	Mary Jane	... Smith	parents
?	Oct 12	Moses	Dix & Wealthy E. Crawford	parents
March 4 1846	Oct 12	Geo. Payson	Elias & Mary Heiner	parents
Jan 20 1843	Nov 8	Thadeus Smyser	Felix T. & Clara Strawinski	parents
Dec 8 1844	Nov 8 1846	Bellini Owen	"	parents
Jan 7 1846	Nov 24 1846	Catharine Amelia	James H. & Rachel F. Watkins	parents
July 14 1840	Dec 16 1846	John Marshall	Robert & Jane Ann Grant	mother
July 18 1842	Dec 16	Mary	"	mother
?	May	Sally	Jacob F. & ... Grove	parents
?	June 4	?	Agustus & ... Clemens	parents
April 8	June 15	Wm. Henry	George F. & Mary Ann Fisher	mother
?	Oct 16	?	Jno. Elliott	parents
?	Oct 16	?	McClain	parents
Sept 15 1844	Nov 6 1844	Laura	R.F. & Eliza M. Maynard	parents
Sept 19 1844	Nov 12 1844	James Lewis	Charles E. & Cath. Hughes	parents
March 5 1842	Dec 1 1844	Laura Jane	Reuben & Sophia M. Watts	mother
Feb 20 1844	Dec 1 1844	John Henry	"	mother

1845

DATE OF BIRTH	DATE OF BAPTISM	NAME	PARENTS	SPONSORS
June 17 1844	Jan 13 1845	Laura Louesa	David & Mary Shotts	mother
Sept 14 1843	Jan 23 1845	Henry Lewis	George H. & Ann B. Diekel	parents
?	Jan 26 1845	George Washington	David J. & C.E. Asprol [Aspral]	parents
Nov 23 1844	Jan 27 1845	Maria Rebecca	Wm. H. & Ann M. Martin	parents
Aug 16 1840	Oct 7	James Henry	James H. & C. J. Bertholf	
July 19 1842	Oct 7	Ruth Emma	"	
Sept 13 1845	Oct 7	Charles Edgar	"	
Oct 21 1848	Oct 7	Albert Seely	"	

FIRST REFORMED CHURCH OF BALTIMORE

DATE OF BIRTH	DATE OF BAPTISM	NAME	PARENTS	SPONSORS
May 3 1844	Jan 27 1845	Ann Rebecca	Wm. D. & Elizabeth Thomas	parents
July 14 1842	Jan 27 1845	Catherine	Joseph & Cath. King	mother
Oct 31 1844	Feb 26 1845	Henry Clay	Jno. M. & Caroline Johannas	parents
Oct 30 1840	March 9 1845	Richard Adam	R.A. & Esther Remare	parents
Nov 24 1844	March 9 1845	Louesa Amelia	"	parents
?	March	?	George Jno. & Christian Gelbach	parents
Aug 17 1844	April 24 1845	Anna Margaretha	Francis L. & Sarah C. Hilberg	parents
Feb 7 1845	May 1 1845	Elizabeth Bowman	Jno. C. & Ariander Alexander	mother
Feb 24 1845	June 26 1845	?	Bernard & Cath. Spangler	mother
May 28 1845	June 29	Alonzo Alexander	Henry & Sphia R. Rodenmayer	parents
Jan 15 1845	July 6	Elizabeth Reed	Henry & Mary Most	parents
July 10 1845	Aug 6	Martha Jane Seesnop	Henry & Mary Ann Richmond	mother
May 20 1843	June 5 1843	Sarah Elizabeth Seesnop	Henry & Mary Ann Richmond	parents
?	July 18	?	Jesse & Sarah Dehoff	parents
Aug 5 1843	Aug 9 1843	David Henry	John and Mary Allen	mother
June 7 1843	Aug 9 1843	Aarne Eliza	Fred. & Mary Bungan [Bunyan, Burgan]	mother
June 25 1843	Aug 9 1843	Edward	Thos. & Sarah Edwards	mother
July 26 1843	Aug 17 1843	Charles Rogers	Charles R. & Malinda A. Diffenderffer	mother
Nov 1 1842	Aug 18 1843	David Springer	David T. & C. E. Aspral	parents
?	Sept 1843	?	Henry & Cath. Shuck	mother
Sept 9 1837	Dec 17 1843	Eliza Jane	Elias & Eliza C. Hale	parents
April 11 1839	Dec 17 1843	George Elias	"	"
Sept 30 1843	Dec 17 1843	Maria C.	"	"
1844				
?	?	?	------Creamer	mother
June 30 1843	Jan 3 1844	George Washington	Conrad & Mary Ann Long	parents
Nov 2 1849	Nov 3	John Jacob	David S. & Eliza Griffin	

FIRST REFORMED CHURCH OF BALTIMORE

DATE OF BIRTH	DATE OF BAPTISM	NAME	PARENTS	SPONSORS
Feb 6 1837	bapt. by Rev. Scheib [?]	Maanda Elizabeth	Conrad & Mary Ann Long	parents
April 2 1843	Jan 4 1844	Elizabeth Ann	J.L. & E.C. Collins	mother
Dec 28 1843	Jan 4 1844	Mary Virginia	Thomas & E. Eliz. Ann Seabrooks	parents
May 30 1842	Jan 4 1844	John Henry	John & Ermeline Hubbard	mother
Aug 28 1842	Feb 17 1844	Wm. Henry	Wm. & Susanna Bersh	parents
June 18 1843	Feb 18 1844	Margt. Eliz. Ridgeway	Madison & Eliz. Jeffres	parents
Feb 8 1844	Feb 19 1844	Moses	James & Sarah Crawford	parents
Dec 15 1843	Feb 27 1844	Aguste Flavilla	Jno. M. & Marg. Hoff	parents
Nov 13 1836	Feb 29 1844	Jno. Francis	Andrew & Marg Keller	parents
Feb 16 1838	Feb 29 1844	Josiah Good	"	"
Aug 13 1841	Feb 29 1844	Mary Catherine	"	"
Feb 22 1844	March 4 1844	Emma Louesa	Wm. & Mary Bell	mother
?	May 24 1842	Sarah Cornelia	Mr. & Mrs. Ensor	Mrs. Ensor
July 25 1841	June 12 1842	Edwin	John & Rebecca Rodenmayer	parents
April 2 1842	July	Cath. Laura	Elias & Mary Heiner	parents
Dec 28 1841	July 2 1842	Louesa	Madison & A. E. Jeffires	mother
March 9 1841	July 14 1842	Wm. J. Harrison	Geo. Gelbach of John Christiana	mother
April 7 1841	July 14 1842	Geo. Thomas	Geo. H. & A.B. Diekel	parents
July 5 1841	July 26 1842	Emma Virginia	G.L. & M.A. Fisher	parents
March 11 1842	Aug 28 1842	Mary Eliza	Geo. L. & M. Hoffman	parents
May 5 1842	Oct 12 1842	Catharine	Thos. S. & Margt. Jones	parents
July 22 1842	Oct 15 1842	Christiana	Christian & Eliz. Rash	parents
Dec 23 1839	Oct 15 1842	William Henry	Henry & Ann Maria Miller	parents
Nov ..	Dec 26 1842	Edwin Walker	Otis & Cath. S. Spear	parents
Feb 15	Nov 15	William Henry	Wm. H. & Cath. R. Ridgely	parents
Oct 1848	Dec 10	Margaret	Dixon & W.E. Crawford	parents

FIRST REFORMED CHURCH OF BALTIMORE

DATE OF BIRTH	DATE OF BAPTISM	NAME	PARENTS	SPONSORS
1843				
Oct 28 1838	Jan 9 1843	Josephine	William & Mary Russel	parents
June 8 1841	Jan 9 1843	Maria Louesa	"	parents
?	Feb 2 1843	Lewis Albert	Lewis & ... Herring	parents
March 7 1830	Feb 2 1843	Octavian Lavertes	Agustus Mathiot & wife	parents
Dec 26 1831	dto.	Susan Matilda	"	parents
Oct 4 1833	dto.	James Haages	"	parents
Oct 23 1839	dto.	Anna Maria	"	parents
Sept 23 1842	dto.	Clara Louise	"	parents
Oct 19 1842	Feb 9	John Abbes	Francis S. & Sarah C. Hilberg	parents
July 28 1841	March 22 1843	Levenia Rebecca	David & Mary Shotts	parents
April 1 1843	April 10 1843	Emma	Frederick & Mar. Achey	parents
Jan 17 1842	April 30 1843	Dixon Crawford	James & Jane Guy	parents
Feb 24 1839	Dec 30 1841	Mary Jane	J.H. & M. Baker	parents
Nov 12 1840	Dec 30 1841	Maria Elizabeth	dto.	parents
1842				
June 23 1841	Feb 10 1841	Adalade	James & Adalade Laudeman	parents
Jan 29 1842	Feb 21 1842	John Joseph	Thomas & Dorothy Murphy	mother
Feb 7 1842	Feb 24 1842	Joseph	Joseph & Sarah Bevan	parents
Jan 1 1842	March 1 1842	Henrietta	Charles & Henrietta Suter	parents
Feb 1 1842	March 2 1842	Isabella Adalade	Jacob & Henrietta Cook	mother
Jan 13 1842	March 20 1842	Agustus Schnebly	G.B. & L. Wilson	parents
June 23 1841	April 5 1842	Mary Jane	Samuel & Margaret Stoneraker	parents
Feb 28 1839	April 18 1842	Mary Ann	John & Mary Curtis	mother
Dec 23 1840	April 18 1842	Al. Catharine	"	mother
May 11 1840	April 18 1842	Margaret	Henry & Cath. Tinkin	mother
April 1 1836	April 18 1842	Marion	Joseph & Cath. King	parents
Nov 23 1838	April 18 1842	Susanna	"	parents
Nov 14 1841	April 10 1842	Mary Louesa	Agustus & Sophia King	mother
Feb 8 1842	May 1 1842	Caroline Agusta	George & Mary Ann Baker	parents
June 25 1839	May 1 1842	Mary Martha	Susan Robinson	mother

FIRST REFORMED CHURCH OF BALTIMORE

DATE OF BIRTH	DATE OF BAPTISM	NAME	PARENTS	SPONSORS
Dec 18 1840	June 21 1841	Ann Elizabeth	Henry & Mary Ann Long	mother
Sept 13 1840	June 21 1841	William Henry	Henry & Elizabeth Jane Schwartz	mother
Jan 24 1832	June 23 1841	Mary Elizabeth	John J. & Susan Myer	parents
Nov 9 1834	June 23 1841	Charles Marshall	John J. & Susan Myer	parents
Aug 27 1838	June 27 1841	Elizabeth	John W. & Ellen Nesbitt	parents
June 26 1840	June 27 1841	Ellen M.	John W. & Ellen Nesbitt	parents
April 24 1839	July 20 1841	Mary Ann	Wm. H. & E. M. Cole	parents
Nov 28 1840	July 20 1841	John Clarence Le Grand	Wm. H. & E. M. Cole	parents
July 5 1841	July 20 1841	George	David & Elizabeth Richter	parents
May 27 1841	July 23 1841	Frances Louesa	Samuel & Mary Linard	mother
Feb 25 1841	Sept 2 1841	John Felix	Jnc. F. & Susanna Durst	mother & Mr. Griffith & wife
Aug 1 1841	Sept 5 1841	James	James & Sarah Crawford	mother
May 4 1841	Sept 5 1841	Elizabeth	Wm. & Isabella Wallance	mother
?	Sept 6 1841	Elenora (adult)	wife of Thos. D. Sultzer	self
?	Sept 6 1841	Wm. H. Harrison	Thos. D. & Elenora Sultzer	parents
May 14 1841	Sept 7 1841	Jacob Wm.	John M. & Margaret Hoff	parents
March 15 1841	Nov 18 1841	Cath. Elizabeth	David & Adaline Mc Coy	mother
Oct 2 1841	Nov 18 1841	John Elias	John & Mary Allen	mother
Aug 10 1841	Nov 18 1841	Mary Elizabeth	Thomas & Sarah Edwards	mother
?	Dec 5 1841	?	Jacob .... Sellers	parents
June 30 1841	Dec 10 1841	Charles Alexander	John & Margaret Smith	parents
April 12 1841	Dec 10 1841	Alexander Gould	W.H. & C.R. Ridgely	parents
July 4 1841	Dec 30 1841	Mary Ann Seesnop	H. & M.A. Richmond	parents
Sept 9 1836	Dec 30 1841	Cath. Franciscus	J.H. & M. Baker	parents
June 16 1848	Dec 13	Louisa	Garrison & Susanna Haten	mother
? 1848	Dec 24	Mary Jefferson	................Kanfelt	parents

FIRST REFORMED CHURCH OF BALTIMORE

Born	Baptized	Name	Parents	Sponsor
Sept 7 1839	March 3 1840	Mary Elizabeth	Henry C. & Margaret Beam	parents
March 25 1840	April 21 1840	James Anna Limes	James L. & Eliz. A. Rogers	mother
Nov 28 1839	June 3 1840	Thomas Penington	...Collins	mother
Nov 20 1839	July 12 1840	Mary Ann	G.L. & A.M. Fischer	parents
Oct 21 1839	July 26 1840	Frances Marion	George & Cath. Elliott	parents
July 3 1840	July 26 1840	Agnes Ellen	James F. & Deborah D. Harvey	mother
Aug 17 1840	Sept 8 1840	Henrietta	Philipp and Elizabeth Thater	parents
June 15 1840	Sept 22 1840	Frederick Matthias	Jacob and Elizabeth Creamer	mother and grandmother
Sept 22 1838	Sept 22 1840	Edward Harris	John & Priscilla Matthias	grandmother Petit
Sept 21 1840	Sept 28 1840	Anna Augusta	John & Sophia Williams	mother
?	Nov 17 1840	Henry Harrison	Michael and Salome Diffenderffer	parents
April 15 1840	Dec 31 1840	Emeline Howard	Henry and Mary Most	parents

1841

Born	Baptized	Name	Parents	Sponsor
Oct 1 1839	Jan 31 1841	Ulric Zwingli	Charles A. & M.L. Oberteuffer	parents
June 2 1840	Feb 2 1841	Mary Susanna	Jno. & Margaret Smith	parents
Nov 2 1840	Feb 2 1841	Mary	Jno. & Barbara Thanda	parents
Jan 3 1841	Feb 9 1841	Jacob	Jno. & Caroline Johannas	parents
	?		Fred & Margaret Achey	parents
	?		Fred & Margaret Achey	parents
Nov 12 1839	March 22 1841	Charles Henry	John R. & Susan Ann Pedrick	mother
Sept 27 1840	March 24 1841	John Henry	Jesse & Sarah Dehoff	parents
?	April 11 1841	Alexenia	J. Holland	self
March 24 1840	June 6 1841	Marion Eliz. Harrison	David and Caroline M. Buckey	parents
?	June 11 1841	?	Levi & ... Wilder	parents
March 16 1841	June 21 1841	Almira Catharine	Conrad & Mary Ann Long	parents
Aug 7 1841	May 5 1842	John	... & Margaret King	parents
?	May 7 1842	Mary Elizabeth	John B. & Adeline Mathiot	parents
?	May 7 1842	Adaline Virginia	John B. & Adeline Mathiot	parents

FIRST REFORMED CHURCH OF BALTIMORE

DATE OF BIRTH	DATE OF BAPTISM	NAME	PARENTS	SPONSORS
Nov 22 1837	June 30 1839	Mary Ann	Henry and Mary Most	parents and grandmother
Dec 6 1838	July 7 1839	Ella	John and Rebecca Rodenmeyer	parents
April 22 1839	Aug 20 1839	Maria Cath. Seesnop	Henry and Mary Ann Richmond	parents
April 26 1839	Aug 20 1839	Thomas Solomon	Thomas S. and Sarah Ann Hubbard	mother
May 27 1839	July 29 1839 by the Rev. Mr. Lochman	William Henry	George and Mary Hoffman	parents
Feb 21 1837	Aug 25 1839	Elizabeth Jane	John and Jane Dohm	parents
Feb 9 1839	Aug 25 1839	Susanna Maria	John and Jane Dohm	parents
June 28 1839	Sept 8 1839	Elias Mayer	Elias and Mary Heiner	parents
Feb 23 1837	Sept 26 1839	Charles	Daniel and Mary Shotts	parents
Feb 14 1839	Sept 26 1839	Susanna	Daniel and Mary Shotts	parents
July 28 1839	Nov 10 1839	Martha Frances	John U. & Susanna Durst	Mr. Daener & parents
Sept 27 1839	Nov 14 1839	Peter Forney	Otis and Cath. S. Spear	parents
Sept 24 1838	Nov 17 1839	Thomas	John and Catharine Elliott	parents
Aug 14 1839	Dec 16 1839	Virginia	Andrew and Catharine Smith	parents
Feb 27 1839	Dec 25 1839	Hamilton Josephus	William and Mary Reifsnider	parents
Dec 15 1839	Dec 30 1839	Cath. Mc. Cubbins	Thomas and Dorothy Murphy	mother

1840

DATE OF BIRTH	DATE OF BAPTISM	NAME	PARENTS	SPONSORS
Dec 6 1839	Jan 16 1840	John Rogers	Charles R. & M.A. Diffenderffer	parents
May 3 1837	Jan 19 1840	James Edgar Stewart	Madison and A. Eliz. Jeffers	mother
July 25 1839	Jan 19 1840	William Henry	"	"
Oct 24 1839	Jan 26 1840	Sophia Elizabeth	Henry F. and Maria Reigart	parents and Mr. Reigart
1820	Jan 26 1840	Ann Maria Gill	adult	self
Aug 5 1825	Jan 25 1840	James L. Hewell	adult	self
Oct 30 1823	Jan 25 1840	Catharine Hewell	adult	self
Aug 1 1840	May 8 1842	Mary	John Elliott & wife	parents
Feb 7 1842	May 8 1842	Susan	John Elliott & wife	parents
Jan 2 1842	May 24 1842	Henry Maynard	Mr. & Mrs. Parish	mother & grandmother Horton

FIRST REFORMED CHURCH OF BALTIMORE

DATE OF BIRTH	DATE OF BAPTISM	NAME	PARENTS	SPONSORS
1839				
Aug 31 1838	Jan 1 1839	Michael	Michael and Salome Diffenderffer	parents
Nov 18 1838	Jan 9 1839	Alexander	John and Mary Allen	parents
April 14 1838	March 3 1839	George Stafford	Jacob and Sarah Boyer	parents
Aug 16 1837	March 31 1839	Anthony	Henry and Amelia H. Groverman	grandfather Groverman
Aug 12 1838	April 4 1839	Michael Nathaniel Jacob	Jacob V. and Amelia Hoffman	M. Hoffman & wife
June 17 1838	April 7 1839	Julia Margaret	George L. & Anna Maria Fisher	parents
Feb 1 1838	April 8 1839	Annett Marion	John and Ann Gade	mother
Feb 27 1839	April 18 1839	William John	Samuel and Mary Linard	mother
Feb 10 1829	April 18 1829	Edwin Ruthwin	John and Catharine Linsey	mother
Feb 16 1839	April 21 1839	George Alexander	John and Jennet Calder	parents
Aug 9 1836	April 21 1839	John Law	John and Jennet Calder	parents
April 19 1833	April 25 1839	Mary Fletcher	Edward and Barbara Greffith	Mr. Keener & wife
May 2 1835	April 25 1839	Casandra	"	"
Aug 24 1839	May 8 1839	George William	James F. and Deborah D. Harvey	mother
Jan 15 1837	May 12 1839	Mary Frances	David and Mary Magdalena Pugh	parents
May 18 1839 [?]	May 14 1839	Charles	Charles and Henrietta Suter	parents
Oct 29 1838	May 26 1839	Charles Henry	Henry and Elizabeth Baker	parents
Jan 30 1839	May 26 1839	Frederick William	George and Mary Ann Baker	parents
Jan 14 1839	May 27 1839	William Henry	Conrad and Mary Ann Long	parents
Jan 18 1839	May 27 1839	Mary Catherine	Henry and Mary Ann Long	parents
April 25 1839	May 28 1839	Edward Coleman	James and Susan Kussear [or Nussear]	parents and grandparents
June 27 1836	June 9 1839	William Foxhall	George and Mary Rishstein	parents
Sept 4 1838	June 9 1839	Retta Jane	"	"
1849				
Dec 31 1845	Jan 10 1849	Mary Jane	David & Cath. Shotts	parents
Oct 1 1848	Jan 10 1849	William	Wm. & Eliz. Tagart [Lagart ?]	parents

FIRST REFORMED CHURCH OF BALTIMORE

DATE OF BIRTH	DATE OF BAPTISM	NAME	PARENTS	SPONSORS
	1838			
Oct 21 1837	Jan 17 1838	Augustus Zacharias	Augustus and Tobitha [?] Hilman	mother
April 13 1836	Jan 31 1838	Rebecca Sophia	Richard and Louesa H. Mott	grandmother & parents
Dec 18 1837	Feb 4 1838	George Peter	George and Mary Ann Baker	parents
Dec 25 1837	Feb 25 1838	Philip	Philip and Elizabeth Thater	parents
Jan 6 1838	Feb 22 1838	Mary Elizabeth	John M. and Margaret Hoff	parents
March 25 1838	April 12 1838	Mary Jane	Charles and Henrietta Suter	parents
April 16 1834	May 13 1838	William Todd	William B. & Louesa Smith	grandmother Smith
Feb 15 1838	May 15 1838	John Michael	Georg and Mary Hoffman	parents
April 21 1838	May 16 1838	Susan Elizabeth	James and Elizabeth Rogers	parents
Sept 26 1835	June 2	John	[no names listed]	parents
July 8 1837	June 8 1838	Julia Baker	Daniel and Caroline Buckey	parents
June 19 1832	June 30 1838	Catharine	Anthony and Maria Miller	mother
April 25 1835	"	Margaret Ann	"	"
July 12 1837	"	Ann Maria	"	"
-	July 3 1838	Susan (a sick grown girl)		-
June 29 1838	July 10 1838	Mary Elizabeth	George and Cath. Elliot	parents
July 8 1838	July 14 1838	Clementine	A. & Sophia Curtois	mother
June 29 1837	Aug 10 1838	Albein Alfred Alcock	David and Sarah Atkinson	mother
Aug 28 1838	Sept 5 1838	James Taylor	Joshua and Harriet Motter	parents
July 8 1838	Sept 8 1838	Sarah Elizabeth	Jacob and Mary Showers	mother and Mrs. Ensor
May 15 1837	Sept 8 1838	Juliett Dusslisiss	Edwin and Susanna R.B. Tarr	mother and Mrs. Duhurst
Aug 17 1838	Oct 30 1838	Cordelia Victoria	Jacob and Henrietta Cook	mother
April 10 1838	Nov 4 1838	Oliver Franklin	Frederick and Elizabeth Smith	parents

FIRST REFORMED CHURCH OF BALTIMORE

DATE OF BIRTH	DATE OF BAPTISM	NAME	PARENTS	SPONSORS
Jan 7 1837	Feb 11 1837	Lloyd	Charles and Henrietta Suter	parents
Jan 11 1837	Feb 15 1837	William Henson	Wm. H. and Elenora M. Cole	parents
Jan 9 1837	Feb 15 1837	Rebecca Amelia	J. and Sarah Ann Frey	parents and grandmother
Feb 27 1837	April 4 1837	Mary Catherine Scesnop	Andrew and Catherine Bowman	mother and grandmother
Aug 29 1836	April 24 1837	Emmerson E.	William and Elizabeth Lange	mother
Dec 2 1834	May 23 1837	Kitty Rogers	Michael N. and Mary B. Diffenderffer	parents
Aug 20 1836	May 23 1837	Baruch Williams	Michael N. and Mary B. Diffenderffer	parents
Jan 16 1837	June 15 1837	Charles August Samuel	Charles A. & Mary L. Oberteuffer	parents
March 19 1837	June 18 1837	James Michael	George and Ann Maria Fischer	parents
Jan 17 1833	July 2 1837	Ellen	Elijah S. and E. S. Freyer	parents
July 15 1835	July 2 1837	James	"	"
May 12 1837	July 2 1837	William	"	"
Aug 7 1847	March 8	Margaret Henrietta	Jacob & Margaret Miller	parents
Feb 15 1849	March 15	Lavenia Valentine	Philip J. & Josephine L. Thomas	mother
Feb 20 1837	Aug 9 1837	Catharine Amanda	John Freberger jun. and Elizabeth	parents
July 2 1837	Sept 10 1837 by Rev. Mr. Backer	John Zwingle	Elias and Mary Heiner	parents
Aug 26 1837	Oct 6 1837	Alva Grove	Otis and Catharine Spear	parents
Nov 24 1836	Oct 9 1837	Margaret Jane	Valentine and Christiane Lutz	mother
June 8 1831	Oct 12 1837	John Edward	J. and Charlotte Chambers	mother
June 10 1833	"	Catharine Jane	"	"
Feb 6 1836	"	William Manion	"	"
June 18 1829	Oct 12 1837	John Isaac	Wm. P. & Mary Ann Miller	mother
March 2 1833	Oct 12 1837	Dolphos Henry	"	"
June 15 1837	Oct 15 1837	John Milton	Henry F. and Maria Reigart	parents and E. Shriver and his wife E. Lydia
Oct 13 1837	Dec 12 1837	James van Buren	Matthew and Sophia Shaw	parents
April 10 1836	Oct 21 1837	Rebecca Hollen	James and Elizabeth Royss	parents

FIRST REFORMED CHURCH OF BALTIMORE

DATE OF BIRTH	DATE OF BAPTISM	NAME	PARENTS	SPONSORS
—	April 5 1836	Mary Elizabeth	John Smith	the parents
Nov 20 1824	April 11 1836	Eugenia Danills	David and Julia Ann Mumma	the parents
Dec 9 1826	"	Sarah	"	"
July 12 1829	"	Eduard Woodyear	"	"
Jan 6 1833	"	Mary Ann	"	"
July 12 1835	"	David Taylor	"	"
Feb 29 1836	April 11 1836	William Henry	William D. and Jane Baden	the parents
Jan 29 1836	April 17 by Rev. B. Kurtz	Martha Virginia	E. and Mary E. Heiner	the parents
Nov 28 1836	April 20 1836	Ellen Francis	Capt. W. Wadlington and Sophia	the parents
April 7 1836	April 25 1836	Caroline Louesa	Benjamin and Margaret Herbaugh	the parents
March 13 1836	May 15 1836	Amelia Indianna	Henry & Amelia H. Groverman	the parents
March 25 1836	July 3 1836	Olivia	John & Rebecca Rodemeyer	the parents
?	April 1	James	Joshua & Mary Ann Van Sant	mother
?	April 1	?	Wm. P. & Marg. Ann Smith	mother
April 1 1847	May 14	Mary	Ralph & Mary Etchberger	mother
April 7 1849	May 14	John Warner	"	mother
April 21 1836	July 1836	Isaac Rennels	Michael and Mary Hoffman	the parents
June 29 1836	August 31 1836	Margaret Frances	William and Mary Russel	the parents
August 1836	Sept 3 1836	William Henry	George and Margaret Webb	the parents
April 21 1836	Sept 18 1836	George Washington	George and Catharina Elliot	the parents
Aug 28 1836	Sept 28 1836 by Rev. Christian Baker	Rosena	Richard and Catherina Miller	the parents
Oct 2 1836	Oct 13 1836	Catharina Elizabeth	George and Mary Ann Baker	the parents
Oct 19 1836	Oct 20 1836	Sarah Elizabeth	Frederick and Margaret Ache	the parents
Oct 10 1836	Nov 10 1836	Charles Heiner	Jacob and Sarah Boyer Boyer	the parents
Oct 13 1836	Nov 17 1836	Henry Jacob	Henry and Mary Long	the parents
March 22 1836	Nov 20 1836	Ann Rebecca	Frederick and Elizabeth Smith	the parents
1837				
Nov 2 1836	Jan 30 1837	Isaac	J. and Eliza Freberger	parents

FIRST REFORMED CHURCH OF BALTIMORE

DATE OF BIRTH	DATE OF BAPTISM	NAME	PARENTS	SPONSORS
Dec 14 1833	Nov 21 1834	Robert Carter	Thomas and Metta Maund	the mother
May 23 1834	May 4 1834	Emily	James and Christina Jones	the parents
	1835			
Sept 16 1834	June 7 1835	Barbara Cornelia	William Cole and his wife	Mrs. Hays
May 16 1835	June 7 1835	Elizabeth Eleonora Virginia	"	Mrs. Ensor
Nov 6 1834	June 19 1835	Albert Jacob	James and Sophia Hanes	Mrs. Long
May 16 1835	June 19 1835	Andrew Jackson	John and Catharine Drane	the parents
July 12 1829	June 20 1835	John Manier	John and Ann Hodgkinson	the mother
Oct 13 1834	June 20 1835	Ann Robinson	John and Ann Hodgkinson	the mother
March 6 1835	July 20 1835	Adelia Amelia	Erasmus and Christianna Peterson	the parents
Aug 3 1834	July 21 1835	Eliza Jane	John and Elizabeth Freeberger	the parents
Feb 1 1834	July 21 1835	Ann Olivia	"	"
July 15 1835	August	Sarah Elizabeth Mc. Colm	Jobe and Sarah Ann German	Matthew and Elizabeth Mc.Colm
April 2 1835	August	William Conrad	Charles Peter Simason	the mother
May 1835	Sept 21 1835	Louisa	Valentine and Christianna Lutz	Miss Thomson
aged 20 month	Nov 29 1835	John Thomas	Fredrick and Eliza Smith	baptized by the Rev. M. Crown of Lebannon (Penna)
April 5 1835		Andrew Jackson	Andrew and Catharine Boroman	baptized by the Rev. Mr. Wm. Miller Methodist clergyman
Oct 6 1834	in the latter part of Dec 1834	Christian Ferdinand	Dietrich and Mary Jane Motz	baptized by the Rev. Albert Helfenstein
28 1835	1835	Mary Elizabeth	Philip and Elizabeth Thater	
	1836			
Jan 11 1836	Feb 23 1836	George Francis	...Yent	the parents
May 12 1835	Feb 23 1836	Elizabeth	...Williams	the parents
May 12 1835	Feb 23 1835	Eduard	"	"

FIRST REFORMED CHURCH OF BALTIMORE

DATE OF BIRTH	DATE OF BAPTISM	NAME	PARENTS	SPONSORS
	1834			
May 5 1833	Feb 19 1834	Davis Tong [Song]	Georg and Mary Rouse	the mother
Jan 31 1831	Feb 19 1834	Layfield	Georg and Mary Rouse	the mother
Dec 26 1833	March 2 1834	John Thomas	Henry and Mary Ann Most	the grandparents
Sept 20 1824	March 17 1834	Virginia	William and Mary Curothers (or Carothers)	the parents
July 11 1826	"	William Murphy	"	"
Dec 11 1827	"	Masoura	"	"
Jan 7 1832	"	Illinois	"	"
Oct 11 1833	March 27 1834	George Milliman	Charles and Ann Diffenderffer	the parents
Aug 7 1833	March 27 1834	Harriot Elizabeth	Carry and Rebecca Chambers	Charles and Ann Diffenderffer
March 12 1834	March 31 1834	Ann Elizabeth Magdalena	William and Mary Russell	Ann Magdlina Fobb (or Tobb)
Oct 22 1833	-	Lewis Henry	John L. Herron and Margaret	Elizabeth Herron
Sept 11 1831	June 7 1834	Carolina Matilda	George and Maria Winckle	the mother
Oct 11 1833	June 8 1834	Ann Cath.	John and Margaret Smith	the mother
Nov 12 1833	July 9 1834	Anna	Daniel and Mary Ann Schatz	the parents
May 25 1834	July 20 1834	John Edward	John and Elizabeth Bunkard [or Bunkerd]	James Edward and Susanna
Feb 6 1834	July 20 1834	William	Jacob and Mary Wunderlich	the mother
Feb 9 1834	July 27 1834	Elionora Cicilia	Georg and Mary Ann Richstein	the parents
May 25 1834	July 27 1834	Ann Rebecca	Georg and Mary Ann Trenken	the parents
May 25 1834	July 27 1834	Margarete Ann	Georg and Mary Ann Trenken	the parents
June 1 1834	July 27 1834	Mary Louisa	Fredrick and Margaret Achey	the parents
Aug 23 1834	Sept 21 1834	John Georg Wash. Drane	Henry and Mary Ann Long	John and Cath. Drane
Nov 8 1833	Oct 10 1834	Thomas Michael	George W. and Susan Powell	Michael Hoffman and his wife
July 11 1834	Oct 12 1834	William Henry	George and Catharine Elliot	the parents
Oct 22 1834	Nov 19 1834	Frederick	Lorentz and Philippina Fishbach	Frederick Simon

DATE OF BIRTH	DATE OF BAPTISM	NAME	PARENTS	SPONSORS
Sept 20 1832	Oct 22 1832	John	John and Ann Gade	the parents
Dec 16 1831	Dec 25 1832	Henry Freyer	Dr. Mott and his wife	Henry and Elizabeth Freyer
1833				
Sept 29 1832	Feb 7 1832	Sarah Marshall	Benjamin and Margaret Harbaugh	
Feb 22 1833	March 12 1833	George Washington Samuel	Andrew and Catharine Bowman	John and Hanna Feuerabend
Aug 9 1832	March 12 1833	Lamech Tubalcain	Richard and Elizabeth Bew	the mother
Nov 12 1833	April 24 1833	Mary Williams	Michael and Mary Diffenderffer	uncle Charles Diffenderffer
Sept 15 1832	June 11 1833	Henrietta Isabel	John B. and Henrietta Magruder	the parents
Jan 20 1833	June 17 1833	John Henry	James and Mary Lloyd	the mother
July 2 1833	June 17 1833	Julia	Henry and Julia Haubert	
May 29 1833	June 24 1833	Dorothea Elisabeth	Thomas and Dorothea Murphy	the mother
July 4 1832	June 27 1833	Wm. George Washington	John and Sarah Baartebeer	the parents
Jan 10 1833	Aug 13 1833	Laura Augusta	Georg and Mary Rodemayer	the parents
Aug 9 1833	Sept 1 1833	Elizabeth Ransaleur	David and Ann Merur	the parents
March 5 1832	Sept 12 1833	John Thomas	John T. and Christiana Newbell	the parents
Sept 9 1833	Oct 8 1833	Sarah Lydia	Otis and Cath. Susanna Speur	the grandmother Mrs. Grove
Oct 13 1833	-	Georg Washington Lafayette	John and Cathrine Drane	the parents
July 12 1833	-	Henry	John and Marg. Miller	the parents
Sept 4 1833		Mary Ann	Henry and Amey Mury	the mother
Feb 21 1833	Oct 27 1833	Mary Cath.	Jacob and Juliann Han	the mother
Feb 10 1833	Nov 3 1833	Albert Bernhardt	John Seidenstricker and his wife	the parents
Oct 9 1833	Nov 14 1833	Eliza Ann	Samuel and Mary Leinard	Mrs. Weidemayer
April 21 1833	Nov 14 1833	Matilda Ann	Erasmus and Christina Peterson	the mother
Oct 6 1833	Dec 11 1833	Ann Caroline	Charles and Sophie Jordan	the grandmother

FIRST REFORMED CHURCH OF BALTIMORE

DATE OF BIRTH	DATE OF BAPTISM	NAME	PARENTS	SPONSORS
May 30 1831	Oct 19 1831	Ann Amelia	George and Margaret Grubb	the mother
Nov 18 1831	Oct 19 entered	George Washington	George and Margaret Grubb	the parents
Feb 20 1831		Andrew Jackson	John and Elizabeth Freeburger	the parents
Sept 28 1831	Dec 11 1831	George	Conrad and Cathrine Broehm	the parents
Oct 28 1831	Dec 11 1831	Ann Mary	John A. Klohr	the parents
1832				
Dec 2 1831	Jan 18 1832	William Hutchins	Daniel and Mary Schatz	the parents
Dec 14 1831	Jan 19 1832	Carolina	Henry and Julianna Haubert	Caroline Haubert
Oct 29 1831	Feb 22 1832	Charles F.	Frank and Margaret Achey	the parents
Feb 20 1832	March 3 1832	Georg Alexander	Alexander and Catharine Sumwalt	Mrs. Duhurst
Feb 23 1832	April 18 1832	Ann Maria Susana	Samuel and Mary Leinard	Maria Spars
dto.		Sarah Lydia	the same	Lydia Mayers
Sept 17 1829	April 18 1832	John Robert	Robert and Lydia Mayers	the mother
Feb 7 1831	April 30 1832	Margaret Jane	Jacob and Henrietta Cook	the parents
March 20 1832	-	Mary Frances	Isaac and Charlotte Baker	the parents
Dec 25 1829	-	William Clare	"	"
March 20 1832	May 23 1832	Mary Ellen	Thomas and Mary Weeden	the mother
Sept 15 1831	June 20 1832	Charlotte Emelia	Charles and Sophia Jordan	Mrs. Foss Mrs. Grane
Feb 24 1830	July 25 1832	Jane Adelaine	Albin and Jane Francis Mellier	Frederick Mierville Adele Susan Sonzer
Sept 8 1831	July 25 1832	Louis Albin	"	Louis Mierville and Marianne
Aug 19 1822	Sept 4 1832	Amelia Elizabeth	John and Elizabeth Zell	the parents
Dec 3 1825	"	Mary Jane	"	"
Nov 19 1829	"	Andre Jackson	"	"
Oct 18 1831	"	Sarah Ann	"	"
Sept 17 1832	Sept 27 1832	Mary Ann	Wm. and Sophia Watlington	Mary Lauderman (grandmother)

FIRST REFORMED CHURCH OF BALTIMORE

DATE OF BIRTH	DATE OF BAPTISM	NAME	PARENTS	SPONSORS
Feb 15 1830	March 11 1830	Daniel Webster	John Myer and his wife	the parents
Feb 18 1828	March 11 1830	George William	dto.	dto.
Oct 2 1829	?	Charles Augustus	Jacob and Margaret Gettier	Elizabeth Bowers
Jan 15 1830	May 2 1830	Maria Louisa	Andrew and Elizabeth Franchi	Angelo Salvador
Feb 25 1830	June 4 1830	Catharine	George and Margaret Weaver	the parents
May 10 1830	July 4 1830	John	James and Christina Jones	the parents
Oct 7 1827	July 6 1830	Elisabeth Catharine	John B. Newbell and his wife Christine	the parents
Jan 20 1830	July 6 1830	July Ann	dto.	dto.
March 8 1830	July 25 1830	Joseph	William Allens and Catharine	Cath. Shaeffer
Feb 14 1829	Aug 14 1830	Felix	Felix and Frena Durst	the parents
June 18 1830	Aug 29 1830	Octavius	John Differnderffer and his wife	the parents
July 1 1830	Sept 7 1830	William Henry	William E. Dorsey and Cath.	the parents
March 31 1830	Nov 1830	Herman	Philip and Elisabeth Shaefer	Herman Neumeyer
Nov 25 1830	Dec 15 1830	Daniel Reinhart	Benjamin and Margaret Herbaugh	the parents
1831				
Nov 16 1830	Feb 16 1831	Margaret Ann	... Miller and his wife Margaret	the parents
March 9 1831	June 3 1831	Amanda Carolina	Erasmus and Christianna C. Peterson	the parents
March 8 1831	June 19 1831	Cath. Elisabeth	John G. and Eliza Tehelmann	the parents
Feb 18 1830	Aug 6 1831	Elizabeth	Daniel and Mary Schatz	the mother
Dec 18 1830	Sept 6 1831	Francis Tobias	George and Maria Rodemayer	the parents
May 11 1831	Sept 20 1831	Charlotte Elizabeth	Henry J. and Rebecca Diffenderffer	the parents
April 12 1831	Sept 20 1831	Charlotte Ann Schlegel	William and Mary Ann Miller	the parents
Feb 18 1831	Sept 29 1831	Eliza Jane	Henry R. and Eliza Rodewald	the parents
July 8 1831	Oct 19 1831	Jacob Waters Penn	Christian F. and Ruth Eichler	the parents

FIRST REFORMED CHURCH OF BALTIMORE

DATE OF BIRTH	DATE OF BAPTISM	NAME	PARENTS	SPONSORS
Dec 10 1824	Oct 14 1827	William Elliot	William Miller and his wife	
Feb 20 1827	Oct 14 1827	James Edward	dto.	
May 18 1829	July 28 1829	Amanda Rebecca	William and Cath. Dorsey	the mother
April 20 1828	July 28 1829	Elizabeth	Charles and Sophia Jordan	Elizabeth Jordan
April 28 1828	August 7 1829	Yanetta or Nancy	John and Sarah Barstekser [Baartekser]	Yanetta Anderson (grandmother)
June 8 1829	Aug 20 1829	Jacob William	David and Elizabeth Spar	Ann Lions
Aug 18 1829	Aug 20 1829	John David	William and Mary Russell	Magdal. Foble
Dec 22 1828	Oct 18 1829	William	Nicolas and Elisabeth Elliot	the parents
Aug 9 1829	Oct 10 1829	Elizabeth Ann	Samuel W. Elwee and his wife	the parents
March 6 1829	Oct 18 1829	Susan Ellen	William and Margaret Steits	the parents
July 2nd 1829	Oct 10 1829	George Helfrich	A. and Mary Helfenstein	the parents
March 7 1828	Nov 9 1829	Elizabeth Ann	John and Elizabeth Weir	the parents
Nov 12 1828	Dec 14 1829	Elizabeth Ann	Jacob and Henrietta Coock	the mother and grandmother

1830

DATE OF BIRTH	DATE OF BAPTISM	NAME	PARENTS	SPONSORS
Aug 10 1828	Jan 5 1830	John Fredrich Uhthoff	Henry and Eliza Rodewald	the parents
Aug 13 1829	Jan 5 1830	William Henry Augustus	dto.	the parents
Nov 18 1827	Jan 12 1830	Elizabeth Ann	Charles P. and Maria Burrows	the father
Feb 1 1826	Jan 12 1830	Jacob Ward	William and Mary Ann Miller	the parents
Sept 25 1829	Jan 12 1830	William Henry	dto.	the parents
Dec 23 1827	Jan 12 1830	Mary Francis	Edwin and Susannah Tarr	the mother
Nov 25 1829	Jan 12 1830	Richard Leving	dto.	dto.
May 12 1829	Jan 22 1830	Susan Jane	John and Margaret Keener	the parents
Jan 23 1830	Feb 11 1830	John William	Jacob and Sarah Boyer	the parents

FIRST REFORMED CHURCH OF BALTIMORE

DATE OF BIRTH	DATE OF BAPTISM	NAME	PARENTS	SPONSORS
Dec 8 1827	?	Frances Jane	Jacob and Elizabeth Weaver	
March 16 1828	May 26 1828	Charles Helfenstein	Greenbury and Mary Duhurst	the parents
Dec 5 1828 [sic]	June 18 1828	Ann Elizabeth	William and Mary Russel	the mother
Dec 2 1827	June 19 1828	Maria Woodside	Benjamin Herbach	the mother
July 21 1828 [sic]	June 23 1828	Ann Mary	Joseph and Cathrine Bonn	Anthony Bonn
Jan 7 1828	June 23 1828	Elizabeth Ann	George and Cathrine Ring	Cath. Kleinauer
April 14 1828		William Albert	Thomas S. and Dorothy Murphy	Eliz. Etchberger
Dec 31 1827		Lewis Thomas	Francis and Mary Gatchair	Maria Magdalena, the grandmother
Sept 26 1827		Mary Magdalena	John Davis Parsons and Margaret	Sarah Etchberger
Feb 20 1828	Aug 25 1828	Margaret Ann	John and Julia Smith	Margaret N. Smith and Wm.
July 23 1828	Aug 25	Joseph Alexander	Joseph and Mary Hugh	John and Julia Smith
June 28 1828	Sept 14 1828	James Wilkes	John and Harriott Schoeneman	the father
July 9 1828	Oct 13 1828	Cathrine	Valentine and Christina Lutz	the parents
Feb 18 1828	Oct 14 1828	Ann Rebecca	Isaac and Charlot Baker	the mother
July 6 1828	Oct 14 1828	Martha Ellen	John and Elizabeth Freeberger	the parents
Sept 27 1828	Dec 21 1828	Catharina Rosalba	John Diffendorfer and his wife	the parents
July 7 1828	?	Catharine	Daniel and Mary Schatz	
Oct 31 1828	Dec 21 1828	?	Georg and Mary Rodemayer	the parents
July 31 1828	Dec 21 1828	Michael Addison	Michael Diffenderffer and his wife	the parents

1829

DATE OF BIRTH	DATE OF BAPTISM	NAME	PARENTS	SPONSORS
Dec 22 1828	Feb 9 1829	William Peter	Samuel and Mary Leinard	Barbara Reiter
Nov 29 1828	Feb 13 1829	Cathrine Martha	Peter and Elizabeth Euler [or Ealer]	the parents
Feb 10 1827	-	Eliza Jane	dto.	the parents
Dec 19 1828	Feb 15 1829	Henry Lewis	James and Christina Jones	the parents

FIRST REFORMED CHURCH OF BALTIMORE 199

DATE OF BIRTH	DATE OF BAPTISM	NAME	PARENTS	SPONSORS
?	Sept 10 1827	Isaac	Samuel Freeman and Mary	the parents
Dec 19 1826	Sept 18 1827	Sarah Ann	John and Sarah Ann Etchberger	Mary Etchberger
Dec 26 1826	Sept 18 1827	William Henry	William and Margaret Lefferman	the mother
July 14 1827	Sept 20 1827	Fanny	Julian and Emilia Nicolet	Felix and Fanny Durst
Sept 24 1826	Sept 16 1827	William Charles	George and Ann Schminke	the parents
Aug 18 1826	Sept 23 1827	Susanna Louisa	John R. and Louisa Chamberlain	Susanna Knipp
Jan 8 1827	Oct 10 1827	John	Joh. Frey Vogel and Philippina	Joh. and Anna Maria Mayer
Sept 15 1827	Nov 27 1827	Francis Michael	George and Mary Rodemayer	the parents
Sept 20 1827	Dec 22 1827	Joseph Henry	Joseph Edwards and Sarah	William B. and Catharine Carter
1828				
Jan 7 1828	Jan 21 1828	Isabel Cath.	Jacob and Sarah Boyer	the parents
June 5 1827	Jan 22 1828	Margaritta Henrietta	Michael Hoffman and his wife	the parents
Jan 25 1826	Feb 19	Maria Louisa	John and Sarah Frey	John and Eliz. Frey (the grandparents)
Nov 22 1827	Feb 19 1828	John Joseph	John and Sarah Frey	dto.
Dec 22 1825		John Hopson	John and Eliz. Leightner	dto.
June 17 1821	Feb 19 1828	John Robinson	John and Ann Hodykinson	the parents
June 1 1823	"	Robert	"	"
July 4 1825	"	Sarah Ann	"	"
March 1 1827	"	Hanna Jane	"	"
Sept 6 1827	March 8 1828	Rachel Matilda	William and Catrina Dorsey	the parents
July 15 1827	March 19 1828	Susanna Jane	Samuel W. and Elizabeth Elwee	Elizabeth Elliot
May 6 1827	April 25 1828	Georgianna	John and Eliza Giesler	Dietrich Giesler (grandfather)
Dec 10 1824	Oct 14 1827	William Elliot	William G. Miller and his wife	—
Feb 20 1827	Oct 14 1827	James Edward	dto.	—

FIRST REFORMED CHURCH OF BALTIMORE

DATE OF BIRTH	DATE OF BAPTISM	NAME	PARENTS	SPONSORS
Sept 6 1826	?	Francis	Jacob and Harriot Wichelhausen	the parents
Sept 25 1826	?	Thomas	Thomas and Christina Lavender	the mother
Aug 7 1826	Jan 29 1827	David Mohler	Abr. Traxel and Sarah	the parents
1827				
May 27 1825	Feb 25 1827	William Edward	Martin and Marg. Bauer	the father and Ann Braun
March 7 1824	March 5 1827	Isaac	Isaac and Elizabeth Petit	the mother
Feb 26 1827	March 5 1827	Mary Ann	"	"
March 10 1827	March 23 1827	Mary Ann Eliz.	Andrew and Eliz. Franchi	Susanna Smith
Dec 26 1826	May 1827	William Henry	Jacob and Martha Brookhard	Sarah Hinkle
May 11 1827	May 17 1827	Henry Adam	Samuel Leinard (?) and Mary	the mother
March 30 1827	May 20 1827	Archibald Lewis	Jacob Cook and Henrietta	the mother
Feb 24 1827	June 5 1827	Amelia	Felix Durst and Irena	the mother
Jan 4 1827	June 5 1827	Mary Elizabeth	Fredrick and Getila Working	the mother
April 23 1826	June 6 1827	Mary Eliza	John and July Smith	Jacob Smith and Henrietta Myers
Oct 8 1826	June 6 1827	William Henry	William Russell and Mary	Magdalina Froble
Feb 10 1827	?	Elizabeth Jane	Peter and Elizabeth Ealer	the parents
March 22 1827	?	Ann Eliza	John Michean & Lutitia	the parents
Jan 9 1827	July 11 1827	Emily Jane	Nicholas Eliott and Elizabeth	the parents
Oct 9 1826	July 11 1827	Eliza Ann	William Stetes and Margaret	the mother
June 8 1827	July 29 1827	Thomas	James Jones and Christine	the parents
July 12 1826	Aug 12 1827	Cathrine	George and Margret Weaver	John H. Allen & Cathrin Lusnop
Aug 5 1818	Sept 18 1827	Catharine	John and Mary Kiplinger	Eliza Keplinger
Feb 13 1820	"	Mary	"	Cath. Grooms
June 11 1823	"	Amanda	"	Susanna Frank
Jan 29 1827	"	John	"	Mrs. Murphy

FIRST REFORMED CHURCH OF BALTIMORE

DATE OF BIRTH	DATE OF BAPTISM	NAME	PARENTS	SPONSORS
July 4 1822	Sept 11 1825	Catharina Louise	Fielding and Cath. Vanhorn	the mother
July 2 1825	Sept 11 1825	Fielding	"	"
Dec 24 1821	Sept 11 1825	Matheus Constantin	Eliza Ann Jones widow	Mrs. Vanhorn
Aug 24 1823	Sept 21 1825	Ann Cath.	John Jer. Mayer and Susan	the parents
Sept 1 1825	Sept 21 1825	Martha Rebecca	"	"
Oct 2nd 1825	Oct 13 1825	Salina Felicity	Francis Gatechair and Mary	Thomas S. Murphy and Dorothea
Oct 27 1825	Oct 30 1825	Johann Ludwig	Johann Schaub and Susanna	Charles (?) Winterich [Hinterich]
Feb 27 1825	?	Carl...	Georg and Marg. Weaver	the mother
July 4 1825	Nov 7 1825	Eliza Ann	George and Mary Rodemayer	the parents
Nov 10 1825	Dec 7 1825	Frederick	Frederick and Maria Laudeman	the grandmother
Nov 28 1825	Dec 11 1825	Juliann	Benjamin and Margaret Harbaugh	Mrs. Rebecca Harbaugh
	1826			
Jan 29 1826	Feb 12 1826	Christianna	John Miller and his wife	the father and Mrs. Christianna Lemate
Feb 7 1826	Feb 20 1826	Andrew Snyder	Herman Bresermann and Elizabeth	the parents
Oct 27 1820	1826	Samuel	William and Catharine Vanwinckle	Josua M. Turner Maria Krebs
Nov 27 1823	1826	William	"	"
Nov 1 1824	Feb 25 1826	Elizabeth	David M. and Ann White	Thomas Burnam, Susan Johns
Dec 21 1825	Feb 26 1826	Edward	John R. and Louisa Chamberlain	Abr. Knup and Margaret
Sept 5 1823	May 31 1826	J. Jacob Henry	John and Elizabeth Miller	Jacob Chrest
Dec 23 1824	Sept 4 1826	William	Valentine Lutz	the mother
Feb 5 1826	Aug 31 1826	Ann Olivia	Charles and Ann Diffenderffer	the parents
Oct 7 1822	Aug 31 1826	Charles	"	"
April 27 1824	Aug 31 1826	Rosina	"	"
Sept 28 1825	Oct 1 1826	Clarissa Juda	Georg and Anna Frey	the parents

FIRST REFORMED CHURCH OF BALTIMORE

DATE OF BIRTH	DATE OF BAPTISM	NAME	PARENTS	SPONSORS
July 31 1824	Aug 5 1824	Thomas Smith	Thomas S. and Dorothea Murphy	Mary Etchberger (grandmother)
July 7 1824	Aug 8 1824	George Henry	John and Louisa Chamberlain	Abraham and Margaret Krupp (or Knapp, K
July 27 1824	Sept 7 1824	Ann Mary	George Locher and wife	the parents
May 2nd 1824	Sept 18 1824	John P.	Jacob Shunk and Elizabeth	John and Ellen Shun
Jan 8 1824	Sept 19 1824	Mary Rebecca	William Russell and Mary	the mother
Dec 18 1823	Sept 21 1824	Selina	Herman and Catharina Neumayer	the parents
Aug 4 1823	Nov 14 1824	Edward	Mathew and Cath. French	Arianna Hart
Oct 30 1823	Nov 14 1824	Margaret Ann	Samuel Childs and Margaret	Arianna Hart
Sept 7 1824	Nov 21	Mary Ann	James Jones and Christina	the parents
Oct 9 1824	Dec 26 1824	William Henry	John Lightner and Rebecca	the parents

1825

DATE OF BIRTH	DATE OF BAPTISM	NAME	PARENTS	SPONSORS
May 7 1824	Jan 14 1825	Emily Augusta Wharton	Edwin and Susanna R.B. Tarr	John J. Mayer
Nov 11 1824	1825	John Mangles	John and Cath. Schoeneman	John Martin Johannes Cath. Bernand
Dec 23 1824	March 3 1825	Repold Carter	Thomas Maund and Metta	Mr. Carter and Metta Pepold
Jan 10 1825		Edward M.	William Dorsey and Cath.	the mother
March 17 1824	April 3 1825	William Thomas	William Newton and Cath.	the mother
April 24 1825	May 8 1825	Alberts	Michael Hoffman and his wife	the parents
Dec 14 1824	May 11 1825	Matthew	John and Elizabeth Weir	the parents
Sept 4 1824	May 27 1825	Andrew Lewis	Julian Nicolet and Emelia	Andrew Lewis Jacot a Emely godparents i Switzerland
Febr 11 1825	May 27 1825	Adalina	Philip A. Sandoz & Mary Ann	Julian and Emelia Nicolet
May 8 1825	Aug 1825	Cornelia Mary Louisa	Moses Conrad and Cath.	Cornelia Vonderschlo
Jan 7 1825	Sept 1 1825	Anna Eliza Clark	George Schminke and Anna	James Clark and Eliza Schminke

FIRST REFORMED CHURCH OF BALTIMORE

DATE OF BIRTH	DATE OF BAPTISM	NAME	PARENTS	SPONSORS
Aug 11 1823	Nov 8 1823	Ernestine Pondoz	Philip A. Sandoz and Mary Ann	Henry Humbert Julia Sweitz
Nov 19 1822	Nov 23 1823	William Albers	Peter and Elizabeth Baker	parents
Sept 20 1819	Dec 29 1823	George Edwin	Martin Bowers and Margaret	William Browny and Nancy
Nov 13 1822	Dec 29 1823	Elmira Ann	Martin Bowers and Margaret	William S. Hall Sus. Bowers
	1824			
April 8 1823	Jan 7 1824	Sarah Jane	William Root and Sarah	Eliza Corwein
Oct 1823	Jan 1 1824	George Peter	John and Margaret Keener	the parents
Dec 24 1823	Jan 23 1824	George Gabriel	George Gabriel Moerche and his wife	parents
Nov 30 1820	Jan 23 1824	John Kirchner	John Kirchner and his wife	William Reinwahl & Louisa
Oct 23 1823	Jan 26 1824	Mary Elizabeth Schaffer	George Rous and Mary	Mary Treis
Sept 25 1823	Feb 6 1824	Eliza Ann	John Weir and his wife Elizabeth	the parents
Aug 29 1822	Feb 8 1824	Thomas Henry August	Benjamin Harbaugh and Margaret	Mrs. Reynolds, the grandmother
Sept 27 1823	Feb 8 1824	Emelia Catherine	"	"
Dec 17 1823	Feb 1 1824	Susan Catharine	Andrew Franchi and Eliza	the parents

baptized Feb 12 an adult by the name of Allen

DATE OF BIRTH	DATE OF BAPTISM	NAME	PARENTS	SPONSORS
Sept 30 1823		Frederica	Fredrick Laudeman and Maria	Mary Laudeman
Dec 13 1823	March 8 1824	Margaret Elizabeth	George and Maria Grubb	John Caucha [?] Elizabeth Eichl
Oct 9 1822	March 12 1824	Thomas Henry	Argelus G.D. Thomas and Rebecca	Mary Neid
July 1 1823	March 12 1824	Philipp Jacob	"	"
April 27 1824	May 24 1824	Rosanna	Charles Diffenderffer and Anna	

June 29 baptized an adult person, Margaret Riteau, who the next day was confirmed

DATE OF BIRTH	DATE OF BAPTISM	NAME	PARENTS	SPONSORS
2nd Christmas day 1824	July 1	Elizabeth	Charles and Margaret Emy	Mary Margaret Mills
Aug 20 1822	July 5 1824	Nicolaus Riyous	William Walker and Elizabeth	the mother

FIRST REFORMED CHURCH OF BALTIMORE

DATE OF BIRTH	DATE OF BAPTISM	NAME	PARENTS	SPONSORS
Nov 30 1922	?	Albert Jacob	Jacob Boyer and Margaret	parents
	1823			
March 13 1821	Feb 5	John Charles	John & Ellen Weaver	parents
Nov 28 1822	Feb 5	Mary Ann	John & Ellen Weaver	parents
Feb 1 1823	March 2nd	William Henry	Michael Diffendorffer and Sarah	parents
April 4	?	John Frederick	Michael Hoffman and his wife	Susann Hoffman
March 15 1823	April 20 1823	Edward Philip	Philip Reigart and Sophia	parents
March 15 1823	April 21 1823	Henry Shaeffer	George and Elizabeth Locher	parents
July 18 1820	June 5 1823	Henry	Bersal Fisher and Barbara	Catb. Ewalt (grandmother)
March 3 1823	June 5 1823	Henry	Robert Lutz and Mary	grandmother
May 31 1822	dto.	Robert	"	mother
Feb 24 1823	dto.	John Henry	John & Catherine Berger	mother
Jan 5 1823	dto.	Ann Elizabeth	William Fairbank and Elizabeth	mother
March 27 1822	June 9 1823	Christopher	William Mumma and Belinda	the mother
March 5 1823	June 9 1823	David	Valentine Lutz and Christina	the parents
Nov 10 1821	June 9 1823	Caroline	dto.	the parents
March 6 1823	June 29 1823	Sarah Jane	Henry and Eliz. Freyer	the parents
May 24 1823	July 17 1823	Jacob	Jacob Lehman and Kitura	John and Cathrine Schoenemann
May 7 1823	July 17 1823	Margaret Elizabeth	Nicolaus and Margaret Lehman	the parents
Feb 24 1823	July 28 1823	Andrew Jackson	William and Barbara Adams	the father
Jan 2 1822	1823	Anna Maria	Isaac and Elizabeth Petit	the mother
June 20	Aug 15	Henrich	Frena Groff	the mother
Nov 3 1822	Aug 17 1823	George Alexander	Henry Freeberger and Sarah	the grandfather
Sept 13 1821	Nov 5 1823	Mary	George Freeberger and Sarah	John Freeberger (grandfather)
Dec 21 1822	Nov 5 1823	John	dto.	dto.

FIRST REFORMED CHURCH OF BALTIMORE

DATE OF BIRTH	DATE OF BAPTISM	NAME	PARENTS	SPONSORS
April 2 1820	April 10 1821	Johann Christian Freedrich	Johannes Eichler & Elizabeth	Sarah Eichler
Sept 1 1819	?	Susan Christianna	Michael Diffenderffer and Salome	the father
April 1 1821	?	George Michael	"	the father
April 20 1821	May 14 1821	Maria Amelia	Carter Hall & Ann	Peter Diffenderffer & wife
April 23 1821	?	Edward Michael	Philip Reigart and Sophia	Dorothea Diffenderffer
Oct 28 1816	June 24 1821	Eliza Maria	James Horton & Elizabeth	Peter Diffenderffer and Catharine
May 19 1821	"	Emma Jane	"	"
April 13 1821	July 1 1821	Sophia Matilda	Henry Albers and Rebecca	parents
April 4 1821	July 3 1821	Elisabeth	Johan Struebert and and Harriet	Cath. Struebert
Oct 17 1819	July 30 1821	John Jacob Myer	John Jer. Myer and Susanna	parents
Feb 27 1821	Aug 20 1821	John	George Weaver and Margaret	mother
? 11 1821	Aug 19 1821	Johann Jacob	David Simon and Cath.	Catharina Simon
July 3 1820	Sept 23	Elisabeth	Peter Bader [Becker] and Elisabeth	parents
March 10 1821	Oct 20 1821	Benjamin	Martin Weisbach & Ester	parents
Oct 22 1821	Nov 5	William Thomas	Gustavus Anderson and Nancy	Margaret Miller
May 2 1821	Nov 13 1821	Eleonora Susanna	Jacob Lehman and Kitura	Jacob Leaman & Wilhelmina
May 26 1821		Susan Placke Henriette	Jacob Winchelhausen & Henriette	Henry C. Nestman Susan Placke Catze [?]
July 11 1821	Nov 30 1821	Daniel Stuller	Peter Glouinger and his wife	parents
March 9 1821	Nov 25 1821	William	William Harst and Rebecca	John Wehr and Elisabeth
June 9 1821	Nov 25 1821	Mathew	John Wehr and Elisabeth	parents
Aug 20 1821	Dec 30 1821	John Henry	John Keener and Margaret	parents
1822				
Oct 30 1821	Jan 1 1822	Julian Felix	Felix Durst and Frena	Julian Nicolet & Amelia
Nov 7 1821	Jan 22 1822	Johannes	Maria Jordan widow	mother
Jan 29 1822	Feb 17 1822	Hanna Elisabeth	Johan Georg Breneifer [or Breneiser] and Margaretha	Georg Ludwig B[T]regerman and Hanna

FIRST REFORMED CHURCH OF BALTIMORE

DATE OF BIRTH	DATE OF BAPTISM	NAME	PARENTS	SPONSORS
Jan 4 1822	Feb 16 1822	Harriot	Lawrence Eisenring and Elisabeth	Harriot Brown
	April 4 1822	Mary Ann Glenn	adult	
July 15 1819	April 23 1822	Mary	Robert Mayers and Lydia	Joseph Reinhard and Barbara
April 19 1822	April 23	Caroline Amanda	John P. Parsons and Mary	Dorothea, her sister
Oct 13 1821	April 29	Mary Elizabeth	Wilhelm Ch. Neal and Mary Christiana	Elizabeth Daughaty
May 13 1822	May 20 1822	Cecilia Carolina	Andrew Franchi and Elizabeth	Susanna Smith (grandmother)
May 20 1822	May 27	Anna Catharina	Johann K[B]ister and Susann	Cath. Steimer & Anna Trafy Glates
April 6 1822	July 6 1822	Friedrich	Friedrich Schaeffer and Catharina	parents
April 1 1822	June 26 1822	Peter	Jacob Lehman and Kitura	Jacob Lehmann & Philippina (grandparents)
born directly after Easter		Mary Ann	Charles Emy and Margaret	Elizabeth Mills
Aug 12 1822	Aug 13 1822	Julian Henry [twins	David Simon and Catharine	Maria Kemp and Cathrine Kramer
	Sept 20 1822	Miss Elis. Forney		
	dto.	Mrs. Ann Maria Beveredge	[both adults	
March 18 1821	Sept 23 1822	Elizabeth	William Adams and Barbara	the father
July 27 1821	Oct 18	Carl Friedrich	James Martiny and Nancy	mother and Carl Fried. Manter
Sept 2 1822	Sept 22	Emily Jane	Georg Rodemayer and Mary	the parents
?	Oct 3	Charles Fredrick	Charles Diffenderffer and Ann	parents
?	Oct 3	Philip Hiss	Georg & Caroline Austin	Rosanna Millimar
Jan 10 1822	Nov 13 1822	Margaret Sarah	James & Elizabeth Cornwein	Margaret Murray
Feb 14 1821	Nov 13 1822	John	William and Sarah Puth [or Peeth or Puck]	Elizabeth Cornwein
Dec 8 1821	Nov 13 1822	Cathrine	Jacob & Elizabeth Shunk	Mary Grimes
March 31 1822	Nov 13 1822	Margaret	Joseph and Ellen Jost	Ellen Shnak
Sept 22 1821	Nov 13 1822	Mathew	William and Ann Christ	Margaret Murray
Dec 8 1822	Nov 24	William	James Jones and Christina	parents
June 13 1822	?	August Julian	Julian Nicolet and Emily	Philip August Saunder Mary Ann

FIRST REFORMED CHURCH OF BALTIMORE

DATE OF BIRTH	DATE OF BAPTISM	NAME	PARENTS	SPONSORS
Nov 25 1859	May 19	MacKall Cox	Wm. & Rebecca Berry	mother
Jan 9 1861	May 19	Mary Charlotte	Wm. C. & Susanna Baker	parents
Dec 28 1860	June 12	Fannie Pickens	Ino. & Susan J. Ryan	parents
May 8 1861	July 24	George Arnold	Englehart & Cecelia J. Frick	parents
May 20 1861	July 29	Augustus Christoph	J.C. & Sophia B. Wheeler	parents
March 29 1861	Sept 30	Anna Elizabeth	George W. & Mary Ann Harvey	parents
March 19 1861	Oct 13	Anna Elsworth	Alexander & Lizzie Shultz	parents
Jan 28 1861	Oct 13	William Shafer	George H. & Mary Locher	parents
Feb 16 1861	Oct 14	Mary Sophia	John & Mary Ann Pomp	mother

1862

DATE OF BIRTH	DATE OF BAPTISM	NAME	PARENTS	SPONSORS
Oct 21 1861	Jan 19	Daniel Jefferson Davis	Cornelius & Marg. Coburn	mother
April 30 1859	Feb 5	Elva Kennedy	August & E.F. Plowman	
Dec 7 1856	March 1	Charles E.	Wm. & Sarah Randal	
March 7 1859	March 1	James Richardson	" " "	
Dec 17 1857	March 4	Firman Goodwin	Benjamin & Christiana Reynolds	
Oct 9 1859	March 4	Mary Frances Parker	" " "	
June 5 1859	April 30	George Barrneh	J.C. & S.B. Wheeler	
Dec 22 1857	April 30	David	Isabella	
Feb 15 1852	May 27	Florence Elias	Henry & Rachael Shaafer	
Nov 1 1857	May 27	Henrietta	" " "	
June 14 1858	Aug 11	Ellen	Wm. & Mary E. Crawford	
Feb 25 1854	Aug 11	Archibald Robinson	James & Cath. J. Balloch	
Nov 22 1856	Aug 11	Kate	" " "	
May 25 1860	Sept 13	Harry Jennings	Wm. Elenora Finley	
July 27 1860	Nov 11	James	Johnson & Fanny Godfrey	
July 20 1860	Nov 18	Ann Elizabeth	Wm. A. & Mary Ann Asprill	

FIRST REFORMED CHURCH OF BALTIMORE

1861

DATE OF BIRTH	DATE OF BAPTISM	NAME	PARENTS	SPONSORS
	Jan		E. S. & Jane O. Fryor	mother
Apr 20 1860	Jan 21	Amelia Handy	Alfred & A. Susiana Buck	parents
Jan 3 1861	Jan 17	Elizabeth	Alfred & Ellen D. Friend	parents
May 20 1860	March 11	Andrew Jeremiah	Andrew J. & Dorothy E. Hubbard	parents
July 29 1860	March 11	Jane Crawford	Wm. Sarah Ann Guy	parents
Dec 13 1860	March 31	Charles McCullough	Joseph & Ellen Vansant	parents
April 25 1860	March 31	Jacob Adae	Dr. J.W. & Susie Houck	parents
July 16 1858	May 15	William	Wm. C. & Mary Ann DeBeet	parents
Nov 15 1858	Feb 18	Mary Frances	James & Mary F. Gourley	
Oct 20 1853	March 11	Ellen Cornelia	Samuel & Elizabeth Mainley	
Aug 17 1856	March 11	James Thomas	" " "	
Dec 25 1856	April 24	Charlotte Emily	Wm & Anna R. Berry	
Feb 17 1859	April 24	Emma Augusta	Jacob & Elizabeth Yeisley	
Feb 12 1859	April 24	George Collins	Joseph & Ellen Vansant	
June 7 1852	April 24	Robert Turner Hamilton	John R. & Eliz. Crozier	
July 27 1855	April 24	Wiona Juliett	" " "	
April 30 1856	April 28	Appalonia Mina Whelan	John H. & Maria Baker	mother
Dec 2 1843	April 28	John Henry Baker	" " "	"
Jan 1 1859	May 5	Mary Grace	Geo. W. & Mary M. Barger	mother
April 6 1859	June 12	Charles Henry	Lewis & M. C. Giderney	
May 1859	June 12	Mary Eliza	Geo. & Mary Gerhold	
July 27 1858	July 31	James	James & Ann M. Hamilton	
March 16 1859	Sept 10	James	James & Cath. Godfrey	
June 28 1854	Sept 10	Eliza Griffin	Charles S. & Julia Hickman	
Aug 9 1859	Oct 16	Samuel Patterson	Moses & Mathilda Guy	
June 7 1859	Oct 16	Anna Martha	John H. & Anna K. Harpel	

FIRST REFORMED CHURCH OF BALTIMORE

DATE OF BIRTH	DATE OF BAPTISM	NAME	PARENTS	SPONSORS
Sept 13 1859	Oct 16	Elizabeth Jane	Cornelius & Marg· Coburn	
June 21 1855	Oct 16	George Eve Anna	George W. & Cath. J. Kraft	
April 8 1859	Oct 16	John Richstein	James L. & Lydia A. Hewell	
March 19 1859	Nov 6	Henrietta	J.G. & Catherina Baker	
Sept 18 1859	Dec 1	Virginia	Wm. P. & Marg. Smith	

1860

DATE OF BIRTH	DATE OF BAPTISM	NAME	PARENTS	SPONSORS
Aug 26 1859	Jan 15	Jerome	Dr. Ed. & Amey Craven	
Oct 23 1857	April 4	William Additer	Wm. A. & Mary Baker	parents
Feb 19 1858	April 4	Martha Louesa Pinkney	Charles H. & Catherine Derr	parents
Nov 21 1857	April 4	Charles Diffenderffer	Geo. W. & Rosena Herring	parents
July 6 1857	April 4	Wm. Berger	Wm. C. & Susanna Baker	parents
Jan 24 1858	May 12	Isabella	Johnston & Fanny Godfrey	
Feb 17 1857	May 12	Mary Elizabeth	David & Elizabeth McCauley	
Dec 3 1857	May 24	James Thomas	John & Margaret Bunch	
April 28 1858	May 28	Mary Ernesta	Reverd. H. & Maria Trail	
March 3 1858	June 6	Netta Arena	Dr. Ed. & Amey Craven	
Jan 11 1857	Aug 5	Zinobia	Charles F. & Rebecca Locher	
Dec 14 1840	Aug 5	Isaac Benj.	Locher	
May 22 1858	Oct 3	John George	Ino. H. & Catharine Harpel	

FIRST REFORMED CHURCH OF BALTIMORE

DATE OF BIRTH	DATE OF BAPTISM	NAME	PARENTS	SPONSORS
April 12 1857	July 5	Ida Kate	James & Abarilla Martin	mother
May 14 1857	July 6	Thomas Simon Murphy	A.J. & Dorothy E. Hubbard	parents
Oct 12 1856	July 6	Henry Groverman	Alfred & A. Indiana Buck	parents
	July 10	Wm. Thomas	Joseph O. & Mary E. Dugan	father
Jan 31 1857	Sept 14	Samuel Vansant	Ephraim & July Ann Daley	
June 20 1857	Oct 11	George	Cornelius & Marg. Coburn	
Feb 16 1857	Oct 18	Mary Ann	Wm. J. & Mary Ann Hart	
Dec 25 1856	Oct 18	Lizzie May	" " " "	
July 7 1857	Nov 2	Mary Margaretta	Geo. & Eliz. Ann Frank	
July 7 1856	Nov 8	Anna Montanye	Dr. Ed. & Amey Craven	
May 10 1857	Dec 28	Mary	Thomas & Josephine Hardester	
July 13 1857	Sept 13 bapt. by Rev. P.S. Davis at St. John's Church, Mt. Washington	George Lewis	Rev. G.L. & Hannah Staley	
Nov 3 1857	Oct 10	Bettie Trissler	Dr. I.W. & Susie Houck	
April 3 1858	Oct 10	Ellen Frances	Capt. John & Mary Ann Pomp	
June 11 1858	Oct 10	James Joseph	William & Sarah Guy	
1858				
Aug 28 1857	Jan 4	Sarah Ann	Wm & Elenora Richstein	
July 6 1857	Jan 4	Wm. Henry	Andrew & Mary Cath. Bentz	
June 5 1856	Jan 10	Josephine Elizabeth	James & Julia Cameron	
Aug 18 1854	Jan 10	Ida	Alexander & Mary Eliz. Shultz	
March 24 1857	Jan 10	Sarah Jane	Matthew & Sarah Jane White	
Oct 20 1857	Feb 12	Allice	J.C. & Sophia B. Sheeler	
July 6 1856	March 5	Caroline Elizabeth	Dr. Warren & Mary A. Welsh	Mr. J.W. Hock & Maggie Lightne
Feb 2 1858	March 5	Edward Jay	" " "	G.S. & Eliz. Griffith
	March 9	?	P.H. & Mary E. Muller	parents
June 28 1857	March 23	Ida Catherine	Geo. L. & Ann Maria Fisher	parents
Aug 28 1853	April 4	John Robert	Ed. G. & Ethlinda Rennons	mother

FIRST REFORMED CHURCH OF BALTIMORE

DATE OF BIRTH	DATE OF BAPTISM	NAME	PARENTS	SPONSORS
		Michael Mary Margaret		
Nov 6 1855	April 6	Sarah Ann	Thomas & Mary Crawford	mother
Oct 7 1855	April 6	Margaret Jane	John & Susan Ryan	mother
Dec 23 1855	May 4	Wm. Washington	John & Marg. A. Pomp	parents
March 14 1856	May 4	Jacob Seltzer	John & Margaret Eigeon	parents
Jan 27 1855	May 11	Hanna Joanna Louisa	Wm. & Catherine Dean	parents
Jan 15 1856	June 8	Melville	Elias & Mary Heiner	parents
Sept 3 1855	June 8	John S.	Wm. S. & Emeline Reese	parents
Feb 23 1856	June 8	Mary Eliza Griffin	John & Melverina McNair	parents
Aug 16 1853	June 8	Charles Jacob	Georg L. & Mary Ann Fisher	parents
Feb 23 1856	July 8	Martha	F.A. & V.R. Uhl	parents
Oct 21 1855	July 20	Ella	H. & Eliz. Ann Bersh	parents
	Oct 10	James	Thomas & Mary Crawford	
Sept 13 1857	Oct 10	Joseph Klapp	Joseph R. & Margaret Milnor	
July 23 1856	Oct 5	David Andrew	Johnsen & Agnes Godfrey	parents
Sept 23 1856	Oct 5	Mary Agnes	Andrew & Agnes Greer	mother
July 2 1856	Oct 12	Elizabeth Smith	Wm. & Sarah Ann Guy	mother
March 26 1856	Oct 12	James Oliver	Moses & Mathilda Guy	parents
Oct 22 1856	Nov 24	Isabella	Daniel W. & Issbella Lowe	mother
Aug 15 1856	Nov 26	Anna Maria	Wm. & Arenia Lowman	mother
April 13 1856	Nov 27	Henry Miller	Benj. & Christina Reynolds	mother
Aug 1856	Dec 2	Wm. Prescott	Joseph & Ellen Vansant	mother
June 10 1856	Dec 15	George Millard	Alexander H. & Sarah A. Heine	mother
April 12 1856	Dec 25	Margaret Ann	Ino. George & Catharine Baker	parents
Oct 20 1855	Dec 28	Mary Elizabeth	Dr. J.W. & Susie Honck	parents
April 11 1856	Dec 29	Emma Margaretta	Robert A. & Cath. Ann Clark	parents

FIRST REFORMED CHURCH OF BALTIMORE

DATE OF BIRTH	DATE OF BAPTISM	NAME	PARENTS	SPONSORS
Oct 6 1840	June 11	Wm. Henry	Alfred & Ann Eliz. Friend	parents
April 26 1842	June 11	Richard Augustus	" " " "	"
Jan 13 1855	June 27	Wm. Finlay	Dr. Wm. L. & Frances A. Finlay	parents
May 14 1855	July 22	Martha	Wm. & Susan McLean	parents
April 29 1855	July 22	Martha Crawford	Wm. & Sarah A. Guy	mother
June 10 1855	Aug 11	George Washingt.	John & Mary Dobbin	mother
March 31 1855	Aug 23	Rose Louesa	Horatio D. & Maria Louesa Hewitt	parents
July 4 1854	Sept 2	John Alexander	James & A.M. Hamilton	parents
April 12 1849	Sept 2	Louis Gibson	Albert J. & Rachel C. Boyer	parents
March 1 1855	Oct 14	Margaret Meredeth	Wm. Prescott & Marg. Smith	parents
March 23 1855	Oct 14	Laura Ellen	Jacob & Marg. Miller	parents
Nov 12 1854	Nov 22	Cornelius DeBeet	George J. & Agnes Bennett	mother
Apr 28 1854	Nov 25	Sarah Frances	Capt. E.C. & C. Phails	

1859

Dec 23 1858	Feb 16	Jacob Parpon Heiner	Elias & Mary Rebecca Magers	

1855

Sept 15 1854	Nov 26	Margaret Ellen	David H. & Eliz. McCauley	mother
Nov 30 1854	Dec 19	Ida Julia	George W. & Eliz. A. League	parents

1856

Sept 14 1855	Jan 26	Grace Amanda	Purwell & Amanda Newman	parents
	Feb 16	Philip Henry	Philip H. & Mary C. Muller	parents
Jan 10 1854	March 8	Judie [Susie] Frances	Dr. J.W. & Susan Honck	parents
Jan 20 1856	March 16	Mary Jane	Ino. & Margaret Bunch	parents
Nov 12 1855	March 16	James	Henry & Eliza Godfrey	parents
March 29 1853	March 24	Wm. Prescott Smith	Thomas & Ann Maria Duncan	parents
Feb 11 1856	March 24	Charles Alfred	Charles A. & Mary Ann Wilson	mother
Dec 10 1855	March 24	Eliza	Peter & Isabella Duncan	parents
June 10 1855	March 24	Dorthia	Thomas & Catherine Godfrey	parents

FIRST REFORMED CHURCH OF BALTIMORE

DATE OF BIRTH	DATE OF BAPTISM	NAME	PARENTS	SPONSORS
	Aug 22		Groften	parents
	Aug 22		Groften	parents
	Aug 22		Henry Baker	parents
Oct 29 1853	Sept 21	Charles Helffenstein	Ino. F. & Mary Lutts	parents
Sept 2 1854	Oct 4	Ella	Elias & Mary Heiner	parents
Aug 9 1854	Oct 7	Ann Maria	Erastus & Marg. Brandt	mother
Dec 13 1853	Oct 7	Charles Wm.	F.L. & Sarah C. Hilberg	mother
Oct 22 1853	Oct 7	Sarah Jane	Ino. E. & Cornelia Allen	
Dec 25 1851	Oct 7	Josephine Jilden	Robert & Jane Grant	mother
	1855			
Sept 5 1854	Jan 1	Frank Baker	Wm. & Ann A. Berry	mother
June 24 1854	Jan 1	Kate Ely	Wm. C. & Susanna Baker	parents
Aug 3 1853	Jan 2	George Herring	E.V. & Julia Dailey	parents
Sept 8 1855	Oct 13	Mary Jane	Jasper R. & Eliza Brown	
Aug 25 1858	Oct 13	Emma Eliza	" " "	
June 22 1858	Oct 17	Richard Lawrence	Rich. L. & Mary Westervelt	
Oct 30 1858	Nov 13	Colburn Knapp	David S. & Eliza Griffin	
Sept 28 1854	Jan 7	Duncan	W.C. & Mary Ann DeBeet	parents
June 20 1853	Jan 14	Carrol Spence	George A. & Terresa Freburger	parents
Oct 14 1854	Jan 16	Charles Henry	Ino. V. & Mary Williams	mother
Sept 11 1853	Feb 15	Charles	Dr. Charles & Ann O. Reese	mother
Dec 1 1854	Feb 27	Henry Hiestand	A.C.N. & Annie Matthews	
June 28 1854	April 8	Imogene	David J. & Mary Aspril	parents
Dec 10 1854	April 8	Margaret Ella	Joseph K. & Marg. Milner	parents
Feb 10 1854	April 8	George Webber	Georg W. & Rosena Herring	mother
Aug 31 1853	April 22	Philip Reigart	Wm. S. & E.M. Reese	parents
May 6 1854	May 6	Alverda	Wm. Sarah E. Randal	mother
Nov 1854	May 6	Ann Louesa Zell	Richard & Susanna Plowman	parents
Oct 16 1853	June 11	Charles Henry	Alfred & Ann Eliz. Friend	parents
April 12 1858	Nov 25	George Balcher	Henry J. & S. J. Michael	

FIRST REFORMED CHURCH OF BALTIMORE

DATE OF BIRTH	DATE OF BAPTISM	NAME	PARENTS	SPONSORS
Feb 22 1853	Feb 22	Ino. Thomas Wash.	Charles J. & Julia Hickman	mother
Feb 6 1854	Feb 22	Charles Edward	Charles & Sophia Keeholtz	mother
born about Jan 1851	March 4	Charles Clifford	A.D. Clemens & wife Caarfeld (?)	
March 27 1852	March 9	Lehman	Alexander & Sophia Duncan	parents
Dec 5 1853	March 9	Ella	" " "	"
May 27 1852	March 9	James	Wm. & Marg Thomas	parents
Jan 29 1854	March 9	Ira Hardy	John G. & Mary P. Johannes	parents
April 29 1853	March 10	Harrie Clarence	Wm. R. & F. H. Constable	mother
Sept 14 1844	March 10	Isabella Harrod	Aug. & Mary Ann Mathiot	parents
Nov 7 1846	March 10	Robert Christian	" " " "	"
Jan 26 1854	March 10	Mary Ella	A.G. & Rachael Mathiot	parents
Feb 17 1853	March 13	Rachael Ann	Wm. H. & Lydia Randel	parents
Oct 6 1849	March 17	Eliza	James W. & Marcella Gorman	mother
Jan 17 1852	March 17	Marcella	" " "	"
Aug 8 1853	April 23	Rentrope	Dr. J.W. & Susan Honck	parents
June 17 1853	April 23	Jacob Alban	Jacob & Marg. Miller	parents
Oct 19 1852	May 1	Wm. Russel	Elias & Rebecca Magers	mother
	May 7	Mary Elizabeth	S.S. & Susan Mills	mother
	May 7	Andrew Francine	" " "	"
May 7 1852	June 16	Edward Winfield	George & Usay (?)	mother
Jan 20 1854	June 28	Robert Andrew Jackson	Robert & Cath. M. Clarke	mother
May 29 1854	July 9	Mary Elizabeth	Dixon & Eliz. Crawford	parents
Aug 4 1852	July 16	Martha Streng	James H. & Cornelia Bertholf	parents
March 30 1853	Aug 3	Wm. Henry	Wm. P. & Margaret Smith	mother
Aug 12 1854	Aug 13	James Wm.	Peter & Isabella Duncan	parents

FIRST REFORMED CHURCH OF BALTIMORE

DATE OF BIRTH	DATE OF BAPTISM	NAME	PARENTS	SPONSORS
Sept 4 1852	June 19	Henry Clay	John P. & Julia Jones	mother
Jan 1 1853	June 26	Malinda	John & Mary Dobbin	parents
Sept 27 1852	July 10	Juliet Amelia	James L. & Lydia A. Hewell	parents
Sept 28 1852	July 16	Aguste Rosena	James & Rosena Johnson	parents
Nov 18 1850	Sept 18	John Jacob	George & Frances Spies	grandmother
Aug 25 1852	Sept 18	Charles Horaesty	Wm. & Rebecca Berry	parents
Aug 4 1853	Oct 9	Mary Elizabeth	Wm. & Susan McClain	parents
May 16 1853	Oct 9	Margaret Jane	Alexnder & Martha Forsyth	mother
May 19 1853	Nov 6	Wm. James	Wm. & Mary C. Hart	parents
Jan 26 1853	Nov 3	Anne Kate	Jacob & Elizabeth Yiesly	parents
Oct 7 1853	Nov 16	John Thomas	Wm. & Sarah Ann Guy	mother
Aug 2 1853	Dec 25	Fanny Erickson	Geo. & Cath. Baker	parents
Dec 22 1853	Dec 25	James Zekel) twins	James D. & Mary Ann Sultzer Johnson	mother
Dec 22 1853	Dec 25	Henry Clay)	" " " "	"

1854

DATE OF BIRTH	DATE OF BAPTISM	NAME	PARENTS	SPONSORS
Nov 7 1848	Jan 6	George Peter	Jno. H. & Susan M. Keener	parents
Sept 13 1850	Jan 6	Wm. Henry	" " "	"
Nov 29 1852	Jan 6	Dashiell	" " "	"
Sept 28 1847	Jan 10	Endocia Elizabeth	Louis & Endocia J. Muller	parents
July 12 1849	Jan 10	Louis Conrad	" " "	"
May 21 1851	Jan 18	Harry Kinnenow	" " "	"
Nov 13 1853	Jan 18	Thomas Edwin	" " "	"
July 14 1852	Jan 22	Alverta	Henry & Sophia R. Rodenmayer	parents
Sept 18 1853	Jan 28	Richard Adolphius	John & Marg. E. Miller	parents
Jan 6 1854	Feb 5	Charles Davis	Phil Henry & Mary C. Muller	parents

FIRST REFORMED CHURCH OF BALTIMORE

DATE OF BIRTH	DATE OF BAPTISM	NAME	PARENTS	SPONSORS
Dec 14 1851	Sept 12	Edwin	Wm. S. & Emiline Reese	parents
Dec 14 1852	Sept 12	?	John E. & Cornelia Allen	mother
July 8 1851	Sept 12	James Morgan	Jno. A. & Georgia Cummingham	mother
Feb 3 1852	Sept 4	Sarah Ann	James A. & Ava E. Hurr	mother
	Nov 16	John Robert	Rescorl	parents
	Nov 14	Alfred Speed	A.C.N. & Matthews	parents
Dec 29 1851	Dec 5	Elenja Ellen	Ino. & Sarah Wise	parents
Sept 2 1852	Dec 14	John Alexander	Peter & J. Duncan	parents
Nov 20 1852	Dec 23	Ida	Samual S. & Susan Mills	parents
1853				
May 22 1852	Jan 1	Ann Maria	John & Cath. Clarke	mother
Jan 3 1852	Jan 15	Willemina Ford	J.M. & C.E. Stephen	parents
April 22 1852	Feb 11	Matilda Irene	Thaddeus & Mary Babeg	mother
Dec 17 1852	Feb 11	Alexander Stephens	Thaddeus & Mary Babeg	mother
July 9 1852	Feb 11	Josephine Eliz. Stephens	Levin & Rebecca Conter	mother
Nov 18 1852	Feb 14	James Edgar	James W. & Cath. Baughn	parents
Jan 18 1853	March 17	John Croft	J. Wm. & Sarah J. Messerschmidt	parents
Dec 7 1841	March 26	Modessa	Isaac B. & Rebecca Jones	parents
Dec 8 1844	March 26	Harriet Rebecca	James H. & Cath. Cridler	parents
March 3 1853	April 23	Thomas Andrew	Henry & Eliza Godfrey	mother
Sept 24 1843	May 22	Edward Wado	Hiram E. & Sarah I. Fox	mother
June 30 1852	May 22	Rosena	Geo. W. & Rosena Herring	mother
?	May 22	?	Moore	mother
Aug 10 1852	June 11	Lina Esten	Washington & Marg. M. Barger	parents
May 25 1851	June 19	Jessie Sarah	John P. & Julia Jones	mother

FIRST REFORMED CHURCH OF BALTIMORE

DATE OF BIRTH	DATE OF BAPTISM	NAME	PARENTS	SPONSORS
Jan 25 1851	Oct 16	Mary Imogene	John & Mary Johannes	mother
Dec 4 1849	Oct 16	Cora	Wm. & Mary Thomas	mother
May ... 1845	Nov 2	Martha Jane	John & Harriet Steele	-
Sept 16 1851	Nov 3	Oberta Jefferson	G.F. & A.M. Fisher	stepmother
May 25 1849	Dec 11	Henry Auguste	Henry & Eliz. A. Bersch	parents
Dec 10 1851	Dec 11 1851	Elizabeth	" " "	"
Dec 2 1851	Dec 21	Andrew	James & Harriet Godfrey	parents

1852

DATE OF BIRTH	DATE OF BAPTISM	NAME	PARENTS	SPONSORS
Nov 20 1851	Jan 21	Sarah Ellen	John and Marg. Hammond	parents
Oct 17 1851	Feb 17	John April	Wm. A. and Mary Baker	parents
Jan 1 1852	Feb 17	Charles	Jno. & Mary Eigeon	parents
June 28 1851	March 17	Matilda Jane Dyer	Benj. & Christina Reynolds	parents
Dec 28 1851	April 26	Dixon Crawford	George & Eliz. Genly	parents
Feb 7 1852	May 30	John Wesley	Ino. & Eliz. Steel	parents
March 12 1852	June 6	John Robert	James & Abrilla Martin	parents
Feb 7 1843	June 6	Righter Levering	Isaac & Emma Weriwag	parents
Jan 3 1850	June 6	Elma	" " "	"
March 24 1852	June 6	Mary Ida	Elias & Mary Heiner	parents
May 9 1852	June 24	Sophia Florence	J.H. & Matilda Barth	mother
June 15	Aug 3	Kate Elizabeth	Wm. & Susan Peffer	parents
July 28 1842	Aug 3	Priscilla	Elijah & Rachael Beufler	parents
Aug 30 1844	Aug 3	Mary Ann	" " "	"
Oct 25 1846	Aug 3	Rebecca	" " "	"
March 1 1849	Aug 3	Caroline	" " "	"
Nov 29 1849	Aug 19	Alice	Jno. & Marg. Hoff	mother
July 28 1852	Aug 19	John Francis	Joseph K. & Marg. Milnor	parents

FIRST REFORMED CHURCH OF BALTIMORE

DATE OF BIRTH	DATE OF BAPTISM	NAME	PARENTS	SPONSORS
Sept 13 1849	May 25	Charles Elijah	Wm. H. & Ann M. Martin	mother
Jan 17 1845	May 25	Agustus Lucas [Ducas]	Augustus D. & Henrietta Clemens	father
June 27 1846	May 25	Mary Ann Jessup	Aug. D. & Henrietta Clemens	father
May 22 1842	May 25	Mary Ellen	Sol. & Mary Charlesworth	aunt
Nov 6 1850	May 25	Charles Frederick	Wm. A. & Leah Rodenmayer	parents
Nov 30 1846	May 31	Emma Louesa	Henry & Sarah Vanderwecken	parents
April 11 1851	May 31	Henrietta	" " "	parents
Nov 22 1850	June 5	Mary Elizabeth	Jacob & Eliz. L. Yiesley	parents
Nov 28 1850	June 15	Theodore James	A.H. & S.J. Robertson	parents
Jan 13 1851	June 15	Wm Benjamin	..... & Rebecca Berry	parents
Dec 25 1850	June 15	Joshua VanSant	Wm. P. & Mary A. Smith	mother
Sept 19 1850	June 29	Emma Frances	Wm. & Ann Cox	mother
Jan 1 1851	June 29	Alice	Richard & Henrietta Armiger	parents
? 1850	July 7	Julia	Richard & Esther Remare	mother
Nov 12 1850	July 23	Geo. Washington Thomas	Robert A. & Cath. Clark	parents
Aug 8 1851	Aug 10	William	Charles & Henrietta Suter	father
April 11 1850	Aug 25	John Wm.	John & Mary Dobbin	mother
June 7 1851	Sept 4	Charles Edmund	Wm. K. & Mrs. Gardner	mother
June 28 1851	Sept 5	Mary Jane	Wm. & Mary Jane Guy	mother
June 11 1850	Sept 19	Alice Whitridge	S. & Georgia Long	mother
Aug 4 1850	Oct 5	Caroline Elizabeth	D.H. & C.T. Berthoef	parents
April 20 1851	Oct 5	Sarah Cath.	Francis L. & S.C. Hilberg	mother
Jan 25 1851	Oct 5	Emma Josephine	Wm. G. & Martha Storch	mother
May 5 1851	Oct 16	Virginia Phillippe	Jno. M. & Caroline Johannes	mother

DATE OF BIRTH	DATE OF BAPTISM	NAME	PARENTS	SPONSORS
April 30 1850	Aug 18	Lewis Cass	Isaac & Mary Ann Phillips	parents
Nov 3 1847	Aug 18	Charles Wesley	" " " "	"
March 12 1845	Sept 2	Mary Jane	Geo. & Eliz. Gurley	mother
?	Sept 9	?	.... Justus	mother
Nov 9 1845	Sept 12	Melvin Pypher	Charles & Jennett Sicken	mother
July 1 1849	Sept 12	Charles Morritz	Charles & Margaret Sicken	mother
May 11 1846	Sept 12	Jannett Melvin	William & Hannah Pypher	mother
May 24 1848	Sept 12	Susan Edward Briant	" " "	"
Sept 16 1850	Sept 19	Samuel	John S. & Mary Steelman	mother
Sept 22 1849	Sept 22 1850	Elizabeth League	W. Barger [Banger] & wife Mary M.	parents
April 4 1850	Sept 23	Sarah Virginia	Levin & R.B. Canter	parents
Sept 9 1848	Oct 29	Maria Leuesa	Alen & Mary Hilbert	mother
Aug 20 1850	Oct 29	Thomas Henry	" " "	"
Jan 1 1850	Nov 1	?	Geo. Eliz. Gray.	mother
Aug 27 1850	Nov 28	Emma Faithful	Charles C. & Julia Hickman	parents
1851				
June 16 1847	Jan	Joseph	Joseph & Cath. King	mother
Nov 27 1850	Jan	George Washington	" " "	"
Jan 20 1851	Jan 29 1851	Anne Bennet	James L. & Lydia A. Hewell	parents
Jan 15 1851	March 9	Francis Edward	Jno. G. & Cath. Baker	parents
Jan 15 1851	March 9	Ida Levenia	" " " "	"
Aug 9 1849	March 19	?	Wm. S. & C.P. Wonderly	parents
June 1 1850	April 3	Harding	E.S. & Jane Freyer	parents
March 18 1851	April 16	Henry Adam Seesnop	Henry & M.A. Richmond	mother
June 17 1850	May 25	Julia	Geo. W. & Rosena Herring	mother

FIRST REFORMED CHURCH OF BALTIMORE

DATE OF BIRTH	DATE OF BAPTISM	NAME	PARENTS	SPONSORS
	1850			
Oct 22 1849	Jan 13 1850	William Reigart	Wm. S. & Emeline Reese	parents
? 1848	Jan 24 1850	Samuel Alton Ready	Sam. D. & Barbara Johnson	mother
June 1 1846	Feb 8 1850	Adiel	Charles A. Oberteuffer & wife	mother
May 7 1849	Feb 8 1850	George Washington	" " "	mother
Oct 17 1849	Feb 8	Michael	Wm. & Eliz. Tagart	mother
Dec 13 1846	Feb 20	Francis Richard	James E. & Anna E. Hurtt	mother
June 26 1849	Feb 20	James Alexander	" " "	mother
Dec 31 1849	March 10	William James	Wm. & Susanna McClean	parents
Aug 14 1849	March 11	Walter Samuel	Wm. & W. Holland	parents
March 17 1850	March 30	William	Robert & Rebecca Elliot	parents
March 17 1850	March 30	Thomas	" " "	"
April 27 1846	March 31	Mary	Allen & Elizabeth Martin	parents
March 17 1848	March 31	John	" " "	"
June 11 1844	March 31	Emma	John & Mary Curtis	parents
Aug 23 1849	May 12	Cecilia Anaretta	John & Mary Lutz	mother
June 6 1849	May 28	David William	Jacob M. & Mary J. Cooper	mother
Sept 6 1847	June 6	David Frey	Ross J. Pennington & Sarah	parents
Aug 15 1849	June 6	Ann Rebecca	" " "	"
Feb 28 1848	July 6	Robert	John & Nancy Aulcorn	parents
Feb 14 1850	July 6	John	" " "	"
Jan 27 1849	July 7	John James	Henry Rodermayer & wife	parents
Dec 31 1849	Aug 18	Charles	Roderick & Jane McRae	parents
Jan 24 1848	Aug 18	Grace Clark	John & Sarah McRae	mother

FIRST REFORMED CHURCH OF BALTIMORE

DATE OF BIRTH	DATE OF BAPTISM	NAME	PARENTS	SPONSORS
1862				
Mar 14	Sep 2	John Sturgen	Alexander H. & Sarah Ann Himes	mother
May 30	Sep 10	Charles Henry William	Henry G. & Caroline Frederick	mother
Oct 2	Sep 10	William Gardner	William & Sophia Deems	parents
1861				
Mar 13	Sep 14	James Jetter	Dr. E. R. & Amey Croven	parents
Dec 7 1861	Sep 24	Mary Margaret	James & Mary Gourley	mother
Aug 17	Oct 8	John Ecklen	Jus. E. & Cornelia Allen	mother
Jun 4 1861	Oct 8	Cornelia	Robert & Jane Grant	mother
Apr 5	Oct 11	Margaret Virginia	Joseph & Ellen Vansant	parents
Feb 26	Oct 11	Virginia Lee	Isaac & Kate Sightner	parents
Oct 1	Oct 11	Georg Shaffner	Danl. S. & Eliza Griffin	parents
Apr 20	Oct 14	William McClellan	Jus. H. & Mary D. Suter	mother
Jun 19	Nov 3	Agnes	Isaac & Mary A. Duncan	mother
Oct 28	Dec 15	Dixon	Wm. & Sarah Ann Guy	
Nov 13	Dec 15	Sarah Eliza	Joseph & Ann Guy	
1863				
Jul 28 1862	Jan 4	Ida Bell	Henry D. & Alverta C. Suck	mother
Feb 16 1862	Jan 18	Loni Milton	Augustus & E. Thelma Plowman	parents
Aug 30 1861	Feb 9	Henrietta Wilhemina Groverman	H. & Indiana A. Buck	parents
Nov 22 1861	Apr 28	Daisey Annie Bell Mette	R.H. & M.L. Noack [Wack] (?)	father's mother (
Jul 1861	May 24	Solomon Louis Bayers	Charles H. & Cath. Bramble	parents
Jun 29 1852	May 24	Howard Aldridge	Com. Drutch	father & Mrs. J. Vansant
Nov 11 1858	May 24	Kate Estelle	Com. Drutch	father & Mrs. J. Vansant
Feb 8	Jun 15	William Albert	Andrew D. & Dor. E. Hubbard	mother
Jun 27	Aug	Florence Heiner	Columbus & Sophia Whqeler	parents
Feb 6	Oct 11	Alfred	Wm. & Mary E. Crawford	mother
Jun 28	Oct 11	Susan Evaline	James & Harriet Magnek	parents
Oct 21 1858	Nov 1	Charles Edward	Philip H. & Mary Cath. Muller	parents
Nov 12 1860	Nov 1	Henry	" " "	"
Aug 14 1862	Nov 1	Warren	" " "	"
Jun 21 1862	Nov 8	Lilia Medes	Benj. & Christiana Reynolds	parents
1864		E.R. Eschbach, Pastor		
Jan 13	Mar 14	William Jackson	Wm. & Marg. J. Harries	mother

FIRST REFORMED CHURCH OF BALTIMORE

DATE OF BIRTH	DATE OF BAPTISM	NAME	PARENTS	SPONSORS
May 12 1857	Mar 21	Carrie Watkins	Horatio D. & Maria L. Hewitt	mother
Sep 16 1863	Mar 21	Alfred Content	Robert K. & Patience F. McMurray	Mrs. Kate Watkins
Oct 16 1863	Mar 21	Robert Franklin	Geo. W. & Elmira Beard	mother
Jan 27 1861	Mar 21	Edward Joseph	Moses & Mathilda Guy	Mrs. Jane Guy
May 20 1863	Mar 21	Albert Kennedy	" " "	"
Jun 28 1857	Mar 21	Kate	Wm. H. & Anna Maria Jjamo	mother
Oct 4 1854	Mar 21	Rebecca	" " "	"
Aug 16 1856	Mar 21	Frederick	" " "	"
Dec 29 1859	Mar 21	Mary	" " "	"
Nov 22 1863	May 3	Mary Elizabeth	E.A. & C.J. Frick	parents
Mar 4 1864	Jun 5	Margaret McLane	Wm. & Sarah Guy	mother
Sep 3 1860	Jun 5	Harry B.	M. & Mary Kidd	mother
Oct 16 1861	Jun 9	Elizabeth Martha	Henry & Rachel Schafer	parents
Dec 2 1863	Jun 8	Henry Melville	" " "	"
Dec 16 1863	Jun 21	Thos. Edwin	Nicolas W. & Mary E. Bull	parents & W. H. Askew
Jun 23	Jul 8	Christiana Griffith	Patrick & Elizabeth Thornton	mother & G.S. Griffith/wife
Feb 1862	Aug 9	Douglas Jerold	Jno. & Emma S. Kessnan (?)	parents
Mar 1863	Aug 9	Lottie	" " "	"
Feb 4	Aug 24	Fanny Frost	Jno. & Mary Ann Pomp	mother
Apr 30	Sep 18	Jno. Jacob	D.W. & Laura Ann Meyer	mother
Feb 12	Sep 18	John Duer	Alex & Mary E. Schultz	parents
Oct 23 1861	Dec 4	Henry Clay	Jos. K. & Margaret Milnor	parents
Feb 24	Dec 4	Elias Heiner	" " "	"
Nov 18	Dec 11	Wm. Henry	John H. & Mary F. Heistel	parents
Mar 13	Dec 18	Mary Elizabeth	Joseph & Ann Guy	mother & grandmother

1865

DATE OF BIRTH	DATE OF BAPTISM	NAME	PARENTS	SPONSORS
Dec 20 1864	Feb 19	Emily	Gottfried & Sophia Weissner	parents & Francis Witt & wife
Nov 11 1863	Mar 13	Lillie May	Georg & Adeline R. Strong	Adelade Lauteman
Oct 6 1864	Apr 16	Charles Lawrence	Jno. H. & Caroline Mouse	parents & Lawrence Doughty
Oct 28 1864	Apr 16	Kate Beckett	Joseph & Ellen Vansant	parents
Jan 14	Apr 16	Charles Ingman	Jos. E. & Harriet E. Magness	parents

FIRST REFORMED CHURCH OF BALTIMORE

DATE OF BIRTH	DATE OF BAPTISM	NAME	PARENTS	SPONSORS
Dec 11 1864	Apr 16	Mary Virginia	Cornelius & Margaret Coburn	mother
Feb 18 1860	Aug 6	Ellen Louisa	" " "	Sahm/parents
Jun 29 1862	Aug 6	Sarah Agnes	" " "	" "
Jul 13 1865	Aug 6	Margaret Phillipena	" " "	" "
Feb 23	Sep 24	Jesse Aitkon	Wm. & Mary E. Crawford	mother
May 18	Sep 24	Goldsboro Sappington	G.S. & E. Griffith	G.S. Griffith, wife & parents
Sep 5	Nov 2	Catharina Elizabeth	E.K. & S. M. Eschbach	parents
	1866			
Feb 25 1865	Jan 7	Frederick Sidney	James E. & Mary E. Young	mother & Jos. Vansant
Oct 12 1865	Feb 10	Wm. Duhmet	Ashton A. & Ann Rebecca Krantz	parents
Jan 1 1857	Apr 1	Rosalie Aarilla	Montmorenei & Mary Jane Price	mother & Mrs. Guffing
Sep 3 1862	Apr 1	Ella Virginia	Jacob W. & Susan Honck	parents
Feb 1 1865	Apr 1	John Mercer Porter	" " "	"
Dec 17 1865	Jun 12	Wm. Howard	Wm. H. & Ann Maria Jjams	mother
Jun 23 1861	Jun 24	Jennie Olive	George A. & Emma R. Honck	parents
Nov 10 1863	Jun 24	Ella Mary	George A. & Emma R. Honck	parents
Mar 20	Jun 24	Laura Emma	" " "	"
May 28 1865	Jun 24	Helen Beata	J.C. & Sophia B. Wheeler	Marg. A. Bryson
Sep 27 1858	Sep 29	Mary Jane Boyl	Robert & Susan Busby	father
Apr 26 1861	Sep 29	Isaiah	" " "	"
Nov 22 1865	Sep 29	Alice	" " "	"
Jan 8	Oct 7	Lillie May	Geo. W. & Elmira Beard	mother
Jul 26	Oct 14	William	Wm. & Sarah Guy	mother
Jan 10	Nov 6	Wm. Henry	Nicolas W. & Mary E. Bull	mother
Nov 2	Dec 29	Charles Eschbach	E. Clark & Cornelia Ann Fales	Mrs. Welch
	1867			
Jan 21	Jan 30	Mary Ross	Fred & Ximena Otto	parents
Jun 15 1866	Feb 14	Clarence Englehart	E.A. & C.J. Frick	parents
Feb 10	Feb 23	Lillie Pancoast	Joe. K. & Maggie A. Milnor	parents
Jan 5	Mar 1	Agnes Virginia	Jhno. H. & Mary F. Heissel [Heistel]	parents & Mich. Young
		Calvert St. Lecture Room of New Church		
Mar 19	May 5	Martha Rebecca	Goldsboro S. & Eleanor Griffith	mother
Sep 20 1866	May 5	Mary	Joseph & Ellen Vansant	parents

FIRST REFORMED CHURCH OF BALTIMORE

DATE OF BIRTH	DATE OF BAPTISM	NAME	PARENTS	SPONSORS
Sep 1856	May 5	Catharina Celia	———— Sarah Wonn	Cornelius J. Gette & wife
Jun 25 1863	May 5	Caroline	John & Rebecca Wilcox	Annie Lightner
Jul 4 1864	May 5	Anna Lettitia	James L. & Emma E. Aspril	mother & W.A. Bake & wife
Jul 19 1866	May 5	James Lightner	" " "	" "
Aug 22 1866	May 5	Dixon	Joseph & Ann Guy	parents & Mrs. Jan Guy
Aug 13 1865	May 20	Charles Edward	Henry & Rachel Schafer	parents
Apr 17	Jun 2	Henry Alexander	Eben. C. & Mary R. Fales	parents & grandpare
Mar 12	Jun 2	Wm. Edward	John E. & Caroline A. Folke	parents & grandpare
May 8	Aug 16	Frances Olevia	John H. & Charlotte E. Anderson	father
Sep 14 1866	Sep 28	Wm. Franklin	Thos. & Mary Ann Hagerty	mother

New Church

Mar 30	Oct 13	James Edwin	Jas. & Harriet Magness	mother
Feb 17	Oct 13	Wm. Edward	A.J. & Naomi M. Lockhart	mother
Feb 12	Oct 13	Ella May	William & Martha Belbin	parents
Sep 19 1866	Oct 13	Anna Dowling	Benj. & Mary Kidd	mother
Aug 4	Oct 13	Eliza Ann	John J. & Eliza S. Kennard	parents
Jan 18 1866	Oct 13	Wm. Passer (?)	Isaac & Jane Lightner	parents

1868

Mar 22 1867	Jan 7	Samuel Edward	Edward & Mary E. Gover	parents
Nov 1 1867	Feb 1	Emma Elizabeth	Thos. Oliver & Sarah F. Kaylor	mother
Nov 25 1867	Mar 17	Thomas	Cornelius & Margaret Coburn	mother
Mar 25	Apr 12	Ellen	Matthew & Sarah White	parents
Jun 4	Jun 23	Allen	Stewart & Mary Hamilton	parents
Dec 24 1852	Jun 13	Elizabeth	Allen & Eliz. Martin	parents
Feb 10 1855	Jun 13	Ellen	" " "	"
Feb 9 1858	Jun 13	Jane	" " " "	"
Jan 22 1861	Jun 13	Sarah	" " "	"
Jun 18 1864	Jun 13	Alice	" " "	"
Mar 18	Jun 16	Abram Mills Eggleston Gordon	Lieut. A.M.E. & Sue M. Gordon	parents
Mar 14	Jun 21	Bessie	Go. W. & Fannie J. Aspriel	parents
Jul 10	Oct 11	David Ross	Fred & Ximena Otto	parents
Aug 13	Oct 11	Joseph	Joseph & Ellen Vansant	parents
Jul 18	Oct 11	Mary Charlesetta	Nicolas & Mary E. Bull	parents
Sep 4	Dec 17	Mary Lizzie	Wm. & Matilda Stahl	Mrs. Lizzie Michel

FIRST REFORMED CHURCH OF BALTIMORE

DATE OF BIRTH	DATE OF BAPTISM	NAME	PARENTS	SPONSORS
1869				
Mar 26 1868	Jan 10	Frances Mary	Ino. W. & Sarah W. Sills	parents
Nov 2 1868	Feb 4	Henry Richmond S.	Wm. T. & Mary Ann Hagerty	mother
Jan 21 1861	Nov 15 1861 (?)	Adam Seasnop B. (by. Rev. Fitzgerald)	Ino. H. & Maria Baker	
Jan 1	Feb 14 (baptized by Rev. Con. C. Cremer)	Mary Susan	Rev. E.R. & Sue M. Eschbach	parents
Oct 2 1868	Mar 28	Lilian Lee	A.J. & Naomi M. Lockhart	mother
Nov 11 1868	Mar 28	Dixon	Wm. & Sarah A. Guy	mother
Jan 4	May 25	Rachel Shorer	E.A. & C. Frick	parents
Dec 18 1868	May 30	Mary Baker	Jas. L. & Emilie E. Aspril	Mrs. Baker
Aug 18	Nov 9	Emily Gertrude	Ino. P. Halbach & Christie E.	parents
May 23	Dec 23	Charles Montgomery	Ino. H. & Charlotte E. Anderson	parents
1870				
Dec 23 1863	May 1	Henry Clay	Ino. T. & Eliza Webster	mother
Mar 12 1857	May 1	Willie Brooks	" " "	"
Apr 14	May 15	Caroline	John & Mathilda Dretell (?)	father & Mrs. Schlag
Feb 6	May 2	Anna Laura	Christian & Anna L. Kehm	parents
Feb 27 1869	Jul 6	Thos. Benj.	Benj. F. & Mary Kidd	mother
Dec 23 1869	Jul 13	Wm. Fred. Philip Zemmerman	Ino. Alex & Ann Maria Hauck (?)	mother
Aug 30	Sep 14	Alphonso Edward	Alfred E. & Susannah Houck	grandmother
Aug 11	Oct 16	Wm. Andrew	F. Thos. & Kate S. Rodenmayer	parents
Jul 2	Oct 16	Bessie Warnick	Matthew & Sarah J. White	parents
Nov 27 1869	Oct 16	Theodore	Theodore & Mary J. Shamer	mother & M.J. Bench
Feb 1	Oct 16	Isabella	Chas. A. & Mary Ann Wilson	Sh. Godfrey
Mar 28	Nov 30	Marrie Elizabeth	Fred & Ximena Otto	parents
Aug 29 1869	Jan 1	Edward Murray	Ino. W. & Sarah W. Sills	parents
1871				
Mar 22 1870	Jan 6	Frederick Hinkelman	Dixon & Josie R. Guy	parents
Jan 3	Jan 15	Edward Loudeman	Capt. John & Mary A. Pomp	grandmother
Jan 3	Jan 15	Maria Myers	" " "	"
Sep 28 1860	Feb 2	Rose May	Sol. & M. Louisa King	parents
Jun 28 1863	Feb 2	John Frey	" " "	"
Dec 16 1865	Feb 2	Bessie Early	" " "	"
Dec 26 1870	Feb 2	Louisa King	Gilbert B. & Cath. Pauline Rathson	parents

FIRST REFORMED CHURCH OF BALTIMORE

DATE OF BIRTH	DATE OF BAPTISM	NAME	PARENTS	SPONSORS
Oct 21 1870	Apr 9	Robert Edward Lee	Joseph & Ellen Vansant	parents
Jun 12 1870	Apr 9	Jessie Blanche	James & Harriet E. Magness	mother
Aug 6 1865	Apr 9	Willie	John L. & Mary Ann Bull	grandparents
May 10 1861	Apr 9	Wm. Winters	" " "	parents
Feb 10	Jun 18	Margaret Joseph	Cornelius & Margaret Coburn	mother
Oct 5 1870	Jun 21	Domi Kate Elizabeth	Jno. D. & Di Domi Quincy	mother
Jun 21	Jul 16	Henry Schillinger	Geo. J. & Mary M. Prechtel	H. Schillinger
Jun 26	Oct 1	Lizzie	Stewart & Mary Hamilton	parents
Jul 4	Oct 2	Emma Virginia	E.A. & C.J. Frick	parents
Jan 9	Nov 1	Naomi Martha	A. Jackson & N. Martha Lockhart	mother
Sep 30	Nov 26	John	Adolph Yocheimer & wife Sophia	D.M. Kohler
Aug 26	Nov 30	Harry Edward	Thos. & Lydia A. Weeks	parents
Aug 27	Nov 30	Charles Nicholas	Nicholas W. & Mary E. Bull	mother
Jul 23 1869	Dec 25	Mary Emma	Charles & Mary Huff	parents
Oct 15	Dec 25	Cora Estelle	" " "	"

1872

DATE OF BIRTH	DATE OF BAPTISM	NAME	PARENTS	SPONSORS
Feb 24 1870	Jan 1	Nelly M. Cannon	Wm. H. & Eliza E. Little	mother
May 8 1871	Jan 1	Susan Elizabeth	" " "	Mrs. Funck
Dec 13 1871	Jan 1	Elizabeth Campbell	Francis D. & Rachel A. Dekker	parents
Dec 29 1871	Mar 21	Martha Virginia R.	Wm. T. & Mary A. Hagerty	M.V. Richmond
Mar 14 1871	Mar 21	Lewis Henry	Lewis H. & Cath. Delia Coleman	parents
Nov 15 1871	Jun 9	Francis Hilberg	F. Thos. & B. Kate Rodenmayer	parents
Dec 1 1871	Jun 9	Mary Virginia	Francis & Mary Cohite	parents
Oct 23 1871	Jun 9	Florence Eugenia	Nathaniel & Selina R. Crow	parents
Mar 27	Jun 9	Hester Estelle	Christian & Amie L. Kehm	parents
Jul 2 1871	Jun 30	John Howard	John P. & Christie E. Halbach	parents
Apr 6 1871	Oct 6	Margaret Adelade	Francis & Cath. M. Lincoln	parents
Sep 24 1871	Oct 6	Fannie Blanche	Dixon & Josephine R. Guy	father

1873

DATE OF BIRTH	DATE OF BAPTISM	NAME	PARENTS	SPONSORS
Jun 25 1872	Feb 9	David Wilmer	John & Amanda Hauer	parents
Jan 6	Apr 10	Chas. Frederick	Chas. A. & Wilhelmina Pfeiffer	parents
Jan 2	Apr 13	Mary Stephenson	Wm. & Sarah Ann Guy	mother
Aug 30 1872	Apr 13	Harriet Elizabeth	James E. & Harriet E. Magness	parents

FIRST REFORMED CHURCH OF BALTIMORE

DATE OF BIRTH	DATE OF BAPTISM	NAME	PARENTS	SPONSORS
Jan 2	Apr 14	Ida Gill	Jno. Wm. & Sarah F. Messersmith	Mrs. Welch
Nov 9 1872	Jul 20	Nellie Stewart	Stewart & Mary Hamilton	mother
Aug 3	Nov 2	Adolf Michael	Adolf & Sophia Yochheim	grandfather
	1874			
Jan 11	Mar 10	Adeline	John F. & Lavinia R. McCoy	Mrs. Shotts
Aug 12, 1872	Apr 4	Sarah Etta	J.B. & Rachel Ann Bigham	Mrs. C. Hardesty
Jun 19 1873	Apr 5	Joseph	Joseph & Ellen Vansant	parents
Sep 4 1873	Apr 5	Richard	Cornelius & Margaret Coburn	grandmother
Feb 26	Apr 5	Agnes Elenora	Charles & Mary Ann Huff	parents
Sep 7 1873	Apr 5	Clara Florence	Thomas R. & Mary E. Wingrove	A.E. Wingrove
Mar 21	May 3	Francis Anton	Geo. Theo. Frances & Charlotte Sophia Waldner	grandfather
Jun 15 1873	May 18	John Dixon	Dixon & Josephine R. Guy	father
Jan 2	May 24	Sarah Catherine	F. Thos. & S. Kate Rodenmayer	parents
Mar 7	Jun 1	Geo. Parker	Wm. B. & Annie C. B. McRea	grandmother
Apr 23	Jun 2	Gilbert Brown	G.B. & Cath. Pauline Rathson	parents
May 25	Jul 7	John Frederick	Geo. F. & Mary M. Prechtel	Mr. F. Prechtel & wife
Feb 22 1873	Oct 25	Ellinor Clarke	John W. & Sarah W. Sills	parents

FIRST REFORMED CHURCH OF BALTIMORE

MARRIAGES

DATE	NAMES	
1862		
Jan 1	Joseph Dume to Elizabeth Kerner	by License
Jan 14	Edmund S. McCoy to Margaretta Jones	"
Mar 23	John W. Rogers to Mary Elizabeth Edwards	"
Mar 27	John Hamilton to Margaret Crawford	"
Jun 2	James E. Magness to Harriet E. Ingman	"
Sep 10	Salim H. Momssen to Elenora Richstein	"
1863		
May 19	William Harris to Margaret J. Lockhart	"
Jun 9	John A. Caumbie to Annie E. Reed	"
Jul 25	Frank R. Gruger, W.S.A. to Carrie Hessgera (?)	"
1864		
Mar 29	Charles F. King to Amelia J.C. Remington	"
Oct 6	Rev. H. J. Comfort to Maggie A. Miller	"
Dec 13	Joseph M. Wittaker to Rebecca M. Boyd	"
Dec 25	Martin Kasmodel to Lizzie Hamand	"
1865		
Apr 6	John Gomley to Jane Frances Mathany	"
Jun 28	Chester S. Marsh to Matilda C. Standiford	"
Sep 14	Robert Clenighen to Ginnie Olive Foyen	"
1866		
Apr 17	William L. Patterson to Mary F. Miller	"
Jun 5	E. Clark Fales to Mary R. Baker	"
Jun 14	Frederick A. Otto to Ximena Ross	"
Jul 24	Wm. Ware to Ms. Catharine F. Baker	"
1867		
Feb 14	Henry J. Nichols to Angie B. Taylen both of Maine	"
Jun 4	Geo. W. Aspril to Fannie J. Lightner	"
Jul 25	Abram M.E. Gordon to Sue W. Jinney	"
1868		
Jan 7	Robert Lautenback M.D. to Endora Nasen	"
Aug 27	Jacob Durst to Catharine Little	"
Sep 7	R. Rewinkel to Ms. Annie Sprole	"

FIRST REFORMED CHURCH OF BALTIMORE

DATE	NAMES	
Oct 20	John Bigham to Rachael Brasheare	by License
Dec 31	Dixon Guy to Josie R. Adams	"
1869		
Jun 15	David L. Bergamosie to Emma J. Wingrove	"
Aug 19	Geo. C. Halton to Mary Harris	"
Nov 3	John E. Tipton to Mary Diffenderffer	"
Nov 11	F. Thomas Rodenmayer to S. Kate Hilberg	"
1870		
Jan 25	Gilbert B. Rathson to Pauline King	"
Mar 8	Chas. H. Bramble to Harriet P. Sanders	"
Apr 14	Geo. Mason Griffith to Emma Stackman	"
Aug 25	Geo. F. Prechtel to Mary M. Schillinger	"
Nov 11	Jacob Rebel to Lizzie Bavarium	"
Nov 23	Francis White to Mary G. Onion	"
Nov 24	James Stuart to Kate Gettier	"
1871		
Oct 10	Wm. F.C. Gerhardt to Hattie E. Elliott	"
1872		
Jan 1	Wm. H.H. Taylor to Ms. Mary S. Locher	"
Mar 21	John H.B. Young to Miss Maggie Brooke	"
Oct 2	Edward F. Brandan to Hannah E. Steube	"
Oct 3	Wm. W. Smith to Belle Hutt	"
1873		
Jan 26	C. W. Bell to Miss Clara McNally	"
Apr 29	Charles M. Rae to Henrietta Siegman	"
Jun 20	John N. Hoffman to Mary A. Dougherty	"
Oct 21	Wm. C. Briely to Laura V. Sinn	"
Dec 3	S. C. Simmons to Georgia A. Houck	"
Dec 21	Geo. F. T. Waldner to Lottie S. Fisher	"
1874		
Jan 8	James Fuller to Mary Wonn	"
Apr 12	Henry Wm. Lewis Waldner to Gertrude Schaeffer	"
May 17	Frederick A. Faost to Catherine Hess	"
May 25	John R. Schaefer to Annie E. M. Glenau	"

DATE	NAMES
1875	
March 20	Francis W. Whitney to Anna Marg. Bohn
April 17	William T. Gilmore to Mary M. Rodgers
April 25	Jacob M. Gammill to Maggie Perry
Sept 4	John W. Cummings to Harriet A. Boyce
Nov 29	Joseph F. McBee to Ariel C. Lee
Dec 2	Charles W. Cherry to Georgie E. Kraft
1876	
Jan 4	Charles Simms to Charlotte A. Crowder
Feb 1	Russ Jones to Annie E. Frazier
Feb 19	Ralph E. Vocke to Mary A.(?) Buchheimer
March 23	Henry L. Wendel to Rosa B. Stone
June 20	Samuel Knott to Eliz. Donahoe
July 5	Lewis Chronister to Annie Ritter
July 20	John H. Huke to Sarah L. Hopple
July 25	Francis R. Kirwin to Emily R. Joseph
Nov 28	Paul Fred. Schminke to Emma C. Messersmith
1877	
Jan 25	Levin Tyler to Mary Feldpusch
Feb 13	John Maguire to Celia Hopkins
March 19	Walter F. Smith to Lena May Crawford
April 2	John W. Geiger to Mary P. Logsdon
May 10	George C. Brown to Rosa Ross Kemp
Oct 2	Frederick N. Troll to Bertha E. Schwartz
Oct 19	B. Frank Welch to Lizzie E. Wayson
Dec 22	J. Harman Smith to Nellie Reisinger
1878	
Jan 30	Isadore de Martore to Susanna Maxfield
April 11	Graves S. Brendel to Kate E. Derr
April 16	J.W. Sefton to Harrie L. Hollida

FIRST REFORMED CHURCH OF BALTIMORE

1878 (con't)   NAMES

June 6	James L. Johnson to Emily T. Massey
July 24	John B. Gheen to Mary E. Wylie
Aug 18	Taylor Buffington to Elvie Sanbower at Shepardstown, West Virginia
Sept 4	Alfred Nagel to Annie E. Rossiter at Blue Bell, Pa.
Sept 12	Wm. C. Weyrauch to Lizzie C. Rehbein
Oct 2	John Watson to Elinor Stewart
Oct 2	Samuel Schillinger to Marietta Newton
Nov 5	Williard M. Smith to Irene Funk
Nov 21	James L. Bradley to Josephine Ferrandini
Dec 25	David S. Wingrove to Clara Belle Stuck

1879

Feb 5	Greenleaf Johnson to Annie E. Baker
May 20	George H. Locher to Mary J. Ronemus
July 1	John G. Wehrman to Katier Brent
Nov 19	Dr. James H. Lewis to Mollie E. Kemp
Nov 20	Robert Wells to Mary N. Bradley
Dec 16	William H. Miller to Annie S. Dorsey

1880

Jan 22	William O. Chaney to Mary E. Christ
March 10	George T. Parker to Ella E. Burgess
April 6	George W. Tracy to Mary E. Curfman
May 18	William H. Griffith to Annie M. Bowers
June 8	James K. Ellis to Carrie B. Curtis
Aug 12	Joseph W. Cockley to Mary C. Leber
Sept 16	Fred Wm. Urbach to Mary E. Kline
Sept 22	Samuel S. Hopple to Ella N. Kelly
Oct 6	Harvey Beard to Mattie E. Grimes
Dec 12	John Peter Brandau to Annie F. O'Neil

1881

May 22	Henry H. Gerhart to Elizabeth Luck
April 21	Joseph K. Kingeley to Meta E. Vietsch
May 11	Wm. N. Zulauf to Amelia C. Rosskamp
May 11	George Adam Klump to Eliz. N. Willis
Jun 5	Wm. D. Cobaugh to Roberta A. Johnson
July 3	George Feldpusch to Frederika Mardaga
Sept 5	Willis Worster to Maggie A. Collins
Oct 26	James A. Murray to Florence I. Derr
Nov 23	Jos. Alonzo Howard to Annie W. Overfield
Dec 1	Solomon Kimmell to Kate M. Lincoln
Dec 31	Edwin E. Thompson to Mary S. G. Diedrich

FIRST REFORMED CHURCH OF BALTIMORE

DATE	NAMES
1882	
Feb 15	James W. Long to Annie A. Wilkening
Feb 21	Richard L. Gray to Mary E. Webster
March 1	George Thomas Elliott to Kate M. Brooks
April 16	Eugene Poezolt to Estelle S. Smith
April 26	Wm. Buchheimer to Sela M. Meikowske
May 7	Hughe G. Shelley to Laura E. Davis
June 14	Charles R. Miller to Minnie R. Kelly
Sept 10	John P. Stenner to Maggie B. Von Waldner
Oct 25	John W. Waldren to Annie C. Schminke
Oct 26	Henry Smith to Augusta Stoll
Nov 7	John Lynch to Esther Boothe
Dec 13	Harry Clay Smith to Emma A. Bradley
1883	
Jan 14	Samuel Johansen to Annie Jetner
April 17	Harry B. Wendler to Alice V. Canby
June 20	George Coburn to Virginia Q. Allison
June 25	Louis Clauss to Dora V. Gaehle
Nov 1	Wm. C. Wellener to Mary E. Blackburn
Nov 4	Jesse Brent to Tillie Deller
Nov 8	Edward H. Shafer to Rosina C. Locher
Nov 13	Charles J. Belbin to Rosa A. Ward
Nov 15	John A. Moore to Bertha G. Sommerville
Nov 26	Henry E. Reville to Kate Parker
Dec 6	Edward G. Staley to Susie Campbell
Dec 18	George F. Godwin to Pauline H. Meikowski
Dec 20	Fayette Bixby to Carrie Cockley
Dec 20	George Esselmann to Emma Scherer
Dec 27	George Guetler to Julia A. Geidt
1884	
Jan 13	George J. Dusel to Lena Sandlass
March 3	Charles W. Hennick to Mary Grupy
March 24	Thomas H. Sommers to Rosa Rehbein
April 15	William McK. Steffey to Rosa E. Sheets
April 22	Joshua N. Richardson to Virginia H. Linhard
May 6	Martin L. Robinson to Emma C. Funk
May 29	William Shorter to Eliz. Cole (colored)
June 10	McIliard S. Cozine to Mary E. Pritchard
June 10	James Dunn to Augusta S. Watson
June 23	Charles Brandau to Elvira G. McFadyen

FIRST REFORMED CHURCH OF BALTIMORE

1884 (con't) — NAMES

Date	Names
Oct 5	Lewis B. Jury to Elizabeth J. Coburn
Oct 30	Henry R. Beans to Barbara A. Buchheimer
Oct 30	Carson Schumacher to Wilhimina E. Buchheimer
Dec 7	James T. Lowe to Sallie V. Preston
Dec 25	James A. DePuey to Emma Lee Funk

1885

Date	Names
Jan 5	Beverly R. Waugh to Lizzie Klaproth
Jan 5	Harry Wilson to Sophia Dennis (colored)
Feb 8	Frederick Turnt to Dorothea K. Hildebrand
Feb 11	Wesley French to Lulu Bertha Seward
Mar 26	Franklin H. Zumpstein to Sarah Jane White
April 15	James W. Bell to Dozilla A. Martin, both of Washington, D.C.
April 5	Bernhard Boehme to Clara R. Schambach
April 27	Samuel M. McAvoy to Alice V. Goss, of Wash. D.C.
May 9	Joseph L. Metcalf to Dora Clarke, both of Rockland, Maine
May 1	Siegfried Hess to Alice K. Frazier
June 11	Clinton S. Johnson to Mary Burns, both of Baltimore Co.
June 23	Richard R. Jenkins to Lydia E. Reason, Balt. & Havre de Grace
June 24	Willie Carman to Nellie E. Magers
June 30	Edgar P. Simons to Miriam S. Holmes of Wash. D.C.
July 16	Charles H.G. Hungerford to Mary Diffenderfer Creney
July 21	George Noble Hurdle to Lillie Nora Cullum, of Balt. and Harford Co.
Aug 30	Samuel J. Bayne to Ella Kellum, both of Balt. Co.
Sept 17	Harry O. Clayton to Mary S. Lindenberg
Dec 20	Henry S. Baker to Lillie Nichalson
Dec 21	William H. Freyer to Margaret A. Kehm

1886

Date	Names
Feb 9	George LeCato to Minnie F. Schall
March 22	Henry C. Schumacher to Blanche Bennett
March 23	Charles Rehbein to Annie Bandel
March 24	George W. Wills to Sarah Ann Crawford
May 25	William H. Mirphy to Katie Helbing
July 12	Charles H. Philips to Elizabeth Naumann, of Philadelphia & Baltimore
Aug 4	Philip D. Warfield to Carrie Dorsey
Sept 2	William A. Hetzel to Elizabeth T. Cockley
Sept 13	Harry C. Heffner to Lillie W. Shock
Sept 22	George B. Alls to Sarah A. Vinyard
Oct 31	Jefferson D. Coburn to Sophia M. Gerboth

FIRST REFORMED CHURCH OF BALTIMORE

DATE	NAMES
1887	
Jan 4	William G. Hammer to Minnie K.L. Schwinn
Jan 15	Albert Payne to M. Emma Marceron of Wash. D.C.
Jan 27	Louis P. Kline to Ida Taylor
Feb 15	Richard E. Cozzens to Mary E. Brady, both of Washington
April 3	Edwin C. Bange to Nora F. Beeker, Hanover, Pa. and Manchester
May 15	Peter Buchheimer to S. Celia Nehren
May 25	James H. Rogers to Belle Z. Rites
June 1	Edward T. Davis to Florence R. Massey
June 1	Henry Clay Smith to Carrie Eirley
June 15	William F. Young to Carrie E. Seebode
June 16	L. Thomas Pennington to Lulu E. Hutt
June 20	Frederick Casper Witte to Annie Margaret Zapp
June 22	Lambert H. Thiess to Mary C. Lephardt
June 25	Edwin D. Loane to Mary Clara Mitten of Westminster
July 3	William B. (?) Snellings to Victoria O'Connor
July 12	Andrew Zuechlag to Emma Bornitz
July 18	John H. Patterson to Theressa K. Sudhause
Oct 3	George Haas Jr. to Evelyn Lee Turley, both of Wash.
Oct 5	George W. Hall to Annie M. Klaproth
Oct 17	William Harlove to Katie Rites
Oct 19	Christian William Kestner to Katie Lee Jackson
Oct 31	William E. Shawgo to Annie C. Bissel
Nov 6	Frank A. Krieager to Florence E. Fry of Glenrock, Pa.
Nov 16	John B. Hunt to Lizzie Crockett
Nov 6	Bernard Lammers to Lottie Buckmiller
Nov 29	William A. Drebing to Mary V. Dunn
Dec 6	Joseph M. Thatcher to Amelia Bowers
Dec 14	Charles A. Bortner to Theoda M. Smith
Dec 21	William Guy Jr. to Ellen L. Garrett
Dec 28	John T. McGahan to Rachel Muller
1888	
Jan 12	John Stengel to Clara L. Grupy
Jan 15	Richard Turnt to Katie M. Vogel
March 13	John A. Burgess to Alice C. Gifford
March 21	George B. Forsyth to Wilhemina Luccabaugh
April 12	George L. Littig to Katie M. Reisinger
April 17	Thomas B. Schall to Stella Mohar
May 9	William H. L. Thorne to Eleanora W. Abbott
June 3	Hamilton A. Glessner to Henrietta Kemp

FIRST REFORMED CHURCH OF BALTIMORE

1888 (cont')	NAMES
June 6	Anthony E. Geidt to Sallie C. Baroux
June 12	Charles J. Bertram to Lizzie Hiltner
June 20	Henry F. Young to Gertrude Amereihu
Aug 8	Ferdinand C. Turnt to Mary E. Cook
Sept 12	Charles W. Smoot to Laura J. Stuck
Oct 9	Charles Robert Johnson to Lettie Commodore, both of Balt. Co.
Oct 14	William E. Fraking to Bertha Lindenberg
Oct 25	Samuel C. Kindig to Annie E. Urbach
Nov 8	William Johnson to Laura Virginia Burns, both Balt. Co.
Nov 22	Donaldson Cologne to Emma Shirley, both Wash. D.C.
Nov 25	George John Koch to Louisa M. Heiller
Dec 5	Charles W. Filler, M.D. to Eva B. Scott
Dec 30	John E. Long to Katie E. Volkmann
1889	
Jan 9	Wm. Stewart Diffenderffer to Estelle Anderson
March 5	Thaddeus S. Taylor to Grace V. Steer
March 18	Julius Wingfield to Helen Bache Nicholson
March 20	Henry E. Schambach to Mary A. Murphy
March 27	John H.G. Rever to Lillie J. Sweaver
April 21	Christian Pannemann to Selma Turnt
April 30	Frank E. Harding to Lulie E. Reed, both of Wash. D.C.
May 16	Howard H. Worthington to Rosa Schminke
June 4	George Owen to Sarah Smith
June 5	Frederick Bartholomay to Georgianna Cunningham
June 21	Sewall A. Musser to Annie Ready of Lewistown, Pa.
July 3	Charles H.G. Keehner (or Kechner) to Maggie Heimbuck
June 26	Julius Fischer to May C. Richarts
July 21	Frederick A. Weisheit to Jennie Guy
Sept 12	Andrew Burga to Nettie E. Mullican, both of Wash. D.C.
Oct 2	William T. Holmes to Mary Lizzetta Rosskamp
Oct 24	George H. Geiger to Ella V. Hammel
Nov 20	Samuel E. Pentz to M. Katie Shallus
Nov 27	Charles Fitzpatrick to Lillian Acton
Dec 5	Charles B. Wantz to Emma V. Rietdorf
Dec 10	John C. Hilberg of Brooklyn to Sarah Cohen of Cin.
Dec 14	Frederick B. Duncan to Sarah J. Tully
1890	
Feb 12	Rev. Joel T. Rossiter to Caroline Elizabeth Welch
Feb 20	John Thomas Daily to Martha K. Waltemeyer, both of Balt. Co.

1890 (con't)

Date	NAMES
March 17	Benjamin Bailey to Jennie Herbert, both of Wash. D.C.
March 23	Frederick H. Meister to Helen E. Kemp
March 27	Thomas Hunter to Annie E. Miller, both of Youngstown, Pa.
April 10	Edward W. Fountain to Mary E. Schriefer
April 23	William O.N. Hammond to Sadie C. Kreps of Greencastle, Pa.
June 9	Charles O. Gunther to Susie Horisberg
June 11	John F. Hesson to Nannie M. Porter
June 24	Charles A. Howell to Mattie Blaney
June 24	George Rosendorn to Rachel L. Ramsey of Pennsylvania
June 25	Robert C. Dorr to Annie C. Buchheimer
July 7	Henry Sporleder to Annie E. Glossner
July 19	Joseph C. Scoggins to Gertrude Amelia Bunting
July 24	William H. Fanning to Mary A. Iglehart, the former of Cin. Ohio
July 30	Alfred Smallwood to Ida S. England
Aug 13	Arthur E. Roberts to Amelia C. Martens
Aug 31	Arnold Siegwart to Amelia Stockhause
Sept 1	Ira A. Harman to Elizabeth I. Baker, both of Wash. D.C.
Sept 7	Henry Hofmann to Christina Waldner
Oct 12	Thomas S. Pocock to Adelaide Lavender, both of Wash.D.C.
Oct 20	Edgar B. Hunt to Annie Kelly
Nov 5	John H. Pillings to Bertha F. Kehn
Nov 18	John W.H. Geiger to Annie Magdalene Melis
Dec 25	John A. Huebner to Margaret K. Vaeth

1891

Jan 10	Hugh Andrew to Laura Correa, both of Ashland, Balt. Co.
Jan 15	Robert A. Krieger to Ella E. Buchheimer
Jan 28	Charles H. Stockhause to Mary L. Haberkorn
Jan 29	James G. Howard to Emma Evans, both of Balt. Co.
Jan 29	J. William Hoover to Nettie Myrtle Huyett, both of Wash. Co., Maryland
Feb 3	Henry P. Rust to Mary A. Gilkey, both of Wash. D.C.
Feb 23	Elmer Zoller to Minnie L. Hogg, both of Philadelphia
Feb 25	George C. Heiligenstadt to Clara M. Phillips
March 4	William Harry Hauer to Mary Christiana
April 9	Charles Watson to Nellie Padgett, both of Wash. D.C.
April 9	Charles J. Hildebrand to Alma A. Pruschak
April 23	John H. Veditz to Elizabeth Held
April 29	John F. Gettemuller to Mary A. Pfau
May 6	John William Snyder to Hattie M. Bell, both of West Va.
May 20	Joseph G. Kline to Mary E. Kelly

FIRST REFORMED CHURCH OF BALTIMORE 237

1891 (con't)	NAMES
May 27	B. Franklin Sherwood to Berhardina Veditz
May 27	Charles H. Waldner to Annie J. Zink
June 16	Robert Glasgow to Amy Scotten, of York and Harford Co.
June 23	George W. Armstrong to Elizabeth Lindenberg
June 30	Charles H. Zinck to Mary L. Wentzel
July 1	Joseph J. Hauer to Laura V. Marine
July 8	Harry H. Kidd to Mabel C. Fisher
July 29	Joseph E. Roelkey to Margant Worman, both of Fred. Co.
Aug 5	Edgar E. Burns to Alverda V. Thomas, both of Balt. Co.
Aug 10	Jesse A. Cornwell to Maggie Cornwell, both of Fairfax Co. Va.
Aug 13	George L. Newman to Caroline C. Cooney
Sept 19	W. Burroughs Taylor to Viola A. Thomas, she from Frederick
Oct 1	William H. Quarles to Rosella Meyers (colored)
Oct 21	John G. Carle to Lillie J. Derr
Oct 25	Joseph T. Hauck to Lizzie F. Rosskamp
Nov 2	Charles D. Welch to Florence A. Earley
Nov 4	John McCullough to Elizabeth S. Black
Nov 25	August Doell to Dora Volkmann
Dec 17	Hugh A. Phillips to Catherine Haas
Dec 24	Thomas Whitelegg to Mary E. Kelly
Dec 25	Guss Werner to Bessie Kershaw
Dec 31	Edward G. Hoover to Mary S. Guy
1892	
Feb 18	Charles Jos. Helfrich to Mary E. Eysler, both of York, Pa.
Feb 19	Jonathan Cilley to Marie Sardy Genesi, both of Wash.D.C.
Feb 20	Edward Dean to Elizabeth Johnson, both of New York
April 2	Benjamin F. Shack to Rosa Jenkins, both of Gloucester Co., Virginia
April 13	Henry Charles Coleman to Katie C. Schambach
April 21	Charles P. Heiller to Julia Koch
April 21	Harvey L. Lambert to Mary Ann Hoover
May 19	William H. Benson to Laura May Hopple
May 23	Ernest E. Heisey to Catherine J. Trostel, both of Lebanon, Pa.
June 16	Allen P. Rogers to Ella B. Hostler
June 29	Charles H. Miller to Lillie Buckman
July 4	Isaiah Chaney to Ella McKnew
July 19	Frank Richards to Maggie Cumor
Aug 16	Charles H. Dale to Carrico Arrico, Rochester, N.Y. & Cin. Ohio
Sept 18	Lewis C. Phillips to Emma Wiedefeld

FIRST REFORMED CHURCH OF BALTIMORE

1892 (con't)   NAMES

Date	Names
Sept 26	Sutton W. Saunders to Katie T. Leek
Sept 27	William H. Clampitt to Annie R. Wood, both of Wash.D.C.
Sept 28	George Waldner to Martha Davis
Oct 25	Harry C. Weiskittle to Daisy M. Grumbine
Oct 26	Dixon Guy to Maggie B. Pierce
Oct 27	John A. Danzeglock to Maggie Hildebrand
Nov 3	Horatio W. Price to Mary E. Davis
Nov 9	G. Carville McCormick M.D. to Ella J. Hedeman
Nov 29	John Young to Ida Scott
Dec 8	William W. Carroll to Ida E. Dougherty
Dec 15	James Guy to Margaret M. Lerch, of Wilmington, Ill. & Buckleystown, Md.
Dec 15	Charles H. Collett to Winfred E. Seitz
Dec 18	Adam Snyder to Helena Reinig

1893

Date	Names
Feb 18	Edmund Burke to Grace N. Thompson, both of Wash. D.C.
Feb 21	Henry Kengla to Mary S. Hazel, both of Wash. D.C.
March 8	Edward Meekius to Emeline Buckman
March 16	Edgar C. Campbell to Bessie R. Carter-
April 11	Thomas White to Minnie A. Plowman, both of Balt. Co.
April 12	George P. Miller to Laura E. Jelko, of Frederick & Baltimore
April 17	Charles Brunger to Maggie Byington, both of Wash. D.C.
April 19	Alan C. Rigney to Grace M. Quynn (?), of Balt. & Frederick
April 23	Adolph F. Slaughter to Bernhardine Kurrelmeyer
April 25	Lawrence F. Whittemore to Florence R. Wernsing
April 30	Edward J. McCleary to Mollie Clifford
May 9	Walter F. Whitehead to Jennie V. Govan
May 16	Edward Hyatt to Charlotte T. Ridgeley
June 14	Charles Yonson to Emma May Martin
June 15	John H. Berens to Maud Frain, both of Wash. D.C.
June 21	Henry Geidt to Camilla M. Wright
June 26	Irving N. Bowden to Bertie C. Luskey, both of Wash.D.C.
July 1	Otis Lee Hood to Florence Eugenia Whiting
July 10	George N. Wilson to Laura M.S.Scheer
July 17	Charles A. Barlow to Susan E. Mullen
July 26	William H. Ash to Martha L. Williams, both of Wash.D.C.
Aug 9	Harry A. Jones to Annie Sanford, both of Wash. D.C.
Aug 17	James J. McGovern to Mary E. Dixon
Aug 22	James J. Murphy to Anita D. Vautier, he of N.Y., she of Wash. D.C.

FIRST REFORMED CHURCH OF BALTIMORE

1893 (con't)	NAMES
Oct 7	Thomas W. Habbojane (?) to Hannah Pacey
Oct 8	Horace Grant Seitz to Annie C. Sharp, both of Wash.D.C.
Oct 24	Otto H. Duker to Emma A. Mehr
Nov 9	Leon C. Yingling to Mary E. White
Nov 15	Nicholas Rogers Merryman to Ella May Belbin
Nov 29	William A. Wells to S. Ella Taylor, he of Aberdeen
Dec 7	Abraham L. Dunham to Mary E. Guy
Dec 18	William E. Sutton to Harriet J. Boon
Dec 31	Joseph H. Wells to Katie M. Kunkel

1894	
Jan 16	Leon H. Sommerfield to Carrie Steiner, he of Washington
Feb 5	George Dalton Crawford to Cora Ann Cherry
Feb 28	William Volkmann to Theresa J. Gorsuch
March 20	Chauncey B. Moorehead to Lela Paca
March 21	William T. Staley to Bessie W. White, he of Fred.Co.
May 23	Thomas W.B.Hussman to Teresa Warmbold
May 30	Charles E. Burkhardt to Mary Schmidt
June 15	William H. Christ to Mamie Freeman
June 20	Edward C. Schwessinger to Marguerite M. Schwinn
July 7	Scott G. Pulliam to Helen B. Tabler, both of Kentucky
July 17	William H. Obenshain to Mary C. Hensley, he of Indiana
Aug 2	Charles C. Hornung to Emma G. Freas, both of Wash.D.C.
Aug 2	John L. Baker to Othelia Christ
Sept 6	Charles L. Brodman to Mary V.S. Adams
Sept 12	John B. Lucas to Mamie Roesch
Oct 10	Charles Denton Mergardt to Julia Wentzel
Oct 17	Thomas E. Biddison to Emma J. Gunther
Nov 28	Thomas M. Shepherd to Annie M. Carter, both of Wash.D.C.
Nov 28	Cody Gemmill to Maggie Brent
Dec 12	William H. Winkelmann to Anna S. Aull
Dec 23	William H. Miller to Minnie Wesselman
Dec 27	George W. Padgett to Emma M. Christ, both of Charles Co.
Dec 28	Hunter Harry O. Snyder to Laura A. Hays, he of West Va. she of Pa.

1895	
Feb 20	Augustus Beck to Maud Gipe, both of York, Pa.
March 13	Sidney O. Fernald to Jennie T. Hudgins, both of Va.
March 20	George L. McDaniel to Ella May Donovan
March 21	William Oscar Plowman to Martha Bull, both of Balt.Co.
April 16	Mylon Roche to Laura Ann McCummum, he of Chicago, she of W.Va.

FIRST REFORMED CHURCH OF BALTIMORE

1895 (con't)   NAMES

Date	Names
April 25	George Harry Elloff to Blanche Teresa Cafferata
April 30	Francis C. Favier to Sarah E. Bigham
May 13	George H. Brown to Sarah E. Carter, both of Wash.D.C.
June 18	Charles W. Glaser to Louise C. Meid
June 20	Henry J. Carle to Matilda Stahl
Aug 28	Henry C. Shaffer to Annie M. Yeatman
Sept 1	Alexander Dischner to Kunigunde Handshuk
Sept 28	James Wilkerson to Mary Boswell, he of Charles Co.
Oct 15	Archie Miles Marshall to Emma Jane Wyatt, both of Va.
Oct 16	Charles H. Macomber to Ida S. Nichols, both of Wash.D.C.
Oct 30	Frank Walter Kreps to Bessie Early King, he of Pittsburg
Nov 6	John C. Armstrong to Mamie Bennett, both of Wash.D.C.
Nov 6	Charles A. Walkling to Catherine E. Christ
Nov 27	William D. Keating to Annie C. Meders
Nov 30	Alphonso O. Stafford to Blanche A. Nugent, both of Wash. D.C.
Dec 2	Arthur W. Nyce to Bernardina Logsdon
Dec 18	James W. Taylor to Margaret J. McCleary

1896

Date	Names
Jan 4	Alexander Golway to Mary Elizabeth Aubinos (Aubinoe) both of Wash.D.C.
Feb 5	Ernest C. Gibson to Blanche H. Thomas, both of Wash.D.C.
Feb 10	Louis H. Gerding to Mary C. Hoffman
Feb 15	Charles T. Bliss to Mary G. Minor
Feb 17	Frederick S. Drew to Anna E. Welch, he of Iowa, she of Wash.D.C.
Feb 19	Daniel A. Weaver to Cora M. Brubaker, both of York, Pa.
Feb 21	Obediah R. Hurley to Jennie Hawn, both of New Jersey
Feb 22	Samuel W. DeVore to Bertha Martin, she of Pa.
Feb 29	Robert E. Russell to Clara Clements, both of Wash.D.C.
Feb 29	Charles W. McCormick to Katie B. Davidson, both of Wash.D.C.
March 2	Thomas O. Probey to Mabel M. Stuart, both of Wash. D.C.
March 5	John W. Conrad to Jessie P. Brown, both of New York
March 25	Augustus L. Boteler to Rosa Allen, he of Frederick, she Balt. Co.
March 26	Thomas D. Shaw to Mary E. Gibbs, both of York Co.,Pa.
April 15	Edmund Geiger Shower M.D. to Marie Elizabeth Otto
April 19	James F. Wiedefeld to Georgiana C. Mattern
April 23	William E. Cooke to Eda V. Zinsser, both of New York
May 21	Walter B. Meehan to Sarah V. Hobbs
May 29	George Chandler to Florence H. Smith, he of Wash., she of N.Y.

FIRST REFORMED CHURCH OF BALTIMORE

1896 (con't) NAMES

June 3	Franklin H. Seitz to Mary Wilhelm
June 9	John C. Wood to Bertha V. Shelton, both of Wash.D.C.
June 17	William Harry Hauer to Mary E. Deppish
July 1	Philip M. Geidt to Mollie A. Haberstumpf
July 16	Henry G. Kernol to Mollie J. Harzog
July 21	John W. Reynolds to Sarah B. Johnson, both of Springfield, Illinois
July 24	Alexander Porter to Carrie E. January
July 28	Frederick W. Wollman to Mary C. Carle
July 30	George Vroom to Minnie Butler, both of Wash. D.C.
Aug 1	Emmett C. Milstead to Minnie L. Downie, both of Wash.D.C.
Sept 14	David Holland to Mary Stewart
Sept 20	Paul Schmidt to Paulina Stockhause
Sept 23	John H. Wilhelm to Laura Rice Hammel
Nov 25	George D. Busch to Arabella H. Redman
Dec 2	William D. Brengle M.D. to Georgia D. Diffenderffer, he of Va.
Dec 3	Henry H. Bye to Clara M. Beeler
Dec 6	Fred Miller to Emma Henkelbein
Dec 10	William F.H.Warnsman to Catherine Bouchet
Dec 20	John Kline to Kate E. Long

1897

Jan 22	Lewis H. Sudik to Alice M. Dehoff, both of York, Pa.
Feb 11	Thomas Blake to Mary E. Ziegler
Feb 17	William H. Glascock to Mamie E. Lyles, both of Wash.D.C.
Feb 17	Albert O.(?) Elliot to Emma L. Carrico, he of Ind. Ter. she of Wash.D.C.
March 6	Charles W. Hall to Sarah A. Popkins, both of Wash. D.C.
March 16	John H. Dobbling to Bertha Gresley, both of York, Pa.
March 30	James R. Thurston to Sarah O. Hogge, both of Va.
April 22	Edwin J. Ryan to Jennie M. Getters, both of Wash. D.C.
April 26	John E. Davis to Avice E. Roberts, both of Wash. D.C.
April 27	Henry W. Sellhausen to Hattie V. Smithsin, both of Wash.D.C.
May 17	George Quinn to Mary Hayden, both of Wash.D.C.
June 2	Joseph H. Ketler to Christina Harelman
June 21	Frank Dellinger to Libbie Tyrrell, both of Wash.D.C.
June 22	William C. Young to Margaret Frost
July 20	Armer G. Abbott to Bessie Ditzel, both of Havre de Grace
July 21	James Edward Wood to Marian Gladys Porter
Aug 14	Caleb H. Ellis to Lottie Ellis, he of Maine, she of Mass.

FIRST REFORMED CHURCH OF BALTIMORE

1897 (con't)	NAMES
Aug 24	Elvin Luskey to Alice Lanham, both of Wash.D.C.
Oct 27	Edward Brooke to Hennie E. Otto, she of Wash.
Oct 27	Samuel W. Yeakle to Alice M. Abrams
Nov 16	John E. Lewis to Maria E. Foley, he of Va. he of Ill.
Nov 21	William H. Sheneman to Mamie T. Kolp, both of Pa.
Nov 25	John W. Rupp to Mary Herzing
Dec 22	John J. Stewart to Annie L. Bleeze, he of Wash. she of Canada
Dec 29	Elias B. Ramsburg to Mary S. Best, both of Frederick, Md.

1898	
Jan 4	Charles McDowell to Lizzie Sechrist, both of Dallastown, Pa.
Feb 8	Harry Friedrich to Katie A. Flaherty, both of Wash. D.C.
April 20	Milton Patterson to Amelia C. Weeden, both of Wash.D.C.
May 11	John T. Wilson to Minnie M. Simpson, both from Altona, Pa.
May 12	Christian G. Reese to Bertha F. Weirs, he of Pa.
May 15	Richard Coburn to Ida Airey
May 16	Frederick Heuse to Martha E. Kline, he of N.Y.
June 3	Broadus W. Preston to May C. Woody, he of Wash., she of Va.
June 6	William J. Musey to Elizabeth Schleigh, he of Hagerstown
June 13	John Thomas Mulligan to Bertha Eliz. Fallon
June 15	John W. Vane to Annie Och, he of Cambridge, Md.
June 21	George Edward Meise to Carrie Eliz. Thomas
June 23	John W. Smith to Ida B. Austine, he of L.Is., she of Glen Rock, Pa.
June 23	Patrick Kelly to Gertrude Clary, she of Smithburg, Md.
June 28	James E. Pierce to Minnie K. Bennett, both of Wash.D.C.
June 30	Jesse Sturtz to Mary L. Hedrick, he of Harford Co.
July 5	Newton Barrett Woodall to Jessie Avaline Riddell, both of Richmond, Va.
July 20	William H. Gilbert to Daisy E. Rieger, both of Wash.D.C.
Aug 9	John R. Gleason to Amy C. Bennett, both of N.J.
Aug 11	Frank C. Wright to Mary E. Quenborg (?), both of Altoona, Pa.
July 25	Dr. Perceval Sherer Rossiter to Isabel P. Jacobi, at Colorado Springs
Aug 17	John Dolan to Josephine Fisher, both of Wash. D.C.
Aug 17	Robert L. Dunn to Edna E. Pollard, he of N.J., she of Wash. D.C.
Sept 3	Samuel Grob to Theresa E. West, he of Pa., she of N.Y.
Sept 7	Adolph Wm. Hildebrand to Anna Mary E. Zabel
Sept 17	Robert L. West to Anna C. Johnson, both of Wash.D.C.
Sept 22	Harry A. Hook to Laura V. Airey

FIRST REFORMED CHURCH OF BALTIMORE

1898 (con't)	NAMES
Sept 29	Leonard C. Grove to Ellen White
Oct 12	A. Lester Tracy to Lillian B. Darlton, both of Wash.D.C.
Oct 17	Henry W. Walters to Ida Seufert, both of N. York
Nov 13	Edward A.B.Harryman to Florence V. Amos
Nov 22	William J. Wright to Emma May D. Loeffler
Nov 24	Robert Andrew Rick to Helen A. Bosley, he of Wash.D.C.
Dec 1	Harry C. Wells to Maggie F. Bates
Dec 1	George Wollman to Minnie Booker
Dec 27	Charles Guetler to Carrie E. Black, both of Balt. Co.
1899	
Jan 30	Silas Walter to Mary E. Green, both of Balt. Co.
Feb 14	Robert Dehuff to Rosie Drane
Feb 25	Holland R. Kibler to Clara T. Austin, both of Wash.D.C.
Feb 27	William H. Bromwell to Anna L. Reilly
March 6	Ralph Westwood Frey to Amelia Emmeda Rupp, both of York,Pa.
April 1	Lewis T. Brown to Nellie M. Murphy, both of Phil.Pa.
April 18	Albert Frederick Holtz to Nellie Schley
April 26	Albert G. Cornwall to Elizabeth A. Dykins, he of Sunbury, she of Muncie, Pa.
May 14	Felix Cunningham to Agnes Eutsey Vanmeeter of Harrisburg, Pa.
May 25	Washington Irving Tuttle to Bessie Corse Richardson
Sept 9	T. Charles McComas to Mae Angelia Yakel
Sept 23	Charles E. Neurath to Lulu M. Kines, he of Wash., she of Va.
Oct 25	Henry A. Huse to Eliz. G. Brent
Oct 30	William Eugene O'Hara to Maggie S. Waldner
Nov 18	Franklin Geoghegan to Edith B. Ward, both of Wash.D.C.
Nov 29	Herbert L. Smith to Florence S. Kabis, both of Altoona, Pa.
Dec 2	Edwin J. Wyall to Gertrude C. Kneuss
Dec 24	Andrew Bohlken to Lena H. Rupp
Dec 27	Charles D. Parke to Anna Mattie Quidland of Spring City, Pa.

ADDENDA

1894	
Oct 3	Charles H. Reiley to Cora Heaps
1895	
Jan 25	Anthony Kennedy to Louisa McCollough (actor and actress)
March 8	William Baxter to Marjory McLean
March 24	James A. Downs to Mable G. King from Parkton and New Freedom
Nov 6	Walter L. Hubbard to Emma V. Booker

FIRST REFORMED CHURCH OF BALTIMORE

DATE	NAMES
1896	
April 9	Henry G. King to Annie E. McWilliams from New Freedom
May 25	Richard N. Thom to Clara Garnet (?) from Phil. & Balt. (colored)
June 3	George M. Harris to Genevieve Whitlock from Wash.D.C.
June 3	Henry Buchsbaum to Mamie Miller
Aug 10	William M. Crunie Jr. to Annie M. Karcher
Oct 21	George H. Wild to Catherine Rouder from Kansas City, Mo. & Balt.
1897	
Jan 4	Rudolph C. Thomas to Marion V. Poole
Jan 18	James C. McKeever to Florence R. Reardon from Wash.D.C.
March 19	John W. Grabill to Alice M. Stevenson from Ridgely, Md.
May 29	Earnest W. Bien to Bessie E. Snyder
June 30	Charles H. Appel to Mary Van Danaker
Sept 21	Walter E. Ovem (or Orem, Obem) to Lillie L. Hartzell
Oct 20	Jacob Brown Halbert to Anna M. Roeder
1898	
May 12	George E. Marshall to Lizzie M. Munck
June 22	Samuel Clinton Wherley to Jane Catherine Hancock, she from Wash.D.C.
Sept 15	Harry E. Simpson to Annie M. Enfield from Bentley Springs, Md.
1899	
Jan 11	Arthur J. Richards to Matilda J. Hoffman from Greensboro, Md.
Feb 15	Albert J. Lemkuhl to Florence H. Muthert
Feb 22	James Edgar Given to Mary Blanche Gees
April 24	Oscar T. Coleman to Mary C. Callahan
June 14	William B. Rutter to Blanche E. Shawn
June 28	George B. Hoffman Jr. to Hattie A. Davis
Oct 29	David Taseell to Sealie Hills (colored)

FIRST REFORMED CHURCH OF BALTIMORE 245

DATE OF BIRTH	DATE OF BAPTISM	NAME	PARENTS	SPONSORS
Jan 7	Nov 18	George Albert	Christian and Annie L. KEHM	
Aug 8, 1876	Nov 18	Mary Florence	Cinnatus and Marietta JELKS	
Aug 8	Nov 18	William Halliway	John F. and Emma J. MYERS	
Nov 30	Dec 18	Christina Catherine	Fred A. and Kate FROST	
Apr 20	Dec 21	Minnie Clara	Henry and Rosa B. WENDEL	
1878				
Oct 19, 1877	Jan 13	Grafton Carlisle	John O. and Eliz. CRAWFORD	
Aug 19, 1873	Jan 13	George Caleb	George C. and Mary HATTON	
Nov 17, 1877	Jan 13	Alexander Bryson	" " " " "	
Oct 12, 1877	Jan 17	Paul Frederick	Paul F. and Emma C. SCHMINKE	
Oct 21, 1876	Jan 29	Charlotte	Charles W. and Georgia E. CHERRY	
Sep 13, 1873	Jan 29	Sarah Elizabeth	Edward and Mary STOWMAN	
Sep 14, 1877	Feb 28	Robert Newton	Daul[Paul?] H. and Mary E. KLINGEL	
Nov 25, 1877	Mar 17	William Clarence	Henry and Marg. HILDEBRAND	
Dec 13, 1877	Mar 31	Christian John Miller	John H. and Annie WILKENNING	
Feb 13	Apr 14	Rosa Otilla	John and Amanda HAUER	
Dec 17, 1877	Apr 25	Franklin Daniel	Char. W. and Mary J. NOELL	
	Apr 19	Louisa ZIEGLER (adult)	Samuel L. ZIEGLER, mother deceased	
	Apr 19	Sarah Francis DYKE (adult)		
	Apr 19	Charles GERHART (adult)		
Jun 1	Jun 3	Vera Montrose	M. Alex and Laura R. GOULD	Mary Smith
Apr 10	Jun 16	Harry (?) William	John W. and Mary P. GEIGER	
Mar 8	Jun 16	John Thomas Ward	John M. and Eliz. M. HAMMAR	
Jun 13	Jul 21	Margaret Franklin	Walter F. and Lena M. SMITH	
Jul 2	Aug 19	Thomas Wilson	William and Lizzie ROUSE	
Aug 11	Sep 8	Charles Edward Fred	Ed. F. and Hannah E. BRANDAU	
Feb 15, 1876	Oct 8	Jessie	Wm. J. and Eliz. G. GETTIER	
Dec 21, 1877	Oct 8	Vernia (?)	" " " " "	
Jun 13, 1870	Oct 13	John Thomas	John W. and Emma V. MICHAEL	
Jan 19, 1874	Oct 13	Daniel Bernard	" " " " "	
Aug 4	Oct 13	Mary Bennetta	Charles W. and Georgie E. CHERRY	
Aug 14	Oct 31	Anna Margaret	William and Mary BROMWELL	
Jun 17	Sep 29	Irene	William W. and Isabel F. SMITH	
Oct 29	Dec 15	Howard Percival	Richard and Maggie SHOOK	
Dec 8	Dec 26	James Isaac	William and Sarah A. GUY	
1879				
Oct 6, 1878	Jan 1	Elias Goldsboro Fectig	Wm. R. and Annie J. MAGERS	
Sep 17, 1878	Feb 23	Louis Reinhold	Geo. F. and Mary M. PRECHTEL	
Jan 21, 1878	Mar 17	Edwin Lang	John R. and Mary E. JACKSON	
Dec 1, 1878	Apr 13	Frederick Joseph	Fred. N. and Bertha E. TROLL	
Feb 20	Apr 13	Dora Lydia	Albert H. and Emma R. ROGERS	
Nov 19, 1878	Apr 13	Edmund Eschbach	Frank T. and S. Kate RODENMAYER	
Mar 13	Apr 16	Rossiter Edwin	Herman H. and Mary C. GITTERMAN	
	Apr 11	Mary E. SOMMERVILLE (adult)		
	May 12	Francis LINCOLN (adult)		
May 3	May 12	John Henry	Justice W. and Anna M. SNYDER	
Apr 30, 1878	May 28	Anna Caroline	John R. and Annie E. SHAFER	
Sep 5, 1878	Jun 10	Howard Rossiter	William and Alice L. SHAFER	Mary Shafer

FIRST REFORMED CHURCH OF BALTIMORE

DATE OF BIRTH	DATE OF BAPTISM	NAME	PARENTS	SPONSORS
Feb 28	Jun 16	Emma Amelia	Henry L. and Rosa B. WENDEL	
May 21	Jun 29	Conrad Most	John and Amanda HAUER	
Feb 4	Jun 26	Lillie	Henry and Marg. D. HILDEBRAND	
Nov 23, 1877	Jul 10	John Louis	Ferdinand and Ursula MOOYER	
Jun 3	Jul 22	William George	Wm. C. and Lizzie C. WEYRAUCH	
Mar 17	Jul 22	George Robert	Christopher and Anna C. LEPHARDT	
Mar 21	Jul 27	Charles William Randolph	Charles and Mary HUFF	
May 23	Aug 3	Mary Ann	John H. and Sarah L. HUKE	
Aug 20	Oct 2	Charles Newton	Saml and Marietta SCHILLINGER	
Jul 28	Oct 19	Frederick Charles	THIESS (mother)	
Jun 29	Oct 20	Lillie Eliza Kerr	Valentine and Martha COOK	
Nov 30	Dec 15	Catherine	Fred. A. and Kate FROST	
Aug 24	Dec 19	Charles Moore	Charles and Eliz. WINAND	
Jul 22	Dec 30	John Edward	Geo. A. and Clementine ABBOTT	

1880

DATE OF BIRTH	DATE OF BAPTISM	NAME	PARENTS	SPONSORS
Jul 22, 1879	Jan 4	Sophia Magdaldne	Adolph and Sophia JOCKHEIM	
Oct 9, 1879	Jan 11	Margaret Ruth	David S. and Clara B. WINGROVE	
Oct 28, 1879	Jan 15	Mary Louisa	John M. and Saloma (Sarah) ROEHLFING	
Feb 28, 1878	Jan 22	Norma Lee	Andrew and Eliz. C. OGLE	
Sep 12, 1879	Jan 22	Clarence Eugene	" " " " "	
Aug 18, 1879	Mar 28	Edgar Meyers	Thomas B. and Annie M. SHALL	
Jan 4	Mar 31	James Alexander	James A. and Minerva McKINLEY	
Feb 26	Apr 1	Annie Iona	Thos. W. and Alma F. BURNS	
Feb 23, 1878	Apr 30	George Davis	John R. and Jennie V. SHEEHAN	
Jul 3, 1879	Mar 4	Edward Water Whitney	Peter and Lucretia C. JOHNSON	
Jan 15	Mar 4	Willie Thomas	Thomas J. and Ernestine F. EATON	
Nov 5, 1879	May 2	Thomas Allfriend	Cincinatus and Marietta JELKS	
	May 26	Minnie Louisa TURNT (adult)		
	May 26	Ferdinand TURNT (adult)		
Nov 5, 1875	May 11	Nannie	Wm. and Sarah A.G. DIFFENDERFER	
May 23, 1878	May 11	Charles Hungerford	" " " " "	
Feb 6	May 11	Sallie Worthington	" " " " "	
May 29, 1878	May 16	Agnus May	Wm. J. and Louisa E. TURNT	
Apr 20, 1871	May 16	Celma Matilda	" " " " "	
Feb 23	May 16	Sarah Rebecca	Cornelius and Marg. COBURN	
Feb 29	Jun 6	Charles Franklin	Charles E. and Maggie McCAULEY	
May 20	Jul 4	Kolma Gerster	Dr. Fred and Emma E. JANSEN	
Jan 16	Jul 18	Mary Alice	John M. and Eliz. M. HAMMAR	
May 30	Jul 22	Lydia Keith	Walter F. and Lena May SMITH	
Jan 12, 1875	Sep 19	Frank	Frank and Maggie SCHRADER	
Jun 13	Sep 21	Anna Maud	Charles W. and Mary J. NOELL	
Dec 26, 1879	Sep 26	Robert Melvin	Christian and Annie L. KEHM	
Jul 14	Oct 7	Walter Chase	Paul F. and Emma C. SCHMINKE	
Jul 7	Oct 10	Ida Johanna	Wm. J. and Louisa TURNT	
Apr 4	Oct 10	Edith May	Graves S. and Kate E. BRENDEL	
Sep 11	Oct 24	Nellie Elizabeth	Jacob M. and Maggie GAMMILL	
Jul 20	Dec 12	Janetta Arthur	John and Agnes BABYLON	

FIRST REFORMED CHURCH OF BALTIMORE

DATE OF BIRTH	DATE OF BAPTISM	NAME	PARENTS	SPONSORS
1875		Adults		
	Mar 26	Clarkeson Eby		
	Mar 26	Robert Levi Henshaw		
	May 23	Marietta Hill		
	Mar 26	Mollie K. Crabbs		
	Jul 23	Charles Augustus Welshoffer		
Nov 4, 1874	Jan 25	Henry	Charles and Henrietta McREA	
Sep 8, 1874	Mar 2	Carrie Warfield	Henry M. and Annie E. BAUTZ	
Nov 30, 1874	Mar 28	Percival Sherer	Rev. J.T. and Nettie S. ROSSITER	
Oct 13, 1874	Mar 28	Joseph Elmer	Wm and Sarah A. GUY	
Feb 14	Mar 28	James Allen	Matthew and Sarah J. WHITE	
Oct 2, 1870	Mar 28	James S. Allison	George and Frances WEBER	Charles Shafer Rosina Locker
Apr 18, 1874	Mar 29	William Henry	Wm. H. and Mary BROMWELL	
Dec 25, 1870	Mar 28	John William	Wm. and Mary KEENE	
Jun 13, 1874	Apr 4	Lewis Rossiter	Jas. E. and Lizzie C. BELL	
Feb 25	Apr 27	George Edward	John and Amanda HAUER	
Jan 19	May 16	Catherine Elizabeth	Adolph and Sophia JOCKHEIM	Mich. Kohler Cath. Haas
Jul 4	Jul 8	Ada	Wm. W. and Nell F. SMITH	Mrs. Mary Smith
Jun 11, 1874	Jul 25	Walter Livingston	John P. and Christie HALBACH	
Aug 15	Sep 1	Margaret	Fred A. and Kate FROST	
Jun 10	Oct 10	Willie Diffenderfer	Joseph and Ellen VANSANT	
Feb 8, 1870	Oct 10	Grace Rutherford	Wm. and Mary E. CRAWFORD	
Apr 8	Oct 10	Mary Elizabeth	Thos. R. and Mary E. WINGROVE	
Jul 9	Oct 13	Ella Blanche	Christian and Anna L. KEEM	
Mar 23	Dec 7	Lulu	Isaac J. and Caroline HOUCK	
Oct 1, 1873	Dec 25	Florence Virginia	Robert S. and Frances V. ONION	
1876				
Sep 27, 1875	Jan 23	John Walter	Charles G. and Maggie McCAULEY	
Apr 26, 1873	Feb 17	William Fennimore COOKE (adult)		
Jul 25, 1875	Mar 8	Catherine Loretta	John and Annie WILKENNING	
Oct 21, 1872	Apr 4	James Oliver	Charles and Margaret STUCK	
Dec 25, 1875	Apr 4	Madge Olevia	" " " "	
Jul 18, 1873	Apr 16	James Edgar	Emma LUDWIG (father dead)	
Jul 19, 1866	Apr 16	Charles Benson	" " " "	
Dec 25, 1875	Apr 16	Bessie	" " " "	
Mar 12, 1866	Apr 16	William Elliot	Jas. E. and Harriet E. MAGNESS	
Oct 12, 1867	Apr 16	Henry Adolphus	Jas. Ed MILLER (mother deceased)	
	Apr 16	Mary Farewell STEWART		
Oct 23, 1873	Apr 17	Louisa Caroline	Wm. and Mary BROMWELL	Mrs. Welch
Feb 2	Apr 17	John Elliot	L.D. and Sarah J. KEYS	
Nov 2, 1875	Apr 20	Mary Jesse	John R. and Annie E. SHAFER	
Mar 13	Jun 11	George Frederick	Geo. F. and Mary M. PRECHTEL	
Oct 24, 1874	Jul 11	Mary Ellen	Saml. F. and Nettie S. ZIEGLER	
Mar 13	Jul 13	Ludolph (?Rudolph) Bosley	Rudolph K. and Mary B. VOCKE	
Jun 20	Aug 6	Geo. Albert	Geo. A. and Anna L. PETERS	
May 12	Aug 27	Anna Emily	Thos. C. and Emily T. WHITSON	
Apr 27	Oct 8	Leah	Frank T. and S. Kate RODEMAYER	
May 5	Oct 9	Alice Amey	Nicholas E. and Mary E. BULL	
Sep 19	Oct 15	Lillian Elizabeth	Edward F. and Hannah E. BRANDAU	
Nov 30, 1875	Nov 30	Jacob Standiford	Charles V. and Mary J. NOELL	
Oct 4	Nov 30	Kate May	Wm. and Alice L. SHAFER	
1877				
	Jan 21	Robert McGREGGOR (adult 38 years)		
Oct 31, 1876	Jan 25	Elsie May	Thomas B. and Annie M. SHALL	
Oct 9, 1876	Feb 5	William Etta Fennimore	Wm. F. and Maud C. COOKE	
Apr 16, 1876	Mar 23	Charles Jelto	Herman H. and Mary C. GITTERMAN	
	Mar 30	Laura WOHN (adult)		
	Mar 30	Olevia WOHN (adult)		
	Mar 30	Isabel F. SMITH (adult)		
May 18, 1876	Apr 1	Catherine Gertrude	Thos. R. and Mary E. WINGROVE	
Nov 30, 1876	Apr 1	Annie May	Charles and Mary HUFF	
Feb 18	May 20	George Goetz	Adolph and Sophia JOCKHEIM	
Jan 31	May 20	Emily Elizabeth	Rev. J.T. and Nettie S. ROSSITER	
Mar 29	Jun 3	Harry A.	John M. and Sarah L. HUKE	
Apr 15	Jun 12	David Charles Henry	David F. and Cath. STONE	
Dec 19, 1876	Jul 15	William Addison Baker	John P. and Christie E. HALBACH	
Mar 30	Jul 27	Paul Clifton	Newton and Emma KING	
Oct 17	Nov 14	William Tobias	Emmanuel and M. LUCCABAUGH	

247

FIRST REFORMED CHURCH OF BALTIMORE

DATE OF BIRTH	DATE OF BAPTISM	NAME	PARENTS	SPONSORS
1881				
Sep 25, 1880	Jan 11	Bertha Lillian	Wm. R. and Annie J. MAGERS	Lillie J. Welch
Apr 28, 1880	Jan 12	Henry Harwood	Harry H. and Annie E. BAUTZ	
May 3, 1880	Feb 11	Harry Ferdinand	John R. and Annie E. SHAFER	
Sep 25, 1880	Feb 11	Elizabeth	Justice W. and Anna M. SNYDER	
Dec 27, 1880	Feb 24	Ida Birdloh	Henry and Marg. HILDEBRAND	
Jan 28	Mar 9	John Andrew	Dixon and Mary A. CRAWFORD	
Dec 16, 1879	Mar 9	John Andrew	John Andrew and Lovinia BLAKE	
Aug 4, 1879	Apr 19	James Clarence	Thomas R. and Mary E. WINGROVE	
Jan 1	Apr 17	Albert Frederick	Albert H. and Emma R. ROGERS	
Mar 6	Apr 24	Florence	Daul B. and Angeline DEHUFF	
Dec 30, 1880	May 1	Charlotte Lana	Adolph and Sophia JOCKHEIM	
Mar 16	May 3	John Peregrine	John W.H. and Rosanna J. GEIGER	
Feb 26	Jun 12	Edna Phronia Emma	Fred. N. and Bertha E. TROLL	
Oct 2, 1880	Jun 12	Louisa Cresselda	Charles and Talitha KNOSKE	
Mar 19, 1877	Jun 20	Nellie Bradford	Capt. Fred. Geo. and Eliz. LUCAS	Mr.&Mrs. Rollkay
Apr 18	Jul 3	Nettie	Frank T. and S. Kate RODENMAYER	
Aug 30	Sep 11	William John	Wm. and Christina HAMMOND	Mrs. Frost
Jun 22	Jul 10	Mary Elizabeth	John G. and Kate WEHRMAN	
Oct 16, 1879	Sep 20	Helena Gertrude	Charles and Christina H. BODE	
Jun 21	Oct 2	Edward Howard	Chas. E. and Maggie McCAULEY	
Aug 11	Oct 2	Samuel Schillinger	Saml. and Marietta SCHILLINGER	
Aug 20	Oct 9	James Massey	James L. and Emily T. JOHNSON	
Jul 17	Oct 12	Anna Margaret	Wm. C. and Lizzie C. WEYRAUCH	
Jul 20	Oct 16	Blanche Estelle	Saml. S. and Ella N. HOPPLE	
Sep 7	Oct 30	Christina Augusta	John M. and Saloma ROHLFING	
Sep 12, 1877	Oct 31	Edith Blanche	Thos. R. and Mary E. WINGROVE	
Oct 21	Dec 7	Alma Frederika	Thos. W. and Alma F. BURNS	
1882				
Feb 28	Apr 9	Henry Karsten	John M. and Louisa BRENT	
Oct 19, 1881	Apr 9	Charles Herbert	Jas. M. and Emma F. HAMMOND	
	Apr 9	Ann Elizabeth	David S. and Clara B. WINGROVE	Annie Wingrove
Apr 4	Apr 26	John Oliver	John Oliver and Eliz. CRAWFORD	
Jun 16, 1881	Apr 27	Catherine Rose	Christopher and Anna C. LEPHARDT	
Jan 4	May 28	John Albert	Ross Nevin and Cath. F. GOSWEILER	
Mar 26	May 28	Grace Edna	Wm. N. and Amelia C. ZULAUF	
Dec 31, 1881	Jun 25	Elvester Gerhart	Henry H. and Eliz. A. GERHART	
Apr 8	Jul 10	Robert Matthiott	Wm. H. and Annie M. GRIFFITH	
Jan 3	Jul 16	Edna Kinnaman	Wm. T. and Mary E. SMART	
Jan 4	Jul 16	Albert Preston	Cincinatus and Marietta JELKS	
Feb 18	Jul 30	Allan Maurice	John M. and Eliz. M. HAMMAR	
Aug 24	Sep 2	James Park	Charles A. and Ella HAVERSTICK	
Aug 17	Sep 3	Thomas Spencer	Fred A. and Kate FROST	Mrs. Hammond
Aug 18	Sep 27	Lillian Elizabeth	Paul F. and Emma C. SCHMINKE	
Feb 27	Oct 8	Helen Rossiter	Thomas R. and Mary E. WINGROVE	
Jul 21	Oct 8	Edith Regina	Albert H. and Emma R. ROGERS	
Sep 20	Oct 29	Catherine Estelle	George and Fredericka FELDPUSCH	
Aug 21	Nov 15	Amelia Alverta	Adam and Emma C. GEHO	
Oct 23	Nov 28	Harry Rossiter	Albert F. and Augusta B. VOLKMAN	

FIRST REFORMED CHURCH OF BALTIMORE

DATE OF BIRTH	DATE OF BAPTISM	NAME	PARENTS	SPONSORS
1883				
Nov 26, 1882	Jan 3	Lillie Idella	James A. and Florence MURRAY	
Feb 20, 1882	Feb 8	George	Nicholas and Marg. ARENZ	
Aug 12, 1882	Mar 6	Lillian May	William E. and Isabel P. STEVENS	
Nov 25, 1882	Mar 6	Howard Edward	Jos. E. and Mary BRENT	
Jan 16	Mar 18	Mary Magdaline	Samuel and Marietta SCHILLINGER	
Jan 9	Mar 25	Frank Horace	Benj. F. and Severa CAMERON	
Feb 23	Apr 25	Owen	Daul B. and Angeline DEHUFF	
Oct 25, 1882	May 13	Mary Christina	Adolph and Sophia JOCKHEIM	Mrs. Ruppel
Dec 1, 1882	May 17	Charles Albert	Wm. and Mary BROMWELL	
Mar 19	May 17	Georgie Rosina	Wm. C. and Lizzie C. WEYRAUCH	
Mar 20	May 17	John Frederick	Christopher and Anna C. LEPHARDT	
Nov 24, 1881	May 20	Ida May	John H. and Sarah L. HUKE	
Jan 27	May 20	Alfred Logsdon	John W. and Mary P. GEIGER	
Mar 18	May 21	Anna Estelle	Henry and Marg. HILDEBRAND	
Apr 8	Jun 3	Frank Swayne	Chas. E. and Maggie McCAULEY	
Jun 18	Jun 26	Mary Elizabeth	Ross Nevin and Cath. F. GOSWEILER	
May 11, 1876	Jul 1	Lela May	Chas. W. and Aldwellah FEIGLEY	
Feb 11, 1878	Jul 1	Bessie White	" " " "	
Jun 18	Jul 1	Mary Alverta	Saml. and Mary MAXFIELD	
Sep 29, 1882	Jul 1	Edward Bradley	Ella D. and George A. BOYER	
May 4	Jul 3	Elfrida May	Christian and Annie L. KEHM	
Jan 15	Jul 3	Katie Anderson	Maggie A. KEHM	
Jun 10	Jul 13	Harry Tranty	Geo. A. and Alice V. KEENE	
Jun 27	Aug 5	Albert Julius	Gustavus and Annie S. MALTER (or MATTER)	
	Sep 16	Albert William	Edwin E. and Mary S. THOMPSON	
Jun 17	Sep 16	Jennie May	Robert and Georgianna HAMMOND	
Jul 24	Oct 9	Alfred Irwin	Paul F. and Emma C. SCHMINKE	
Aug 5	Oct 14	Elizabeth Katie	John M. and Louisa BRENT	
Aug 13	Nov 21	Philip	Wm. and Eliz. VOLKMANN	
Nov 12	Dec 25	John Frederick	Wm. and Christina HAMMOND	
Oct 22	Dec 31	Inez	George Knox and Maria L. PEREGOY	
1884				
Oct 1, 1883	Jan 10	George William	Wm. Geo. and Louisa MEYER	
Nov 11, 1883	Jan 13	Reynolds Kraft	James L. and Emily T. JOHNSON	
Nov 11, 1883	Jan 13	Warren Samuel	Saml. S. and Ella N. HOPPLE	
Sep 1, 1882	Jan 13	Janette Francis	Robert G. and Louisa LAWRIE	
Sep 15, 1883	Jan 14	Frederick Christian	John and Saloma ROHLFING	
Oct 19, 1879	Jan 28	Howard Lawrence	John and Anna B. SMALTZEL	
Jan 14	Feb 14	Emma Agnus	David S. and Clara B. WINGROVE	
Feb 14	Feb 24	John Lowe	Wm. E. and Isabel P. STEVENS	
Jul 27, 1883	Mar 18	Harry	Henry H. and Eliz. A. GERHART	
Feb 22	Mar 19	Robert Giles	Robert G. and Louisa LAWRIE	
Apr 4, 1881	Apr 17	Benjamin Franklin	George and Mary J. UNGLAUB	
Jul 15, 1883	Apr 17	Clarence Albert	" " " " "	
Jul 8, 1883	Apr 21	Wilhelmina Julia	Wm. and Selma M. BUCHHEIMER	
Feb 22	Apr 24	William Octavius	Charles Ross and Annie E. DIFFENDERFER	
Dec 27, 1883	May 15	Reginald LeGrand	Graves S. and Kate E. BRENDEL	

250 FIRST REFORMED CHURCH OF BALTIMORE

DATE OF BIRTH	DATE OF BAPTISM	NAME	PARENTS	SPONSORS
Sep 19, 1883	May 20	Charles Augustus	Harry C. and Emma A. SMITH	
Nov 14, 1883	May 20	Irene Attick	Ella Dahlgren and Geo. H. BOYER	
Feb 9	Jun 2	Leanna Allison	George and Virginia COBURN	
May 21, 1883	Jun 27	Percy Williams	Thomas B. and Annie M. SCHALL	
Apr 26	Jun 27	Ann Louisa Canby	Harry B. and Alice V. WENDLER	
May 7	Aug 3	Sophie Minnie	Chas. F.W. and Mary Ann HUSSMAN	
Mar 1, 1882	Aug 3	William Thomas	John Hamilton and Estelle R. CORREA	
May 28	Aug 3	John Hamilton	" " " " " "	
Apr 5	Aug 24	Sophia Madeline	George F. and Mary M. PRECHTEL	
Jun 15	Aug 30	Maud Louise	Lewis G. and Lizzie A. ONION	
May 8, 1870	Sep 8	Oliver Morris (adult)	Nelson C. and Carrie L. THOMAS	
Mar 11	Sep 21	William Joel Rossiter	John H. and Sarah L. HUKE	
Sep 6, 1883	Sep 21	John Preston	John F. and Emma J. MYERS	
Jun 7	Sep 26	Anna Louisa Wood	Andrew J. and Anna L. HAMMAR	
Aug 27	Nov 2	Walter	Emil and Annie STOCKHAUSEN	
Feb 17	Nov 30	John Hawkins Patterson	Chas. L. and Carrie FEIGE	
Aug 22	Dec 8	William Harman	Wm. J. and Annie M. GRIFFITH	
Dec 4	Dec 25	Verina Rose	Louis and Dora V. CLAUSS	

1885

DATE OF BIRTH	DATE OF BAPTISM	NAME	PARENTS	SPONSORS
Oct 28, 1884	Jan 4	Earle Blackburn	Wm. C. and Mary E. WELLENER	
Sep 2, 1884	Jan 5	Florence Derr	James A. and Florence I. MURRAY	
Jul 4, 1839 (or 1809)	Jan 10	George Austin McCOMAS (adult)		
Jul 1884	Jan 11	Gertrude Wells	James Edgar and Ida R. McCRONE	
Jul 29, 1884	Jan 11	Aubrey Sommerville	John A. Bertha G. MOORE	
Feb 26, 1884	Jan 16	Elma Beatrice	Joseph Charles and Elma J. SCOGGINS	
Oct 30, 1884	Jan 29	Mary Ann Schultz	Frederick D. and Mary Ann WESTERFELD	
Mar 9, 1883	Feb 1	Isabella Shaw	James and Ellen Watt MANN	
Dec 6, 1884	Feb 1	Margaret Watt	" " " " "	
Jul 21, 1883	Feb 1	Bertie May	Charles R. and Minnie R. MILLER	
Dec 12, 1884	Feb 4	Edward	Joseph E. and Mary BRENT	
Jan 19	Feb 5	James Homewood	James Homewood and Charlotte Esther MARRIOTT	
Jan 16	Feb 15	Charles Henry	John P. and Maggie B. STENNER	
Nov 22, 1884	Feb 22	Georgie Virginia	George A. and Alice V. KEENE	
Feb 9	Mar 1	Ferdinand Mardoga	George and Frederika FELDPUSCH	
Mar 3	Mar 4	Lewis	Wm. and Eliz. VOLKMANN	
Aug 20, 1884	Mar 8	Clara Grace	John C. and Mary M. KAUFMAN	
Nov 19, 1884	Apr 5	Catherine	John Thomas and Margaret HARE	
Jun 27, 1884	Apr 5	Elizabeth Martin	John M. and Eliz. M. HAMMAR	
Jan 22, 1884	Apr 5	Eva Virginia Valient	Thomas R. and Mary E. WINGROVE	
Oct 21, 1884	Apr 7	Bessie Gordon	Albert H. and Emma R. ROGERS	
Feb 22, 1883	Apr 7	Annie Brittingham	George W. and Mary G. HOPKINS	
Jan 25	Apr 12	William Thomas	Robert and Georgianna HAMMOND	
Mar 26	Apr 30	Ella Lile	John G. and Kate WEHRMAN	
Dec 19, 1884	May 6	Albert Summers	Wm. C. and Lizzie C. WEYRAUCH	
Dec 29, 1884	May 6	Anna Margaret	Thomas H. and Rosa SOMMERS	
Dec 29, 1884	May 6	Christopher Franklin	Christopher and Anna C. LEPHARDT	
Mar 12	May 6	George Edwin	Wm. and Mary BROMWELL	

FIRST REFORMED CHURCH OF BALTIMORE

DATE OF BIRTH	DATE OF BAPTISM	NAME	PARENTS	SPONSORS
May 3, 1883	May 11	Laura Helen	Nelson O. and Annie E. ROBOSSON	
Feb 2	May 12	Emma Clara	John and Anna B. SMALTZEL	
Feb 19	May 24	Paul Hudson	Rev. Louis F. and Ella B. ZINKHAU(or N)	
Nov 23, 1884	May 25	Rosina Shafer	Frank T. and S. Kate RODENMAYER	
Apr 3	Jun 4	Magdalena	John and Saloma ROHLFING	
Sep 3, 1881	Jun 14	Daisy Bell	John L. and Eleanor STONE	
Nov 23, 1882	Jun 14	Myrtle Maud	" " " " "	
Dec 29, 1884	Jun 14	Pearl Estelle	" " " " "	
Sep 7, 1883	Jun 16	Mabel Adele	Wm. Edward and Matilda F. ALBAUGH	
Mar 5	Jun 20	Julia Day	Thomas C. and Annie O. MEDINGER	
Jun 29, 1879	Jun 25	Willie Solomon	W. Newton and Emma KING	
Oct 10, 1883	Jun 25	Pauline	" " " " "	
Jun 4	Jul 4	Rose Campbell	Edward G. and Susie STALEY	
Feb 2	Jul 12	Edwin Eugene Alexander	Edwin E. and Mary S. THOMPSON	
Feb 14	Jul 19	George Frederick	George Frederick and Anna NICHOLS	
Jun 16	Jul 22	Joseph Charles	Joseph Charles and Elma J. SCOGGINS	
May 27	Aug 2	Darthey Louisa	John M. and Louisa BRENT	
May 27	Aug 30	Lola Jenette	John W. H. and Rosanna J. GEIGER	
Dec 12, 1884	Aug 30	Solomon	William and Estelle C. COLLMUS	
Feb 9	Aug 31	Robert Johnston	Nelson C. and Carrie L. THOMAS	
Feb 16	Sep 3	Estelle Magdalene	Alfred P. and Mary A. HART	
Jun 1	Sep 6	James Franklin	William and Sarah Jane BAKER	
Jul 28, 1874	Sep 22	Bertha Sarah	Alfred P. and Mary A. HART	Mrs. Zetsman
Sep 29	Oct 25	Nettie Margaret	Wm. and Christina HAMMOND	
Sep 29	Oct 25	Jessie	Fred A. and Kate FROST	
Aug 11	Oct 25	Edith Amelia	Charles and Talitha KNOSKE	
Oct 9	Nov 3	Harry Himmelwright	Harry H. and Barbara BEANS	
Oct 14	Nov 3	Carson Schier	Carson S. and Minnie E. SCHUMACHER	
Sep 15	Nov 10	Bessie Campbel	Joseph and Annie GUY	
Sep 2	Nov 11	Harry Ehl	Adam K. and Emma C. GEHO	
Apr 27, 1884	Dec 1	Edith Clare	Solomon and Kate M. KIMMELL	
Jun 16	Dec 3	Claude Augustus	Charles Ross and Annie E. DIFFENDERFFER	
Dec 4	Dec 4	Anton Earnest	George and Julia A. GUETLER	

1886

Apr 18, 1873	Jan 3	William George	August and Elizabeth SCHULTZ	
Sep 30, 1877	Jan 3	Matilda Elizabeth	" " " " "	
Jan 11, 1880	Jan 3	George John	" " " " "	
Nov 20, 1883	Jan 3	Alfred Herman	" " " " "	
Nov 13, 1885	Jan 21	Gertrude Griffith	Charles H.D. and Mary D. HUNGERFORD	
Jan 9	Jan 28	Herman Ezra	John V. and Minnie M. RICHARDSON	
Nov 21, 1885	Jan 29	Mary Locher	Edward H. and Rosina C. SHAFER	
Feb 25, 1885	Feb 7	William	Frederick and Dora K. TURNT	
Jan 19	Mar 21	Helen Harman	J. Harman and Nellie SMITH	
Nov 12, 1885	Apr 11	Benjamin Franklin	John P. and Margaret HARE	
Feb 5	Apr 26	Gertrude Weiner	Louis and Dora V. CLAUSS	
Mar 9	Apr 26	Milton Gaehle	Thomas W. and Alma F. BURNS	
Oct 31, 1885	Apr 26	Elsie Frederica	Martin and Alma A. WURST	Julia Bruckner
Jun 28, 1875	Apr 26	John Robert	Moses and Celia T. CRAWFORD	Grace J. Crawford
Feb 26	May 23	Genevieve Louise	John Thomas and Marie Louise CLAGGETT	

FIRST REFORMED CHURCH OF BALTIMORE

DATE OF BIRTH	DATE OF BAPTISM	NAME	PARENTS	SPONSORS
Apr 1	May 23	Edward Oscar	Henry and Augusta SMITH	
	Apr 23	Laura May HOPPLE (adult)		
Aug 29, 1882	Jun 10	Richard Rose	Edwin S. and Annie TARR	Mrs. Mary Massey
May 6	Jun 13	Maud Irene	Thomas R. and Mary E. WINGROVE	
Dec 23, 1885	Jul 11	George Cleveland	Charles and Florence M. BURGAU	
May 1	Jul 11	Harry Rankin	John H. and Estelle R. CORREA	
May 3	Jul 27	Lola May	Wm. Edward and Matilda F. ALBAUGH	
Nov 7, 1885	Aug 15	Wilfred Rogers	John and Emily NOBEL	
Oct 26, 1885	Sep 25	Grace Algie	John W. and Mary P. GEIGER	
Jul 2	Oct 10	Elmer Franklin	Nicholas and Tillie KRIEAGER	
Sep 2, 1885	Oct 10	Willie Augustus	James A. and Emma Lee DePUEY	
Jul 2	Oct 10	Arthur Ockert	Fred N. and Bertha E. TROLL	
May 18, 1884	Oct 10	Bertha	William and Louisa TURNT	
May 19	Oct 10	Frank Antonie	" " " "	
Jul 26	Oct 14	John Henry Schultze	Fred D. and Mary Ann WESTERFELD	
Dec 13, 1882	Oct 28	Georgie Matilda	Harry G. and Georgie E. JAVIUS	
Sep 9	Oct 28	Harry Tranty	George A. and Alice V. KEENE	
Oct 9	Nov 7	Louis Bringman	Wm. and Cath. BRINGMAN	Lulu Schwin
Jan 20, 1884	Dec 6	Nowland Bennett Edgar	Percival and Francina B. GWYNN	
Aug 20	Dec 16	Andrew Hamilton	Henry T. and Nellie REHBEIN	
Sep 5	Dec 16	Lydia Ann	Thomas H. and Rosa SOMMERS	

1887

DATE OF BIRTH	DATE OF BAPTISM	NAME	PARENTS	SPONSORS
Sep 12, 1886	Jan 1	William Alfred	William and Sarah Jane BAKER	
Dec 6, 1886	Jan 9	Carrie Elanora	Samuel S. and Ella N. HOPPLE	
Mar 19, 1886	Mar 17	David Dorncifer	Jos. Thomas and Louisa Eliz. HAUCK	
Jan 6	Mar 23	Annie Margaret	Charles and Annie REHBEIN	
Jan 29, 1886	Mar 30	Lilian Emma	Bernhard and Clara R. BOEHME	
Jan 14	Apr 10	George Howell	Albert H. and Emma R. ROGERS	
Aug 27, 1886	Apr 10	Grace Virginia	George and Virginia COBURN	
Nov 5, 1882	Apr 17	Willie Christopher	Francis and Christina NICHOLSON	
Mar 22, 1885	Apr 17	Charles Sylvester	" " " "	
Jan 2	Apr 17	Minnie Christian	Henry S. and Lillie BAKER	
Dec 27, 1886	May 4	Rosina	William and Mary BROMWELL	
	Apr 8	Mary Isabel TOMLINSON (adult)		
	Apr 8	Mrs. Eliz. Irene HELTZEL (adult)		
	Apr 8	Mrs. Lydia HOPPLE (adult)		
	Apr 8	Lillie Estella URBACH (adult)		
	Apr 8	Charles YONSON (adult)		
May 5	Jun 10	Opie	Martin L. and Emma C. ROBINSON	
	May 27	Capitola Lenora McCLEARY (adult)		
Mar 23	Jun 28	Lulie Amelia	Robert G. and Louisa LAWRIE	
May 25	Jun 26	Malinda	John W. and Louisa BRENT	
Mar 18	Jul 3	Arthur Edmund	George W. and Sarah Ann WILLS	
Dec 1, 1884	Jul 10	Alice Lillian	James Alfred and Lillian Frances BRADLEY	
Jan 22	Jul 21	Augusta Golden	Joseph Charles and Emma J. SCOGGINS	
Dec 12, 1886	Jul 22	Anna Schall	George H. and Minnie F. LECATO	
Jul 22	Jul 23	Margaretta	Wm. A. and Eliz. T. HELTZEL	
Nov 29, 1885	Jul 29	Rossiter Magers	James Edgar and Ida R. McCRONE	

FIRST REFORMED CHURCH OF BALTIMORE

DATE OF BIRTH	DATE OF BAPTISM	NAME	PARENTS	SPONSORS
Jun 15, 1886	Jul 31	Elizabeth Alice	Willie and Nellie E. CARMAN	
Jul 16	Jul 31	William Girard	George and Lena SCHWINN	
Jul 25, 1886	Aug 14	Harry Sayen (?)	Maurice L. and Lizzie L. ROSSITER	
Aug 31	Sep 21	George Philip	George and Julia A. GUETLER	
Oct 20	Oct 21	Franklin White	Franklin H. and Sadie ZUMSTEIN	
May 9	Sep 30	Clarence Rossiter	David and Kate McCULLOUGH	
Dec 7, 1886	Oct 9	Margaret Forsythe	John M. and Lizzie M. HAMMER	
Jul 10	Oct 23	Lizzie Rebecca	Daniel B. and Angeline DEHUFF	
Oct 11	Nov 9	Frederick Augustus	Charles W. and Minnie FADER	
Oct 27	Dec 11	Mark Herbert	George W. and Lizzie V. SHULER	
Sep 21	Dec 15	Bertha Sophie	John M. and Kate REHLING	
Dec 6	Dec 18	Louisa Boland	Wm. G. and Minnie K. L. HAMMER	Lulu and Mr. Boland

1888

DATE OF BIRTH	DATE OF BAPTISM	NAME	PARENTS	SPONSORS
Aug 14, 1887	Jan 1	Mary Anna	Philemon D. and Carrie S. WARFIELD	
Apr 28, 1887	Jan 5	Christopher Albert	Christopher and Anna C. LEPHARDT	
Aug 8	Jan 24	Emma Frances	Charles F.W. and Mary Ann HUSSMAN	
Dec 25, 1887	Feb 5	John Thomas	John Thomas and Catherine HAVE or HARE	
Sep 4, 1887	Feb 5	Catherine	Martin and Annie Eliz. LEBER	
Nov 11, 1887	Feb 8	Edna Leora	Harry V. and Mary Ellen SNYDER	
Nov 28, 1887	Mar 6	Marguerite Clagett	Edward G. and Susie STALEY	
Jul 10, 1885	Mar 30	Sallie Frey	W. Newton and Emma KING	Mrs. Frey
Jan 2	Apr 1	John Herman Walter	Henry and Augusta SMITH	
Nov 28, 1887	Apr 1	Thomas David	Thomas R. and Mary E. WINGROVE	
Jan 11	Apr 2	Carl	George and Frederika FELDPUSCH	
Feb 18	Apr 12	Goldie Marie	Charles R. and Minnie MILLER	
Apr 6	Apr 17	David	Wm. and Christina HAMMOND	
Dec 11, 1887	Apr 22	Fannie Catherine	Christian B. and Susanna Eliz. LERMAN	
Oct 4, 1887	Apr 25	Grover Cleveland	Dominick and Emma HORLITZ	
Jan 20	Apr 26	Florence Corinne	Frederick and Levina BURKHARDT	
Feb 10	May 10	Rosa Adeline	Thomas H. and Rosa SOMMERS	
Mar 16	May 10	Anna Catherine Lambert	Henry and Mary C. THIESS	
Nov 23, 1887	May 17	Lewis Daniel Dietrick	Adolph and Sophia JOCKHEIM	
Apr 4	May 20	Emilie Georgette	James L. and Emily T. JOHNSON	
Feb 20, 1877	May 21	Elizabeth	Frederick August and Dorethea W. WERNER	
Dec 12, 1878	May 21	Albert	" " " " "	
Mar 17, 1881	May 21	Dorethee	" " " " "	
Feb 20, 1886	May 21	Charles	" " " " "	
Dec 13, 1887	Jun 12	Ira Day	Ira Day and Lydia KAHNEY	
Apr 17	Jun 15	Bessie May	William F. and Carrie E. YOUNG	
Aug 4	Aug 19	Louisa Caroline Johanna	Frederick C. Annie M. WITTE	
Jul 14	Aug 21	Mary Wilhemina	Frederick August and Dorethee W. WERNER	
Jul 30	Aug 26	Viola May	William and Katie HARTLOVE	
May 14, 1887	Aug 26	William Franklin	Joseph Franklin and Mary Alice ARNOLD	
Dec 12, 1886	Sep 2	Howard Elmer	Martin and Alma Augusta WURST	
Jun 15	Sep 2	Augusta Henrietta	" " " " "	
Jul 26	Sep 2	Robert	Thomas W. and Alma F. BURNS	
Sep 14	Oct 2	Frederick Albert	Frederick A. and Kate FROST	
May 10	Oct 14	James Van Dyke Stewart	Charles Ferd. Gaston and Claribel Wright BENOIT	

FIRST REFORMED CHURCH OF BALTIMORE

DATE OF BIRTH	DATE OF BAPTISM	NAME	PARENTS	SPONSORS
Aug 10	Oct 14	Clara Estella	William E. and Annie C. SHAWGO	
Sep 9	Oct 16	Louie Julius	Louis and Dora V. CLAUSS	
Feb 2	Oct 18	George	Henry T. and Nellie REHBEIN	
Jul 24	Oct 21	Thomas Vernon	L. Thomas and Lula E. PENNINGTON	
Aug 5, 1887	Oct 24	Nellie Ray	John L. and Eleanora STONE	
Sep 21	Oct 25	Elizabeth Hammar	George A. and Alice V. KEENE	
Jun 26	Oct 26	Robert Harrison	Robert Emory and Mary Eliz. ECCLESTON	
Nov 18, 1886	Nov 1	Beulah May	Wm. C. and Mary E. WELLENER	
Aug 9	Nov 4	Maud Elizabeth	George and Emma ESSELMANN	
Sep 6	Nov 4	Henry William	George Wm. and Cora SNYDER	
Dec 22, 1887	Nov 7	Edna Estelle	Adam K. and Emma C. GEHO	
Sep 26	Nov 13	Alice Catherine	Ross Nevin and Catherine F. GOSWEILER	
Apr 12	Nov 15	Joseph Charles	James Fletcher and Allie Lee SCOGGINS	
Dec 11	Dec 30	Lillian Annie	George and Lizzie HENDERSON	

1889

DATE OF BIRTH	DATE OF BAPTISM	NAME	PARENTS	SPONSORS
Nov 8, 1888	Jan 1	Mary Catherine	Ferdinand A. and Carrie A. ULRICH	
Oct 22, 1888	Feb 3	Bennetta Catherine	Charles and Talitha KNOSKE	
Jul 22, 1888	Feb 24	Charles Ervin	Charles A. and Theoda M. BORTNER	
Nov 16, 1885	Feb 24	Heister Clymer	William Charles and Elizabeth SMITH	
Oct 16, 1887	Feb 24	Mary Emma	" " " "	
Jan 12	Feb 24	Chadwick Murray	" " " "	
Oct 28, 1888	Feb 28	William Leslie	Charles T. and Mabel M. BAKER	
Jan 5	Mar 3	George Leon	William W. and Isabel F. SMITH	
Feb 22	Mar 7	Lillian Verona	William A. and Mary V. DREBING	
Nov 24, 1888	Mar 8	Royston Beverly	Samuel C. and Annie E. KINDIG	
Feb 10, 1888	Mar 8	William Christian	George W. and Annie M. HALL	
	Mar 18	Joseph Mitchell THATCHER (adult)	William A. and Mary Wilhemina KEHM	
Sep 7, 1888	Mar 18	Linden Aurelius	Joseph M. and Amelia THATCHER	
Mar 6, 1884	Mar 18	Walter Caryl	Sheppard C. and Hester A. HALL	
Jun 24, 1887	Mar 18	Jesse Albert	" " " "	
Oct 29, 1888	Apr 21	Walter Melchior	Frederick N. and Bertha E. TROLI (or TROLL)	
Jan 17	Apr 21	Alice White	Albert H. and Emma R. ROGERS	
Jan 18	May 5	Annie Catherine	Granville O. and Mary S. BANKERT	
Feb 20	Apr 22	James William	William and Ellen L. GUY	
	Apr 12	Mary Elizabeth THATCHER (adult)		
	Apr 19	Betzie Louisa THOMAS (adult)		
	Apr 19	Eleanor PETERMAN (adult)		
	Apr 19	Mrs. Harriet PRYN (adult)		
	Apr 19	Mrs. Katherine Glessner IRVIN (adult)		
	Apr 19	Gaston BENCIT (adult)		
	Apr 19	Abraham SEIDENSTRICKER (adult)		
Mar 7	Jun 9	James Russell	William R. and Annie J. MAGERS	
Jan 3	Jun 9	Don Francis Greenleaf	Edwin G. and Mary B. HUDSON	
Oct 5, 1888	Jun 20	William Lester	John G. and Pattie V. HAMMEL	
Mar 31	Jun 25	Harry Morrison	Harry Morrison and Clara Eliz. STONESIFER	
Sep 18, 1888	Jul 4	Hazel Adelaide	Llewllyn W. and Clara May WALKER	
Jun 14, 1888	Jul 4	James Edwin	Alfred N. and Lebbie A. HURLEY	
Jun 16	Jul 11	William James	John Thomas and Rachel McGAHAN	

FIRST REFORMED CHURCH OF BALTIMORE

DATE OF BIRTH	DATE OF BAPTISM	NAME	PARENTS	SPONSOR
Apr 4	Jul 12	Edward Rudolph	Carson S. and Minnie E. SCHUMACHER	Mrs. Budheimer
May 27	Jul 16	James Alfred	Charles W. and Laura J. SMOOT	Mrs. Wingrove
Jun 26	Sep 16	Grace	David and Kate McCULLOUGH	
May 26	Oct 3	Anna May	Harry R. and Barbara A. BEANS	Annie Bucheimer
Aug 27	Nov 14	Mary Louise	George L. and Katie M. LITTIG	Mrs. Reisinger
Nov 12	Nov 14	J. Frank Morrison	John E. and Katie E. LONG	
Jul 4	Dec 15	Catherine	Charles and Annie REHBEIN	
Aug 2	Nov 21	Elizabeth	Henry T. and Nellie REHBEIN	Mrs. Lephardt
Sep 10	Dec 25	Robert Calvin	George Harrison and Laura Margaret EHRMAN	
Nov 5	Dec 25	Lottie Priscilla	" " " " "	"

1890

DATE OF BIRTH	DATE OF BAPTISM	NAME	PARENTS	SPONSOR
Nov 20, 1889	Jan 5	Katie Werner	John M. and Louisa BRENT	
Nov 22, 1889	Jan 5	James Edwin	George and Frederika FELDPUSCH	
Dec 5, 1889	Jan 7	Edgar Victor	Harry Victor and Mary E. SNYDER	
Jul 3, 1889	Jan 12	James Mewburn	James Mewburn and Emma F. HAMMOND	
Dec 3, 1889	Jan 12	Edgar Cockley	Wm. A. and Eliz. T. HELTZEL	
Nov 29, 1889	Jan 13	Lillian Elizabeth	James H.C. and Mary GARING	
Jul 30, 1887	Jan 19	Pauline Hannah	Wm. and Selma M. BUCHHEIMER	
Nov 21, 1888	Feb 9	Louetta	Samuel A. and Sarah F. BURKE	
Feb 15	Mar 16	Henry	John P. and Maggie B. STENNER	
Dec 29, 1889	Mar 15	Edna Viola	William A. and Mary V. DUNN	Mrs. Dunn
Aug 31, 1889	Mar 26	Mary Olevia	Alfred P. and Mary A. HART	Mrs. Zetzman
Mar 11, 1890	Apr 6	Frank Harper	Thomas S. and C. Alice GREENAWALT	
Sep 9, 1881	Apr 6	Addie Gertrude	Samuel A. and Sarah F. BURKE	
Feb 6	Apr 6	Edward Nicholas	Nicholas and Catherine Matilda KRIEAGAR	
Jan 22	Apr 6	Guy McDonald	Charles W. and Minnie C. STACKS	Jane Lichtner
Feb 11	Apr 6	Bertha Gertrude	Henry S. and Lillie BAKER	
Mar 29	Apr 7	Helen Eliza	Howard H. and Rosa WORTHINGTON	Eliza Harmon
Mar 19	Apr 8	Margaret Caroline	Wm. F. and Annie Laura KRAETER	Eliz Krater
May 19, 1889	Apr 14	John Louis	John Louis and Maggie K. RASCH	
Feb 14	Apr 14	Mary Caroline	William and Mary Caroline BROMWELL	
Mar 2	Apr 29	Frank Gordon	Samuel W. and Elizabeth Jones DERR	
May 26	Jun 15	Rosa May	George W. and Emma Virginia SCHMALZEL	
Apr 25	Jun 16	Bernard Schambach	Bernard C. and Clara R. BOEHME	
Dec 19, 1888	Jun 22	Clarence Funk	John L. and Emma C. WEAVER	
Apr 21	Jul 6	Esther Louise	William E. and Elbertha PRAKING	Mrs. Lindenberg
May 30, 1887	Jul 18	Mary Susan	John L. and C. Virginia KNODE	
Jan 25	Jul 18	Harriet Spielman	" " " " "	"
Oct 12, 1887	Jul 18	Magdalene Susan	William H. and Ella E. KNODE	
Apr 23, 1887	Jul 22	Ellenora Reese	William and Estelle C. COLLMUS	
May 30, 1889	Jul 22	William	" " " " "	
May 29	Sep 9	Nellie	William F. and Carrie E. YOUNG	
Jul 27	Sep 28	James William	James S. and Ellen H. GANTZ	
Jul 23, 1889	Oct 12	Elmer Reuben	Thomas R. and Mary E. WINGROVE	
Jul 30	Oct 12	Gertrude Louisa	Joseph E. and Mary BRENT	
Mar 8	Oct 13	Henrietta Emma	Frederick A. and Jennie WEISHEIT	
Mar 27	Oct 28	James Arthur	Charles W. and Minnie FADER	Mrs. Theiss
Oct 27	Oct 28	Samuel Wilbert	Charles Henry and Francis M. HARE	

FIRST REFORMED CHURCH OF BALTIMORE

DATE OF BIRTH	DATE OF BAPTISM	NAME	PARENTS	SPONSORS
Sep 10	Nov 16	Alfred Henry	C.F. Gaston and Claribel W. BENOIT	Mrs. E.F. Hunter
Jul 27	Nov 17	Washington Franklin	Samuel A. and Sarah F. BURKE	
Oct 23	Nov 18	William, George, Charles	William E. and Annie C. SHAWGO	
Oct 1	Nov 25	Frederick August	Frederick August and Dorethee W. L. WERNER	
Nov 16	Nov 27	Eldridge Price	Thomas W. and Alma F. BURNS	
Aug 3	Dec 1	Arthur Morris	Rev. Louis F. and Alman B. ZINKHAN (or ZINKHAU)	
Oct 14	Dec 14	Florence Estelle	Martin and Alma Augusta WURST	
	1891			
Jan 9	Jan 20	Edward Hazelton	William and Christina R. HAMMOND	
Nov 21, 1890	Jan 22	Alice	Lewis G. and Elizabeth A. ONION	V.C. Wilson
Nov 7, 1890	Jan 27	Susie Harvey	George A. and Alice V. KEEN	
Jan 5	Feb 8	Goldsborough Sappington Griffith	Rev. Joel T. and C. Eliz. ROSSITER	G.S. Griffith
Aug 12, 1890	Feb 19	Victoria Elenora	Charles B. and Emma V. WANTZ	
Feb 10	Mar 15	Raymond Rossiter	John H.G. and Lillie J. REVER	
Jan 15	Mar 29	Frederick Allen	Franklin H. and Sarah J. ZUMSTEIN	
Feb 12	Apr 12	Bessie Marie	George L. and Kate M. LETTIG	
	Mar 27	Annie Zapparah HOLLAND (adult)		
	Mar 27	Ella Cochran OTTO		
Nov 27, 1890	Apr 16	Frances Katie Virginia	John Louis and Maggie K. RASCH	
Mar 2	Apr 16	Anna Margaret	Henry T. and Nellie REHBEIN	
Jan 1	Apr 30	Charles Wesley	Charles W. and Laura J. SMOOT	
Apr 22	May 24	Florence Marguerite	John T. and Margaret HARE	
Feb 22	May 24	Lela May	Daniel B. and Angeline DEHUFF	
Jun 8	Jun 21	George William	Julius and May C. FISCHER	
Apr 21	Jun 23	Thomas Price	Abraham R. and Mollie E. McCLEARY	
Jun 4	Jun 28	Annie	Arnold and Amelia SIEGWART	
Mar 16, 1890	Jul 10	Ruth Penwood	John G. and Pattie V. HAMMEL	
May 10	Jul 26	Louis Staley	John F. and Anna Mary HESSON	
May 10	Jul 26	Lillian Gladys	" " " " "	
Aug 18, 1889	Aug 24	Rose Annie	John D. and Ida Gertrude ENGELBRECHT	
Mar 26	Aug 24	John Henry	" " " " "	
Dec 30, 1890	Oct 12	Ehrman Dauphin	Thomas S. and C. Alice GREENAWALT	
Jul 4	Oct 11	Marguerite Anna	Charles O. and Susie GUNTHER	
Sep 7	Oct 25	Justis William	John and Saloma ROHLFING	
Nov 6, 1890	Oct 25	Myrtle Marie	John T. and Magdalena GILES	
Oct 11	Nov 1	George John	George W. and Lizzie G. HENDERSON	
Jun 16	Dec 8	James Elsworth	Joseph Franklin and Mary Alice ARNOLD	Mr. & Mrs. Rogers
Oct 27, 1889	Dec 8	John Henry	" " " " "	
Sep 7	Dec 27	Anna Marguerite	George W. and Lizzie V. SHULER	
	Dec 31	Dixon Guy	Frederick A. and Jennie WEISHEIT	Dixon Guy
	1892			
Dec 20, 1891	Jan 11	Helen	Richard and Maggie SHOOK	
Sep 19, 1891	Jan 21	Margaret	David and Kate McCULLOUGH	
Oct 9, 1891	Jan 23	William Janney	Samuel C. and Annie E. KINDIG	Lillie Uhrbach
Dec 18, 1891	Jan 24	Lizzie Mary	Charles H. and Annie J. WALDNER	
Dec 27, 1891	Jan 27	Thomas Sommers	William and Mary Caroline BROWNELL	
Jan 9	Feb 11	Berhardina	John P. and Maggie B. STENNER	Mrs. Sherwood
Feb 23	Mar 6	Schall Wilhelm	John G. and Pattie V. HAMMEL	

FIRST REFORMED CHURCH OF BALTIMORE 257

DATE OF BIRTH	DATE OF BAPTISM	NAME	PARENTS	SPONSORS
Oct 15, 1891	Mar 6	Myrtle Rossiter	Edgar B. and Annie HUNT	
Dec 28, 1891	Mar 7	Annie Kate	George C. and Clara M. HEILIGENSTADT	
Jan 20	Mar 13	Edith Amanda	Wm. Harry and Mary HAUER	
Mar 13	Apr 3	Margaretta	Frederick Casper and Annie M. WITTE	
	Apr 15	Bertie Threasa MONOSMITH (adult)		
	Apr 15	John Wesley MONOSMITH (adult)		
Oct 12, 1891	Apr 17	Richard Edward	Benjamin S. and Mary E. DALLAM	Mrs. Griffin
Dec 19, 1891	Apr 17	Raymond Wilmer	Samuel S. and Ella N. HOPPLE	
Feb 27	Apr 18	Ralph	Martin L. and Emma C. ROBINSON	
Mar 18	Apr 14	Carrall Thomas	James H. and Belle Z. ROGERS	
Oct 26, 1891	May 3	Edna Alma	Charles J. and Alma A. HILDEBRAND	
Apr 4	May 15	Henry Leroy	Joseph J. and Laura V. HAUER	
Apr 23	May 18	Dora Elenora	Lambert Henry and Mary C. THEISS	
Feb 8	May 18	Henry Lambert	Charles W. and Minnie FADER	
May 11, 1891	May 29	Bessie May	John L. and Eleanora STONE	
Jun 12	Jun 26	Christina Catherine	William and Christina HAMMOND	Christina Frost
Jul 17, 1891	Jun 26	Alice Louise	William H. and Katie MURPHY	
May 24	Jul 10	Katie Elizabeth	August and Dora DOELL	
Aug 3, 1891	Jul 13	Grace Lizzie	George W. and Annie M. HALL	
Jul 27, 1890	Jul 13	Lizzie May	" " " " " "	
Jan 1	Jul 19	Mary Arabel	Richard R. and Lydia E. JENKINS	
Jul 19, 1890	Aug 1	Bessie Marie	William A. and Mary W. KEHM	
Jul 18	Sep 21	Mary Catherine	Charles H. and Mary L. STOCKHAUSEN	
Sep 17	Oct 16	Annie Margaret	George W. and Mary C. ZAPP	Annie Zapp
Jul 27	Nov 11	Edith Marian	John G. and Lillie J. CARLE	
Sep 8	Nov 13	Mary Ellen	William H. and Laura May BENSON	
Aug 9	Nov 13	Ida Dorsey	Joseph P. and Georgianna PEARSON	
Nov 16	Nov 27	Clara May	Julius and May C. FISCHER	Lena Keim
Oct 24	Nov 27	Charles Henry	Charles H. and Annie J. WALDNER	
Apr 5	Dec 4	Frank Allan	Samuel P. and Martha M. WHITE	Allan White

1893

DATE OF BIRTH	DATE OF BAPTISM	NAME	PARENTS	SPONSORS
May 9, 1892	Jan 22	Leah Lucille	Lewis V. and Annie B. TIPTON	
Oct 18, 1892	Jan 31	Mary Ellen	George A. and Alice V. KEEN	
Nov 20, 1892	Feb 22	Nellie Irene	George L. and Kate M. LITTIG	Mrs. Smith
Jun 20, 1887	Mar 9	Edna Viola	George Wash. and Mary Jane EBY	
Jun 11, 1892	Mar 9	Helen Beatrice	George Wash. and Bertha May BLANEY	
Oct 26, 1892	Mar 9	John Gourley	John and Eliz. S. McCULLOUGH	
Sep 30, 1892	Mar 14	Edna May	Charles L. and Sarah ROHRBAUGH	
Aug 29, 1892	Mar 20	Fannie Eliz. Dalrymple	James Edgar and Ida R. McCHONE	
Dec 23, 1887	Mar 20	Annie Louise	" " " " " "	
Jan 11	Mar 23	Theresa Louisa	Arnold and Amelia SIEGWART	
Feb 13	Mar 29	Helena Regina	Charles and Annie REHBEIN	
Oct 11, 1892	Apr 2	Clara Estelle	Charles W. and Laura J. SMOOT	
Feb 15	Apr 2	Bessie Leasetta	Joseph T. and Lizzie F. HAUCK	
Apr 23, 1892	Apr 2	Morris Lee	William T. and Mary Lizzetta HOLMES	Bertha Holmes
Feb 10	Apr 2	Louisa Margaretta	Charles P. and Julia HEILLER	
Mar 9	Apr 5	Helen	Nellie and Henry T. REHBEIN	Margaret Rehbein
Mar 7	Apr 20	Paul Gaeble	Louis and Dora V. CLAUSS	
Feb 14	May 28	Karl Henry	Henry F. and Bessie M. KIMKEL	

FIRST REFORMED CHURCH OF BALTIMORE

DATE OF BIRTH	DATE OF BAPTISM	NAME	PARENTS	SPONSORS
Dec 5, 1891	Jun 4	John Lewis	George Harrison and Laura Margaret EHRMAN	
Mar 19	Jun 12	Blanche Henrietta	William A. and Mary W. KEHM	
May 8	Jun 18	Charles Leslie	Harvey L. and Mary Ann LAMBERT	
Aug 16, 1888	Jun 18	William Carl	Jesse Addison and Mary Emma METZ	Mrs. Smallwood
Apr 23	Jun 18	Ida Smallwood	" " " " "	
Apr 4	Jun 25	Irvin Baroux	Anton E. and Sallie C. GEIDT	
Jun 6	Jul 9	Raymond Andrew	James S. and Ellen H. GANTZ	
Aug 11	Aug 13	Abell Herbert	John G. and Pattie V. HAMMEL	
Mar 28	Oct 8	Rose Myrtle	Arthur Conrad and Alice BEEFELT	
Sep 23	Oct 15	Harry (or Harvy) Carle	George W. and Lizzie G. HENDERSON	
Oct 6	Nov 2	Elsie Elizabeth	Wm. F. and Annie Laura KRAETER	
Oct 23	Dec 5	Dudley	Martin L. and Emma C. ROBINSON	
Oct 20	Dec 18	Helena Fredricka	Adam and Helena SNYDER	
Nov 1	Dec 25	Mary Agnes Durst	Rev. Joel T. and Caroline Elizabeth ROSSITER	
Jul 27	Dec 24	John August	John A. and Maggie DOUZEGLOCK	
Nov 19	Dec 25	John	John and Ida V. YOUNG	
Nov 15	Dec 31	Robert Giles	William H. and Katie MURPHY	Mr. & Mrs. Lowry

1894

DATE OF BIRTH	DATE OF BAPTISM	NAME	PARENTS	SPONSORS
Sep 26, 1893	Jan 11	Mildred Marie	Harry C. and Daisy M. WEISKITTLE	
Feb 23, 1888	Jan 21	Carrie Brown	John H. and Estelle CORREA	
Sep 7, 1892	Jan 21	Eleanora	" " " " "	
Nov 19, 1893	Jan 21	Walter Beauregard	George W. and Emma Virginia SCHMALZEL	
Mar 12, 1812	Jan 21	Mary JONES (adult)		
Dec 6, 1893	Jan 14	William Henry	Charles H. and Lillie MILLER	Wm. H.Buckman
Sep 3, 1893	Jan 14	John Andre Shultz	James Mewburn and Emma F. HAMMOND	
Dec 24, 1893	Feb 5	Virginia Hazel	Lewis G. and Elizabeth A. ONION	
Jan 19	Feb 11	Ruth Aurelia	Geo. B. and Nettie A. COVELL	
Dec 20, 1893	Feb 13	Philip Claude	Charles H. and Annie J. WALDNER	
Jun 24, 1893	Feb 18	Charles Gardner	Joseph L. and Julia V. THOMPSON	
Sep 8, 1893	Feb 27	Raymond Elvene	John and M. Mary BAPTISTE	
Jan 24	Mar 11	Alice Catherine	George H. and Ella V. GEIGER	Mrs. Roelke
Feb 10	Mar 15	Martha Elmina	Edward J. and Mary A. McCLEARY	
Feb 15	Mar 25	Fredericke Amelia	Charles H. and Mary L. STOCKHAUSEN	
May 8, 1893	Mar 25	Anna Laura Bertram	Harry Bertram and Hughena Thomson JOSEPH	
Jun 27, 1893	Mar 25	Edna May	Thomas S. and C. Alice GREENAWALT	
Dec 7, 1893	Mar 25	James Henry	Conrad and Hattie Eliz. WEGAU	Annie Greek
Feb 10	Mar 29	Henry Horst	William and Mary Caroline BROMWELL	
Nov 8, 1893	Mar 29	Lulu Mamie Catherine	John Louis and Maggie K. RASCH	
Mar 11, 1889	Mar 29	Thomas Tenant	Charles M. and Florence M. BURGAU	
Oct 18, 1887	Mar 29	Minnie Hester	" " " " "	
Dec 12, 1893	Apr 3	Myrtle Louisa	James Thomas and Gertrude Agnes McCLURE	
Mar 27	Apr 7	Dora	Frederick Caspar and Annie M. WITTE	
Feb 14	Apr 8	William Albert	Henry and Camilla M. GEIDT	
	Mar 23	Hughena Thomson JOSEPH (adult)		
Feb 27	Apr 25	Harry Raymond	William and Ellen L. GUY	
Jun 1, 1890	Apr 27	Ruth Olinda	Harry R. and Barbara A. BEANS	
Oct 18, 1892	Apr 27	Lilbourn Irvine	" " " " "	
Oct 19, 1893	May 7	Berhardina	John and Carrie M. TODD	Mrs. Kiely

FIRST REFORMED CHURCH OF BALTIMORE

DATE OF BIRTH	DATE OF BAPTISM	NAME	PARENTS	SPONSORS
Apr 9	May 24	William Claude	Joseph J. and Laura V. HAUER	
Mar 26	Jun 3	Harry Edgar	William H. and Laura May BENSON	
May 30	Jun 13	John	William and Christina HAMMOND	
Apr 3, 1892	Jun 19	Ethel Weaver	Jas. Jonothan and Ida J. JACKSON	
Jun 15, 1893	Jun 19	Alma Gertrude	" " " " "	
May 26	Jul 11	Alice Caroline	William Henry and Margaret Alice FREYER	
Aug 1, 1889	Jul 12	Edgar Percival	Edgar Percival and Francina Bouchelle GWYNN	
May 2, 1893	Jul 13	Mabel Estelle	Samuel N. and Allie MASON	
May 2	Jul 29	Charles Henry	Charles Henry and Mary Eleanor VODITZ	
Jul 25	Sep 7	Alma Marie	Dixon and Maggie B. GUY	
Jan 7, 1885	Sep 7	William Watson	George Q. and Mary J. KENNARD	
Aug 20	Sep 15	George Henry	John L. and Eleanora STONE	
Jul 25	Sep 16	Margaret Keys	William Brooks and Margaret WEBSTER	
Jul 13	Sep 18	John William Lester	Wm. and Sarah Eliz. ZIMMERMAN	
Jun 30	Sep 18	Joseph Gehring	Joseph G. and Mary E. KLINE	
May 18	Sep 30	Nellie Catherine	George W. and Lizzie V. SHULER	
Sep 1	Oct 3	Earle Joseph	Thomas H. and Rosa SOMMERS	
Jun 30	Oct 15	Joseph Elmer	Frederick A. and Jennie WEISHEIT	
Aug 5	Nov 11	Ella May	Charles M. and Florence M. BURGAU	
Dec 3	Dec 4	Charles Frederick	John T. and Magdalena GILES	
Apr 3	Dec 5	Gladys	Samuel and Marietta SCHILLINGER	
Sep 11	Dec 9	Mary Cath Bertha Goldsborough	David and Maria M. GLOAG	
Nov 24	Dec 23	Frederick August	August and Dora DOELL	
Oct 26	Dec 25	Mary Parker	John and Ida V. YOUNG	

1895

DATE OF BIRTH	DATE OF BAPTISM	NAME	PARENTS	SPONSORS
Nov 18, 1894	Jan 7	Alice May	Charles and Emma May YONSON	
Nov 7, 1894	Jan 13	Bernard William	John G. and Lillie J. CARLE	
Oct 5, 1894	Jan 22	Melton Ross	Ross Nevin and Cath. F. GOSWEILER	
Aug 21, 1894	Jan 22	William Herbert	Thomas G. and Blanche E. DORSEY	
Oct 10, 1894	Jan 27	Sarah Violetta	Leon C. and Mary E. YINGLING	
Feb 13	Feb 14	Howard Schminck	Howard H. and Rosa WORTHINGTON	
Oct 15, 1894	Feb 14	Margaret Florence	Charles H. and Florence Christina WINKELMANN	
Dec 10, 1893	Feb 17	William Arthur	William F. and Emma J. WARNER	
Jun 29, 1894	Feb 18	John	David and Kate McCULLOUGH	
Jan 19	Mar 26	Raymond Duchheimer	Robert A. and Ella E. KRIEGER	
Mar 2	Mar 26	Matthew Patterson	William T. and Bessie W. STALEY	
Aug 17, 1894	Apr 25	Mildred Lenore	Charles O. and Susie GUNTHER	
	Apr 12	Annie Minerva GEORGE (adult)		
Mar 19, 1892	May 24	Thomas Lowry	Thomas Sinclair and Alice GERMAN	
Dec 21, 1894	May 24	Margaret Ellen	" " " " "	
	Jun 2	Theoda May BORTNER (adult)		
Feb 20	Jun 19	Anton Karl	Harry C. and Daisy M. WEISKITTEL	
May 2	Jun 20	Helen	William G. and Minnie K.L.HAMMER	
May 25	Jul 12	Edith Amanda	James Thomas and Gertrude Agnes McCLURE	
Feb 1, 1894	Jul 12	James Everette	George A. and Alice V. KEEN	
Jan 29	Jul 14	Norma Virginia	John L. and Julia V. THOMPSON	
Aug 1	Aug 21	Marie Agnes	Adam and Helena SNYDER	
Jun 19	Sep 1	Marguerite	John A. and Maggie DANZEGLOK	
Mar 14	Oct 6	Bertha Carnes	Joseph H. and Katie M. WELLS	

FIRST REFORMED CHURCH OF BALTIMORE

DATE OF BIRTH	DATE OF BAPTISM	NAME	PARENTS	SPONSORS
Aug 22	Oct 20	John Earle Howard	George and Julia A. GUETLER	
Sep 20	Oct 27	James William Graydon	Cody and Maggie GEMMILL	
Sep 14	Dec 23	Cornelia Owen	John H.G. and Lillie J. REVER	
Dec 11	Dec 25	Ida Virginia	John and Ida Virginia YOUNG	
Nov 17	Dec 26	Lawrence Henry	Lawrence F. and Florence R. WHITTEMORE	
Jul 22	Dec 29	Herbert Carter	John William and Iva Cath. LIST	
1896				
May 9, 1895	Jan 11	Margaret Thelma	David and Virginia FOARD	
Jul 26, 1892	Jan 12	William Eowell	Willie and Nellie E. CARMAN	
Sep 26, 1895	Jan 26	Margaret Sybilla	William H. and Anna S. WINKELMANN	
Apr 1, 1895	Feb 5	Caroline Augusta	Frederick A. and Jennie WEISHEIT	
Dec 13, 1895	Feb 9	Walter Carroll	William A. and Elizabeth T. HELTZEL	
Sep 24, 1895	Feb 11	Bertha Lowe	George A. and Alice V. KEEN	
Sep 24, 1895	Feb 11	Katie Huey	" " " " " "	
Apr 29	Mar 12	Robert Gamble Rankin	John H. and Estelle R. CORREA	
Jan 24	Mar 16	John Laub	Charles H. and Lillie MILLER	
Feb 20	Mar 29	Jerome Montford	Charles E. and Mary BURKHARDT	
	Apr 3	Miss Ella CAMPBELL (adult)		
	Apr 3	Miss Mollie Johanna HERZOG (adult)		
	Apr 3	John Charles PETERMAN (adult)		
	Apr 3	James William SADLER (adult)		
Feb 18	Apr 5	Mary Martha	Nicholas Rogers and Ella May MERRYMAN	
Sep 14, 1895	Apr 5	Albert Herman	Thomas W.B. and Thresa HUSSMAN	
Aug 22, 1894	Apr 5	Elmer Louis	Charles W. and Laura J. SMOOT	
Feb 13	Apr 5	Mary Isabel	Harrey (or Harvey) L. and Mary Ann LAMBERT	
Apr 27, 1895	Apr 6	William Guy	Edward G. and Mary S. HOOVER	
Apr 5, 1895	Apr 6	Isabella Cushman	John F. and Savannah HOLLODAY	
Oct 1, 1895	Apr 6	Mary Charlotte	George P. and Laura E. MILLER	
Mar 16	Apr 12	William Alfred	John and Catherine STRAUSS	
Apr 5	May 31	Maurice Webster	Rev. Joel T. and Caroline Elizabeth ROSSITER	
Dec 19, 1895	Jun 24	Edna Margaret	Thomas E. and Emma S. BIDDISON	
Sep 1, 1895	Jun 30	Ferdinand George	Lambert Henry and Mary C. THIESS	
Jan 24, 1894	Jul 5	Ethel	Chas. Ferd. Gaston and Claribel Wright BENOIT	
Jul 16	Sep 16	Gladys Eleanora	Joseph G. and Mary E. KLINE	
May 13	Sep 20	Claudius Earl	Edwin C. and Lenora F. BAUGE	
May 6, 1893	Sep 23	Grace Marie	Oliver and Barbara Rowena WEISER	
Dec 15, 1895	Sep 23	Emily Catherine	" " " " " "	
Sep 7	Oct 25	Joseph Edward Guy	Dixon and Maggie B. GUY	
Jul 21	Oct 4	Charles Calvin	Charles Henry and Cath. Eliz. WALKLING	
Sep 9	Oct 11	Raymond Lawrence	Conrad H. and Elizabeth GEWECKI	
Sep 4	Oct 11	John Russell McCleary	James Wm. and Margaret J. TAYLOR	
Oct 11	Nov 15	Charles Chapman	George W. and Lizzie G. HENDERSON	
	Nov 27	Henry Howard BYE (adult)		
Feb 23, 1895	May 5 [?]	Paul	Martin L. and Emma C. ROBINSON	
Jan 10, 1893	Dec 28	Florence Marie	Thomas and Mary Elizabeth WHITELEGG	
Apr 6	Dec 28	Ethel Lyle	" " " " "	

FIRST REFORMED CHURCH OF BALTIMORE

DATE OF BIRTH	DATE OF BAPTISM	NAME	PARENTS	SPONSORS
1897				
Sep 27, 1896	Jan 17	Emmeline Euphina May	David and Mary M. GLOAG	Victor & May Edwards
Jul 9, 1896	Jan 31	Wilhemina Hilbert	William H. and Annie L. KNICKMAN	Miss Hilbert
Nov 20, 1896	Feb 1	Myrtle Elizabeth	Harry M. and Clara Eliz. STONESIFER	
Jan 25	Feb 21	Emma Louise	Jacob and Katie BENNETT	Emma L. Miller
Jan 9	Feb 28	Raymond Henry	Louis H. and Mary C. GERDING	Henry Gerding
Sep 18, 1896	Mar 21	Milton	John A. and Maggie DAUZEGLOCK	
Sep 19, 1896	Apr 18	William Henry	James F. and Georgiana M. WIEDEFELD	Maggie Stevenson
Feb 26	Apr 18	Harry Leroy	Harry Cromwell and Florence Rebecca THOMAS	
Oct 7, 1896	Apr 18	William Raymond	Charles W. and Laura J. SMOOT	
	Apr 18	Horace Levering ROSSITER (adult)		
Apr 9	May 5	John Matthew	Francisco or Cody and Maggie GEMMILL	
Apr 1	May 9	Elmer	John and Ida Virginia YOUNG	
Apr 9	May 17	Harry Eberle	William Harry and Mary E. HAUER	Mrs. Amanda Hauer
Jul 1	Aug 1	Edna Margaret	Adam and Helena SNYDER	Mrs. Margaret Noppenberger
Jun 20	Aug 1	William Alfred	Charles W. and Louise C. GLASER	William Glaser
Apr 2	Aug 15	William Harman	John and Eliz. S. McCULLOUGH	Wm. H. Black
Jul 13	Aug 22	Edward Francis	Fred. and Anna MILLER	Charles F.A. Henkelt---?
May 27	Aug 25	Grace Catherine	George W. and Jennie Cath. WALZ	Cath. Feldpusch
Jan 15	Aug 29	Alice Stevens	George A. and Alice V. KEEN	
Aug 27	Sep 5	Annie Celinda	James Wm. and Margaret J. TAYLOR	
Aug 29	Sep 6	Charles Richmond	William and Christina HAMMOND	Mrs. Frost
Jul 29	Sep 22	Charles Leroy	Charles E. and Maggie McCAULEY	
Jul 12	Sep 23	Esther Carter	John H. and Laura Rice WILHELM	
Mar 6	Oct 3	James William McKinley	William A. and Mary V. DREBING	Dora Dunn
Jun 15	Oct 10	William Cornelius	William T. and Bessie W. STALEY	Mrs. Sarah White
Aug 1	Oct 10	Samuel Field	William Watters and Lillie Estelle PARSONS	Clara S. Mergardt
Jul 16	Oct 29	Helen Louise	Christian and Selma PANNEMANN	
Nov 18	Dec 29	Emma Clara	Nicholas Rogers and Ella May MERRYMAN	
1898				
Aug 31, 1897	Jan 23	Flora Adahl	William H. and Anna S. WINKELMANN	Florence M. Winkelmann
Jan 24	Feb 9	Clayton Edward	James Thomas and Gertrude Agnes McCLURE	Louisa C. Yeakle
Jan 28	Feb 15	Elizabeth	William F.H. and Catherine WARNSMAN	Elizabeth Boucher
Nov 25, 1897	Feb 17	Henry Burton	Henry H. and Clara Mills BYE	
Sep 7, 1897	Mar 3	Raymond Henry	Philip M. and Mollie A. GEIDT	Magd. Strohrman
Dec 17, 1897	Mar 13	George	Charles H. and Annie J. WALDNER	George Mehl
Nov 29, 1897	Mar 23	Henry Charles	Harry C. and Daisy M. WEISKITTEL	
Feb 4	Apr 10	Adeline Margaret	Henry G. and Mollie J. KERNDL	Mrs. Kerndl
Nov 24, 1894	Apr 10	George Harrison	George Harrison and Laura M. EHRMAN	
Dec 27, 1897	Apr 10	Alice Lucelle	Paul E.C. and Mollie PYERITZ	Bessie Staley
Apr 12	May 1	Charles Norris	Julius and May C. FISCHER	
	Apr 8	Nellie Blanch BRANDEL (adult)		
Mar 7	May 29	Emma Augusta	Walter Lawrence and Mamie WESTPHAL	
May 6	Jun 5	William Christian	William Christian and Margaret YOUNG	Cinda Brightwell
Jul 31, 1897	Jul 5	Isadore	Isadore and Minnie L. BRIGHTWELL	

FIRST REFORMED CHURCH OF BALTIMORE

DATE OF BIRTH	DATE OF BAPTISM	NAME	PARENTS	SPONSORS
Jun 7	Jul 10	Lillian May	John and Ida Virginia YOUNG	
Jun 10	Jul 10	Matilda Gebhart	Henry J. and Matilda Marie CARLE	
Jun 7	Jul 31	Henry August	Francisco and Maggie GEMMILL	
Jul 18	Sep 6	George Elkins	George Lambert and Ella May McDANIEL	
Jul 7	Sep 6	Richard William	Richard Ed McClone and Kartha Edra SANDS	
Aug 10	Sep 11	Joseph Maurice	Joseph H. and Laura V. HAUER	
Feb 11	Sep 14	Charles Otto	Charles O. and Susie GUNTHER	
Sep 12	Oct 9	Leroy Henry	Henry and Camilla M. GEIDT	
Oct 4	Oct 10	Lester George	Howard H. and Rosa WORTHINGTON	
Oct 9	Nov 8	Charles Henry	Lambert Henry and Mary C. THEISS	Mrs. Lephardt
Jun 28	Nov 10	Hazel Estelle	Jesse A. and Emma K. SACHSE	
Dec 10	Nov 26	Alan Davis	Horation William and Mary E. PRICE	Harry Price
Nov 7	Dec 11	Mamie Matilda	George W. and Lizzie G. HENDERSON	

1899

DATE OF BIRTH	DATE OF BAPTISM	NAME	PARENTS	SPONSORS
Sep 13, 1898	Jan 8	Ralph Derr	John G. and Lillie J. CARLE	
Oct 14, 1898	Jan 8	Robert Washington	James Edward and Marian Gladys WOOD	
Jan 5	Feb 6	Emma Irene	George W. and Emma Va. SCHMALZEL	
Dec 14, 1898	Feb 9	George John	George and Martha WALDNER	Mrs. Schafer
Nov 27, 1898	Mar 23	Estella May	William Henry and Mary E. HAUER	Mrs. Hauer
Apr 4, 1892	Mar 28	Margaret Elizabeth	Lewis Plitt and Margaret Elizabeth WALTERS	
Jun 27, 1895	Mar 28	Louisa	" " " "	" "
Feb 21	Mar 28	Lewis Plitt	" " " "	" "
Feb 1	Apr 18	Mortimer Vernon	William R. and Emma L. HANDY (or HAUDY)	
Nov 17, 1896	Apr 23	John Lewis	John L. and Eleanora STONE	
Jan 5, 1896	Apr 23	Howard Edward	" " " " "	
Aug 22, 1898	Apr 30	Howard Rossiter	Joseph Albert and Pauline Rosalie TAYLOR	
Aug 6, 1898	Apr 30	Herbert Elmer	Samuel W. and Alice M. YEAKLE	
	May 21	Mrs. Belle JACOBS (adult)		
	May 21	Lionel Mark JACOBS (adult)		
Mar 11	May 28	Elizabeth	William Dykes and Agnes May BOURNE	
May 6	Jun 25	Myrtle Estelle	Harry A. and Laura V. HOOK	Annie M. Hook
Jul 9, 1882	Jul 12	Harrison Benjamin	Perry Ellsworth and Emma APPLEBY	Miss Edwards
Feb 14, 1884	Jul 12	William Ellsworth	" " " " "	" "
Jan 24, 1886	Jul 12	Emma Agnes	" " " " "	" "
Dec 13, 1889	Jul 12	Oliver Lemuel	" " " " "	" "
Nov 2, 1892	Jul 12	Berdie Irene	" " " " "	" "
Feb 24, 1894	Jul 12	Robert Ambrose	" " " " "	" "
Mar 13, 1896	Jul 12	Otto Eugene	" " " " "	" "
Apr 14, 1897	Jul 12	Bessie Shower	" " " " "	" "
Mar 8	Jul 12	May Edwards	" " " " "	" "
Nov 1, 1896	Sep 15	Irma Isabel	John H.G. and Lillie J. REVER	
Jan 12, 1898	May 24	William Dorritee	George Harvey and Blanche Teresa ELLOFF	
Dec 6, 1898	May 24	John Edgar	Joseph G. and Mary E. KLINE	Edgar Hunt
Jun 1	Oct 10	Ida Ismay	John Donniker and Amelia RAEMER	Mrs. Raemer
Sep 20	Nov 6	Mary Charlotte	Charles Denton and MERGARTH	Mrs. Ida Smallwood
Aug 11	Dec 7	Marie Sessions Voight	William Walters and Lillie Estella PARSONS	
Aug 13	Dec 17	Olive Vicla	Henry Fred Wm and Julia Viola WEBER	
Oct 11	Dec 22	James William	James William and Margaret J. TAYLOR	

ADDENDA

1892

DATE OF BIRTH	DATE OF BAPTISM	NAME	PARENTS	SPONSORS
Feb 17	Oct 3	Emilie Viola	Samuel A. and Sarah F. BURKE	
Aug 3	Oct 26	Charles Wilbert	John W. and Leah BOLLINGER	died 1-29-93

FIRST REFORMED CHURCH OF BALTIMORE

DATE OF BIRTH	DATE OF BAPTISM	NAME	PARENTS	SPONSORS
1893				
Jun 5, 1890	Feb 2	Permelia Ashcom	Chas. R. and Mary Louisa SPENCER	Eva Spencer
Sep 11, 1892	Feb 2	Charles Attwill	" " " " " "	
Feb 20	Mar 26	Mary Emma	John B. LUCAS	(died late autumn)
Sep 3, 1890	Jul 29	Clarwell Nelson	Alfred E. and Dora Grace SHORTT	
Oct 1, 1891	Jul 29	Sadie Grace	" " " " " "	
Jul 11	Jul 29	Earnest Clayton	" " " " " "	
Dec 8, 1892	Jul 29	Viola Caroline	James W. and Sarah SHORTT	
Dec 24, 1892	Sep 24	Nellie May	Fred. B. and Maggie GOVE	
1894				
Sep 15, 1893	Jan 4	Robert Norris	Harry and Katie McGINITY	died
Jul 26, 1893	Jan 15	Caroline Louisa	John F. and Mary HORICHS	
Jun 1, 1892		Joseph Orndorff	Rev. Charles W. and Harvera LEVAN	
Aug 6	Sep 30	Clarence Vernon	Alpha E. and Fannie WHERLEY	
May 30	Jul 1	Charles William	Henry and Annie FERSTERMAN	Chas. Fersterman
1895				
Aug 24, 1894	Jan 13	Lottie Bell	Fred. B. and Margret GOVE	
Nov 27, 1894	Feb 6	Frances Edward	John W. and Leah BOLLINGER	
Nov 23, 1894	Feb 10	Mary Florence	Chas. and Mary L. SPENCER	Millie Irene Duglass
Nov 1, 1894	Feb 24	Susanna	Lewis and Mary SPUCK	Susanna Deckring
Mar 18	Mar 24	Alice Margret	Edw. W. and Augusta WAGNER	
Jul 18	Aug 18	Caroline Susanna	Edward and Mary GUTMAN	
Jul 18	Aug 18	Doretha Louisa	" " " "	died
Oct 30	Dec 28	Hilda Annetta	Harry and Catherine McGINITY	
Sep 24	Oct 6	Gerald Wilberforce	Rev. Charles W. and Harvene LEVAN	Dr. G.L. STALEY
Dec 3	Dec 29	Arthur Henry	William and Susanna DEERING	
1896				
Sep 26, 1895	Jan 7	Paul Edwin	James W. and Catherine SHORTT	
Dec 29, 1895	Jan 7	Harry Rowley	Alfred E. and Dora G. SHORTT	
Nov 6, 1895	Feb 25	Albert Jefferson	Frederick D. and Mary C. NALL	died 2-26-1896
Jul 13	Sep 12	Ashton Gamble	Samuel W. and Sophia M. KIRK	
Jul 3, 1895	Oct 7	Walter Skillman	Wm. and Carrie BRIGHTMAN	died April 1897
May 17, 1894	Nov 28	Katie Ruth	Saml. and Catherine BARNHILL	
Sep 1, 1895	Dec 5	Layra Katie	Jas. and Ella HARRIS	died
Aug 22, 1894	Apr 14, 1895	Robert Noah	Melanthon and Savilla C. MYERS	
1897				
Jul 23, 1864	Jan 20	Lynne Rebecca METCALF (adult)	John and Julia	
Aug 25, 1892	Jan 27	Allen Lee	William L. and Ida SLAYSMAN	
Jan 5	Mar 4	Thomas Hopkins	Chas. R. and Mary L. SPENCER	
Dec 16, 1889	Sep 2	Esther Lenor	Henry Charles WALDVOGEL and Louisa	
Aug 21, 1891	Sep 2	Harry George	" " " " "	
Aug 21, 1892	Sep 2	Raymond Frederick	" " " " "	
Oct 10, 1894	Sep 2	Marion Louisa	" " " " "	
Oct 17, 1896	Sep 2	Hugo Wesley	" " " " "	
Aug 4, 1896	Mar 31	Frank Adams	Edward W. and Augusta WAGNER	died 9-3-1897
Aug 12	Sep 19	George Oscar	John N. and Florence SMITH	
Oct 13	Nov 21	Jennie Elizabeth Delinger	John H. and Minnie KRAFT	

FIRST REFORMED CHURCH OF BALTIMORE

DATE OF BIRTH	DATE OF BAPTISM	NAME	PARENTS	SPONSORS
Oct 23	Nov 28	Agnes Roselea	John and Margaret DEISE	
1898				
Nov 4, 1893	Jan 13	Louisa Scheldt	Chas. Lewis and Sarah W. CROSS	
Jul 23, 1896	Jan 13	Sarah Jane	" " " " "	
Sep 29, 1896	Jan 18	Chas. Edward	Chas. Edward and Clara HOFFMAN	*died Jan 19*
Jul 4, 1897	Feb 22	William Leroy	Wm. Walter and Lillie REYNOLDS	
	Apr 3	William Dorsey BRIGHTMAN (adult)		
Jun 5	Jul 24	Florence Elizabeth	William C. and Lillian P. OURSLER	*died*
Oct 29, 1897	Aug 14	Chester	Henry C. and Louisa WALDVOGEL	
Aug 16	Oct 9	Edgar Earnest	Earnest William and Bessie Ellen BIEN	
Oct 4, 1895	Oct 9	Gladdys Frost	William L. and Ida J. SLAYSMAN	
Sep 7, 1897	Oct 9	William Hawry	" " " " "	
May 27	Oct 23	Carl Staley	Carl H. and Mary T. APPEL	
1899				
Nov 25, 1898	Jan 15	Lillian Katherine	Fred. G. and Elizabeth BICKEL	Katharns Hurst
Nov 8, 1898	Jan 29	John Edwin	Artis J. and Katherine FISSEL	
Nov 26, 1898	Feb 12	Margaret Iona	Albert F. and Sarah V. SHARER	Alpha and Fannie Wherley
May 2, 1898	Feb 22	Grace Elizabeth	Samuel W. and Sophia M. KIRK	
Apr 2	Jun 29	Mildred Lee	James and Mary MAGUIRE	*died July 1*
Dec 29, 1895	Sep 10	Jessie	William Carswell and Margory BAXTER	
Nov 3, 1896	Sep 10	William Carswell	" " " " "	
Nov 28, 1898	Sep 10	Mary McGillivray	" " " " "	
Jul 13	Nov 12	Ethel Staley	Jane Catherine and S. Clinton WHERLEY	
Jul 20	Dec 31	John Hilary	James and Catherine GLASCOE (colored)	

FIRST REFORMED CHURCH OF BALTIMORE

BURIALS

DATE OF DEATH	NAME	AGE	PLACE OF BURIAL
1875			
Feb 27	George H. Locher Jr.	20 years	Greenmount
Mar 30	Emanuel Middlekauf	57 years	Loudon Park
Apr 12	Lydia McAllister	55 years	Greenmount
Apr 17	William T. Haggerty	37 years	Loudon Park
Apr 19	Mary F. Durst	20 years, 2 Mo. 4 days	Greenmount
May 23	Lizzie Abbess	35 years	Baltimore Cem.
Jul 10	Joseph Hershey Frick	3 years, 7 days	" "
Sep 1	Jesse Crawford	11 years	Greenmount
Sep 22	Charles Welshofifer	50 years	Loudon Park
Oct 4	Mrs. Susan Meeks		" "
Nov 22	Mrs. Sarah Abbess	66 years	Baltimore Cem.
1876			
Jan 13	Mrs. Sarah Smith	53 years	Meth. Cem. Phila. Road
Mar 5	Gotleib Schanseil	51 years	Balti. Cem.
May 7	William F. Cooke	39 years	Greenmount
Jun 16	Ella Blanche Kehm	11 mo.	Balti. Cem.
Sep 14	Margaret Joseph	89 years	Presby. Cem.
Oct 9	Willie D. Vansant	1 yr 3 mo 27 d	Greenmount
Oct 26	Henrietta Cockey	77 years	Westminster, Md.
Nov 7	John B. Himbury	65 years	Frederick, Md.
Nov 23	John Aulabaugh	66 years	Balt. Cem.
Dec 4	L.D. Keys	28 years	" "
Dec 29	James Ensor	81 years	Greenmount
1877			
	James Garland		Balt. Cem.
Feb 20	Mamie Smith Harris	3 years 14 d.	Meth. Cem. Phila. Road
Feb 22	Edward Stewart Shook	7 wks.	Balti. Cem.
Mar 19	Madge Oleria Strick	2 years, 2mo, 20 d.	Greenmount
Mar 2	Francis Hilberg Rodenmeyer	5 years, 3 mo, 16d.	"
Apr 4	Alice Amy Bull	10 mo. 20 d.	"
Jun 21	Emily Eliz. Rossiter	4 mo., 20 d.	Woodward Hill, Lancaster, Pa.
Jun 25	David Chas. H. Stone	2 mo. 9 d.	Near Westminster, Md.
Jun 29	Henry Rehbein	61 years 4 mo.	Balt. Cem.
Jul 3	Mrs. Mary Ann Vansant	72 years	Greenmount
Jul 22	Mrs. Carrie S. Reese	21 years	"
Jul 26	Harry McRea, Jr.	2 years, 8 mos. 21d.	"

FIRST REFORMED CHURCH OF BALTIMORE

DATE OF DEATH	NAME	AGE	PLACE OF BURIAL
Jul 28	John Miller	50 years	Western Cem.
Jul 30	Thomas Elliott	25 years	Presby. Cem.
Aug 9	Colby K. Griffing	18 yrs. 10 mos.	Greenmount
Aug 28	Anna May Huff	9 mos.	Loudon Park
Oct 27	Maggie Lincoln	7 years	Loudon Park
Nov 3	Daniel A. Meyers	40 years	Greenmount
Nov 27	Col. S. Sands Mills	45 years	Greenmount
Dec 6	James Sargus	36 years	Loudon Park

1878

Jan 14	Mrs. Mary Cockey	86 years	Balt. Cem.
Mar 19	Peter Feldpusch	14 yrs. 4 mos. 11 d.	Balt. Cem.
Mar 25	Bessie Magness	2 years 3 mos.	Balt. Cem.
Apr 10	Nicholas E. Bull	45 years	Western Cem.
May 6	Geo. B. Michael	61 years	Aberdeen, Md.
May 22	Elias Magers	68 years	Greenmount
Jun 10	Mrs. Catherine Jones	91 years	Loudon Park
Jul 11	Benjamin A. Hoffman	29 yrs. 5 mos. 2 d.	Loudon Park
Aug 6	Christian Bowers	23 years	Balt. Cem.
Oct 15	David Wilmer Hauer	6 yrs. 3 mos. 19d.	Balt. Cem.
Nov 18	Mary Florence Jelks	2 yrs. 3 mos.	Balt. Cem.
Nov 20	Rosa Otilla Hauer	3 mos.	Balt. Cem.
Dec 6	George Edward Hauer	2 yrs. 8 mos.	" "
Dec 28	James Isaac Guy	18 d.	Balt. Cem.

1879

Jan 10	Charles J. Gitterman	2 yrs. 9 mos.	Western Cem.
Jan 13	Edward Lephardt	2 yrs. 6 mos. 20 d.	Balt. Cem.
Jan 16	James Edward Miller	54 years	Greenmount
Feb 7	Louisa C. Bromwell	3 yrs. 3 mos. 12 d.	Balt. Cem.
Mar 2	Emaline Urbach	58 years	Mt. Olivet
Mar 17	Sarah C. Rodenmayer	5 yrs. 2 mos. 13 d.	Greenmount
Mar 19	Emma Weitzel	25 years	Shrewsbury, Pa.
Apr 1	John Hauer	46 years	Balt. Cem.
May 5	Margaret Jane Jennings	30 years	Balt. Cem.
May 13	John Henry Snyder	10 d.	Balt. Cem.
Jul 21	John G. Carle	38 years	Balt. Cem.
Jul 23	James Oliver Strick	6 yrs. 6 mos.	Greenmount
Jul 24	Dora Lydia Rogers	5 mos. 4 d.	Loudon Park
	John Frederick Rohlfing	1 yr. 9 mos.	Balt. Cem.
	Francis Lincoln	54 years	Loudon Park
Sep 14	Jane Algie	88 years	Greenmount

FIRST REFORMED CHURCH OF BALTIMORE

DATE OF DEATH	NAME	AGE	PLACE OF BURIAL
Nov 23	Sarah F. Messersmith	46 years	Greenmount
Aug 15	Mollie E. Crabbs	22 years	---
Aug 21	Mary E. Frick	16 years	Manchester, Md.
1880			
May 10	Herman H. Gitterman	34 yrs. 4 mos. 18 d.	York, Pa.
May 18	Jane Crawford Guy	20 years	Balt. Cem.
May 31	George Dehuff	2 years	Shrewsberry, Pa.
Jun 27	Charles F. McCauley	5 mos.	Mt. Olivet
Jun 27	Mary M. Wells	31 years	Loudon Park
Nov 1	J. Engel	25 years	Balt. Cem. a stranger
Nov 13	Lizzie Benson	28 years	Greenmount
Nov 28	George Fred. Prechtel	4 mos. 8 days	Balt. Cem.
Dec 1	Clarence E. Ogle	1 mo. 2 days	Balt. Cem.
1881			
Jan 12	John Bowers	21 years 5 d.	Balt. Cem.
Apr 20	James C. Wingrove	20 mos.	Loudon Park
Apr 26	Louis H. Hildebrand	15 yrs. 9 mos. 18 d.	Western Cem.
May 5	Joseph Guy	4 years	Balt. Cem.
May 16	George Davidson Guy	1 yr. 7 mos. 25 d.	Balt. Cem.
Jul 23	Eugenia Heiner	33 yrs. 4 mos. 15 d.	Greenmount
Feb 5	Dudley A. Randall	75 years	Greenmount
Jul 28	Taylor Price	32 years	Greenmount
Aug 7	Walter Chase Schminke	1 year 22 d.	Greenmount
Sep 7	Edwin H. Tarr	1 year	Greenmount
Sep 7	Edward A. Server	33 years	Balt. Cem.
Nov 3	Edith Blanche Wingrove	4 yrs. 1 mo. 20 d.	Loudon Park
Nov 17	Elizabeth Horton	91 years	Greenmount
1882			
Jan 6	James H. Barrett	8 mos.	Greenmount
Jan 18	Mrs. Elizabeth Wingrove	58 yrs. 5 mos.	Loudon Park
Feb 14	Mrs. Ann C. Richardson	80 years	Balt. Cem.
Mar 27	Sarah Rebecca Coburn	2 yrs. 2 mos. 2 d.	Greenmount
Apr 21	Louis R. Prechtel	3 yrs. 7 mos.	Balti. Cem.
Apr 26	John Oliver Crawford	21 years	Balti. Cem.
May 7	Henry Karsten Brent	2 mos. 8 d.	Balti. Cem.
May 12	William D. Minton	5 yrs. 11 mos. 11 d.	Balti. Cem.
May 27	Edward Roby Marsten	24 years	Greenmount
July 11	Samuel S. Schillinger	10 mo. 2 d.	Baltimore Cemetery
July 14	Ferdinand A. Mooyer	52 years	Baltimore Cemetery
Jul 25	Louisa Wilson	75 years	Greenmount
Aug 12	Mary Ann Klingel	39 years	Gettysburg, Pa.

FIRST REFORMED CHURCH OF BALTIMORE

DATE OF DEATH	NAME	AGE	PLACE OF BURIAL
Aug 24	Juliet D. McCord	45 yrs. 3mos. 6 d.	Greenmount
Aug 6	John Albert Gosweiler	7 mos.	Loudon Park
Sep 3	James P. Haverstick	9 d.	Western Cem.
Oct 9	Lillian Eliz. Schminke	1 mo. 10d.	Greenmount
Oct 10	William Crawford	56 years	Greenmount
Oct 22	Frederick C. Lindenberg	56 years	Balt. Cem.
Nov 11	Salome D. Diffenderfer	87 years	Greenmount
Nov 25	Jos. Wilbur Underwood	23 years	Greenmount
Dec 1	Harry Rossiter Volkman	1 mo.	Balt. Cem.
Dec 13	William S. Locher	21 yrs. 10 mos. 13 d.	Greenmount
Dec 22	Mrs. Ann Sills	77 years	Balt. Cem.
1883			
Jan 28	Fanny Frey Lichtner	93 years	Greenmount
Jan 29	Louis Bishop Zinkhan	3 yrs. 4 mo.	Balt. Cem. *very sad—*
Jan 29	James Garfield Zinkhan	1 yr. 5 mo.	" " *their only children*
Mar 8	Lillian May Stevens	7 mos.	Balt. Cem.
Apr 4	Octavius Diffenderfer	53 years	Greenmount
Apr 11	James H. Delahay	60 years	Loudon Park
Apr 24	Katie B. Lukehardt	22 years	Balt. Cem.
May 6	Charles F. Rodenmayer	33 years	Greenmount
Jun 25	Charlotte Von Waldner	35 years	Western Cem.
Jul 2	Mrs. Mary L. Brent	35 years	Hookstown, Md.
Jul 12	Mrs. Mary Ellen Bull	49 years	Greenmount
Sep 2	Campbell Parker Brent	3 yrs. 5 mos.	Balt. Cem.
Oct 13	Elliott L. Knoske	12 yrs. 11 mos. 12 d.	Greenmount
Nov 17	Erasmus Uhler	65 years	Greenmount
Nov 18	William H. Little	44 years	Hagerstown, Md.
Nov 27	Harry Tranty Keene	4 mos. 16 d.	Balt. Cem.
Dec 26	Philip Volkmann	4 mos. 19 d.	Cem. on Trap Road
Dec 31	Samuel Charles Wehrman	4 mos. 27 d.	Loudon Park
1884			
Mar 19	Bertie Lillian Magers	3 years 5 mos.	Greenmount
Mar 28	Alfred Irvin Schminke	8 mos.	Greenmount
Apr 10	Hon. Joshua Vansant	81 years	Greenmount *Ex-mayor*
May 12	Kate Anderson Kehm	1 year 6 mos.	Balt. Cem.
May 19	William J. Lammers	18 yrs. 1 d.	Balt. Cem.
Jun 6	Henry Haas	52 years	Loudon Park
Aug 30	Blanche Eliz. Loane	47 years	Loudon Park
Sep 1	Maud Louise Onion	11 weeks	Greenmount
Sep 1	Louisa Stockhausen	13 years	Balt. Cem.

FIRST REFORMED CHURCH OF BALTIMORE

DATE OF DEATH	NAME	AGE	PLACE OF BURIAL
Sep 9	Oliver Morris Thomas	15 years	Greenmount
Sep 24	Annie L. Hammar	23 years	Balt. Cem.
Oct 2	Anna L. Wood Hammar	4 mos.	Balt. Cem.
Oct 4	John F. Diffenderfer	65 years	Greenmount
Nov 6	Julia Hickman	66 years	Loudon Park
Nov 28	Mrs. E.S. Quincy	78 years	Greenmount

1885

Jan 2	Englehart A. Frick	55 years	Manchester, Md.
Jan 11	George Austin McComas	46 years	Loudon Park
Jan 18	Edwin S. Tarr	85 years	Greenmount
Jan 20	Charles Brandau Esq.	28 years	Balt. Cem.
Feb 5	Paul Fred. Schminke	31 years	Greenmount
Feb 9	Sallie W. Diffenderfer	5 years	Greenmount
Mar 3	William H. Griffith	35 years	Greenmount
Mar 5	Lewis Volkmann	2 d.	Cem. on Trapp Road
Apr 14	Mrs. Augusta P. Volkman	25 years	Balt. Cem.
May 17	Mrs. Sarah Harris	65 years	Balt. Cem.
Apr 25	Mrs. Elizabeth Welshoffer	65 years	Loudon Park
Jun 6	George Truscott	69 years	Frederick, Md.
Jun 17	Willie H. Funk	24 yrs. 10 mo.	Hagerstown, Md.
Jun 26	Willie Solomon King	6 years	Greenmount
Jun 27	J. Daniel Stoll	69 years	Cedar Hill
Jul 6	James Homewood Marriott	5 mos. 16 d.	Loudon Park
Jul 26	Mrs. Lydia M. Rogers	64 years	Balt. Cem.
Sep 6	Catherine Hare	9 mos. 17 d.	Baltimore Co.
Sep 27	William G. Meyer	48 years	Greenmount
Oct 7	Mrs. Olivia Kime	40 years	Greenmount
Oct 31	Miss Eliza Smith Frazier	84 years	Balt. Cem.
Dec 6	Anton Ernest Guetler	2 d.	Balt. Cem.

1886

Jan 27	Mrs. Rachel Bighau	38 years	Mt. Olivet
Feb 12	Mary Rebecca Magers	62 years	Greenmount
Feb 19	August Schultz		Trapp Road
Feb 19	Margaret Hammond	59 years	Balt. Cem.
Mar 7	Gertrude Griffith Hungerford	3 mos. 24 d.	Greenmount
Mar 15	Dietrich H. Radecke	79 years	Balt. Cem.
Mar 19	Clinton Taylor Mettee	3 years	Mt. Olivet
Apr 8	Georgia Rosina Weyraugh	3 yrs 18 d	Balt. Cem.
Apr 19	William Hildebrand	8 years	Western Cem.
Apr 20	Joseph Charles Scoggins	9 mos. 4 d.	Loudon Park
May 20	George H. Locher	61 years	Greenmount

FIRST REFORMED CHURCH OF BALTIMORE

DATE OF DEATH	NAME	AGE	PLACE OF BURIAL
Jun 27	Rose Campbell Staley	1 yr. 19 d.	Greenmount
Jun 29	Edith A. Knoske	10 mos. 18 d.	Mechanicstown
Jul 13	Sally V. Medinger	6 weeks	Greenmount
Jul 17	John F. Davids	22 yrs. 6 mos.	Balt. Cem
Aug 2	Blanche Bradley	10 mos.	Loudon Park
Aug 22	Henry Brown	81 years	Loudon Park
Aug 27	William Gifford	53 years	Greenmount
Aug 27	Ada M. Henry	40 years	Loudon Park
Sep 29	Grace Algie Geiger	11 mos.	Loudon Park
Oct 30	William A. Rodemeyer	70 years	Greenmount
Nov 6	Thomas W. Dorsey	33 years	Glenwood D.C.
Nov 22	Thomas C. Medinger	26 years	Greenmount
Dec 10	John Henry Schultze	5 mos.	Balt. Cem.

1887

DATE OF DEATH	NAME	AGE	PLACE OF BURIAL
Jan 8	Mrs. Mary Ann LaCompte	84 years	Balt. Cem.
Jan 10	Theodore Tarr	53 years	Greenmount
Feb 19	Nathalie Benoit	10 mos. 19 d.	Greenmount
Feb 26	Mrs. Leah Rodenmayer	66 years	Greenmount
Apr 2	Dr. Charles F. Percival	70 years	Frederick, Md.
Apr 10	J. Henry Hussman	20 years	Old Trapp Road
Jun 20	Mrs. Maggie Young	34 years	Greenmount
Aug 4	John Frey King	25 years	Greenmount
Aug 29	Roderick McRae	75 years	Greenmount
Sep 4	Sarah Catherine Hoover	20 yrs. 2 mos. 11 d.	Hagerstown
Sep 16	George Arenz	5 yrs. 7 mos.	Balt. Cem.
Oct 19	Margaretta Heltzel	2 mos. 19 d.	Oxford, Pa.
Oct 21	Franklin White	1 d.	Loudon Park
Oct 24	Martha A. Krantz	45 years	Loudon Park
Nov 10	Philip A. Gluck	45 years	Greenmount
Nov 23	William D. McCord	66 years	Greenmount

1888

DATE OF DEATH	NAME	AGE	PLACE OF BURIAL
Jan 25	George Gordon Hopkins	2 yrs. 7 mos.	Balt. Cem.
Jan 30	William Goodrich	25 yrs. 10 mos. 13 d.	Clearspring, Md.
Feb 25	Jacob Coker Fester	7 yrs. 4 mos. 22 d.	near Seitzland, Pa.
Feb 25	Charles Parker Fester	3 yrs. 3 mos. 24 d.	" " "
Mar 4	Christian G. Wilkenning	70 years	Balt. Cem.
Mar 19	Francis Thomas Rodenmayer	41 years	Greenmount
Mar 21	David Johnson	41 years	Balt. Cem.
Apr 11	Thomas Spencer Frost	5 yrs. 7 mos. 24 d.	Western Cem.
May 25	Mrs. Katie Rehling	24 years	Loudon Park
Jun 25	David Henry Westerfeld	10 mos.	Balt. Cem.

FIRST REFORMED CHURCH OF BALTIMORE

DATE OF DEATH	NAME	AGE	PLACE OF BURIAL
Jul 27	Francis A. Von Waldner	62 years	Balt. Cem.
Jul 30	Alfred H. Tarr	47 years	Greenmount
Aug 5	John Smalzel	65 years	Balt. Cem.
Aug 6	Henry W. Marston	43 years	Greenmount
Aug 13	Sallie Cooke	46 years	Greenmount
Sep 6	Miss Mary A. Smith	70 years	Balt. Cem.
Sep 11	Mrs. Josephine Delahay	64 years	Loudon Park
Sep 13	Mrs. Rosanna J. Geiger	32 years	Balt. Cem.
Sep 15	Mrs. Jane H. Edwards	49 years	Balt. Cem.
Sep 24	Bertha Sophie Rehling	1 year	Loudon Park
Sep 23	Hannah Francis Staley		Loudon Park
Oct 2	Bennetta Sherer Rossiter	44 years	Woodward Hill, Lan. Pa.
Oct 9	John F. Huke	33 years	Loudon Park
Oct 27	William Henry Stone	12 d.	Loudon Park
Oct 25	Rosanna Belbin	32 years	Mt. Olivet
Oct 31	Miss Elizabeth Smith	69 years	Balt. Cem.
Nov 1	H. William Siemonn	40 years	Greenmount
Nov 20	Anna Margaret Winkelmann	61 years	Loudon Park
Nov 28	Herbert A. Ehrman	6 yrs. 3 mos.	Seitzland, Pa.
Nov 27	Alice Catherine Gosweiler	2 mos.	Loudon Park
Dec 27	Mrs. Alice Hunter Wright	53 years	Loudon Park
Dec 30	Mrs. Elma June Scoggins	28 years	Loudon Park
1889			
Jan 9	William Heltzel	2 mos.	Oxford, Pa.
Jan 28	Miss Sarah E. Reigart	64 years	Friends Cem.
Feb 9	Miss Emma F. Schambach	19 yrs. 6 mos.	Cedar Hill Cem.
Feb 24	Edna Leora Snyder	1 yr. 3 mos.	Rose Hill Hagerstown
Mar 12	Lillian Verona Kindig	3 wks.	Mt. Olivet
Apr 1	Mrs. Dora M. Thiess	52 years	Mt. Carmel
Jun 12	George Leon Drebing	5 mos.	Balt. Cem.
Jun 19	Levin Tyler	58 years	Balt. Cem.
Jun 28	Oliver Edward Soelkey	2 yrs. 2 mos. 24 d.	Loudon Park
?	Mrs. Alice Luck Smith	29 years	Lorraine Cem
	Body found at Nenevehm 10 miles from Johnstown, Pa.		
Jul 2	Bennetta Cath. Knoske	9 mos.	Mechanicstown, Pa.
Jul 21	William Lester Mamell	9 mos.	York, Pa.
Oct 10	Henry Veditz	54 years	Balt. Cem.
Oct 4	Mrs. Annie Griffith	38 years	Balt. Cem.
Nov 18	Mary Louise Littig	3 mos.	Mt. Olivet
Nov 23	John Farrell	34 (?) years	Balt. Cem.

FIRST REFORMED CHURCH OF BALTIMORE

DATE OF DEATH	NAME	AGE	PLACE OF BURIAL
Dec 5	Richard Cockey	70 years	Loudon Park
1890			
Feb 18	John H. Kelly	58 years	Loudon Park
Feb 22	Miss Mary McMullen	71 years	Balt. Cem.
Mar 29	William E. Shawgo	27 years	Mt. Olivet
Apr 10	Robert Rossiter Feister	1 yr. 10 mos.	Sissels Church, Pa.
May 2	Harry McRae	37 years	Greenmount
Jun 14	Mrs. Clara R. Boehme	26 years	Cedar Hill Cem.
Jun 14	Mrs. Allillian R. Bushong	25 years	St. Peters Cem.
Jun 26	George W. Moffitt	45 years	Balt. Cem.
Jun 29	Emilie Georgette Johnson	2 yrs. 2 mos. 25 d.	Greenmount
Jul 13	Ann Plowman	98 years	Balt. Cem.
Jul 16	Francis Marguerite McClelland	6 wks.	Western Cem.
Jul 24	Mrs. Isabel Kelly	53 years	Loudon Park
Jul 27	Elnora Reese Collmus	3 yrs. 3 mos. 4 d.	Greenmount
Sep 14	William C. Heiligenstadt	70 years	Balt. Cem.
Sep 27	Lawrence Kohler	30 years	Balt. Cem.
Oct 11	Mrs. Sarah A. Frey	88 years	Greenmount
Oct 23	Mrs. Mary J. Berans (Bevans)	55 years	Loudon Park
Nov 4	Mrs. Jane McRae	83 years	Greenmount
Nov 6	Loretta Burke	2 years	Hightstown, N.J.
Nov 11	Louis Philip Porter	27 yrs. 7 mos. 9 d.	Loudon Park
Nov 25	William A. Rodenmoyer	21 years	Greenmount
Nov 30	Wm. H. Yeakle	51 years	Soldiers Park
Dec 29	Carrie E. Hopple	4 years 21 d.	Loudon Park
1891			
Jan 15	Fredirika Waldner	62 years	Balt. Cem.
Jan 29	Edward Hazelton Hammond	20 d.	Western Cem.
Feb 6	John S. Richardson	54 years	Mt. Olivet
Feb 12	Edward Roelkey	54 years	Loudon Park
Feb 16	Wilhelmia Haebel	9 yrs. 1 mo.	Stone Church, Pikesville
Apr 30	Mrs. Catharine Kindig	84 years	Western Cem.
May 15	Mrs. Louisa Hauck	38 years	Loudon Park
Jun 7	William Turnt	6 yrs. 4 mos. 10 d.	Loudon Park
Jun 25	Mrs. Anne Rebecca Diffenderffer	70 years	Greenmount
Jul 5	Joseph Howard Giles	2 yrs. 4 mos.	Balt. Cem.
Jul 10	Michael Hoover	26 yrs. 7 mos. 20 d.	East Berlin, Pa.
Jul 12	William H. Fritter	23 years	Loudon Park
Jul 13	Joseph E. Benson	54 years	Greenmount
Aug 28	Mary May Drebing	3 mos.	Balt. Cem.

FIRST REFORMED CHURCH OF BALTIMORE

DATE OF DEATH	NAME	AGE	PLACE OF BURIAL
Aug 29	Alice Onion	9 mos.	Loudon Park
Aug 28	Charles A. Davids	72 years	Balt. Cem.
Aug 29	Mrs. Mary Brent	41 years	Balt. Cem.
Oct 2	Florence J. D. Chappell	54 years	Greenmount
Oct 16	Harvy B. Clayton	35 years	Mt. Olivet
Oct 25	Jesse L. Porter	27 years	Loudon Park
Nov 4	Mrs. Augusta S. Dunn	26 years	Balt. Cem.
Nov 12	Charles Kerndl	68 years	Balt. Cem.
Nov 21	Mrs. Sarah M. Schley	68 years	Frederick, Md.
Nov 22	Mrs. Elizabeth J. Jory	32 years	Greenmount
Nov 29	W. Harry Cook	41 years	Greenmount
Dec 1	Matilda E. Schultz	14 years 2 mos.	Trapp Road
Dec 5	Capt. James Jones	81 years	Balt. Cem.
Dec 7	Mrs. Catherine Shook	69 years	Balt. Cem.
Dec 7	James Alfred Smoot	2 yrs. 6 mos.	Mt. Carmel Cem.
Dec 11	David Hammond	3 yrs. 8 mos. 5 d.	Western Cem.
Dec 26	Henry Hildebrand	54 years	Western Cem.
Dec 26	George Wm. Fischer	6 mos.	Western Cem.

1892

DATE OF DEATH	NAME	AGE	PLACE OF BURIAL
Jan 3	Mrs. Ella Server	74 years	Balt. Cem.
Jan 9	Charles McRae	42 years	Greenmount
Jan 22	Miss Annie E. Hussman	19 years	St. Mathews Cem.
Jan 26	Mrs. Elizabeth A. Mayes	68 years	Loudon Park
Feb 7	John Philip Kern	22 years	Holy Cross Cem.
Feb 22	Lotta Zenetta Mace	2 mos.	Balt. Cem.
Apr 19	Mrs. Mattie S. Ziegler	60 years	Hagerstown
May 2	Alfred Henry Benoit	1 yr. 8 mos. 22 d.	Loudon Park
May 10	John W. Otto	46 years	Greenmount
May 8	James Vandyke Stewart Benoit	3 yrs. 7 mos. 24 d.	Loudon Park
May 18	Annie B. Hopkins	9 yrs. 3 mos.	Balt. Cem.
May 22	John Hilberg	50 years	Greenmount
Jun 11	Miss Margaret D. Lightner	62 years	Greenmount
Jul 7	Edith Amanda Hauer	5 mos. 8 d.	Balt. Cem.
Jul 10	Carrol Thomas Rogers	5 mos.	Cedar Hill Cem.
Jul 10	Mrs. Mary Hauer	20 years	Balt. Cem.
Jul 14	Grace Lizzie Hall	9 mos.	Balt. Cem.
Jul 14	Schall Wilhelm Hammel	5 mos.	York, Pa.
Aug 7	Lewis Daniel Jochheim	4 yrs. 9 mos.	Loudon Park
	Lillie May Hall		Balt. Cem.
Sep 26	Mrs. Mary A. Taylor	60 years	Mt. Olivet
Dec 27	Thomas Sommers Bromwell	1 years	Balt. Cem.

FIRST REFORMED CHURCH OF BALTIMORE

DATE OF DEATH	NAME	AGE	PLACE OF BURIAL
1893			
Jan 11	Frances Katie Virginia Rasch	2 yrs. 1 mo. 5 d.	Balt. Cem.
Jan 28	Mary Magdaline Schillinger	10 yrs. 12 d.	Balt. Cem.
Feb 3	Mrs. Mary L. Wentzel	62 years	Balt. Cem.
Feb 11	Mrs. Charlotte Chambers	84 years	Loudon Park
Mar 1	Henry Richmond	80 years	Loudon Park
Apr 14	William H. Server	75 years	Balt. Cem.
May 20	Annie Iona Burns	13 yrs. 3 mos. 4 d.	Loudon Park
Jul 5	Mary Eliz. Gosweiler	10 years	Loudon Park
Jul 14	William Guy	64 years	Balt. Cem.
	Hugh A. Philipps		Loudon Park
Jul 19	George A. Kelly	17 years	Loudon Park
Aug 4	Richard S. Brooks	10 mos.	Balt. Cem.
Aug 21	Elizabeth McLanahan	35 years	Greenmount
Sep 10	Harry D. Smith	41 years	Balt. Cem.
Sep 19	Euphrasia F. Cooke	74 yrs. 8 mos. 13 d.	Greenmount
Dec 7	Alice Louise Murphy	2 yrs. 5 mos.	Balt. Cem.
Dec 11	Phoebe Margaurite Freyer	1 yr. 10 mos.	Balt. Cem.
Dec 13	Raymond Wilmer Hopple	2 years	Loudon Park
Dec 25	Elizabeth Katie Brent	10 yrs. 4 mos. 20 d.	Balt. Cem.
1894			
Jan 12	Dudley Robinson	2 mos. 15 d.	Lorraine Cem.
Feb 4	Nellie Irene Littig	14 mos. 10 d.	Mt. Olivet
Feb 10	Abell Herbert Hammell	6 mos.	York, Pa.
Feb 9	Alex. D. Michael	66 years	Greenmount
Feb 12	Clara Bell Wingrove	34 years	Loudon Park
Feb 26	H.H. Fuhrman	70 years	Stites Church, Pa.
Mar 3	Henry Shook	90 years	Balt. Cem.
Mar 7	Howard E. Wurst	6 yrs. 2 mos. 23 d.	Balt. Cem.
Mar 8	Mrs. Elizabeth Griffith	74 years	Greenmount
Apr 1	Harry G. Javius (or Jarius)	46 years	Alexandria, Va.
Apr 3	Myrtle Louisa McClure	3 mos. 3 wks.	Greenmount
May 2	Mrs. Emma Barrett	45 years	Greenmount
May 9	Emil Stockhausen	53 years	Balt. Cem.
May 25	Ludwig Albert Wentzel	69 years	Balt. Cem.
Jul 14	Mrs. Annie McKewen	27 years	Loudon Park
Jul 21	Virginia Hazel Onion	7 mos.	Loudon Park
Aug 17	Charles Gardner Thompson	15 mos.	Balt. Cem.
Sep 17	George Henry Stone	1 mo.	Loudon Park
Oct 3	Susanna R.B. Tarr	91 years	Greenmount
Oct 8	Edward P. Bevans	24 years	Mt. Carmel Cem.

FIRST REFORMED CHURCH OF BALTIMORE

DATE OF DEATH	NAME	AGE	PLACE OF BURIAL
Nov.3	John A. Long	37 years	Swartzes Cem.
Nov 6	George Fischer	70 years	Western Cem.
Dec 10	Mrs. Anna V. Canby	67 years	Mt. Olivet
1895			
Jan 5	Mrs. Wilhemina Forsyth	27 years	Stetzes church, Pa.
Jan 16	Mrs. Anna Stockhausen	41 yrs. 9 mos.	Balt. Cem.
Feb 10	Walter B. Schmalzel	14 mos.	Balt. Cem.
Feb 22	Mrs. Laura Mary Scheer Wilson		Loudon Park
Feb 22	Elder Samuel F. Ziegler	68 years	Rose Hill, Hagerstown
Mar 6	Blanche H. Kehm	2 years	Balt. Cem.
Mar 10	Robert Giles Murphy	15 mos.	Balt. Cem.
Mar 16	Mrs. Sophia M. Schillinger	80 years	Balt. Cem.
Mar 26	Charles Frederick Giles	3 mos. 22 d.	Balt. Cem.
Mar 26	John Wolf	35 years	Loudon Park
Mar 30	William Reisinger	83 years	Mt. Olivet
May 12	Mrs. Margaret Landis	82 years	Balt. Cem.
May 15	Mrs. Mary Fuller	50 years	Loudon Park
Jun 20	Julia Annie Pohler	15 years	Balt. Cem.
Jul 24	Mrs. Cath. Zinn Zacharios	80 years	Frederick
Aug 18	Charles M. Burgau	39 years	Mt. Carmel
Aug 28	Mrs. Belle Z. Rogers	28 years	Cedar Hill Cem.
Aug 12	Miss Martha Lowe	80 years	Bay View
Sep 10	William B. Carter	70 years	York, Pa.
Sep 20	Cincinnatus Jelks	53 years	Balt. Cem.
Sep 25	Mary P. Young	11 mos.	Balt. Cem.
Oct 1	Mrs. Annie E. Michael	62 years	Greenmount
Oct 3	Sophia B. Baker	25 years	Greenmount
Oct 18	George Young	62 yrs. 1 mo. 3 d.	Balt. Cem.
Nov 7	Christina Gafford Groome	65 years	Fullerton
Nov 8	Agnes May Kraetor	4 mos.	St. Matthews Cem.
Nov 5	Lloyd Lowndes Miller	2 wks.	Loudon Park
Dec 24	George P. Emrich	54 years	Mt. Carmel
Dec 27	Annie Wingrove	48 years	Loudon Park
1896			
Jan 11	Mrs. Mary A. Snyder	56 years	Balt. Cem.
Jan 14	John H. Gosweiler	70 years	Loudon Park
Jan 15	Viola Marie Hoover	3 yrs. 2 mos.	Balt. Cem.
Feb 18	William A. Gruenawald	24 years	-
Apr 24	Mrs. Mary Jones	81 years	Balt. Cem.
Jul 9	Elmer Warner	12 years	Hampden

FIRST REFORMED CHURCH OF BALTIMORE

DATE OF DEATH	NAME	AGE	PLACE OF BURIAL
Jul 12	Hanson Cormack	82 years	Greenmount
Jul 18	Lawrence Matthew Fisher	3 mos.	Balt. Cem.
Jul 22	William H. Belbin	34 years	Mt. Olivet
Jul 26	Katie Huey Keen	10 mos. 2 d.	Mt. Carmel
Jul 31	Bertha Lowe Keen	10 mos. 7 d.	Mt. Carmel
Jul 30	Marie Agnes Snuder	1 year	Balt. Cem.
Sep 14	Christian H. Weber	50 years	Loudon Park
Oct 23	Gover Stem	10 years	Carroll Co., Md.
Oct 23	Mrs. Minnie Florence LeCato	31 years	Prospect Hill, York, Pa.
Oct 30	Mrs. Susan E. Bians	51 years	Loudon Park
Nov 24	William H. Herbert	54 years	Quakertown, Pa.
Dec 29	Mrs. Annie C. Fales	78 years	Balt. Cem.
1897			
Jan 5	Mary C. Ijams	80 years	Loudon Park
Feb 4	John R. McCleary	52 years	Union Cem., New Freedom
Feb 12	Mrs. Catherine Spear	86 years	Greenmount
Feb 18	Miss Lillie Becker	23 years	Balt. Cem.
Mar 21	Mrs. Sarah A. Benson	87 years	Greenmount
Mar 22	Frederick Tollberg	38 years	St. Matthews Cem.
Apr 21	Gladys Eleanora Kline	9 mos. 5 d.	Loudon Park
May 6	John Matthew Gemmill	4 wks	Balt. Cem.
May 23	Charles Stuck	68 years	Greenmount
Jun 14	William H. Karsten	24 years	Balt. Cem.
Jun 22	Mrs. Lizzette Rosskamp	75 years	Balt. Cem.
Jul 7	Emmeline Euphina May Gloag	9 mos. 10 d.	Mt. Olivet
Jul 21	Howard Laurence Schmalzel	17 years	Balt. Cem.
Jul 27	Margaret D. Meltee (or Mettee)	42 years	Mt. Olivet
Sep 8	Charles Richard Hammond	10 d.	Western Cem.
Nov 3	Thomas B. Schall	53 years	Prospect Hill, York, Pa.
Dec 1	William Derr	75 years	Mt. Olivet, Frederick, Md.
1898			
Jan 12	William Turnt	65 yrs. 10 mos. 13 d.	Loudon Park
Jan 16	John H. (or W.) Geiger	46 years	Loudon Park
Jan 18	Mrs. Marietta Jelks	42 years	Balt. Cem.
Mar 2	Mrs. Thomasina Q. Escavalle		Greenmount
Mar 5	Naomi Belbin	4 yrs. 9 mos.	Mt. Olivet
Mar 8	John G. Holzman	28 years	Mt. Carmel
Mar 25	J. Edward Cook	33 years	St. Pauls Germ. Cem.

FIRST REFORMED CHURCH OF BALTIMORE

DATE OF DEATH	NAME	AGE	PLACE OF BURIAL
Mar 29	Mrs. Minnie Weisheit	34 years 7 mos.	Loudon Park
Apr 3	Mrs. Mary A. Vocke	50 years	Balt. Cem.
Apr 27	Mrs. Rosa Sommer	39 years	Balt. Cem.
Apr 23	Mervin Edwin Stacks	31 yrs. 4 mos. 23 d.	Prospect Hill, York, Pa.
May 13	Solomon King	76 years	Greenmount
Jun 1	Mrs. Margaret Ann Stuck	64 years	Greenmount
Jun 29	Nelson Clark Thomas	58 years	Greenmount
Jul 1	James Wm. McKinley Drebing	1 yr. 3 mos. 25 d.	Balt. Cem.
Jul 10	Isadore Brightwell	11 mos.	Western Cem.
Jul 20	Earle Joseph Sommers	3 yrs. 10 mos.	Balt. Cem.
Aug 14	Frederick William Urbach	77 years	Loudon Park
Aug 16	J. Edgar McCrone	45 years	Loudon Park
Sep 26	Alexander Meikowski	76 years	Balt. Cem.
Oct 8	Annie Schumacher	5 d.	Loudon Park
Oct 18	Bertha Schwartz	77 years	Oak Hill, D.C.
Nov 19	Vernon Webb Billmire	24 years	Greenmount
Dec 19	Elizabeth Dougherty	88 years	Old Glendy Cem.
Dec 21	John Plennhoff	21 years	St. Matthews Cem.
Dec 30	Mrs. Mary Schmink	59 years	Balt. Cem.
Dec 31	Leon C. Yingling	35 years	Loudon Park

1899

DATE OF DEATH	NAME	AGE	PLACE OF BURIAL
Jan 1	Adolph Jochheim	54 years	Loudon Park
Jan 16	Mary C. Kraproth	79 years	Balt. Cem.
Jan 20	Mrs. Sarah Wonn	87 years	Loudon Park
Jan 27	Mrs. Mary Burkhardt	26 yrs. 8 mos. 25 d.	Balt. Cem.
Mar 18	Mrs. Ann E. Hall	74 years	Greenmount
Mar 26	Warren E. Cooke	60 years	Greenmount
Mar 28	John C. Cockey	74 years	Loudon Park
Apr 7	Charles Norris Fischer	1 year	Western Cem.
May 1	Mrs. Mary E. Gosweiler	70 years	Loudon Park
May 5	Mrs. Sophie Jochheim	49 years	Loudon Park
May 9	Lewis Selby Allen	29 years	Freedom, Carroll Co.
May 18	Charles Clapham Henderson	2 yrs. 7 mos. 4 d.	Balt. Cem.
Jul 22	Mamie Matilda Henderson	8 mos. 15 d.	Balt. Cem.
Oct 4	Margaret Myers	80 years	Prospect Hill, York, Pa.
Nov 4	William M. Chambers	64 years	Mt. Olivet
Nov 2	Russell R. McCord	33 years	Greenmount
Nov 9	Mary Charlotte Mergaroth	1 mo. 19 d.	Balt. Cem.
Nov 12	Augustus Theodore Zetzman	56 years	U.S. cemetery

FIRST REFORMED CHURCH OF BALTIMORE

DATE OF DEATH	NAME	AGE	PLACE OF BURIAL
Nov 30	William Fred. Volkmann	57 years	Schwartzs Cem.
Dec 2	Charles P. Oyler	45 years	Balt. Cem.
Dec 12	Justus W. Snyder	67 years	Balt. Cem.
Dec 27	Frank Bird Perry	19 years	Greenmount

ADDENDA

1893

Jan 29	Charles Wilbert Bollinger	5 mos. 26 d.	York Co.
Oct 26	William Carlton Bollinger	1 yr. 2 mos. 23 d.	York Co.
Mar 2	Mrs. Mary Lucas		Balt. Cem.
May 25	Sophia Anna Rutter	34 years	

1894

Jan 5	Robt. Norris McGinity	3 mos. 25 d.	York, Pa.
Oct 31	William John McKee McLean	5 yrs. 11 mos. 11 d.	Greenmount
Nov 25	Virginia Annie Brightman	5 yrs. 1 mo. 28 d.	Western Cem.

1895

Feb 27	Wilhelmina Unger	66 yrs. 10 mos. 10 d.	Western Cem. (Lutheran)
Jun 30	Norman Robb Hook	8 yrs. 20 mos. 2 d.	Greenmount
Oct 15	George Courtland Elmer Herbert	5 mos. 13 d.	Balt. Cem.

1896

Mar 2	Grace Elizabeth Lucas	8 mos. 13 d.	Balt. Cem.
Mar 15	Adaline Thompson	67 years	Greenmount
Mar 31	James Tyson Williams	1 yr. 9 mos. 5 d.	Howard Co.
Sep 3	Rose Daumann	26 yrs. 11 mos. 24 d.	St. Pauls Cem.
Nov 18	Harry Joseph Werneth	2 yrs. 11 mos. 22 d.	Western Cem. (Presbyterian)
Dec 7	Laura Katie Harris	1 yr. 3 mos. 26 d.	Mt. Calvary Cem.

1897

Sep 3	Frank Adams Wagner	1 year 29 d.	Loudon Park

1898

Jan 19	Chas. Edward Hoffman	1 yr. 3 mos. 29 d.	Balt. Cem.

1899

Mar 9	Sarah D. Hook	57 yrs. 2 mos. 16 d.	Greenmount
Mar 18	Rosina Schaffer Rodenmayer	14 yrs. 2 mos. 27 d.	Greenmount
Jul 1	Mildred Lee Maguire	3 mos.	Mt. Olivet Cem.

FIRST REFORMED CHURCH OF BALTIMORE

Entries are given in the following order:
Name and country of origin, dates of Birth, Death and Burial.

1802

Wilhelm List, from Hessia not far from Kassel, 54 years old; d. July 14; bur. July 15, 1802.

Wilhelm, son of Friedrich Morganthal and Maria Katharina, nee Rudolph; b. Oct. 24, 1801; d. July 18; bur. July 19, 1802.

George Philipp Traub, born in Ober-Ringelheim, left shore of the Rhine; d. July 21; bur. July 22, 1802.

Friedrich, son of Christian Krömer and Elisabeth, nee Winkert, 6 months old; d. July 23; bur. July 23, 1802.

Theresia Dorothea, daughter of Peter Benson and Rebecca, nee Herklotz; b. June 8, 1801; d. Aug. 12; bur. Aug. 13, 1802.

Lüder Albers, born in Bremen, Lower Saxony, Deacon of the German-Reformed Church since ... (Funeral sermon Aug. 22); b. Aug. 12, 1772; d. Aug. 15; bur. Aug. 16, 1802.

Regina Simon, nee Herman, 22 years old, (Funeral sermon Aug. 29); d. Aug. 19; bur. Aug. 19, 1802.

Christian, son of Herman Neumeier and Elisabeth, nee Rieserin; b. Nov. 16, 1801; d. Aug. 25; bur. Aug. 25, 1802.

Rahel Friberger, nee Mathaes, 35 years and 32 days old; b. July 28, 1767; d. Sept. 1; bur. Sept. 2, 1802.

Ludwig, son of Carl Friedrich Zoller and Maria; d.1802.

Johann, son of Johann Ewald and Katharina, nee Pingel, 17 years, 1 mo., 3 days old; b. Oct. 12, 1785; d. Sept. 8; bur. Sept. 8, 1802.

Johann Stremel, born in Berlenberg, County of Wittgenstein-Berlenburg (Funeral sermon Oct. 10); b. May 28, 1759; d. Sept. 26; bur. Sept. 27, 1802.

Martha Elisabeth Elliger, formerly Schweinebraten, nee Werner, born in Kassel; b. 1753; d. Oct. 6; bur. Oct. 6, 1802.

Johann, son of Jacob Simon and Katharina; b. 1800; d. Oct. 13; bur. Oct. 13, 1802.

Johann Schley, born in Freilaubersheim, Palantinate (Funeral sermon Nov. 28); b. Nov. 5, 1724; d. Nov. 17; bur. Nov. 19, 1802.

Alexander, son of Georg Watel and Anna Margaretha; b. Oct. 19, 1801; d. Dec. 23; bur. Dec. 25, 1802.

1803

Johann Hintske from Ober-Riethen in Lower Hessia, Germany, 49 years, 4 mo. old; b. May 23, 1753; d. March 2; bur. March 4, 1803.

Anna Christina Schmettenberg, nee Herminghaus, from the Unter-Lüttwinghaus ?, Lower Palatinate in Germany, 31 years old; b. March 8, 1772; d. April 3; bur. April 4, 1803.

Johann Henrich, son of Wilhelm and Susanna Riem; b. Jan. 31, 1803; d. June 24; bur. June 25, 1803.

Katharina, daughter of Jacob Terretiner (mother died in childbirth); b. Sept. 1802; d. July 17; bur. July 18, 1803.

Jacob, son of Bernhard Zoelle and Anna, nee Waker; b. July 5, 1803; d. July 19; bur. July 20, 1803.

Johanna, daughter of Bernhard Zoelle and Anna, nee Waker; b. July 5, 1803; d. July 19; bur. July 20, 1803.

Peter Keener, born in Switzerland, 70 years, 6 mo. old (Funeral sermon, July 31); b. Jan. 12, 1733; d. July 24; bur. July 25, 1803.

Margaretha, daughter of Johannes Freyburger; b. Aug. 25, 1802; d. Aug. 31; bur. Aug. 31, 1803.

Helena Carolina, daughter of Peter Schmachtenberg and Wilhelmina, nee Weck; b. Dec. 29, 1802; d. Aug. 5; bur. Aug. 6, 1803.

Georg Bernhard, son of Ludwig Schneider and Christina, nee Kitz; b. May 26, 1802; d. Aug. 2; bur. Aug. 2, 1803.

Katharina von Hemeschen, nee Geyser, 18 years, 7 mo. old (Funeral sermon Aug. 14); b. Jan. 7, 1785; d. Aug. 7; bur. Aug. 8, 1803.

Veronica Keeports, nee Moser, born in Philadelphia, 43 years, 21 days old; b. July 27, 1760; d. Aug. 18; bur. Aug. 19, 1803.

Sophia Katharina, daughter of Peter Benson and Rebecka; b. Dec. 23, 1802; d. Sept. 2; bur. Sept. 3, 1803.

Peter, son of Peter Schmachtenberg and Wilhelmina; b. Dec. 29, 1802; d. July 29; bur. July 30, 1803.

1804

Anna Zoelle, nee Wackring, died in childbirth; b. Nov. 3, 1762; d. Feb. 11; bur. Feb. 13, 1804.

Martin Pauli from Germany near Hanau and born in Büchingen, died of an illnes of the chest; b. Nov. 3, 1762, d.1804.

Georg Heinrich Bleichroth from Schwier in Germany, died of consumption; b. 1755; d.1804.

Peter Jung, born near Zweibrücken in Germany, died of consumption; b. 1781; d. April 16; bur. April 18, 1804.

Johannes Hoffmann, born in Friedrichstown, Maryland, died of consumption; b. Dec. 3, 1777; d. May 10; bur. May 12, 1804.

Adelheid Peters, born in Amsterdam; b. 1761; d. Sept. 22; bur. Sept. 23, 1804.

Anna Zelle, nee Wackring; b. Nov. 3, 1762; d. Nov. 11; bur. Nov. 13, 1804.

Philipp Sengstake from Bremen, Germany; d. Dec. 12; bur. Dec. 14, 1804.

1805

Peter Miller, born in Baltimore; b. June 10, 1788; d. March 22; bur. March 23, 1805.

Margaretha, daughter of Jacob Cronmiller and Christina; b. Nov. 13, 1804; d. April 14; bur. April 15, 1805.

Anna Robert, born near Annapolis; b. 1740; d. June 14; bur. June 26, 1805.

Johann Richstein, from the area of Wittgenstein in Germany; b. April 23, 1776; d. Sept. 22; bur. Sept. 24, 1805.

Samuel, son of Johann Schweitzer and Anna Maria Juliana; b. Sept. 20, 1802; d. Sept. 20; bur. Sept. 21, 1805.

Wilhelm Christian Richstein from the area of Wittgenstein in Germany, b. Aug. 21, 1782; d. Nov. 24; bur. Nov. 25, 1805.

1806

Elisabeth Schaum; b. 1742; d. Jan 24; bur. Jan. 25, 1806.

Leonmhard Bange from the area of Wittgenstein in Germany; b. Nov. 28, 1780; d. Apr. 11; bur. April 12, 1806.

Johann Friderich, son of the late Christian Friedrich Eichler and Salome; b. Feb. 13, 1799; d. July 7; bur. July 8, 1806.

Johann, son of Heinrich von Newkerck and Catharina; b. Dec. 17, 1804; d. July 20; bur. July 21, 1806.

Nelly Appold, born in Yorck; b. March 1, 1781; d. Aug. 9; bur. Aug. 10, 1806.

Anna Maria, daughter of Johann Zollig; b. March 11, 1805; d. Aug. 15, bur. Aug. 16, 1806.

Louisa, daughter of Augustine Schütt; b. Feb. 18, 1806; d. Sept. 21; bur. Sept. 22, 1806.

Heinrich Sengstack, captain from Bremen; b. 1764; d. Oct. 18; bur. Oct. 18, 1806.

Dorothea Bintzel, born in Lancaster; b. March 23, 1750; d. Dec. 12; bur. Dec. 13, 1806.

1807

Johannes, son of Christian Krämer; b. Nov. 16, 1805; d. Feb. 1, bur. Feb. 2, 1807.

Maria, daughter of Abraham Lefeber; b. Feb. 6, 1806; d. March 11; bur. March 12, 1807.

Philip Emig, born in Saarbrück in Germany; b. April 6, 1743; d. March 22; bur. March 23, 1807.

Heinrich, son of Jung; b. Dec. 25, 1800; d. March 28; bur. March 29, 1807.

Heinrich, son of Jacob Krall; b. Oct. 10, 1806; d. April 4; bur. April 5, 1807.

Nancy Fige; b. Jan. 1780; d. April 11; bur. April 12, 1807.

David, son of Heinrich Hachenbracht; b. Oct. 1806; d. June 6; bur. June 7, 1807.

Heinrich Jäger; b. Dec. 23, 1733; d. June 8; bur. June 9, 1807.

Wilbur Busch; b. 1756; d. June 9; bur. June 10, 1807.

Mother and son; d. June 29; bur. June 30, 1807.

Maria Elizabeth Bell; b. 1764; d. July 3; bur. July 4, 1807.

Wilhelm, son of Wilhelm Thomson; b. Jan. 26, 1806; d. July 19; bur. July 20, 1807.

Johan Georg, son of Mr. Forney; b. Oct. 30, 1806; d. July 26; bur. July 27, 1807.

Wilhelm, son of Thomas Bollman; b. Aug. 3, 1806; d. Aug. 2; bur. Aug. 2, 1807.

John Jacob Hildebrand from Zweibrücken; b. March 1, 1729; d. Aug. 5; bur. Aug. 6, 1807.

Dorothea Louisa, daughter of Georg Reider; b. March 13, 1806; d. Aug. 11; bur. Aug. 12, 1807.

Johan Georg Geisler from Hambrechen; b. Sept. 1765; d. Sept. 3; bur. Sept. 4, 1807.

Jacob, son of Friderich Dehmar; b. June 28, 1807; d. Sept. 4; bur. Sept. 5, 1807.

Barbara Tinger (or Finger); b. 1748; d. Sept. 6; bur. Sept. 7, 1807.

Johan Georg, son of J. Georg Breneisen; b. March 2, 1806; d. Sept. 10; bur. Sept. 11, 1807.

Wilhelm, son of Beniamin Sitler; b. Nov. 30, 1806; d. Sept. 20; bur. Sept. 21, 1807.

Margaretha, daughter of Mr. Tomson; b. May 5, 1802; d. Sept. 23; bur. Sept. 24, 1807.

Joseph, son of Christian Mumma; b. Dec. 24, 1802; d. Nov. 5; bur. Nov. 6, 1807.

James Kelly, from the Eastern Shore; b. Sept. 15, 1793; d. Dec. 6; bur. Dec. 7, 1807.

A child of Captain Williams; b. Sept. 19, 1807; d. Dec. 19; bur. Dec. 20, 1807.

1808

Elisabeth, wife of Philip German, nee Kurtz, from Yorck; b. Feb. 20, 1786; d. Dec. 29; bur. Dec. 31, 1808.

A child of Mr. Gade; 4 months old; d. 1808.

Maria Friderica Starck from Hannover, born in Wittgenstein, Berlenberg; b. Oct. 12, 1750; d. Jan. 18; bur. Jan. 20, 1808.

Johann Laucht from Altcronau near Schwartzenfeld in Hessia; b. Oct. 1738; d. Jan. 23; bur. Jan. 24, 1808.

Ludwig Wilhelm, son of Ludwig Schneider; b. March 29, 1807; d. March 14; bur. March 15, 1808.

Johann Herbert from the Rheinpfalz (Palantinate); b. 1773; d. April 14; bur. April 15, 1808.

Beniamin, son of Beniamin Sibler (or Sitler); b. July 21, 1804; d. May 20; bur. May 22, 1808.

Peter Harthinck, Dutch Vice Admiral from Wageningen, Holland (Netherlands); b. 1767; d. June 8; bur. June 9, 1808.

Maria Elisabeth Groverman, a Lutheran who was buried at the Lutheran Cemetery; b. July 20, 1807; d. June 14; bur. June 15, 1808.

Philip Zinsmaier, a Lutheran from Baltimore, buried at the Lutheran Cemetery, b. Sept. 29, 1770; d. June 17; bur. June 18, 1808.

Peter Schmachtenberg from the Lower Palantinate; b. Sept. 1770; d. July 1; bur. July 2, 1808.

Anna Elisabeth, child of Johan Homrichshausen; b. May 16, 1807; d. July 13; bur. July 14, 1808.

Degariera, daughter of Jacob Steiger; b. Dec. 13, 1807; d. July 21; bur. July 23, 1808.

Albert Louis, son of Mr. Zwissler (Lutheran Cemetery); b. Jan. 30, 1808; d. Aug. 2; bur. Aug. 3, 1808.

Herman Warking from Germany, Lutheran burial at Schields Cemetery; b. March 3, 1743; d. Sept. 9; bur. Sept. 10, 1808.

Daniel Pauli from Mariath (?) near Hanau in Germany; b. 1777; d. Sept. 14; bur. Sept. 15, 1808.

A child of Mr. Langenfelder; b. Jan. 17, 1808; d. Sept. 27; bur. Sept. 28, 1808.

Johanna Florina, a daughter of Mr. Böhm, b. Feb. 26, 1806; d. Oct. 12; d. Oct. 13, 1808.

Maria, daughter of Peter Feige; b. June 17, 1805; d. Oct. 13; bur. Oct. 14, 1808.
Mr. Jacob Hildebrand, b. Dec. 25, 1768; d. Oct. 17; bur. Oct. 18, 1808.
Johann Lindenfelder from Friedrichs County, Maryland; b. 1777; d. Oct. 21; bur. Oct. 23, 1808.
Maria Fletscher; b. June 24, 1761; d. Nov. 24; bur. Nov. 25, 1808.
Georg Daniel, son of Mr. Wolf; b. Oct. 22, 1791; d. Dec. 4; bur. Dec. 5, 1808.
Elisabeth, child of Mr. West; b. April 6, 1808; d. Dec. 7; bur. Dec. 8, 1808.
Catharina, daughter of Absalom Chrisbin (or Christian); b. June 17, 1807; d. Dec. 7; bur. Dec. 8, 1808.
Wilhelm Bollman from Habenhausen by Bremen in Germany; b. April 21, 1787; d. Dec. 28; bur. Dec. 29, 1808.

1809

Mariana, child of Georg Lucas; b. Oct. 17, 1808; d. Feb. 3; bur. Feb. 4, 1809.
Mr. Warner (without a preacher); d. Feb. 17; bur. Feb. 18, 1809.
Johannes Ewald from Zweibrücken in Germany; b. March 6, 1751; d. March 16; bur. March 17, 1809.
Adelheid, daughter of Nocolaus Hacke; b. Jan. 10, 1808; d. March 30; bur. March 31, 1809.
Michael Diefendörfer (was trustee of our community and died suddenly in his sleep); b. July 29, 1744; d. April 9; bur. April 11, 1809.
Sally, wife of John Forney, Jr.; b. Sept. 9, 1773; d. May 6; bur. May 7, 1809.
Mrs. Orrick, daughter of Ch. Kühner; d. July 3; bur. July 4, 1809.
Georg Fischer from Yorck County; b. 1767; d. Aug. 7; bur. Aug. 8, 1809.
Johan Diederich, son of Mr. Geisler; b. 1808; d. Aug 25; bur. Aug. 25, 1809.
Johan Friederich, son of Beniamin Bausman; b. Feb. 11, 1808; d. Aug. 25; bur. Aug. 26, 1809.
Christian Zingling from Haringen in Giessen; b. July 4, 1775; d. Aug. 28; bur. Aug. 28, 1809.
Maria, daughter of Johan Krämer; b. Oct. 14, 1808; d. Sept. 23; bur. Sept. 24, 1809.
Elisabeth, daughter of Heinrich Arnold Wilmsen; b. Feb. 8, 1808; d. Sept. 24; bur. Sept. 25, 1809.
Johan Jacob Gensberg from Oberwildern in Nassau Dillenberg; b. June 4, 1767; d. Oct. 1; bur. Oct. 7, 1809.
Wilhelm, son of Stephanus Grof; b. Feb. 11, 1808; d. Oct. 28; bur. Oct. 29, 1809.
Wilhelm Heinrich Hartwig; b. April 4, 1787; d. Nov. 27; bur. Nov. 29, 1809.
Peter Berckert; b. July 18, 1750; d. Dec. 25; bur. Dec. 26, 1809.

1810

Johannes Zoll, born in Adams County, Pa.; b. Aug. 15, 1788; d. Jan. 10; bur. Jan. 11, 1810.

Heinrich Hirschberger, born in Hägerstown; b. March 17, 1785; d. Jan. 21; bur. Jan. 22, 1810.

Nancy Freiberger; b. 1775; d. Jan. 30; bur. Jan. 31, 1810.

Catharina Hirschberger, born in Lancaster; b. 1745; d. April 28; bur. April 29, 1810.

Catharina Kraus; b. 1772; d. April 30; bur. May 1, 1810.

Heinrich, son of Mar. Leybrand; b. 1801; d. May 13; bur. May 14, 1810.

Martin Weisbach from the Middle Palantinate: Goggenheim, District Altsey; b. Feb. 11, 1739; d. July 7; bur. July 8, 1810.

Johanna Sophia, daughter of Peter Diefendörfer; b. Sept. 18, 1809; d. July 24; bur. July 25, 1810.

Jacob Mesmer; d. July 25; bur. July 26, 1810.

Johan Forney; b. March 17, 1776; d. Aug. 9; bur. Aug. 10, 1810.

Heinrich Schreiber, born in Nassau Siegen; b. July 22, 1757; d. Aug. 17; bur. Aug. 18, 1810.

Johan Eberhard, son of Michael Warnecke; b. Feb. 22, 1809; d. Sept. 26; bur. Sept. 27, 1810.

Friedrich, son of Mr. Spier; b. July 26, 1809; d. Sept. 28; bur. Sept. 29, 1810.

Johannes Meier from Altenkronau in Germany; b. 1761; d. Oct. 2; bur. Oct. 2, 1810.

Carl Jung; b. Oct. 5, 1786; d. Oct. 7; bur. Oct. 8, 1810.

Maria Magdalena Schauf born in Lower Palatinate; b. July 1745; d. Oct. 15; bur. Oct. 16, 1810.

Johannes Schweitzer; b. March 7, 1759; d. Nov. 11; bur. Nov. 11, 1810.

Charlotta, daughter of Mr. Ström; b. Oct. 7, 1809; d. Dec. 4; bur. Dec. 5, 1810.

Dorothea Louisa, daughter of George Diederich Geisler, buried at the Lutheran Cemetery; b. April 2, 1805; d. Dec. 19; bur. Dec. 19, 1810.

1811

Catharina Elisabeth Schalli, from Herborn in Nassau Dillenburg; b. Sept. 2, 1747; d. April 11; bur. April 17, 1811.

Salome Friederichs, from Gundershofen in Nassau Dillenburg; b. 1746; d. April 13; bur. April 14, 1811.

Charlotta Miller from Hamburg, died on the street, was buried at the Lutheran Cemetery; b. Nov. 3, 1792; d. April 11; bur. April 24, 1811.

Ludwig Schneider from Niederscholten in Nassau Siegen; 47 years old; d. May 5; bur. May 6, 1811.

Anna Spanhof, from the Oldenburg area; 51 years old; d. May 6; bur. May 7, 1811.

Catharina Weickert; b. Sept. 1754; d. May 15; bur. May 16, 1811.

Elisabeth Hummer, was an adopted child born in Manoff(?); b. Jan. 1792; d. June 4; bur. June 5, 1811.

Georg, son of Jacob Miller, buried at the Lutheran Cemetery; b. March 14, 1793; d. June 13; bur. June 14, 1811.

Heinrich Meinhaus; d. June 16; bur. June 16, 1811.

Susanna Fobel; b. March 21, 1789; d. June 16; bur. June 17, 1811.

Andreas Treppert from Lancaster, Pa.; b. Aug. 22, 1764; d. July 6; bur. July 7, 1811.

Georg Frantz Bange, Leader (Vorsteher) of this congregation; b. Oct. 27, 1778; d. July 10; bur. July 11, 1811.

Elisabeth, child of Frantz Riedesel; b. Oct. 5, 1800; d. July 24; bur. July 25, 1811.

Catharina, child of Heinrich Becker; b. Dec. 10, 1810; d. July 31; bur. Aug. 1, 1811.

Child of Jacob Lange; b. July 29, 1811; d. Aug. 3; bur. Aug. 4, 1811.

Catharina, daughter of Jacob Derr; b. July 23, 1795; d. Aug. 19; bur. Aug. 19, 1811.

Sarah, daughter of Friedich Warner; b. Feb. 23, 1807; d. Aug. 20; bur. Aug. 21, 1811.

Hyronimus Lesch from Neuwird in Germany; b. 1766; d. Aug. 25; bur. Aug. 26, 1811.

Maria Juliana Schweitzer; b. 1755; d. Sept. 1; bur. Sept. 2, 1811.

Catharina Sophia, child of Heinrich Koch, buried at the Lutheran Cemetery; b. March 4, 1800; d. Sept. 9; bur. Sept. 10, 1811.

Johan Heinrich Colmer, buried at the Lutheran Cemetery; b. Jan. 17, 1800; d. Sept. 10; bur. Sept. 11, 1811.

Elisabeth Bordly; b. 1800; d. Sept. 16; bur. Sept. 17, 1811.

FIRST REFORMED CHURCH OF BALTIMORE 287

Casiana, child of Christian Gelbach; b. July 1810; d. Sept. 17; bur. Sept. 18, 1811.

James Wearum, an Englishman; d. Sept. 21; bur. Sept. 22, 1811.

Maria Müllerin, nee Franck; b. April 7, 1780; d. Oct. 5; bur. Oct. 6, 1811.

Susanna Müllerin; b. Sept. 17, 1794; d. Oct. 6; bur. Oct. 7, 1811.

Henrich Herr from Meribach, Germany; b. 1737; d. Oct. 23; bur. Oct. 24, 1811.

Elisabeth, child of Adam Schwab; b. Oct. 20, 1811; d. Oct. 28; bur. Oct. 29, 1811.

Catharina Weisbach; b. July 4, 1761; d. Nov. 5; bur. Nov. 6, 1811.

Thomas Scherry; b. March 26, 1785; d. Nov. 17; bur. Nov. 18, 1811.

Anna Catharina Rund, born in the Berlenburg area; b. 1740; d. Dec. 7; bur. Dec. 8, 1811.

Heinrich, child of Mr. Kring; b. July 11, 1811; d. Dec. 27; bur. Dec. 28, 1811.

1812

Samuel Binsel; b. Aug. 30, 1788; d. Jan. 15; bur. Jan. 16, 1812.

Sally, child of Peter Getier; b. Oct. 24, 1809; d. Jan. 21; bur. Jan. 22, 1812.

Wilhelmina Lug (or Luy), born in Büdingen in the area of Ysenburg; b. March 1, 1794; d. Jan. 25; bur. Jan. 27, 1812.

Barbara Reid; b. 1780; d. Jan. 28; bur. Jan. 29, 1812.

Joseph, son of John Schunck, buried at the Methodist Cemetery; b. June 16, 1798; d. Jan. 30; bur. Jan. 31, 1812.

Elisabeth, child of Mr. Web; age 6 months; d. Feb. 8; bur. Feb. 9, 1812.

Johannes, child of Johan Alsfeld; b. March 8, 1810; d. Feb. 10; bur. Feb. 11, 1812.

John Alsfeld, born near Cassel; b. March 16, 1772; d. March 31; bur. April 1, 1812.

Jacob, child of Mrs. Fusch; b. Nov. 5, 1811; d. April 1; bur. April 2, 1812.

Small child of Mr. Mecharco; d. April 7; bur. April 8, 1812.

Child of Johann Mumma; d. April 24; bur. April 25, 1812.

Small child of Georg Vogelman; d. April 31; bur. May 1, 1812.

Mr. Duncker from Hagensburg; 50 years old; d. May 12; bur. May 13, 1812.

Johan Friederich Gebhard, born in Duderstadt, buried at the Lutheran Cemetery; b. 1760; d. May 24; bur. May 26, 1812.

Martin Fletscher; b. Sept. 30, 1756; d. June 29; bur. June 30, 1812.

David Mumma; b. 1787; d. July 12; bur. July 12, 1812.

Christian Stöver; b. Aug. 24, 1760; d. July 15; bur. July 16, 1812.

Amelia Jane, child of Peter Diefendörfer; b. March 26, 1812; July 18; bur. July 19, 1812.

Jacob, child of Friedrich Detmar; b. July 5, 1812; d. Aug. 2; bur. Aug. 3, 1812.

Sophia, daughter of Johan Feige; d. Aug. 3; bur. Aug. 4, 1812.

Jacob Seltzer from the middle Palatinate, near Manheim; b. April 23, 1759; d. Aug. 16; bur. Aug. 17, 1812.

Margaratha, daughter of Mr. Wäsche, buried at the Lutheran Cemetery; b. Feb. 27, 1811; d. Aug. 21; bur. Aug. 22, 1812.

Elisabeth, daughter of James Thomson; b. May 12, 1811; d. Aug. 22; bur. Aug. 23, 1812.

Andreas, son of Andreas Wolf; b. Dec. 12, 1811; d. Aug. 24; bur. Aug. 25, 1812.

Louisa Catharina, daughter of Mr. Schwab; b. July 10, 1811; d. Aug. 26; bur. Aug. 27, 1812.

Wilhelm Reiter, son of Ludwig Reiter; b. April 13, 1811; d. Sept. 7; bur. Sept. 8, 1812.

Louisa, child of Heinrich Becker; b. June 4, 1811; d. Sept. 15; bur. Sept. 16, 1812.

Weily, child of Caspar Heinrich Peters; b. Nov. 12, 1811; d. Sept. 18; bur. Sept. 18, 1812.

Jacob Boose; b. 1790; d. Sept. 22; bur. Sept. 23, 1812.

Anna Catharina Borman from Elbenrod by Giessen Kassel; b. Aug. 26, 1751; d. Oct. 3; bur. Oct. 4, 1812.

Louisa, daughter of David Forney; b. 1794; d. Oct. 20; bur. Oct. 21, 1812.

Johan Ludwig, child of Jacob Seltzer; b. Sept. 7, 1811; d. Oct. 22; bur. Oct. 23, 1812.

Johanna, child of Mr. Zellers; b. Aug. 24, 1811; d. Nov. 13; bur. Nov. 14, 1812.

Johan Keller from Canton Basel in Switzerland; b. March 2, 1751; d. Dec. 26; bur. Dec. 28, 1812.

Johan Scherer; about 53 years old; d. Dec. 30; bur. Dec. 31, 1812.

1813

Sarah Mumma, born in Philadelphia; b. Aug. 29, 1761; d. Dec. 30; bur. January 1, 1813.

Georg, son of Johan Fush; b. Dec. 23, 1809; d. Jan. 27; bur. Jan. 28, 1813.

Mr. Miller from Bremen (or Barmen); about 60 years old; d. Feb. 1; bur. Feb. 2, 1813.

Emilia Carolina, child of Heinrich Berghaus; b. Feb. 5, 1812; d. Feb. 8; bur. Feb. 9, 1813.

Christiana Adelheid, child of Nicolaus Hacke; b. Feb. 16, 1810; d. March 15; bur. March 16, 1813.

George Dob from Hagen near Münster in Germany; b. May 31, 1763; d. March 28; bur. March 30, 1813.

Wilhelm, child of Georg Richstein; b. Dec. 16, 1811; d. April 1; bur. April 2, 1813.

Christina, daughter of Caspar Zode; 5 years old; d. May 18; bur. May 19, 1813.

Philip, son of Andreas Wolf; b. Dec. 13, 1807; d. June 5; bur. June 6, 1813.

Wilhelm, son of Friedrich Krämer; b. Feb. 7, 1813; d. July 14; bur. July 15, 1813.

Maria Margaretha, child of Friederich Delmore; b. Aug. 13, 1805; d. July 26; bur. July 27, 1813.

James, child of Johan Freiburger; b. March 15, 1813; d. Aug. 7; bur. Aug. 8, 1813.

Maria Schneider; b. 1797; d. Aug. 14; bur. Aug. 15, 1813.

Heinrich Kammerer from Pittsburg; b. July 26, 1794; d. Sept. 12; bur. Sept. 13, 1813.

David, child of Mr. Keilholtz (or Krilholz); b. Jan. 9, 1813; d. Sept. 13; bur. Sept. 14, 1813.

Elisabeth Lobstein from the Palantinate; b. 1747; d. Sept. 14; bur. Sept. 15, 1813.

Child of Mr. Wilms; bur. Oct. 9, 1813.

Johann, son of Johan Maier; 13 years old; bur. Oct. 12, 1813.

Charlotte Marfibius; bur. Oct. 13, 1813.

Wilhelmine Jordan from Solingen in Niederbergen; b. Nov. 23, 1789; d. Oct. 30; bur. Oct. 31, 1813.

Catharina Maria, child of Mr. Schwab (or Schmal); b. Aug. 22, 1812; d. Nov. 15; bur. Nov. 16, 1813.

Arnold Schmids from the area of Mörs (Möss), a ... master in the community; b. Oct. 16, 1767; d. Dec. 20; bur. Dec. 22, 1813.

Wilhelm, child of Wilhelm Kamp; b. Feb. 14, 1813; d. Dec. 26; bur. Dec. 28, 1813.

Henrich Ewald; b. March 5, 1788; d. Jan. 9; bur. Jan. 10, 1814.

Johan Heinrich Fuselbach aus Mussen in Oranien Nassau; b. 1768; d. Jan. 19; bur. Jan. 20, 1814.

William Lefever; b. March 16, 1786; d. Jan. 21; bur. Jan. 22, 1814.

Beniamin Bausman, born in Philadelphia county; b. July 23, 1786; d. Feb. 2; bur. Feb. 3, 1814.

Henrich Orth; b. March 24, 1773; d. March 15; bur. March 16, 1814.

Margaretha, child of Johan Fush; b. Jan. 10, 1813; d. May 7; bur. May 8, 1814.

Jacob Miller; b. Feb. 13, 1754; d. May 17; bur. May 18, 1814.

Jacob Hartman from Switzerland; b. 1730; d. July 6; bur. July 7, 1814.

Philip German from Odernheim in the Middle Palatinate; b. Jan. 19, 1749; d. July 11; bur. July 13, 1814.

Catharina Fush; b. 1787; d. July 23; bur. July 24, 1814.

David, son of Mr. Jordan; b. Sept. 5, 1813; d. July 28; bur. July 29, 1814.

Maria Elgert; b. July 22, 1768; d. Aug. 19; bur. Aug. 20, 1814.

Louisa Sophia, child of Johan Krauth; b. Sept. 15, 1813; d. Sept. 5; bur. Sept. 6, 1814.

Peter Hahn, from near Zweibrücken; b. 1768; d. Sept. 8; bur. Sept. 9, 1814.

Jacob Daub, a soldier from Lebanon County; b. 1793; d. Sept. 29; bur. Sept. 30, 1814.

Louisa Richstein from Witgenstein, Germany; b. Sept. 28, 1739; d. Oct. 17; bur. Oct. 18, 1814.

Jacob Weber from Friederichstadt; d. Oct. 31; bur. Nov. 1, 1814.

Child of Heinrich Becker; d. Oct. 30; bur. Oct. 31, 1814.

Johan Hubert from Lancaster; d. Nov. 7; bur. Nov. 8, 1814.

Friederich Johnson from Preussisch Minden; b. 1747; d. Nov. 10; bur. Nov. 11, 1814.

Maria Johnson from Bamberg; b. Aug. 25, 1751; d. Nov. 16; bur. Nov. 17, 1814.

Valentin Sanders, from Hirschfeld in Hessen; b. Aug. 6, 1774; d. Nov. 30; bur. Dec. 1, 1814.

Johan Dom; b. Aug. 6, 1776; d. Dec. 17; bur. Dec. 18, 1814.

Fransciscus Krusen; b. 1795; d. Dec. 20; bur. Dec. 22, 1814.

FIRST REFORMED CHURCH OF BALTIMORE

1815

Elisabeth Lehman; b. April 5, 1788; d. Jan. 5; bur. Jan. 7, 1815.

Philip Jacob Schade; b. April 27, 1754; d. Jan. 6; bur. Jan. 6, 1815.

Heinrich, child of Heinrich Meier; b. April 11, 1814; d. Jan. 7; bur. Jan. 8, 1815.

Philip Beutel; b. April 29, 1778; d. Jan. 15; bur. Jan. 6, 1815.

Martin Henze; b. Oct. 26, 1758; d. March 27; bur. March 28, 1815.

Dieterich Rottermeier from Schwachhausen near Bremen; b. Dec. 1773; d. April 20; bur. April 21, 1815.

Johan Feige from Germany; b. July 4, 1781; d. June 25; bur. June 26, 1815.

Anna Catharina, child of Michel Haussmann; b. May 1, 1814; d. July 20; bur. July 21, 1815.

Heinrich Maier from Preussisch Minden; b. Jan. 1, 1787; d. July 25; bur. July 26, 1815.

Maria Barbara Christi; 74 years old; d. July 25; bur. July 26, 1815.

Dorothea, child of Mr. Schäfer; b. Feb. 12, 1815; d. Aug. 2; bur. Aug. 3, 1815.

Maria, child of Mr. Boyer; b. Jan. 19, 1815; d. Aug. 3; bur. Aug. 4, 1815.

Nicolaus Jacob, child of Nicolaus Lehman; b. Dec. 27, 1814; d. Aug. 4; bur. Aug. 5, 1815.

Anna Maria, child of Daniel Fobel; b. Sept. 17, 1812; d. Aug. 29; bur. Aug. 30, 1815.

Wilhelm Peters; b. 1792; d. Sept. 27; bur. Sept. 28, 1815.

Barbara Lauch from Alt Cronau in the district Schwarzenfel in Hessen; b. Feb. 2, 1782; d. Oct. 2; bur. Oct. 3, 1815.

Maria Kiefer from Solingen; b. 1781; d. Oct. 14; bur. Oct. 15, 1815.

Maria, child of Mr. Dieffendörfer; b. 1810; d. Oct. 22; bur. Oct. 23, 1815.

Martin Borman from Pennsylvania; b. Nov. 11, 1793; d. Nov. 8; bur. Nov. 9, 1815.

Johan Hoffman; b. March 13, 1795; d. Nov. 25; bur. Nov. 26, 1815.

Wilhelm Rhode from Cassel; b. June 15, 1777; d. Dec. 9; bur. Dec. 10, 1815.

1816

Dr. Johan Friederich Schwartz from Hannover, buried at the Lutheran Cemetery; b. Dec. 10, 1756; d. Jan. 7; bur. Jan. 9, 1816.

Friederich Wilhelm Kramer from Bremen, buried at the Lutheran Cemetery; b. 1790; d. Jan. 12; bur. Jan. 13, 1816.

Dr. Ernst Heinrich Zoller, from Zweibrücken in Germany; b. March 6, 1764; d. Jan. 18; bur. Jan. 21, 1816.

Joh. Michel Dosch from Weissbach in Germany, at the Lutheran Cemetery; b. Sept. 1, 1767; d. Jan. 26; bur. Jan. 27, 1816.

Johan Zahner from the area of Schwartzenfeld in Hessia; b. 1744; d. Jan. 25; bur. Jan. 27, 1816.

Georg Schrot, Lutheran Cemetery; b. April 13, 1768; d. Jan. 27; bur. Jan. 28, 1816.

Michel, child of Michel Kemperling; b. Nov. 10, 1815; d. Feb. 7; bur. Feb. 8, 1816.

Ferdinand, child of Mr. Fuhrman, at the Lutheran Cemetery; b. Oct. 2, 1815; d. Feb. 7; bur. Feb. 8, 1816.

Elisabeth Miller, at the Baptist Cemetery; b. 1747; d. Feb. 14; bur. Feb. 15, 1816.

Baltzer Bentzel from Germany; b. 1753; d. March 5; bur. March 6, 1816.

Maria Anna, child of Richard Luis; b. Sept. 17, 1815; d. March 28; bur. March 29, 1816.

Wilhelmina Heinrich, nee Hugfeld, from Marburg, b. Jan. 9, 1794; d. April 27; bur. April 28, 1816.

Tobias Wolf; b. 1759; d. April 27; bur. April 28, 1816.

Jacob, child of Mr. Putzhard; b. July 3, 1815; d. June 9; bur. June 9, 1816.

Thomas Frast; b. March 17, 1767; d. June 17; bur. June 18, 1816.

Anna Maria, child of Mr. Metlack; b. April 2, 1816; d. July 2; bur. July 3, 1816.

Elisabeth, child of Mr. Schwahl; b. Dec. 11, 1815; d. July 24; bur. July 25, 1816.

Daniel Fobel from Arfeld in Wittgenstein; b. 1783; d. July 27; bur. July 28, 1816.

Barbara Jung from the Zweibrücken area; b. 1749; d. July 28; bur. July 29, 1816.

Catharina Rotter; b. 1789; d. Aug. 7; bur. Aug. 8, 1816.

Christina, daughter of Jacob Seltzer, Jr.; b. March 28, 1816; d. Aug. 10; bur. Aug. 11, 1816.

Heinrich, son of Johan Berger; b. Aug. 6, 1815; d. Aug. 10; bur. Aug. 11, 1816.

Daniel Conrad, son of Mr. Geisler; b. Jan. 2, 1803; d. Aug. 27; bur. Aug. 17, 1816.

Juliana Comfort from Yorck County; b. Jan. 9, 1794; d. Aug. 28; bur. Aug. 28, 1816.

Johan Forney; d. Aug. 30; bur. Aug. 30, 1816.

Maria Butscher, born in Witgenstein; b. Aug. 6, 1784; d. Sept. 12; bur. Sept. 13, 1816.

Wilhelm, child of Nicolaus Matthäus; b. Oct. 2, 1815; d. Sept. 14; bur. Sept. 15, 1816.

Friederich, child of Georg Keller; b. July 11, 1811; d. Sept. 21; bur. Sept. 23, 1816.

Jacob Heinrich, child of Georg Keller; b. Feb. 9, 1813; d. Oct. 8; bur. Oct. 10, 1816.

David Mumma; b. Feb. 17, 1751; d. Oct. 30; bur. Oct. 31, 1816.

Nicolaus Job, from the Palatinate in Germany; b. July 4, 1728; d. Nov. 3; bur. Nov. 4, 1816.

Baltzer Binsel; b. 1781; d. Nov. 8; bur. Nov. 9, 1816.

Thomas, child of Georg Lucas; b. March 13, 1816; d. Dec. 2; bur. Dec. 3, 1816.

Julia Feige, nee Meren, from Montgomery County; b. July 11, 1778; d. Dec. 3; bur. Dec. 4, 1816.

Child of Mr. Carder; 5 weeks old; d. Dec. 4; bur. Dec. 5, 1816.

Jacob Crosh; b. Aug. 13, 1795; d. Dec. 18; bur. Dec. 19, 1816.

1817

Peter, child of Mr. Zinszoner (or Zinsgoner); b. June 7, 1815; d. Jan. 19; bur. Jan. 20, 1817.

Georg, child of Mr. Keller, b. April 2, 1810; d. Jan. 20; bur. Jan. 23, 1817.

Wilhelm Heinrich, child of Mr. Welshofer; b. Sept. 18, 1816; d. March 2; bur. Mar. 3, 1817.

Friederich Warner from Germany; b. Jan. 16, 1764; d. March 5; bur. March 7, 1817.

Susanna, wife of John Flush; b. 1790; d. March 12; bur. March 13, 1817.

Heinrich Tausch; b. July 22, 1791; d. March 17; bur. March 19, 1817.

Elisabeth, child of Friederich König; b. June 14, 1815; d. March 23; bur. March 25, 1817.

FIRST REFORMED CHURCH OF BALTIMORE

Carl Wilhelm Ferdinand Focke from Germany; b. Feb. 3, 1786; d. March 31; bur. April 2, 1817.

Wilhelm, child of Georg Schleig; b. Jan. 31, 1816; d. April 9; bur. April 10, 1817.

Daniel Heilig; b. April 15, 1808; d. May 13; bur. May 14, 1817.

Georg, child of Mr. Reiter; b. Dec. 20, 1814; d. June 1; bur. June 2, 1817.

Lucius Narrold from Fuhren in Graubünden, Switzerland; b. Dec. 22, 1788; d. Jan. 8; bur. Jan. 9, 1817.

Jacob Wolf; b. July 25, 1748; d. June 9; bur. June 10, 1817.

Anna Catharina Thomae from Kirchheim by Hessen Marburg; b. March 28d, 1751; d. June 10; bur. June 11, 1817.

Susanna Hartman from Baumhold in Zweibrücken, Germany; b. 1740; d. June 21; bur. June 22, 1817.

Caspar Charles, child of Caspar Peters; b. Aug. 1815; d. July 2; bur. July 3, 1817.

Catharina Elisabeth, child of Ludwig Schröder; b. Aug. 4, 1816; d. July 4; bur. July 5, 1817.

Friederich, child of Anthony Schäfer; b. March 22, 1816; d. July 6; bur. July 7, 1817.

David Fuhrman; b. Dec. 1744; d. July 22; bur. July 23, 1817.

Sabina, child of the late Schmachtenberg; b. March 19, 1807; d. Aug. 5; bur. Aug. 6, 1817.

August, child of Georg Keller; b. April 26, 1817; d. Aug. 20; bur. Aug. 21, 1817.

Wilhelm, child of Michel Hofman; b. May 25, 1817; d. Aug. 21; bur. Aug. 22, 1817.

Anna Maria, child of Carl Volck; b. June 26, 1817; d. Aug. 24; bur. Aug. 25, 1817.

Johan Friederich, child of Friederich Fock(?); b. Aug. 19, 1816; d. Aug. 25; bur. Aug. 26, 1817.

Jacob Morris, child of Georg Breneisen; b. Jan. 19, 1815; d. Sept. 15; bur. Sept. 16, 1817.

Jacob, child of Jacob Seltzer; b. June 17, 1817; d. Sept. 25; bur. Sept. 26, 1817.

Mariana, child of Mr. Florens from Elsass; 1 year old; d. Oct.; bur. Oct., 1817.

Margaretha Neit; b. April 15, 1815; d. Oct. 16; bur. Oct. 17, 1817.

Child of Mr. Matlack (or Hatlack); d. Oct. 16; bur. Oct. 17, 1817.

FIRST REFORMED CHURCH OF BALTIMORE 295

Anna Elisabeth, daughter of Johan Schmnid; b. June 28, 1810; d. Nov. 8; bur. Nov. 9, 1817.

Christian Keener, Senr.; b. Aug. 1757; d. Nov. 21; bur. Nov. 23, 1817.

Thomas, child of Thomas Schmid; b. May 1, 1817; d. Nov. 23; bur. Nov. 24, 1817.

Johan, child of Johan Kramer, Jun.; b. April 15, 1815; d. Dec. 10; bur. Dec. 11, 1817.

Elisabeth Osborn, nee Cohler, buried at the Lutheran Cemetery; b. August 1759; d. Dec. 12; bur. Dec. 13, 1817.

1818

Job Reyli, stepson of Ludwig Schröder; b. June 10, 1798; d. Jan. 6; bur. Jan. 7, 1818.

Jacob Kleinauer from Rostock/Mecklenburg; b. Nov. 1772; d. Jan. 13; bur. Jan. 14, 1818.

Friederich Detmore from Germany; b. 1767; d. Feb. 19; bur. Feb. 20, 1818.

Jacob Simon from Zweibrücken; b. 1731; d. Feb. 19; bur. Feb. 20, 1818.

Johan Jacob Schultz from Otterndorf, Germany, buried at the Lutheran Cemetery; b. July 20, 1774; d. May 13; bur. May 14, 1818.

Christina Drost from Hundsleben, Thüringen, buried at the Lutheran Cemetery; b. about 1758; d. May 26; bur. May 27, 1818.

David Friederich, child of Wilhelm Reiter; b. May 28, 1817; d. June 1; bur. June 2, 1818.

Daniel Klein; b. May 24, 1795; d. June 9; bur. June 10, 1818.

Mrs. Kähre; d. Aug. 1; bur. Aug. 2, 1818.

James Götz; b. 1795; d. Aug. 6; bur. Aug. 6, 1818.

William Thomas Knight, son of John Knight; b. Aug. 16, 1817; d. Aug. 14; bur. Aug. 15, 1818.

Charles Keller, son of George Keller; b. June 1, 1818; d. Aug. 14; bur. Aug. 15, 1818.

1851

Richard Diffenderfer; about 70 years; d. Feb. 1851.

John Clifford; d. Feb. 1851.

Lewis C. Muller; 62 years old; d. Feb. 19, 1851.

William Tagart; 30 years old; d. March 1851.
A. Hughes; 60 years old; d. March 1851.
Mrs. Frazier; 51 years old; d. March 1851.
Mrs. Capt. Lauderman; 33 years old; d. April 3, 1851.
Elisha R. Sinners; 74 years old; d. April 5, 1851.
Harding Freyer; 1 year old; d. April 6, 1851.
--- Stansbury; 17 years old; d. April 15, 1851.
Catharina Rash; 34 years old; d. April 19, 1851.
Mr. Jones; 30 years old; d. May 1851.
Mr. Cook; 40 years old; d. May 1851.
Mr. Ball; 55 years old; d. May 29, 1851.
Child of Mr. Vandervecker; 6 months old; d. May 29, 1851.
Jane Freyer; 80 years old; d. June 3, 1851.
Child of Mrs. Pypher; 3 years old; d. June 7, 1851.
Child of Mr. Edwards; 4 years old; d. June 8, 1851.
David Mumma; 49 years old; d. June 8, 1851.
Mr. Conder's mother; 70 years old; d. June 15, 1851.
Child of Elizabeth Tagart; 1 1/2 years old; d. June 20, 1851.
Brother of Mrs. White; 40 years old; d. July 1, 1851.
Mrs. Elizabeth Nussear (or Nusslar); 70 years old; d. July 6, 1851.
Mrs. Janey Cull; 50 years old; d. July 8, 1851.
Mrs. Steelman's mother; 60 years old; d. July 20, 1851.
John Martin; 30 years old; d. Aug. 1, 1851.
Henrietta Suter; 43 years old; d. Aug. 10, 1851.
John Miller; 70 years old; d. Aug. 13, 1851.
William Suter; 5 days old; d. Aug. 30, 1851.
Mrs. Robinson; 80 years old; d. Sept. 1, 1851.
Mrs. Cummings; 58 years old; d. Sept. 7, 1851.
Martha Guy; 10 years old; d. Oct. 4, 1851.
Charles Suter; 46 years old; d. Nov. 19, 1851.
Nathaniel Lightun(?); 62 years old; d. Dec. 5, 1851.
Mr. A. Groverman's daughter; 2 years old; d. 1851.

Son of Mr. Robertson; 1 year 19 days old; d. Dec. 17, 1851.
James Edwards; 70 years old; d. Dec. 21, 1851.

1852
Emily Robertson; 27 years old; d. Jan. 8, 1852.
Annie Remane; 4 years old; d. March 10, 1852.
William Singleton; 51 years old; d. March 17, 1852.
Ross Pennington's child; 2 years old; d. March 18, 1852.
Sam. Parsons, Jun.; 24 years old; d. March 21, 1852.
Mr. Wilhelm's child; 8 years old; d. March 25, 1852.
William Joseph; 30 years old; d. April 13, 1852.
Ellen Watlington; 16 1/2 years old; d. May 9, 1852.
Mrs. Elizabeth West; 72 years old; d. June 13, 1852.
Mrs. Smith (John Smith's mother); 83 years old; d. June 20, 1852.
Elizabeth Reynolds; 84 years old; d. June 27, 1852.
James Landerman; 18 years old; d. June 27, 1852.
Robert Allen; 6 years old; d. July 1852.
John Miller's mother-in-law; 42 years old; d. July 1852.
Ross Pennington's child; d. Aug. 1852.
John McColman; 70 years old; d. Aug. 24, 1852.
Mrs. Echberger's child; 6 years old; d. Nov. 1852.
Mr. Mill's child; 5 weeks old; d. Dec. 1852.
Henry Spillman's child; 5 years old; d. Dec. 25, 1852.
Wm. H. Martin's wife; 31 years old; d. Dec. 29, 1852.

1853
Fred. Cook's wife; 33 years old; d. Jan. 12, 1853.
Child of Mr. Stephens; 10 months old; d. Jan. 11, 1853.
Mary Lainhart; 77 years old; d. Jan. 18, 1853.
Mrs. Godfrey; 55 years old; d. Jan. 11, 1853.
Mr. Jones (High Str.); 24 years old; d. Jan. 27, 1853.
Mrs. Sills' father; 80 years old; d. Feb. 18, 1853.

Mr. Craggs; 27 years old; d. Feb. 18, 1853.
Dr. J. W. Honek's mother; 65 years old; d. Feb. 18, 1853.
William Klessner; 55 years old; d. March 1853.
Wm. Randal's child; 1 1/2 years old; d. April 1853.
Child of Mr. Barger; 10 months old; d. June 11, 1853.
Laura Tarman; 25 years old; d. June 24, 1853.
Mrs. Jud. E. Allen's child; d. June 24, 1853.
Mrs. Mary Ann Shotts; 47 years old; d. July 22, 1853.
Mrs. Z. and L. Tarman's child; 6 days old; d. 1853.
Mr. Caldwell; 26 years old; d. Aug. 15, 1853.
Mrs. Uhl's sister; 30 years old; d. Nov. 1853.
Mrs. Nasen's mother - Mrs. Coombs; 56 years old; d. Nov. 1853.
Capt. Wm. C. Nasen; 44 years old; d. Dec. 25, 1853.
Mr. Seesnop; 45 years old; d. Dec. 30, 1853.
James Zekel Johnson; 9 days old; d. Dec. 30, 1853.

1854
Mary Ann Johnson; 23 years old; d. Jan. 16, 1854.
Thos. Edwin Muller; 7 weeks old; d. Jan. 29, 1854.
Child of Mrs. Hays; 13 months old; d. Jan. 22, 1854.
John Keener; 85 years old; d. Jan. 22, 1854.
Nicholas E.[or B.] Boyer; 2 1/2 years old; d. Jan. 28, 1854.
Chas. Clifford Clemens; 3 years old; d. March 4, 1854.
Mrs. Miller's child (Mrs. Uhl's sister); 6 months old; d. March 18, 1854.
Eveline Duvall; 21 years old; d. May 3, 1854.
Mary Smith (daughter of Wm. Best S.); 5 1/2 years old; d. May 6, 1854.
Mr. Gray's wife (Chestnut St.); 34 years old; d. May 16, 1854.
Old Mrs. Cranford; 86 years old; d. June 15, 1854.
Old Mrs. Hamilton (5th St.); 72 years old; d. June 23, 1854.
Child of C. & S. Keelhitz; 5 months old; d. June 28, 1854.
Mrs. Henry Miller (Point); 50 years old; d. Sept. 1854.
Mr. Carsen; 30 years old; d. Sept. 29, 1854.

Mr. James Cranford; 47 years old; d. Oct. 2, 1854.
Mrs. Keller, near Penn. Avenue; 40 years old; d. Sept. 1854.
Mr. Jones (Water St.); 27 years old; d. Oct. 16, 1854.
Mr. Lutz's child; 1 year old; d. Oct. 25, 1854.
Mr. David (or Daniel) Diffenderfer Vaughn; 37 years old; d. Oct. 28, 1854.
Miss Amelia Lambert; 15 years old; d. 1854.
Wm. H. Cobsen; 81 years old; d. Dec. 7, 1854.
Christian Rash; 55 years old; d. Nov. 1854 (at sea).
George Rodenmayer; 67 years old; d. Dec. 8, 1854.
Henry C. Sultzer; 31 years old; d. Dec. 18, 1854.
John Matthias; 80 years old; d. Dec. 26, 1854.
Miss Catharine Boyer; 66 years old; d. Dec. 30, 1854.

1855
Jacob Alban, child of J. & M. Müller; 18 months old; d. Jan. 1, 1855.
Child of Mr. Joseph; 3 years old; d. Jan. 26, 1855.
Leopold Dousee; 78 years old; d. Jan. 27, 1855.
Virginia E. Johannes; 3 1/2 years old; d. Feb. 2, 1855.
Ella Heiner; 6 months old; d. Feb. 20, 1855.
Charles Reese; 2 1/2 years old; d. Feb. 21, 1855.
Mrs. Wm. Finley; 56 years old; d. April 12, 1855.
Mrs. Craggs; 75 years old; d. June 3, 1855.
Charles Davis Muller; 17 months; d. June 4, 1855.
Charles F. Diffenderffer; 34 years old; d. July 20, 1855.
Child of Mrs. Hauer (Frederick); 5 years old; d. July 21, 1855.
Malinda Dobbin; 2 1/2 years old; d. Aug. 10, 1855.
Child ----, d. 1855.
Mrs. Dugan, wife of Joseph O.; 26 years old; d. Sept. 1855.
John Joseph; 30 years old; d. Sept. 1855.
Emily Williams; 4 years old; d. Nov. 13, 1855.
Robert Elliot (son-in-law of Mr. Joseph); 33 years old; d. Nov. 21, 1855.
Mrs. Margaret Kaylor; 75 years old; d. Dec. 10, 1855.

Burte Fisher (daughter of Georg L. Fisher); 4 years old; d. Dec. 11, 1855.
Lewis Howell Randall (son of Wm. Randall); 4 years old; d. Dec. 12, 1855.
John Abbes; 56 years old; d. Dec. 13, 1855.
Mrs. Grace McRae; 73 years old; d. Dec. 14, 1855.
Thomas Joseph; 74 years old; d. Dec. 19, 1855.
Julia Maynard; 9 1/2 years old; d. Dec. 28, 1855.

1856
Dr. Charles S. Davis; 61 years old; d. Feb. 27, 1856.
Rose Louesa Hewitt; 1 year old; d. March 12, 1856.
Luorie Ruskell; 26 months old; d. March 17, 1856.
Barbara Riddell; 84 years old; d. May 8, 1856.
George Kaylor; 79 years old; d. May 9, 1856.
Child of Mr. Joseph; 2 years old; d. May 11, 1856.
Henry Welshoffer; 75 years old; d. July 1856.
Louis Gibson Boyer; 7 years old; d. July 1856.
Child of Philip Pyfer; 9 months old; d. August 1856.
Mrs. Lobleman; 65 years old; d. August 22, 1856.
Mrs. Berger's mother; 94 years old; d. August 1856.
Emily Naker; 31 years old; d. Sept. 25, 1856.
Mary Elizabeth Honeck; 14 months old; d. Dec. 28, 1856.

1857
Richard Owen Maynard; 8 years 3 months old; d. Jan. 15, 1857.
Mary Elizabeth Phillips; 3 years 4 months old; d. March 4, 1857.
Harry Hilberg; 1 year old; d. March 16, 1857.
Laura Diffenberger; 25 years old; d. March 18, 1857.
Mrs. Agnes Bennett; 35 years old; d. April 1, 1857.
George Sebastian Hewell; 2 years old; d. April 11, 1857.
Mr. Gettier; 75 years old; d. April 16, 1857.
Young Kunse; 15 years old; d. April 19, 1857.
Mrs. Shaw (at Mrs. E. Bixler's); 80 years old; d. April 21, 1857.

Martha Uhl (daughter of J. A. Uhl); 14 months old; d. April 22, 1857.
George, son of G. W. Herring; 3 years old; d. April 25, 1857.
Son of Jacob Yeisley; 19 months old; d. June 25, 1857.
Harvey, son of G. D. Bennett; 1 year old; d. June 26, 1857.
Charles Diffenderffer; 76 years old; d. June 27, 1857.
Philip Reigart; 74 years old; d. July 9, 1857.
Mrs. Charlotte Baker; about 50 years old; d. July 3, 1857.
Child of Mrs. Clarke; 20 months old; d. July 3, 1857.
Edwin S. J. Allen; 11 years old; d. July 29, 1857.
Mrs. Sarah Boyer; 57 years old; d. Aug. 2, 1857.
Mr. Bardorf (Concord St.); about 38 years old; d. July 24, 1857.
Child of Mr. Cox; 4 months old; b. Sept. 15, 1857.
Mrs. von Holland (sister of Richstein); 56 years old; d. Oct. 5, 1857.
Mrs. Berthorf; about 39 years old; d. Nov. 4, 1857.
Child of Mr. Eikert; 22 months old; d. Nov. 5, 1857.
Mrs. Merideth (Baldersten St.); 24 years old; d. Dec. 4, 1857.
Mr. Hart (son-in-law of Mrs. Miller); 32 years old; d. Dec. 6, 1857.
Mrs. Ann Jane Silvester; about 28 years old; d. Nov. 1857.
Mr. Meredith, R. B.; 30 years old; d. Dec. 26, 1857.
Miss Margaret Meyers; 70 years old; d. Dec. 27, 1857.

1858
Grandchild of Mr. Lutz (Point); 18 months old; d. Jan. 18, 1858.
Mrs. Elizabeth Friend; about 36 years old; d. Jan. 20, 1858.
Mrs. Millitts, sister of A. Matthew (?); about 65 years old; d. Jan. 26, 1858.
Miss Harriet Eliz. Page; 21 years old; d. Feb. 15, 1858.
Mrs. Hanna; 43 years old; d. March 3, 1858.
Wm. Russell; 65 years old; d. March 6, 1858.
Miss Georgianna Ball; 27 years old; d. March 9, 1858.
Wm. Miller, son of Jacob; 18 years old; d. March 11, 1858.
Miss Mary Elizabeth Yeakle; 24 years old; d. April 7, 1858.
Mrs. Frances Durst; 64 years old; d. April 8, 1858.

Mr. John Miller's wife; 30 years old; d. May 1, 1858.
Child of Mrs. Williams (Mr. Dorr's daughter); 3 years old; d. May 4, 1858.
Mrs. Mary Miller (East Fayette St.); 54 years old; d. May 29, 1858.
Mrs. Catherine Wolf; 65 years old; d. May 30, 1858.
Mrs. Letitia Snyder; 38 years old; d. July 10, 1858.
Child of Mr. McCauly; in its 2nd year; d. July 10, 1858.
Mr. Dolbin; d. July 1858.
David J. Aprill; 42 years old; d. Sept. 2, 1858.
Mrs. Susan Keener; 64 years old; d. Sept. 1858.
Old Lady, a Mrs. Giles; 75 years old; d. Oct. 31, 1858.
Sherburn L. Moore; 10 years old; d. Nov. 5, 1858.
Mr. Campbell (corner Lomb./Frederick); 30 years old; d. Dec. 3, 1858.
Henry Miller; about 56 years old; d. Dec. 15, 1858.
Mrs. Bowie; about 60 years old; d. Dec. 24, 1858.

1859

Jacob Paysen Heiner Magus; about 2 months old; d. Feb. 1859.
Charles Hardesty and Frank Baker, children of Wm. and Ann Rebecca Berry; d. 1859.
Felix Durst; about 35 years old; d. March 7, 1859.
James Cameron; about 40 years old; d. April 22, 1859.
Daughter of Albert J. Boyer; in her 9th month; d. May 18, 1859.
Berthorf; about 10 years old; d. May 21, 1859.
Humes; 39 years old; d. May 21, 1859.
Charlotte McCord; about 30 years old; d. Oct. 7, 1859.
Miss Eliza Ann (?) Joseph; about 30 years old; d. 1859.

1860

Wm. Prescott Vansant; d. Jan. 8, 1860.
John A. Vaughn; nearly 14 years old; d. Jan. 12, 1860.
James Joseph Guy (or Grey); 19 months old; d. Feb. 25, 1860.
Edward Diffenderffer; about 36 years old; d. Feb. 26, 1860.

Mrs. Scharper; about 76 years old; d. April 2, 1860.
Ellen Frances Pomp; 18 months old; d. May 1, 1860.
Miss Eliza Letetia Asprill; 21 years old; d. May 24, 1860.
Child of G. W. & M. M. Barger; about 3 years old; d. June 1860.
Child of Mr. & Mrs. Lyer (?); about 5 months old; d. June 29, 1860.
Child of Mr. & Mrs. Crozier; about 10 years old; d. July 5, 1860.
Mrs. Martha E. Hatchesen; 64 years old; d. July 7, 1860.
Child of J. Dobbin; d. Sept. 8, 1860.
William Joseph; 70 years old; d. Sept. 28, 1860.
Child of Wm. Nasen; 9 months old; d. Nov. 26, 1860.
Joshua Cockey; about 56 years old; d. Nov. 29, 1860.
Wm. Richstein; about 26 years old; d. Dec. 1860.

1861
George Franck; about 66 years old; d. Jan. 5, 1861.
Jane Olive Fryer; about 48 years old; d. Jan. 19, 1861.
Christiana Gelbach; about 43 years old; d. Jan. 27, 1861.
Hannah Kraig; about 52 years old; d. Feb. 1, 1861.
Jacob Shaffner; about 81 years old; d. Feb. 12, 1861.
Maggie Lighum (or Lightner); about 21 months old; d. April 5, 1861.
Old Mrs. Hamilton; about 82 years old; d. July 18, 1861.
Lewis A. Diffenderffer; about 36 years old; d. June 1861.
Henry Weisinger; 15 years, 8 months old; d. Aug. 8, 1861.
Mrs. Henry G. Freberger; about 63 years old; d. Aug. 28, 1861.
Mrs. Sophia M. Kraut; about 18 years old; d. Aug. 30, 1861.
Dr. Charles S. Reese; about 37 years old; d. Sept. 25, 1861.
Mrs Elizabeth Frances Porter (or Portor); about 52 years old; d. Oct. 25, 1861.
Mrs. Jacob Miller; about 42 years old; d. Nov. 12, 1861.
Mrs. Elizabeth Locher; about 68 years old; d. Dec. 1861.
Emma G. Uhl; about 18 years old; d. Dec. 31, 1861.

1862

Wm. C. Baker; 32 years old; d. June 23, 1862.

Son of Geo. W. & Rosena Herring; a few weeks old; d. 1862.

Wm. Bowie; 39 years old; d. Nov. 1862.

Child of Joseph and Ann Guy (or Grey); 8 days old; d. Dec. 19, 1862.

1863 - Rev. E. R. Echbach

Mrs. Joseph (widow); about 59 years old; d. Jan. 29, 1863.

John Hamilton, son of James and Ann Hamilton; 8 years, 7 months old; d. Jan 30, 1863.

Ida Isabella, child of Capt. Chas. Miller; 3 years, 2 months old; d. Feb. 10, 1863.

Mr. J. Harpel; about 30 years old; d. March 7, 1863.

James Henry Phillips; about 26 years old; d. March 22, 1863.

Ida, daughter of Alex and Elizabeth Shultz; about 6 years old; d. March 23, 1863.

Mrs. Eliza Ann Rupp, wife of Jacob Rupp; 58 years old; d. March 25, 1863.

Sarah Eliza, daughter of Wm. C. & Rosa A. Crawford; about 6 months, 21 days old; d. March 26, 1863.

Mrs. L. S. Moore; about 54 years old; d. April 24, 1863.

Mrs. Maria L. Frail; about 29 years old; d. April 24, 1863.

Mrs. Amelia A. Groverman; about 54 years old; d. May 2, 1863.

George Schaffner Griffin, son of D. & E. Griffin; about 8 months old; d. June 2, 1863.

George S. Booser; about 53 years old; d. June 3, 1863.

George P. Keener; about 40 years old; d. June 16, 1863.

George Zobleman, died at Georgetown, D.C.; about 65 years old; d. June 13, 1863.

Charles L. Wiesner, son of Gottfried Wiesner; about 13 years old; d. June 22, 1863.

Henry Groverman Buck, son of Alfred and Indiana Buck; about 7 years old; d. June 26, 1863.

Elizabeth Wiesner, daughter of Gottfried Wiesner; 1 year, 11 months, 20 days old; d. July 5, 1863.

Frances Edward Uhl, son [sic] of F. A. & P. Uhl; about 14 years old; d. July 13, 1863.

Mrs. R. Elliot; 36 years old; d. Aug. 16, 1863.

Jacob Rupp; 64 years old; d. Sept. 25, 1863.

Lydia Jane, daughter of George & Cath. Welch; 7 years, 3 months old; d. Oct. 16, 1863.

Rev. Elias Heiner, D.D., for nearly 28 years Pastor of the Congregation; 53 years old; d. Oct. 20, 1863.

Charles A. Kreider; 33 years old; d. Dec. 11, 1863.

1864 - Pastor Rev. E. R. Eschbach

Andrew R. Brunner; 30 years old; Jan. 5, 1864.

Dixon Guy (or Grey), son of Wm. & Sarah Guy (or Grey); 1 year, 4 months old; d. March 6, 1864.

William Schaeffer; 35 years old; d. March 14, 1864.

Andrew Uhl, brother of F. A. Uhl; 48 years old; d. June 9, 1864.

John A. Diffenderffer; 54 yeas old; d. June 27, 1864.

Jas. B. Kauffelt; 44 years old; d. July 18, 1864.

Lottie Kerman, daughter of J. & Emma S. Kerman; 9 months old; d. August 9, 1864.

Mrs. Dorothy Murphy; 65 years old; d. Sept. 7, 1864.

Susie, child of George S. & Laura A. Roberts; 13 months old; d. Sept. 13, 1864.

Miss Elizabeth Etchberger; 69 years old; d. Sept. 12, 1864.

William Haurand (or Hamand); 28 years old; d. Oct. 16, 1864.

Charles M. Cullough, son of Jos. & Ellen Vansant; 4 years old; d. Nov. 6, 1864.

Margaret Virginia, daughter of Jos. & Ellen Vansant; about 2 years, 6 months old; d. Nov. 19, 1864.

William J., son of Wm. & Maggie Harries; about 1 year old; d. Dec. 27, 1864.

1865

Maggie R. Startzman; 1 year, 6 months old; d. Jan. 20, 1865.

Eliza Ann, wife of Julius Schneider; 44 years old; d. Jan. 24, 1865.

Matilda Abbot; about 70 years old; d. Feb. 10, 1865.

Margaret A., wife of Rev. H. J. Comfort; about 35 years old; d. March 15, 1865.

Mrs. Elizabeth McColm; 82 years old; d. March 16, 1865.

Mrs. Dorothy E., wife of Andrew J. Hubbard; 28 years old; d. March 31, 1865.
Alverda Smith; 22 years old; d. April 2, 1865.
Daisy A. B. M. Trail, daughter of R. H. & M. L. Trail; 4 years old; d. July 20, 1865.
Mrs. Ann Diffenderffer; 65 years old; d. Aug. 9, 1865.
Wm. Albert; son of Art D. F. Hubbard; 3 years old; d. Aug. 14, 1865.
Mrs. Phoebe Schaffner, wife of Jacob S.; 82 years old; d. Sept. 17, 1865.
Mrs. Laura A., wife of George Roberts; 26 years old; d. Sept. 26, 1865.
Sol. Louis, son of Charles H. & Cath. Bramble; 3 years, 7 months old; d. Oct. 3, 1865.
Dr. F. E. B. Hintze; 63 years old; d. Oct. 12, 1865.
Mrs. Mary Locher, wife of Geo. H. Locher; 44 years old; d. Nov. 20, 1865.

1866

Henry Michael; 73 years, 1 month old; d. Feb. 3, 1866.
Mary Ann, wife of Gottlieb Locy (or Faey); 49 years old; d. Feb. 10, 1866.
Jacob Hummel; 65 years old; d. April 18, 1866.
Wm. H. Ljame (or Jjame); 48 years old; d. April 19, 1866.
David J. Ross; 46 years old; d. April 20, 1866.
Margaret Phillippina, daughter of Sahm; 1 year old; d. May 1, 1866.
John Elliott; 1 year old; d. May 15, 1866.
Frank, son of John and Hettie V. Hilberg; 8 months old; d. June 24, 1866.
Mrs. Ann Eva Shriver, mother of C. E. Jones; 79 years old; d. June 27, 1866.
Willie, son of S. B. Sommers; 8 months, 2 weeks old; d. June 30, 1866.
Emma Eudora, daughter of Edward L. & Mary E. Gover; about 9 months old; d. July 6, 1866.
Mrs. Elizabeth McConnell; about 80 years old; d. Aug. 5, 1866.
Mrs. Anna M. Hilberg; about 83 years old; d. Aug. 17, 1866.
Cromwell, son of Frank & Jane Lemon; about 2 years old; d. Sept. 18, 1866.
Mrs. Mary Heiner, wife of the late Dr. Heiner; 53 years old; d. Sept. 18, 1866.
Lewis Hewell (or Hervell), former Capt. of police; about 68 years old; d. Sept. 24, 1866.
Lizzie May, daughter of Mary C. Hart; about 10 years old; d. Oct. 3, 1866.

Mrs. Sarah Beard; about 52 years old; d. Oct. 27, 1866.

Edwin Askew, son of Susan Askew; about 28 years old; d. Nov. 5, 1866.

Miss Elizabeth Diffenderffer, sister of Doctor M.D.; about 80 years old; d. Nov. 10, 1866.

Henry Bersch (or Busch); about 80 years old; d. Nov. 21, 1866.

Mrs. Elizabeth Morry (or Money); about 89 years old; d. Nov. 22, 1866.

1867

David, son of Wm. & Mary Vandaniker; about 13 months old; d. Jan. 1, 1867.

Mrs. Elizabeth League; 64 years, 3 months old; d. Jan. 2, 1867.

Mrs. Ann Maria, wife of David Hartzell; about 58 years; d. Jan. 6, 1867.

Joseph D. Matthews; about 58 years old; d. Jan. 9, 1867.

Laura Emma, daughter of Geo. A. & Emma K. Honck; about 10 months old; d. Jan. 15, 1867.

Mary Ross, daughter of Fred and Ximena Otto; about 11 days old; d. Feb. 1, 1867.

Daniel S. Griffing; about 50 years old; d. Feb. 4, 1867.

Isaac Phillips; about 60 years old; d. Feb. 17, 1867.

Lillie Pancoust, daughter of Jos. K. & Maggie A. Milnor; about 1 month old; d. March 11, 1867.

Greenbury Wilson, about 68 years old; d. April 12, 1867.

Mrs. Georgettea Schley; about 60 years old; d. April 13, 1867.

Mrs. Margaret Sturgeon; about 80 years old; d. May 1, 1867.

William P. Lightner; about 47 years old; d. Sept. 29, 1867.

Annie L., infant daughter of Wm. & Annie J. Harris; 23 months, 13 days old; d. Oct. 13, 1867.

Mrs. Mary R., wife of E. C. Falls, Jr.; about 25 years old; d. Oct. 17, 1867.

John Aspril; about 80 years old; d. Nov. 7, 1867.

William Taggert, grandson of David Shotto; about 18 years old; d. Nov. 12, 1867.

Anna Dawling (or Darling), daughter of Benj. & Mary Kidd; 1 year, 2 months old; d. Nov. 13, 1867.

Virginia Smith, alias Vara Montrose; about 28 years; d. Nov. 15, 1867.

1868

Mrs. Charlotte Clockgether; about 69 years old; d. Jan. 23, 1868.

Mrs. Catherine Seesnop; about 78 years old; d. March 26, 1868.

Mrs. Catherine Reigart, wife of Philip Reigart; about 77 years old; d. June 1, 1868.

Mrs. Catherine J. Durst (or Barron); about 53 years old; d. June 18, 1868.

Mrs. Elizabeth J. Kaylor, wife of John Kaylor; about 51 years old; d. July 3, 1868.

Rachel Jenson, daughter of Geo. D. & D. D. Dumey; about 1 1/2 months old; d. Aug. 21, 1868.

Wm. Edward, son of A. D. & Naomi M. Lockhart; about 18 months old; d. Aug. 27, 1868.

George Heiner Crawford, about 21 years old; d. Oct. 18, 1868.

Moses Crawford; about 23 years old; d. Dec. 4, 1868.

Mary Lizzie, infant daughter of Wm. & Matilda Stahl; 14 months old; d. Dec. 23, 1868.

1869

Isabella, daughter of Wm. C. & Louisa Mason; 7 years old; d. Jan. 1, 1869.

Helen Augusta Harrman; about 17 1/2 years old; d. Jan. 9, 1869.

Mrs. Ann Catharine Bramble, wife of Chas. Bramble; about 34 years old; d. Jan. 13, 1869.

Wm. L. Keller; about 43 years old; d. March 4, 1869.

Mrs. Emma Besh; about 23 years old; d. March 4, 1869.

Miss Mary R. Crider; about 39 years old; d. March 8, 1869.

Miss Mary Ann Seltzer; about 56 years old; d. March 11, 1869.

David Ross, son of Fred and Lina Otto; about 10 months old; d. May 11, 1869.

Mary Baker, daughter of Jos. L. & Emilie E. Aspril; about 6 months old; d. June 11, 1869.

Wm. Thomas Crawford; about 17 years old; d. June 16, 1869.

Mrs. Catherine Smith; about 72 years old; d. July 16, 1869.

Mrs. Margaret Spies; about 82 years old; d. Aug. 26, 1869.

Rose Ann Crawford, wife of Wm. C.; about 29 years old; d. Aug. 26, 1869.

Geo. W. Aspril; about 25 years old; d. Sept. 30, 1869.

Margaret Ann Garland; about 33 years old; d. Oct. 20, 1869.

Moses Guy; about 37 years old; d. Oct. 29, 1869.

1870

Levi S. Bowie; about 80 years old; d. Jan. 17, 1870

Laura Virginia Schlodtfeld; about 19 years old; d. Feb. 7, 1870.

Solomon Bramble; 36 years old; d. Feb. 18, 1870.

Emma, daughter of Henry and Sophia Schillinger; 14 years, 19 days old; d. Feb. 25, 1870.

Kate Beckett, daughter of Jos. & Ellen Vansant; 5 years, 5 months old; d. March 22, 1870.

Joseph, son of Joseph & Ellen Vansant; 1 year, 7 months old; d. March 24, 1870.

James, son of Matthew Shaw; 33 years old; d. April 17, 1870.

Mary Charlesetta, daughter of Nicola & Mary E. Bull; 2 years old; d. May 19, 1870.

Mrs. James L. Aspril; about 27 years old; d. May 21, 1870.

Thomas Wingmore; about 60 years old; d. May 31, 1870.

Mrs. Susan Edwards; 77 years old; d. June 6, 1870.

John Blake; 76 years old; d. June 20, 1870.

Mrs. Sarah Ensor; 69 years old; d. June 26, 1870.

Richard Brooks; 54 years old; d. July 5, 1870.

Angeline League; 33 years old; d. Sept. 3, 1870.

Alfred E. Honck; 25 years old; d. Sept. 13, 1870.

Dr. Michael Diffenderffer; 80 years old; d. Sept. 17, 1870.

Dixon, son of Wm. and Sarah Guy; 2 years old; d. Oct. 2, 1870.

1871

Mrs. Mary Ann Pomp, wife of Capt. John Pomp; 38 years old; d. Jan. 15, 1871.

Alexander Levy; 35 years old; d. Feb. 3, 1871.

Howard, son of ---; 17 months old; d. Feb. 28, 1871.

Willie Dechnast, son of A. A. Krantz; 5 1/2 years old; d. March 9, 1871.

Theodore, son of Theodore & Mary J. Shamer; 15 months old; d. March 16, 1871.

Edward Louderman, son of Capt. Thom Pomp; 2 1/2 months old; d. March 24, 1871.
John Martin, son of A. A. & A. K. Krantz; 17 months old; d. April 5, 1871.
Grandchild of Mrs. E. F. Cooke; 2 years old; d. May 2, 1871.
Howard Lee, son of Wm. & Sarah E. Randall; 4 yeas old; d. May 6, 1871.
Robert James, son of Wm. & Mary Moore; 5 years old; d. May 10, 1871.
Mrs. Nancy Vance; 71 years old; d. May 15, 1871.
Mrs. Mary Brandau; 53 years old; d. June 11, 1871.
Honey Groverman; 68 years old; d. Sept. 1, 1871.
Robert C. Elliott; 17 years old; d. Sept. 30, 1871.
Lizzie, daughter of Stewart & Mary Hamilton; 5 months old; d. Dec. 1, 1871.
Susan Askero; 70 years old; d. Dec. 19, 1871.

1872
Wm. Lafevre Eben, son of --- Eben; 3 years, 7 months old; d. Jan. 26, 1872.
Infant son of George Hays; 3 weeks old; d. Feb. 7, 1872.
Elma Poultney, daughter of C. B. & Marg. A. Kleibackers; 19 months, 2 days old; d. Feb. 28, 1872.
Anna Martha Wilson; 83 years old; d. April 3, 1872.
Mrs. Barbara Kepler; 85 years old; d. April 13, 1872.
Benjamin F. B. Constable; 33 years old; d. May 31, 1872.
Mrs. Catharine Klotz; 58 years old; d. June 8, 1872.
Walter C. Hayes; 53 years old; d. June 18, 1872.
Charles Nicholas, son of Nicholas & Mary E. Bull; 1 year old; d. July 3, 1872.
Mrs. Margaret Smith; 56 years old; d. July 7, 1872.
Augustus Mathirt; 73 years old; d. July 15, 1872.
Jacob F. Decker; 79 years old; d. Aug. 12, 1872.
Geo. McDonald Chambers; 33 years old; d. Nov. 16, 1872.
John B. Mathirt; 70 years old; d. Dec. 9, 1872.

1873
Miss Mary Welshoffer; about 50 years old; d. Jan. 4, 1873.

James M. Hook; 47 years old; d. Feb. 16, 1873.
Stewart Hamilton; 28 years old; d. March 25, 1873.
Mrs. Mary A. Philips; 65 years old; d. May 8, 1873.
Richard Brooks; 28 years old; d. June 1, 1873.
James Myers; 52 years old; d. July 1, 1873.
Susan E. Ingman; 62 years old; d. Oct. 11, 1873.
Otis Spear; 72 years old; d. Nov. 1, 1873.
Willie H., son of Henry H. & Annie E. Bautz; 2 1/2 years old; d. Nov. 18, 1873.
Maria Cath. C. Richmond; 35 years old; d. Dec. 7, 1873.
J. Emory Lipton (or Tipton); 35 years old; d. Dec. 29, 1873.

1874
Mrs. Caroline Rehm; 38 years old; d. Jan. 8, 1874.
August Pomplitz; 48 years old; d. Feb. 5, 1874.
W. H. Rehm; 40 years old; d. March 1, 1874.
Nettie Massey; 20 years old; d. April 21, 1874.

1875
George H. Locher, Jr.; 20 years old; bur. Feb. 27, 1875 in Greenmount.
Emanuel Middlekauf; 57 years old; bur. March 30, 1875 in London [Loudon] Park.
Lydia McAllister; 55 years old; bur. April 12, 1875 in Greenmount.
Wm. J. Hagerty; 37 years old; bur. April 17, 1875 in London [Loudon] Park.
Mary F. Durst; 20 years, 2 months, 4 days old; bur. April 19 in Greenmount.
Miss Lizzie Abbess; 35 years old; bur. May 23, 1875 in Baltimore Cemetery.
Joseph Hershey Frick; 3 years, 7 days old; bur. July 10, 1875 in Baltimore Cemetery.
Jesse Crawford; 11 years old; bur Sept. 1, 1875 in Greenmount.
Charles Welshoffer; 50 years old; bur. Sept. 22, 1875 in London [Loudon] Park.
Mrs. Susan Meeke; bur. Oct. 4, 1875 in London [Loudon] Park.
Mrs. Sarah Abbess; 66 years old; bur. Nov. 22, 1875 in Baltimore Cemetery.

1876

Mrs. Sarah Smith; 53 years old; bur. Jan. 13, 1876 in Methodist Phil. Road Cemetery.

Gottleib Schausiel; 51 years old; bur. March 5, 1876 in Baltimore Cemetery.

William F. Cooke; 39 years old; bur. May 7, 1876 in Greenmount.

Ella Blanche Kehm; 11 months old; bur. June 16, 1876 in Baltimore Cemetery.

Margaret Joseph; 89 years old; bur. Sept. 14, 1876 in Presbyterian Cemetery.

Lillie D. Vansant; 14 years, 3 months, 27 days old; bur. Oct. 9, 1876 in Greenmount.

Henrietta Cockey; 77 years old; bur. Oct. 26, 1876 in Westminster, Maryland.

John B. Himbury; 65 years old; bur. Nov. 7, 1876 in Frederick, Maryland.

John Aulbaugh; 66 years old; bur Nov. 23, 1876 in Baltimore Cemetery.

L. D. Keys; 28 years old; bur. Dec. 4, 1876 in Baltimore Cemetery.

James Ensor; 81 years old; bur. Dec. 29, 1876 in Greenmount.

1877

James Garland; bur. in 1877 in Greenmount.

Marie Smith; bur. Feb. 20, 1877 in Methodist Cemetery.

Edward Stewart Shook; 7 weeks old; bur. Feb. 22, 1877 in Baltimore Cemetery.

Maggie Olivia Stuck; 2 years, 2 months, 20 days old; bur. March 19, 1877 in Greenmount.

Francis Hilberg Rodenmayer; 5 years, 3 months, 16 days old; bur. March 2, 1877, in Greenmount.

Alice Amey Bull; 10 months, 28 days old; bur. April 4, 1877, in Greenmount.

Emily Elizabeth Rossiter; 4 months, 20 days old; bur June 21 in Woodward Hill.

David Charles Henry Stone; 2 months, 9 days old; bur. June 25, 1877 near Westm. Cememtery.

Index

-A-

ABBES, Ann Elizabeth, 160
  John, 300
  Martha, 160
  Sarah C., 157
ABBESS, Lizzie, 265, 311
  Sarah, 265, 311
ABBOT, Matilda, 305
ABBOTT, Armer G., 241
  Clementine, 246
  Eleanora W., 234
  George A., 246
  John Edward, 246
ABRAHAMS, Peggi, 48
  Rebecca, 57
ABRAMS, Alice M., 242
ACHE, Frederick, 191
  Margaret, 191
  Sarah Elizabeth, 191
ACHENBACH, Anna Elisabeth, 39, 45, 80, 83, 90
  Anna Katharina, 45
  Anna Louisa, 106
  Anna Maria, 80
  Johann Kraft, 39, 45
  Johannes, 106
  Kraft, 46, 80, 90, 106
  Margareth, 144
ACHEY, Charles F., 195
  Emma, 184
  Frank, 195
  Fred, 186
  Frederick, 184
  Fredrick, 193
  Mar., 184
  Margaret, 186, 193, 195
  Mary Louisa, 193
ACKLAND, James, 170
  Julia A., 165
ACTON, Lillian, 235

ADAM, Elisabeth, 44
ADAMS, Alex, 66
  Alexander, 16, 24, 76
  Andrew Jackson, 204
  Barbara, 204, 206
  Catharina, 24
  Cathrina, 16
  David, 156
  Elizabeth, 206
  James, 16
  Johannes, 66
  Josie R., 229
  Mary V., 239
  Samuel, 54
  William, 146, 204, 206
ADKINSON, Elisabeth, 80
  Maria, 80
ADLERMUSH, Dorothea, 70
AFTERHEIDE, Maria Elisabeth, 142
AIKEN, Harriet E., 158
  Robert E., 158
AIREY, Ida, 242
  Laura V., 242
ALANER, Alexander, 19
  Cathrina, 19
  Elisabeth, 19
  Mary, 19
ALBAUGH, Daniel J., 172
  Lola May, 252
  Mabel Adele, 251
  Matilda F., 251, 252
  William Edward, 251, 252
ALBERGER, Hiob, 46
  Rebecca, 46
  Samuel, 46
ALBERS, Eva, 35, 39, 121
  Eva Barbara, 41
  Henric Nicolaus, 35
  Henry, 205

Luder, 39, 279
Ludwig, 39
Lueder, 35, 56
Mathilde Elisabeth, 41
Rebecca, 205
Salomon Gottlieb, 57
Sophia Matilda, 205
ALBRECHT, Elisabeth, 46
  Mr., 103
ALERS, Heinrich Wilhelm, 115
ALEXANDER, Ariander, 182
  Elizabeth Bowman, 182
  John C., 182
ALFORD, Elizabeth, 152
ALGIE, Jane, 266
ALLBERGER, Eliza, 147
ALLEN, ---, 203
  Alexander, 188
  Cathrin Lusnop, 200
  Cornelia, 177, 178, 181, 213, 216, 221
  David Henry, 182
  Edwin Larr, 181
  Edwin S. J., 301
  Elenezar N., 150
  Ino. E., 213
  James Edwards, 178
  John, 155, 178, 182, 185, 188
  John E., 158, 177, 178, 181, 216
  John Ecklen, 221
  John Elias, 185
  John H., 200
  Jud E., 298
  Jus. E., 221
  Lewis Selby, 277
  Mary, 152, 178, 182, 185, 188
  Mary Ella, 177

Index

Robert, 297
Rosa, 240
Sarah Jane, 158, 213
ALLENBACH, Johan, 87
ALLENS, Catharine, 196
  Joseph, 196
  William, 196
ALLISEN, Heinrich, 138
ALLISON, Robert, 156
  Virginia Q., 232
ALLS, George B., 233
ALLSPACH, ---, 77
  Barbara, 14, 19
  Cathrina, 52
  David, 14, 16, 19
  Frantz, 14
  Friedrich, 14
  Susanna, 14
ALMER, Alexander, 19, 76
  Cathrina, 19
  Elisabeth, 19
  Mary, 19
ALNS, Lewis, 162
ALPACHTNER, ---, 77
ALSFELD, Elisabeth, 97
  Johann, 287
  Johannes, 97, 287
  John, 287
ALSFELT, John, 139
AMELUNG, John P. W., 145
AMEREIHU, Gertrude, 235
AMEY, Susan, 146
AMOS, Balinda P., 157
  Florence V., 243
AMY, Henry, 149
ANDERSEN, Annie, 165
ANDERSON, Charles Montgomery, 225
  Charlotte E., 224, 225

Edward, 130
Estelle, 235
Frances Olevia, 224
Gustavus, 130, 205
Ino. H., 225
John H., 224
Nancy, 130, 205
William Thomas, 205
Yanetta, 197
ANDOL, Carolina, 109
  Gregorius, 109
  Maria, 109
ANDRE, Rebecca, 85
ANDREE, Michael, 122
  Rebecca, 139
ANDREW, Hugh, 236
ANDREWS, Mary Ann, 159
ANDSENS, Mary Ann, 159
ANSPACH, Dr., 172
  Elisabeth, 144
  F. A., 172
  Johan Adam, 96
  Maria Catharina, 96
  Miss, 82
ANTONIO, Henry, 149
APPEL, Carl H., 264
  Carl Staley, 264
  Charles H., 244
  Mary T., 264
APPLEBY, Berdie Irene, 262
  Bessie Shower, 262
  Emma, 262
  Emma Agnes, 262
  Harrison Benjamin, 262
  May Edwards, 262
  Oliver Lemuel, 262
  Otto Eugene, 262
  Perry Ellsworth, 262
  Robert Ambrose, 262

William Ellsworth, 262
APPOLD, Ann, 147
  Nelly, 281
APRILL, David J., 302
ARD, Catharina, 83
  Johan, 83
  Maria, 83
  Nancy, 83
ARDIN, David, 168
ARENZ, George, 249, 270
  Marg., 249
  Nicholas, 249
ARGELUS, G. D.
  Thomas, 203
  Philipp Jacob, 203
  Rebecca, 203
  Thomas, 203
ARMIGER, Alice, 218
  Henrietta, 218
  Richard, 164, 218
ARMSTRONG, George W., 237
  James, 149
  John C., 240
ARNETT, James W., 170
ARNOLD, James Elsworth, 256
  Joh. Adam, 22
  Joh. Anton, 22
  Johann, 9
  John Henry, 256
  Joseph Franklin, 253, 256
  Margaretha, 22
  Mary Alice, 253, 256
  Rebecca, 55
  Sarah, 163
  William Franklin, 253
ARQUIT, Ely, 148
ARRICO, Carrico, 237
ARSPACH, Constantina, 91
  Johan Friederich, 91

Index

ASH, William H., 238
ASKEN, Thomas W., 146
ASKERO, Susan, 310
ASKEW, Edwin, 307
  Susan, 307
  W. H., 222
ASPRAL, C. E., 182
  C.E., 181
  David J., 181
  David Springer, 182
  David T., 182
  George Washington, 181
ASPRIEL, Bessie, 224
  Fannie J., 224
  Go. W., 224
ASPRIL, Ann Elizabeth, 207
  Anna Lettitia, 224
  David J., 213
  Emilie E., 225, 308
  Emma E., 224
  George W., 228, 308
  Imogen, 213
  James L., 224, 225, 309
  James Lightner, 224
  John, 307
  Joseph L., 308
  Mary, 165, 213
  Mary Ann, 207
  Mary Baker, 225, 308
  William A., 207
ASPRILL, Eliza Letetia, 303
ASPROL, C.E., 181
  David J., 181
  George Washington, 181
AST, William F., 171
ATKINSON, Albein Alfred Alcock, 189
  David, 189
  Sarah, 189

ATWELL, Samuel B. (T.), 150
AUBINOE, Mary Elizabeth, 240
AUBINOS, Mary Elizabeth, 240
AUCHY, Frederick, 150
AUGUSTIN, Anna Elisabeth, 11
  Anna Elisabetha, 8
  Christof Henrich, 11
  Christoph Henrich, 8
  Margaretha, 138
  Margretha, 8
  Susanna Henrietha, 11
AUGUSTUS, Johannes, 4
AUL, Rachael, 150
AULABAUGH, John, 265
AULBAUGH, John, 312
AULCORN, John, 220
  Nancy, 220
  Robert, 220
AULL, Anna S., 239
AULT, Hanna, 154
AUSTIN, Caroline, 206
  Clara T., 243
  Georg, 206
  Philip Hiss, 206
AUSTINE, Ida B., 242
AYRES, Elizabeth, 168

-B-
BAARTEHER, John, 194
  Sarah, 194
  William George Washington, 194
BAARTEKSER, John, 197
  Nancy, 197
  Sarah, 197
  Yanetta, 197
BABEG, Alexander Stephens, 216

  Mary, 216
  Matilda Irene, 216
  Thaddeus, 216
BABLER, Charlotta, 134
  Christina, 104, 117, 134
  Georg, 104, 117, 134, 141
  Jacob, 104
BABYLON, Agnes, 246
  Janetta Arthur, 246
  John, 246
BACHER, Adelheit, 95
  Christian C., 95
BACHLEY, John, 51
BACHMAN, Cathrina, 15
  Joh. Georg, 15
BACKER, Mr., 190
BAD, David, 24
  Elisabeth, 24
  Margaretha, 24
BADEN, Jane, 191
  William D., 191
  William Henry, 191
BADER, Dominic, 56
  Elisabeth, 62, 205
  Johann, 3
  Johannes, 14, 62
  Margareth, 14
  Margaretha, 3, 62
  Mr., 89
  Peter, 205
  Susanna, 14
  Wilhelm Philip, 89
BADLER, Christina, 122
BAHM, Hanna, 54
BAHNERT, Joh. George, 30
  Mr., 30
BAHSAGE, Hannah, 54
BAIER, Johannes, 52
  Ludwig, 64
BAILEY, Benjamin, 236

Josiah, 149
Montgomery H., 154
BAIN, Helen, 158
BAIRD, Robert, 150
BAIRLEY, John, 171
BAKEN, John Henry, 154
BAKER, Adam Seasnop B., 225
Ann Rebecca, 198
Annie E., 231
Appalonia Mina Whelan, 208
Bertha Gertrude, 255
Caroline A., 173
Caroline Agusta, 184
Cath., 215, 219
Cath. Franciscus, 185
Catharina Elizabeth, 191
Catharine, 211
Catharine F., 228
Catherine, 152, 209
Chadwick Murray, 254
Charles Henry, 188
Charles T., 254
Charlot, 198
Charlotte, 195, 301
Christian, 191
Daniel, 153
Elizabeth, 188, 203
Elizabeth I., 236
Fanny Erickson, 215
Francis Edward, 219
Frederick William, 188
George, 184, 188, 189, 191, 215
George Peter, 189
Henrietta, 164, 209
Henry, 150, 188, 213
Henry S., 233, 252, 255
Ida Levenia, 219
Ino. George, 211
Ino. H., 225

Isaac, 195, 198
isaac, 147
J. G., 209
J. H., 184, 185
James Franklin, 251
John April, 217
John G., 219
John H., 208
John Henry, 157, 208
John L., 239
Kate Ely, 213
Lillie, 252, 255
M., 184, 185
Mabel M., 254
Margaret Ann, 211
Maria, 208, 225
Maria Elizabeth, 184
Mary, 209, 217
Mary Ann, 184, 188, 189, 191
Mary Charlotte, 207
Mary Frances, 195
Mary Jane, 184
Mary R., 228
Minnie Christian, 252
Mrs., 225
Peter, 203
Sarah Jane, 251, 252
Sophia B., 275
Susanna, 207, 209, 213
W. A., 224
William, 251, 252
William A., 165, 209, 217
William Additer, 209
William Albers, 203
William Alfred, 252
William Berger, 209
William C., 168, 207, 209, 213, 304
BALD, Cardo, 121
Catharina, 40
Christian, 40

Jacob, 40
BALEY, Rosina, 157
BALHRAUER, Cathrina, 52
BALL, Eliza, 145
Georgianna, 301
Mr., 296
BALLAUF, Mathilda, 166
BALLOCH, Archibald Robinson, 207
Cath. J., 207
James, 207
Kate, 207
BALTZER, John, 145
BAMBERGER, Arnold, 7
Elisabeth, 7
Johannes, 7
BAMFLER, Johann, 56
BAMPFLER, Catharina, 39
Catharina Elisabeth, 39
Johannes, 39
BANCKERT, Abraham, 120
Catherina, 141
Jacob, 117
Maria, 117
Peter, 120
BANCKS, Maria Margaretha, 49
BANDEL, Annie, 233
Georg W., 157
BANGE, Catharina, 100
Edwin C., 234
Elisabeth, 90, 97
Franciscus, 100, 140
Frantz, 97
Georg, 97, 139
Georg Frantz, 286
Georg Franz, 40, 41
Johan Georg, 90
Johann Georg, 47

Index

Johann George, 40
Johanna Maria, 47
Katharina, 41, 47
Leonhard, 38, 41, 47
Leonmhard, 281
Maria Susanna, 90
Wilhelm, 100
BANGER, Daniel, 29
Elizabeth League, 219
Mary M., 219
W., 219
BANKERT, Anna, 127
Annie Catherine, 254
David, 127
Granville O., 254
Mary S., 254
Peter, 127
BANKS, Mary, 149
BANTZ, Catharina, 64
Johannes, 55
BAPTISTE, John, 258
M. Mary, 258
Raymond Elvene, 258
BARBINI, Charles, 52
BARCHED, Clara, 171
BARCKER, Julian, 140
BARDORF, Mr., 301
BARE, Elisabeth, 98
Jacob, 98, 116
Johannes Steg, 98
Juliana, 116
BARETT, Isabella G., 166
BARGER, Elizabeth League, 219
G. W., 303
George W., 208
Georgianna Ida, 177
Lina Esten, 216
M. M., 177, 303
Marg. M., 216
Mary Grace, 208

Mary M., 208, 219
Mr., 298
W., 219
Washington, 161, 177, 216
BARGETT, John, 55
BARGNET, Mary Ann, 146
BARLES, Anna Catharina, 35
Henrich, 35
BARLET, Maria Elisabeth, 114
BARLOW, Charles A., 238
BARNHILL, Catherine, 263
Katie Ruth, 263
Samuel, 263
BAROUX, Sallie C., 235
BARRETT, Emma, 274
James H., 267
John L., 166
Rachael, 159
BARRON, Catherine J., 308
Sarah C., 166
Sarah F., 166
BARSTEKSER, John, 197
Nancy, 197
Sarah, 197
Yanetta, 197
BARTH, J. H., 217
Matilda, 217
Sophia Florence, 217
BARTHAUER, Anna Regina, 81
Johan Conrad, 81
Johanna Louisa, 81
BARTHAUFER, Johan Konrad, 94
Johanna Regina, 94
BARTHAUSEN, Johan Conrad, 98

Johan Henrich Christoph, 98
Johanna Regina, 98
BARTHOLOMAY, Frederick, 235
BARTLING, Thomas E., 160
BASSLER, Fritz, 53
BATES, Maggie F., 243
BATTEE, John Walter, 178
Richard, 178
Susan, 178
BATTERSON, David, 123
Georg, 123
Louisa, 123
Maria, 123
BAUER, Christina, 15
Elisabeth, 15, 144
Eva, 102
Herta, 15
Joh. Georg, 15
Johannes, 15, 22
Marg., 200
Margaret, 23
Martin, 23, 200
Wilhelm, 15, 102
Wilhelm Cutherish, 102
Willhelm, 51
William Edward, 200
BAUGE, Claudius Earl, 260
Edwin C., 260
Lenora F., 260
BAUGHN, Cath., 216
James Edgar, 216
James W., 216
BAURMAN, Beniamin, 94
Elisabeth, 94
Johan, 94
Maria Elisabeth, 94

318 Index

BAUSMAN, Beniamin, 112, 284, 290
  Benjamin, 89
  Elisabeth, 89
  George Washington, 112
  Johan, 89
  Johan Friederich, 284
  Johann Friderich, 89
  John, 112
BAUSMANN, Beniamin, 107
  Johan, 107
  Lorentz, 55
  Sophia Dorothea, 107
BAUTZ, Annie E., 247, 248, 311
  Carrie Warfield, 247
  Harry H., 248
  Henry H., 247, 311
  Henry Harwood, 248
  Willie H., 311
BAVARIUM, Lizzie, 229
BAXTER, Jessie, 264
  Margory, 264
  Mary McGillivray, 264
  Sarah, 139
  William, 243
  William Carswell, 264
BAYER, Catharina, 6
  Cathrina, 17
  Georg, 6
  Georg Phillip, 6
  Jacob, 14, 148
  Ludwig, 14, 17, 52
  Maria, 14, 17
BAYERLE, Conrad, 22
  Georg, 22
  Magdalena, 22
BAYLY, Mary Jane, 165
BAYNE, Samuel J., 233
BEACH, Sarah, 142
BEAGOR, Richard, 55

BEALL, Sarah, 147
BEAM, Henry C., 186
  Margaret, 186
  Mary Elizabeth, 186
BEAN, Elias, 44
  Elisabeth, 44
  Robert, 44
BEANS, Anna May, 255
  Barbara, 251
  Barbara A., 255, 258
  Harry H., 251
  Harry Himmelwright, 251
  Harry R., 255, 258
  Henry R., 233
  Lilbourn Irvine, 258
  Ruth Olinda, 258
BEAR, Rebecca, 151
BEARD, Eliza, 162
  Elmira, 222, 223
  George W., 222, 223
  Harriet, 157, 163
  Harvey, 231
  Lillie May, 223
  Robert C., 169
  Robert Franklin, 222
  Sarah, 307
BEARTCHEER, Christopher, 152
BEATTY, Cornelia Ann, 156
BEAYOR, Richard, 55
BECK, Appollonia, 99
  Augustus, 239
  Johann, 99
BECKER, Adelheid, 81, 133
  Adelheit, 86, 106
  Captain, 65
  Carl Friederich, 114
  Catharina, 90, 94, 102, 122, 286

  Charlotta Christina Philippina, 47, 76
  Christian L., 174
  Christian Ludwig, 80, 81
  Christina, 52
  Elisabeth, 90, 91, 102, 113, 205
  Heinrich, 90, 94, 102, 286, 288, 290
  Johan, 90
  Johan Heinrich, 91, 138
  Johann Jost, 36
  John Peter, 127
  Lillie, 276
  Louisa, 102, 288
  Mariana, 102
  Martin, 67
  Peter, 90, 91, 102, 113, 122, 127, 139, 205
  Rosina, 113
  Simon, 114
BECKERIN, Adelhein, 85
BECKIER, Conrad, 20
  Elisabeth, 20
  Peter, 20
BECKLI, Heinrich, 83
  Maria, 83
BEEBE, Jeremiah T., 164
BEEFELT, Alice, 258
  Arthur Conrad, 258
  Rose Myrtle, 258
BEEKER, Nora F., 234
BEELER, Clara M., 241
BEERMAN, Amalia, 142
BEGT, Catharina, 16
  David, 16
  Peter, 16, 75
BEILEFELD, Elisabeth, 139
BEILS, Johan Francis, 123
  William, 123
BEITEL, Maria Katharina, 79

Index

Philipp, 79
Phillip, 57
BEIZEL, Anna Gertraud, 46
  Johannes, 46
  Magdalena, 46
  Peter, 46
  Philip, 46
BELBIN, Charles J., 232
  Ella May, 224, 239
  Martha, 224
  Naomi, 276
  Rosanna, 271
  William, 224
  William H., 276
BELL, C. W., 229
  Emma Louesa, 183
  Hattie M., 236
  James H., 247
  James W., 233
  Jemina R., 168
  Lewis Rossiter, 247
  Lizzie C., 247
  Margaret, 151
  Maria Elizabeth, 282
  Mary, 183
  Mary Ann, 145
  Richard, 142
  William, 183
BELTZ, Anna Elisabeth, 26
  Elisabeth, 76
  George, 26, 76
  Jacob, 71
  Wilhelm, 71
BELZ, Georg, 35
  George, 38
  Maria Elisabeth, 35, 38
  Wilhelm, 35
BENCKER, Louisa, 86
BENCKERT, Johanna, 97
  Johannes, 97

Peter, 97
BEND, Elisabeth, 32
  Joh. George, 30
  Johann, 32
  John, 30
  Margaretha, 30, 32
BENDER, Barbara, 6
  Daniel, 6
  Gottfried, 6
  Jacob, 55
  Louisa, 22
  Margretha, 6
  Maria Elisabetha, 6
  Peter, 22
BENFER, Anna Elisabeth, 80
  Catharina, 86
  Johann, 80
  Johannes, 43, 86
  Kath., 80
  Katharina, 43
  Tobias, 86
BENGEL, John, 60
BENJAMIN, Salomon, 140
BENKERT, Hanna, 45
  Nicolaus, 45
  Peter, 45
BENNER, Louis, 76
BENNET, Geo. J., 169
BENNETT, Agnes, 212, 300
  Alfred, 171
  Amy C., 242
  Blanche, 233
  Cornelius DeBeet, 212
  Emma Louise, 261
  G. D., 301
  George, 146
  George J., 212
  Harvey, 301
  Jacob, 261

Katie, 261
Mamie, 240
Minnie K., 242
BENNIWEL, Elisabeth Burr, 137
  Jacob Hardy, 137
  James Baly, 137
  Leydi Schally, 137
  Mr., 137
  Schally Kelim, 137
BENOIT, Alfred Henry, 256, 273
  C. F. Gaston, 256
  Charles Ferd. Gaston, 253, 260
  Claribel W., 256
  Claribel Wright, 253, 260
  Ethel, 260
  Gaston, 254
  James Van Dyke Stewart, 253
  James Vandyke Stewart, 273
  Nathalie, 270
BENSEMAN, Johan Friederich, 126
BENSON, Catharina, 138
  Elisabeth Anna, 47
  Harry Edgar, 259
  Joseph E., 272
  Laura May, 257, 259
  Lizzie, 267
  Mary Ellen, 257
  Peter, 39, 42, 44, 47, 279, 280
  Rebecca, 39, 42, 44, 47, 279
  Rebecka, 280
  Sarah A., 276
  Sophia, 77
  Sophia Katharina, 42, 280
  Theresia Dorothea, 39, 279

William H., 237, 257, 259
BENTLEY, Thomas, 154
BENTZ, Andrew, 210
  Charlotta, 134
  Mary Cath., 210
  William Henry, 210
BENTZEL, Baltzer, 292
  Johann, 57
  Maria Sophia, 62
BENZEL, Elisabeth, 79
  Johann, 79
  Louise, 79
  Malzer, 65
  Sophia, 65
BENZEN, Joh., 69
  Margaretha Adelheid, 33, 69
  Peter, 33
  Rebecca, 33, 69
BEOHEME, Aug. C. H., 159
BERANS, Mary J., 272
BERBAY, Anna Maria, 15
  John, 15
  Juliana, 15
BERCKERT, Peter, 284
BERCKHAUS, Anna, 109
  Emilia Carolina, 109
  Heinrich, 109
BERCKMANN, Sophia, 57
BERENS, John H., 238
BERG, Peggy, 56
  Wilhelm, 67
BERGAMOSIE, David L., 229
BERGER, Catherine, 204
  Diedrich, 14
  Heinrich, 133, 292
  Jacob Alexander, 125
  Johan, 125, 133, 292
  Johannes, 140
  John, 204
  John Henry, 204
  Joseph B., 167
  Margareth, 14
  Maria, 133
  Mary, 14, 75
  Mrs., 300
BERGHAUER, Johan Conrad, 113
  Sophia, 113
BERGHAUS, Emilia Carolina, 289
  Heinrich, 289
BERGMAN, Anna Maria Elisabeth, 90
  Conrad, 90, 112, 130, 133
  Elisabeth, 90, 130
  Jacob, 130
  Otilia Margaretha, 133
BERHORF, ---, 302
BERKEIMER, Michael L., 166
BERKLY, Jeminiah, 54
BERNAND, Cath., 202
  John Martin Johannes, 202
BERNARDS, James, 23
BERNED, ---, 77
  Andreas, 3
  Barbara, 3
  Elisabeth, 3
BERNED(IN), Elisabetha, 3
BERNET, ---, 77
  Andreas, 13
  Elisabeth, 13, 54
  Wilhelm, 13
BERNHARD, Anna, 17, 21, 133
  Carl, 17
  Elisabeth, 44
  Jacob, 17
BERNHARDT, Anna, 23
  Heinrich, 23
  Jacob, 23, 26
  Susanna, 26
BERNY, Betzie, 51
BERRY, Ann Rebecca, 302
  Anna A., 213
  Anna R., 208
  Charles Hardesty, 302
  Charles Horaesty, 215
  Charlotte Emily, 208
  Frank, 302
  Frank Baker, 213
  MacKall Cox, 207
  Rebecca, 207, 215, 218
  William, 207, 208, 213, 215, 302
  William Benjamin, 218
BERSCH, Elizabeth, 217
  Elizabeth, A. 217
  Elizabeth Ann, 179
  Heinrich, 144
  Henry, 160, 179, 217, 307
  Henry Auguste, 217
  Mary Ann, 179
  William, 157
BERSH, Elizabeth Ann, 211
  Ella, 211
  H., 211
  Henry, 127, 132
  Johanna Amalia Maria, 127
  Maria, 127
  Susanna, 183
  William, 132, 183
  William Henry, 183
BERTHAUER, Johan Christian, 89
  Johan Conrad, 89
  Johanna Regina, 89
BERTHOEF, C. T., 218

Index

Caroline Elizabeth, 218
D. H., 218
BERTHOLF, Albert Seely, 181
C. J., 181
Charles Edgar, 181
Cornelia, 214
James H., 181, 214
James Henry, 181
Martha Streng, 214
Ruth Emma, 181
BERTHORF, Mrs., 301
BERTRAM, Charles J., 235
BERTRANT, Joseph, 94
Rosina, 94
BESH, Emma, 308
BEST, Mary S., 242
Peter, 75
William, 298
BESTOLAY, John, 172
BETCHER, Catharine, 179
Henry, 179
John Henry, 179
BETEFUHR, Eliza Wilhelmina, 144
BETSON, Harriet, 150
BETTEE, Richard, 159
BETZ, Mary, 52
BEUFLER, Caroline, 217
Elijah, 217
Mary Ann, 217
Priscilla, 217
Rachael, 217
Rebecca, 217
BEUTEL, Philip, 291
BEUTZEL, Frederick, 151
BEVAN, Joseph, 184
Sarah, 184
BEVANS, Edward, 274

Mary J., 272
BEVER, Gerhardt Henry, 153
BEVERBACH, Jacob, 56
BEVEREDGE, Ann Maria, 206
BEW, Elizabeth, 194
Lamech Tubalcain, 194
Richard, 194
BIANS, Susan E., 276
BICHLEY, Henry L., 154
BICKEL, Elizabeth, 264
Fred G., 264
Lillian Katherine, 264
BIDDEL, Abraham, 116
Elisabeth, 116
Eva Maria, 116
Johan, 116
Richard, 116
BIDDINGER, William, 172
BIDDISON, Edna Margaret, 260
Emma S., 260
Thomas E., 239, 260
BIEN, Bessie Ellen, 264
Earnest W., 244
Earnest William, 264
Edgar Earnest, 264
BIER, Catharina, 128
Jacob, 128
Sophia Barbara, 128
Susanna, 128
BIERLERIN, Sabina Elis., 56
BIGHAM, J. B., 227
John, 229
Rachel Ann, 227
Sarah E., 240
Sarah Etta, 227
BIGHAU, Rachel, 269
BILLMIRE, Vernon Webb, 277

BINDER, Henrich, 22, 76
BINDERIN, Maria, 53
BINGEL, Cathrina, 52
Widow, 61
BINNIX, Mary C., 180
Thomas H., 180
William Clagget, 180
BINNS, Thomas Lee Sim, 149
BINSEL, Baltzer, 293
Jacob, 83
Johan, 83
Louisa, 83
Samuel, 287
BINTZEL, Dorothea, 22, 281
Joh. Georg, 22
Johannes, 22
Samuel, 22
BIRGENHAM, Frantz Henrich Wilhelm, 36
Tabitha, 36
BIRGMAN, Conrad, 99, 139
Elisabeth, 99
Friederich Jacob Wilhelm, 99
BISSEL, Annie C., 234
BISTER, Anna Catharina, 206
Johann, 206
Susann, 206
BISTOR, Johan, 145
BITCH, Samuel, 55
BIXBY, Fayette, 232
BIXLER, E., 300
Louis A., 161
BLACK, Carrie E., 243
Elizabeth S., 237
William H., 261
BLACKBURN, Mary E., 232
BLADEN, Martha A., 161

Index

BLAKE, John, 309
  John Andrew, 248
  Lovinia, 248
  Thomas, 241
BLANCHORD,
  Elizabeth A., 166
BLANCK, J. Arends, 143
BLANEY, Bertha May, 257
  George Washington, 257
  Helen Beatrice, 257
  Mattie, 236
BLATIN, Irene, 140
BLATNER, Fanny, 141
  Mathias, 126
  Vrena, 126
BLECHRODT,
  Elisabeth, 29
  Henrich, 29, 67
  Mr., 65, 67
BLEEZE, Annie L., 242
BLEICHROTH, Georg
  Heinrich, 11, 280
  Maria Cathr., 11
  Mr., 59
  Sophia Dorothea, 11
BLERHRODT,
  Elisabeth, 25
  Henrich, 25
  Sophia Juliana, 25
BLISS, Charles T., 240
BLOCK, Johannes, 25
  Sophie, 25
BLOOD, William, 167
BLOODGOOD, Sylvanis, 158
  Sylvanus, 158
BLOT, Elisabeth, 86
  Johann, 56
BOBERT, Andreas, 14
BOCHMEG, George
  Friderich, 62

BOCHMER, George
  Friderich, 62
BOCK, Anna, 114
  Mr., 122
BODE, Charles, 248
  Christina H., 248
  Helena Gertrude, 248
BODEN, Elizabeth Ann, 167
BODENSICK, Henrich, 57
BODIN, Maria, 81
BODLEY, John, 147
BOEHME, Bernard C., 255
  Bernard Schambach, 255
  Bernhard, 233, 252
  Carl Ludwig, 51
  Charles L., 174
  Clara R., 252, 255, 272
  Lilian Emma, 252
  Susanna, 5
BOEHMER, Elisabeth, 24
  Friderich, 24
BOEM, Georg, 18
  Sara B., 18
BOHLKEN, Andrew, 243
BOHM, Anna Elisabetha, 4
  Catharina, 4
  Elias, 13
  Georg, 13, 14
  Joh. Willy, 13
  Johanna Florina, 283
  Maria, 13
  Mary, 14
  Mr., 283
  Phillip, 4
  Sara, 13, 14
  Willy, 12, 13
BOHMER, Sara, 65
  Widow, 65

BOHN, Anna Marg., 230
BOK, Anna, 8
  Johannes, 8
BOLAND, Louisa, 253
  Lulu, 253
  Mr., 253
BOLBIN, Madame, 88
BOLGIANO, John, 154
BOLK, Cardo, 143
BOLLINGER, Charles
  Wilbert, 262, 278
  Frances Edward, 263
  John W., 262, 263
  Leah, 262, 263
  William Carlton, 278
BOLLMAN, Anna
  Catharina, 88
  Heinrich, 88
  Johan Georg, 98
  John Thomas, 107
  Margareth, 107
  Thomas, 98, 107, 282
  Wilhelm, 282, 284
BOLMAN, Barbara, 85
  Mariana, 85
  Thomas, 85
BOND, Cathrina, 51
  John, 153, 163
  Joseph, 148
BONDONY, Sara, 54
BONI, Claus, 53
BONIFACE, George C., 170
BONIS, Sarah Ann, 147
BONN, Ann Mary, 198
  Anthony, 149, 198
  Cathrine, 198
  Joseph, 198
BONNES, Anna, 85
  Christina, 85
  Thomas, 85
BONNET, Anna, 85

Christina, 85
Thomas, 85
BONTON, Wilhelmine, 40
BOOCHEL, Elisabeth, 15
  Ida, 15
  Matheiss, 15
BOOKER, Emma V., 243
  Minnie, 243
BOOKMAN, Henry, 165
BOOL, Maria Louisa, 162
BOON, Harriet J., 239
BOORER, Carl, 20
BOOS, Anna Elisabetha, 8
  Anna Margretha, 8
  Nicolaus, 8
BOOSE, Jacob, 288
BOOSER, George S., 304
BOOSS, Adam, 11
  Cathrina, 11
  Elisabeth, 11
  Henrich, 60
  Nicolaus, 52
BOOSS(IN), Anna Margareth, 60
BOOTHE, Esther, 232
BORDLY, Elisabeth, 286
BORMAN, Anna, 139
  Anna Catharina, 288
  Johan Heinrich, 101
  Martin, 291
BORNET, Elisabeth, 54
BORNITZ, Emma, 234
BORNS, Catharina, 7
BOROMAN, Andrew, 192
  Andrew Jackson, 192
  Catharine, 192
BORTNER, Charles A., 234, 254
  Charles Ervin, 254
  Theoda M., 254
  Theoda May, 259
BOSCH, Cath., 35

Catharina, 30
Jacob, 30
Samuel, 35
Wilhelm, 30
BOSH, Anna Maria, 68
  Joh., 68
BOSH(EN), N., 59
BOSHERT, Jacob, 84
BOSLEY, Helen A., 243
BOSS, Cathrina, 12
  Elisabeth, 12
  Nicolaus, 12
  Peter, 52
BOSSER, Cathrina, 51
BOSSERT, Jacob, 84
BOSSSER, Cathrina, 77
BOSWELL, Mary, 240
BOTELER, Augustus L., 240
BOTER, Helena Johanna, 91
BOUCHER, Elizabeth, 261
BOUCHET, Catherine, 241
BOUIS, Sarah Ann, 147
BOURFORD, Georg, 7
  Paley, 7
  Sahra, 7
BOURNE, Agnes May, 262
  Elizabeth, 262
  William Dykes, 262
BOWDEN, Agnes M., 159
  Irving N., 238
BOWER, Barbara, 159
BOWERS, Amelia, 234
  Annie M., 231
  Christian, 266
  Elizabeth, 196
  Elmira Ann, 203
  George Edwin, 203

John, 267
Margaret, 203
Martin, 203
Sus., 203
BOWIE, Levi S., 309
  Mrs., 302
  William, 304
BOWMAN, Andrew, 190, 194
  Catharine, 194
  Catherine, 190
  George Washington Samuel, 194
  Mary Catherine Scesnop, 190
BOYCE, Harriet A., 230
BOYD, Rebecca M., 228
BOYER, Albert J., 212, 302
  Albert Jacob, 204
  Ann Maria, 168
  Anna Maria, 130
  Catharine, 299
  Charles Heiner, 191
  Edward Bradley, 249
  Ella D., 249
  Ella Dahlgren, 250
  George A., 249
  George H., 250
  George Stafford, 188
  Heinrich Ludewig, 134
  Irene Attick, 250
  Isabel Cath., 199
  Jacob, 119, 130, 134, 148, 188, 191, 197, 199, 204
  John W., 164
  John William, 197
  Louis Gibson, 212, 300
  Margaret, 204
  Margaretha, 119, 130, 134
  Maria, 119, 291
  Michael, 119

Mr., 291
Nicholas B., 298
Nicholas E., 298
Rachel C., 212
Sarah, 188, 191, 197, 199, 301
BOYES, Sarah, 40
BOYS, Sarah, 50
BRACH, Anna Gertraud, 44
Benjamin, 44
Ferdinand, 57
BRACKENBRIDGE, Fanny, 163
BRADLEY, Alice Lillian, 252
Blanche, 270
Emma A., 232
James Alfred, 252
James L., 231
Lillian Frances, 252
Mary N., 231
BRADY, Mary E., 234
BRAKIN, Davis, 151
Thomas, 149
BRAMBLE, Ann Catharine, 308
Cath., 221, 306
Charles, 308
Charles H., 221, 229, 306
Sol. Louis, 306
Solomon, 309
Solomon Louis Bayers, 221
BRAMBLY, Thomas, 151
BRAND, Christina, 52
Wilhelm, 117
BRANDAN, Edward F., 229
BRANDAU, Charles, 232, 269
Charles Edward Fred, 245

Ed. F., 245
Edward F., 247
Hannah E., 245, 247
John Peter, 231
Lillian Elizabeth, 247
Mary, 310
BRANDEL, Nellie Blanch, 261
BRANDT, Ann Maria, 213
Erastus, 213
Marg., 213
BRANNAN, Bridget, 171
BRANT, Erastus, 168
William M., 159
BRASHEARE, Rachael, 229
BRAUER, Friederich, 44, 116
BRAUN, Amelia, 40
Ann, 200
Anna Maria, 41
Elisabeth, 40
Eva Margaretha, 45
Henrich, 40, 43, 45
Henrich Wilhelm, 41
Jacob, 131, 135, 143
Joh. Henrich, 40, 41
Johan Heinrich, 131
Margaretha, 82
Maria, 82, 135, 139
Maria Elisabeth, 40, 41, 45, 114, 115, 131
Mary, 131
Michael, 107, 108
Sophia, 114
BRAUNIN, Anna Maria, 141
Maria Elisabeth, 99
BRECHTLY, Elisabetha, 3
Mathias, 3

BRECNSCHITT, Conrad, 36
BREGERMAN, Georg Ludwig, 205
Hanna, 205
BREIDENHARTH, Maria, 51
BREKET, Maria Magdalena, 7
BREMERMAN, Amalie, 117
Amelia, 127
Anna Sophia, 136
Anthony Henry, 127
Herman, 117, 120, 127, 136, 142
Sophia Maria, 131
Wilhelm Friederich, 117
Wilhelmina Elisabeth, 120
BREMERMANN, Andrew Snyder, 201
Elizabeth, 201
Herman, 201
BRENDEL, Edith May, 246
Friderich, 27
Graves S., 230, 246, 249
Kate E., 246, 249
Reginal LeGrand, 249
BRENECHER, Johan Georg, 86
Margaretha, 86
Mariana, 86
BRENEIFER, Hanna Elisabeth, 205
Johan Georg, 205
Margaretha, 205
BRENEISEN, Anna Elisabeth, 135
Bernhard, 135
Georg, 294
Hyronimus, 135
J. Georg, 282

Jacob Morris, 135, 294
Johan Georg, 282
Margaretha, 135
BRENEISER, Hanna Elisabeth, 205
Johan Georg, 205
Margaretha, 205
BRENESSER, Johan Georg, 86
Margaretha, 86
Mariana, 86
BRENGLE, William D., 241
BRENSFEILD, Ann Maria, 172
BRENT, Campbell Parker, 268
Darthey Louisa, 251
Edward, 250
Elizabeth G., 243
Elizabeth Katie, 249, 274
Gertrude Louisa, 255
Henry Karsten, 248, 267
Howard Edward, 249
Jesse, 232
John M., 248, 249, 251, 255
John W., 252
Joseph E., 249, 250, 255
Katie Werner, 255
Katier, 231
Louisa, 248, 249, 251, 252, 255
Maggie, 239
Malinda, 252
Mary, 249, 250, 255, 273
Mary L., 268
BRENZEN, Anna Maria, 38
Jacob, 37, 38
BRETT, Catharine, 165
BREUNING, Georg, 140
BREWER, Lewis, 144

BREWITT, John, 51
BRIAN, James N., 170
BRIBBEN, Anna Maria, 33
Johann, 33
BRIELY, William C., 229
BRIGHTMAN, Carrie, 263
Virginia Annie, 278
Walter Skillman, 263
William, 263
William Dorsey, 264
BRIGHTWELL, Cinda, 261
Isadore, 261, 277
Minnie L., 261
BRILL, Friedrich, 52
BRINGMAN, Cath., 252
Louis, 252
William, 252
BRITTEN, Anna Elisabeth, 138
Catharina, 27
Johann, 27
Maria Phillipina, 27
BRITTINGHAM, Joseph, 56
BRITTON, Elisabeth, 49
Maria Philippa, 132
Maria Sophia, 128
Michael, 123
Phillipina, 119
Sophia, 144
BROADERS, Anna L., 160
BROCHEL, Elisabeth, 15
Ida, 15
Matheiss, 15
BRODBECK, Rudolph, 59
BRODMAN, Charles L., 239
BROEHM, Cathrine, 195

Conrad, 195
George, 195
BROMWELL, Anna Margaret, 245
Charles Albert, 249
George Edwin, 250
Henry Horst, 258
Louisa C., 266
Louisa Caroline, 247
Mary, 245, 247, 249, 250, 252
Mary Caroline, 255, 256, 258
Rosina, 252
Thomas Sommers, 256, 273
William, 245, 247, 249, 250, 252, 255, 256, 258
William H., 243, 247
William Henry, 247
BROOKE, Edward, 242
Maggie, 229
BROOKHARD, Jacob, 200
Martha, 200
William Henry, 200
BROOKHART, Peter, 151
BROOKS, John, 59
Kate M., 232
Richard, 309, 311
Richard S., 274
BROON, Joseph O., 151
BROWN, Casper R., 167
Catherine, 138
Elisabeth, 52
Eliza, 213
Emma Eliza, 213
Eva Margaretha, 57
George C., 230
George H., 240
Harriot, 206
Henry, 270

Jasper R., 213
Jessie P., 240
Lewis T., 243
Mary Jane, 213
Thomas, 52
BROWNY, Nancy, 203
William, 203
BRUBAKER, Cora M., 240
BRUCHS, Maria Magdalena, 8
Ruland, 8
Wilhelm, 8
BRUCKNER, Julia, 251
BRUDER, Henrich, 76
Magdalena, 12
Wilhelm, 12
BRUNGART, Elisabeth, 139
BRUNGER, Charles, 238
BRUNNER, Andrew R., 305
Mary, 145
BRURIEN, Charles P., 157
BRUSHWEELER, William, 150
BRUTZEL, Johannes, 12
BRYAN, Thomas E., 172
BRYDEN, Henrietta M., 157
BRYSON, Marg. A., 223
BUCH, Georg, 14, 18
George, 28, 64
Jana, 14
Joan, 18
Joseph Matthias, 28
Priscilla, 18
BUCHEIMER, Annie, 255
BUCHHEIMER, Annie C., 236
Barbara A., 233

Ella E., 236
Mary A., 230
Pauline Hannah, 255
Peter, 234
Selma M., 249, 255
Wilhelmina Julia, 249
Wilhimina E., 233
William, 232, 249, 255
BUCHLEY, Ann A., 172
BUCHSBAUM, Henry, 244
BUCK, A. Indiana, 210
A. Susiana, 208
Alfred, 170, 208, 210, 304
Amelia Handy, 208
Francis, 160
H., 221
Henrietta Wilhemina, 221
Henry Groverman, 210, 304
Indiana, 221, 304
BUCKEY, Caroline, 189
Caroline M., 186
Daniel, 189
David, 186
Eviline Virginia, 156
Harriet E., 159
Jacob M., 159
Julia Baker, 189
Marion Elizabeth Harrison, 186
BUCKMAN, Emeline, 238
Lillie, 237
William H., 258
BUCKMILLER, Lottie, 234
BUCKNALL, Benjamin, 145
BUDHEIMER, Mrs., 255
BUFFINGTON, Taylor, 231
BUHADS, Dorothea, 81
Friederich, 81

BUKOFFSKY, Geo., 169
BULER, Adelheit, 95
Ch. L., 106
Christian C., 95
BULHAUS, Mrs., 67
BULHAUSS, Polly, 23
BULL, Alice Amey, 247, 312
Alice Amy, 265
Chales Nicholas, 226
Charles NIcholas, 310
Eliza, 145
John L., 226
Martha, 239
Mary Ann, 226
Mary Charlesetta, 224, 309
Mary E., 222, 223, 224, 226, 247, 309, 310
Mary Ellen, 268
Nicholas, 310
Nicholas E., 247, 266
Nicholas W., 226
Nicola, 309
Nicolas, 224
Nicolas W., 222, 223
Thomas Edwin, 222
William Henry, 223
William Winters, 226
Willie, 226
BUNCH, Ino., 212
James Thomas, 209
John, 209
Margaret, 209, 212
Mary Jane, 212
BUNDONGIN, Susanna, 80
BUNGAN, Aarne Eliza, 182
Fred., 182
Mary, 182
BUNKARD, Elizabeth, 193

Index

John, 193
John Edward, 193
BUNKERD, Elizabeth, 193
John, 193
John Edward, 193
BUNTING, Gertrude Amelia, 236
BUNYAN, Aarne Eliza, 182
Fed., 182
Mary, 182
BURCK, Davy, 21
Elisabeth, 21
William, 21
BURDONGIN, Susanna, 80
BURGA, Andrew, 235
BURGAN, Aarne Eliza, 182
Fred., 182
Mary, 182
BURGAU, Charles, 252
Charles M., 258, 259, 275
Ella May, 259
Florence M., 252, 258, 259
George Cleveland, 252
Minnie Hester, 258
Thomas Tenant, 258
BURGESS, Ella E., 231
John A., 234
BURGIN, Sally, 142
BURK, David, 54
George, 68
BURKE, Addie Gertrude, 255
Edmund, 238
Elizabeth, 146
Ellen E., 173
Emilie Viola, 262
Loretta, 272
Samuel A., 255, 256, 262

Sarah F., 255, 256, 262
Washington Franklin, 256
BURKER, Louetta, 255
Samuel A., 255
Sarah F., 255
BURKHARDT, Charles E., 239, 260
Elisabeth, 23
Florence Corinne, 253
Frederick, 253
Henrich, 23
Jerome Montford, 260
Levina, 253
Mary, 260, 277
BURKITT, John, 56
BURLAM, Elisabeth, 51
BURLAND, Elisabeth, 51
BURMAN, Anna, 139
BURNAM, Thomas, 201
BURNETT, Caroline P., 168, 171
BURNHAM, Magdalena C., 171
Thomas, 148
BURNS, Alma F., 246, 248, 251, 253, 256
Alma Frederika, 248
Annie Iona, 246, 274
Edgar E., 237
Eldridge Price, 256
Laura Virginia, 235
Mary, 233
Milton Gaehle, 251
Robert, 253
Thomas W., 246, 248, 251, 253, 256
BURRER, Barbara, 51
BURROWS, Charles P., 197
Elizabeth Ann, 197
Maria, 197
BUSADS, Dorothea, 81
Friederich, 81

BUSBY, Alice, 223
Isaiah, 223
Mary Jane Boyl, 223
Robert, 223
Susan, 223
BUSCH, Abraham, 138
Eliza, 165
Friederich, 124
George D., 241
Henry, 307
Sophia, 162
Wilbur, 282
BUSCHEN, Rebecca, 141
BUSHONG, Allillian R., 272
BUSSEL, Jennett, 155
BUSTIN, Rebecca, 54
BUSTLIN, Rebecca, 54
BUT, Johann George, 56
BUTCHER, James H., 162
BUTLER, Minnie, 241
BUTSCHER, Maria, 293
BYE, Clara Mills, 261
Henry Burton, 261
Henry H., 241, 261
Henry Howard, 260
BYINGTON, Maggie, 238
BYT, Catharina, 16
David, 16
Peter, 16, 75

-C-
CAFFERATA, Blanche Teresa, 240
CAFFREE, Ann, 147
CAHN, Mary, 51
CALDER, George Alexander, 188
Jennet, 188
John, 188
John Law, 188

CALDWELL, Elizabeth J., 170
  Mr., 298
CALENSTEIN, Friederich August, 103
  Justina, 103
CALFUS, Lewis, 54
CALLAHAN, Mary C., 244
CAMBPELL, Robert, 150
CAMERON, Benj. F., 249
  Benjamin F., 163
  Frank Horace, 249
  James, 168, 210, 302
  Josephine Elizabeth, 210
  Julia, 210
  Rose A., 170
  Severa, 249
CAMPBELL, Edgar C., 238
  Ella, 260
  John, 147
  Laura Ann, 161
  Mr., 302
  Peter, 150
  Priscilla, 151
  Susan, 169
  Susie, 232
CANBY, Alice V., 232
  Anna V., 275
CANE, Miss, 146
CANN, Eliza Ann, 154
CANNON, Neemi, 51
CANTER, Ida Elexenia, 175
  Leven, 163
  Levin, 219
  R. B., 219
  Rebecca B., 175
  Sarah Virginia, 219
CAPITO, Anna Maria Gertraude, 36
  Christian, 35, 96
  Elisabeth, 35, 57, 96
  Georg, 140
  Maria Elisabeth, 66
CAPLERN, Catherina, 138
CAPLES, Mary Cath., 172
CARDER, Mr., 293
CARL, Rahel, 45
  Rebecca, 45
  Robert, 45
CARLE, Bernard William, 259
  Edith Marian, 257
  Henry J., 240, 262
  John G., 237, 257, 259, 262, 266
  Lillie J., 257, 259, 262
  Mary C., 241
  Matilda Gebhart, 262
  Matilda Marie, 262
  Ralph Derr, 262
CARLSON, Neils, 145
CARMAN, Elizabeth Alice, 253
  Nellie E., 253, 260
  William Howell, 260
  Willie, 233, 253, 260
CARNIGHAM, Catharina, 86
  Georg Peter, 45
  Jacobus, 41
  James, 41, 45, 49, 86
  Johann, 49
  Joseph, 86
  Katharina, 41, 45, 49
CAROTHERS, Illinois, 193
  Mary, 193
  Masoura, 193
  Virginia, 193
  William, 193
  William Murphy, 193
CARPENTER, Catharina, 49, 91
  Katharina, 57
CARPETON, Maria Elisabeth, 52
CARR, Ann M., 168
  Geo. M. N., 170
  Jennet, 170
CARRICO, Emma L., 241
CARROL, Anna Fortine, 39
CARROLL, Emily Jane, 156
  Thomas, 151
  William W., 238
CARRUTHERS, William, 147
CARSEN, Mr., 298
CARSOLL, Maria D., 170
CARTER, Annie M., 239
  Bessie R., 238
  Catharine, 199
  Laban W., 173
  Mr., 202
  Sarah E., 240
  Susannah, 51
  William B., 199, 275
CARWELL, Maria D., 170
CASE, Emerson J., 158
CASEY, Henry, 149
CASHEL, ---, 77
  Catharina, 64
  Jacob, 39
  Johann, 24
  Johannes, 27, 35, 39
  Lydia, 24
  Magdalena, 24, 35, 39
  Maria, 27
  Salome, 27
CASPARI, Elisabeth, 105
  Harriet, 105
  Jacob, 105, 141

Index

Josephus Jacobus, 118
Mr., 118
CASPEL, Catharina, 55
CASSEL, ---, 77
Johann, 24
John, 22
John Georg, 22
Lydia, 24
Magdalena, 22, 24
CATTRIDER, Angeline, 164
CATZ, Susan Placke, 205
CAUCHA, John, 203
CAULK, William, 167
CAUMBIE, John A., 228
CAUNSELMAN, Elisabeth, 15
Freidrich, 15
Margareth, 15
CAVANS, ---, 75
Elisabeth, 12
John, 12
Wilhelm, 12
CHALT, Margaret, 164
CHAMBELAIN, George Henry, 202
John, 202
Louisa, 202
CHAMBERLAIN, Edward, 201
John C., 147
John R., 199, 201
Louisa, 199, 201
Susanna Louisa, 199
CHAMBERS, Carry, 193
Catharine Jane, 190
Charlotte, 190, 274
George McDonald, 310
Harriot Elizabeth, 193
J., 190
John, 150
John Edward, 190

Rebecca, 193
William M., 277
William Manion, 190
CHANDLER, George, 240
CHANEL, Isaiah, 237
CHANEY, William O., 231
CHAPMAN, Rachel, 52
CHAPPELL, Florence J. D., 273
CHARLES, Catharina, 28
CHARLESWORTH, Mary, 218
Mary Hellen, 218
Sol., 218
CHARRON, John B., 157
CHASE, Catharine, 165
CHASHEL, Catharina, 55
CHERRY, Charles W., 230, 245
Charlotte, 245
Cora Ann, 239
Georgie E., 245
Mary Bennetta, 245
CHESBOROUGH, Isaac M., 152
CHESBROUGH, Ellis S., 155
CHILCOAT, Josuah, 55
CHILDS, Margaret, 202
Margaret Ann, 202
Robert E. R., 167
Samuel, 202
CHIVERL, Alexander B., 157
CHREST, Jacob, 201
CHRISBIN, Absalom, 84, 115, 284
Anna Maria, 84
Catharina, 84, 284
Sophia, 115
Wilhelm, 100

CHRISH, Mrs., 131
CHRIST, Ann, 206
Anna, 37, 44
Cathrine E., 240
Emma M., 239
Johannes, 44
Mary E., 231
Mathew, 206
Othelia, 239
Wilhelm, 37, 44
William, 206
William H., 239
CHRISTFIELD, Absalom, 48
Anna, 48
Anna Maria, 48
CHRISTI, Maria Barbara, 291
CHRISTIAN, Absalom, 284
Catharina, 284
CHRISTIANA, Mary, 236
CHRISTIN, Elizabeth, 141
CHRONISTER, Lewis, 230
CHUBB, Thomas J., 163
CHURCH, Anna, 48
Nancy, 57
CILLEY, Jonathan, 237
CIMGIN, John, 51
CISSEL, Benjamin C., 172
CLAGGETT, Genevieve Louise, 251
John Thomas, 251
Marie Louise, 251
CLAMPITT, William H., 238
CLARES, Wille, 58
CLARIC, Wille, 58
CLARIDGE, Margaret Ann, 166
CLARK, Cath., 218
Cath. Ann, 211

Index

Emma Margaretta, 211
George Washington Thomas, 218
James, 202
John, 159
Robert A., 211, 218
William, 163
CLARKE, Ann Maria, 216
Cath., 216
Cath. M., 214
Dora, 233
Eliza, 149
John, 216
Mrs., 301
Ray S., 167
Robert, 214
Robert A., 164
Robert Andrew Jackson, 214
CLARY, Gertrude, 242
CLASS, Rosina, 56
CLAUS, Barbara, 3
Johanna Maria, 27
Petronella, 30
Rosina, 27, 30
Rosina Josepha, 30
Stephen, 27, 30, 55, 70
Wilhelm, 3
CLAUSS, Dora V., 250, 251, 254, 257
Gaehle, 257
Gertrude Weiner, 251
Louie Julius, 254
Louis, 232, 250, 251, 254, 257
Paul, 257
Verina Rose, 250
CLAUSSEN, Johann Peter, 45
CLAUTICES, Henry C., 171
CLAYTON, Harry O., 233
Harvy B., 273

CLEAVEN, Elizabeth, 148
CLEMENS, A. D., 214
Agustus Ducas, 218
Agustus Lucas, 218
Aug. D., 218
Augustus, 181
Augustus D., 157, 218
Caarfeld, 214
Charles Clifford, 214, 298
Henrietta, 218
Mary Ann Jessup, 218
CLEMENTS, Clara, 240
CLENAU, Catharina, 84
CLENIGHEN, Robert, 228
CLERKSON, Thomas, 52
CLIFFE, mary, 164
CLIFFORD, John, 295
Mollie, 238
CLIFT, Susan, 162
CLIM, Margaretha, 138
CLINE, Margaretha, 138
CLING, Polly, 57
CLOCKGETHER, Charlotte, 308
CLOUD, Amanda Jane, 156
COACK, Friederich, 140
COBAUGH, William D., 231
COBERTS, Jakob, 2
COBSEN, William H., 299
COBURN, Cornelius, 207, 209, 210, 223, 224, 226, 227, 246
Daniel Jefferson Davis, 207
Elizabeth J., 233
Elizabeth Jane, 209
Ellen Louisa, 223
George, 210, 232, 250, 252
Grace Virginia, 252

Jefferson D., 233
John, 179
Leanna Allison, 250
Lucinda, 179
Marg., 207, 209, 210, 246
Margaret, 223, 224, 226, 227
Margaret Joseph, 226
Margaret Phillipena, 223
Mary Virginia, 223
Richard, 227, 242
Sarah Agnes, 223
Sarah Rebecca, 246, 267
Thomas, 179, 224
Virginia, 250, 252
COCHEN, Lucretia Jane, 160
COCHER, Henrich, 116
COCHERAN, Martha, 57
COCHM, Lucretia Jane, 160
COCHRAN, James M., 165
COCKEY, Henrietta, 265, 312
John C., 144, 277
Joshua, 150, 303
Mary, 150, 266
Richard, 272
COCKLEY, Carrie, 232
Elizabeth T., 233
Joseph W., 231
COCOCK, Elizabeth Ann, 197
Henrietta, 197
Jacob, 197
CODWALD, Margaretha, 92
COHEN, Sarah, 235
COHITE, Francis, 226
Mary, 226
Mary Virginia, 226
COHLER, Elisabeth, 295

COHN, James E., 170
COLE, Barbara Cornelia, 192
　Christiana, 155
　E. M., 185
　Elenora M., 190
　Elizabeth, 232
　Elizabeth Eleonora Virginia, 192
　Hynson Hammilton, 148
　John Clarence Le Grand, 185
　Mary Ann, 185
　Sarah, 52
　William, 192
　William H., 185, 190
　William Henson, 190
COLEMAN, Cath. Delia, 226
　Henry Charles, 237
　John, 166
　Lewis H., 226
　Lewis Henry, 226
　Oscar T., 244
COLLETT, Charles H., 238
COLLIFLOWER, William H., 156
COLLINS, Ann V., 167
　E. C., 183
　Elizabeth Ann, 183
　J. L., 183
　John C., 154
　Maggie A., 231
　Thomas Penington, 186
COLLMUS, Ellenora Reese, 255
　Elnora Reese, 272
　Estelle C., 251, 255
　Solomon, 251
　William, 251, 255
COLLODIN, ---, 38
　Barbara, 56

　Margaretha, 56
COLMER, Jacob Heinrich, 286
COLOGNE, Donaldson, 235
COLT, George, 173
COLTON, Frederick, 170
　John, 170
COMFORT, H. J., 228, 305
　Jacob, 133
　Johannes, 133
　Juliana, 133, 293
　Margaret A., 305
COMMODORE, Lettie, 235
CONDER, Mr., 296
CONN, Henry, 146
CONOWAY, Edward C., 160
CONRAD, Cath., 202
　Cornelia Mary Louisa, 202
　Elisabetha, 4
　John W., 240
　Moses, 202
CONSTABLE, Benjamin F. B., 310
　F. H., 214
　Harrie Clarence, 214
　William R., 214
CONTER, Josephine Elizabeth Stephens, 216
　Levin, 216
　Rebecca, 216
CONWAY, Marja Ann, 171
COOCK, Georg, 138
COOK, Alexander C., 156
　Ann Maria, 158
　Archibald Lewis, 200
　Cordelia Victoria, 189
　Eber F., 154

　Elanora R. C., 156
　Fred., 297
　Frederick, 152
　Henrietta, 184, 189, 195, 200
　Isabella Adalade, 184
　J. Edward, 276
　Jacob, 184, 189, 195, 200
　John F., 164
　Josephine L., 163
　Lillie Eliza Kerr, 246
　Margaret, 145
　Margaret Jane, 195
　Martha, 246
　Martha Ann, 155
　Mary E., 235
　Mary S., 150
　Mr., 296
　Valentine, 246
　W. Harry, 273
COOKE, E. F., 310
　Euphrasia F., 274
　Maude C., 247
　Sallie, 271
　Warren E., 277
　Wiliam F., 265
　William E., 240
　William Etta Fennimore, 247
　William F., 247, 312
　William Fennimore, 247
COOMBS, Mrs., 298
COONEY, Caroline C., 237
　Isabel, 172
COOPER, David William, 220
　Elizabeth, 148
　Jacob M., 162, 220
　John, 15
　Margaret, 159
　Mary J., 220

Index

COPENS, Henrich, 54
COPES, Ann E., 169
CORDES, Maria, 48
COREL, Anna Maria, 84
  Johann, 84
  Maria, 84
CORMACK, Hanson, 276
CORNWALL, Albert G., 243
CORNWEIN, Elizabeth, 206
  James, 206
  Margaret Sarah, 206
CORNWELL, Jesse A., 237
  Maggie, 237
CORREA, Carrie Brown, 258
  Eleanora, 258
  Estelle, 258
  Estelle R., 250, 252, 260
  Harry Rankin, 252
  John H., 252, 258, 260
  John Hamilton, 250
  Laura, 236
  Robert Gamble Rankin, 260
  William Thomas, 250
CORRIN, Cath., 5
CORROLVING, Elisabeth, 120
CORWEIN, Eliza, 203
COSMAN, Christian, 91
COURTOIS, Bernard Amand, 152
  Rebeca Ann, 157
COURTOUS, Bernard Amand, 152
COUSIUS, Elisabetha, 6
COVELL, George B., 258
  Nettie A., 258
  Ruth Aurelia, 258
COX, Ann, 218

Emma Frances, 218
Mr., 301
Sabre, 153
William, 218
COZINE, McIliard S., 232
COZZENS, Richard E., 234
CRABBS, Mollie E., 247, 267
CRADEL, Anton, 54
CRAGGS, Mrs., 298, 299
CRAIG, Margaretha, 141
CRANFORD, James, 299
  Mrs., 298
CRAUSSE, Jacob, 142
CRAVEN, Amey, 209, 210
  Anna Montanye, 210
  Ed., 209, 210
  Jerome, 209
  Netta Arena, 209
CRAWFORD, Alfred, 221
  Celia T., 251
  Clara, 177
  Dix, 181
  Dixon, 160, 183, 214, 248
  Elisabeth, 34
  Elizabeth, 214, 245, 248
  Ellen, 207
  Eva Greta, 30
  George, 177
  George Dalton, 239
  George Heiner, 308
  Grace J., 251
  Grace Rutherford, 247
  Grafton Carlisle, 245
  James, 177, 183, 185, 211
  Jesse, 265, 311
  Jesse Aitkon, 223
  John Andrew, 248
  John O., 245
  John Oliver, 248, 267
  John Robert, 251

Lena May, 230
Margaret, 183, 228
Maria Magdalena, 30
Martha, 162
Mary, 211
Mary A., 248
Mary E., 207, 221, 223, 247
Mary Elizabeth, 214
Moses, 181, 183, 251, 308
Richard, 30, 34
Rosa A., 304
Rose Ann, 308
Sarah, 183, 185
Sarah Ann, 211, 233
Sarah Eliza, 304
Susan, 159
Thomas, 169, 211
W. E., 183
Wealthy E., 181
William, 207, 221, 223, 247, 268
William C., 304, 308
William Thomas, 308
CREAGH, Duncan, 151
CREAMER, ---, 182
  Elizabeth, 186
  Frederick Matthias, 186
  Jacob, 186
CRECSIUS, Willy, 11
CREDER, Mary R., 308
CREIDER, Maria, 140
CREM, Perry C., 168
CREMER, Con. C., 225
CRENEY, Mary Diffenderfer, 233
CRESEIUS, ---, 77
CREVER, Jacob, 144
CRIDLER, Cath., 216
  Harriet Rebecca, 216
  James H., 216
CRISFIELD, Sophia, 150

Index 333

CROCKETT, Lizzie, 234
CROMER, Cath. H., 163
  James L., 162
CROMWELL, Harry, 261
  Harry Leroy, 261
CRONEY, Margaretha, 142
CRONMILLER,
  Catharina, 29, 64
  Christina, 29, 281
  Elisabeth, 25, 64
  Jacob, 29, 45, 281
  Jenny, 45
  Joseph, 48
  Lydia, 39
  Margaretha, 25, 31, 34, 39, 45, 48, 281
  P., 64
  Philipp, 45
  Phillip, 25, 29, 31, 34, 39, 48, 55
  Rebecca, 34
  Samuel, 45
  Sarah, 31
  Thomas, 45
CRONMULLER, Johan Phillip, 100
  Lidiana, 91
  Margaretha, 85
  Philip, 85, 91, 100
CROOK, Eliza A., 158
CROSH, Jacob, 293
CROSS, Charles Lewis, 264
  Louisa Scheldt, 264
  Sarah Jane, 264
  Sarah W., 264
CROUSE, Edwin Henry, 171
  Elizabeth, 161
CROUSIUS, Elisabeth, 6
CROVEN, Amey, 221
  E. R., 221
  James Jetter, 221
CROW, Florence Eugenia, 226
  Mary, 146
  Nathaniel, 226
  Selina R., 226
CROWDER, Charlotte A., 230
CROWN, M., 192
CROZIER, Elizabeth, 208
  John R., 208
  Mr., 303
  Mrs., 303
  Robert Turner Hamilton, 208
  Wiona Juliett, 208
CRUHSIUS, ---, 77
  Elisabeth, 5
  Philipp, 6
  Phillip, 5
CRUIT, John, 164
CRULLE, Ann Maria, 155
CRUNIE, William M., 244
CRUSH, Catharina, 29
  Jacob, 29
  Robert, 29
CRUSIUS, ---, 77
  Elisabeth, 23
  Gustaf, 29
  M., 19
  Philip, 23
  Philipp, 2
  Phillip, 5, 62
  Willy, 14
CULENSTEIN,
  Friederich August, 103
  Justina, 103
CULL, Janey, 296
CULLUM, Lillie Nora, 233
CUMINGS, Sarah J., 164
CUMMINES, Ann P., 154
CUMMINGHAM, Georgia, 216
  James Morgan, 216
  John A., 216
CUMMINGS, John W., 230
  Mrs., 296
CUMMINS, Eleanor P., 155
  Mary Ann, 149
CUMOR, Maggie, 237
CUNNINGHAM, Felix, 243
  Georgianna, 235
  Jane, 147
  John, 158
  Julia Ann, 158
CUNNINS, Robert P., 158
CUNZ, Daniel, 2
CUNZELMANN, Joh., 5
  Maria, 5
  Susanna, 5
CURFMAN, Mary E., 231
CUROTHERS, Illinois, 193
  Mary, 193
  Masoura, 193
  Virginia, 193
  William, 193
  William Murphy, 193
CURRAU, Salome, 89
CURTIS, Al. Catharine, 184
  Carrie B., 231
  Emma, 220
  John, 184, 220
  Mary, 184, 220
  Mary Ann, 184
CURTOIS, A., 189
  Clementine, 189
  Sophia, 189

Index

-D-

DAELLEN, Allen, 114
DAER, Jacob, 56
DAILEY, E. V., 213
  George Herring, 213
  Julia, 213
DAILY, Ephraim B., 167
  John Thomas, 235
DAIRS, Ezekiel, 153
DALE, Charles H., 237
  James, 164
DALEY, Ann, 171
  Ephraim, 210
  July Ann, 210
  Samuel Vansant, 210
DALLAM, Benjamin S., 257
  Mary E., 257
  Richard Edward, 257
DALLIGER, Catharina, 10
  Christian, 10
  Christina, 10
DALLWICK, Edward, 152
DAMUTH, Mrs., 63
DANAKER, Mary Van, 244
DANNE, Abraham, 143
DANNER, Elisabeth, 107
  Jacob, 52
  Mec., 107
DANZEGLOCK, John A., 238
DANZEGLOK, John A., 259
  Maggie, 259
  Marguerite, 259
DARLTON, Lillian B., 243
DASHIELS, Ann, 150
DAUB, Jacob, 290
DAUBE, Heinrich, 102
  Johan, 102
  Maria Juliana, 102
DAUGHATY, Elizabeth, 206
DAUMANN, Rose, 278
DAUNER, Jacob, 52
DAUZEGLOCK, John A., 261
  Maggie, 261
  Milton, 261
DAVIDS, Charles A., 273
  John F., 270
DAVIDSON, Katie B., 240
DAVIS, Benjamin, 51
  Charles, 153
  Charles S., 300
  Danie E., 173
  Edward T., 234
  Elisabeth, 19
  Elizabeth, 156, 157
  Ellen, 145
  Hattie A., 244
  Jacob, 52
  John E., 241
  Joseph, 19
  Josiah, 169
  Laura E., 232
  Martha, 238
  Mary Ann, 167
  Mary Cath., 168
  Mary E., 238
  P. S., 210
  William, 19
DE (VON) CLOT, Wilehms, 140
DE BALKE, Cuerdo, 141
DE CARNAP, Caspar, 55
DE MARTORE, Isadore, 230
DEAL, Barbara, 57
  Henrich, 142
DEAN, Catherine, 211
  Edward, 237
  Hanna Joanna Louisa, 211
  William, 211
DEBEET, Agnes M., 169
  Duncan, 213
  Duncan H., 173
  Mary Ann, 208, 213
  W. C., 213
  William, 163, 208
  William C., 208
DEBEETS, Deborah, 155
DECHANT, Wilhelm, 139
DECKER, Anna Maria, 27, 31
  Elisabeth, 43
  Friderich, 27
  Georg, 27
  George, 31, 35, 55
  Jacob, 27, 35
  Jacob F., 158, 179, 310
  Johannes, 35
  Julia Ann, 179
  Louis, 179
  Lydia, 35
  Margaret, 144
  Margaretha, 35
  Sally, 31
  Susanna, 27, 31, 35, 130
DECKERIN, Magdalena, 54
DECKRING, Susanna, 263
DEEMS, Barbara, 64
  Sophia, 221
  William, 221
  William Gardner, 221
DEERIG, Arthur Henry, 263
  Susanna, 263
  William, 263

Index

DEFANO, Maria, 141
DEFARE, Maria, 141
DEFFRES, James E., 172
DEGEN, Anna
  Catharina, 4
  Catharina, 4
  Frohna, 22
  Georg, 4, 22, 51
  George, 24
  Maria Elisabeth, 63
  Peter, 22
  Salome, 72
  Susanna, 24
  Veronica, 24
DEGMEIER, Ludewig, 82
DEGROFT, Jane, 145
DEHLERS, Herman, 19
DEHMAR, Friderich, 282
  Jacob, 282
DEHOFF, Alice M., 241
  Jesse, 182, 186
  John Henry, 186
  Sarah, 182, 186
DEHUFF, Angeline, 248, 249, 253, 256
  Daniel B., 253, 256
  Daul B., 248
  Daul P., 249
  Florence, 248
  George, 267
  Lela May, 256
  Lizzie Rebecca, 253
  Owen, 249
  Robert, 243
DEIS, Peter, 64
DEISE, Agnes Roselea, 264
  John, 264
  Margaret, 264
DEKER, Georg, 22
DEKKER, Elizabeth Campbell, 226
  Francis D., 226
  Rachel A., 226
DELAHAY, James H., 268
  Josephine, 271
DELGER, Anna Maria, 8
  Johannes, 8
DELLAHAY, James U., 162
DELLER, Elisabeth, 143
  Tillie, 232
DELLET, Dr., 136
  Henrietta, 136
  Philippina, 136
DELLINGER, Frank, 241
DELMORE, Friederich, 289
  Maria Margaretha, 289
DEMMITT, Joshua, 171
DEMPSEY, Ann L., 154
DENNER, Louis, 30, 76
DENNIS, Sophia, 233
DEPEN, Sophia, 136
DEPOSS, Lacinda Ann, 148
  Lucinda Ann, 148
DEPPISH, Mary E., 241
DEPUEY, Emma Lee, 252
  James A., 233, 252
  Willie Augustus, 252
DERINGER, Calhoun M., 161
DERR, Catharina, 72, 286
  Catherine, 209
  Charles H., 209
  Elisabeth, 106
  Elizabeth Jones, 255
  Florence I., 231
  Frank Gordon, 255
  Jacob, 42, 79, 286
  Johann Wilhelm, 79
  Kate E., 230
  Lillie J., 237
  Maria, 79
  Martha Louesa Pinkney, 209
  Michael, 113, 121
  Samuel W., 255
  William, 276
DERRY, Mary P., 158
DERZEBACH, Cath., 69
  Catharina, 24
  Elisabeth, 24
  George, 66
  Joh., 69
  Johannes, 24, 26, 28, 34, 77
  Mr., 66
DERZENBACH, Catharina, 32
  Joh., 32
  Susanna, 32
DESPER, Elisabeth, 143
DETMA, Elisabeth, 42, 45, 49
  Friedrich, 42, 45, 49
  Johannes, 42
  Maria Margaretha, 49
DETMAR, ---, 77
  Barbara, 23
  Catharina, 95
  Christoph, 23, 61
  Elisabeth, 95
  Friedrich, 95, 288
  Jacob, 288
  Phillip Henrich, 23
DETMOR, ---, 77
  Christian, 89
  Christoph, 33, 71
  Elisabeth, 89, 104, 113
  Frid., 71
  Friederich, 33, 56, 89, 104, 113
  Jacob, 104

Index

Margaretha, 33, 71
Phil., 28
Sophia, 33, 71
Wilhelm, 113
DETMORE, Friedeich, 295
Margaretha, 49
DEVERBACH, Jacob, 56
DEVINNY, Margaretha, 142
DEVIS, Anna Maria, 4
Barbara, 5
Benjamin, 4
Mathias, 4, 73
Nancy, 5
William, 5
DEVISION, Joseph, 76
DEVISON, Elizabeth, 8
Joh. George, 8
Joseph, 8
DEVORE, Samuel W., 240
DEWALT, Juliana Mary, 20
DEWIS, Francis, 55
Job, 60
DEWLING, Mary, 168
DICHART, Elisabeth, 18
Henrich, 18, 75
Susanna, 18
DICK, Elisabeth, 138
Georg Friedrich, 54
DICKEL, B., 175
Charles Zwingle, 175
G. H., 175
Henry, 156
DICKHUT, Friederich Wilhelm, 89
Georg, 89
Johanna, 89
DICKINSON, Amos, 36
DICKLE, Barbara, 178

G. Henry, 178
John William, 178
DIDIER, Heinrich, 82
Michael, 119
DIEDER, Jacob, 76
DIEDRICH, Mary S. G., 231
DIEFENBERGER, Maria, 142
DIEFENDORFER, Amelia Handy, 96
Amelia Jane, 288
Amilia Jane, 103
Carl, 90
Carl Friederich, 9
Catharina, 8, 95, 126
Charles Rogers, 116
Daniel, 8, 19, 59, 103
Dorothea, 9, 16, 19
Elisabeth, 19, 20, 95
Emily Julie, 103
Jacob, 16
Johan, 90, 96, 104, 134
Johan Robert, 134
Johanna Sophia, 285
John, 116, 121
Lonihe, 8
Lonine, 75
Louisa, 60
Louise, 75
Michael, 9, 16, 19, 60, 103, 116, 284
Michael Nicolaus, 104
Peter, 52, 86, 95, 103, 285, 288
Samuel, 17
Sophia, 116, 142
Susanna Sophia, 95
DIEFENDORFTER, Dorothea, 7
Michael, 7
Nicolaus Henrich, 7

DIEFFENDERFFER, Ann Elisbeth, 128
Charlotte, 128
Mary Ann Maxell, 128
Richard, 128
DIEFFENDOERFER, Anna Margaretha, 33
Catharina, 33, 37
Dan., 33, 35
Daniel, 25, 27, 32
Dorothea, 25, 28, 32, 35, 39
Elisabeth, 25, 27, 32, 33, 35
Eva, 56
Friederich Meyer, 37
Juliana, 32
Maria, 33
Michael, 25, 28, 32, 35, 39
Nicolaus, 28
Peter, 37
William, 33
DIEFFENDORFER, Catharina, 23
Dorothea, 22, 23
Johan Michael, 22
Maria, 291
Michael, 23, 66
Mr., 291
Peter, 23, 33
DIEFFENDORFFER, Michael, 63
DIEKEL, A. B., 183
Ann B., 181
George H., 181, 183
George Thomas, 183
Henry Lewis, 181
DIEL, Christian, 51
Elisabeth, 115
Henrich, 115
Henrietta, 115
DIETMAR, ---, 77
Christoph, 60

Index   337

DIEV, Anna Maria, 15
　Jacob, 15
　Vallentin, 15
DIFFENBERGER,
　Laura, 300
DIFFENDEERFFER,
　Baruch William, 190
　Kitty Rogers, 190
　Mary B., 190
　Michael N., 190
DIFFENDERFER, Ann, 174
　Annie E., 249
　Charles, 174
　Charles Hungerford, 246
　Charles Ross, 249
　Edward, 174
　Elizabeth A., 178
　Henrich, 44
　John F., 269
　Katharina, 44
　Nannie, 246
　Octavius, 268
　Peter, 44, 45
　Richard, 295
　Sallie W., 269
　Sallie Worthington, 246
　Salome D., 268
　Sarah A. G., 246
　William, 178, 246
　William Octavius, 249
DIFFENDERFERR,
　John, 146
DIFFENDERFFER,
　Amelia Hamly, 153
　Ann, 193, 201, 206, 306
　Ann Elizabeth, 156
　Ann Olivia, 201
　Anne Rebecca, 272
　Annie E., 251
　Catharine, 158, 205
　Charles, 160, 179, 193,
　　194, 201, 203, 206, 301
　Charles F., 299
　Charles Fredrick, 206
　Charles R., 182, 187
　Charles Rogers, 155, 182
　Charles Ross, 251
　Charlotte Elizabeth, 196
　Claude Augustus, 251
　Daniel, 2
　Dorothea, 205
　Edward, 302
　Elizabeth M., 179
　Elizabeth, 307
　George Michael, 205
　George Milliman, 193
　Georgia D., 241
　Henry Harrison, 186
　Henry J., 196
　Henry Oliver, 152
　Johannes Augustus, 49
　John, 198
　John A., 305
　John Rogers, 187
　Katharina, 49
　Lewis A., 303
　M. A., 187
　Malinda A., 182
　Mary, 179, 194, 229
　Mary Ann, 151
　Mary William, 194
　Mathilda E., 157
　Michael, 186, 188, 194,
　　198, 205, 309
　Michael Addison, 198
　Peter, 2, 49, 205
　Rebecca, 196
　Rosanna, 203
　Rosena M., 159
　Rosina, 201
　Salome, 186, 188, 205
　Susan Christianna, 205
　William Stewart, 235
DIFFENDOERFFER,
　Georg, 40
　Katharina, 40
　Peter, 40
DIFFENDORFER,
　Catharina Rosalba, 198
　Dorothea, 41, 75
　Eva Barbara, 41
　Michael, 41, 75
　Peter, 41
　Sophia, 75
DIFFENDORFFER,
　Charlotte, 167
　Michael, 2, 204
　Sarah, 204
　William Henry, 204
DIFFERENDERFFER,
　John, 196
　Octavius, 196
DILL, Nicolaus, 120
　Nikalaus, 53
DILLEHUNT, Solomon
　S., 163
DILLEN, Hanna, 45
　Maria Eva, 45
　Nicolaus, 45
DILLING, Henry, 169
DINHART, Henrich, 75
DINJES, Philip, 55
DINSMORE, Elizabeth, 168
DISCHNER, Alexander, 240
DITMAR, ---, 77
　Anna Maria, 19
　Barbara, 17, 19
　Christoph, 16, 17, 19
　Elisabeth, 84, 101
　Friederich, 84
　Friedrich, 101
　Georg, 101
　Jacob, 84
　Johannes, 17

Index

DITMORE, Elizabeth, 129
DITTMAN, Elisabeth, 43
  Heinrich, 43
  Katharina, 43
  Katherina, 77
  Wilhelm, 43
DITZEL, Bessie, 241
DIX, Mary C., 162
DIXON, Margaret, 165
  Mary E., 238
  William H., 161
DOB, Anna, 142
  George, 289
DOBBIN, George Washington, 212
  J., 303
  James Wesley, 178
  John, 161, 178, 212, 215, 218
  John William, 218
  Malinda, 215, 299
  Mary, 212, 215, 218
  Mary A., 178
DOBBLING, John H., 241
DOBLER, Jacob, 121
  Magdalena, 121
DOBLIN, Mr., 302
DOELL, August, 237, 257, 259
  Dora, 257, 259
  Frederick August, 259
  Katie Elizabeth, 257
DOERR, Anna Margaretha, 4
  Catharina, 4
  Henrich, 4
DOFT, Elisabella, 80
  Johann Georg, 80
  Wilhelmina, 80
DOHM, Elizabeth Jane, 187
  Jane, 187
  John, 140, 151, 187
  Susanna Maria, 187
DOLAN, John, 242
DOLDER, Christian, 21
DOLIKER, James, 111
DOM, Johan, 290
DOMI, Michael, 104
  Mr., 104
DOMINI, Michael, 139
DONAHOE, Elizabeth, 230
DONALDSON, Francis, 179
  Martha, 179
  Noah, 179
DONIS, Carl, 145
DONOVAN, Ella May, 239
DONSCA, Leopold, 119
DONSEE, Elisabeth, 87
  Friederike Sophie, 50
  Johann, 50
  Leopold, 50, 82, 87
  Maria, 82
  Sophia, 82, 87
DONSER, Elisabeth, 87
  Leopold, 87
  Sophia, 87
DORGENBERG, Johann, 2
DORNBUSCH, Michael, 118
DORNIN, Johan, 100
  Margaretha, 100
  Maria Magdalena, 100
DORR, Mr., 302
  Robert C., 236
DORR(IN), Catharina, 8
  Widow, 59
DORSCHHEIMER, Jacob, 87
DORSER, Elisabeth, 87
  Leopold, 87
  Sophia, 87
DORSEY, Alice Euphenia, 177
  Amanda Rebecca, 197
  Annie S., 231
  Bazel John, 52
  Blanche E., 259
  Carrie, 233
  Cath., 196, 197, 202
  Cathrina, 199
  Edward M., 202
  Elizabeth, 177
  Hannah Ann, 166
  James, 52
  Juliet E., 159
  Rachel Matilda, 199
  Thomas G., 259
  Thomas W., 270
  William, 197, 199, 202
  William D., 177
  William E., 196
  William Henry, 196
  William Herbert, 259
DOSCH, Joh. Michael, 292
DOTTE, Elisabeth, 51
DOTTER, Elisabeth, 11
  Maria, 19
DOUGHERTY, Elizabeth, 277
  Ida E., 238
  John W., 162
  Julia, 161
  Mary A., 229
DOUGHTY, Lawrence, 222
DOUSEE, Leopold, 299
DOUZEGLOCK, John A., 258
  John August, 258
  Maggie, 258
DOWNIE, Minnie L., 241

Index

DOWNS, James A., 243
DOWY, Jerry, 169
DOYL, John, 52
DRABERT, Andreas, 54
DRAM, Mary, 152
DRANE, Andrew Jackson, 192
  Cath., 193
  Catharine, 192, 194
  George Washington Laffayette, 194
  John, 192, 193, 194
  Mary, 152
  Rebecca, 54
  Rosie, 243
DREBERT, Andreas, 54
  Christian, 55, 66
DREBING, George Leon, 254, 271
  James William McKinley, 261, 277
  Mary May, 272
  Mary V., 254, 261
  William A., 234, 254, 261
DREHER, Sophia, 45
DREIER, Catharina, 124
  Chartarina, 144
  Elisabeth Margaretha, 124
  Joseph, 124, 143
DRETELL, Caroline, 225
  John, 225
  Mathilda, 225
DREW, Frederick S., 240
DREYER, John H., 174
DRIESS, George, 23
  Maria Elisabeth, 23
DRIETER, James, 111
DRISSLER, Maria, 18
  Maria Magd., 18
  Maria Margareth, 18
  Vallentin, 18

DRITTER, Jacob, 58
DROST, Christian, 295
DROTZEBACH, Cathrina, 18, 20
  Johann Georg, 20
  Johannes, 18, 20, 77
  Margareth, 18
DRUTCH, Com., 221
  Howard Aldridge, 221
  Kate Estelle, 221
DUCHART, Henrich, 11, 51
DUCK, Christoph, 54
DUCKHARDT, Henrich, 30
DUFELD, Michael, 133
DUFT, George, 56
DUGAN, Joseph O., 162, 210, 299
  Mary E., 210
  Mrs., 299
  William, 144
  William Thomas, 210
DUGLASS, Millie Irene, 263
DUHURST, Charles Heflenstein, 198
  Ellen M., 161
  Greenbury, 198
  Mariana, 126
  Mary, 198
  Mr., 126
  Mrs., 195
DUKE, E., 1, 2
DUKEHEART, Henry, 129
  Mary Ann, 129
DUKER, Otto H., 239
DUKHEART, Thomas, 144
DULEY, Isabella, 148
DULING, George, 162

DUMBOLTON, James A., 154
DUME, Joseph, 228
DUMEY, D. D., 308
  George D., 308
  Rachel Jenson, 308
DUMPHREY, Elizabeth, 154
DUNBECKER, Adam, 140
DUNCAN, Agnes, 221
  Alexander, 214
  Ann Maria, 177, 212
  Cornelia, 177
  Eliza, 212
  Ella, 214
  Frederick B., 235
  Isaac, 221
  Isabella, 165, 212, 214
  J., 216
  James Smith, 177
  James William, 214
  John Alexander, 216
  Lehman, 214
  Mary A., 221
  Peter, 165, 212, 214, 216
  Sophia, 214
  Susanna, 177
  Thomas, 161, 177, 212
  William, 177
  William Prescott Smith, 212
DUNCKER, Johan, 87
  Mr., 287
DUNEK, Mary, 146
DUNHAM, Abraham L., 239
DUNN, Ann M., 161
  Augusta S., 273
  Edna Viola, 255
  James, 232
  Mary V., 234, 255

Index

Mrs., 255
Robert L., 242
William A., 255
DUNNING, John, 139
DURHAM, Lucy, 160
William E., 150
DURHURST, Mrs., 189
DURIAN, John, 109
Maria, 109
DURST, Amelia, 200
Anna Catharina, 111
Catharina Justina, 121
Catherine J., 308
Elisabeth, 131
Elizabeth, 156
Fanny, 111, 199
Felix, 116, 121, 126, 131, 196, 199, 200, 205, 302
Felix V., 169
Frances, 301
Frena, 131, 196, 205
Irena, 200
Jacob, 228
Johan Felix, 111, 141
Johan Ulrich, 126
John F., 185
John Felix, 185
John U., 155, 187
Julian Felix, 205
Martha Frances, 187
Mary A., 170
Mary F., 265, 311
Susanna, 185, 187
Veronica, 116, 121
Vrene, 126
DUSEL, George J., 232
DUSIUS, Barbara, 69
DUVALL, Eveline, 298
DYKE, Sarah Francis, 245
DYKES, Catherine, 154
Mary Ann, 154

DYKINS, Elizabeth, 243

-E-

EALER, Cathrine Martha, 198
Elisabeth, 198
Elizabeth, 200
Elizabeth Jane, 198, 200
Peter, 148, 198, 200
EARING, Susanna, 141
EARLEY, Florence A., 237
EARLONGHED, Bennetta, 172
EATON, Ernestine F., 246
Thomas J., 246
Willie Thomas, 246
EAVANS, ---, 75, 77
Elisabeth, 17, 54
John, 17
EBAUGH, Kitty Ann, 170
Rachael, 170
EBBART, Phillip, 75
Willy, 75
EBBECKE, Johann Friederich, 39
EBBERT, ---, 78
Elisabeth, 19
Magdalena, 19
Willy, 19
EBEN, William Lafevre, 310
EBERHARD, Georg, 136
Jacob, 17
Johannes, 11
EBERHARDIN, Elisabeth, 51
EBERSIN, Salome, 20
EBERT, Cathrina, 14
Jacob, 14
Johan, 112
Johannes, 14
John, 112

Margaretha, 112
EBERWEIN, Catharina, 113
Wilhelm, 113
EBHART, ---, 78
Harthman, 54
EBHERT, Cathrina, 14
Magdalena, 14
Willy, 14
EBY, Clarkeson, 247
Edna Viola, 257
George Washington, 257
Mary Jane, 257
ECCLESTON, Mary Elizabeth, 254
Robert Emory, 254
Robert Harrison, 254
ECHBACH, E. R., 304
ECHBERGER, Mrs., 297
ECHEL, Wilhelm, 88
ECKEL, Mr., 88
Wilhelm, 88
ECKERT, Catharina, 111
Johan, 124, 141
Mr., 111
ECKMAN, John G., 158
EDES, Mary Ruth Lee, 147
EDWARD, James, 193
Susanna, 193
EDWARDS, Cath., 180
Edward, 182
Elizabeth, 164
George, 153
Henry, 150
James, 297
Jane H., 271
Johann, 23
Johannes, 23
Joseph, 199
Joseph Henry, 199
Louesa, 176

Index 341

Magdalena, 23
Mary, 155
Mary Elizabeth, 185, 228
May, 261
Miss, 262
Mr., 296
Paul, 52
Sarah, 176, 182, 185, 199
Sarah Catharine, 180
Susan, 309
Susanna, 164
Thomas, 176, 180, 182, 185
Thomas B., 157
Victor, 261
William H., 169
EGE, Fredrick, 145
EGENS, Anna Magdalena, 63
Friederich, 63
EGERIN, Mrs., 53
EHLIART, Harthman, 54
EHRENBERG, Maria Magd., 46
Phillip, 56
EHRMAN, George Harrison, 255, 258, 261
Herbert A., 271
John Lewis, 258
Laura M., 261
Laura Margaret, 255, 258
Lottie Priscilla, 255
Louisa M., 165
Mary, 151
Robert Calvin, 255
EICHELBERGER, Eliza Henrietta, 149
Mary, 172
EICHERLIN, Salome, 86
EICHL, Elizabeth, 203
EICHLER, Christian F., 196
Christian Friedrich, 281

Elizabeth, 205
Jacob Waters Penn, 196
Johann Christian Freedrich, 205
Johann Friderich, 281
Johannes, 205
Ruth, 196
Salome, 281
Sarah, 118, 205
EIGENBROD, Anna Maria, 96
Catharina, 96
Jacob, 96
EIGEON, Charles, 217
Jacob Seltzer, 211
John, 161, 211, 217
Margaret, 211
Mary, 217
EIKERT, Mr., 301
EILER, Anna, 101
George, 145
EILERT, John, 140
EIRDELER, Christian, 24
EIRICH, ---, 36
Elisabeth, 55
EIRLEY, Carrie, 234
EISELIN, Catharina, 31
Friderich, 31
Friederich, 37
Salome, 37
EISENBRAUT, Lisette D., 156
EISENRING, Elisabeth, 206
Harriot, 206
Lawrence, 206
EISLIN, Eva Margaretha, 40
Friedrich, 40, 46
Salome, 40, 46
ELDER, Anna Maria, 101
Georg, 101

John, 101
ELESTON, Frances, 160
ELGERT, Elisabeth, 79
Georg, 99
James, 43, 77
Johannes, 43
Maria, 43, 79, 86, 99, 290
Nicolaus, 43, 79, 86, 99
Susanna, 86
ELI, David, 62
ELINS, Widow, 58
ELIOTT, Emily Jane, 200
Margaret, 200
Nicholas, 200
ELKERT, Hartmann, 26
ELLEN, Johan, 141
ELLGER, Hartman, 56
ELLIGER, Martha Elisabeth, 279
ELLIOT, Albert O., 241
Cath., 189
Catharina, 191
Catharine, 193
Elisabeth, 45, 76, 132, 197
Elizabeth, 199
George, 189, 191, 193
George Washington, 191
Hartman, 45
Henrich, 45
John, 306
Mary, 132
Mary Elizabeth, 189
Nicholas, 132
Nicolas, 197
R., 305
Rebecca, 220
Robert, 164, 220, 299
Thomas, 220
William, 197, 220
William Henry, 193
ELLIOTT, Cath., 186

Catharine, 187
Frances Marion, 186
George, 152, 186
George Thomas, 232
Hattie E., 229
John, 181, 187
Mary, 187
Nicholas, 152
Robert C., 310
Susan, 187
Thomas, 160, 187, 266
ELLIS, Caleb H., 241
James K., 231
Lottie, 241
Margaret, 170
ELLOFF, Blanche Teresa, 262
George Harry, 240
George Harvey, 262
William Dorritee, 262
ELRICH, Elisabeth, 44, 55
ELWEE, Elizabeth, 199
Elizabeth Ann, 197
Samuel W., 197, 199
Susanna Jane, 199
EMICH, Elisabeth, 41, 44, 47
Henrich, 41
Nicolaus, 41, 44, 55
Peter, 44
Susanna, 41
EMIG, Anna Cathr., 30
Anna Maria, 32
Baltzer, 36
Barbara, 24, 114
Elisabeth, 30, 32, 35, 36, 82, 91, 92, 103, 114
Georg, 114
George, 35
Heinrich, 91, 103
Henrich, 24, 30, 32, 82
Joh. George Valentin, 32

Joh. Hen., 35
Johannes, 24, 91
Johannes Valentin, 34
Juliana, 82
Maria, 114
Maria Magdalena, 88
Mr., 88, 114
Nicolaus, 32, 36, 92
Nikolaus, 34
Peggy, 36
Philip, 103, 282
Phillip, 75
Sarah, 114
Smauel, 103
EMMETT, Thomas, 172
EMMONS, Charles, 168
EMRICH, Elisabeth, 35
George P., 275
Johannes, 35
EMY, Charles, 203, 206
Elizabeth, 203
Margaret, 203, 206
Mary Ann, 206
ENFIELD, Annie M., 244
ENGEL, J., 267
ENGELBRECHT, Ida Gertrude, 256
John D., 256
John Henry, 256
Rose Annie, 256
ENGLAND, Ida S., 236
ENSLY, Latheysy, 139
ENSOR, James, 265, 312
Mr., 183
Mrs., 183, 189
Sarah, 309
Sarah Cornelia, 171, 183
Temperence, 153
ENTLER, Joseph W., 146
Mary Ann, 147
Rebecca, 152

ERB, Johann Christian, 89
Lucia Dorothea, 89
ERECKSON, Federal, 146
ERHARDT, Barbara, 64
Nicolaus, 64
ERNEST, Master, 24
ERNST, Georg, 129
Maria, 129
ESCAVALLE, Thomasina Q., 276
ESCHBACH, Catharina Elizabeth, 223
E. K., 223
E. R., 174, 221, 225, 305
Mary Susan, 225
S. M., 223
Sue M., 225
ESSELMANN, Emma, 254
George, 232, 254
Maud Elizabeth, 254
ETCHBERGER, Aley, 132
Dorothy, 144
Elizabeth, 198, 305
Elizabeth Ann, 154
John, 132, 199
John Warner, 191
Mary, 191, 199, 202
Mary Magdalena, 150
Ralph, 191
Rebecca Marbaret, 132
Sarah, 151
Sarah Ann, 199
ETCHERBERG, Sarah, 198
ETSCHBERGER, ---, 75
Catherina, 8
Cathrina, 17
Elisabeth, 31
Jacob, 16
Joh., 31

Index

Johann Wilhelm, 38
Johannes, 22
Magdalena, 16
Maria, 8, 17, 22, 33
Simon, 38
Wilhelm, 16, 33, 60
Wolfgang, 8, 17, 19, 21, 22, 33, 59, 60
EULER, Cathrine Martha, 198
Elisabeth, 198
Eliza Jane, 198
Peter, 198
EULERT, Anna Catharina, 32
Friderich, 32
Friederich, 33
EVALD, John, 52
EVANS, ---, 77
Davis, 161
Elisabeth, 20
Emma, 236
Johann, 76
John, 20
Joseph, 166
Sarah Ann, 153
EVATT, Ellanorah, 171
EVEN, Friderich, 65
Friderich, 60
EVERHART, Meranda, 161
EVERWINE, Margaret, 170
EWALD, Anna Barbara, 40
Baltzer, 32
Barbara, 144
Cath., 32
Catharina, 27, 37, 88, 110
Catharina Margaretha, 27, 40
Catherina, 18, 141
Cathrina, 22

Hanrich, 110
Henrich, 290
Jacob, 37, 110
Joh. Henrich, 22
Johan, 88
Johann, 40, 279
Johannes, 18, 27, 32, 37, 88, 284
John, 22
Katharina, 279
Mr., 64
EWALT, Cath., 204
EWERWEIN, Heinrich, 139
EYEN, Anna Magdalena, 23
Catharina, 27
Cathrina, 21, 23
Charlotta Magdalena, 18
Friedrich, 18, 21, 23, 27, 51, 77
Gottlob Samuel, 21
Maria Salome, 27
EYRA, Carl Friedrich, 14
Cathrina, 14, 16
Friedrich, 14, 16, 77
Maria Cathrina, 16
EYSLER, Mary E., 237

-F-

FABER, Johann Christoph, 3
Johann Wilhelm, 3
John Christian, 1, 174
John Theobald, 3
Margaretha, 3
FACHSKORN, William, 141
FADER, Charles W., 253, 255, 257
Frederick Augustus, 253
Henry Lambert, 257
James Arthur, 255

Minnie, 253, 255, 257
FAEY, Gottlieb, 306
Mary Ann, 306
FAGE, Mary, 172
FAHEY, Charles, 171
FAIGE, Robert, 107
Sarah, 107
FAILES, Sarah Ann, 154
FAIRBANK, Ann Elizabeth, 204
Elizabeth, 204
William, 204
FALES, Annie C., 276
Charles Eschbach, 223
Cornelia Ann, 223
E. Clark, 223, 228
Eben C., 224
Henry Alexander, 224
Mary R., 224
FALLON, Bertha Elizabeth, 242
FALLS, E. C., 307
Mary R., 307
FANCHI, Andrew, 206
Cecilia Carolina, 206
Elizabeth, 206
FANESTOCK, Ann, 150
FANNING, William H., 236
FANTZ, Jacob, 31, 70, 76
Joh. Jacob, 31
Maria Magdalena, 70
FAOST, Frederick A., 229
FARDWELL, Ann M., 170
FARR, Johan, 103
FARRALL, Charles, 165
FARRELL, John, 271
FASSBINDER, Hedwig, 37
Peter, 37
FAUBEL, John Jacob, 160

Wilhelm, 56
FAUPEL, Jacob, 40
FAUST, Margaretha, 91
  Maria, 116
  Theobald, 14, 91, 101
FAUT, ---, 78
  Anna Magdalena, 28
  Catharina, 28, 32, 36, 39
  Catherine, 76
  Henrich, 76
  Magdalena, 36
  Theob., 36, 39, 70, 72
  Theobald, 28, 32, 39, 56, 69, 76
FAUTZ, ---, 78
  Catharina, 25
  Jacob, 25
  Theobald, 25
FAVIER, Francis C., 240
FEGER, Cathrina, 54
FEICE, Catharina, 91
  Louisa, 91
  Peter, 91
FEIGE, Anna, 48
  Carrie, 250
  Catharina, 91
  Charles L., 250
  Friederich, 48
  Georg, 95
  Gotfried, 95, 103
  James Hackerus, 116
  Johan, 108, 288, 291
  Johann Friederich, 48
  John, 116
  John Hawkins Patterson, 250
  Julia, 103, 293
  Juliana, 95
  Louisa, 91
  Maria, 284
  Mariana, 103
  Nancy, 108, 116

Peter, 91, 284
Sophia, 108, 288
FEIGIN, Sophia, 39
FEIGL, Gottfried, 103
  Julia, 103
  Mariana, 103
FEIGLEY, Aldwellah, 249
  Bessie White, 249
  Charles W., 249
  Lela May, 249
FEIL, Friederich, 80
  John, 4
FEISTER, Robert Rossiter, 272
FEIT, Conrad, 34
  Jacob, 34
FELDNER, Rebecka, 54
FELDPUISCH,
  Frederika, 255
  George, 255
  James Edwin, 255
FELDPUSCH, Carl, 253
  Cath., 261
  Catherine Estelle, 248
  Ferdinand Mardoga, 250
  Fredericka, 248, 250
  Frederika, 253
  George, 231, 248, 250, 253
  Mary, 230
  Peter, 266
FENNELL, Nancy, 57
FERNALD, Sidney O., 239
FERRANDINI, Josephine, 231
FERRELL, Eleanor E., 163
FERSTERMAN, Charles, 263
  Charles William, 263
FESTER, Charles Parker, 270
  Jacob Coker, 270

FEUERABEND, Hanna, 194
  John, 194
FEYE, Johan, 96
  Mariana, 96
  Nancy, 96
FEYER, Friederich, 57
FEYL, Johan, 96
  Mariana, 96
  Nancy, 96
FIEGE, Maria Sophia, 46
FIELD, Wilhelm, 64
FIELDS, William, 38
FIGE, Friederich, 138
  Johan, 85
  Johannes, 85
  Nancy, 85, 282
FILIARSIN, Barbara, 81
FILINGIN, Barbara, 81
FILLER, Charles W., 235
FINDERS, Phillip, 56
FINGER, Barbara, 282
FINLAY, Frances A., 168, 212
  William, 212
  William L., 212
FINLEY, Harry Jennings, 207
  William, 299
  William Elenora, 207
FISCHBACH, Anna Maria, 41
FISCHER, A. M., 186
  Ann E., 156
  Ann Maria, 190
  Charles Norris, 261, 277
  Clara May, 257
  Elisabeth, 29, 37
  G. L., 186
  Georg, 89, 284
  George, 190, 275
  George William, 256, 273

Index

James Michael, 190
Julius, 235, 256, 257, 261
Mary Ann, 186
Mary C., 261
May C., 256, 257
Wilhelm Presler, 89
FISHBACH, Frederick, 193
  Lorentz, 193
  Philippina, 193
FISHER, A. M., 217
  Ann Maria, 210
  Anna Maria, 188
  Barbara, 204
  Basel, 144
  Bersal, 204
  Burte, 300
  Charles Jacob, 211
  Emma Virginia, 183
  G. F., 217
  G. L., 183
  Georg L., 300
  George, 154
  George F., 181
  George L., 175, 188, 210, 211
  Georgianna, 181
  Henry, 204
  Ida Catherine, 210
  James D., 150
  Johannes, 73
  John Haas, 175
  Josephine, 242
  Julia Margaret, 188
  Lawrence Matthew, 276
  Lottie S., 229
  M. A., 175, 183
  Mabel C., 237
  Mary Ann, 181, 211
  Mary E., 171
  Oberta Jefferson, 217
  Susah, 156

William Henry, 181
FISSEL, Artis J., 264
  John Edwin, 264
  Katherine, 264
FITZGERALD, Rev., 225
FITZPATRICK, Charles, 235
FLACHSKAMP, Clara, 111
  Margaretha, 111, 119
  Maria, 119
  Wilhelm, 111, 119, 142
FLAHERTY, Katie A., 242
FLAX, Johannes, 24
  Magdalena, 24
FLEMMING, Ann Eliza, 164
  Elyah, 52
  James R., 163
FLETSCHER, Anna Maria, 19
  Maria, 284
  Martin, 19, 287
  Rebecca, 138
FLORENS, Mariana, 294
  Mr., 294
FLORI, John Conrad, 51
FLORINA, Johanna, 283
FLOTZER, Anna Maria, 31
  Christof Michael, 9
  Martin, 31
  Sarah, 31
FLUSH, John, 293
  Susanna, 293
FOARD, David, 260
  Margaret Thelma, 260
  Virginia, 260
FOBB, Ann Magdlina, 193
FOBEL, Anna, 114
  Anna Charlotta, 44
  Anna Maria, 114, 291

Daniel, 89, 99, 114, 122, 291, 292
Elisabeth, 99
Heinrich, 102
Helena, 44, 50
Johann Wilhelm, 50
Johannes, 110, 122
Michael, 102
Mr., 99
Susanna, 99, 286
Susanna Rebecca, 134
W., 102
Wilhelm, 44, 50, 109, 110, 134
William, 114
FOBLE, Magdal., 197
  Mary, 147
  Rebecca, 153
FOBLER, Rebecca, 153
FOCHE, Frederick, 117
  Julia Elisabeth, 117
FOCK, Friederich, 294
  Johan Friederich, 294
FOCKA, Louisa, 145
FOCKE, Aletta, 132
  Anna Henrietta, 88
  Carl Wilhelm, 79
  Carl Wilhelm Ferdinand, 79, 294
  Edward Lewis, 132
  Fredrick, 132
  Friederich, 79, 98, 134
  Friedrich, 43, 88
  Henrich Justus, 98
  Johan Friederich, 134
  Johann Peter, 79
  Johann Peter Friederich, 43
  Louisa, 145
  Metta, 43, 79
  Rebecca Frederica, 132
FOERMANN, Minta, 56

FOGELMAN, Catharina, 118, 123
  Georg, 118, 123, 141
  Susanna, 123
FOGLEMAN, Susan, 171
FOLCK, Anna Elisabeth, 82
  Carl, 82, 91
  Johan Friederich, 91
  Margaretha, 82, 91
FOLEY, Maria E., 242
FOLK, John E., 173
FOLKE, Caroline A., 224
  John E., 224
  William Edward, 224
FORD, Catharine M., 163
  Edmond, 51
  Joshua, 52
FORDER, Peter, 153
FORNE, Johan, 85
  Johan Heinrich, 85
  Sarah, 85
FORNEIR(IN), Barbara, 28
FORNEN, Adam, 30
  Barbara, 30
  Johannes, 30, 76
FORNER, Joh., 22
FORNEY, ---, 37, 78
  Abraham, 48
  Adam, 59, 62, 65
  Anna Barbara, 24, 38, 66
  Barbara, 24, 96
  Catharina, 84
  Charlotte, 38
  David, 288
  Elisabeth, 38, 40, 48, 50, 84, 206
  Eva, 96
  Ewis, 49
  Jacob, 49, 96
  Job., 65
  Johan, 84, 285, 293
  Johan Georg, 282
  Johann, 38, 40, 50, 76
  Johann Georg, 49
  Johannes, 24, 76
  John, 284
  Louisa, 288
  Maria, 48, 55
  Maria Elisabeth, 24, 38
  Mathias N., 148
  Mr., 66, 282
  Nicolaus, 38, 40
  Sally, 284
  Sara, 76
  Sarah, 40, 50
  Susanna, 55
  Widow, 32
  Wilhelm, 76
FORNISEN, Anna Barbara, 40
FORNY, ---, 78
  Adam, 11
  Anna-Catharina, 11
  Barbara, 11
  Elisabeth, 11
  Johannes, 11
FORRESTER, Georg, 54
FORSYTH, Alexander, 162, 176, 215
  George B., 234
  Margaret, 176
  Margaret Jane, 215
  Martha, 176, 215
  Wilhemina, 275
FORTER, Margareth, 20
  Samuel, 20, 61
FORTINE, Anna Martha, 101, 112
  Georg, 112
  Johannes, 101
  Nicolaus, 101
  Nikolaus, 112
FORTNEY, Anna Maria, 31
  Elisabeth, 35
  Rachel, 35
  Rahel, 31
  Wilhelm, 31, 35, 76
FORTUNE, Nicolaus, 139
FOSS, Catharine Emily, 151
  Mrs., 195
FOSTER, William, 168
FOUNTAIN, Edward W., 236
FOWBLE, Elizabeth, 149
FOX, Edward Wado, 216
  Hiram E., 216
  Sarah I., 216
FOXCROFT, Nicholas, 161
FOY, Elisabeth, 51
  John, 138
FOYE, Friederich, 144
FOYEN, Ginnie Olive, 228
FOYER, Emma R., 172
FRAIL, Maria L., 304
FRAIN, Maud, 238
FRAKING, Elbertha, 255
  Esther Louise, 255
  William E., 235, 255
FRANCES, Francis Anton, 227
  George Theo., 227
FRANCHI, Andrew, 196, 200, 203
  Elizabeth, 196, 200, 203
  Maria Louisa, 196
  Mary Ann Elizabeth, 200
  Susan Catharine, 203
FRANCIS, William P., 166
FRANCISCUS, Catharina, 64
  Cathrina, 10
  Georg, 6, 10

Index

George, 62
Joh. Georg, 8
Johannes, 6
Margaretha, 10
Margretha, 6
FRANCISUS, Georg, 8
Margretha, 8
FRANCK, Elisabeth, 48
George, 162, 303
Margaretha, 48
Maria, 287
Peter, 48
FRANK, Elizabeth Ann, 210
George, 210
Mary Margaretta, 210
Susanna, 200
FRANKLIN, Miss, 156
FRANS, Johann, 25, 76
Katharina, 25
FRANTZ, ---, 78
Abraham, 8, 13, 17, 25, 26, 28, 61
Anna, 25
Catharina, 26, 28
Catherina, 8
Cathrina, 13
Elisabeth, 82
Henrich, 28
Joh. Georg, 13
Mr., 63
Sara, 26
FRANZ, ---, 78
Abraham, 19
Cathrina, 19
Johannes, 19
FRAST, Thomas, 292
FRAUCHI, Andrew, 145
FRAUD, Willy, 22
FRAZIER, Alice K., 233
Annie E., 230
Eliza Smith, 269

Mrs., 296
FREAS, Emma G., 239
FREBERGER, Benjamin Franklin, 178
Catharine Amanda, 190
Eliza, 191
Elizabeth, 178, 190
Henry G., 303
Isaac, 191
J., 191
John, 178, 190
Mary Elizabeth, 178
FREBURGER, Carrol Spence, 213
George A., 213
Johann, 87
Johannes, 87
Nancy, 87
Terresa, 213
FREDERICK, Caroline, 221
Charles Henry William, 221
Henry G., 173, 221
FREEBERGER, Ann Maria, 156
Ann Olivia, 192
Eliza Jane, 192
Elizabeth, 192, 198
George Alexander, 204
Henry, 204
John, 192, 198, 204
Martha Ellen, 198
Mary, 204
Sarah, 204
FREEBURGER, Andrew Jackson, 195
Elizabeth, 195
Henry G., 168
Johann, 57
John, 148, 151, 195
FREEMAN, Isaac, 199
Jane, 151

Mamie, 239
Mary, 199
Samuel, 199
FREI, Elisabet, 53
FREIBERGER, Charlotte, 147
John, 148
Nancy, 285
FREIBURGER, James, 289
Johan, 289
Susanna, 52
FRENCH, Anna Jane, 171
Cath., 202
Edward, 202
Mathew, 202
Wesley, 233
FRESE, Johan Friederich, 134
Julia, 117
Rebecca, 134
FRESH, Sarah, 150
FREUDENBERGER, Henrich, 54
FREY, Adam, 14
Anna, 201
Anna Maria, 14, 121
Clarissa Juda, 201
Elisabeth, 81, 121
Elizabeth, 199
Georg, 201
Gottfried, 14
Heinrich, 105
Henrich, 121
J., 190
Jacob, 89
Joh. Adam, 14
Johann, 81
John, 199
John B., 147
John Joseph, 199
Luisana Henrietta, 121

Index

Maria Louisa, 199
Mrs., 253
Nancy, 141
Ralph Westwood, 243
Rebecca Amelia, 190
Rebecca Sophia, 121
Sarah, 199
Sarah A., 272
Sarah Ann, 190
FREYA(ER), Johannes, 54
FREYBURGER, Johannes, 280
  Margaretha, 280
FREYER, Alice Caroline, 259
  E. S., 176, 190, 219
  Elijah S., 177, 190
  Elijah Samuel, 176
  Elizabeth, 204
  Elizabeth Ann, 155
  Ellen, 190
  Emma Rachel, 176
  Eugene Henry, 177
  Harding, 219, 296
  Henry, 204
  James, 190
  Jane, 176, 177, 219, 296
  Jane Olive, 176
  Margaret Alice, 259
  Maria, 140
  Phoebe Margaurite, 274
  Rebecca S., 156
  Sarah Jane, 204
  William, 190
  William H., 233
  William Henry, 259
FREYMILLER, Barbara, 52
FRIBERGER, Rahel, 279
FRIBURGER, Anna Margaretha, 41

George, 37
Heinrich, 80, 89
Henrich, 33, 37, 41, 45
Jacob, 102
Johannes, 41
Margaretha, 33, 37, 41, 45, 80, 89
Mr., 102
Rahel, 41
Rosina, 89
Samuel, 45
Wilhelm, 80
FRICK, C., 225
  C. J., 222, 223, 226
  Cecelia J., 207
  Clarence Englehart, 223
  E. A., 222, 223, 225, 226
  Emma Virginia, 226
  Englehart, 207
  Englehart A., 269
  George Arnold, 207
  Joseph Hershey, 265, 311
  Mary E., 267
  Mary Elizabeth, 222
  Rachel Shorer, 225
FRIEBURGER, Carl, 118
  Henrich, 118
  James, 111
  Johan, 111
  John, 111
  Margaretha, 111
  Margarethe, 111
  Nancy, 111
FRIED, Henrich, 61
FRIEDERICHS, David, 106, 112, 137
  Maria, 136
  Mr., 120
  Salome, 286
FRIEDRICH, Harry, 242
FRIEN, Nancy, 169

FRIEND, Alfred, 156, 172, 179, 208, 212, 213
  Alfred Diffenderffer, 179
  Ann Elizabeth, 179, 212, 213
  Charles Henry, 213
  Elizabeth, 208, 301
  Ellen D., 208
  Richard Augustus, 212
  William Henry, 212
FRIGAL, William, 52
FRIGGER, Eliza Ann, 152
FRITTER, William H., 272
FROBLE, Magdalina, 200
FROHLENIER,
  Elisabeth, 25
  Georg, 25
  George, 76
  Susanna, 25
FROST, Catherine, 246
  Christina, 257
  Christina Catherine, 245
  Fred A., 245, 246, 247, 248, 251
  Frederick A., 253
  Frederick Albert, 253
  Jessie, 251
  Kate, 245, 246, 247, 248, 251, 253
  Margaret, 241, 247
  Mrs., 248, 261
  Thomas Spencer, 248, 270
  Veronica, 88
  William, 171
FRUBERGER, Charlotte, 147
  John, 148
FRUBURGER, John, 151
FRUM, Catharine, 162
  Sarah, 163

FRY, Florence E., 234
FRYBURGER, Charlotte, 49
  Johann, 49
  Nancy, 49
FRYER, Jane Olive, 303
FRYOR, E. S., 208
  Jane O., 208
FUHRMAN, Carl, 121, 136
  Charles, 142
  David, 294
  Ferdinand, 121, 292
  H. H., 274
  Jacob, 136
  Margaretha, 121, 136
  Mr., 292
FUHRMANN, Andreas, 26
  Anna, 26
  Anna Maria, 24, 48
  Carl, 42
  Carl Theodor, 41
  Johann Jacob, 26
  Leonhard, 34, 48
  Leonhart, 24
FULLER, James, 229
  Josiah, 153
  Mary, 275
FULLHARDT, Elisabeth, 55
FUNCK, Mrs., 226
FUNCKERT, Christian, 31
FUNK, Emma C., 232
  Emma Lee, 233
  Franz, 47
  Irene, 231
  Maria, 47
  Willie H., 269
FUSCH, Jacob, 287
  Mrs., 287

FUSELBACH, Barbara, 99
  Jacob, 99
  Johan, 99
  Johan Heinrich, 290
FUSH, Catharina, 109, 290
  Georg, 289
  Jacob, 109
  Johan, 109, 111, 289, 290
  Margaretha, 111, 290
FUSS, John, 142
FUSSELL, Philena F., 168

-G-
GABE, Fannie, 170
GABLE, John, 156
GADE, Ann, 188, 194
  Annett Marion, 188
  Ida, 175
  John, 175, 188, 194
  Maria Louesa, 168
  Mr., 283
GAEHLE, Dora V., 232
GAITHER, Menerva, 170
GALBGA, Francis, 148
GALE, George, 171
  James H., 148
  Martha, 148
GALLOWAY, Eleanor, 163
GALT, Washington, 158
GAMBER, Anna Barbara, 14
  Conrad, 14
  Sara, 14
GAMMILL, Jacob M., 230, 246
  Maggie, 246
  Nellie Elizabeth, 246
GANDERMAN, Mr., 106
GANTZ, Adam, 9
  Ellen H., 255, 258

  James S., 255, 258
  James William, 255
  Maria, 105
  Raymond Andrew, 258
GARD, E. H., 162
  Margaret, 162
GARDENER, Cathrina, 14, 22
  Daniel, 17
  Phillip, 17, 22, 75
  Willy, 14, 75
GARDINER, Cathrina, 52
  Sarah, 52
GARDNER, Casandra, 54
  Cathrina, 20
  Charles Edmund, 218
  Joh. Jacob, 20
  Marinda, 176
  Mrs., 218
  Phillip, 20
  William K., 176, 218
  William Kingsbury, 176
GARING, James H. C., 255
  Lillian Elizabeth, 255
  Mary, 255
GARLAND, James, 265, 312
  Margaret Ann, 309
GARMANN, John, 55
GARNET, Clara, 244
GARRETT, Ellen L., 234
  Margaret, 150
GARRETTSEN, Elizabeth M., 163
GARRISON, David G., 163
  Eliza, 146
  Rebecca, 46
GARTERBECK, Rebecca, 87
GASCHA, Barbara, 2
  Margaretha, 2

Peter, 2
GATCHAIR, Francis, 198
　Lewis Thomas, 198
　Maria Magdalena, 198
　Mary, 198
GATCHELL, Caroline D., 171
GATECHAIER, Francis, 132
　Francis George, 132
　Mary, 132
GATECHAIR, Francis, 201
　Mary, 201
　Salina Felicity, 201
GATSCHLER, Johan, 136
　Mr., 136
GAUL, Anna Maria, 89
GAURIG, Susanna, 55
GAUS, Catharina, 115
　Jakob, 115
GAUSS, Regina, 112
GEATY, Ellen, 169
GEBHARD, Catharina, 95
　Friedrich, 45
　Johan Friederich, 95, 287
　Katharina, 45
GECKLER, William G., 163
GEDDIS, Margaret Ann, 164
GEES, Mary Blanche, 244
GEHLBACH, Christian, 45
GEHO, Adam, 248
　Adam K., 251, 254
　Amelia Alverta, 248
　Edna Estelle, 254
　Emma C., 248, 251, 254
　Harry Ehl, 251
GEIDT, Anthony E., 235
　Anton E., 258

Camilla, 262
Camilla M., 258
Henry, 238, 258, 262
Irvin Baroux, 258
Juia A., 232
Leroy Henry, 262
Mollie A., 261
Philip M., 241, 261
Raymond Henry, 261
Sallie C., 258
William Albert, 258
GEIGER, Alfred Logdsdon, 249
　Alice Catherine, 258
　Anna Elisabeth, 63
　Charles, 171
　Elisabeth, 98
　Ella V., 258
　George H., 235, 258
　Grace Algie, 252, 270
　Harry William, 245
　Jacob, 144
　Joh., 7
　John H., 276
　John Peregrine, 248
　John W., 230, 245, 249, 252, 276
　John W. H., 236, 248, 251
　Lola Jenette, 251
　Mary P., 245, 249, 252
　Rosanna J., 248, 251, 271
GEISER, Anna Maria, 140
GEISLER, Adelheid Elisabeth, 43, 48, 49
　Adelheid Elisbeth, 37
　Daniel Conrad, 292
　Diederich, 87
　Dietrich George, 37
　Dorothea Louisa, 48, 285
　Elisabeth, 49, 87
　Eliza, 150
　Friderica, 37

Friderike, 43
Friederike, 49
Georg, 43, 49, 143
Georg Diederich, 48, 49
George Diederich, 285
George Diederich, 56
Georgianna, 158
Jacob, 43
Johan Diederich, 87, 284
Johan Georg, 282
Johann George, 37
Mr., 284, 292
GEISSENDOERFFER, Elisabeth, 48
GEISSLER, Daniel Conrad, 42
　Georg Diedrich, 42
　George, 65
　Johann Friederich, 65
GELBACH, Casisana, 99, 287
　Cath., 132
　Christian, 99, 110, 122, 132, 182, 287
　Christiana, 183, 303
　Elisabeth, 122
　George, 150, 183
　George John, 182
　John Jackson, 132
　Sally, 99
　Sarah, 110
　Sophia, 110
　William J. Harrison, 183
GELLI, Elisabeth, 142
GELTZER, George, 66
　Geroge, 24
　Vallentin, 52
GEMMILL, Cody, 239, 260, 261
　Francisco, 261, 262
　Henry August, 262
　James William Graydon, 260

Index

John Matthew, 261, 276
Maggie, 260, 261, 262
GENESI, Marie Sardy, 237
GENLY, Dixon Crawford, 217
  Elizabeth, 217
  George, 217
GENSBERG, Andreas, 46
  Jacob, 46
  Johan Jacob, 284
  Katharina, 46
GENTIL-MAJER, Johann Michael, 11
GEORG, Anna Maria, 12
  Henrich, 12
GEORGE, Annie Minerva, 259
GEORGHEGAN, Franklin, 243
GERARD, Peter Johan, 143
GERASS, Peter Johan, 143
GERBOTH, Sophia M., 233
GERDING, Henry, 261
  Louis H., 240, 261
  Mary C., 261
  Raymond Henry, 261
GERDNER, Susan, 167
GERHARDT, William F. C., 229
GERHART, Charles, 245
  Elizabeth A., 248, 249
  Elvester, 248
  Harry, 249
  Henry H., 231, 248, 249
GERHOLD, George, 208
  Mary, 208
  Mary Eliza, 208
GERLACH, Carolina, 144
GERMAN, Alice, 259

Anna, 115
Catharina, 64
Elisabeth, 85, 283
Elizabeth, 169
Friederich, 115
Jobe, 192
Joh., 67
Johan Daniel, 87
Johannes, 68
Magdalena, 56
Margaret Ellen, 259
Margaretha, 67
Michael, 71, 85, 97
Michel Philip, 115
Nikolaus, 87
Philip, 39, 85, 87, 89, 115, 134, 283, 290
Phillip, 36
Rebecca, 87
Sarah Ann, 192
Sarah Elizabeth McColm, 192
Thomas Lowry, 259
Thomas Sinclair, 259
Wilhelm Philip, 85
GERMANN, Catharina, 26, 31
  Elisabeth, 26
  Johannes, 26, 31
  Magdalena, 31
GERWIN, Maria, 54
GESSLER(IN), Cathrina, 17
GETIER, Elis., 103
  Elisabeth, 142
  Peter, 287
  Sally, 287
GETTELMORA, Georg, 16
  Magdalena, 16
  Vallentin, 16
  Wilhelm, 16

GETTEMULLER, John F., 236
GETTER, Cornelius J., 224
GETTERS, Jennie M., 241
GETTIER, Charles Augustus, 196
  Eliza G., 245
  Jacob, 196
  Jessie, 245
  Kate, 229
  Margaret, 196
  Mr., 300
  Vernia, 245
  William J., 245
GETZ, Friederich, 143
GEWECKE, Conrad H., 260
  Elizabeth, 260
  Raymond Lawrence, 260
GEYSER, Katharina, 44, 280
GHEEN, John B., 231
GIBBEN, John Francis, 177
GIBBS, Margaretha, 143
  Mary E., 240
  Susanna, 138
GIBS, Susanna, 88
GIBSEN, Elisabeth, 141
GIBSON, Ernest C., 240
  James, 88
GIDDIER, Margaret, 152
GIDDLEMAN, Ellen, 148
GIDERNEY, Charles Henry, 208
  Lewis, 208
  M. C., 208
GIESLER, Dietrich, 199
  Eliza, 199
  Georgianna, 199
  John, 199
GIESSLER, John, 54

Index

GIFFORD, Alice C., 234
  William, 270
GILBERT, William H., 242
GILES, Charles Frederick, 259, 275
  John T., 256, 259
  Joseph Howard, 272
  Magdalena, 256, 259
  Mrs., 302
  Myrtle Marie, 256
GILKEY, Mary A., 236
GILL, Ann Maria, 187
GILLARD, Joh., 130
GILLIGAN, Edward, 171
GILMORE, William T., 230
GIPE, Maud, 239
GIPSON, Lydia, 162
GISCHE, Johannes, 3, 73
GITTERMAN, Charles J., 266
  Charles Jelto, 247
  Herman H., 245, 247, 267
  Mary C., 245, 247
  Rossiter Edwin, 245
GIVEN, James Edgar, 244
GLADENER, Adam, 15
  Cathrina, 15
  Elisabeth, 15
GLASCOCK, William H., 241
GLASCOE, Catherine, 264
  James, 264
  John Hilary, 264
GLASER, Charles W., 240, 261
  Louise C., 261
  William, 261
  William Alfred, 261
GLASGOW, Adaline, 157
  Robert, 237

GLASSNER, John, 148
GLATES, Anna Trafy, 206
GLEASON, John R., 242
GLENAU, Annie E. M., 229
GLENN, Mary Ann, 149, 206
GLESNER, Catharine, 146
GLESSNER, Hamilton A., 234
GLOAG, David, 259, 261
  Emmeline Euphina May, 261, 276
  Maria M., 259
  Mary Cath. Bertha G., 259
  Mary M., 261
GLONINGER, John, 149
GLOSSNER, Annie E., 236
GLOUINGER, Peter, 205
GLOVER, William, 154
GLUCK, Philip A., 270
GOBEL, Elisabeth, 53
GOBER, Margareth, 18
GODFREY, Agnes, 211
  Andrew, 217
  Cath., 208
  Catherine, 212
  David Andrew, 211
  Dorothy, 212
  Elizabeth, 212, 216
  Fanny, 207, 209
  Harriet, 217
  Henry, 212, 216
  Isabella, 168, 209
  James, 165, 207, 208, 212, 217
  John, 169
  Johnsen, 211
  Johnson, 170, 207
  Johnston, 209

  Mary Ann, 169
  Mrs., 297
  Sh., 225
  Thomas, 212
  Thomas Andrew, 216
GODWIN, George F., 232
GOHRING, Anna Barbara, 45
GOIN, Sarah, 55
GOLE, Susan M., 172
GOLWAY, Alexander, 240
GOMLEY, John, 228
GONYARD, Joseph, 55
GOODRICH, William, 270
GOOTFRIED, Anna, 18
GORDON, A. M. E., 224
  Abram M. E., 228
  Abram Mills Eggleston Gor, 224
  Sue M., 224
GORE, Benjamin, 153
GORMAN, Eliza, 214
  James W., 161, 214
  Marcella, 214
GORMLY, James, 54
GORNELY, James, 54
GORSUCH, Theresa J., 239
GORTHENER, Phillip, 52
GOSBURY, Edward, 174
  Elizabeth, 174
GOSNELL, Hoper, 54
GOSS, Alice V., 233
GOSWEILER, Alice Catherine, 254, 271
  Cath. F., 248, 249, 259
  Catherine F., 254
  John Albert, 248, 268
  John H., 275
  Mary E., 277

Index 353

Mary Elizabeth, 249, 274
Melton Ross, 259
Ross Nevin, 248, 249, 254, 259
GOTTRY, Josua, 61
GOTZ, James, 295
GOUGH, William, 139
GOULA, John H., 169
GOULD, Laura R., 245
  M. Alex, 245
  Samuel F., 164
  Samuel J., 164
  Vera Montrose, 245
GOUNLY, Ann, 173
GOURGARD, Joseph, 55
GOURLEY, James, 208
  Mary, 169
  Mary F., 208
  Mary Frances, 208
GOVAN, Jennie V., 238
GOVE, Fred. B, 263
  Fred. B., 263
  Lottie Bell, 263
  Maggie, 263
  Margret, 263
  Nellie May, 263
GOVER, Edward, 224
  Edward L., 306
  Emma Eudora, 306
  Mary E., 224, 306
  Samuel Edward, 224
GOVERMAN, Amelia Indiana, 170
GRABER, Allen, 114
  Daniel, 114, 126
  Johan David, 119
  Johan Henrich, 126
GRABILL, John W., 244
GRAEBER, Daniel, 141
GRAF, Catharina, 123
  Elisabeth Margaretha, 96
  Heinrich, 123

Stephanus, 88, 96
  Wilhelm, 88
GRAFF, Ann Levinia, 151
GRAFFT, William, 51
GRAHAM, Mary A. A., 171
GRAIN, Eduart, 105
  Georg Washington, 105
  Joseph, 105
GRAMMER, Anna Elisabeth, 45, 79
GRANCHET, ---, 78
  Andreas, 8
  Maria, 8
GRANE, Mrs., 195
GRANT, Cornelia, 221
  Eleisa, 36
  Elisabeth, 36
  Ethlan A., 172
  Jane, 213, 221
  Jane Ann, 178, 181
  John, 36, 56, 153
  John Marshall, 181
  Josephine Jilden, 213
  Margaret, 150
  Marion, 178
  Mary, 181
  Mary Ann, 147
  Robert, 178, 181, 213, 221
GRASTAN, Sara, 52
GRAY, Catharine, 158
  Charles Wesley, 177
  Elizabeth, 177, 219
  George, 177, 219
  Heziah, 161
  John, 56
  Josuah, 54
  Laura Virginia, 177
  Leonard W., 172
  Mary, 52
  Mary Elizabeth, 177
  Mr., 298

Rebecca Ann, 177
Richard L., 232
William L., 158
GRAYHIT, ---, 78
  Andreas, 59
GREEK, Annie, 258
GREEN, Ann M., 161
  Cornelius, 156
  Josias, 56
  Julius, 56
  Mary E., 243
  Susan, 160
GREENAWALT, Alice, 256
  C. Alice, 255, 258
  Edna May, 258
  Ehrman Dauphin, 256
  Frank Harper, 255
  Thomas S., 255, 256, 258
GREER, Agnes, 211
  Andrew, 211
  Mary Agnes, 211
GREFFITH, Barbara, 188
  Casandra, 188
  Edward, 188
  Mary Fletcher, 188
GREGLER, Elizabeth, 55
GREGOR, John M., 168
GRENCHETT, ---, 78
  Andreas, 6
  Maria, 6
GRERSETSCH, Helena, 3
  Johannes, 3
GRESLEY, Bertha, 241
GREULICH, Cathrina, 17
  Herman, 17
  Jacob, 17
GREUZET, Andreas, 2
GREY, Ann, 304
  Dixon, 305
  James Joseph, 302

Joseph, 304
Richard, 170
Sarah, 305
William, 305
GRIDY, Barbra, 53
GRIFFER, Heinrich, 140
GRIFFIN, Colburn Knapp, 213
D., 3304
Dan. S., 221
Daniel S., 163
David S., 182, 213
E., 3304
Elizabeth, 182, 221
Georg Shaffner, 221
George Schaffner, 304
John Jacob, 182
Mary Ann, 166
Mrs., 257
GRIFFING, Colby K., 266
Daniel S., 307
GRIFFIS, James, 154
GRIFFITH, Annie, 271
Annie M., 248, 250
E., 223
Eleanor, 223
Elizabeth, 210, 274
G. S., 210, 222, 223, 256
George Mason, 229
Goldsboro Sappington, 223
Goldsborough S., 156
Goldsborow S., 223
Harriot, 151
Martha Rebecca, 223
Mary B., 146
Robert Matthiott, 248
William H., 231, 248, 269
William Harman, 250
William J., 250
GRIMES, Mary, 206
Mattie E., 231

GRIN, Sarah, 55
GROASON, Samuel, 52
GROB, Agnes, 135
Georg, 118, 135
Margaretha, 118, 135
Samuel, 242
Sarah Anna, 118
GRODENER, Phillip, 75
Willy, 75
GROF, Catharina Susanna, 104
Stephanus, 88, 104, 284
Wilhelm, 88, 284
GROFF, Catharina, 131
Frena, 204
Henrich, 204
Henry, 131
Jacob Forney, 119
Stephanus, 119
Susanna Catharina, 131
GROFTEN, ---, 213
GRONAU, Christian, 56
GROOME, Christina Gafford, 275
GROOMS, Cath., 200
GROSS, Sarah, 130
Wilhelm, 13
GROULEY, James, 221
Mary, 221
Mary Margaret, 221
GROVE, Catherine, 152
Jacob F., 181
Leonard C., 243
Mrs., 194
Sally, 181
GROVERMAN, A., 296
Amelia A., 304
Amelia H., 180, 188, 191
Amelia Indianna, 191
Anthony, 188
Frances, 180
Henry, 153, 180, 188, 191

Honey, 310
Maria Elisabeth, 283
Michael Diffenderffer, 180
GRUBB, Agnes, 155
Ann Amelia, 195
George, 195, 203
George Washington, 195
Margaret, 195
Margaret Elizabeth, 203
Maria, 203
Sarah Ann, 154
GRUBER, Anna, 143
Anna Maria, 105, 118, 130
Daniel, 105
Elisabeth, 118, 136
Jacob, 118, 130, 143
Johan Jacob, 130, 136
Martin, 118, 136
Mary, 143
Michael, 123
GRUENAWALD, William A., 275
GRUGER, Frank R., 228
GRULER, Daniel, 141
GRUMBINE, Daisy M., 238
GRUN, Magdalena, 136
GRUND, Adam, 11, 16
Cathrina, 11
Christina, 11
Jacob, 11
GRUPY, Clara L., 234
Mary, 232
GUETLER, Anton Earnest, 251
Anton Ernest, 269
Charles, 243
George, 232, 251, 253, 260
George Philip, 253
John Earle Howard, 260

Julia A., 251, 253, 260
GUFFING, Mrs., 223
GULDENER, Friederich, 10
GUNDERMAN, Mr., 106, 136
GUNTER, Charles O., 262
Charles Otto, 262
Susie, 262
GUNTHER, Charles O., 236, 256, 259
Emma J., 239
Marguerite Anna, 256
Mildred Lenore, 259
Susie, 256, 259
GURLEY, Elizabeth, 219
Eliza Patterson, 177
Elizabeth, 177
George, 177, 219
Mary Jane, 219
GUTEBACH, Catharina, 52
GUTMAN, Caroline Susanna, 263
Doretha Louisa, 263
Edward, 263
Mary, 263
GUY, Albert Kennedy, 222
Alma Marie, 259
Ann, 221, 222, 224, 304
Annie, 251
Bessie Campbel, 251
Dixon, 221, 224, 225, 226, 227, 229, 238, 256, 259, 260, 305, 309
Dixon Crawford, 184
Edward Joseph, 222
Elizabeth Smith, 211
Ellen L., 254, 258
Fannie Blanche, 226

Frederick Hinkleman, 225
George Davidson, 267
Harry Raymond, 258
James, 184, 238
James Isaac, 245, 266
James Joseph, 210, 302
James Oliver, 211
James William, 254
Jane, 184, 222, 224
Jane Crawford, 208, 267
Jennie, 235
John, 227
John Thomas, 215
Joseph, 173, 221, 222, 224, 251, 267, 304
Joseph Edward, 260
Joseph Elmer, 247
Josephine R., 226, 227
Josie R., 225
Maggie B., 259, 260
Margaret McLane, 222
Martha, 296
Martha Crawford, 212
Mary E., 239
Mary Elizabeth, 222
Mary Jane, 218
Mary S., 237
Mary Stephenson, 226
Mathilda, 208, 211, 222
Moses, 208, 211, 222, 309
Samuel Patterson, 208
Sarah, 210, 212, 222, 223, 305, 309
Sarah A., 225, 245, 247
Sarah Ann, 208, 211, 215, 221, 226
Sarah Ann R., 166
Sarah Eliza, 221
William, 166, 208, 210, 211, 212, 215, 218, 221, 222, 223, 225, 226, 234,

245, 247, 254, 258, 274, 305, 309
GUYEN, John R., 146
GWYNN, Edgar Percival, 259
Francina B., 252
Francina Bouchelle, 259
Nowland Bennett Edgar, 252
Percival, 252

-H-
HAACK, Anna Maria, 37
Maria, 37
Nicolaus, 37, 56
HAACKE, Hermann Wilhelm, 44
Sophia, 44
HAAKE, Lucia Sophia, 49
Nicolaus, 49
Sophia, 49
HAAN, Adam, 46
Eva, 46
Peter, 46
HAAS, Cath., 247
Catherine, 237
George, 234
Henry, 268
HAASE, George, 71
HAASEN, Anna J., 160
HABBARD, Edward, 148
HABBOJANE, Thomas W., 239
HABER, Catharina, 138
Maria, 143
HABERKORN, Mary L., 236
HABERSTUMPF, Mollie A., 241
HABLISTON, Heinrich, 107
Henrietta, 56
HABLITZ, Johan, 138

HABURG, Anna, 47
HACHENBACH, Anna Maria, 118
  Louisa, 118
HACHENBRACHT, David, 83, 282
  Heinrich, 83, 282
  Henrich, 57
  Louisa, 83
HACK, Anna Maria, 71
  Nic., 71
  Sarah, 159
HACKE, Adelheid, 284
  Adelheit, 86
  Carolina Wilhelmina, 115
  Christiana Adelheid, 289
  Christiana Adelheit, 95
  Nicolaus, 39, 86, 115, 122, 289
  Nicolaus Philip, 39
  Nocolaus, 284
  Rebecca, 122
  Sophia, 39, 86, 95, 115, 122
HADDAWAY, Alfred, 155
HADKE, Gregorius, 117
  Johan Gregorius, 117
HADLEY, George W., 160
HAEBEL, Wilhelmia, 272
HAFEKOST, Henrich, 143
HAFF, Catharina, 36
HAFFERNING, Margaret, 170
HAGAN, Susan, 150
HAGELIN, Catherine Elizabeth, 178
  Charles M., 159, 176, 178
  Charles Magnus, 176
  Mary, 176, 178
HAGEMANN, Carl, 57

HAGEN, John R., 146
HAGENER, David, 36, 71
  George, 67
  Jacob, 36, 70
  Mr., 67
HAGERMAN, Maria M., 143
HAGERTY, Henry Richmond S., 225
  Martha Virginia R., 226
  Mary A., 226
  Mary Ann, 224, 225
  Thomas, 224
  William Franklin, 224
  William J., 311
  William T., 225, 226
HAGG, Elizabeth, 164
HAGGERTY, William T., 265
HAGON, Susan, 150
HAHN, Christian, 143
  Elisabeth, 43
  Peter, 15, 34, 290
HAIFEL, Peter, 18
HAIKE, July Ann, 130
  Nicholaus, 130
  Sophia, 130
HAINES, Margaret R., 172
HAISS, Cathrina Mary, 22
  Maria Cath., 22
  Theobald, 22
HALBACH, Christie, 247
  Christie E., 225, 226, 247
  Emily Gertrude, 225
  Ino. P., 225
  John Howard, 226
  John P., 226, 247
  Walter Livingston, 247
  William Addison Baker, 247
HALBERT, Jacob Brown, 244

HALE, Elias, 182
  Elizabeth C., 182
  Elizabeth Jane, 182
  George Elias, 182
  Maria C., 182
HALEY, Catharina, 140, 142
HALL, Ann, 205
  Ann E., 277
  Annie M., 254, 257
  Carter A., 129
  Charles W., 241
  Georg Heinrich, 107
  George W., 234, 254, 257
  Grace Lizzie, 257, 273
  Hester A., 254
  James, 168
  Jesse Albert, 254
  Lillie May, 273
  Lizzie May, 257
  Maria Amelia, 205
  Martha, 154
  Royston Beverly, 254
  Sheppard C., 254
  Walter Caryl, 254
  William, 107
  William French, 129
  William S., 203
HALL(IN), Anna Maria, 11
HALLER, Elisabeth, 52
HALTON, George C., 229
HALZ, Cath., 36
HAMAND, Lizzie, 228
  William, 305
HAMILTON, A. M., 212
  Allen, 224
  Ann, 304
  Ann M., 208
  Dilly, 135
  Edwin, 160
  Elisabeth, 135

Hugh, 163
James, 168, 208, 212, 304
John, 228, 304
John Alexander, 212
Julia, 179
Lizzie, 226, 310
Martin, 135
Mary, 224, 226, 227, 310
Mrs., 298, 303
Nellie Stewart, 227
Stewart, 224, 226, 227, 310, 311
William Henry Augustus, 179
William J., 160, 179
Wilson, 135
HAMMAR, Allan Maurice, 248
Andrew J., 250
Anna L., 250
Anna L. Wood, 269
Anna Louisa Wood, 250
Annie L., 269
Elizabeth M., 245, 248, 250
Eliza M., 246
Elizabeth Martin, 250
John M., 245, 246, 248, 250
John Thomas Ward, 245
Mary Alice, 246
HAMMEL, Abell Herbert, 258
Ella V., 235
John, 172
John G., 254, 256, 258
Laura Rice, 241
Pattie V., 254, 256, 258
Ruth Penwood, 256
Schall Wilhelm, 256, 273
William Lester, 254
HAMMELL, Abell Herbert, 274

HAMMENMANN, Friedrich, 146
HAMMER, ---, 114
Carl, 114
Friderich, 138
Friederich, 96, 114
Helen, 259
John M., 253
Lizzie M., 253
Louisa Boland, 253
Margaret Forsythe, 253
Minnie K. L., 253, 259
Sophia, 96
William G., 234, 253, 259
HAMMOND, Charles Herbert, 248
Charles Richard, 276
Charles Richmond, 261
Christian, 251
Christina, 248, 249, 253, 257, 259, 261
Christina Catherine, 257
Christina R., 256
David, 253, 273
Edward Hazelton, 256, 272
Emma F., 248, 255, 258
Georgianna, 249, 250
James M., 248
James Mewburn, 255, 258
Jennie May, 249
John, 217, 259
John Andre Shultz, 258
John Frederick, 249
Marg., 217
Margaret, 269
Mrs., 248
Nettie Margaret, 251
Robert, 249, 250
Sarah Ellen, 217
William, 248, 249, 251, 253, 256, 257, 259, 261

William John, 248
William O. N., 236
William Thomas, 250
HAN, Jacob, 194
Juliann, 194
Mary Cath., 194
HANCKE, Friedericke, 143
HANCOCK, Jane Catherine, 244
William, 76
HANCOD, William, 76
HANDSHUK, Kunigunde, 240
HANDY, Elenora, 181
Emma L., 262
Mortimer Vernon, 262
Samuel J., 181
Sarah Rebecca, 181
William R., 262
HANECKE, Friedericke, 143
HANEOD, Elisabeth, 21
Wally, 21
William, 21
HANES, Albert Jacob, 192
James, 192
Polly, 52
Sophia, 192
HANNA, James, 148
Mrs., 301
HANSON, Sophia, 145
HAPER, David, 171
HAPS, Catharina, 113
Elisabeth Maria, 113
Lehman, 113
HARBAUGH, Benjamin, 194, 201, 203
Emelia Catherine, 203
Juliann, 201
Margaret, 194, 201, 203
Rebecca, 201

358   Index

Sarah Marshall, 194
Thomas Henry August, 203
HARDESTER,
  Josephine, 210
  Mary, 210
  Thomas, 171, 210
HARDESTY, C., 227
HARDICH, Jacob, 62
  Maria Clara, 62
HARDING, Frank E., 235
HARDIS, Sophia, 56
HARDMAN, Elisabeth, 15
  Johannes, 15
  Lorentz, 15, 75
HARE, Benjamin Franklin, 251
  Catherine, 250, 253, 269
  Charles Henry, 255
  Florence Marguerite, 256
  Francis M., 255
  John P., 251
  John T., 256
  John Thomas, 250, 253
  Margaret, 250, 251, 256
  Samuel Wilbert, 255
HARELMAN, Christina, 241
HARGOOD, Elisabeth, 55
HARLOVE, William, 234
HARMAN, Ira A., 236
  Jacob J., 171
HARMON, Eliza, 255
HARPEL, Anna K., 208
  Anna Martha, 208
  Catharine, 209
  Ino. H., 209
  J., 304
  John George, 209
  John H., 208
HARPER, Doctor, 146

HARPT, Christian, 139
HARRIES, Maggie, 305
  Marg. J., 221
  William, 221, 305
  William J., 305
  William Jackson, 221
HARRINGTON,
  Ellengder Jane, 160
  Joshua S., 165
HARRIS, Annie J., 307
  Annie L., 307
  Ella, 263
  Ellen D. B., 166
  George M., 244
  James, 263
  John, 12
  Joseph, 158
  Laura Katie, 278
  Layra Katie, 263
  M. A. V., 171
  Mamie Smith, 265
  Mary, 155, 229
  Nathaniel, 12
  Rachel, 176
  Samuel, 176
  Samuel M., 163
  Sarah, 12, 269
  William, 228, 307
  William Henry, 176
HARRISON, Ethalinda E., 167
HARRMAN, Helen Augusta, 308
HARRYMAN, Edward A. B., 243
HARST, Rebecca, 205
  William, 205
HART, Alfred P., 251, 255
  Bertha Sarah, 251
  Estelle Magdalene, 251
  James M., 167
  Lizzie May, 210, 306

  Mary A., 251, 255
  Mary Ann, 210
  Mary C., 215, 306
  Mary Olevia, 255
  Mr., 301
  Samuel, 147
  William, 166, 215
  William J., 210
  William James, 215
HARTHINCK, Peter, 283
HARTHMAN, Jacob, 13
HARTHMANN, Mary, 52
HARTLOVE, Katie, 253
  Viola May, 253
  William, 253
HARTLY, Richard, 146
HARTMAN, Elisabeth, 140
  Jacob, 290
  Susanna, 294
HARTMANN, Cathrina, 19
  Jacob, 20, 28
  Joh. Henrich, 19
  Willy Jacob, 19
HARTWIG, Wilhelm Heinrich, 284
HARTZELL, Ann Maria, 307
  David, 307
  Lillie L., 244
HARVEY, Agnes Ellen, 186
  Anna Elizabeth, 207
  Deborah D., 186, 188
  George W., 207
  George William, 188
  James F., 155, 186, 188
  Mary Ann, 207
HARZOG, Mollie J., 241
HASE, Elisabeth, 36
  Georg, 95

Index 359

George, 36
Joh., 72
Johanna Margaretha, 32
Johannes, 37
Maria Catharina, 36
Peter, 37, 72
HASENBEG, Anna Maria, 118
Louisa, 118
HASHELBACH, Anna, 33
Elisa, 33
Johann, 33
Magdalena, 33
HASIN, Christiana, 141
HASLAM, Martha Jane, 155
HASLANE, Martha Jane, 155
HASSELBACH, Anna Magdalena, 33
Barbara, 33, 40, 48
Carl, 33
Carl Schwarz, 33
Catherina, 22
George, 33
Henrich, 40
Johann, 23, 38, 48
Johann Georg, 40
Johann George, 56
Johannes, 22, 38, 51
Magdalena, 23
Maria, 22
Maria Magdalena, 23
Peter, 48
HASSLER, Mr., 112
HASSON, Eduard, 48
Esther, 48
Johann, 48
HATCHESEN, Martha E., 303
HATEN, Garrison, 185
Louisa, 185

Susanna, 185
HATLACK, Mr., 294
HATTINGTON, Fanny, 21
William, 21
HATTON, Alexander Bryson, 245
George C., 245
George Caleb, 245
Mary, 245
HAUBERT, Carolina, 195
Caroline, 195
Henry, 194, 195
Julia, 194
Julianna, 195
HAUCK, Ann Maria, 225
Bessie Leasetta, 257
David Dorncifer, 252
Ino. Alex, 225
Jos. Thomas, 252
Joseph T., 237, 257
Lizzie F., 257
Louisa, 272
Louisa Elizabeth, 252
William Frederick Philip, 225
HAUDY, Emma L., 262
Mortimer Vernon, 262
William R., 262
HAUER, Amanda, 226, 245, 246, 247, 261
Conrad Most, 246
David Wilmer, 226, 266
Edith Amanda, 257, 273
Estella May, 262
George Edward, 247, 266
Harry Eberle, 261
Henry Leroy, 257
John, 226, 245, 246, 247, 266
Joseph H., 262
Joseph J., 237, 257, 259

Joseph Maurice, 262
Laura V., 257, 259, 262
Mary, 257, 273
Mary E., 261, 262
Mrs., 262, 299
Nicholas D., 158
Rosa Otilla, 245, 266
William, 261
William Claude, 259
William Harry, 236, 241, 257
William Henry, 262
HAUER(IN), Anna Elisabetha, 8
Rauben, 8
HAURAND, William, 305
HAUSER, Jacob, 3
Johannes, 3
Margaretha, 3
HAUSHOLDER, Maria, 55
HAUSSMANN, ---, 75
Anna Catharina, 291
Michel, 291
HAVE, Catherine, 253
John Thomas, 253
HAVERSTICK, Charles A., 248
Ella, 248
James P., 268
James Park, 248
HAWKING, Anna, 138
HAWN, Jennie, 240
HAY, Jacob, 55
HAYDEN, Mary, 241
HAYES, Walter, 310
Walter C., 310
HAYFAL, Peter, 18
HAYS, Aaron, 52
David, 161, 177
Frances Ann, 177
George, 310

Index

Laura A., 239
Mrs., 298
Simeon James, 177
HAZEL, Mary S., 238
HEADELICK, Elisabeth, 81
   Jacob, 81
   Maria, 81
HEADINGER,
   Catharina, 143
HEAGY, John J., 169
HEALY, Catherine, 148
HEAPS, Cora, 243
HECKMAN, Elisabeth, 28
   Henrich, 28
   Lorentz, 28, 75
   Michael, 105
HECKMANN, Elisabeth, 38
   George Wilhelm, 38
   Lorenz, 66
   Wilhelm, 38
HEDEMAN, Ella J., 238
HEDRICH, Christina, 146
HEDRICK, Mary L., 242
HEERING, Elisabeth, 39
   Ludwig, 34, 39
HEES, Anna Maria, 47
HEFFELE, Leon, 156
HEFFNER, Harry C., 233
HEGADY, John, 20
HEGENER, Barbara, 24
   Jacob, 24
   Johann Henrich, 24
HEIDEBACH, Mr., 94
HEIDELBACH, Georg, 145
HEIDMAN, Elisabeth, 21
   Jacob, 21
   Lorenz, 21
HEIG, Elisabeth, 12
   Jacob, 12

Sophia, 12
HEIL, Elisabeth, 89, 143
   Johan, 89
HEILIG, Daniel, 294
HEILIGENSTADT,
   Annie Kate, 257
   Clara m., 257
   George C., 236, 257
   William C., 272
HEILLER, Charles P., 237, 257
   Julia, 257
   Louisa M., 235
   Louisa Margaretta, 257
HEILMAN, Maria, 51
HEILMANN, Katharina, 43
   Marie, 43
HEIMBUCK, Maggie, 235
HEIN, Salomo, 31
   Veronica, 31
HEINE, Alexander H., 211
   George Millard, 211
   Sarah A., 211
HEINER, Cath. Laura, 183
   Charles, 156
   Dr., 306
   E., 191
   Elias, 174, 177, 181, 183, 187, 190, 211, 213, 217, 305
   Elias Mayer, 187
   Elisabeth, 12
   Ella, 213, 299
   Eugenia, 177, 267
   George Payson, 181
   John, 12
   John Zwingle, 190
   Joseph, 12
   Martha Virginia, 191

   Mary, 177, 181, 183, 187, 190, 211, 213, 217, 306
   Mary E., 191
   Mary Ida, 217
   Melville, 211
HEINERT, E., 154
HEINRICH, Wilhelmina, 292
HEINSMAN, Anna Maria, 17
   Elisabeth, 17
   Samuel, 17, 77
HEINTZMANN, Anna Maria, 26, 31
   Friderich, 26, 66
   Jacob, 32, 68
   Maria, 32
   Samuel, 26, 32, 66, 68, 77
HEINZMAN, Anna Maria, 11
   Cathrina, 11
   Samuel, 11
HEISEY, Ernest E., 237
HEISLING, Thomas, 56
HEISLUNG, Peggy, 38
   Thomas, 38
HEISS, Carlus, 4
HEISSEL, Agnes Virginia, 223
   John H., 223
   Mary F., 223
HEISSEN, Charlotte Christine, 29
   Cornelius, 29, 55
   Elisabeth, 29
HEISSON, Elisabeth, 56
HEISTEL, Agnes Virginia, 223
   John H., 222, 223
   Mary F., 222, 223
   William Henry, 222
HELBING, Katie, 233
HELD, Elizabeth, 236

Index

HELFENSTEIN, A., 197
  Albert, 128, 174, 192
  Christian Albert, 174
  George Helfrich, 197
  Mary, 174, 197
HELFRICH, Charles Jos., 237
HELM, ---, 75
HELMES, James, 52
HELMESH, Henrich, 56
HELMESS, Henrich, 56
HELMTON, Johan Christopher, 146
HELTZEL, Edgar Cockley, 255
  Elizabeth Irene, 252
  Elizabeth T., 252, 255, 260
  Margaretta, 252, 270
  Walter Carroll, 260
  William, 271
  William A., 252, 255, 260
HELVESTINER, Lewis B., 167
HEMMICK, Mary A., 166
HEMPHILL, Alexander, 150
HENCK, Friderich, 67
HENDELICK, Elisabeth, 81
  Jacob, 81
  Maria, 81
HENDERSON, Charles Chapman, 260
  Charles Clapham, 277
  George, 254
  George John, 256
  George W., 256, 258, 260, 262
  Harry Carle, 258
  Harvy Cole, 258
  Lillian Annie, 254
  Lizzie, 254
  Lizzie G., 258, 260, 262
  Lizzie W., 256
  Mamie Matilda, 262, 277
  Robert, 165
HENIG, Barbara, 13, 15
  Christoph, 13, 14
  Elisabeth, 13
  Jacob, 17
  Joh. Carl, 17
  Maria Barbara, 17
  Peter, 15
  Phillip, 15, 75
HENKE, Henry, 152
HENKELBEIN, Emma, 241
HENKELS, Wilhelmina, 80
HENKELT---, Charles F. A., 261
HENKLE, Ellen, 148
HENNECKER, Conrad, 34
  Eva, 34
HENNICK, Charles W., 232
HENNIG, Barbara, 18
  Christoph, 18
  Joseph, 18
HENRICH, Allbrecht, 52
  Anna, 42
  Georg, 10
  Isaak, 42, 57
  Johann, 10
  Johannes, 42
  Regina, 42
  Sofia, 10
  Sophie, 42
HENRY, Ada M., 270
  Georg, 138
  Margaret, 165
  Sarah, 152
  Sophia, 56
  Susanna, 155
HENSHAW, Robert Levi, 247
HENSLEY, Mary C., 239
HENSMANN, Anna Maria, 8
  Johannes, 8
  Samuel, 8, 77
HENTZ, Magdalen, 143
HENZE, Martin, 291
HEPFELD, Wilhelmina, 104
HERALD, Jeremiah Dietrich, 152
HERBACH, Benjamin, 198
  Maria Woodside, 198
HERBAUGH, Benjamin, 191, 196
  Caroline Louesa, 191
  Daniel Reinhart, 196
  Margaret, 191, 196
HERBERT, Gabriel, 159
  George Courtland Elmer, 278
  Jennie, 236
  Johann, 283
  William H., 276
HERDESTER, Josua, 51
HERITAGE, Henry, 165
HERKLOTZ, Rebecca, 39, 42, 47
HERMAN, Conrad, 79
  Elsie, 79
  Johann, 22
  Phillip, 52
  Regina, 279
HERMANN, Andreas, 65
  Anna, 84
  Anna Maria, 65
  Eva, 65
HERMINGHAUS, Anna Christina, 280

Christina, 41
HERON, John L., 193
  Lewis Henry, 193
  Margaret, 193
HERR, Anna Maria, 20, 22, 24, 27, 37
  Augustus, 32
  Elenora, 20
  Friderich, 65
  Heinrich, 287
  Jacob, 66
  Jacob Friderich, 27
  Maria, 22, 32, 141
  Mr., 65
  P., 66
  Peter, 2, 20, 22, 24, 26, 27, 32, 37, 54
  Wilhelm, 37
HERRGUTH, Georg, 100
HERRING, Charles Diffenderffer, 209
  Edward Diffenderffer, 179
  G. W., 301
  Geo. W., 304
  Georg W., 159
  George, 301
  George W., 179, 209, 213, 216, 219
  George Webber, 213
  John Lewis, 152
  Julia, 219
  Julia A., 167
  Julia Ann, 158
  Lewis, 184
  Lewis Albert, 184
  Ludwig, 18, 44
  R. M., 179
  Rosena, 209, 213, 216, 219, 304
HERRMAN, Johan, 126
  Maria, 126

HERRMANN, Andreas, 26, 34
  Elisabeth, 34
  Eva, 34
HERRON, Elizabeth, 193
HERSCHN, Phillip, 66
HERSCHU, Phillip, 66
HERTZ, Wilhelmina, 41
HERVELL, Lewis, 306
HERZ, Helena, 144
HERZING, Mary, 242
HERZOG, Mollie Johanna, 260
HESS, Catherine, 229
  Johannes, 47, 54
  Siegfried, 233
HESSEGERA, Carie, 228
HESSON, Anna Mary, 256
  John F., 236, 256
  Lillian Gladys, 256
  Louis Staley, 256
HETZEL, William A., 233
HEUDORFER, Hans Jacob, 112
  Mr., 112
HEUSE, Frederick, 242
HEWELL, Anne Bennet, 219
  Catharine, 187
  George Sebastian, 300
  James L., 187, 209, 215, 219
  John Richstein, 209
  Juliet Amelia, 215
  Lewis, 306
  Lydia A., 209, 215, 219
  Sarah Elizabeth, 161
HEWITT, Carrie Watkins, 222
  Horatio D., 168, 212, 222
  Maria L., 222
  Maria Louesa, 212
  Rose Louesa, 212, 300

HEYDY, Joh. Wily, 10
HEYE, Anna Maria, 57
  Heyl, 57
HEYER, Christian, 20
HEYLMANN, Maria, 79
HIANTS, Christian, 123, 143
  Mariana, 123
HICKMAN, Cath., 179
  Charles, 179
  Charles C., 219
  Charles E., 161
  Charles J., 214
  Charles Jacob, 179
  Charles S., 208
  Elisabeth, 153
  Eliza Griffin, 208
  Emma Faithful, 219
  Emoson, 179
  George Washington, 179
  Ino. Thomas Washington, 214
  Julia, 179, 208, 214, 219, 269
HICKMANN, Nancy, 57
HICKSON, Anna Maria, 32
  Thomas, 32
HIESCH, Anna Maria, 15
  Cathrina, 15
  John, 15, 75
HIESH, Charles, 142
  George, 64
HIESS, M., 13
HIETZMAN, Elisabeth, 153
HIGH, Joseph, 148
HILBERG, Anna M., 306
  Charles William, 213
  F. L., 176, 213
  Francis L., 157, 179, 182, 218
  Francis Lewis, 176

Index 363

Francis S., 184
Frank, 306
Harry, 300
Hettie V., 306
John, 273, 306
John Abbes, 184
John C., 235
Martha Isabella Julia, 179
S. C., 218
S. Kate, 229
Sarah C., 176, 179, 182, 184, 213
Sarah Cath., 218
HILBERT, Alen, 219
James A., 162
Maria Leuesa, 219
Mary, 219
Miss, 261
Thomas Henry, 219
HILDEBRAND, Adolph William, 242
Alma A., 257
Anna Estelle, 249
Cathrina, 17
Charles J., 236, 257
Dorothea K., 233
Edna Alma, 257
Henry, 245, 246, 248, 249, 273
Ida Birdloh, 248
Jacob, 14, 54, 284
Johan Christian, 140
John Jacob, 282
Lillie, 246
Louis H., 267
Maggie, 238
Marg., 245, 248, 249
Marg. D., 246
Margaretha, 140
Mstr., 29
Polly, 52
William, 269

William Clarnece, 245
HILDEBRANDT, Andreas, 138
HILERG, Anna Margaretha, 182
HILL, Cathrina, 11
Christoph, 11, 15
Henrich, 57
Juliana, 11, 15
Marietta, 247
Mary Jane, 162
Susanna, 15
HILLESIN, Cathar., 22
HILLMANN, Elisabeth, 44
HILLS, Sealie, 244
HILMAN, Augustus, 189
Augustus Zacharias, 189
Tobitha, 189
HILTNER, Lizzie, 235
HILTON, Susan H., 149
HIMBURY, John B., 265, 312
HIMES, Alexander H., 221
John Sturgen, 221
Sarah Ann, 221
HIMMELREICH, Elisabeth, 24
Maria, 24
Samuel, 24
HINCKE, Caroline, 149
HINCKELS, Wilhelmine, 56
HINCKH, Caroline, 149
HINCKLE, Caroline, 149
HINDEL, Anthony, 84
Catharina, 84
HINDLE, Priscilla, 149
HINKLE, Sarah, 200
HINTERWICH, Charles, 201
HINTSKE, Johann, 280

HINTZ, Carl, 81, 116
Friderich Ernst Becker, 81
Henrietta, 81, 116
Magdalen, 143
HINTZE, Carl, 56
F. E. B., 306
Henrietta, 107
HIPNER, Conrad, 172
HIRKSON, Anna Maria, 32
Thomas, 32
HIRSCHBERGER, ---, 75
Catharina, 285
Heinrich, 285
Johannes, 13
Maria, 13
Wolfgand, 13
HITT, Andreas, 91, 139
Mariana, 91
Sarah, 91
HOBBS, Armstead R., 171
Sarah V., 240
HOBLITZ, Dominick, 253
Emma, 253
Grover Cleveland, 253
HOBURG, Sophie, 42
HOCK, J. W., 210
HODGES, Mary, 148
HODGKINSON, Ann, 192
Ann Robinson, 192
John, 192
John Manier, 192
HODYKINSON, Ann, 199
Hanna Jane, 199
John, 199
John Robinson, 199
Robert, 199
Sarah Ann, 199
HOECKMANN, Anna, 48
HOENS, Barbara, 35
Johannes, 35

Martin, 35
HOFF, Alice, 217
  Auguste Flavilla, 183
  Jacob M., 185
  John, 217
  John M., 183, 185, 189
  Marg., 183, 217
  Margaret, 185, 189
  Mary Elizabeth, 189
HOFFHIND, Mary, 143
HOFFMAN, ---, 75
  Aaron, 149
  Alberts, 202
  Amelia, 188
  Anna L., 177
  Barbara, 46
  Benjamin A., 266
  Charles Edward, 264, 278
  Charlotte, 36
  Clara, 264
  Daniel, 25
  Elizaabeth, 157
  Frederick Broaders, 177
  Georg, 189
  George, 25, 187
  George B., 244
  George L., 183
  Henry, 174
  Isaac Rennels, 191
  Jacob, 25, 37, 46
  Jacob V., 188
  Johan, 291
  Johan Georg Lochman, 122
  John Frederick, 204
  John Michael, 189
  John N., 229
  John Thomas, 155
  M., 183
  Margaritta Henrietta, 199
  Maria, 112, 142
  Mary, 174, 187, 189, 191
  Mary C., 240
  Mary Eliza, 183
  Marya, 127
  Matilda J., 244
  Michael, 119, 122, 127, 130, 191, 193, 199, 202, 204
  Michael Nathaniel Jacob, 188
  Michel, 123
  Nicholas, 155
  Polly, 129
  Susann, 204
  Susanna, 37, 46, 151
  Valentine, 145
  Wilhelm, 123
  Wilhelm Henrich, 127
  William, 160, 177
  William Henry, 187
HOFFMANN, Dorothea, 69
  Henrich, 27
  Jacob, 28
  Johannes, 28, 281
  Maria, 44, 47, 48
  Michael, 69
HOFFNAGLE, Lydia, 168
HOFL, Cathrina, 11
  Johannes, 11
HOFMAN, Anna Catharina, 116
  Barbara, 12
  Cathrina, 17
  Henrietta, 97
  Jacob, 12, 85, 97, 101
  Jacob Valentin, 101
  Johan Casper, 143
  Johannes, 17
  Juliana, 85
  Maria, 144
  Michael, 12, 101, 110, 116
  Michel, 294
  Susanna, 110
  Wilhelm, 294
HOFMANN, Henry, 236
  Jacob, 51
HOFSATTER, Elisabeth, 59
HOGG, Minnie L., 236
HOGGE, Sarah O., 241
HOGNER, Elizabeth, 157
  Fielding, 149
HOH, Catharina, 25
  Elisabeth, 25
  Francisus, 29
  Johannes, 25, 29
HOHRMAN, Leonhard, 22
HOLBROOK, Mary C., 166
HOLL, Cathrina, 16, 19
  Jacob, 19
  Johannes, 19, 23
  John, 16
  Maria Cathr., 23
  Maria Cathrina, 23
  Maria Magdalena, 16
  Mr., 64
HOLLAND, Albert, 163
  Alexenia, 186
  Annie Zapparah, 256
  David, 241
  Elexenia, 159
  Elizabeth, 150
  J., 186
  John W., 155
  Kate Elizabeth, 179
  Orilla M., 179
  Richard R., 159
  W., 220
  Walter Samuel, 220
  William, 158, 179, 220
HOLLER, Elisabeth, 9

Index

Franciscus, 9
HOLLIDA, Harrie L., 230
HOLLODAY, Isabella Cushman, 260
  John F., 260
  Savannah, 260
HOLMAN, Wilhelm, 92
HOLMES, Anna, 55
  Bertha, 257
  Mary Lizzeta, 257
  Miriam S., 233
  Morris Lee, 257
  Susan M., 162
  William James, 52
  William T., 235, 257
HOLMS, Marie, 55
HOLTZ, Albert Frederick, 243
HOLZ, Gesche Margaret, 174
  Henry Fred., 174
  Martina, 174
  Wilhelm, 22
HOLZENBERGER, Johannes, 13
HOLZMAN, John G., 276
HOMMERICH-SHAUSEN, Johan Wilhelm, 91
HOMRICH, Anna Elisabeth, 83
  Shausen, 83
HOMRICHSHAUS, Georg Wilhelm, 103
  Johan, 103
  Maria, 103
HOMRICHSHAUSEN, Anna Elisabeth, 283
  Johan, 283
HOMRIGHAUS, Johannes, 49
  Polly, 49
  Sarah, 49

HOMRIGSHAUSEN, Johan, 91
  Johannes, 91
  Maria, 91
HONCK, Alfred E., 309
  Ella Mary, 223
  Ella Virginia, 223
  Emma K., 307
  Emma R., 223
  Georg A., 307
  George A., 223
  J. W., 211, 212, 214
  Jacob W., 167, 223
  Jennie Olive, 223
  John Mercer Porter, 223
  Judie Frances, 212
  Laura Emma, 223, 307
  Mary Elizabeth, 211
  Rentrope, 214
  Susan, 212, 214, 223
  Susie, 211, 212
HONDERLICH, Elisabeth, 99
  Johan Jacob, 99
  Johannes, 99
HONECK, Mary Elizabeth, 300
HONEK, J. W., 298
HONEY, Franziska, 84
HOOD, Carl Gerhard, 88
  Georg Walther, 88, 138
  Otis Lee, 238
  Susanna, 88
HOOK, Annie M., 262
  Harry A., 242, 262
  Henry, 145
  James M., 311
  Laura V., 262
  Mrytle Estelle, 262
  Norman Robb, 278
  Sarah D., 278
HOOKER, Tabitha, 27

HOOPERT, Maria, 144
HOOVER, Edward G., 237, 260
  J. William, 236
  Mary Ann, 237
  Mary S., 260
  Michael, 272
  Sarah Catherine, 270
  Viola Marie, 275
  William Guy, 260
HOPEWELL, John P., 155
HOPKINS, Annie B., 273
  Annie Brittingham, 250
  Celia, 230
  George Gordon, 270
  George W., 250
  Gerrard, 54
  James, 167
  Margaret M., 160
  Mary G., 250
  Sarah, 146
HOPPE, Henrich Justus, 98
  Justus, 132
  Justus Ludwig Heinrich, 44
HOPPLE, Blanche Estelle, 248
  Carrie E., 272
  Carrie Elanora, 252
  Ella N., 248, 249, 252, 257
  Laura May, 237, 252
  Lydia, 252
  Raymond Wilmer, 257, 274
  Samuel S., 231, 248, 249, 252, 257
  Sarah L., 230
  Warren Samuel, 249
HORDEN, Elisabeth, 95
  Heinrich Peter, 95

Index

HORICHS, Caroline Louisa, 263
John F., 263
Mary, 263
HORISBERG, Susie, 236
HORMANS, Beta, 138
HORN, Cath., 56
HORNER, Christina, 22
Elisabeth, 22
Johannes, 22
Margretha, 9
Susanna, 54
HORNRICHHAUSER, Johannes, 43
HORNUNG, Charles C., 239
HORTEN, Laura F., 167
HORTON, Elizabeth 205, 267
Elizabeth M., 158
Elizabeth Marie, 205, 267
Emma Jane, 205
James, 205
Miss, 187
HOSERMAN, Elizabeth J., 155
HOSS, ---, 75
Alfred, 161
Dorothea, 10
Friederich, 10
Johannes, 10
HOSTADTER, Carolina, 108
HOSTEDTER, Carolina, 91, 113
Michael, 95, 113
HOSTEDTERIN, Catharina, 83
HOSTLER, Ella B., 237
HOUCK, Alfred E., 225
Alphonso Edward, 225
Bettie Trissler, 210
Caroline, 247

George A., 172
Georgia A., 229
I. W., 210
Isaac J., 247
J. W., 208
Jacob Adae, 208
Lulu, 247
Susannah, 225
Susie, 208, 210
HOWARD, Angeline, 163
Anna, 42
Cinithia, 149
Henrich, 42
James G., 236
Johannes, 42
Joseph Alonzo, 231
Joshua, 161
HOWELL, Catherine, 159
Charles A., 236
HOY, Maria Magdalena, 49
HOYLE, George A., 166
HOYT, Martha, 169
HRUTSCHA, Phillip, 52
HUBBARD, A. J., 210
Andrew D., 221
Andrew J., 170, 208, 306
Andrew Jeremiah, 208
Art D. F., 306
Dor. E., 221
Dorothy E., 208, 210, 306
Ermeline, 183
John, 183
John Henry, 183
Mary M., 169
Sarah Ann, 187
Thomas S., 187
Thomas Simon Murphy, 210
Thomas Solomon, 187
Walter L., 243
William Albert, 221, 306

HUBER, Hanses Rudolf, 53
HUBERT, Johan, 290
HUBLITZ, Elisabeth, 91
Elisabeth Wilhelmina, 91
Johan, 83, 91, 138
Johann, 49
HUCK, Jacob, 51
Maria, 43
HUCKIN, Elisabetha, 51
HUD, ---, 78
Elisabeth, 9
Jacob, 6, 9
Ursula, 6
HUDGINS, Jennie T., 239
John K., 164
HUDSON, Don Francis Greenleaf, 254
Edwin G., 254
Mary B., 254
HUE, Isabella, 172
HUEBNER, John A., 236
HUEY, James, 170
HUFF, Agnes Elenora, 227
Anna May, 266
Annie May, 247
Charles, 226, 227, 246, 247
Charles William Randolph, 246
Cora Estelle, 226
Mary, 226, 246, 247
Mary Ann, 227
Mary Emma, 226
HUG, Elisabeth, 12
Jacob, 12
Sophia, 12
HUGFELD, Wilhelmina, 292
HUGH, Conrad, 28
Joseph, 198
Joseph Alexander, 198

Mary, 198
Susanna, 28
HUGHES, A., 296
Cath., 181
Charles E., 159, 181
Emily, 155
James Lewis, 181
Mary Ann, 167
HUKE, Harry A., 247
Ida May, 249
John F., 271
John H., 230, 246, 247, 249, 250
Mary Ann, 246
Sarah, 247
Sarah L., 246, 249, 250
William Joel Rossiter, 250
HUKEN, Ursula, 4
HULER, Anna, 142
HULL, Johann, 2
HUMBERT, Henry, 203
HUMEL, Jacob, 133
Mariana, 133
HUMES, ---, 302
HUMMEL, Jacob, 142, 306
HUMMER, Elisabeth, 286
HUMPHREYS, Joshua, 145
Mary Ann, 165
HUND, ---, 75
Anna, 6
Johannes, 6
HUNGERFORD, Charles H. D., 251
Charles H. G., 233
Gertrude Griffith, 251, 269
Mary D., 251
HUNT, Anne P., 170
Annie, 257
Edgar, 262

Edgar B., 236, 257
John B., 234
Myrtle Rossiter, 257
HUNTER, E. F., 256
Thomas, 236
HUNTZIGERIN, Anna, 53
HUPFELD, Charlotta Rosina, 41
Henrich, 41
Katharina, 41
Rosina Henrietta Dorothea, 41
HUPFELDER, Charlotte, 30
Henrich, 30
Rosina, 30
Susanna Henrietta, 30
HUPFIELD, Charlotta Christina Philp, 76
Henrich, 76
HURD, Jacob, 20
HURDLE, George Noble, 233
HURLEY, Alfred N., 254
Elijah, 154
James Edwin, 254
Lebbie A., 254
Obediah R., 240
HURR, Ava E., 216
James A., 216
Sarah Ann, 216
HURST, Katharns, 264
Susan, 169
William, 145
HURTHLY, John, 54
HURTT, Anna E., 220
Francis Richard, 220
James A., 160
James Alexander, 220
James E., 220
HUSCH, John, 75
HUSE, Henry A., 243

HUSSMAN, Albert Herman, 260
Annie E., 273
Charles F. W., 250, 253
Emma Frances, 253
J. Henry, 270
Mary Ann, 250, 253
Sophie Minnie, 250
Thomas W. B., 239, 260
Thresa, 260
HUSSONG, Margaret, 152
HUTCHESON, William, 167
HUTCHINS, Mary, 149
HUTH, Anna Margaretha, 140
HUTT, Belle, 229
Lulu E., 234
HUYETT, Nettie Myrtle, 236
HYATT, Edward, 238
HYMNES, Alexander H., 170

-I-
IGLEHART, Mary A., 236
IJAMS, Mary C., 276
ILGENFRITZ, Johan, 97
Margaretha, 97
Rebecca, 97
Samuel, 97
Waschington, 97
ILGENFRONTZ, Johan, 97
Margaretha, 97
Rebecca, 97
Samuel, 97
Waschington, 97
IMMESSEN, ---, 43
Elisabeth, 44
Friederike, 49

Index

IMMOHARD, John, 166
INGENOHL, Clemens, 65
  Mrs., 63
INGLES, Abraham, 141
INGMAN, Harriet E., 228
  Susan E., 311
IRVIN, Katherine Glessner, 254
IRWIN, Ann, 168
  Henry, 146
ISERLO, Caspar, 51
IVANS, Johann, 76

-J-

JACKLE, Isabel, 169
JACKSON, A., 226
  Alma Gertrude, 259
  Edwin Lang, 245
  Ethel Weaver, 259
  Ida J., 259
  James Jonathan, 259
  Jane, 151
  John R., 245
  Kattie Lee, 234
  Mary E., 245
  Naomi Martha, 226
JACOB, Georg, 138
JACOBI, Isabel P., 242
  Louisa, 102
JACOBS, Belle, 262
  Lionel Mark, 262
  Mary, 152
JACOT, Andrew Lewis, 202
  Emely, 202
JADE, Johannes, 46
JAGER, Heinrich, 282
JAMES, Anna Maria, 99
  Cath. Ann, 171
  Catherine, 146
  Cecelia A., 157
  Charles, 111

Elisabeth, 111
Friederich, 99
  Margaretha Reid, 111
  Mary E., 171
JANNINGS, Mary, 159
JANSEN, Anna Maria, 90
  Emma E., 246
  Fred., 246
  Friederich, 90
  Kolma Gerster, 246
JANTZ, Anna Maria, 30
  Jacob, 30, 76
JANTZIN, Anna, 53
JANUARY, Carrie E., 241
JARIUS, Harry G., 274
JATHO, John Henry W., 153
JAVIUS, Georgie E., 252
  Georgie Matilda, 252
  Harry G., 252, 274
JEFFERS, A. Elizabeth, 187
  James Edgar Stewart, 187
  Madison, 187
  William Henry, 187
JEFFIRES, A. E., 183
  Louesa, 183
  Madison, 183
JEFFRES, Elizabeth, 183
  Madison, 183
  Margt. Elizabeth Ridgeway, 183
JELKO, Laura E., 238
JELKS, Albert Preston, 248
  Cincinatus, 246, 248
  Cincinnatus, 275
  Cinnatus, 245
  Marietta, 245, 246, 248, 276
  Mary Florence, 245, 266
  Thomas Allfriend, 246

JELL, Mr., 66
JENKINS, Lydia E., 257
  Mary Arabel, 257
  Richard B., 257
  Richard R., 233
  Rosa, 237
JENNINGS, Elleanora, 172
  Marella B., 161
  Margaret Jane, 266
  Mary Louesa, 178
  Orilla M., 158
  Robert, 178
  Samuel J., 171
  Susan, 178
JENSFEILD, Arnold, 165
JERVIS, Hannah, 147
JESAIAS, Anna Maria, 15
  Joh. Theis, 15
  Rebecka, 15
JESSOP, Priscilla Ann, 162
JETNER, Annie, 232
JEWEL, Alse, 54
JINNEY, Sue W., 228
JISSEN, Elizabeth Jane, 166
JJAME, William H., 306
JJAMO, Anna Maria, 222
  Frederick, 222
  Kate, 222
  Mary, 222
  Rebecca, 222
  William H., 222
JJAMS, Ann Maria, 223
  William H., 223
  William Howard, 223
JOB, Dorothea, 41
  Nicolaus, 104, 116, 293
JOCHHEIM, Adolph, 277
  Lewis Daniel, 273
  Sophie, 277

Index

JOCKHEIM, Adolph, 246, 247, 248, 249, 253
  Catherine Elizabeth, 247
  Charlotte Lana, 248
  George Goetz, 247
  Lewis Daniel Dietrick, 253
  Mary Christina, 249
  Sophia, 246, 247, 248, 249, 253
  Sophia Magdaline, 246
JOHANNAS, Caroline, 186
  Jacob, 186
  John, 186
JOHANNES, Allen, 178
  Caroline, 169, 178, 182, 218
  Henry Clay, 182
  Ira Hardy, 214
  Jno. G., 159
  John, 217
  John G., 178, 214
  John M., 147, 178, 218
  John Martin, 178
  John W., 182
  Jus., 159
  Mary, 217
  Mary Imogene, 217
  Mary P., 178, 214
  Virginia E., 299
  Virginia Phillippe, 218
JOHANSEN, Samuel, 232
JOHNS, Isaac D., 145
  Susan, 148, 201
JOHNSEN, Arthur Thomas, 167
  James D., 168
JOHNSON, Anna C., 242
  Auguste Rosena, 215
  Barbara, 220
  Charles Robert, 235
  Clinton S., 233
  David, 270
  Edward Water Whitney, 246
  Elizabeth, 237
  Emilie Georgette, 253, 272
  Emily T., 248, 249, 253
  Erasmus, 140
  Friederich, 290
  Greenleaf, 231
  Henry Clay, 215
  James, 215
  James D., 215
  James L., 231, 248, 249, 253
  James Massey, 248
  James Zekel, 215, 298
  Lucretia, 246
  Maria, 290
  Mary Ann, 298
  Mary Ann Sultzer, 215
  Mr., 112
  Peter, 246
  Reynolds Kraft, 249
  Roberta A., 231
  Rosena, 215
  Samuel Alton Ready, 220
  Samuel D., 220
  Sarah B., 241
  William, 235
JOHNSTON, Samuel D., 160
JOICE, Nathan, 54
JONES, Ann Maria, 163
  C. E., 306
  Catharine, 183
  Catherine, 266
  Christian, 192
  Christina, 196, 198, 202, 206
  Christine, 200
  Danford D., 148
  Eliza Ann, 201
  Emily, 192
  Harry A., 238
  Henry C., 171
  Henry Clay, 215
  Henry Lewis, 198
  Isaac B., 216
  James, 192, 196, 198, 200, 202, 206, 273
  Jessie Sarah, 216
  John, 196
  John P., 165, 215, 216
  Julia, 215, 216
  Levering, 155
  Maheus Constantin, 201
  Margaret, 148
  Margaretta, 228
  Margt., 183
  Mary, 258, 275
  Mary Ann, 202
  Modessa, 216
  Mr., 296, 297, 299
  Rebecca, 170, 216
  Russ, 230
  Sarah, 157
  Thomas, 200
  Thomas L., 157
  Thomas S., 183
  William, 153, 206
JOPPERT, Anna Barbara, 28
  Anna Maria, 28
  Christian, 28
JORDAN, Ann Caroline, 194
  Anna Maria, 120
  Carolina, 136
  Charles, 194, 195, 197
  Charlotte Emelia, 195
  David, 112, 290
  Elizabeth, 197
  Friederica, 137

Herman, 147
Johannes, 205
John, 112, 120, 142
Maria, 205
Maria Elisabeth, 118
Mr., 137, 290
Sophia, 195, 197
Sophie, 194
Wilhelmina, 112
Wilhelmine, 289
JORY, Elizabeth J., 273
JOSEPH, Ann, 178
 Anna Laura Bertram, 258
 Eliza Ann, 302
 Emanuel, 159
 Emily R., 230
 Francisco, 164
 Harry Bertram, 258
 Hughena Thomson, 258
 James, 165
 John, 166, 299
 Margaret, 265, 312
 Mary J., 180
 Mary Jane, 178
 Mr., 299, 300
 Mrs., 304
 Rebecca, 164
 Thomas, 300
 William, 159, 178, 180, 297, 303
JOST, Ann, 206
 Joseph, 131
 Margaret, 206
 William, 206
 William Henry, 131
JUB, Nicolaus, 104
JUGEL, Charlotte, 54
JUN, Elisabeth, 38
 Johann, 38, 76
 Sara, 38, 76
JUNG, Abraham, 48

Anna, 48
Barbara, 292
Carl, 285
Georg, 51, 52
Heinrich, 282
Hen., 68, 69
Henrich, 34
Jacob, 35, 42, 144
Magdalena, 35, 42
Maria Barbara, 34, 69
Peggi, 48
Peter, 42, 280
Sarah, 34, 82
Sophie, 27
JUNGE, Johann Abraham, 57
JUNT, Elisabet, 53
JUPPERT, Anna Barbara, 28
 Anna Maria, 28
 Christian, 28
JURY, Lewis B., 233
JUSTUS, ---, 219
JVENS, Elisabeth, 10
 Jean, 10
 Maria, 10
 William, 10

-K-
KABIS, Florence S., 243
KABORZ, Jacob, 62
KAF, Georg, 122
 Louisa, 122
KAHL, Gottfried, 21
KAHN, Christian, 142
 Daniel, 64
KAHNEY, Ira Day, 253
 Lydia, 253
KAHRE, Mrs., 295
KAISER, Caspar, 30
 Johannes, 30
 Marie, 30

Mr., 66
KAISERIN, Catharina, 56
KAKEBART, Rebecca, 152
KALCKBRONNER, Maria, 114
 Mr., 114
KALETIN, Barbara, 40
KALEY, Catharina, 140
KALL, Anna Florentina, 41
 Cath. Wilhelmina, 41
 Katharina Wilhelmina, 56
KAMMER, Charlotte, 36
 Elisabeth, 44
 Henrich, 27
 Margaretha, 24
 Maria, 27, 44, 47
 Marie, 32, 36
 Michael Lucas, 47
 Peggy, 56
 Phillip, 24, 27, 32, 36, 44, 47
 Phillip Jacob, 32
 Salome, 24, 72
KAMMERER, Heinrich, 289
KAMP, Wilhelm, 112, 120, 289
 Wilhelm Friederich, 120
 William, 112
KANFELT, Mary Jefferson, 185
KANN, Daniel, 142
KAPP, Anna Maria, 41
 Johannes, 41
 Joseph, 41
KARBER, Catharina, 85
KARCHER, Annie M., 244
KARL, Elisabeth, 102
 John, 112
 Mr., 102

Index

Rosina, 112
Roxana Louisa, 102
KARPENTER, Katharina Elis., 46
KARRE, James J., 169
KARSTEN, William H., 276
KARTHAUS, Christine, 47
KASMODEL, Martin, 228
KASSTEL, Johannes, 54
KASTEL, Johannes, 54
KAUB, ---, 73
  Barbara, 3
  Elisabetha, 3
  Wilhelm, 3
KAUDEN, Elisabeth, 39
  George, 39
  Sophia, 39
KAUDER, George, 37, 56
  Sophia, 106, 143
KAUDERER, A., 175
  Barbara, 175, 178
  Christian, 33
  Elisabeth, 46
  Jacob, 178
  John, 175, 178
  Louesa Catherine, 175
  Margaret Jane, 175
  S. J., 175
KAUDERIN, Anna Elisabeth, 40
KAUFFELT, James B., 305
KAUFMAN, Clara Grace, 250
  Jesse A. D., 172
  John C., 250
  Mary M., 250
KAUFNER, John Friederich, 153
KAUP, Abraham, 125
  Anna Margaretha, 125

KAUS, ---, 73
KAUTERER, Anna Elisabeth, 98
  Georg, 98
  Wilhelm, 98
KAYLOR, Elizabeth J., 308
  Emma Elizabeth, 224
  George, 300
  John, 308
  Margaret, 299
  Sarah F., 224
  Thomas Oliver, 224
  William, 152
KAYSER, Mr., 67
  William, 67
KEAM, Mary, 51
KEATING, William D., 240
KECHNER, Charles H. G., 235
KEEFER, Justus, 159
KEEHNER, Charles H. G., 235
KEEHOLTZ, Charles, 214
  Charles Edward, 214
  Sophia, 214
KEELHITZ, C., 298
  S., 298
KEEN, Alice Stevens, 261
  Alice V., 256, 257, 259, 260, 261
  Bertha Lowe, 260, 276
  George A., 256, 257, 259, 260, 261
  James Everette, 259
  Katie Huey, 260, 276
  Margaretha, 4
  Mary Ellen, 257
  Susie Harvey, 256
KEENE, Alice V., 249, 250, 252, 254

  Elizabeth Hammar, 254
  George A., 249, 250, 252, 254
  Georgie Virginia, 250
  Harry Tranty, 249, 252, 268
  John William, 247
  Mary, 247
  William, 247
KEENER, Carl Schwab, 43
  Christian, 43, 295
  Dashiell, 215
  George P., 304
  George Peter, 203, 215
  John, 130, 197, 203, 205, 298
  John H., 162, 215
  John Henry, 205
  Margaret, 130, 197, 203, 205
  Peter, 280
  Sarah Ann, 130, 156
  Susan, 302
  Susan Jane, 197
  Susan M., 215
  Susanna, 43
  William Henry, 215
KEENEY, Susan J., 169
KEEPORTS, Veronica, 280
KEERL, Henry A., 158
KEFT, Marlina Ann, 155
KEHM, Amie L., 226
  Anna L., 225
  Anna Laura, 225
  Anne L., 247
  Annie L., 245, 246, 249
  Bessie Marie, 257
  Blanche H., 275
  Blanche Henrietta, 258
  Christian, 225, 226, 245, 246, 247, 249

Elfrida May, 249
Ella Blanche, 247, 265, 312
George Albert, 245
Hester Estelle, 226
Kate Anderson, 268
Katie Anderson, 249
Maggie A., 249
Margaret A., 233
Mary W., 257, 258
Mary Wilhemina, 254
Robert Melvin, 246
William A., 254, 257, 258
William Christian, 254
KEHN, Bertha F., 236
KEIDEL, Anna Maria, 89
Catherina Margaretha, 89
Michael, 102
Nicolaus, 89, 102
Rebecca, 102
KEIER, Catharina, 84
KEIFEL, Anna Maria, 89
Anthony, 143
Catherina Margaretha, 89
Nicolaus, 89
KEILHOLTZ, Anna Cath., 103
Anna Catharina, 84
Carl, 119
Carolina, 101
David, 112, 289
Heinrich, 90, 101
Jacob, 81
Maria, 81, 90, 101
Mr., 112, 119, 289
KEILHOLZ, Elisabeth, 35
Henrich, 35
Joh., 36
Johann, 37, 42
Katharina, 42
Margaretha, 36
Maria, 35

KEILIG, ---, 75
KEILS, Johannes, 97
KEIM, Friderich, 23
Friedrich, 54
Juliana, 23
Lena, 257
Maria Magdalena, 23
KEITHLEY, Emily E., 164
KELLER, Andrew, 183
Ann Barbara, 174
Ann Mary, 174
Anna Louisa, 136
Anne E., 160
August, 137, 294
Barbara, 30
Carl, 125
Charles, 295
Charlotta, 18
Christian, 174
Christoph, 136
Christoph Gerhard, 136
Elisabeth, 91, 100, 107, 111, 137
Friederich, 107, 293
Georg, 91, 100, 107, 111, 125, 137, 293, 294
George, 133, 295
Jacob Heinrich, 293
James Henrich, 111
Jenny, 91
Joh., 30
Johan, 288
Johannes, 13, 18
John, 12
John Francis, 183
Josiah Good, 183
Magdalena, 13, 18
Marg., 183
Maria Magd., 30
Mary Catherine, 183
Mary Margaretta, 174

Mr., 293
Mrs., 299
Nancy, 133
Sarah Anna, 133
William L., 308
William Tell, 174
KELLERIN, Elisabeth, 56
KELLEY, Mary A., 159
Mary Ann, 167
KELLUM, Ella, 233
KELLY, Annie, 236
Charlotta, 115
Eliza, 153
Ella N., 231
George A., 274
Georgianna, 178
Henry R., 1, 73
Isabel, 272
James, 55, 282
John, 115
John H., 272
Lewis, 115
Mary, 173
Mary Ann, 147
Mary E., 236, 237
Minnie R., 232
Patrick, 242
Rebecca, 178
Thomas, 178
KELNER, Anna Louisa, 92
Catharina Sophia, 92
Johan Christoph, 92
KEMP, Anna Maria Catharina, 103
Helen E., 236
Henrietta, 234
Katharine Elisabeth, 127
Maria, 127, 206
Maria Elisabeth, 103
Mollie E., 231
Rosa Ross, 230

Index

William, 103, 127
KEMPERLING, Christina, 106, 110
David, 106
Michael, 106, 110, 120
Michel, 139, 292
KENGERIN, Christina, 80
KENGLA, Henry, 238
KENNARD, Eliza Ann, 224
Eliza S., 224
George Q., 259
John J., 224
Mary J., 259
William Watson, 259
KENNEDY, Anthony, 243
Peter F., 168, 171
KENNY, James, 170
KENT, Friederich, 23
Maria Magdalena, 23
KENY, Johann Henrich, 24
Juliana, 24
KEP, William, 90
KEPLER, Barbara, 109, 134, 310
Georg, 134
Johan, 134
John, 109, 118
Sarah, 118
Wilhelm, 109
KEPLINGER, Eliza, 200
KEPP, Johanna Margaretha, 32
KERMAN, Emma S., 305
J., 305
Lottie, 305
KERN, Anna, 67
John Philip, 273
Mr., 86
KERNAN, John, 173
KERNDL, Adeline Margaret, 261

Charles, 273
Henry G., 261
Mollie J., 261
Mrs., 261
KERNER, ---, 76
Barbara, 18
Cath. V., 171
Catherina, 18
Elenora, 171
Elizabeth, 228
Jacob, 18
Mary Christiana, 152
KERNOL, Henry G., 241
KERR, Gerog, 113
Johannes, 30
Joseph B., 172
Magdalena, 113
Maria, 30, 113
KERSCH, Heinrich, 129
Maria, 129
KERSEY, Mary C., 170
KERSHAW, Bessie, 237
KESLER, Mathias, 141
KESSNAN, Douglas Jerold, 222
Emma S., 222
John, 222
Lottie, 222
KESTNER, Christian William, 234
KETLER, Joseph H., 241
KETTLEWELL, John, 151
KETTY, Betty, 76
KEYS, Emma, 173
James, 164
John Elliot, 247
Josephine A., 158
L. D., 247, 265, 312
Mary Ann, 163
Sarah J., 247
KEYSER, Henry, 146

Louise, 57, 79
KEYWORTH, Robert W., 165
KIBLER, Holland R., 243
KIBORZ, ---, 78
Peter Georg, 4
KIDD, Anna Darling, 307
Anna Dawling, 307
Anna Dowling, 224
Benj., 224, 307
Benj. F., 225
Benjamin, 168
Harry B., 222
Harry H., 237
M., 222
Mary, 222, 224, 225, 307
Mary Jane, 170
Thomas Benj., 225
KIEFER, Daniel, 144
Henrich, 76
Maria, 291
KIEGERIN, Elisabeth, 54
KIEGERNI, Elisabeth, 54
KIELY, Mrs., 258
KIEM, Johannes, 77
Johannes Henrich, 42
Susanna, 42
Wilhelm, 42
KIEMAN, Anna Margareta, 38
Anna Margaretha, 38
Betty, 76
Ketty, 38
Mr., 38
KIENER, Anna Margaretha, 4
Catharina, 4
Christoph, 16
Johannes, 4, 73
Melchior, 69
Peter, 4

Index

KIERNAN, Anna Margaretha, 38
  Catharina, 36
  Elisabeth, 36
  Ketty, 38
  Mr., 38
KIERSTED, Luke, 146
KIERSTER, Luke, 146
KIESS, Anna Margareth, 52
KIFFECK, Christina, 86
KIFSTEIN, Catharina, 38
KILSCH, Christina, 86
KIMBERLY, Christina, 127
  Henry Williams, 127
  Michael, 127
KIME, Olivia, 269
KIMKEL, Bessie M., 257
  Henry F., 257
  Karl Henry, 257
KIMMEL, S., 168
KIMMELL, Edith Clare, 251
  Kate M., 251
  Solomon, 231, 251
KIMMELMEIER, Anna Maria, 37
KINDIG, Annie E., 254, 256
  Catharine, 272
  Lillian Verona, 254, 271
  Samuel C., 235, 254, 256
  William Janney, 256
KINER, Cath., 20
  Frederick, 76
  Friedrich, 20
  Juliana Appolonia, 20
KINES, Lulu M., 243
KING, Agustus, 184
  Anna M., 169
  Bessie Early, 225, 240
  Cath., 184, 219
  Catherine, 182
  Charles F., 228
  Emma, 247, 251, 253
  Georg, 141
  George Washington, 219
  Henry G., 244
  John, 186
  John Frey, 225, 270
  Joseph, 182, 184, 219
  M. Louisa, 225
  Mable G., 243
  Margaret, 186
  Marion, 184
  Mary, 51
  Mary Louesa, 184
  Newton, 247
  Paul Clifton, 247
  Pauline, 229, 251
  Rose May, 225
  Sallie Frey, 253
  Sol., 225
  Solomon, 277
  Sophia, 184
  Susan R., 157
  Susanna, 184
  W. Newton, 251, 253
  Willie Solomon, 251, 269
KINGELEY, Joseph K., 231
KINSELL, Catharine, 145
KIPLINGER, Amanda, 200
  Catharine, 200
  John, 200
  Mary, 200
KIPP, Elisa, 57
  William A., 145
KIRBY, John W., 165
KIRCHNER, Johan, 144
  John, 203
KIRK, Ashton Gamble, 263
  Georg W., 157
  Grace Elizabeth, 264
  Samuel W., 263, 264
  Sophia M., 263, 264
KIRWIN, Francis R., 230
KISTER, Anna Catharina, 206
  Johann, 206
  Susan, 206
KITZ, Christiane, 48
  Christina, 40, 45, 280
KIZ, Cathrina, 55
KLA, Johan, 96
KLAPROTH, Annie M., 234
  Lizzie, 233
KLASS, Georg, 10
KLEIBACKERS, Elma, 310
KLEIN, Anna Maria, 29, 33, 36
  Anthony, 54
  Catharina, 56
  Daniel Dieffendoerfer, 29
  Elisabeth, 33
  Jacob, 29, 33
  Louisa, 36
  Maria, 36
KLEINAUER, Cath., 198
  Jacob, 295
KLEISEN, Cathrina Sal., 54
KLERER, Jacob, 63
KLERIE, Jacob, 143
KLESSNER, William, 298
KLIEN, Daniel, 295
KLINE, Gladys Eleanora, 260, 276
  John, 241
  John Edgar, 262
  Joseph G., 236, 259, 260, 262
  Joseph Gehring, 259

Index 375

Louis P., 234
Martha E., 242
Mary E., 231, 259, 260, 262
KLINGEL, Daul H., 245
Mary Ann, 267
Mary E., 245
Paul H., 245
Robert Newton, 245
KLOCKGETHER, Emma S., 173
KLOHR, Ann Mary, 195
John A., 195
KLOTZ, Catharine, 310
KLUMP, George Adam, 231
KNAB, Jacob, 51
KNABS, Sarah, 56
KNAPP, Abraham, 41, 202
Colbey, 154
Margaret, 202
KNEELAND, Sarah Jane Elizabeth, 158
KNEUSS, Gertrude C., 243
KNICKMAN, Annie L., 261
Wilhemina Hilbert, 261
William H., 261
KNIGHT, John, 295
William Thomas, 295
KNIGT, Cathrina, 12
Jacob, 12
Mary, 12
KNIPP, Luisa Ann, 147
Susanna, 199
KNODE, C. Virginia, 255
Ella E., 255
Harriet Spielman, 255
John L., 255
Magdalene Susan, 255
Mary Susan, 255
William H., 255

KNODT, Daniel, 79
Elisab., 79
Johann, 79
KNOSKE, Bennetta Cath., 271
Bennetta Catherine, 254
Charles, 248, 251, 254
Edith A., 270
Edith Amelia, 251
Elliott L., 268
Louisa Cresselda, 248
Talitha, 248, 251, 254
KNOTT, Ellen, 149
Lucretia, 148
Samuel, 230
KNUGG, Abraham, 131
Irma Cath., 131
Margaretha, 131
KNUP, Abr., 201
Abraham, 141
Margaret, 201
KNUPP, Abraham, 43, 56, 202
Katharina Wilhelmina, 50
Margaret, 202
KOBOLD, Anna, 22
Hanna, 21, 26
Johann George Hartmann, 26
Johannes, 21
Ludwig, 21, 22, 26
Peter, 22
KOBOLT, Luis, 54
KOCH, Andreas, 86
Catharina Sophia, 286
Dorothea, 47
Friederich, 106
George John, 235
Heinrich, 110, 286
Julia, 237
Sophia, 47
KOCHIN, Elisabeth, 121

KOETHEN, Mary Ann, 167
KOHLENBERG, Wilhelmina, 44
KOHLER, Carolina Sophia, 137
D. M., 226
Johann, 48
Lawrence, 272
Michael, 113, 247
Mr., 99, 137
Susanna, 137
KOHLHAUSEN, Dorothea, 48
KOHLHAUSS, Dorothea, 143
KOHLINGER, Maria Elisabeth, 47
KOHLSTADT, Beniamin, 116
Elisabeth, 116
KOLLEDIN, Barbara, 48
KOLLER, Georg, 138
KOLP, Mamie T., 242
KONIG, Catharina, 96, 139
Cathrina, 14
Elias, 14
Elis., 103
Elisabeth, 293
Friederich, 103, 293
Georg, 116
Heinrich, 103
Joh. Georg, 14
Margareth, 14
Thomas, 14
KONRADT, Nicolaus, 19
KOP, John, 141
KORRELVINK, Maria Elisabeth, 140
KORTEN, Susanna, 55
KOSER, Margaretha, 66

KOUDERER, Elisabeth, 127
  Georg, 127
  Henrich, 127
KRAETER, Annie Laura, 255, 258
  Eliz, 255
  Elsie Elizabeth, 258
  Margaret Caroline, 255
  William F., 255, 258
KRAETOR, Agnes May, 275
KRAFT, Anna Cathrina, 15
  Cath., 22
  Cath. J., 209
  Catharina, 30
  Cathrina, 27
  Elisabeth, 48
  Friedrich, 98
  George Eva Anna, 209
  George W., 209
  Georgie E., 230
  J. Christian, 167
  Jacob, 30
  Jennie Elizabeth Delinger, 263
  Joh. Wilhelm, 22
  Johann Wilhelm, 27
  Johannes, 34
  John H., 263
  John Henrich, 22
  Kathrina, 44, 48
  Margareth, 98
  Maria Katharina, 44
  Meyl Cathrina, 15
  Minnie, 263
  Mr., 63
  Nicolaus, 38
  Sophia, 90
  Wilhelm, 15, 27, 30, 34, 38, 44, 48, 54
KRAHIN, Elisabeth, 32

KRAIG, Hannah, 303
KRAISS, Jacob, 16
KRALL, Heinrich, 81, 282
  Jacob, 81, 282
  Johann Jacob, 46
  Maria, 46, 81
KRAM, Frederick, 76
KRAMER, Catharina, 25, 82
  Cathrine, 206
  Christian, 82, 91, 134, 282
  Elisabeth, 90, 94, 99
  Friederich, 25, 99, 105, 120, 133, 134
  Friederich Wilhelm, 292
  Friedrich, 91, 289
  Georg, 124
  Henrietta, 113
  Johan, 82, 90, 99, 113, 124, 139, 284, 295
  Johann, 94
  Johannes, 82, 282
  John, 112
  Margaretha, 134
  Maria, 82, 90, 105, 113, 120, 284
  Maria Elisabeth, 90, 91
  Maria Elisabetha, 25
  Mariana Elisabeth, 120
  Marta, 82
  Martha, 91
  Mr., 87, 108
  Theobald, 12
  Wilhelm, 289
KRANTZ, A. A., 309, 310
  A. K., 310
  Ann Rebecca, 223
  Ashton A., 223
  John Martin, 310
  Martha A., 270
  William Duhmet, 223
  Willie Dechnast, 309

KRAPF, John, 149
KRAPROTH, Mary C., 277
KRASS, Catharina, 25
  Johann Phillip, 25
  Wilhelm, 25
KRAUS, Catharina, 285
  Elisabeth, 92
  Jacob, 92
  Maria, 92
  Rachel, 92
  Samuel, 92
KRAUSS, David, 133
  Elisabeth, 133
  Jacob, 133
KRAUT, Elisabeth, 120
  Johan, 120
  John Beniamin, 120
  Sophia M., 303
KRAUTH, Johan, 290
  Louisa Sophia, 290
KREBS, Elisabeth, 51
  Maria, 201
KREGLER, Barbara, 94
  Johann, 94
  Johann Georg, 94
KREIDER, Charles A., 305
  Maria, 107
KREIGER, Robert A., 236
KREITER, Maria, 141
KREMER, ---, 76
KREPS, Frank Walter, 240
  Sadie C., 236
KRESS, Mr., 63
KRESSMANN, Catharina, 24, 28
  Georg, 24, 28
  Jacob, 24
  Wilhelm, 28
KREUDEL, Henrich, 11

Index 377

KREUSER, Dorothea Elizabeth, 152
KRIEAGAR, Catherine Matilda, 255
Edward Nicholas, 255
Nicholas, 255
KRIEAGER, Elmer Franklin, 252
Frank A., 234
Nicholas, 252
Tillie, 252
KRIEG, Elisabeth, 136
Friderich, 136
Georg Friederich, 136
KRIEGER, Ella E., 259
Raymond Buchheimer, 259
Robert A., 259
Velten, 54
KRIENER, Daniel, 17
KRILER, ---, 75
KRILHOLZ, David, 289
Mr., 289
KRILIG, Cathrina, 11
Herman, 11
Johannes, 11
KRILIY, Cathrina, 11
Herman, 11
Johannes, 11
KRING, Heinrich, 287
Mr., 287
KRINGELING, Carolina, 94
Christina, 94
Michael, 94
KROMER, Anna, 138
Anna Katharina, 45, 49
Christian, 40, 279
Elisabeth, 41, 279
Friederich, 40, 77
Friedrich, 279
Johann, 49

Katharina, 49
KRUP, Abraham, 110, 115
Margaretha, 110
Susanna, 115
KRUPP, Abraham, 202
Margaret, 202
KRUSEN, Franscicus, 290
KRYLOR, Barbara, 94
Johan, 94
Johann Georg, 94
KUBERTZ, Michael, 9
KUBORTZ, ---, 78
Michael, 9
KUBORZ, ---, 78
Jacob, 62
Mrs., 63
KUFNER, Michael, 16
KUHBOARD, Jacob, 2
KUHBORTZ, Feronica, 8
Georg, 8
Jacob, 8
KUHNER, Andreas, 62
Anna Maria, 56
Ch., 284
Christian, 13, 20, 27, 30, 32, 61, 63, 67
Christina, 13, 17
David, 32
Johann Georg, 17
Johann Joseph, 27, 67
Margareth, 13
Maria Catharina, 34
Michael, 13, 17, 60, 66
Samuel, 17
Sara, 20
Susanna, 13, 27, 32, 34
Sussanna, 34
KUMMER, Maria, 105
KUNER, Christina, 21
Elisabeth, 19, 21
John, 130

Margaret, 130
Michael, 21
Sarah Ann, 130
KUNIKE, Margaretha, 28
Samuel, 28
KUNKEL, Katie M., 239
KUNSE, Young, 300
KUNTZ, Abraham, 16
Elisabeth, 85
Henrich, 16
John, 144
Magdalena, 16
KUNZ, Catharina, 55
KUPFELD, Charlotta Christina Phillipina, 47
Henrich, 47
Henrich Helfreich, 47
Henrich Hielfreich, 47
KUPFELDER, Charlotte, 39
Henrich, 39
Johann Margaretha, 39
KUPP, Johannes, 34
Margaretha, 34
KURRELMEYER, Bernhardine, 238
KURTZ, B., 191
Elisabeth, 85
KURZ, Daniel, 21
KUSK, Anna, 9
Catharina, 9
Richard, 9
KUSSEAR, Edward Coleman, 188
James, 188
Susan, 188

-L-

LABROGNOR, Mary, 153
LACHER, Catharina Corneliche, 91
Cornelius Wilhelm, 91

Index

Nicolaus Constantin, 91
LACOMPTE, Mary Ann, 270
LAGART, Elizabeth, 188
  Helen, 159
  William, 188
LAIER, Michael, 115
LAIG, George, 157
LAINHART, Mary, 297
LAMB, Ann, 150
LAMBART, Daniel D., 177
  Maria, 177
  Mary Louesa, 177
LAMBERT, Amelia, 299
  Charles Leslie, 258
  Harrey L., 260
  Harvey L., 237, 258, 260
  Mary Ann, 258, 260
  Mary Isabel, 260
  Mary Lizzie, 168
  Rosa, 171
  Thomas, 154
LAMM, Jacob, 20
LAMMERS, Bernard, 234
  William J., 268
LAMUTH, Elizabeth, 55
  Mrs., 63
LANDERMAN, James, 297
LANDIS, Margaret, 275
LANE, Mary, 165
LANG, Abraham, 99
  Hemes Thomas, 99
  Johannes, 99
  Maria, 99
LANGE, Conrad, 91
  Dorothea, 34
  Elisabeth, 85, 114
  Elizabeth, 190
  Emmerson E., 190
  Heinrich, 85

  Jacob, 85, 91, 114, 123, 138, 286
  Johannes, 34, 123
  Sarah, 123
  Sophia, 114
  Wilhelm, 34
  William, 190
LANGENFELDER, Mr., 283
LANGFORD, Jane B., 151
LANGKEN, Sophia, 148
LANHAM, Alice, 242
LANKFORD, Julia, 160
  Sarah, 154
LANKFORES, Sarah, 154
LANOHAN, John, 165
LARGE, Conrad, 91
  Jacob, 91
LARMEN, Zeakiah, 167
LARONETTO, Margaretha, 141
LARR, Charlotte L., 170
LARUE, Francis, 13
  Janet Anna, 13
  Maga, 13
LASHIR, Catharina Corneliche, 91
  Cornelius Wilhelm, 91
  Nicolaus Constantin, 91
LAUBER, Georg Mannes, 57
LAUCH, Barbara, 291
  Michael, 107
LAUCHT, Johann, 283
LAUDEMAN, Adalade, 184
  Edward, 88
  Frederica, 203
  Frederick, 201
  Fredrick, 203
  Friederich, 87
  Jacob, 87

  James, 184
  James William, 88
  Maria, 87, 201, 203
  Mary, 203
  Mr., 87, 88
  Sophia, 88, 150
LAUDEMANN, ---, 78
  Christian, 23
  Margaretha, 23
  Nancy, 23
LAUDENSLAGER, Ann L., 147
  Susanna S., 145
LAUDERMAN, Adeline, 179
  Clinton Wright, 179
  James, 179
  Mary, 195
  Mrs., 296
LAUHEMAN, George, 64
LAUHEMANN, ---, 78
  Anna, 27
  Christian, 27
  George, 27
  Mr., 64
LAUTEMAN, ---, 78
  Adeline, 222
  Christian, 76
LAUTEMANN, Anna, 29, 38, 76
  Christian, 29, 68
  Henrich, 38
  Joh, 76
  Joh., 38
  Joh. Christian, 29
  Johann Christian, 68
LAUTEN, Anna, 76
LAUTENBACK, Robert, 228
LAUTERING, Louisa, 83
LAUTERJUNG, Louise, 57

Index 379

LAUTESUNG, Louisa, 83
LAUTN, Anna, 76
  Anna Katharina Elisabeth, 45
LAUZATTELN, Sophia, 143
LAVENDER, Adelaide, 236
  Christina, 200
  Thomas, 200
LAWLER, Margaret, 164
LAWRENCE, Ann, 150
LAWRIE, Janette Francis, 249
  Louisa, 249, 252
  Lulie Amelia, 252
  Robert G., 249, 252
  Robert Giles, 249
LAWSON, Luisa, 128
  Robert, 128
  Sarah, 128
LAY, Valentin, 91
LAZARETH, Mary J., 161
LE BURN, Ambroose, 155
LE FEBER, Abraham, 82
  Elisabeth, 82
  Maria, 82
LE FEVRE, Abraham, 23
  Elisabeth, 23
  Nikolaus, 23
LE ROU, Catharina, 101
  James, 101
LEAGNER, Marcellus, 161
LEAGUE, Angeline, 309
  Elizabeth A., 212
  Elizabeth, 307
  Emerson, 178
  George W., 212
  Ida Julia, 212
  Julia, 178
  Marcellus, 161, 178
  Mary M., 161
LEAKIN, Julia, 160
LEAMAN, Jacob, 205
  Wilhelmina, 205
LEAVER, Elisabeth, 56
LEBER, Annie Elizabeth, 253
  Catherine, 253
  Martin, 253
  Mary C., 231
LECATO, Anna Schall, 252
  George, 233
  George H., 252
  Minnie E., 252
  Minnie Florence, 276
LECOMPTE, Cordelia F., 169
LEDLEY, Susan, 147
LEE, Ariel C., 230
LEEHRIN, Catharina, 51
LEEK, Katie T., 238
LEFEBER, Abraham, 282
  Maria, 282
LEFEVER, William, 290
LEFFERMAN, Margaret, 199
  William, 199
  William Henry, 199
LEHHARD, Friedrich, 47
  Johanna Maria, 47
LEHMAN, Carolina, 92
  Caroline, 147
  Cathrine, 147
  Christian, 106, 137
  Christian B., 253
  Eleonora Susanna, 205
  Elisabeth, 65, 118, 291
  Fannie Catherine, 253
  Jacob, 21, 92, 106, 118, 131, 204, 205, 206
  Johan Christian, 106
  John, 65
  John George, 131
  Ketura, 131
  Kitura, 204, 205, 206
  Lewis, 160
  Louis William, 129
  Margaret, 158, 204
  Margaret Elizabeth, 204
  Margaretha, 106, 129, 137
  Nicolaus, 118, 129, 133, 141, 143, 204, 291
  Nicolaus Jacob, 118, 291
  Nikolaus, 137
  Peter, 206
  Philippina, 92, 106, 131
  Susanna Elizabeth, 253
LEHMANN, Anna, 39
  Barbara, 39
  Catharina, 39
  Charlotte, 62
  Jacob, 37, 55, 206
  John, 39
  John Jacob, 34
  Johann Jacob, 37
  Martha, 62
  Philippina, 206
  Phillipine, 34, 37
LEHRS, John, 169
LEIBRAND, Henrich, 42
  Johann, 81
  Johannes, 42, 47
  Maria, 42, 47, 81
  Samuel, 81
LEIBRANDT, Johannes, 55
LEIGHTNER, Elizabeth, 199
  John, 199
  John Hopson, 199
LEIL, Elisabeth, 42

LEINARD, Ann Maria Susana, 195
  Eliza Ann, 194
  Henry Adam, 200
  Mary, 194, 195, 198, 200
  Samuel, 194, 195, 198, 200
  Sarah Lydia, 195
  William Peter, 198
LEITHNER, Georg, 21
LEMATE, Christianna, 201
LEMKUHL, Albert J., 244
LEMMER, Valentin, 32
LEMMON, Benjamin F., 173
LEMON, Cromwell, 306
  Frank, 306
  Jane, 306
LENA, Anna, 52
LENDER, Ferdinand Ludewig, 86
LENGENFELDER, Anna, 43
  Elise, 43
  Johann, 43
  Wilhelm, 43
LENHARD, Sara, 56
LEOBOLD, ---, 78
  Dorothea, 6
  John, 6
LEONARD, F., 35
  Johanna Maria, 35
LEOPOLD, ---, 78
  Dorothea, 7
  Johannes, 7
  Regina, 8
  W. Carl, 8
LEOPOLD(IN), Anna Regina, 10
LEPARD, Elisabeth, 89
  Friederich, 89

LEPHARDT, Anna C., 246, 248, 249, 250, 253
  Catherine Rose, 248
  Christopher, 246, 248, 249, 250, 253
  Christopher Albert, 253
  Christopher Franklin, 250
  Edward, 266
  George Robert, 246
  John Frederick, 249
  Mary C., 234
  Mrs., 255, 262
LEPNER, Harriat, 141
LEPRESH, Joseph, 55
LERCH, Margaret M., 238
LERROIW, Carolina, 91
  David, 91
  Jacob, 91
LESCH, Hieronimus, 46
  Hyronimus, 286
  Maria, 46, 80
LESTER, Christian, 141
LETHNER, M., 19
LETTIG, Bessie Marie, 256
  George L., 256
  Kate M., 256
LEUT, Leander, 168
LEUTHOLD, Maria, 71
LEVAN, Charles W., 263
  Gerald Wilberforce, 263
  Harvene, 263
  Harvera, 263
  Joseph Orndorff, 263
LEVEDY, ---, 73
LEVELY, ---, 73
  Catharina, 5
  Wilhelm, 5
LEVERING, George, 149
LEVI, Johanna, 143
LEVON, Carolina, 116

  Johan, 116
  Maria Johanna, 116
LEVT, Leander, 168
LEVY, Alexander, 309
LEWIS, Anna Maria, 132
  George, 210
  Jackson, 165
  James H., 231
  John, 147
  John E., 242
  Louisa, 167
  Martin, 156
  Mary, 132
  Mary Ann, 132
LEXEE, Catharina, 140
LEYBRAND, Georg, 91
  Heinrich, 101, 285
  Johan, 91, 101
  Mar., 285
  Maria, 91, 101, 142
LICHTHOLD, Andreas, 51
LICHTHOLT, Andreas, 14
  Carolus Andreas, 14
  Cathrina, 14
LICHTNER, Fanny Frey, 268
  Jane, 255
LID, Anna Maria, 5, 11
  Henrich, 11
  Peter, 5, 11
LIGHT, Mary, 155
LIGHTERN, Maggie, 303
LIGHTNER, Annie, 224
  Cath. M., 159
  Fannie J., 228
  Isaac, 224
  Jane, 224
  John, 202
  Maggie, 210
  Margaret D., 273

Rebecca, 202
William Henry, 202
William P., 307
William Passer, 224
LIGHTUN, Nathaniel, 296
LIGHUM, Maggie, 303
LILLY, Alonzo, 147
LINARD, Elizabeth, 161
  Frances Louesa, 185
  Mary, 185, 188
  Samuel, 185, 188
  William John, 188
LINCOLN, Cath. M., 226
  Francis, 226, 245, 266
  Kate M., 231
  Maggie, 266
  Margaret Adelade, 226
LINDENBERG, Bertha, 235
  Elizabeth, 237
  Fredeick C., 268
  Mary S., 233
  Mrs., 255
LINDENFELDER, Johann, 284
LINDOR, Jacob, 20, 76
LINDSEY, Emma V., 172
LINGENFELD, ---, 67
LINGENFELDER, Elisabeth, 66
  Johannes, 34
  Sarah, 34
LINHARD, Virginia H., 232
LINK, Mary F., 172
LINKEN, Mary Ann, 171
LINSEY, Catharine, 188
  Edwin Ruthwin, 188
  John, 188
LINTHICUM, Elizabeth A., 160
LINTON, Samuel, 166

LINVILLE, Elizabeth, 165
  Thomas, 164
LIONS, Ann, 197
LIPTON, J. Emory, 311
LIST, Herbert Carter, 260
  Iva Cath., 260
  John William, 260
  Wilhelm, 279
LISTON, Henrich, 21
  Leggin, 21
  Margareth, 21
LITTEL, Susanna, 128
LITTIG, George L., 234, 255, 257
  Kate M., 257
  Katie M., 255
  Louise, 271
  Mary Louise, 255
  Nellie Irene, 257, 274
LITTLE, Catharine, 228
  Elizabeth E., 226
  Heinrich, 102
  Johanna, 140
  Nelly M. Cannon, 226
  Susan Elizabeth, 226
  William H., 226, 268
LJAME, William H., 306
LLOYD, James, 194
  John Henry, 194
  Mary, 194
LOANE, Blanche Elizabeth, 268
  Edwin D., 234
LOBLE, Barbara, 5, 6
  Wilhelm, 5, 6
LOBLEMAN, Mrs., 300
LOBSTEIN, Andreas, 29
  Elisabeth, 29, 289
  Susanna, 29
LOCHER, Ann Mary, 202
  Charles F., 209
  Elizabeth, 204, 303

George, 202, 204
George H., 207, 231, 265, 269, 306, 311
Heinrich, 85
Henry Shaeffer, 204
Isaac Benj., 209
Margaretha, 139
Mary, 207, 306
Mary S., 229
Michael, 97
Rebecca, 209
Rosina C., 232
William S., 268
William Shafer, 207
Zinobia, 209
LOCHMAN, Mr., 187
LOCK, Henry N., 154
LOCKER, Rosina, 247
LOCKHART, A. D., 308
  A. J., 224, 225
  Lilian Lee, 225
  Margaret J., 228
  N. Martha, 226
  Naomi, 225
  Naomi M., 224, 308
  Naomi Martha, 226
  William Edward, 224, 308
LOCKNER, Charles F., 170
LOCY, Gottlieb, 306
  Mary Ann, 306
LOEFFLER, Emma May D., 243
LOGSDON, Bernardina, 240
  Mary P., 230
LOGUS, Rebecca, 140
LOHL, Johannes, 10
  Salome, 10
LOHR, Christian, 6
  Henrich, 6
  Johann Carl, 55

382 Index

Johannes, 6
Maria Catharina, 6
LOHRA, Anna Maria, 8
  Catharina, 8
  Christina, 8, 10
  Henrich, 8, 10
  Joh., 8
  Johannes, 10
LOKERD, Mary, 52
LONEHART, Daniel D., 177
  Maria, 177
  Mary Louesa, 177
LONEY, Francis B., 160
LONG, Alice Whitridge, 218
  Almira Catharie, 186
  Ann Eizabeth, 185
  Anna Maria, 178
  Conrad, 178, 181, 182, 183, 186, 188
  Elizabeth A., 151
  George Washington, 182
  Georgia, 218
  Henry, 152, 185, 188, 191, 193
  Henry Jacob, 191
  Hugh, 54
  J. Frank Morrison, 255
  Jacob, 181
  James W., 232
  John A., 275
  John E., 235, 255
  John George Washington Drane, 193
  Kate E., 241
  Katie E., 255
  Maanda Elizabeth, 183
  Mary, 191
  Mary Ann, 178, 181, 182, 183, 185, 186, 188, 193
  Mary Catherine, 188
  S., 218

William Henry, 188
LONGLY, Samuel, 56
LOOS, Barbara, 6, 9
  Johann Arnold, 6
  Ursula, 6
LORA, Barbara, 52
  Christiane, 52
  Christina, 11
  Elisabeth, 11
  Johannes, 11
LORAIN, Maria Catherina, 59
LORCH, Henrich, 2
LORENTZ, Ferdinand, 15
LORESH, Valentine, 2
LORSBACH, Hermann, 10
LORSMAN, Georg, 76
LOS, Barbara, 28
  Jacob, 28
  Joh:, 28
  Ursula, 28
LOSSMAN, Georg, 22, 76
  Johannes, 22
  Maria Cath., 22
LOUDERGOUNG, Wilhelmina, 141
LOUDEROUNG, Wilhelmina, 141
LOUIS, Benedict, 80
  Columbia, 80
  Eduart, 123
  Elisabeth, 80
  Uronia, 123
LOURY, Mary Ann, 156
LOWE, Daniel W., 169, 211
  Isabella, 211
  James T., 233
  Martha, 275
LOWELY, Wilhelm, 11
LOWMAN, Anna Maria, 211

Arenia, 211
William, 211
LOWNEY, Elisabeth, 54
LOWOLY, ---, 60
LOWRIE, Caroline, 152
LOWRIG, Francis, 143
LOWRY, Mr., 258
  Mrs., 258
LUCAS, Carolina, 91, 108, 113
  Christiana, 113
  Elizabeth, 248
  Fred. George, 248
  Georg, 91, 122, 293
  George, 284
  Grace Elizabeth, 278
  Johan David, 108
  John B., 239, 263
  Josua, 108, 113
  Mariana, 91, 284
  Mary, 278
  Mary Emma, 263
  Nellie Bradford, 248
  Thomas, 122, 293
LUCCABAUGH, Emmanuel, 247
  M., 247
  Wilhemina, 234
  William Tobias, 247
LUCI, Elisabeth, 54
LUCK, Elizabeth, 231
LUCKER, Carolina, 95
  Georg, 95
LUDI, Anna Regina, 81
LUDWIG, Carl, 5
  Catharina, 5
  Charles Benson, 247
  Emma, 247
  James Edgar, 247
LUER, Elisabeth, 54
LUG, Catharina, 104
  Nicolaus, 104

Index

Valentin, 104
Wilhelmina, 287
LUIS, Maria Anna, 119, 292
Richard, 119, 292
LUKEHART, Katie B., 268
LUKER, Carolina, 109
LUSBY, Margaret Ann, 152
LUSKEY, Bertie C., 238
Elvin, 242
LUTHNER, M., 19
LUTTS, Charles Helffenstein, 213
Ino. F., 213
Mary, 213
LUTTZ, Eliza Jane, 166
LUTZ, Adreas, 15
Andreas, 16, 52, 60
Anna, 15
Caroline, 204
Catharina, 90, 96, 126
Cathrine, 198
Cecilia Anaretta, 220
Christiane, 190
Christianna, 192
Christina, 198, 204
David, 204
Henrich, 45
Henry, 204
Johan Georg, 90
Johan Jacob Gottlieb, 96
John, 220
Katharina, 45
Louisa, 192
Margaret Jane, 190
Mary, 204, 220
Mr., 299, 301
Robert, 204
Susanna, 15
Tobias Wolf, 126

Valentin, 90, 96, 126, 139, 201
Valentine, 146, 190, 192, 198, 204
William, 201
LUY, Wilhelmina, 287
LUZ, Carl, 116
Catharina, 116, 122
Valentin, 116, 120, 122
LYER, Mr., 303
Mrs., 303
LYLES, Mamie E., 241
LYNCH, John, 232
LYNN, Louisa, 171
LYON, Ira C., 169
LYONS, Sarah Jane, 165
LYPOLD, ---, 78
Johannes, 11

-M-

M CLASKY, Joseph, 54
MAAKBEIN, Catharina, 56
MABEE, Delvene, 175
Elexenia, 175
Julia, 168
Mary, 175
Thaddeus, 161
Thadeus, 175
MABS, Anna Elisabetha, 8
Elisabeth, 8
Friederich, 8
MC CAULEY, Elijah G., 158
MAC MAS, Lucas, 51, 52
MCALLISTER, Elizabeth, 163
Lydia, 265, 311
MCAROY, Sarah H., 169
MACAULY, David H., 168
MCAVOY, Samuel M., 233

MCBEE, Joseph F., 230
MCCAFFERTY, Charles, 170
MACCALLA, Magdalena, 14
William, 14
MCCALLE, James, 51
MACCALLESTER, John, 12
Joseph, 12
Loyd, 12
Mary, 12
Sarah, 12
MCCALLISTER, Mary, 52
MCCALLOS, Elisabeth, 10
Magdalene, 10
Wilhelm, 10
MCCANN, Eliza Ann, 154
MCCAULEY, Charles E., 246, 248, 249, 261
Charles F., 267
Charles Franklin, 246
Charles G., 247
Charles Leroy, 261
David, 209
David H., 212
Edward Howard, 248
Elizabeth, 209
Frank Swayne, 249
John Walter, 247
Maggie, 246, 247, 248, 249, 261
Margaret Ellen, 212
Mary Elizabeth, 209
MCCAULY, Mr., 302
MCCLAIN, ---, 181
Mary Elizabeth, 215
Susan, 215
William, 159, 215
MCCLEAN, Susanna, 220
William, 220

Index

William James, 220
MCCLEARY, Abraham R., 256
  Capitol Lenora, 252
  Edward J., 238, 258
  John R., 276
  Martha Elmina, 258
  Mary A., 258
  Mollie E., 256
  Thomas Price, 256
MCCLELLAND, Francis Marguerite, 272
MCCLERY, Margaret J., 240
MCCLURE, Clayton Edward, 261
  Edith Amanda, 259
  Gertrude Agnes, 258, 259, 261
  James Thomas, 258, 259, 261
  Myrtle Louisa, 258, 274
MCCOLM, Elizabeth, 192, 305
  Emily V., 161
  Matthew, 192
MCCOLMAN, John, 297
MCCOMAS, George Austin, 250, 269
  T. Charles, 243
MCCONNEL, Elizabeth, 306
MCCONNELL, Elizabeth A., 160
MCCORD, Charlotte, 302
  Julit D., 268
  Russell R., 277
  William D., 170, 270
MCCORMICK, Charles W., 240
  G. Carville, 238
MCCOY, Adaline, 185
  Adeline, 227
  Alexander, 153

Cath. Elizabeth, 185
David, 185
Edmund S., 228
John F., 227
Lavinia R., 227
MCCREDEN, Mary, 154
MCCRONE, Annie Louise, 257
  Fannie Elizabeth Dalrymple, 257
  Gertrude Wells, 250
  Ida R., 250, 252, 257
  J. Edgar, 277
  James Edgar, 250, 252, 257
  Rossiter Magers, 252
MCCULLOUGH, Clarence Rossiter, 253
  David, 253, 255, 256, 259
  Elizabeth S., 257, 261
  Grace, 255
  John, 237, 257, 259, 261
  John Gourley, 257
  Kate, 253, 255, 256, 259
  Louisa, 243
  Margaret, 256
  William Harman, 261
MCCUMMUM, Laura Ann, 239
MCDANIEL, Ella May, 262
  George Elkins, 262
  George L., 239
  George Lambert, 262
MCDONALD, Ann, 148
  Catharine, 148
  Charlotte, 150
  Elizabeth Cath., 151
  Smuel, 151
MACDONNEL, Catharina, 114
  Johan, 114
  Johan Wilhelm, 114

MCDOWELL, Charles, 242
  Emily V., 165
MACE, Lotta Zenetta, 273
MACELROY, Dorothea, 142
MCFADYEN, Elvira G., 232
MCGAHAN, John T., 234
  John Thomas, 254
  Rachel, 254
  William James, 254
MCGIBBON, Aratus Alexander, 147
MCGINGAN, Sarah Elizabeth, 161
MCGINITY, Catherine, 263
  Harry, 263
  Hilda Annetta, 263
  Katie, 263
  Robert Norris, 263, 278
MCGOVERN, James J., 238
MCGREGGOR, Robert, 247
MACHAUX, Henrietta, 56, 81
MACINSKY, William, 54
MCKEEVER, James C., 244
MACKELFRESH, Thomas, 51
MACKELTAY, Doroth., 101
MCKEWEN, Annie, 274
MCKINLEY, James A., 246
  James Alexander, 246
  Minerva, 246
MACKINSEY, Benjamin, 18
  John, 18
  Susanna, 18

Index 385

MCKNEW, Ella, 237
MCLANAHAN, Elizabeth, 274
MCLEAN, John, 177
  Margaret, 180
  Marjory, 243
  Martha, 212
  Mary Ann, 158
  Susan, 177, 180, 212
  Susanna, 180
  William, 177, 180, 212
  William John McKee, 278
MCMANNS, John H., 155
MCMULLEN, Mary, 272
MCMURRAY, Alfred Content, 222
  Patience F., 222
  Robert K., 222
MCNAIR, John, 211
  Mary Eliza Griffin, 211
  Melverina, 211
MACNALLEN, Rebecca, 142
MCNALLY, Clara, 229
MCNAMARA, Margaret, 169
MACOMBER, Charles H., 240
MCPHERSON, John, 165
MCRAE, Charles, 220, 273
  Grace, 300
  Grace Clark, 220
  Harry, 272
  Jane, 220, 272
  John, 220
  Roderick, 220, 270
  Sarah, 220
MCREA, Annie C. B., 227
  Charles, 247
  George Parker, 227
  Harry, 265
  Henrietta, 247
  Henry, 247
  William B., 227
MCWILLIAMS, Annie E., 244
MADENHEIMERIN, Susanna, 58
MADERI, ---, 75
MADERN, Jacob, 59
MADEWELL, Alexander, 21
  Hannah, 21
  Sandy, 21
MADISON, Maria, 149
MAGEE, Mary Ann, 152
MAGENHEIMERIN, Catharina, 51
MAGERS, Annie J., 245, 248, 254
  Bertha Lillian, 248
  Bertie Lillian, 268
  Elias, 154, 214, 266
  Elias Goldsboro Fectig, 245
  James Russel, 254
  Mary Rebecca, 269
  Nellie E., 233
  Rebecca, 214
  William R., 245, 248, 254
  William Russel, 214
MAGES, Elias, 212
  Jacob Parpon Heiner, 212
  Mary Rebecca, 212
MAGGS, Elias, 167
MAGI, Jacob, 124
  Maria, 124
MAGNEK, Harriet, 221
  James, 221
  Susan Evaline, 221
MAGNESS, Bessie, 247, 266
  Charles Ingman, 222
  Harriet, 222, 224, 226
  Harriet E., 226, 247
  Harriet Elizabeth, 226
  James, 224, 226
  James E., 226, 228, 247
  James Edwin, 224
  Jessie Blanche, 226
  Jos. E., 222
MAGROTH, Henriatta, 146
MAGRUDER, Henrietta, 194
  Henrietta Isabel, 194
  John B., 151, 194
MAGUIRE, James, 264
  John, 230
  Mary, 264
  Mildred Lee, 264, 278
MAGUS, Jacob Paysen Heiner, 302
MAIER, Albert, 117
  Elisabeth, 117
  Heinrich, 117, 291
  Johan, 289
  Johann, 289
  Ludewig Bernhard, 117
  Otilia, 117
MAINLEY, Elizabeth, 208
  Ellen Cornelia, 208
  James Thomas, 208
  Samuel, 208
MAINLY, Samuel, 168
MAJER, Anna Margaretha, 3
  Balthasar, 3, 73
  Barbara, 3
  Catharina, 3, 4
  Friderich, 3, 4
  Friedrich, 3, 4, 77
  Jacob, 2, 3, 77
  Johannes, 3
  Margaretha, 2
  Philip Jacob, 3

Index

MAJOR, John, 52
MAKINSON, Daniel, 169
MALONEY, James M., 172
MALTER, Albert Julius, 249
  Annie S., 249
  Gustavus, 249
MAMMELL, William Lester, 271
MANGOLD, Salome, 40, 46
MANN, Anna Maria, 21
  Ellen Watt, 250
  Euphrania Frances, 154
  Euphrasia Frances, 154
  Eurydice, 156
  Isabella Shaw, 250
  James, 250
  Johannes, 18
  Margaret Watt, 250
  Susanna, 18
MANND, Thomas, 147
MANNING, Alexander M., 156
  Richard, 161
MANNS, William che, 171
MANSON, John, 151
MANTER, Carl Fried., 206
MARBEL, Francis, 11, 18
MARCERON, Emma, 234
MARDAGA, Frederika, 231
MARETENEL, George W., 171
MARFIBIUS, Charlotte, 289
MARFILIUS, Helena, 44, 50
MARG, Christina, 11
  Elisabeth, 11
  Nicolaus, 11

Wilhelmina, 11
MARGRET, John, 142
MARIAM, Harriot J., 153
MARINE, Laura V., 237
MARIS, Christina, 47
MARKER, Henry, 169
MARRIOTT, Charlotte Esther, 250
  James Homewood, 250, 269
MARRY, Margaretha, 134
MARSH, Chester S., 228
MARSHALL, Amelia, 153
  Archie Miles, 240
  Cornelia, 158
  George E., 244
MARSILIUS, Anna Charlotta, 44
  Helena, 44
MARSTEN, Edward Roby, 267
MARSTON, Henry W., 271
MARTENS, Amelia C., 236
MARTIN, Abarilla, 210
  Abrilla, 217
  Alice, 224
  Allen, 220, 224
  Ann H., 181
  Ann M., 218
  Benedict, 147
  Bertha, 240
  Charles Elijah, 218
  Dozilla A., 233
  Elizabeth, 220, 224
  Ellen, 224
  Emma May, 238
  Frantz, 9
  Ida Kate, 210
  Isabella, 146
  James, 210, 217
  Jane, 224

John, 220, 296
John Robert, 217
Joseph, 51
Maria Rebecca, 181
Mary, 155, 220
Mary Ann, 177
Sarah, 224
William H., 158, 168, 177, 181, 218, 297
William John Worth, 177
MARTINETTE, Simon D., 168
MARTINY, Carl Friedrich, 206
  James, 206
  Nancy, 206
MARZIN, Margaretha, 100
MASCHBERGER, David, 20
MASE, Ethelenda F., 172
MASEN, Carton, 162
MASERI, ---, 75
  Catharina, 6
  Jacob, 6
  Maria, 6
MASON, Allie, 259
  Carton, 162
  Isabella, 308
  Louisa, 308
  Mabel Estelle, 259
  Samuel N., 259
  William C., 308
MASSEY, Emily T., 231
  Florence R., 234
  Mary, 252
  Nettie, 311
MATHAES, Rahel, 41, 279
MATHANY, Jane Frances, 228
MATHAUS, Johann, 105
  Nikolaus, 105

MATHER, Elizabeth, 145
MATHEWS, Johann, 105
　John, 151
　Nikolaus, 105
MATHIAS, Elisabeth, 132
　Nicolaus, 132
MATHIOT, A. G., 214
　Adaline Virginia, 186
　Adeline, 186
　Agustus, 184
　Anna Maria, 184
　Aug., 214
　Augustus, 148
　Augustus G., 165
　Clara Louise, 184
　Isabella Harrod, 214
　James Haages, 184
　John B., 151, 157, 186
　Mary Ann, 214
　Mary Elizabeth, 186
　Mary Ella, 214
　Mary Julie, 166
　Octavian L., 170
　Octavian Lavertes, 184
　Rachael, 214
　Robert Christian, 214
　Susan Matilda, 171, 184
MATHIRT, Augustus, 310
　John B., 310
MATHIST, John B., 157
MATLACK, Mr., 294
MATTER, Albert Julius, 249
　Annie S., 249
　Gustavus, 249
MATTERN, Georgiana C., 240
MATTHAES, Johann, 43
MATTHAUS, Nicolaus, 119, 293
　Wilhelm, 119, 293

MATTHEUS, Anna Elisabeth, 123
　Friederich, 112
　Nicolaus, 123
　Nikolaus, 112
MATTHEW, A., 301
MATTHEWS, A. C. N., 213, 216
　Aldred Speed, 216
　Annie, 213
　Frances, 164
　Henry Hiestand, 213
　Joseph D., 307
　Mary, 144
　Nicholas, 159
　Nicolaas, 140
MATTHIAS, Edward Harris, 186
　John, 186, 299
　Priscilla, 186
MAUL, Maria, 57, 96
MAUND, Metta, 192, 202
　Repold Carter, 202
　Robert Carter, 192
　Thomas, 192, 202
MAURER, Elisabeth, 49
　Maria Margareth M., 54
　Philippina, 142
　Phillipina Elisabeth, 49
MAXFIELD, Mary, 249
　Mary Alverta, 249
　Samuel, 249
　Susanna, 230
MAY, Melvina E., 163
　Robert, 163
　Thomas, 142
MAYBURY, Elizabeth, 151
MAYER, Ann Cath., 201
　Anna Maria, 54, 199
　Balthasar, 58
　Barbara, 58

　Catharina, 95
　Cathrina, 52
　Elisabeth, 11
　Elizabetha, 58
　Friederich, 9
　Friedrich, 60, 77
　Geo. Friedrich, 75
　Georg Washington, 58
　Henrich, 10
　Henry, 52
　Jacob, 16, 58, 77
　Joh., 199
　John J., 202
　John Jer., 201
　Katharina, 44, 49
　Margaretha, 58
　Martha Reecca, 201
　Mary Ann, 152
　Susan, 201
MAYERS, John Robert, 195
　Lydia, 195, 206
　Mary, 206
　Robert, 195, 206
MAYES, Elizabeth A., 273
MAYNARD, Eliza, 177
　Eliza M., 181
　Julia, 300
　Laura, 181
　R. F., 177, 181
　Richard F., 158
　Richard Owen, 177, 300
MAYS, Martha Ann, 153
MEADES, Mary Ann, 177
　Mary Cath., 177
　William W., 177
MEASONDIN, Catharina, 9
　Johann Arnold, 9
　Michael, 9
MECDONNEL, Catharina, 94

388 Index

Charlotta, 94
MECHARCO, Mr., 287
MECKI, Catharina, 89
MECKINGS, John H., 168
MECNALETN, Rebecca, 142
MEDERS, Annie C., 240
MEDINGER, Annie O., 251
  Julia Day, 251
  Sally V., 270
  Sophia B., 170
  Thomas C., 251, 270
MEEGHEIMER, Johanna, 12
MEEHAN, Walter B., 240
MEEK, Georg, 12
  Mary, 12
  Susan, 311
  Thomas, 12
MEEKIUS, Edward, 238
MEEKS, Josephine E., 162
  Susan, 265
MEERFIELD, Miss, 91
MEHL, George, 261
MEHR, Emma A., 239
MEID, Louise C., 240
MEIER, Anna, 101
  Catharina, 101
  Emanuel, 53
  Friederich W., 85
  Heinrich, 291
  Johan, 101
  Johannes, 285
  Margaretha, 45
  Salome, 85
  Sophia, 85
MEIER, Eva, 55
MEIERS, Sarah, 139
MEIKOWSKE, Sela M., 232

MEIKOWSKI, Alexander, 277
  Pauline H., 232
MEILS, Johannes, 97
MEIN, Michael, 55
MEINER, Mary Ann, 147
MEINHAUS, Heinrich, 286
MEISE, George Edward, 242
MEISTER, Frederick H., 236
  Johannes, 76
MEKIN, James, 120
  Juliana, 120
MEKY, Jacob, 108
  Johanna Catharina, 108
  Maria, 108
MELIS, Annie Magdalene, 236
MELLACK, John, 121
  Thomas Kean, 121
MELLEN, Catharin Ann, 153
MELLIER, Adlphus, 149
  Albin, 195
  Jane Adelaine, 195
  Jane Francis, 195
MELTEE, Margaret D., 276
MENZIES, James, 172
MERCHANT, Susannah, 150
MERCIL, Carolina Dorothea, 115
  Georg, 115
  Maria, 115
  Rebecca Catharina, 115
MERDEL, John, 7
  Sahra, 7
MEREDITH, Mr., 301
MEREICA, Georg, 146
MEREN, Julia, 293

MERFIELD, Hannah, 143
MERGARDT, Charles Denton, 239
  Clara S., 261
MERGAROTH, Mary Charlotte, 277
MERGARTH, Charles Denton, 262
  Mary Charlotte, 262
MERIDETH, Mrs., 301
  R. B., 171
MERIGE, Georg Gabriel, 85
MERRIL, Carolina Dorothea, 115
  Georg, 115
  Maria, 115
MERRYMAN, Ann, 146
  Cath., 176
  Ella May, 260, 261
  Emma Clara, 261
  Mary Louesa, 176
  Mary Martha, 260
  Nicholas, 176
  Nicholas Rogers, 239, 261
  Sarah Elizabeth, 167
MERUR, Ann, 194
  David, 194
  Elizabeth Ransaleur, 194
MERYMAN, Wesley Martin, 176
MESENHEIMER, Cath., 3
  Georg, 3
  Georg Peter, 3
MESMER, Jacob, 285
MESSERSCHMIDT, J. William, 216
  John Croft, 216
  Sarah J., 216
MESSERSMITH, Emma C., 230
  Ida Gill, 227

Index

J. William, 166
John William, 227
Sarah F., 227, 267
METCALF, John, 263
  Joseph L., 233
  Julia, 263
  Lynne Rebecca, 263
METLACK, Anna Maria, 292
  Mr., 292
METSTRUFF, Johann, 138
METTEE, Clinton Taylor, 269
  Margaret D., 276
METTI, Martin, 121
METZ, Ida Smallwood, 258
  Jesse Addison, 258
  Mary, 151
  Mary Emma, 258
  William Carl, 258
METZDORFF, Rachael A., 169
METZGER, Helena, 141
  John, 142
MEYER, Barbara, 52
  Carl, 48
  Catherina, 143
  D. W., 222
  Elisabeth, 48
  Frederich, 2
  Friederich Wilhelm, 138
  Friedrich, 7, 77
  George William, 249
  Henrich, 48
  Jakob, 2
  Johannes, 55
  John Jacob, 222
  Laura Ann, 222
  Louisa, 249
  Magdalena, 76
  Margareth, 52
  Margaretha, 55
  Philipine, 55
  Phillip, 22
  William G., 269
  William George, 249
MEYERS, Daniel A., 266
  Jacob, 61, 77
  Margaret, 301
  Rosella, 237
MICHAEL, Alex. D., 274
  Annie E., 275
  Daniel Bernard, 245
  Emma V., 245
  George B., 266
  George Balcher, 213
  George Daniel, 35, 70
  Henrietta, 148
  Henry, 306
  Henry J., 213
  Johan, 107
  John Thomas, 245
  John W., 245
  Ludwig, 35, 70
  S. J., 213
MICHEAN, Ann Eliza, 200
  John, 200
  Lutitia, 200
MICHEL, Johann, 53
  John, 144
MIDDLEKAUF, Emanuel, 311
  Emmanuel, 265
MIERLE, Johannes, 56
MIERVILLE, Albin, 195
  Frederick, 195
  Jane Adelaine, 195
  Jane Francis, 195
  Louis, 195
  Louis Albin, 195
  Marianne, 195
MILL, Mr., 297
MILLEMAN, Eveline, 148
MILLER, Adam, 42
  Alonzo, 156
  Amanda Jane, 180
  Ann Elizabeth, 180
  Ann Maria, 189
  Anna, 261
  Anna Christin, 109
  Anna Maria, 183
  Annie E., 236
  Anthony, 189
  Bertie May, 250
  Caroline A., 161
  Catharina, 87, 191
  Catharine, 189
  Catherine Ann, 164
  Cathrina, 11
  Charles, 304
  Charles H., 237, 258, 260
  Charles R., 232, 250, 253
  Charlotta, 286
  Charlotte Ann Schlegel, 196
  Christiana, 162
  Christianna, 201
  Christoph, 121
  Dolphos Henry, 190
  Edward Francis, 261
  Elisabeth, 27, 81, 82, 84, 87, 109, 114, 122, 126, 139, 140, 149, 153, 201, 292
  Elizabeth A., 160
  Emma L., 261
  Fred., 241, 261
  Georg, 142, 286
  George P., 238, 260
  Godrey S., 161
  Goldie Marie, 253
  Henry, 143, 169, 183, 298, 302

Index

Henry Adolphus, 247
Ida Isabella, 304
J. Jacob Henry, 201
Jacob, 67, 81, 179, 180, 190, 212, 214, 286, 290, 301, 303
Jacob Alban, 214
Jacob W., 162
Jacob Ward, 197
James Ed., 247
James Edward, 197, 199, 266
Johan, 109, 122, 126, 145
Johann, 42
John, 114, 194, 201, 215, 266, 296, 297, 302
John H., 167
John Isaac, 190
John Laub., 260
John Nicolaus, 141
Justina, 121
Katharina, 41, 45, 49, 56
Laura E., 260
Laura Ellen, 212
Lillie, 258, 260
Lloyd Lowndes, 275
Lloyd M., 163
Maggie A., 228
Mamie, 244
Marg, 215
Marg., 194, 212, 214
Margaret, 179, 180, 190, 196, 205
Margaret Ann, 189, 196
Margaret Henrietta, 190
Margaretha, 45, 80
Maria, 81, 189
Maria Barbara, 27
Maria Catharina, 122
Mary, 302
Mary A., 168
Mary Ann, 190, 196, 197

Mary C., 166
Mary Charlotte, 260
Mary F., 228
Mary Frances, 179
Mathias, 27
Michael, 107
Minnie, 253
Minnie R., 250
Mr., 289
Mrs., 298, 301
Peter, 281
Richard, 191
Richard Adolphius, 215
Rosena, 191
Salome, 138
Sandy, 54
Sophie, 42
Susanna Maria, 11
Wilhelm, 97, 109, 114, 122
Wilhelm Hermann, 126
William, 192, 196, 197, 301
William Byers, 180
William Elliot, 197, 199, 247
William G., 199
William H., 160, 231, 239
William Henry, 183, 197, 258
William P., 190
MILLIMAR, Rosanna, 206
MILLITS, Mrs., 301
MILLS, Andrew Francine, 214
Elizabeth, 206
Ida, 216
James L., 166
Mary Elizabeth, 214
S. S., 214
S. Sands, 266
Samuel S., 179, 216

Samuel Sands, 179
Susan, 179, 214, 216
Susanna, 146
MILNER, Joseph K., 213
Marg., 213
Margaret Ella, 213
MILNOR, Elias Heiner, 222
Henry Clay, 222
James P., 172
John Francis, 217
Jos. K., 222, 223
Joseph K., 217, 307
Joseph Klapp, 211
Joseph R., 211
Lillie Pancoast, 223
Lillie Pancoust, 307
Maggie A., 223, 307
Marg., 217
Margaret, 211, 222
MILROY, Anna A., 164
MILSTEAD, Emmett C., 241
MINIER, Eberhart, 53
MININGER, Catharina, 146
MINKIN, Maria Elisabeth, 142
MINNA, Barbara, 16, 21
Cathrin, 13
Cathrina, 11, 16
Christian, 11, 16, 76, 77
David, 15, 16, 18, 21, 77
Johannes, 12, 13
Juliana, 21
Margareth, 13
Maria Barbara, 15
Maria Cathrina, 13
Martin, 12
Sara, 13, 15
Sarah, 12, 18
Susanna, 16

Wilhelm, 11, 16
MINNER, Abraham, 21
MINOR, Mary G., 240
MINTON, William D., 267
MIRPHY, William H., 233
MISCHER, Cathrina, 21
　Elisabeth, 21
　Samuel, 21
MISLER, Cath., 131
MITCHEL, Maria, 166
MITCHELL, Francis J., 163
MITSCHEL, Josua, 4
　Sara, 4
MITTEN, Daniels, 161
　Mary Clara, 234
MOCK, Cathrina, 51
MOERCHE, George Gabriel, 203
MOFFAT, Patrick, 171
MOFFITT, George W., 272
MOGENTHAL, Wilhelm, 77
MOHAR, Stella, 234
MOHLER, Anna, 53
　Anna Maria, 29
　David, 29
　Elisabet, 53
　Elisabeth, 61
　Jacob, 2, 29, 53, 54, 65
　Johannes, 63
　Kath., 29
　Ludwig, 53
　Peter, 29, 54
　Sarah, 29, 66
　Weinbert, 54
MOHLERIN, Miss, 53
MOHLERS, Elisabetha, 4
　Jacob, 4
　Weinbertus, 4
MOLLS, Phillip, 76

Willy, 21, 76
MOMSSEN, Salim H., 228
MONEY, Elizabeth, 307
MONGAN, Isabella, 162
MONK, Mary, 56
MONLI, Susanna, 109
MONOSMITH, Bertie Threasa, 257
　John Wesley, 257
MONTAGNE, Samuel, 147
MONTAGNO, Richard, 168
MONTROP, Sarah P., 163
MONTROSE, Vara, 307
MOOR, Henrich, 17
MOORE, ---, 216
　Aubrey Sommerville, 250
　Bertha G., 250
　Eliza, 167
　Georg, 49
　John A., 232, 250
　L. S., 304
　Laurendia, 179
　Maria Margaretha, 49
　Mary, 310
　Robert James, 310
　Sherburn L., 179, 302
　Sherburn Langdon, 179
　Wilhelm, 49
　William, 310
MOOREHEAD, Chauncy B., 239
MOOYER, Ferdinand, 246
　Ferdinand A., 267
　John Louis, 246
　Ursula, 246
MORAN, Charles S., 154
MORCHEN, Gabriel, 39
MORE, William W., 148
MOREHEAD, William H., 169

MORELAND, Elizabeth A., 165
MORF, Christina, 11
　Elisabeth, 11
　Nicolaus, 11
　Wilhelmina, 11
MORFILINER, Heinrich, 102
MORFILIUS, Lene, 56
MORG, Christina, 11
　Elisabeth, 11
　Nicolaus, 11
　Wilhelmina, 11
MORGAN, Charles, 146
　William L., 155
MORGANTHAL, Friedrich, 279
　Maria, 279
　Wilhelm, 279
MORGENSTERN, Michael, 59
MORGENTHAL, Friederich, 40
　Maria Catharina, 40
　Wilhelm, 40
MORREY, Elizabeth, 307
MORRIS, William, 51
MORRISON, Elen, 154
　James, 56
MORROW, William, 169
MOSER, Veronica, 280
MOST, Elizabeth Reed, 182
　Emeline Howard, 186
　Henry, 182, 186, 187, 193
　John Thomas, 193
　Mary, 182, 186, 187
　Mary Ann, 187, 193
MOSTS, Henry, 152
MOTT, Dr., 194
　Elizabeth, 194
　Gulielma M., 163
　Henry Freyer, 194

Louesa H., 189
Rebecca Sophia, 189
Richard, 189
MOTTER, Harriet, 189
James Taylor, 189
Joshua, 189
MOTZ, Christian Ferdinand, 192
Diedrich, 152
Dietrich, 192
Mary Jane, 192
MOUCK, Mary, 56
MOUSE, Caroline, 222
Charles Lawrence, 222
John H., 222
MUAGE, Adansla A., 157
MUCK, Margaretha, 48
MUDGE, Adansla A., 157
MUELLER, Adam, 33
Catharina, 6, 33
J., 35
Jac., 35
Jacob, 33
Johannes, 33
Margareth, 33
Maria, 33, 35
Nikolaus, 6
MULLEN, Susan E., 238
MULLER, ---, 38
Adam, 37, 56, 62, 67
Carl, 4
Carl Henrich, 4
Catharina, 8, 36, 94
Cathrina, 21
Charles Davis, 215, 299
Charles Edward, 221
Christian, 21, 76
Conrad, 55
Daniel, 56
Elisabeth, 67
Endocia Elizabeth, 215

Endocia J., 215
Eva, 3
Henrich, 21
Henry, 221
J., 299
Jacob, 36
Jacob Alban, 299
Johannes, 3
Justina Maria, 126
Kinnenow, 215
Lewis C., 295
Louis, 215
Louis Conrad, 215
M., 299
Maria, 9, 36
Maria Magdalena, 4
Mary C., 212, 215
Mary Cath., 221
Mary E., 210
Nicolaus, 3, 8, 51, 59
P. H., 210
Phil Henry, 215
Phil. Henry, 168
Philip H., 212, 221
Philip Henry, 212
Phillip, 9
Rachel, 234
Rebecca, 67
Sophia, 37
Susanna, 36
Thomas Edwin, 215, 298
Warren, 221
MULLERIN, Anna, 53
Cath., 39
Maria, 287
Susanna, 287
MULLICAN, Nettie E., 235
MULLIGAN, John Thomas, 242
MULLNIX, Basil, 170
MUMA, Abraham, 22, 61

Catharina, 66
Catherina, 8
Christ., 69
Christian, 8, 66, 77
David, 9, 22, 63, 77
Elisabeth, 8
George, 69
Johann David, 9
Margaretha, 63
Sara, 9, 22, 63
Susanna, 52
MUMMA, Anna Catharina, 37
Belinda, 204
Catharina, 23, 26
Christian, 23, 26, 29, 37, 42, 77, 282
Christopher, 204
David, 26, 30, 34, 39, 44, 62, 178, 191, 288, 293, 296
David Taylor, 191
Eduard Woodyear, 191
Elisabeth, 44, 87, 100
Elizabeth, 131
Eugenia Danills, 191
George, 29, 147
Jacob, 30
Johan, 100
Johann, 23, 87, 287
Johann George, 39
Johanna, 105
Johannes, 44
John, 131
John Jacob, 178
Joseph, 42, 282
Julia, 178
Julia Ann, 191
Katharina, 42
Margaret, 178
Margaretha, 87
Mary Ann, 191
Michael, 87, 100

Priscilla, 178
Samual, 105
Samuel, 26
Sara, 26, 30
Sarah, 34, 39, 100, 161, 191, 288
Susanna, 160
William, 147, 204
MUNA, Cathrina, 11
  Christian, 11, 77
  Wilhelm, 11
MUNCK, Lizzie M., 244
MUNNA, David, 76, 77
  Elizabeth, 76
  Sarah, 76
MUNNICH, Maria Elisabeth, 46
MUNSON, Georgianna, 162
MURPHY, Alice Louise, 257, 274
  Cath. McCubbins, 187
  Dennis, 148
  Dorothea, 194, 201, 202
  Dorothea Elisabeth, 194
  Dorothy, 184, 187, 198, 305
  Dorthey E., 170
  Elizabeth, 54
  James J., 238
  John Joseph, 184
  Katie, 257, 258
  Mary A., 235
  Mrs., 200
  Nellie M., 243
  Robert Giles, 258, 275
  Thomas, 144, 184, 187, 194
  Thomas S., 198, 201, 202
  Thomas Smith, 202
  William Albert, 198
  William H., 257, 258
MURRAY, Florence, 249

Florence Derr, 250
Florence I., 250
James A., 231, 249, 250
Juliana, 138
Lillie Idella, 249
Margaret, 206
Sarah, 171
William, 172
MURRY, Margaretha, 134
MURY, Amey, 194
  Henry, 194
  Mary Ann, 194
MUSEY, William J., 242
MUSLIN, Margareth, 54
MUSSELMAN, Christian, 165
MUSSER, Sewall A., 235
MUTH, George, 159
  Philip, 102
MUTHERT, Florence H., 244
MUTTER, Adam, 25
  Anna Maria, 25
  Rebecca, 25
MYER, Anne C., 158
  Araminta, 165
  Catherine S., 146
  Charles Marshall, 185
  Daniel Webster, 196
  George William, 196
  John, 196
  John J., 185
  John Jacob, 205
  John Jer., 205
  Martha R., 169
  Mary Elizabeth, 185
  Susan, 185
  Susanna, 205
  Susanna M. Barbara, 160
MYERS, Emma J., 245, 250

Henrietta, 200
James, 311
John F., 245, 250
John Jerimer, 128
John Preston, 250
Margaret, 277
Maria, 142
Melanthon, 263
Robert Noah, 263
Savilla C., 263
Susanna, 128
Susanna Maxill Barbara, 128
William Halliway, 245

-N-
NACE, Amanda, 148
NAGEL, Alfred, 231
NAKER, Emily, 300
NALL, Albert Jefferson, 263
  Frederick D., 263
  Mary C., 263
NALLS, Ann Maria, 170
NARROLD, Lucius, 294
NASEN, Endora, 228
  Mrs., 298
  William, 303
  William C., 298
NAUBEN, Georg, 76
  George, 39
NAUBER, Georg, 76
NAUGEN, George H., 163
NAUMANN, Elizabeth, 233
NEAL, Mary Christiana, 206
  Mary Elisabeth, 206
  Wilhelm Ch., 206
NEFF, Marlina Ann, 155
NEHREN, S. Celia, 234
NEID, Mary, 203

Index

NEILL, Mary C., 150
NEIPERT, Anna Maria, 33
　Elisabeth, 30
　Georg, 30
　Johannes, 33
NEIS, Christina, 3
　Christoph, 3
NEIT, Catharina, 124
　Jacob Thomas, 124
　John, 124
　Margaretha, 124, 294
　Wilhelm Alexander, 124
NELHY, Anna Maria, 14
　Vallentia, 75
　Vallentin, 14
NELSON, Anna Maria, 18
　George, 148
　Joh. Georg, 18
　Vallentin, 18
NEPPARD, Catherine, 144
NESBITT, Elizabeth, 185
　Ellen M., 185
　John W., 185
NESTMAN, Henry C., 205
NETZ, Anna Maria, 47
　Rebecca, 47
NEUKIRCH, Catharina, 84, 94, 132
　Heinrich, 84
　Henrich, 94
　Henry, 132
　Johan Konrad Heinrich, 94
　Joseph, 132
　Maria Catharina Philippina, 84
NEUMAYER, Cath., 132
　Catharina, 130, 202
　Elizabeth, 149
　Henrietta, 130
　Herman, 132, 202
　Hermann, 130
　Selina, 202
　Susannah, 149
NEUMEIER, Anna Christian, 120
　Anna Margaretha, 102
　Catharina, 85, 91, 111
　Christian, 279
　Elisabeth, 279
　Herman, 85, 102, 111, 120, 279
　Juliana, 111
　Susanna, 85
NEURATH, Charles E., 243
NEWBALL, John, 148
NEWBELL, Christian, 194
　Christine, 196
　Elisabeth Catharine, 196
　John B., 196
　John T., 194
　John Thomas, 194
　July Ann, 196
NEWMAN, Amanda, 212
　George L., 237
　Grace Amanda, 212
　Purnell, 169
　Purwell, 212
　Thomas, 140
NEWTON, Cath., 202
　Cathrine, 174
　Isaac, 174
　Marietta, 231
　William, 174, 202
　William Thomas, 202
NEYMEIER, Anna Maria, 49
　Catharina, 49
　Georg Henrich, 46
　Herman, 46
　Hermann, 49
　Katharina Elis., 46
NEYMEYER, Hermann, 57
NICHALSON, Lillie, 233
NICHOLAS, Christian, 139
NICHOLS, Anna, 251
　George Frederick, 251
　Henry J., 228
　Ida S., 240
NICHOLSON, Charles Sylvester, 252
　Christina, 252
　Francis, 252
　Helen Bache, 235
　Willie Christopher, 252
NICKOLSON, Nicolaus, 140
NICODEMUS, Cathrina, 54
　Kathrina, 44, 48
NICOLAI, Caroline, 165
NICOLET, Amelia, 205
　August Julian, 206
　Emelia, 202
　Emilia, 199
　Emily, 206
　Fanny, 199
　Julian, 199, 202, 205
　Julian Nicolet, 206
NIEDHAM, Cathrine, 149
NIGHT, Basche, 55
NIKOLAI, Herman Wilhelm, 152
NILES, Elizabeth, 153
NILLEN, John, 20
NIMMO, John E., 162
NIPPERT, Anna Elisabeth, 126
NOACK, Daisey Annie Bell Mette, 221
　M. L., 221
　R. H., 221

Index

NOBEL, Emily, 252
  John, 252
  Wilfred Rogers, 252
NOBLE, Marinda, 154
NOELL, Anna Maud, 246
  Charles W., 245, 246, 247
  Franklin Daniel, 245
  Jacob Standiford, 247
  Mary J., 245, 246, 247
NOLL, Amy, 10
  Christina, 4
  Elisabeth, 4
  Joseph, 10
  Michael, 4
  Thomas, 10
  Wilhelm, 4
NOMOHAN, John, 166
NOPPENBERGER, Margaret, 261
NOPPS, Catharina, 55
NORTON, Miss, 146
NOSHER, Eduart, 127
  James, 126
  John, 126, 127
NUGENT, Blanche A., 240
NUNLEE, Martha, 171
NUSSEAR, Edward Coleman, 188
  Elizabeth, 296
  James, 188
  Susan, 188
NUSSLAR, Elizabeth, 296
NYCE, Arthur W., 240

-O-

OBEM, Walter E., 244
OBENSHAIN, William H., 239
OBERMAN, ---, 60
OBERTEUFFER, Adiel, 220
  Charles A., 186, 190, 220
  Charles August Samuel, 190
  George Washington, 220
  M. L., 186
  Mary L., 190
  Ulric Zwingli, 186
OBERTEUFFERT, Charles A., 154
OBHOLD, Johann Andreas, 51
OCH, Annie, 242
O'CONNOR, Victoria, 234
ODELL, Benjamin L., 172
ODENBACH, Elisabeth, 51
ODERWALT, Anna Maria Elizabeth, 153
O'DONNELL, Cath., 158
OGLE, Andrew, 246
  Clarence E., 267
  Clarence Eugene, 246
  Elizabeth C., 246
  Norma Lee, 246
O'HARA, William Eugene, 243
OHRENDORF, Catharina, 28
  Conrad, 14, 24
  M., 60
OLER, Louis, 57
OMERA, Elizabeth, 147
ONEHORN, Anna Catharina, 133
  Catharina, 133
  Fuling, 133
  Wilhelm Heinrich, 133
O'NEIL, Annie F., 231
ONION, Aice, 273
  Alice, 256
  Elizabeth A., 256, 258
  Elizabeth Ann, 163
  Florence Virginia, 247
  Frances V., 247
  Lewis G., 250, 256, 258
  Lizzie A., 250
  Mary G., 229
  Maud Louise, 250, 268
  Robert S., 247
  Virginia Hazel, 258, 274
  William J. H., 163
OPP, Frantz, 63
  Louise, 63
ORACELL, Georg, 115
  Maria, 115
  Rebecca Catharina, 115
OREM, Perry C., 168
  Walter E., 244
ORRICK, Mrs., 284
ORRLOFF, Jno. C., 171
ORT, Anna Cathar., 70
  Johannes, 56
  Matheus, 69
  Mattheus, 70
  Matthias, 56
ORTELBERGER, Maria Elis., 38
  Rebecca, 38
  Samuel, 38
ORTH, Eduart Laurentz, 115
  Henrich, 115, 290
  Mr., 117
ORTIN, Johanna Maria, 47
OSBORN, Elisabeth, 295
OSTERLOHR, Anna Catharina, 138
OTTER, Eleanor, 165
OTTERBEIN, Philip, 1
OTTO, Charlotta Henrietta, 104
  David Ross, 224, 308
  Ella Cochran, 256
  Fred., 223, 224, 225, 307, 308

Frederick A., 228
Georg Heinrich, 104
Hennie E., 242
John W., 273
Lina, 308
Marie Elizabeth, 240
Marrie Elizabeth, 225
Mary Ross, 223, 307
Wilhelmina, 104
Ximena, 223, 224, 225, 307
OURSLER, Florence Elizabeth, 264
Lillian, 264
William C., 264
OUTHENRIETH, Johannes, 52
OVEM, Walter E., 244
OVERFIELD, Annie W., 231
OWEN, George, 235
OWENS, Alice A., 172
OWINGS, Ann Rebecca, 171
OYLER, Charles P., 278

-P-
PACA, Lela, 239
PACEY, Hannah, 239
PADGETT, George W., 239
Nellie, 236
PAGE, Elizabeth H., 179
Harriet Elizabeth, 301
Mary Augusta, 179
Washington A., 179
PAHMER, Joseph F., 156
PANCKERT, Jacob, 112
Johanna, 112
Peter, 112
PANNDEBER, Sarah, 5
PANNEBEDER, Margretha, 5

Maria, 5
Peter, 5
PANNEMANN, Christian, 235, 261
Helen Louise, 261
Selma, 261
PANTZ, Elisabeth, 44
Johannes, 44
Kathrina, 44
Margaretha, 44
PARISH, Henry Maynard, 187
Mr., 187
Mrs., 187
PARISOT, Johann Baptiste, 144
PARKER, Charles D., 243
George T., 231
Jonathan, 152
Joshua H., 165
Kate, 232
Mary Frances, 207
PARKERSEN, Elisabeth, 120
Robert, 120
PARKS, Rachel, 139
PARLEY, John, 154
PARSONS, Caroline Amanda, 206
John Davis, 198
John P., 206
Lillie Estella, 262
Lillie Estelle, 261
M., 159
Margaret, 198
Marie Sessons Voight, 262
Mary, 206
Mary Magdalena, 198
Samuel, 157, 297
Samuel Field, 261
William Walters, 261, 262
Williams W., 155

PASCAULT, ---, 78
Ester, 12
Lewis, 12
Louis, 129
Mary, 12, 129
PASS, Friederich, 112
Henrietta, 112
Philippina, 112
PASSOULT, ---, 78
Anna Maria, 20
Lewis, 20, 76
Mary, 20
Pauseault, 76
PATMAN, Elisabeth, 89
John, 89
Salome, 89
PATRICK, George, 163
James Fritz, 52
PATT, Elisabeth, 91
Katharina, 40
PATTERSON, Elisabeth, 129
Georg, 129
John H., 234
Maria, 137
Milton, 242
Robert, 129
William L., 228
PATTIN, Anna Katharina, 47
PATTON, Elizabeth, 163
PAULI, Daniel, 283
Johanna, 139
Martin, 280
PAULUS, Anna Margreta, 22
PAUSEAULT, ---, 78
Lewis, 51
PAUSMANN, Anna Maria, 31
Catharina, 24, 27, 71
Dorothea Sophia, 27

Index   397

Elisabeth, 24, 71
Elizabeth, 34
Johann Phillip, 27
Johannes, 24, 27
Joseph, 27
Lorentz, 24, 27, 31
Lorenz, 34, 68, 71
Maria, 24, 27
Mr., 63
PAYNE, Albert, 234
PEARSON, Georgianna, 257
  Ida Dorsey, 257
  Joseph P., 257
PEDRICK, Charles Henry, 186
  John R., 154, 186
  Susan Ann, 186
PEETH, John, 206
  Sarah, 206
  William, 206
PEFFER, Kate Elizabeth, 217
  Susan, 217
  William, 164, 217
PEIFFERIN, Anna Margaretha, 51
PEIN, Ephemia, 146
PEN, Jacob, 114
  Johan, 114
  John, 114
  Margaretha, 114
PENCEL, Johannes, 6
  Maria Dorothea, 6
PENDEL, John, 87
PENINGTON, Thomas, 156
PENKERT, Esther, 55
PENN, Elizabeth, 159
PENNCKERT, Anna, 83
  Elisabeth, 83
  Peter, 83

PENNEL, John, 55
PENNIMAN, Clarissa H., 148
  Louisa M., 156
PENNINGTON, Ann Rebecca, 220
  David Frey, 220
  L. Thomas, 234, 254
  Lula E., 254
  Mary L., 154
  Ross, 297
  Ross J., 161, 220
  Sarah, 220
  Thomas Vernon, 254
PENOON, Cathrina, 51
PENSEL, Catharina, 5
  Dorothea, 5
  Johannes, 5
PENTZ, Samuel E., 235
PEPOLD, Metta, 202
PERCIVAL, Charles F., 270
PEREGOY, George Knox, 249
  Inez, 249
  Maria L., 249
  Welthy Ann, 164
PERRY, Frank Bird, 278
  Maggie, 230
  Mary S., 158
PETER, Amalia Elisabet, 67
  Anna Elisabeth, 6
  Anna Maria, 17, 53
  Cathrina, 19, 52
  Daniel, 6, 9, 17, 19, 67
  Elisabeth, 9, 19
  Henrich, 17
  Jacob, 17
  Johann, 47
  Margretha, 6
PETERMAN, Eleanor, 254

John Charles, 260
PETERS, Adam, 29
  Adelheid, 281
  Anna Elisabeth, 23, 62
  Anna L., 247
  C. G., 180
  Caspar, 294
  Caspar Charles, 294
  Caspar Heinrich, 108, 288
  Christian George, 180
  Daniel, 23, 24, 58, 62, 67
  David, 119
  David A., 158
  David Alexander, 180
  Dorothea, 70
  Elisabeth, 23, 24, 29, 34, 62
  Elizabeth, 180
  George A., 247
  George Albert, 247
  Jacob, 59
  Johannes, 34
  Margaretha, 58
  Maria, 123
  Michael, 29, 34
  Mr., 31
  Rudy, 108
  Sarah, 119
  Weily, 108, 288
  Wilhelm, 291
  William Henrich, 119
PETERSON, Adelia Amelia, 192
  Amanda Carolina, 196
  Christianna, 192
  Christianna C., 196
  Christina, 194
  Erasmus, 192, 194, 196
  John, 150
  Matilda Ann, 194
PETIT, Anna Maria, 204
  Elizabeth, 200, 204

Isaac, 200, 204
Mary Ann, 200
PETRI, Anton, 11
　Cathrina, 11
　Joh. Georg, 11
　Wilhelmina, 145
PETTET, Isaac, 145
PETTITT, Mary Ann, 161
PEUCHERT, Anna, 83
　Elisabeth, 83
　Peter, 83
PFAU, Mary A., 236
PFEIFER, Joh., 69
　P., 69
　Sarah, 69
PFEIFFER, Charles A., 226
　Charles Frederick, 226
　Nicolaus, 57
　Wilhelmina, 226
PFISSLER, Vallentin, 51
PFISTER, Johannes, 20, 76
　Nanzy, 20
　Serowol, 20
PHAILS, C., 212
　E. C., 212
　Sarah Frances, 212
PHEIL, Cathrina, 17
　Susanna, 17
　Willy, 17
PHELFIS, Martha, 51
PHELPS, Martha, 51
PHIBS, Anna, 98
　Elisa, 98
　James, 98
PHILIPPS, Hugh A., 274
PHILIPS, Charles H., 233
　Henry S., 151
　Mary A., 311
PHILLIPS, Charles Wesley, 219

Clara M., 236
Hugh A., 237
Isaac, 219, 307
James Henry, 304
Lewis C., 237
Lewis Cass, 219
Mary Ann, 153, 219
Mary Elizabeth, 300
Patience, 54
PHIPPIN, William B., 167
PHUMFREY, Greenberry A., 166
PICKETT, Eliza R., 159
PIEN, Elisabeth, 142
　Friederich, 142
PIERCE, David, 148
　James E., 242
　Maggie B., 238
PIERSON, Henriatta, 162
PIETERS, Mr., 30
PILLINGS, John H., 236
PINDALL, William J., 162
PINGEL, Catharina Margaretha, 40
　Katharina, 279
PINLY, William, 172
PIPPEL, Anna Gertraud, 46
PLENNHOFF, John, 277
PLOWMAN, Ann, 272
　Ann Louesa Zell, 213
　August, 207
　Augustus, 172, 221
　Catharine, 157
　E. F., 207
　E. Thelma, 221
　Elva Kennedy, 207
　Loni Milton, 221
　Minnie A., 238
　Richard, 160, 179, 213
　Sarah Jane, 179
　Susanna, 179, 213

　William Oscar, 239
POCOCK, Thomas S., 236
POEZOLT, Eugene, 232
POHLER, Julia Annie, 275
POLLARD, Edna E., 242
POLLOCK, Elizabeth, 164
POLLUCH, Maria, 57
POMP, Edward Loudeman, 225
　Edward Louderman, 310
　Elisabeth, 26
　Ellen Frances, 210, 303
　Fanny Frost, 222
　John, 170, 207, 210, 211, 222, 225, 309
　Marg. A., 211
　Maria Myers, 225
　Mary A., 225
　Mary Ann, 207, 210, 222, 309
　Mary Sophia, 207
　Nicholas, 174
　Thom, 310
　William Washington, 211
POMPLITZ, August, 311
POMZ, Cathrine, 54
POOL, Susan, 159
POOLE, Marion V., 244
POPKINS, Sarah A., 241
POPPE, Henrich, 142
POPPIN, Carolina, 115
PORCK, Polly, 49
PORPER, Juliana Charlotte, 31
PORTER, Alexander, 241
　Elizabeth Frances, 303
　Jesse L., 273
　Louis Philip, 272
　Marian Gladys, 241
　Nannie M., 236
　Susan F., 167

Index 399

PORTOR, Elizabeth Frances, 303
POSEY, Sophia Maria, 152
POSICKE, Henrich, 88
  Magdalena, 88
  Wilhelm, 88
POST, David, 84
POTT, Elisabeth, 138
POTTEN, Anna Elisabeth, 80
POULTNEY, C. B., 310
  Elma, 310
  Marg. A., 310
POWDER, Francina, 161
POWELL, George W., 151, 193
  Susan, 193
  Thomas Michael, 193
POWIL, William, 51
PRAWBAUGH, Charity, 141
PRECHTEL, F., 227
  George F., 227, 229, 245, 247, 250
  George Fred., 267
  George Frederick, 247
  George J., 226
  Henry Schillinger, 226
  John Frederick, 227
  Louis R., 267
  Louis Reinhold, 245
  Mary M., 226, 227, 245, 247, 250
  Sophia Madeline, 250
PRESBURY, Louisa, 152
PRESTON, Broadus W., 242
  Sallie V., 233
PRICE, Alan Davis, 262
  Charlotte, 147
  Eliza J., 153
  Elizabeth, 145

  Ephraigm, 159
  Harry, 262
  Horatio W., 238
  Horation William, 262
  Mary E., 262
  Mary Jane, 223
  Montmorenei, 223
  Rosalie Aarilla, 223
  Samuel, 159
  Taylor, 267
  Thomas C., 165
PRIGNON, Mary, 144
PRITCHARD, Mary E., 232
PROBEY, Thomas O., 240
PROLDENIER, Elisabeth, 76
PROLDENIEZ, Elisabeth, 45
PROPSTIN, Theodor Conrad, 46
PRUSCHAK, Alma A., 236
PRYN, Harriet, 254
PUCK, John, 206
  Sarah, 206
  William, 206
PUGH, David, 188
  Mary Frances, 188
  Mary Magdalena, 188
PULLIAM, Scott G., 239
PULSGROVE, Friderike, 47
  Maria Margaretha, 47
PUMPHREY, Elizabeth, 154
  George S., 154
PURVIANNA, Cloe, 52
PUTH, John, 206
  Sarah, 206
  William, 206
PUTZHARD, Jacob, 119, 292

  Mr., 119, 292
PYERITZ, Alice Lucelle, 261
  Mollie, 261
  Paul E. C., 261
PYFER, Philip, 300
PYPHER, Hannah, 219
  Janett Melvin, 219
  Mrs., 296
  Susan Edward Briant, 219
  William, 219

-Q-
QUARLES, William H., 237
QUENBORG, Mary E., 242
QUIDLAND, Anna Mattie, 243
QUINCEY, Sarah J., 168
QUINCY, Di Domi, 226
  Domi Kate Elizabeth, 226
  E. S., 269
  Ellen D., 172
  John D., 226
  Lizzie A., 169
  William H., 166
QUINN, George, 241
QUYNN, Grace M., 238

-R-
RABBOW, Marie, 56
RACHE, Jacob, 148
RADCLIFFE, John, 142
RADECKE, Dietrich H., 269
RAE, Charles M., 229
  John, 153
RAEMER, Amelia, 262
  Ida Ismay, 262
  John Donniker, 262
  Mrs., 262
RAHM, Catharina, 4

Jacob, 3, 4
Regina, 6
Ursula, 3, 4
RAHNER, Joseph F., 156
RAMSBURG, Elias B., 242
RAMSEY, Elizabeth, 148
　Rachel L., 236
RANDAL, Alverda, 213
　Charles E., 207
　James Richardson, 207
　Mary Frances Parker, 207
　Sarah, 207
　Sarah E., 213
　William, 207, 213, 298
RANDALL, Dudley A., 267
　Howard Lee, 310
　Lewis Hewell, 175
　Lewis Howell, 300
　Peggy, 56
　Sarah Ann, 175
　Sarah E., 175, 310
　William, 161, 175, 300, 310
RANDEL, Lydia, 214
　Rachael Ann, 214
　William H., 214
RANDLE, William H., 166
RASCH, Frances Katie Virginia, 256, 274
　John Louis, 255, 256, 258
　Lulu Mamie Catherine, 258
　Maggie K., 255, 256, 258
RASH, Catharina, 296
　Christian, 180, 183, 299
　Christiana, 183
　Elizabeth, 180, 183
　William Lawrence, 180
RASOELL, William, 147
RASSEL, Johannes, 54

RASSELL, William, 147
RATHROB, Barbara, 10
　Jacob, 10
RATHSON, Cath.
　Pauline, 225, 227
　G. B., 227
　Gilbert B., 225, 229
　Gilbert Brown, 227
　Louisa King, 225
RATIEN, Dietrich, 19, 76
　Henrich Dietrich, 19
　Richard, 41
　Wilhelmina, 41, 113
RATTIG, ---, 78
　Christian, 20
　Jacob, 20
　Magdalena, 20
RAU, Elisabeth, 105
　John Christian, 105
RAYLI, ---, 78
　Anna Maria, 8
　Catharina, 8
　Conrad, 8
RAYLY, ---, 78
　Georg, 5
　Juliana, 5
　Peter, 5
REACKE, Johan Heinrich, 98
READY, Annie, 235
REARDON, Florence R., 244
REASON, Lydia E., 233
REB, Adam, 3
　Catharina, 3
REBEL, Jacob, 229
REBER, James, 82
REBOLD, Jacob, 4
　Josua, 4
　Sara, 4
RECK, George, 137
　Maria, 137

　Mariana, 137
REDER, Cathrina, 11
　Jacob, 11
　Michael, 11
　Regina, 11
REDETT, Matheus, 68
REDGAVE, Eliza, 174
　Elizabeth, 174
　John, 174
REDIG, ---, 78
　Anna Maria, 6
　Christian, 6
　Maria, 6
REDMAN, Arabella H., 241
REDSIL, Daniel, 174
　George Frans, 174
　Jacob, 174
　Magdalena, 174
REED, Annie E., 228
　Jacob, 145
　John, 170
　Lulie E., 235
　Mary, 157
REELY, Eva, 51
REES, Katharina, 46
REESE, Ann O., 213
　Carrie S., 265
　Charles, 213, 299
　Charles S., 303
　Christian G., 242
　E. M., 213
　Edwin, 216
　Emeline, 211, 220
　Emeline M., 179
　Emiline, 216
　John S., 211
　Philip Reigart, 213
　Sophia Reigart, 179
　William Reigart, 220
　William S., 158, 179, 211, 213, 216, 220

Index

REESIDES, James, 159
REHBEIN, Andrew Hamilton, 252
  Anna Margaret, 256
  Annie, 252, 255, 257
  Annie Margaret, 252
  Catherine, 255
  Charles, 233, 252, 255, 257
  Elizabeth, 255
  George, 254
  Helen, 257
  Helena Regina, 257
  Henry, 265
  Henry T., 252, 254, 255, 256, 257
  Lizzie C., 231
  Margaret, 257
  Nellie, 252, 254, 255, 256, 257
  Rosa, 232
REHLING, Bertha Sohie, 271
  Bertha Sophie, 253
  John M., 253
  Kate, 253
  Katie, 270
REHM, Caroline, 311
  W. H., 311
REHMAN, Daniel, 61
REHTER, Johannes, 8
REICHARD, Johannes, 56
REICHART, Michael, 52
REICHTER, Margaretha, 55
REID, Barbara, 287
REIDER, Dorothea Louisa, 282
  Georg, 282
REIFSNIDER, Hamilton Josephus, 187
  Mary, 187
  William, 187
REIGARD, Philip, 142
REIGART, Catherine, 308
  Edward Michael, 205
  Edward Philip, 204
  Emmeline Mathilda, 129
  Heinrich Fenelon, 121
  Henry F., 190
  John Milton, 190
  Maria, 190
  Philip, 129, 158, 204, 205, 301, 308
  Sarah E., 271
  Sophia, 121, 129, 204, 205
  Wmeline M., 158
REIGEL, Maria Juliana, 57
REIGERT, Milton Job, 116
  Philip, 116, 126
  Sophia, 116, 126
  Sophia Christiana, 126
REIL, Mr., 91
  Wilhelm Heinrich, 91
REILE, Katharina, 43
REILEY, Charles H., 243
REILI, Adam, 83
  Susanna, 83
REILLY, Anna L., 243
REILY, Adam, 87
  Catharina, 102
  Conrad, 87
  Maria, 143
REINGER, Hans Jacob, 53
  Leonhart, 53
REINGERIN, Anna, 53
REINHARD, Barbara, 206
  Elisabeth, 96
  Joseph, 206
  Maria Catharina, 96
REINIG, Helena, 238
REINWAHL, Louisa, 203
  William, 147, 203
REIS, Anna Maria, 4
  Johannes, 4
  Rudolph, 4
  Ulrich, 4
REISER, Sarah Anna, 138
REISINGER, Katie M., 234
  Mrs., 255
  Nellie, 230
  William, 275
REISS, Friedrich, 14
  Johannes, 15
  Maria Magdalena, 15
  Ulrich, 15
REIT, Mr., 91
  Wilhelm Heinrich, 91
REITENAUER, Maria, 14
REITER, Andreas Friedrich, 86
  Catherina Louise, 80
  David Friedrich, 123, 295
  Dorothea, 47
  Dorothea Catharina, 80, 86, 95, 100, 110
  Dorothea Sophia, 47
  Friederich, 86, 95
  Georg, 47, 80, 86, 95, 100, 110, 117, 294
  Georg Friederich, 95
  Johan Georg, 100
  Johanna, 102
  Ludewig, 102, 140
  Ludewig Friederich, 109
  Ludwig, 288
  Mr., 117, 123, 294
  Wilhelm, 102, 288, 295
  Wilhelm Heinrich, 102
  Wilhelm Ludewig, 109

Wilhelmina Henrietta, 110
REITTER, Anna Maria, 4
  Mathias, 4
REITZ, Catharina, 102
RELY, Margaretha, 146
REMANE, Annie, 297
REMARE, Esther, 178, 182, 218
  Esther Anna, 178
  Julia, 218
  Louesa Amelia, 182
  R. A., 178, 182
  Richard, 218
  Richard Adam, 182
REMINGTON, Amelia J. C., 228
RENCUS, Ed. G., 167
RENDEL, Elizabeth, 145
RENDER, Barbara, 88
RENER, Ali, 56
RENHOLTZ, Catharina Elisabeth, 108
  James, 108
  Susanna, 108
RENNER, Anna Maria, 52
  Maria, 52
RENNERS, Christina, 88
  Johann, 88
RENNONS, Ed. G., 210
  Ethlinda, 210
  John Robert, 210
RENTZ, Heinrich, 140
RENTZE, Friederich August, 103
  Heinrich, 103
  Wilhelmina, 103
RENZEL, Conrad, 55
REPDOGER, Catharina, 23
  Nelle, 76
  Nette, 23, 76

Phillip, 23
REPOLD, Georg, 41
  Michael, 81
REPP, Johanna Margaretha, 32
RERRIG, Maria, 10
RESCORL, John Robert, 216
RETGREVE, Elizabeth, 129
  Heinrich Hoffman, 129
  John, 129
RETTER, Christina, 6
  Elisabeth, 6
  Henrich, 6
RETTIG, ---, 78
  Anna Maria, 11, 17, 19
  Catharina, 10
  Cathrina, 17
  Christian, 11, 17, 61
  Daniel, 19
  Johann Christian, 10
REUTER, Johan, 108
REVEER, Mary F., 169
REVEN, Christoph, 14
REVER, Cornelia Owen, 260
  Gerhardt Henry, 153
  Irma Isabel, 262
  John H. G., 235, 256, 260, 262
  Lillie J., 256, 260, 262
  Raymond Rossiter, 256
REVILLE, Henry E., 232
REWINKEL, R., 228
REYLI, Job, 295
REYLY, ---, 78
  Catharina, 10
  Conrad, 10
  Joh. Georg, 15
REYNOLDS, Benjamin, 162, 176, 207, 211, 217, 221

Christiana, 207, 221
Christiane, 176
Christina, 211, 217
Elizabeth, 297
Firman Goodwin, 207
Henry Miller, 211
John W., 241
Lilia Medes, 221
Lillie, 264
Margaret Elizabeth, 176
Matilda Jane Dyer, 217
Mrs., 203
William Leroy, 264
William Walter, 264
RHADY, Maria, 142
RHOAD, Elisabeth, 141
RHODE, Abraham, 98
  Chatharina, 143
  Conrad, 98
  Kraul, 98
  Louisa, 147
  Wilhelm, 291
RHODS, Henry, 157
RICHARD, Michael, 118
RICHARDS, Arthur J., 244
  Frank, 237
  Mary T., 147
RICHARDSON, Ann C., 267
  Bessie Corse, 243
  Elisabeth, 55
  Elizabeth, 168
  Herman Ezra, 251
  John, 169
  John S., 272
  John V., 251
  Joshua N., 232
  Minnie M., 251
RICHARTS, May C., 235
RICHMOND, H., 185

Henry, 176, 177, 182, 187, 219, 274
Henry Adam Seesnop, 219
Laura Rebecca Seesnop, 176
M. A., 185, 219
M. V., 226
Maria Cath. C., 311
Maria Cath. Seesnop, 187
Martha Jane Seesnop, 177, 182
Mary, 157
Mary Ann, 176, 177, 182, 187
Mary Ann Seensop, 185
Sarah Elizabeth Seesnop, 182
RICHSTEIN, ---, 301
  Cath., 131
  Catharina, 82, 83, 115
  Eleanora, 210
  Elenora, 228
  Elionora Cicilia, 193
  Elisabeth, 115
  Frau, 109
  Friederike Sophie, 50
  Georg, 47, 83, 115, 131, 193, 289
  Johann, 47, 50, 82, 281
  John, 119
  Katharine, 50, 127
  Louisa, 290
  Margaret, 131
  Margaretta, 157
  Mary Ann, 193
  Michael, 133
  Mr., 109
  Sarah Ann, 210
  Wilhelm, 109, 289
  Wilhelm Christian, 281
  William, 171, 210, 303
RICHTER, Abraham, 40
  Anna, 40
  Katharina, 40
  Margaretha, 42, 55
  Sophia, 44
RICHTERIN, Sophia Louisa, 56
RICHTERN, Sophia, 49
RICHTLER, Elias, 152
RICHTSTEIN, Catharina, 89, 91, 95
  Christina, 91
  Georg, 137
  Johan Georg, 91
  Johann, 87
  Mariana, 137
  Michael, 100
RICHTSTIEN, Georg, 101
RICK, Robert Andrew, 243
RICKS, Elisabeth, 118
  Georg, 118
RICMOND, Henry, 156
RIDDELL, Barbara, 300
  Jessie Avaline, 242
RIDDLER, Beal D., 172
RIDER, Appolona, 157
  Margaret, 152
  Mary Ann, 162
RIDESEL, Franciscus, 140
  Frantz, 91
  Magdalena, 91
RIDGELEY, Charlotte T., 238
RIDGELY, Alexander Gould, 185
  C. R., 185
  Cath. R., 183
  Richard G., 149
  Ruth, 145
  W. H., 185
  William H., 183
  William Henry, 183
RIEBSAM, William P., 152
RIED, Elisabeth, 111
  Margarethe, 111
RIEDBUHL, Cath., 95
RIEDECKER, Frantz, 111
  Magdalena, 111
  Margaretha, 111
RIEDENSEL, Elisabeth, 100
  Frantz, 100
  Magdalena, 100
RIEDESEL, Elisabeth, 286
  Franciscus, 122
  Frantz, 122, 286
  Maria, 122
RIEGART, Henry F., 187
  Maria, 187
  Sophia Elizabeth, 187
RIEGER, Daisy E., 242
RIEGT(EN), ---, 59
RIEHM, Elisabeth, 52
  Maria Cathar., 70
RIEM, Christoph, 60
  Engelhard, 38
  Joh. Engelhard, 38
  Johann Henrich, 280
  Susanna, 38, 280
  Wilhelm, 38, 280
RIEMAN, Daniel, 52
RIEMANN, Daniel, 75, 76
RIES, Adam, 60
  Carl, 67
  Johann Jacob, 7
  Maria Magdalena, 7
  Ulrich, 7
RIESCH, Anna, 76
  Christian, 76
  Joh, 76
RIESERIN, Elisabeth, 279
RIESH, Catharina, 32

Christian, 38
Daniel, 38
Else, 32, 38
Henrich Jac., 38
Jacob, 32
Karl, 32
Marie Cath., 38
RIESS, ---, 59
  Adam, 29
  Jacob, 29
RIET, Johannes, 49
  Maria Margaretha, 49
RIETDORF, Emma V., 235
RIETER, Susanna, 128
  Susanna Dorothea, 128
  Wilhelm Ludwig, 128
RIGBY, Susanna, 142
RIGHT, Elz. J. P., 150
RIGNEY, Alan C., 238
RIGOR, Henrich, 52
RILEY, Amy, 167
  John, 167
RINBY, Lydia, 166
RING, Cath., 148
  Cathrine, 198
  Eliza Ann, 149
  Elizabeth Ann, 198
  George, 198
RINGOLD, Mary, 149
RINMANN, Anna Maria, 19
  Catherina, 18
  Cathrina, 19
  Daniel, 18, 19, 75, 76
  Henrich, 18
RISCHSTEIN, Cath., 36
  Wilhelm, 35
RISHSTEIN, Anna Katharina, 47
  George, 188
  Mary, 188

Retta Jane, 188
William Foxhall, 188
RISTHER, David, 157
RISTON, Christina, 40
  Elisabeth, 40
  Johann Georg, 40
  Katharina, 40, 43
  Wilhelmina, 40
RISTOR, Mary, 51
RITCHER, David, 185
  Elizabeth, 185
  George, 185
RITEAU, Margaret, 203
RITENOUR, Elisha P., 155
RITES, Belle Z., 234
  Katie, 234
RITTER, Anna, 97
  Annie, 230
  Hanna, 129
  Helena Carolina, 97
  Jacob, 97, 129, 138
  John, 52
  Mary Jain, 129
RITTERIN, Maria, 51
ROACHE, Evaline, 170
ROBBES, Catharina, 91
ROBERT, Anna, 281
ROBERTS, Arthur E., 236
  Avice E., 241
  George, 306
  George S., 305
  Jacob, 147
  Jane, 171
  Laura A., 305, 306
  Susie, 305
ROBERTSON, A. H., 176, 218
  Archibald John, 176
  Emily, 297
  Jeanne, 38
  Mr., 297

S. J., 218
Sarah T., 176
Susanna, 99
Theodore James, 218
ROBINS, Mary J., 162
ROBINSON, Dudley, 258, 274
  Emma C., 252, 257, 258, 260
  Gustavus, 162
  Martin L., 232, 252, 257, 258, 260
  Mary Martha, 184
  Mrs., 296
  Nancy, 55
  Opie, 252
  Paul, 260
  Ralph, 257
  Samuel, 55
  Susan, 184
  Thomas, 150
ROBOSSON, Laura Helen, 251
  Nelson O., 251
ROBSEN, William H., 162
ROCHE, Mylon, 239
ROCKES, Catharina, 56
RODE, Catharina, 107
  Wilhelm, 107
RODEMAYER, Alverta, 215
  Ann Maria, 154
  Eliza Ann, 201
  Emily Jane, 206
  Francis Michael, 199
  Francis Thomas, 177
  Francis Tobias, 196
  Frank T., 247
  Georg, 194, 198, 206
  George, 128, 196, 199, 201
  Henry, 215
  John, 152

Index

July Ann, 128
Laura Augusta, 194
Leah, 177, 247
Maria, 196
Mary, 128, 194, 198, 199, 201, 206
S. Kate, 247
Sophia R., 215
William, 177
RODEMEIER, Anna Maria, 110
Georg, 110, 125, 136
Maria, 110
Wilhelm Andreas, 136
RODEMEYER, William A., 270
RODENMAYE, F. Thomas, 227
S. Kate, 227
Sarah Catherine, 227
RODENMAYER, Alonzo Alexander, 182
B. Kate, 226
Charles F., 268
Charles Frederick, 218
Edmund Eschbach, 245
Edwin, 183
Elizabeth Ann, 162
F. Thomas, 225, 226, 229
Francis Hilberg, 226, 312
Francis Thomas, 270
Frank T., 245, 248, 251
George, 132, 299
George C., 155
Henry, 132, 182
John, 183
Kate S., 225
Leah, 218, 270
Mary, 132
Nettie, 248
Rebecca, 183
Rosina Schaffer, 278

Rosina Shafer, 251
S. Kate, 245, 248, 251
Sarah C., 266
Sophia R., 182
William A., 218
William Andrew, 225
RODENMEYER, Ella, 187
Francis Hilberg, 265
John, 187
Rebecca, 187
RODENMOYER, William A., 272
RODER, Christina, 19
Johannes, 19
RODERMAYER, Henry, 220
John James, 220
RODEWALD, Eliza, 196, 197
Eliza Jane, 196
Fredrick Charles Henry, 148
Henry, 197
Henry R., 196
John Fredrich Uthoff, 197
William Henry Augustus, 197
RODGERS, Mary M., 230
RODIN, Eduard, 124
Jane, 124
Mariana, 124
RODMEYER, John, 191
Olivia, 191
Rebecca, 191
ROEDER, Anna M., 244
ROEHRE, Agnese, 34
Andreas, 34
Joh. Jacob, 34
Phillipine, 34
ROELKE, Mrs., 258
ROELKEY, Edward, 272

Joseph E., 237
ROESCH, Mamie, 239
ROESSLER, Gotthelf T. R., 167
ROGAN, Alice, 156
ROGERS, Albert Frederick, 248
Albert H., 245, 248, 250, 252, 254
Alice White, 254
Allen P., 237
Anna Pickhaver, 176
Belle Z., 257, 275
Bessie, 250
Carrall Thomas, 257
Carrol Thomas, 273
Dora Lydia, 245, 266
Edith Regina, 248
Elizabeth A., 186
Elizabeth, 189
Emma, 248
Emma R., 245, 248, 250, 252, 254
Fanny, 171
George Howell, 252
Jacob S., 176
James, 189
James Anna Limes, 186
James H., 234, 257
James L., 186
John W., 228
Lydia M., 176, 269
Margaret, 149
Mary Gordon, 176
Mr., 256
Mrs., 256
Nicholas, 260
Susan Elizabeth, 189
William Cummings, 176
ROHBAUGH, Charles L., 257
Edna May, 257

Sarah, 257
ROHLFING, Christiana Augusta, 248
Frederick Christian, 249
John, 249, 251, 256
John Frederick, 266
John M., 246, 248
Justis William, 256
Magdalena, 251
Mary Louisa, 246
Saloma, 246, 248, 251, 256
Salomna, 249
Sarah, 246
ROHMAN, Daniel, 61
ROHRBACH, Adam, 8
Anna Maria, 8
Johannes, 8
Magdalena, 4
Michael, 4
ROHRICH, Andreas, 46
ROHTER, Anna Henrietta, 79
ROIGART, Heinrich Fenelon, 121
Philip, 121
Sophia, 121
ROLAND, Rosina, 55
ROLEY, Patrick, 164
ROLLINS, Eliza, 153
ROLLKAY, Mr., 248
Mrs., 248
ROMAN, Joseph, 154
RONEMUS, Mary J., 231
ROOT, Elizabeth Ann, 131
Sarah, 131, 203
Sarah Jane, 203
William, 131, 203
RORE, Rachel, 55
RORER, Hanss, 53
Martin, 53
RORERIN, Elisabet, 53

Ursula, 53
ROSENBROCK, Ama J., 180
Caroline, 180
Christian, 160, 180
ROSENDORN, George, 236
ROSER, Margaretha, 66
ROSS, David J., 306
Rosanna, 164
Ximena, 228
ROSSIETER, Nettie S., 247
ROSSITER, Annie E., 231
Bennetta Sherer, 271
C. Elizabeth, 256
Caroline Elizabeth, 258, 260
Emily Elizabeth, 247, 265, 312
Goldsborough Sappington Griffith, 256
Harry Sayen, 253
Horace Levering, 261
J. T., 247
Joel R., 174
Joel T., 235, 256, 258, 260
Lizzie L., 253
Mary Agnes Durst, 258
Maurice L., 253
Maurice Webster, 260
Nettie S., 247
Perceval Sherer, 242
Percival Sherer, 247
ROSSKAMP, Amelia C., 231
Lizzette, 276
Lizzie F., 237
Mary Lizzetta, 235
ROSSMEIER, Louisa, 140
ROTEMEIER, Georg, 101, 118
Georg Carl, 118

Johannes, 101
Maria, 101
ROTEMUND, Diederich, 139
ROTFROD, Anna Maria, 10, 12
Georg, 10, 12
Joseph, 12
ROTHE, Catharina, 92
Wilhelm, 92, 138
ROTHER, Anna Engel, 45
ROTHROCK, Johan, 91
ROTHROD, Anna Maria, 10, 12, 18
Georg, 10, 12, 18, 20
Jacob, 20
Joseph, 12
Maria, 20
Phillip, 18
ROTHRUCK, Mrs., 65
ROTTEMNUND, Wilhelmina, 144
ROTTER, Catharina, 292
Jacob, 121
Johanna, 121
ROTTERMEIER, Dieterich, 291
Michael, 121
ROTTERMUND, David Heinrich, 106
Diederich, 97, 106
Rebecca Louise, 97
Wilhelmina, 106
Wilhelmine, 97
ROUDER, Catherine, 244
ROUNTREE, Mary Ann, 168
Susanna, 157
ROUS, George, 203
George L., 146
Mary Elizabeth Schaffer, 203

ROUSE, David Song, 193
  Davis Tong, 193
  George, 193
  Layfield, 193
  Lizzie, 245
  Mary, 193
  Thomas Wilson, 245
  William, 245
ROWEN, Ann, 155
ROY, Susanna, 46, 47, 49
ROYERS, Margaret, 149
ROYSS, Elizabeth, 190
  James, 190
  Rebecca Hollen, 190
RUAB, Adam Gottlie, 85
  Magdalena, 85
RUDDACH, Washington, 164
RUDOLPH, Maria Catharina, 40
  Maria Katharina, 279
RUHSTEIN, Cath., 131
  Georg, 131
  Margaret, 131
RUND, Anna Catharina, 287
RUPLEY, Admiral, 157
  Margaret R., 155
RUPP, Amelia Emmeda, 243
  Eliza Ann, 304
  Jacob, 304, 305
  John W., 242
  Lena H., 243
RUPPEL, Mrs., 249
RURHE, Johanna, 160
RURKE, Johanna, 160
RUSK, Catharina, 56
RUSKELL, Luorie, 300
RUSSEL, Ann Elizabeth, 198
  Josephine, 184
  Margaret Frances, 191
  Maria Louesa, 184
  Mary, 184, 191, 198
  William, 184, 191, 198
RUSSELL, Ann Elizabeth Magdalena, 193
  John David, 197
  Mary, 193, 197, 202
  mary, 200
  Mary R. F., 167
  Mary Rebecca, 202
  Robert E., 240
  William, 147, 193, 197, 202, 301
  William Henry, 200
RUST, Henry P., 236
RUTGERS, Anna Catharina, 95
  Christiana Jacobina, 95
  Wilhelm Samuel, 95
RUTIEN, Dietrich, 76
RUTTER, Sophia Anna, 278
  William B., 244
RUTTERS, Elisabeth, 9
  Salomon, 9
RYAN, Edwin J., 241
  Fannie Pickens, 207
  Ino., 207
  John, 169, 211
  Margaret Jane, 211
  Mary C., 172
  Sarah, 167
  Susan, 211
  Susan J., 207
RYNE, Elizabeth, 150

-S-
SAAR, Samuel, 55
SACHSE, Emma K., 262
  Hazel Estelle, 262
  Jesse A., 262
SADLER, James William, 260
SAHM, Margaret Phillippina, 306
SALTZER, Sebastian, 91
SALVADOR, Angelo, 196
SANBOWER, Elvie, 231
SANDER, ---, 60, 61
  Anna Sophia, 46
  Johann Valentin, 46, 48
  Johannes, 16
  Margareth, 16
  Maria Elisabeth, 16
  Maria Sophia, 46
  Valentin, 44
SANDERS, Abellina, 110
  Beniamin, 110
  Charlotta, 84
  Elisabeth, 110
  Harriet P., 229
  Johan Georg, 90
  Maria, 110
  Maria Elizabeth, 147
  Sophia, 84, 90, 113
  Valentin, 84, 85, 90, 103, 106, 108, 290
SANDLASS, Lena, 232
SANDONCKIN, Maria Margareth, 52
SANDOZ, Adalina, 202
  Ernestine Pondoz, 203
  Mary Ann, 202, 203
  Philip A., 202, 203
  Philip Augustus, 146
SANDS, Kartha Edra, 262
  Richard Ed., 262
  Richard William, 262
SANFORD, Annie, 238
SARGUS, James, 266
SAUDERS, Banjamin, 149
  Maria Elizabeth, 147
SAUER, Georg, 141

Index

SAUERWEIN, Peter, 22
SAUNDER, Mary Ann, 206
  Philip August, 206
SAUNDERS, Sutton W., 238
SAUR, Samuel, 55
SAURIN, John, 149
SAUTER, Johan Georg, 90
  Margaretha, 90
SAUTHER(IN), Sara, 10
SAVAGE, Lycurgus E., 167
SAVILLE, Ann Jane, 164
SAY, Maria Elisabeth, 91
SBEITZ, Feronica, 9
  Maria, 9
  Michael, 9
SCARF, Hannah, 153
SCELZ, ---, 75
  Johannes, 7
  Maria, 7
  Robert, 7
SCETZ, ---, 75
SCHA, Rettpheli, 88
SCHAAF, Johannes, 96
  Maria Magdalena, 96
SCHADE, Martin G., 147
  Philip Jacob, 291
SCHAEFER, John R., 229
  Ludwig, 56
SCHAEFFER, Anthony, 131
  Catharina, 206
  Catherine, 146
  Friedrich, 206
  Gertrude, 229
  Henrietta Mary, 146
  Jacob, 149
  Maria, 131
  Sophia, 131

William, 305
SCHAF, Helena, 97
  Mr., 97
  Rebecca Althaus, 97
SCHAFER, Amalia, 142
  Anthony, 294
  Balsar, 21
  Baltzer, 18
  Balzer, 75
  Cathrina, 18, 20
  Charles Edward, 224
  Daniel, 21
  Dorothea, 291
  Elisabeth, 20
  Elizabeth Martha, 222
  Friederich, 294
  Georg, 18, 20, 21
  Georg Andreas, 113
  Henry, 222, 224
  Henry Melville, 222
  Lina, 18
  Mary, 146
  Mr., 113, 291
  Mrs., 262
  Rachel, 222, 224
SCHAFFER, Jacob, 16
  Margareth, 16
  Mary, 16
SCHAFFNER, Jacob S., 306
  Phoebe, 306
SCHALL, Annie W., 250
  Margareth, 52
  Minnie F., 233
  Percy Williams, 250
  Thomas B., 234, 250, 276
SCHALLER, Anna Catharina, 84
  Franziska, 84
  Georg, 84
SCHALLI, Catharina Elisabeth, 285

SCHALLY, Adam, 70, 108
  Catharina, 142
  Cathrina, 21
  Elisabeth, 55
  Jacob, 21, 23, 54, 63
  Johann Daniel, 23
  John, 55
  Susanna, 21, 23
SCHAMALZEL, Emma Virginia, 258
  George W., 258
  Walter Beauregard, 258
SCHAMBACH, Clara R., 233
  Emma F., 271
  Henry E., 235
  Katie C., 237
SCHANDING, Elisabeth, 140
SCHANSEIL, Gotleib, 265
SCHAPER, Anna Engel, 45
  Anna Katharina Elisabeth, 45
  Henry, 178
  Rachel, 178
  Rosina, 154
  Wilhelm Adolf, 45
  William Henry, 178
SCHAPEY, Rosina, 154
SCHARDING, Elisabeth, 140
SCHARF, J. Thomas, 2
SCHARPER, Anna Henrietta, 79
  Mrs., 303
  Wilhelm Adolph, 79
SCHATZ, Anna, 193
  Catharine, 198
  Daniel, 193, 195, 196, 198
  Elizabeth, 196
  Mary, 195, 196, 198

Mary Ann, 193
William Hutchins, 195
SCHATZER, Balzer, 10, 75
  Eleanor, 10
  Sarah, 10
SCHAUB, Johann, 201
  Johann Ludwig, 201
  John, 144
  Susanna, 201
SCHAUF, Helena, 42
  Johann, 49
  Maria Magdalena, 49, 285
SCHAUF., Johann, 48
SCHAUM, Anna Maria, 35
  Elisabeth, 281
SCHAUSIEL, Gottlieb, 312
SCHAVER, Anna, 76
  Diane, 76
  Johannes, 76
SCHEER, Laura M. S., 238
SCHEIB, Henry, 156
SCHEIERLY, Wilhelm, 96
SCHEITHAUER, Henrich, 25, 30, 41
  Jacob, 25
  Juliana Margaretha, 30
  Margaretha, 25, 30, 41
SCHEL, Dorothea, 115
SCHELLY, Maria, 143
SCHENEMAN, John, 147
SCHENKEL, Johannes, 55
SCHEPPERT, Thomas, 88
SCHERER, Elisabeth, 23, 44
  Johan, 288
  Johann Carl, 20
  Johannes, 20, 23, 26, 31, 36, 44
  Juliana Catharina, 31
  Maria, 44, 56, 79
  Maria E., 20
  Maria Elisabeth, 23, 26, 31, 36
  Maria Magdalena, 25
  Mathildis, 36
  Peter, 26
SCHERRY, Thomas, 287
SCHERTEL, Susanna, 42
SCHESROY, Esther, 48
SCHIEG, Cathrina Margareth, 21
  Conrad, 18, 21
  Elisabeth, 21
SCHIEL, Carl, 63
SCHILINGER, Mary M., 229
SCHILLER, Christopher, 141
SCHILLINGER, Charles Newton, 246
  Emma, 309
  Gladys, 259
  H., 226
  Henry, 309
  Marietta, 246, 248, 249, 259
  Mary Magdaline, 249, 274
  Samuel, 231, 246, 248, 249, 259
  Samuel S., 267
  Sophia, 309
  Sophia M., 275
SCHIMP, John, 146
SCHLACKEN, Sophia Eleonora, 152
SCHLAG, Mrs., 225
SCHLEGEL, Anna Maria, 3
  Elisabetha, 3
  Ernst Carl, 51
  Henrich, 3
  John, 3
SCHLEICH, Catharina, 109
  Georg, 109
  Johan Georg, 109
SCHLEIF, Johannes, 6
SCHLEIG, Catharina, 116
  Ernst, 126
  Georg, 116, 122, 126, 294
  Wilhelm, 122, 294
SCHLEIGH, Elizabeth, 242
SCHLEY, Anna Maria, 18, 48
  Cathrina, 18, 21
  Georgetta, 307
  Johann, 279
  Johannes, 18, 21, 65
  John, 12
  Nellie, 243
  Sarah M., 273
  Sophia, 21, 65
SCHLODTFELD, Laura Virginia, 309
SCHLOTZ, Johannes, 5
SCHLUSSELBERGER, Elisabeth, 100
SCHMACHTENBERG, Anna Susanna, 46
  Helena Carolina, 42, 280
  Peter, 42, 46, 83, 280, 283
  Sabina, 83
  Wilhelmina, 42, 46, 280
  Wilhelmine, 83
SCHMACHTENBERGER, Wilhemina, 139
SCHMACHTENBERGS, Wilhemina, 139
SCHMACHTENERG, Sabina, 294

410 Index

SCHMAL, Catharina, 30, 96, 106
Catharina Maria, 106, 289
Elisabeth, 30, 121
Johan, 96, 107, 136, 140
Johan Beniamin, 116
John, 106, 116
Louisa, 96, 106, 107, 116, 121, 136
Louisa Catharina, 107
Michael, 30, 124
Mr., 121, 289
SCHMALZEL, Emma Irene, 262
Emma Virginia, 255, 262
George W., 255, 262
Howard Laurence, 276
Rosa May, 255
Walter B., 275
SCHMECK, Anna Maria, 10
Peter, 10
Sara, 10
SCHMELLENBERG, Christina, 41
Peter Caspar, 41
Wilhelmina Carolina, 41
SCHMETTENBERG, Anna Christina, 280
SCHMID, ---, 75
Abraham, 12
Adam, 92
Anna, 5, 15
Anna Elisabeth, 98
Anna Maria, 4, 7, 13, 16, 17, 22
Barbara, 107
Beddy, 52
Catharina, 107
Cathrina, 52
Christina, 80, 89, 106
Christophe, 16
Daniel, 88, 89

Elisabeth, 12, 88, 133
Friederich Christian, 144
Georg, 22
Jacob, 11, 16, 17, 22, 80
Jenny, 84, 92
Joh. Peter, 7
Johan, 83, 89, 91, 97, 98, 106, 108
Johann, 80, 81, 92
Johann Adam, 84
Johann Phillip, 5
Johannes, 5, 16, 17
John, 133
Juliana, 133
Margareth, 12
Margaretha, 124
Maria, 133
Maria Margaretha, 84
Martha, 12
Martin, 53
Nicolaus, 104
Peter, 7, 13
Sally, 112
Sara, 13
Sarah, 88
Sophia, 106
Thomas, 107, 124, 295
William, 12
SCHMIDS, Arnold, 289
Elisabeth, 139
SCHMIDT, Anna Maria, 8
Barbara, 51
Catharina, 5, 7
Christian, 30
Christina, 37, 39
Christine, 34
Elisabeth, 7, 30
Eva, 51
Jacob, 23
Joh., 34
Joh. Arnold, 69

Johann, 37, 50
Johann Arnold, 36
Johannes, 24
Konrad, 2
M. Magdalena, 24
Magdalena, 23
Maria, 23
Maria Catharina, 36
Maria Louisa, 69
Maria Magd., 30
Mary, 239
Mena, 129
Mrs., 65
Paul, 241
Peter, 59
Philipp, 23
Roland, 73
Rouland, 7
Ruland, 8
Susanna, 36
Uland, 5, 73
SCHMIDTEN, Christina, 43
SCHMIDTS, Johannes Arnold, 33
Maria Louise, 33
Susanna, 33
SCHMINK, Mary, 277
SCHMINKE, Alfred Irvin, 268
Alfred Irwin, 249
Ann, 199, 202
Anna Eliza Clark, 202
Annie C., 232
Eliza, 202
Emma C., 245, 246, 248, 249
George, 199, 202
Lillian Elizabeth, 248, 268
Paul F., 245, 246, 248, 249
Paul Fred., 230, 269
Paul Frederick, 245

Index   411

Rosa, 235
Walter Chase, 246, 267
William Charles, 199
SCHMINOKE, George, 142
SCHMIROKE, George, 142
SCHMITH, Mary, 138
SCHMITZ, Arnold, 39, 46, 47, 49
Peter, 49
Susanna, 46, 47, 49
SCHMNID, Anna Elisabeth, 295
Johan, 295
SCHMOK, Peggy, 55
SCHMOLL, Conrad, 20, 22
Johann Conrad, 9
SCHNAUFER, Mr., 98, 100
SCHNECK, Elisabeth, 70
Jacob, 70
SCHNEDIER, Christine, 34
Hieronimus, 34
Maria Elisabeth, 34
SCHNEEMANN, Joh. Andreas Christian, 44
SCHNEIDER, Andreas, 84
Anna Maria, 63
Carl, 95
Catharina, 5, 27, 37, 64
Christian, 125
Christiane, 48
Christina, 40, 45, 84, 86, 98, 280
Daniel, 27, 64
Elisabeth, 40, 95, 125
Elizabeth Ann, 305
Georg Bernhard, 40, 280
Herman, 85

Herrman, 138
Hieronimus, 40
Hieronymus, 38
Jacob, 125
James, 84
Johan, 143
Johanna Ludwig, 45
Johannes, 6
Julius, 305
Katharina, 41
Leonhard, 38
Ludewig, 83, 84, 85, 86, 125
Ludwig, 40, 45, 48, 98, 280, 283, 286
Ludwig Wilhelm, 86, 283
Margaretha, 85
Maria, 289
Maria Sara, 13
Michael, 97, 109
Pastor, 146
Peter, 27, 64
Simon Carl, 48
Wilhelm, 95, 98
SCHNEIDERN, Katharina, 47
SCHOARF, Carl, 14
SCHOENEBERGER, Johann, 49
SCHOENEMAN, Cath., 202
Harriott, 198
James Wilkes, 198
John, 198, 202
John Mangles, 202
SCHOENEMANN, Cathrine, 204
John, 204
SCHOMAK, Michael, 70
SCHOP, ---, 61
SCHOPER, Henry, 159
SCHORR, Anna, 76
Diane, 20, 76

Johannes, 20, 76
Maria, 20
SCHRADER, Frank, 246
Maggie, 246
SCHRADERIN, Catharina Elisabeth, 92
Sophia Margaretha, 92
SCHREIBER, Catharina, 104
Heinrich, 285
Michael, 58
SCHREIN, Rebecca, 138
SCHRENK, Catharina, 94
Johann Marris, 94
SCHRIEFER, Mary E., 236
SCHRIYAD, Johannes, 13
SCHROBB, Sarah, 5
SCHRODER, Catharina, 10
Catharina Elisabeth, 137, 294
Henrich, 17
Hermann, 10
Johannes, 10
Ludewig, 137, 143
Ludwig, 294, 295
SCHROEDER, Charles Frederick, 180
Daniel, 42
Elisab., 79
Elisabeth, 42
H., 180
Harriet, 180
Harriet Krider, 180
Nicolas, 148
P., 180
Philip, 180
Philip Korkhaus, 180
Sophia, 42
Susanna, 65
SCHROETER, Carl, 86
Georg, 86

412 Index

Ludwig Georg, 86
SCHROT, Georg, 292
SCHUDI, Barbara, 5, 8
  Nicolaus, 5, 8
SCHUDY, ---, 78
  Barbara, 6, 9
  Elisabeth, 8
  Emanuel, 8
  Magdalena, 8
  Martin, 8
  Nicolaus, 6, 9, 11
  Winberth, 8
SCHUECK, ---, 75
SCHUG, Conrad, 18, 52
SCHULTZ, Uliana, 51
  Alex, 222
  Alfred Harman, 251
  August, 251, 269
  Catharina, 98
  Elizabeth, 251
  George John, 251
  Heinrich, 98
  Johan Jacob, 295
  John Duer, 222
  John H., 167
  Mary E., 222
  Matilda E., 273
  Matilda Elizabeth, 251
  Salome, 98
  William George, 251
SCHULTZE, John
  Henry, 270
SCHULZ, Conrad, 46
  Elisabeth, 46
  Theodor Conrad, 46
SCHUMACHER, Annie, 277
  Carson, 233
  Carson S., 251, 255
  Carson Schier, 251
  Edward Rudolph, 255
  Henry C., 233

Minnie E., 251, 255
SCHUMACK, Catharina, 56
SCHUNCK, Anna, 26, 28, 37, 44
  Anna Maria, 28
  Elisabeth, 134
  Henrietta, 125
  Jacob, 26, 125
  Johannes, 26, 28, 37, 44
  John, 287
  Joseph, 37, 287
  Michael, 125
  Philip, 134
  Samuel, 37
  Sophia, 134
SCHUNK, Anna, 22
  Anna Margareta, 22, 76
  Joh., 71
  Johannes, 22
  Maria, 76
  Samuel, 71
SCHUPPAR, Anna Ottila, 65
SCHURCK, Anna, 101
  Mr., 101
  Philip, 101
SCHUREK, Henrietta, 125
  Jacob, 125
  Michael, 125
SCHUSTER, Georg, 60
  Lena, 60
SCHUTT, Augustine, 281
  Louisa, 281
SCHUY, Cathrina Margareth, 21
  Elisabeth, 21
SCHWAB, Adam, 287
  Catharina Maria, 289
  Elisabeth, 287
  Louisa Catharina, 288

Mr., 288, 289
  Susanna, 43
SCHWAHL, Elisabeth, 292
  Mr., 292
SCHWARTZ, Anna Magdalena, 23, 28
  Bertha, 277
  Bertha E., 230
  Carl, 17, 18, 28
  Carl Gottlob, 23
  Cathrina, 54
  Elizabeth Jane, 185
  Henrich, 51
  Henry, 185
  Johan Friederich, 291
  William Henry, 185
SCHWARZ, Anna Magdalena, 33
  Carl, 22, 33
  Carl Gottlob, 21
  George, 64
  Susanna, 65
SCHWEINEBRATTEN, Martha Elisabeth, 279
SCHWEITZER, Anna Maria Juliana, 281
  Daniel, 27
  Elisabeth, 91, 138
  Jacob, 48
  Joh. Britton, 128
  Johan, 139
  Johann, 281
  Johannes, 27, 285
  Maria Juliana, 27, 286
  Michael, 128, 144
  Philip, 91
  Regina, 48
  Samuel, 281
  Sophia, 128
SCHWELK, Catharina, 56
SCHWENGEL, Barbara, 46

Index

SCHWESSINGER, Edward C., 239
SCHWIN, Lulu, 252
SCHWINGEL, Barbara, 51
  Georg, 55
  John, 12
SCHWINN, George, 253
  Lena, 253
  Marguerite M., 239
  Minnie K. L., 234
  William Girard, 253
SCHWOB, Benedict, 13
  Margareth, 13
SCOGGINS, Allie Lee, 254
  Augusta Golden, 252
  Elma Beatrice, 250
  Elma J., 250, 251
  Elma June, 271
  Emma J., 252
  James Fletcher, 254
  Joseph C., 236
  Joseph Charles, 250, 251, 252, 254
SCOTT, Eva B., 235
  Ida, 238
  Mary C., 165
SCOTTEN, Amy, 237
SCROGGINS, Joseph Charles, 269
SEABROOK, Eliza., 167
SEABROOKS, E.
  Elizabeth Ann, 183
  Mary Virginia, 183
  Thomas, 183
SEBLER, Jacob, 125
SECHRIST, Lizzie, 242
SEDLIMEYER, Christoph, 51
SEEBODE, Carrie E., 234
  Charles F., 171

SEELTZER, Mary Ann, 168
SEEMAN, Andrew H., 162
SEESNOP, Catherine, 308
  Maria, 154
  Mary Ann, 156
  Mr., 298
SEFTON, J. W., 230
SEGENSSER, Martin, 14, 17, 77
SEGENTZER, Margareth, 16
  Martin, 16, 77
  Michael, 16
SEGERHINDIN, Johann Georg, 7
  Margaritha, 7
  Martin, 7, 77
SEGESSERS, Martin, 77
SEGESTER, Johannes, 3
  John Peter, 3
  Marg., 4
  Margaretha, 3
  Martin, 3, 4, 77
SEGESTERIN, Anna Maria, 51, 77
SEIBEL, Ludwig, 5
SEIDENSTRICKER, Abraham, 254
  Albert Bernhardt, 194
SEIP, William, 156
SEITZ, Franklin H., 241
  Horace Grant, 239
  Winfred E., 238
SELBER, Jacob, 125
SELER, Johan, 97
SELGER, Leonard, 112
SELLERS, Anna, 48
  Elisabeth, 48
  Jacob, 185
  Johann, 48

SELLHAUSEN, Henry W., 241
SELSER, Jacob, 140
SELTZER, Adam, 159, 176
  Adam Heck, 176
  Anna Elisabeth, 126
  Anna Maria, 114, 135
  Anna Maria Charlotta, 114
  Catharina, 144
  Christian, 141
  Christina, 104, 122, 292
  Elizabeth, 172
  Jacob, 104, 107, 114, 122, 137, 288, 292, 294
  Johan Ludwig, 107, 288
  Ludewig, 126
  Ludwig, 135
  Margaret, 161, 176
  Maria, 107, 114
  Mary Ann, 308
  Michael, 111, 117, 135
  Miss, 112
  Sidney Norris, 176
SENGSTACK, Heinrich, 281
SENGSTAKE, Philipp, 281
SEOBOLD, Carl, 61
SERTIMEYER, Christoph, 51
SERVER, Edward A., 267
  Ella, 273
  William H., 274
SETTER, Carolina, 83
SEUFERT, Ida, 243
SEUMERING, Elizabeth, 140
SEWARD, Lulu Bertha, 233
SEWCHEN, Joseph, 76
SEWCHON, Elisabeth, 20

Joseph, 20
Thomas, 20
SHAAFER, Florence Elias, 207
Henrietta, 207
Henry, 207
Rachael, 207
SHACK, Benjamin F., 237
SHAEFER, Elisabeth, 196
Herman, 196
Philip, 196
SHAEFFER, Cath., 196
George A., 163
SHAFER, Alice L., 245, 247
Anna Caroline, 245
Annie E., 245, 247, 248
Charles, 247
Dorothea, 118
Edward H., 232, 251
Harry Ferdinand, 248
Howard Rossiter, 245
John R., 245, 247, 248
Kate May, 247
Mary, 245
Mary Jesse, 247
Mary Locher, 251
Mr., 118
Rosina C., 251
William, 245, 247
SHAFFER, Elizabeth, 157
Henry C., 240
SHAFFNER, Eliza, 163
Jacob, 303
Juliet, 161
Margaret, 157
Mathias, 158
SHALL, Annie M., 246, 247
Edgar Meyers, 246
Elsie May, 247
Thomas B., 246, 247

SHALLIG, John, 55
SHALLUS, M. Katie, 235
SHAMER, Mary J., 225, 309
Theodore, 225, 309
SHANAMAN, John, 149
SHAPPARD, John J., 166
SHARER, Albert F., 264
Margaret Iona, 264
Sarah V., 264
SHARP, Annie C., 239
SHAW, James, 149, 309
James van Buren, 190
Matthew, 190, 309
Mrs., 300
Sophia, 190
Thomas D., 240
SHAWGO, Annie C., 254, 256
Charles, 256
Clara Estella, 254
George, 256
William, 256
William E., 234, 254, 256, 272
SHAWN, Blanche E., 244
SHEBLE, Jacob D., 157
SHEDEL, Agnes Jane, 149
SHEEHAN, George Davis, 246
Jennie V., 246
John R., 246
SHEELER, Allice, 210
Cath. M., 168
J. C., 210
Sophia B., 210
SHEETS, Rosa E., 232
SHELL, Charles D., 156
SHELLEY, Hugh G., 232
John, 161
SHELTON, Bertha V., 241

SHENEMAN, William H., 242
SHEPHERD, Thomas M., 239
SHEPPARD, Mathilda Ann, 156
SHERER, Elias, 55
Emma, 232
SHERWOOD, B. Franklin, 237
Mrs., 256
SHEUTE, Daniel, 165
SHIER, William, 145
SHIMP, John, 146
SHINEMANN, Abraham, 51
SHIRLEY, Emma, 235
SHLIGH, Mary, 51
SHLIY, John, 52
SHOCK, Lillie W., 233
SHOEMAKER, John A., 162
SHOFER, Anna, 127
Anthony, 127
SHOFFNER, Catharine, 154
SHOLL, Mary Elisabeth, 52
SHOOK, Catherine, 273
Edward Stewart, 265, 312
Helen, 256
Henry, 274
Howard Percival, 245
Maggie, 245, 256
Richard, 245, 256
SHORTER, William, 232
SHORTT, Alfred E., 263
Catherine, 263
Clarwell Nelson, 263
Dora Grace, 263
Earnest Clayton, 263
Hary Rowley, 263
James W., 263

Paul Edwin, 263
Sadie Grace, 263
Sarah, 263
Viola Carolina, 263
SHOTT, David, 307
SHOTTS, Cath., 188
Charles, 187
Daniel, 149, 187
David, 181, 184, 188
Laura Louesa, 181
Levenia Rebecca, 184
Mary, 181, 184, 187
Mary Ann, 298
Mary Jane, 188
Mrs., 227
Susanna, 187
SHOWER, Edmund Geiger, 240
SHOWERS, Jacob, 189
Mary, 189
Sarah Elizabeth, 189
SHRAD, Dorothea, 118
SHRECK, John, 147
SHREYER, M., 52
SHRIVER, Ann Eva, 306
E., 190
E. Lydia, 190
Edward, 155
SHUCK, Barbara, 168
Cath., 182
Catharine, 179
Elenora Virginia, 179
Henry, 157, 179, 182
SHUGH, Mr., 156
SHULER, Anna Marguerite, 256
George W., 253, 256, 259
Lizzie V., 253, 256, 259
Mark Herbert, 253
Nellie Catherine, 259
SHULTZ, Alex, 304
Alexander, 207, 210

Anna Elsworth, 207
Elizabeth, 304
Ida, 210, 304
Lizzie, 207
Mary Elizabeth, 210
SHUNK, Cathrine, 206
Elizabeth, 206
Ellen, 202, 206
Jacob, 202, 206
John, 202
John P., 202
SHURTZ, Catharina, 99
Friederich, 99
Louisa, 99
SHUUTZ, Catharina, 99
Friederich, 99
Louisa, 99
SIBLER, Abraham, 90
Beniamin, 283
Catharina, 90
SICKEN, Charles, 219
Charles Morritz, 219
Jennett, 219
Margaret, 219
Melvin Pypher, 219
SIEBER, Cath. Margar., 34
Catharina, 24
Catharina Maria, 28
Johann Friderich, 24
Johannes, 34
Philipp, 28
Phillip, 24, 28, 34
SIEGMAN, Henrietta, 229
SIEGWART, Amelia, 256, 257
Annie, 256
Arnold, 236, 256, 257
Theresa Louisa, 257
SIEMERS, Mary Elizabeth, 160

SIEMONN, H. William, 271
SIGAND, Albert, 22
Maria, 22
SIGHTNER, Isaac, 221
Kate, 221
Virginia Lee, 221
SILLE, Beniamin, 122
Catharina, 122
SILLS, Ann, 268
Edward Murray, 225
Ellinor Clarke, 227
Frances Mary, 225
Ino. W., 225
John W., 227
Mrs., 297
Sarah W., 225, 227
SILVA, John Enos, 166
SILVESTER, Ann Jane, 301
George Thomas, 164
Mary A. E., 169
SIM, Robert, 168
SIMASON, Charles Peter, 192
William Conrad, 192
SIMMERING, Catharina, 88
Elisabeth, 95
Wilhelm, 88
SIMMON, Earl, 143
SIMMONS, Margaret, 151
S. C., 229
SIMMOR, Earl, 143
SIMMS, Charles, 230
SIMON, Anna Katharina, 49
Anna Maria, 40
Carolina, 87
Cath., 36, 205
Catharina, 87, 97, 105, 205
Catharine, 206

Conrad Herman, 79
David, 41, 49, 87, 97, 105, 127, 134, 205, 206
Elisabeth, 25, 41
Frederick, 193
Friederich, 105
Henry, 206
Jacob, 25, 30, 36, 40, 46, 79, 87, 134, 279, 295
Johann, 279
Johann Jacob, 205
Johannes, 46
Julian, 206
Juliana, 25, 67
Katharina, 46, 49, 79, 279
Katherine, 127
Mariana, 97
Regina, 279
Wilhelm, 87
William, 127
SIMONICH, Henrich, 127
SIMONS, Edgar P., 233
SIMPSEN, Elizabeth, 162
SIMPSON, Caroline, 169
  Elizabeth, 162
  Harry E., 244
  Maria A., 164
  Minnie M., 242
SINCLAIR, Elisabeth, 134
  Mary A., 151
  Mathies, 134
  Wilhelm, 134
SINGLETON, William, 297
SINN, Laura V., 229
SINNERS, Elisha R., 296
SINSENICH, Nancy, 38
SINSNER, Fredrick, 129
  Luisa, 129
SIRICH, John Henry, 161
SISNOP, Adam, 138

SISSEN, Elizabeth Jane, 166
SITLER, Abraham, 90
  Beniamin, 282
  Catharina, 90
  Wilhelm, 282
SITTER, Abraham, 138
SITTLER, Abraham, 98
  Samuel, 98
SKAR, Elisabeth, 86
  Georg, 86
  Magdalena, 86
SKINNER, Samuel J., 153
SKURE, Eva, 99
  Robert, 99
SKYSTER, Ephraim, 59
SLADE, John S., 153
SLATER, John M., 150
SLAUGHTER, Adolph E., 238
  Columbia, 153
SLAYSMAN, Allen Lee, 263
  Gladdys Frost, 264
  Ida, 263
  Ida J., 264
  William Hawry, 264
  William L., 263, 264
SLEIIN, Michael, 100
SLEMMER, Jane, 159
SLICER, William, 145
SLIGH, John, 52
SLON, Elisabeth, 9
  James, 9
  John, 9
SMALLWOOD, Alfred, 236
  Ida, 262
  Mrs., 258
SMALTZEL, Anna B., 249, 251
  Emma Clara, 251

  Howard Lawrence, 249
  John, 249, 251
SMALZEL, John, 271
SMART, Enda Kinnaman, 248
  Mary E., 248
  William T., 248
SMIDT, John, 52
SMITH, Ada, 247
  Alice Luck, 271
  Alverda, 306
  Andrew, 187
  Ann Barbara, 156
  Ann Cath., 193
  Ann Rebecca, 191
  Anna Maria, 127
  Augusta, 252, 253
  Bell F., 247
  Catharine, 187
  Catherine, 308
  Cathrine, 145
  Charles Alexander, 185
  Charles Augustus, 250
  Christina, 127
  Conrad, 2
  Edwad Oscar, 252
  Elizabeth, 145, 189, 191, 192, 254, 271
  Emma A., 250
  Ephraim, 52
  Estelle S., 232
  Florence, 263
  Florence H., 240
  Frederick, 189, 191
  Fredrick, 192
  George D., 159
  George Oscar, 263
  Harriet, 169
  Harry C., 250
  Harry Clay, 232
  Harry D., 274
  Heister Clymer, 254

Index   417

Helen Harman, 251
Henry, 232, 252, 253
Henry Clay, 234
Herbert L., 243
Irene, 245
Isabel F., 245, 247, 254
J. Harman, 230, 251
Jacob, 149, 200
Jacob Stephen, 151
James Wilson, 168
Johanna E., 150
John, 127, 142, 185, 186, 191, 193, 198, 200, 297
John B., 153
John Herman Walter, 253
John N., 263
John Thomas, 192
John W., 242
Josephine E., 162
Joshua VanSant, 218
Julia, 198
July, 200
Lena M., 245
Lena May, 246
Louesa, 189
Lydia Keith, 246
Marg., 209, 212
Marg. Ann, 191
Margaret, 185, 186, 193, 214, 310
Margaret Ann, 198
Margaret Franklin, 245
Margaret Meredeth, 212
Margaret N., 198
Marie, 312
Mary, 148, 245, 247, 298
Mary A., 218, 271
Mary Ann, 149
Mary B., 152
Mary Elizabeth, 191, 200
Mary Emma, 254
Mary Jane, 181

Mary Susanna, 186
Mr., 297
Mrs., 189, 257
Nellie, 251
Oliver Franklin, 189
Sarah, 145, 235, 265, 312
Sophia, 151
Susanna, 200, 206
Theoda M., 234
Virginia, 160, 187, 209, 307
Walter F., 230, 245, 246
William, 158
William B., 152, 189
William Charles, 254
William Henry, 214
William Leslie, 254
William P., 191, 209, 214, 218
William Prescott, 212
William Todd, 189
William W., 229, 245, 247, 254
Williard M., 231
Wnn., 198
SMITHSIN, Hattie V., 241
SMITHSON, Susanna M., 160
SMOOT, Charles W., 235, 255, 256, 257, 260, 261
   Charles Wesley, 256
   Clara Estelle, 257
   Elmer Louis, 260
   James Alfred, 255, 273
   Laura J., 255, 256, 257, 260, 261
   William Raymond, 261
SMULLY, Margaret, 162
SNEIDER, Georg, 52
SNELLINGS, William B., 234
SNIFEL, Josephine, 156

SNUDER, Marie Agnes, 276
SNYDER, Adam, 238, 258, 259, 261
   Ann, 145
   Anna M., 245, 248
   Bessie E., 244
   Cora, 254
   Edgar Victor, 255
   Edna Leora, 253, 271
   Edna Margaret, 261
   Elizabeth, 248
   George William, 254
   Harry V., 253
   Harry Victor, 255
   Helena, 258, 259, 261
   Helena Fredricka, 258
   Henrietta, 149
   Henry William, 254
   Hunter Harry O., 239
   John Henry, 245, 266
   John William, 236
   Justice W., 245, 248
   Justus W., 278
   Letitia, 302
   Maria Agnes, 259
   Mary A., 275
   Mary E., 255
   Mary Ellen, 253
SOB(IN), Dorothea, 9
SOELKEY, Oliver Edward, 271
SOLLER, John, 2
SOMMER, Elisabeth, 34
   Rosa, 277
SOMMERFIELD, Leon H., 239
SOMMERLOCK, John F., 170
SOMMERS, Anna Margaret, 250
   Earle Joseph, 259, 277
   Lydia Ann, 252

Index

Rosa, 250, 252, 253, 259
Rosa Adeline, 253
S. B., 306
Thomas H., 232, 250, 252, 253, 259
Willie, 306
SOMMERVILLE, Bertha G., 232
Mary E., 245
SONZER, Adele Susan, 195
SOUTHCOMB, Sarah A., 155
SPAMER, Henry, 164
SPANGLER, Bernard, 182
Cath., 182
Margaret Ann, 158
SPANHOF, Anna, 286
SPANHOFF, Reinhardt, 70
SPAR, David, 197
Elizabeth, 197
Jacob William, 197
SPARR, David, 149
SPARS, Maria, 195
SPEAR, Alva Grove, 190
Cath. S., 183, 187
Catharine, 190
Catherine, 276
Edwin Walker, 183
Otis, 152, 183, 187, 190, 311
Peter Forney, 187
SPECK, Anna Maria, 30
Catharina, 61
Henrich, 30, 38, 72, 101
Johann Henrich, 30
Johannes, 54, 61
Johannes Nikolaus, 66
John, 61
Maria, 38, 42, 47, 81
Mary, 55

Wilhelm, 66
Wilhelm August, 38
SPED, Eva, 75
Eva Barbara, 75
Herta Barbara, 75
SPEIL, Eva, 75
Eva Barbara, 75
Herta, 11
Herta Barbara, 11, 75
Wilhelm, 11
SPEILERN, Elisabeth, 55
SPEK, Catharina, 4
Johannes, 4
Magdalena, 4
SPENCE, Frederick, 160
Georg W., 167
Mary Brown, 150
SPENCER, Charles, 264
Charles Attwill, 263
Charles R., 263
Eva, 263
Mary Florence, 263
Mary L., 263, 264
Mary Louisa, 263
Permelia Ashcom, 263
Stephen, 56
Thomas Hopkins, 263
SPENER, Mary Brown, 150
SPENSER, Abel, 147
SPERRY, Marianna, 161
SPEUR, Cath. Susanna, 194
Otis, 194
Sarah Lydia, 194
SPICER, Levinia, 158
Susannah, 54
SPIER, Friedrich, 285
Mr., 285
SPIES, Carl Ludewig, 108
Catharina, 140
Christian, 120

Frances, 215
Friederich, 96
Georg, 120
Georg W., 164
George, 215
Johan, 96, 108
Johann, 81
Johann P., 57
John Jacob, 215
Louisa, 81
Margaret, 308
Margaretha, 81, 96, 108
Nancy, 120
Peter, 135
Wilhelm Tell, 135
SPIESSSER, Daniel, 27
Maria Salome, 27
SPILLMAN, Henry, 297
SPILMAN, Henry, 161
SPLEICH, Anna Catharina, 96
Georg, 96, 139
Georg Henrich, 96
SPORLEDER, Henry, 236
SPRANG, Carl Alexander, 105
Christiana, 105
Georg, 105
SPROLE, Annie, 228
SPRUNG, Christian, 117
Georg, 87, 95, 117, 141
Isabella, 117
Jacobina Catharina Charlo, 87
Johanna Christina, 87, 95
SPUCK, Lewis, 263
Mary, 263
Susanna, 263
SRAD, Joh. Nicholas, 5
Maria Eva, 5
Wilhelm, 5
STACK, Christian, 59

Index 419

Magdalena, 59
STACKMAN, Emma, 229
STACKS, Charles M., 255
  Guy McDonald, 255
  Mervin Edwin, 277
  Minnie C., 255
STAFFORD, Alphonso O., 240
  Mary, 148
  Sarah, 148
STAHL, Mary Lizzie, 224, 308
  Matilda, 224, 240, 308
  William, 224, 308
STALEY, Bessie, 261
  Bessie W., 259, 261
  Edward G., 232, 251, 253
  G. L., 210, 263
  Hannah, 210
  Hannah Francis, 271
  Marguertie Clagett, 253
  Matthew Patterson, 259
  Rose Campbell, 251, 270
  Susie, 251, 253
  William Cornelius, 261
  William T., 239, 259, 261
STAMMER, Sally, 25
STANDIFORD, Matilda C., 228
STANFORD, Elizabeth, 154
STANSBURG, Fanny B., 164
  George W., 160
STANSBURY, ---, 296
  Edith Scott, 157
STARCK, Maria Friderica, 283
STARR, Edward G., 157
  J. Taylor, 171
  Thomas W., 155
  William Henry, 150

STARTZMAN, Maggie R., 305
STAUBER, Catharina, 36
  Christian, 36
  Henrietta, 36
STAUTZ, Cecilia, 134
STAYLONG, John, 169
STEADMAN, John, 164
STECK, Ada Romanus, 180
  Mary C., 180
  P. Roman, 180
STEEG, Anna Maria, 31, 76
  Catharine, 76
  Michael, 64
STEEL, Elizabeth, 217
  Ino., 217
  John Wesley, 217
STEELE, Eduard, 52
  Harriet, 217
  John, 165, 217
  Martha Jane, 217
STEELMAN, John S., 219
  Mary, 219
  Mrs., 296
  Samuel, 219
STEENHUIS, Henrich, 42
  Margaretha, 42
  Maria, 42
STEER, Grace V., 235
STEFFEY, William McK., 232
STEGENSFER, Martin, 77
STEGENSSER, Ester, 19
  Margareth, 19
  Martin, 19
STEIDS, Lorentz, 51
STEIGER, Andreas, 2, 23
  Andrew, 2
  Cathrina, 51

  Degariera, 283
  Jacob, 283
  Maria, 23
STEIMER, Cath., 206
STEIN, Anna Maria, 24
  Catharina, 55
  Georg, 118
  Johan Michael Ruden, 107
  Johannes, 24, 67
  Margaretha, 123
  Margaretha Ruden, 107
  Maria Magdalena, 24
  Peter, 123, 143
  Ruden, 107
  Sophia, 123
STEINER, Carrie, 239
STEINFORT, Johan, 100
STEINMAN, John, 148
STEITS, Hanna, 51
  Margaret, 197
  Maria, 52
  Susan Ellen, 197
  William, 197
STEITZ, ---, 75
  Laurenz, 67
  Lorentz, 31
  Michael, 61
  Wilhelm, 31
STEITZER, ---, 58
STEIVER, Catharine, 144
STEIWERS, Susanna, 145
STELMES, Henrich, 39
STEM, Gover, 276
STEMDER, Johann, 24
  Magdalena, 24
  Margaretha, 24
  Sara, 24
STEMLER, Johann, 24, 26
  Johannes, 65
  Magdalena, 24, 26

Margaretha, 24
Phillipine, 26
Sara, 24
STENGEL, John, 234
STENNER, Berhardina, 256
  Charles Henry, 250
  Henry, 255
  John P., 232, 250, 255, 256
  Maggie, 256
  Maggie B., 250, 255
STEPHEN, C. E., 216
  J. M., 216
  Willemina Ford, 216
STEPHENS, Mr., 297
  Virginia B., 172
STETCHER, Anna Emilia, 23, 62
  Jacob, 23, 62
  Margaretha, 23
STETHJOR, Jacob, 16
  Margareth, 16
  Peter, 16
STEUBE, Hannah E., 229
STEUCK, Maria Magd., 14
  Nicolaus, 14
STEVEINS, Christiana, 148
STEVENS, A., 175
  Christopher Columbus, 175
  Elizabeth, 175
  Isabel P., 249
  James J., 166
  John Lowe, 249
  Josephine Elizabeth, 175
  Lillian May, 249, 268
  Lucinda Baptist, 175
  Mary, 161, 175
  Matilda, 175
  Rebecca B., 163, 175
  Thomas Murphy, 175
  Virginia Baptist, 175
  William E., 249
STEVENSEN, James C., 163
STEVENSON, Alice M., 244
  Lydia, 155
  Maggie, 261
STEWART, Ann B., 148
  Elinor, 231
  John J., 242
  Mary, 159, 241
  Mary Farewell, 247
  Sarah, 168
STIBBENS, Daniel, 159
STICK, Jacob, 136
STIERLE, Johannes, 46, 56
STIETZ(EN), Lorentz, 59
STILLIT, John, 102
STIMPEL, Anthony, 97, 108, 139
  Heinrich, 97
  Margaretha, 97, 108
  Sophia, 108
STINE, Frederick, 150
STINER, James, 156
STIRLING, Robert, 147
STITGER, Elisabeth, 18
  Jacob, 18
  Mary, 18
STITTLEMYER, Jonathan, 144
STO--, Johannes, 3
STOCK, Maria Magdalena, 139
  Metta, 43, 79
STOCKER, James J., 162
  James T., 162
STOCKHAUSE, Amelia, 236
  Charles H., 236
  Paulina, 241
STOCKHAUSEN, Anna, 275
  Annie, 250
  Charles H., 257, 258
  Emil, 250, 274
  Fredericke Amelia, 258
  Louisa, 268
  Mary Catherine, 257
  Mary L., 257, 258
  Walter, 250
STOCKIN, ---, 88, 98
STODDARD, Mary E., 165
  William, 161
STOERCKEL, Maria, 46
STOFFELMAN, Gesina, 69
  Hen., 69
STOFFELMANN, Anna Julianna Dorothea, 31
  Gesina, 31
  Henrich, 31
STOHLER, Anna Catharina, 8
  Catharina, 9
  Joh., 8
  Johannes, 7, 9
  Maria Cathy, 7
STOHLIN, Cathrina, 10
STOLL, Augusta, 232
  Georg, 139
  J. Daniel, 269
STONA, ---, 75
  Elisabeth, 5
  Tomas, 6
STONART, ---, 75
STONE, Bessie May, 257
  Cath., 247
  Daisy Bell, 251
  David Charles H., 265
  David Charles Henry, 247, 312

Index

David F., 247
Eleanor, 251
Eleanora, 254, 257, 259, 262
George Henry, 259, 274
Howard Edward, 262
John L., 251, 254, 257, 259, 262
John Lewis, 262
Myrtle Maud, 251
Nellie Ray, 254
Pearl Estelle, 251
Rosa B., 230
William Henry, 271
STONERAKER, Margaret, 184
Mary Jane, 184
Samuel, 184
STONESIFER, Clara Elizabeth, 254, 261
Harry M., 261
Harry Morrison, 254
Myrtle Elizabeth, 261
STOPPS, Catharina, 55
STORCH, Antonetta Milcha, 179
Emma Josephine, 218
Martha, 176, 179, 218
Martha Cath., 176
William G., 176, 179, 218
William Geo., 160
STORER, Carolina, 143
STORM, Henry, 159
STOUFFER, Mathilda A., 156
STOUT, Jospeh, 148
STOVER, Christian, 288
STOVERTAWN, Margareth, 13
STOWMAN, Edward, 245
Mary, 245
Sarah Elizabeth, 245

STRAAKBEIN, Catharina, 56
STRACKBEIN, Kath., 80
Katharina, 43
STRAUUS, Catherine, 260
John, 260
William Alfred, 260
STRAWINSKI, Bellini Owen, 181
Clara, 177, 181
Felix J., 177
Felix T., 181
Justus Frisby, 177
Thadeus Smyser, 181
STREMEL, Johann, 279
STREMMEL, Dav. Friederich, 47
Friederich, 47
Friedrich, 57
Georg Ludwig, 40
Johann, 39
Katharina, 46
STREPPERT, Andreas, 94
Catharina, 94
Joseph, 94
STRIBECK, Catharina, 3
Peter, 3
STRIBEK, Anna Catharina, 9
Catharina, 9
Peter, 9
STRICK, James Oliver, 266
Madge Oleria, 265
STRIEBECK, Betzie, 52
STRIEBEL, Cathrina, 13
Johannes, 13, 75
Peter, 13
STROHMAN, Magd., 261
STROM, Charlotta, 285
Mr., 285

STRONG, Adeline R., 222
Georg, 222
Lillie May, 222
STRUEBERT, Cath., 205
Elisabeth, 205
Harriet, 205
Johan, 205
STUART, James, 229
Mabel M., 240
STUCK, Caspar, 17, 52
Charles, 247, 276
Clara Belle, 231
James Oliver, 247
Laura J., 235
Madge Olevia, 247
Maggie Olivia, 312
Margaret, 247
Margaret Ann, 277
STULLER, Daniel, 205
STUND, ---, 75
Anna, 8
Anna Regina, 8
Joh., 8
STURE, Eva, 99
Robert, 99
STURGEN, Sarah A., 170
STURGEON, Margaret, 307
STURM, Elisbeth, 144
STURTZ, Jesse, 242
STUTZ, ---, 75
Lorentz, 12
Magdalena, 12
Suhsannah, 12
STUTZER, David, 10
Georg, 10
Hermann, 10
Judith, 10
Wilhelm, 10
STUVER, Catharina, 121
SUCK, Alverta C., 221

Henry, 221
Henry D., 221
Ida Bell, 221
SUDHAUSE, Theressa K., 234
SUDIK, Lewis H., 241
SUHRMANN, Anna Maria, 27
Leonhard, 27
SUIS, Maria Anna, 119
Richard, 119
SULLIVAN, Daniel, 52
SULTZER, Elenora, 180, 185
Elora, 176
Henry C., 299
John Frederick, 180
John Sebastian, 176
Mary Frances, 180
Thomas D., 176, 180, 185
Thomas Dukart, 156
William H., 185
SUMWALD, Alexander, 151
SUMWALT, Alexander, 195
Catharine, 195
Georg Alexander, 195
SUSNAB, Adam, 90, 108
Catharina, 90, 108
Elisabeth, 108
Heinrich, 90
SUSRAB, Adam, 83, 90, 108, 111, 122
Agnese, 111
Catharina, 83, 90, 108
Elisabeth, 108
Heinrich, 90
Johan Adam Henrich, 83
Maria Catharina, 111
Mariana, 122
SUSSNOP, Adam, 129
Cath., 129

Maria, 129
SUTER, Charles, 178, 179, 184, 188, 189, 190, 218, 296
Edward Payson, 178
Elisabeth, 42, 45
Henrietta, 178, 179, 184, 188, 189, 190, 218, 296
Jacob, 126
John H., 170
Jus. H., 221
Lloyd, 190
Maria, 126
Mary D., 221
Mary Jane, 189
Sarah Ann, 179
Wilhelm, 126
William, 218, 296
William McClellan, 221
SUTHERLAND, Ann Eliza, 164
SUTTEN, Samuel, 171
SUTTER, George, 175
Lucinda, 175
Mary Frances, 175
SUTTON, Ann, 147
William E., 239
SUTTS, Kate, 169
SWAGER, Susanna, 152
SWARZ, John, 52
SWAYER, Susanna, 152
SWEARS, Catherina, 140
SWEAVER, Lillie J., 235
SWEITZ, Julia, 203
SWOP, Mary, 51
SWORMSTEAD, Luther K., 148

-T-
TABLER, Helen B., 239
TAGART, Elizabeth, 188, 220
Elizabeth, 296

Michael, 220
William, 188, 220, 296
TAGGERT, William, 307
TAMKIN, Elisabeth, 5, 75
TANEYHILL, Samuel, 164
TANG, Sarah, 82
TANY, Elisabeth, 42
Sarah, 47, 56
TARMAN, L., 298
Laura, 298
Z., 298
TARNER, Rebecca, 145
TARNEX, Rebecca, 145
TARR, Albert H., 271
Alfred Hall, 175
Annie, 252
Edwin, 189, 197, 202
Edwin H., 267
Edwin S., 175, 177, 252, 269
Edwin Sturges, 175
Emily Augusta Wharton, 202
Ida Estella Diffenderffer, 177
Juliett Dusslisiss, 189
Mary Francis, 197
Richard Leving, 197
Richard Rose, 252
Susanna, 175, 177
Susanna R. B., 189, 202, 274
Susannah, 197
Theodore, 270
TARTELL, Mary, 169
TASEELL, David, 244
TAUSCH, Heinrich, 293
TAYLEN, Angie B., 228
TAYLER, Eizabeth E., 156
Joseph, 172

Index   423

TAYLOR, Annie Celinda, 261
Cathrina, 52
Eliza Jane, 166
Elizabeth, 166
Howard Rossiter, 262
Ida, 234
James, 171
James W., 240
James William, 260, 261, 262
John Russell McCleary, 260
Joseph Albert, 262
Margaret J., 260, 261, 262
Mary A., 273
Pauline Rosalie, 262
S. Ella, 239
Thaddeus S., 235
W. Burroughs, 237
William H. H., 229
TEBLEMANN, John George, 150
TEGELER, Lena, 153
TEGLMEYER, August, 126
TEHELMANN, Cath. Elisabeth, 196
Eliza, 196
John G., 196
TENNISON, Robert, 159
TENRINSON, Robert, 159
TERRELTON, Elisabeth, 43
Jeremias, 43
Katharina, 43
TERRETINER, Jacob, 280
Katharina, 280
TERRY, Hester E., 151
THAETER, Philip, 149

THAMERD, Rosetta B., 172
THANDA, Barbara, 186
John, 186
Mary, 186
THATCHER, Amelia, 254
Joseph M., 234, 254
Joseph Mitchell, 254
Linden Aurelius, 254
Mary Elizabeth, 254
THATER, Elizabeth, 186, 189, 192
Henrietta, 186
Mary Elizabeth, 192
Philip, 189, 192
Philipp, 186
THEDDIER, Abraham, 62
THEISS, Dora Elenora, 257
Jacob, 15
Johannes, 15
Lambert Henry, 257
Magdalena, 15
Mary C., 257
Mrs., 255
THEPERT, Nancy, 87
THIELS, Elisabeth, 139
THIESS, Anna Catherine Lambert, 253
Charles Henry, 262
Dora M., 271
Ferdinand George, 260
Frederick Charles, 246
Henry, 253
Lambert H., 234
Lambert Henry, 260, 262
Mary C., 253, 260, 262
THOM, Richard N., 244
THOMAE, Anna Catharina, 294
Georg Friedrich, 41
Helfrich, 41, 47

Rosina Henrietta Dorothea, 41
THOMAS, Alverda V., 237
Ann Maria, 158
Ann Rebecca, 182
Betzie Louisa, 254
Blanche H., 240
Carrie Elizabeth, 242
Carrie L., 250, 251
Cath., 168
Christian K., 156
Cora, 217
Edmund, 147
Elizabeth, 182
Florence Rebecca, 261
Georg, 146
Harry Cromwell, 261
Harry Leroy, 261
James, 214
James L., 155
Josephine L., 190
Katharina, 45
Lavenia Valentine, 190
Marg., 214
Margaret, 190
Margell, 161
Martin, 148
Mary, 147, 217
Mary M., 161
Nelson C., 250, 251
Nelson Clark, 277
Oliver Morris, 250, 269
Philip F., 163
Philip J., 163, 190
Robert Johnston, 251
Rudolph C., 244
Samuel L., 169
Viola A., 237
William, 158, 214, 217
William D., 182
THOMASON, Roberts, 38

Index

THOMPSON, Adaline, 278
　Albert William, 249
　Charles Gardner, 258, 274
　Edwin E., 231, 249, 251
　Edwin Eugene Alexander, 251
　Grace N., 238
　Isaac Henry, 177
　John, 161
　John H., 161, 177
　John L., 259
　Joseph L., 258
　Julia V., 258, 259
　Martha, 168
　Mary Ann, 177
　Mary S., 249, 251
　Norma Virginia, 259
　Rachel Ann, 165
　Richard B., 157
THOMSON, Agnes, 54
　Clementina, 148
　Elisabeth, 12, 106, 288
　Hatti, 106
　James, 86, 92, 106, 288
　Margaretha, 92
　Miss, 192
　Mr., 113
　Nelson Adam, 106
　Salome, 86
　Sofia, 86
　Sophia, 92, 106
　Susanna, 113
　Tobias, 106
　Wilhelm, 282
THORNE, William H. L., 234
THORNTON, Christiana Griffith, 222
　Elizabeth, 222
　Patrick, 222
THURALL, Mark, 146
THURSTON, James R., 241
TICL, Anna Elisabeth, 40
　Jacob, 40
TILGE, Heinrich, 144
TILGHMAN, Weathy E., 160
　William J., 163
TINGER, Barbara, 282
TINKIN, Cath., 184
　Henry, 184
　Margaret, 184
TIPTON, Annie B., 257
　J. Emory, 311
　John E., 229
　Leah Lucille, 257
　Lewis V., 257
TOBB, Ann Magdlina, 193
TOBEL, Anna Charlotta, 44
　Elisabeth, 89
　Helena, 44, 80, 89
　Wilhelm, 44, 89
TODD, Berhardina, 258
　Carrie M., 258
　John, 258
　Mary, 145
TOLLBERG, Frederick, 276
TOMIN, Elisabeth, 75
TOMLINSON, Mary Isabel, 252
TOMPANKS, Elisabeth, 52
TOMSON, Anna Barbara, 45
　James, 45
　Margaretha, 282
　Mr., 282
　Sophia, 45
TOPKEN, Carolina, 92
　Dethart, 92
　Gerhart, 139
TOWBLE, Elizabeth, 149
TOWSANS, Catharina, 140
TRACY, A. Lester, 243
　George W., 231
TRAIL, Daisy A. B. M., 306
　H., 209
　M. L., 306
　Maria, 209
　Mary Ernesta, 209
　R. H., 306
TRAIN, Ewis, 49
TRAUB, George Philipp, 279
TRAVOLET, Sarah, 52
TRAXEL, Abr., 200
　David Mohler, 200
　Sarah, 200
TREGERMAN, Georg Ludwig, 205
　Hanna, 205
TREIL, Anna Maria, 4
　Johannes, 4
TREIS, Mary, 203
TRENKEN, Ann Rebecca, 193
　Georg, 193
　Margarete Ann, 193
　Mary Ann, 193
TRENTON, Rosa, 168
TREPPERT, Andreas, 94, 286
　Catharina, 94
　Joseph, 94
TRICE, Fredrick, 146
TRIEBURGER, John, 111
　Margaretha, 111
　Margarethe, 111
TRIPPEL, Christoph, 43

Index

TROHLENIEN, Elisabeth, 28
TROHLENIER, George, 76
TROKLENIEN, Elisabeth, 28
TROKNIER, Susanna, 64
TROLDENIER, Elisabeth, 56, 76
George, 174
TROLI, Bertha E., 254
Frederick N., 254
Walter Melchoir, 254
TROLL, Arthur Ockert, 252
Bertha E., 245, 248, 252, 254
Edna Phronia Emma, 248
Fred. N., 245, 248, 252
Frederick Joseph, 245
Frederick N., 230, 254
Walter Melchior, 254
TROMBAUER, Peter, 7
TROSTEL, Catherine J., 237
TROTZ, Adrian Christian, 91
Helena Johanna, 91
Maria, 91
TROXEL, Amanda, 169
TRUESMAN, Arianna, 147
TRUGS, Johanna Katharina, 42
TRUMBO, David, 108
Henrietta, 108
Maria, 3
Peter, 3
TRUSCOTT, George, 269
TSCHINKERS, Mariana, 97
TSCHUDI, ---, 78
Anna, 25, 53
Anna Maria, 53

Barbara, 25
Elisabet, 53
Margaretha, 57
Martin, 25, 53
Weinbert, 2, 53
TSCHUDJ, Elisabeth, 3
Winbert, 3
TSCHUDY, ---, 78
Anna, 142
Barbara, 5, 29, 36, 70
David, 28
Elisabet, 53, 58
Emanuel Martin, 59
Jacob, 5
Margaretha, 81
Martin, 28, 36, 58, 70, 145
Mr., 81
Nicholas, 2
Nicolaus, 5, 28, 29, 51
Weinbert, 60
TSCHUNDY, Jacob, 63
Nicolaus, 63
TULBY, Margaretta, 167
TULLY, Sarah J., 235
TURF, Cath., 95
Johannes Georg, 95
TURLEY, Evelyn Lee, 234
TURNER, Barbara Ann, 149
Josua M., 201
TURNT, Agnus May, 246
Bertha, 252
Celma Matilda, 246
Dora K., 251
Ferdinand, 246
Ferdinand C., 235
Frank Antonie, 252
Frederick, 233, 251
Ida Johanna, 246
Louisa, 252
Louisa E., 246

Minne Louisa, 246
Richard, 234
Selma, 235
William, 251, 252, 272, 276
William J., 246
TUTTLE, Washington Irving, 243
TWEEDELL, Mary A., 161
TYCON, H., 175
Laura Virginia, 175
M. J., 175
TYLER, Levin, 230, 271
TYRELL, Libbie, 241

-U-

UDI, Catharina, 83
UHL, Andreas, 137, 141
Andrew, 305
Catharina, 137
Emma G., 303
F., 175
F. A., 211, 304, 305
Frances Edward, 304
Francis Edward, 175
J. A., 301
Martha, 211, 301
Mrs., 298
P., 304
P. R., 175
V. R., 211
UHLER, Catharina, 127
Erasimus, 127
Erasmus, 268
Marya Elisabeth, 127
UHLHORN, Philip C., 160
UHRBACH, Lillie, 256
ULRICH, Anna Margaretha, 68
Carrie A., 254
Ferdinand A., 254

Index

Joh Gottf., 68
Mary Catherine, 254
Susanna, 51
UNDERWOOD, Joseph Wilbur, 268
UNDEUTSCH, Johan, 100
Metta, 100
Nicolaus, 100
UNGER, Wilhelmina, 278
UNGLAUB, Benjamin Franklin, 249
Clarence Albert, 249
George, 249
Mary J., 249
URBACH, Annie E., 235
Emaline, 266
Fred William, 231
Frederick William, 277
Lillie Estella, 252
UTER, Katharina, 40
UYSSNEL, Elisabeth, 139

-V-
VAETH, Margaret K., 236
VALENTINE, Rosina, 56
VALIANT, James H., 164
VALLENTIN, Maria, 54
VAN DER HEIDE, Maria Elisabeth, 92
VAN HORN, Ann Elizabeth, 130
Catharine, 130
Fielding, 130
VAN NEUKIRCH, Hart, 124
Maria, 124
William, 124
VAN SANT, James, 191
Joshua, 191
Mary Ann, 191
VANCE, James H., 167
John, 159

Nancy, 310
VANDANIKER, David, 307
Mary, 307
William, 307
VANDERWECKEN, Emma Louesa, 218
Henrietta, 218
Henry, 218
Sarah, 218
VANDEVECKER, Mr., 296
VANE, John W., 242
VANHORN, Cath., 201
Catharina Louise, 201
Fielding, 149, 201
VANMEETER, Agnes Eutsey, 243
VANSANT, Charles M. Cullough, 305
Charles McCullough, 208
Ellen, 208, 211, 221, 222, 223, 224, 226, 227, 247, 305, 309
George Collins, 208
J., 221
Jos., 223
Joseph, 208, 211, 221, 222, 223, 224, 226, 227, 247, 305, 309
Joshua, 268
Kate Beckett, 222, 309
Lillie D., 312
Margaret Virginia, 221, 305
Mary, 223
Mary Ann, 265
Robert Edward, 226
Robert Edward Lee, 226
William Prescott, 211, 302
Willie D., 265
Willie Diffenderfer, 247
VANTZ, Jacob, 113

VANWINCKLE, Catharine, 201
Samuel, 201
William, 201
VAUGHAN, Daniel Diffenderfer, 299
David Diffenderfer, 299
VAUGHN, Daniel D., 168
John A., 302
VAUTIER, Anita D., 238
VEDITZ, Berhardina, 237
Henry, 271
John H., 236
VEIT, Andreas, 13
Appolona, 13
Elisabeth, 13
VERDEROK, Peter, 54
VEWEEN, John, 19
Mary, 19
Rachel, 19
VICTOR, David, 151
VIETSCH, Meta E., 231
VINYARD, Sarah A., 233
VIZE, Rachel, 153
VOCKE, Ludoph Bosley, 247
Mary A., 277
Mary E., 247
Ralph E., 230
Rudolph Bosley, 247
Rudolph E., 247
VODITZ, Charles Henry, 259
Mary Eleanor, 259
VOGEL, Joh. Frey, 199
John, 199
Katie M., 234
Philippina, 199
VOGELMAN, Catharina, 110
Georg, 110, 287
Johannes, 110

VOIGD, David Rittenhaus, 114
  Georg Washington, 113
  Mr., 113
VOLCK, Anna Margaretha, 105
  Anna Maria, 105, 294
  Carl, 105, 124, 294
  Johan, 124
  Simon Carl, 48
VOLEMAN, Albert F., 248
  Augusta B., 248
  Harry Rossiter, 248
VOLKMAN, Elizabeth, 250
  Harry Rossiter, 268
  Lewis, 250
  William, 250
VOLKMANN, Augusta P., 269
  Dora, 237
  Elizabeth, 249
  Katie E., 235
  Lewis, 269
  Philip, 249, 268
  William, 239, 249
  William Fred., 278
VON BREMEN, Anna Gertraud, 33, 68
  Daniel, 33, 56, 68
  Maria Sabina Elis., 33
VON CARNUP, Caspar Wilhelm, 26
  H., 26
VON DURNBURY, Franciscus, 141
VON HEMESCHEN, Katharina, 280
VON HEMESSEN, Andreas Jacob, 44
  Eduard, 44, 77
  Katharina, 44

VON HOLLAND, Mrs., 301
VON HOLLEN, Amalia, 131
  Christoph, 115
  Christopher, 131
  Henrietta, 115
VON HOXAR, Henry, 168
VON KAP, Bernhard John, 131
  Henriette, 131
  Hetty, 131
  John Frederick Christophe, 131
VON KAPF, Christoph, 82
  Emilie, 119
  H., 91, 105, 119
  Heinrich Christoph, 82
  Henrietta Esther, 82, 91
  Hetti Henrietta, 105
  Johan Bernhard, 105
  Johanna Maria, 91
  Miss, 91
  Mr., 82
VON KAPFF, Esther H., 151
  Mary Jane, 152
VON KAPP, Eliza Margaret, 148
VON NEWKERCK, Catharina, 281
  Heinrich, 281
  Johann, 281
VON WALDNER, Charlotte, 268
  Francis A., 271
  Maggie B., 232
VONDERSCHLOT, Cornelia, 202
VROOM, George, 241

-W-
WACK, Daisey Annie Bell Mette, 221
  M. L., 221
  R. H., 221
WACKE, Elisabeth, 94
  Wilhelm, 94
WACKRING, Anna, 280, 281
WADDEL, Georg, 48
  Johan Robert, 133
  Johann Jacob, 49
  Margaretha, 49, 133
  Mr., 133
WADDLE, Margaretha, 97
  Mr., 97
WADLINGTON, Ellen Francis, 191
  Sophia, 191
  W., 191
WADNER, Fredirika, 272
WAESCHE, Friederich, 113
  H., 81
  K., 81
  Metta Henrietta, 81
  Wilhelmina Elisabeth, 113
WAGENER, Anna Maria, 54
WAGER, Anna Maria, 6
  Hanna, 6
  Phillip, 6
WAGES, Luck, 54
WAGNER, Alice Margret, 263
  Augusta, 263
  Edward W., 263
  Frank Adams, 263, 278
  Juliana, 24
  Katharina, 46, 79
  Martha A., 166

Susanne, 168
WAHL, Elisabeth, 48
WAITE, Lonesa, 163
WAKER, Anna, 43
WALDNER, Annie J., 256, 257, 258, 261
  Charles H., 237, 256, 257, 258, 261
  Charles Henry, 257
  Charlotte Sophia, 227
  Christina, 236
  Francis Anton, 227
  George, 238, 261, 262
  George F. T., 229
  George John, 262
  Henry William Lewis, 229
  Lizzie Mary, 256
  Maggie S., 243
  Martha, 262
  Philip Claude, 258
WALDREN, John W., 232
WALDVOGEL, Chester, 264
  Esther Lenor, 263
  Harry George, 263
  Henry C., 264
  Henry Charles, 263
  Hugo Wesley, 263
  Louisa, 263, 264
  Marion Louisa, 263
  Raymond Frederick, 263
WALKER, Anna, 280
  Clara May, 254
  Elizabeth, 203
  Hazel Adelaide, 254
  Llewllyn W., 254
  Nicolaus Riyous, 203
  William, 203
WALKLING, Cath. Elizabeth, 260
  Charles A., 240
  Charles Calvin, 260

Charles Henry, 260
WALL, William, 145
WALLANCE, Elizabeth, 185
  Isabella, 185
  William, 185
WALLUER, George, 174
WALS, Beniamin Gottlieb, 120
  Christiophia Rosina, 120
WALSCH, Metta, 147
WALTEMEYER, Martha K., 235
WALTER, Heinrich, 119
  John A. W., 155
  Silas, 243
WALTERS, Henry W., 243
  Lewis Plitt, 262
  Louisa, 262
  Margaret Elizabeth, 262
WALTON, Electa, 149
WALZ, George W., 261
  Grace Catherine, 261
  Jennie Cath., 261
WAMPLER, Johanna, 82
  Leonhard, 130
  Ludwig, 82
  Maria, 130
  Sybilla, 130
WAMSSLER, Leonhard, 130
  Maria, 130
  Sybilla, 130
WAND, Joseph, 118
WANTZ, Charles B., 235, 256
  Emma V., 256
  Victoria Elenora, 256
WARD, Anna Maria, 106, 121
  Catharina, 106
  Edith B., 243

Johannes, 121
John S., 155
Rosa A., 232
Thomas, 106, 121
WARDEL, Margaretha, 90
WARE, William, 228
WAREN, Maria, 23
  Thomas, 23
  Wilhelm, 23
WARFIELD, Carrie S., 253
  Mary Ann, 253
  Philemon D., 253
  Philip D., 233
WARKE, Elisabeth, 94
  Wilhelm, 94
WARKING, Herman, 283
WARMBOLD, Teresa, 239
WARNECKE, Johan Eberhard, 285
  Michael, 285
  Michel, 138
WARNER, Elisabeth, 42
  Ellen, 178, 180
  Elmer, 275
  Emma J., 259
  Fanny, 117
  Friederich, 56, 82, 117, 293
  Friedich, 286
  Friedrich, 42
  Joseph, 178, 180
  Josephine Mason, 178
  Maria, 139
  Mary Jane, 180
  Mr., 284
  Sarah, 82, 286
  Thaddeus, 158
  William Arthur, 259
  William F., 259

Index

WARNSMAN, Catherine, 261
  Elizabeth, 261
  William F. H., 241, 261
WARREN, Anna Maria, 12
  Collen K., 160
  Georg, 17
  Johannes, 12, 75
  Maria, 17
  Mary A., 167
  Thomas, 12, 17, 51
WARWING, Mary E., 167
WASCHE, Friederich, 108
  Margaratha, 288
  Margaretha, 108
  Mr., 288
WASHINGTON, Jane, 152
WASMUS, Charles Fr., 146
WATEL, Alexander, 39, 77, 279
  Anna Margaretha, 39, 279
  Georg, 39, 279
  Johann Georg, 43
  Margaretha, 43
WATERS, Mary B., 159
WATKINS, Catharine Amelia, 181
  James H., 181
  Kate, 222
  Rachel F., 181
WATLINGTON, Ellen, 297
  Mary A., 170
  Mary Ann, 195
  Sophia, 195
  William, 195
WATSON, Augusta S., 232
  Charles, 236

John, 231
WATTERS, Samuel Field, 261
  William, 261
WATTINGTON, William, 150
WATTS, Caroline, 160
  Elizabeth H., 164
  Harriet, 100
  Heinrich, 100
  John Henry, 181
  Laura Jane, 181
  Margaretha, 100
  Mary F., 167
  Reuben, 181
  Sophia W., 181
WAUGH, Beverly R., 233
WAUSSMAN, ---, 75
WAUSSMANN, Anna Maria, 10
  Salome, 10
  Samuel, 10
WAYSON, Lizzie E., 230
WEARUM, James, 287
WEAVER, Carl, 201
  Catharine, 196
  Cathrine, 200
  Clarence Funk, 255
  Daniel A., 240
  Elizabeth, 149, 198
  Ellen, 204
  Emma C., 255
  Frances Jane, 198
  Georg, 57, 201
  George, 196, 200, 205
  Heinrich, 142
  Henry, 152
  Jacob, 198
  John, 147, 148, 204, 205
  John Charles, 204
  John L., 255
  Marg., 201

Margaret, 196, 205
  Margret, 200
  Mary Ann, 204
  Priscilla, 148
  Sarah, 145
WEB, Elisabeth, 287
  Mr., 287
WEBB, George, 191
  Margaret, 191
  William Henry, 191
WEBBER, Thomas, 169
WEBER, Anna, 48, 101, 105
  Anna Elisabeth, 45
  Anna M., 33
  Anna Margaretha, 39
  Anna Maria, 135
  Bernhard, 40
  Charlotta, 5
  Charlotte, 16
  Christian H., 276
  Daniel, 5, 16
  David, 61, 83
  Elisabeth, 5, 55
  Eva Margaretha, 45, 99, 107
  Frances, 247
  Georg, 82, 99, 107, 115, 135
  George, 247
  Heinrich, 105
  Henry Fred William, 262
  Jacob, 290
  James S. Allison, 247
  Johan Heinrich, 107
  Johan Jacob, 115
  Johan Wilhelm, 83
  Johann, 48
  Johann Georg, 45
  Johann Wilhelm, 48
  Johanna, 87, 94, 139
  Johannes, 16, 62

Index

Julia Viola, 262
Ludwig, 5
Marg., 38
Margaretha, 43, 49, 82, 115
Maria Elisabeth, 99
Michael, 126
Nancy, 83
Oliva Viola, 262
Wilhelm, 43, 57, 82, 101, 105
Wilhelmina, 103, 140
WEBER(IN), Barbara, 10
WEBERIN, Anna Elisabeth, 80, 90
WEBSTER, Eliza, 225
Henry Clay, 225
Ino. T., 225
Margaret, 259
Margaret Keys, 259
Mary E., 232
William Brooks, 259
Willie Brooks, 225
WECH, Cornelia, 138
Wilhelmina, 42
WECHSLER, Anna, 43
WECHZ, Cornelia, 138
WECK, Anna, 138
Carolina, 42
Caroline, 48
Johanna Catharina, 83
Wilhelm, 48
Wilhelmina, 46, 280
WEDMAN, Elisabetha, 6
Lorentz, 6
Phillip David, 6
Susanna Elisabetha, 6
WEEDEN, Amelia C., 242
Mary, 195
Mary Ellen, 195
Thomas, 150, 195

WEEKS, Harry Edwad, 226
Lydia A., 226
Thomas, 226
WEG(IN), Maria, 6
WEGAU, Conrad, 258
Hattie Elizabeth, 258
James Henry, 258
WEGENER, Cathrina, 54
WEHR, Caleb, 128
Elisabeth, 128, 205
John, 128, 205
Mathew, 205
WEHRMAN, Ella Lile, 250
John G., 231, 248, 250
Kate, 248, 250
Mary Elizabeth, 248
Samuel Charles, 268
WEIB, Elisabet, 53
WEIBEL, Anna, 9
Catharina, 9
Daniel, 9, 10
Maria Elis., 40, 45
WEICKERT, Catharina, 286
WEIDEMAYER, Frederick, 145
Mrs., 194
WEIDEMEIER, Georg, 144
WEIDENER, Christina Sophia, 17
Georg, 15
Henrich, 17
Maria W., 17
WEIDNER, Carl Herm., 20
Carl Hermann, 20
Johanna Maria, 44
Maria, 20
WEIGAND, Anna Catharina, 136

Conjunda, 9
Mariana, 136
Peter, 9, 114, 136
WEIHMANN, Anna Barbara, 29
Henrich, 29
WEIKMANN, Jacob, 55
WEIR, Eliza Ann, 203
Elizabeth, 197, 202, 203
Elizabeth Ann, 197
John, 197, 202, 203
Matthew, 202
WEIRS, Bertha F., 242
WEISAMBEL, Anna Catharina, 83
WEISBACH, Anna Catharina, 35
Anna Maria, 135
Benjamin, 205
Catharina, 287
Ester, 205
Esther, 135
Johann George, 35
Johannes, 35
Maria Catharina, 23
Maria Katharina, 57
Martin, 23, 35, 135, 205, 285
WEISER, Barbara Rowena, 260
Emily Catherine, 260
Grace Marie, 260
Oliver, 260
WEISHAMPEL, Christian, 157
WEISHEIT, Caroline Augusta, 260
Dixon Guy, 256
Frederick A., 235, 255, 256, 259, 260
Henrietta Emma, 255
Jennie, 255, 256, 259, 260
Joseph Elmer, 259

Minnie, 277
WEISINGER, Caroline, 173
　Henry, 303
WEISKITTEL, Anton Karl, 259
　Daisy M., 259, 261
　Harry C., 259, 261
　Henry Charles, 261
WEISKITTLE, Daisy M., 258
　Harry C., 238, 258
　Mildred Marie, 258
WEISS, Barbara, 4
　Johannes, 4
　Sara, 4
WEISSBACH, Cathrina, 21
　Joh. Jacob, 17
　Maria Barbara, 21
　Maria Cath., 17
　Maria Cathrina, 14
　Martin, 14, 17, 21
WEISSNER, Emily, 222
　Gottfried, 222
　Sophia, 222
WEITZEL, Emma, 266
WEKSON, Mr., 142
WELCH, Annie E., 240
　B. Frank, 230
　Caroline Elizabeth, 235
　Cath., 305
　Charles D., 237
　George, 305
　Lillie J., 248
　Lydia Jane, 305
　Mrs., 223, 227, 247
　Warren, 170
WELLENER, Beulah May, 254
　Earle Blackburn, 250
　Mary E., 250, 254

William C., 232, 250, 254
WELLER, Eve, 54
　George P., 165
　Johan, 92
　Maria, 92
　Nancy, 92
WELLS, Ann., 52
　Bertha Carnes, 259
　Harry C., 243
　Joseph H., 239, 259
　Katie M., 259
　Mary M., 267
　Robert, 231
　William A., 239
WELM, ---, 75
　Catharina, 9
　Conrad, 9
　Elisabeth, 9
　Magdalena, 9
　Peter, 9
WELSCH, Anna Catharina, 138
　Barbara, 18
　Jacob, 7
WELSH, Caroline Elizabeth, 210
　Edward Jay, 210
　Henrich, 75
　Mary A., 210
　Warren, 210
WELSHOFER, Adline, 135
　Elisabeth, 135
　Heinrich, 141
　Henrich, 135, 136
　Maria, 135, 136
　Wilhelm Heinrich, 293
　Wilhelm Henrich, 136
WELSHOFFER, Charles, 311
　Charles Augustus, 247
　Elizabeth, 269

Henry, 300
　Mary, 310
WELSHOFIFER, Charles, 265
WENDEL, Emma Amelia, 246
　Henry, 245
　Henry L., 230, 246
　Minnie Clara, 245
　Rosa B., 245, 246
WENDLER, Alice V., 250
　Ann Louisa Canby, 250
　Harry B., 232, 250
WENGELING, Carolina, 94
　Christina, 94
　Michael, 94
WENTWORTH, Thomas J., 150
WENTZEL, Julia, 239
　Ludwig Albert, 274
　Mary L., 237, 274
WERING, Carl, 105
WERIWAG, Elma, 217
　Emma, 217
　Righter Levering, 217
WERLE, Catharina, 34
　Johannes, 34
WERNER, Albert, 253
　Anna Maria, 92
　Charles, 253
　Dorethee, 253
　Dorethee W., 253
　Dorethee W. L., 256
　Dorothea W., 253
　Elizabeth, 253
　Frederick August, 253, 256
　Friederich, 92, 104
　Friedrich, 47
　Guss, 237
　Katharina, 47

Martha Elisabeth, 279
Mary Wilhemina, 253
Sally, 92
Sara, 104
Sarah, 47
WERNETH, Harry Joseph, 278
WERNSING, Florence B., 238
WERTENBERGER, Jacob, 75
WESSELMAN, Minnie, 239
WEST, Anna Margaretha, 49
Dorothea, 70
Elisabeth, 49, 88, 92, 284
Elizabeth, 297
Georg Wilhelm, 92
Johan, 88, 92
Johann, 49
Johannes, 121
John, 109, 121
Maria Magdalena, 88
Mr., 284
Rebecca t., 154
Robert L., 242
Sarah, 157
Theresa E., 242
WESTERFELD, David Henry, 270
Fred D., 252
Frederick D., 250
John Henry Schultze, 252
Mary Ann, 250, 252
Mary Ann Schultz, 250
WESTERVELT, Mary, 213
Rich. L., 213
Richard Lawrence, 213
WESTON, Cathrina Elisabeth, 55

WESTPHAL, Emma Augusta, 261
Mamie, 261
Walter Lawrence, 261
WESTZ, Johann, 57
WETTERSTEIN, Elisabeth, 87
Jacob, 87
Sarah, 87
WEYAND, Anna Maria, 31
Johann George, 31
Peter, 31
WEYGART, Elisabeth, 96
Maria, 96
Peter, 96
WEYRAUCH, Albert Summers, 250
Anna Margaret, 248
Georgie Rosina, 249
Lizzie C., 246, 248, 249, 250
William C., 231, 246, 248, 249, 250
William George, 246
WEYRAUGH, Georgia Rosina, 269
WEYSSMANN, Maria, 6
Samuel, 6
WHEELER, Augustus Christoph, 207
Columbus, 221
Florence Heiner, 221
George Barrneh, 207
Helen Beata, 223
J. C., 207, 223
Joseph C., 170
S. B., 207
Sophia, 221
Sophia B., 207, 223
WHEN, Rahel, 55
WHERELEY, Ethel Staley, 264

Jane Catherine, 264
S. Clinton, 264
WHERLEY, Alpha, 264
Alpha E., 263
Clarence Vernon, 263
Fannie, 263, 264
Samuel Clinton, 244
WHI, Hanna, 10
WHISEL, Maria Anna, 143
WHITE, Allan, 257
Ann, 201
Bessie, 225
Bessie W., 239
David H., 147, 201
Elizabeth, 201
Ellen, 224, 243
Francis, 229
Frank Allan, 257
Franklin, 270
James Allen, 247
Maria Ann, 166
Martha M., 257
Mary Ann, 159
Mary E., 239
Matthew, 210, 224, 225, 247
Mrs., 296
Rachel E., 159
Samuel P., 257
Sarah, 224, 261
Sarah J., 225, 247
Sarah Jane, 210, 233
Theodor W., 166
Thomas, 238
WHITEHEAD, Walter F., 238
WHITELEGG, Ethel Lyle, 260
Florence Marie, 260
Mary Elizabeth, 260
Thomas, 237, 260

Index

WHITING, Florence Eugenia, 238
WHITLOCK, Genevieve, 244
WHITMORE, Jacob, 151
WHITNEY, Francis W., 230
   Miss, 155
   Richard, 155
WHITSON, Anna Emily, 247
   Emily T., 247
   Thomas C., 247
WHITTEMORE, Florence R., 260
   Lawrence, 260
   Lawrence F., 238, 260
   Lawrence Henry, 260
WICHELHAUSEN, Francis, 200
   Harriot, 200
   Jacob, 200
WIEDEFELD, Emma, 237
   James F., 240
WIEDFELD, Georgianna M., 261
   James F., 261
   William Henry, 261
WIEN, Georg, 138, 143
   Johannes, 61
WIER, Mary E., 167
WIESNER, Charles L., 304, 3304
   Elizabeth, 304
   Gottfried, 304
WIGART, Andrew, 157
WILBY, Emaline J., 168
WILCKE, Johanna, 136
WILCOX, Caroline, 224
   John, 224
   Rebecca, 224
WILD, Appolinia, 91

Elisabeth, 115
George H., 244
Jacob, 91, 109
Margaretha, 91
Rebecca, 97
Susanna Mathilda, 109
WILDER, Levi, 186
WILDERMAN, Jacob, 54
   Margaretha, 54
WILHELM, Adeline, 125
   Anna Maria, 107
   Catherine, 146
   Eleonora, 125
   Esther Carter, 261
   Georg Alexander, 125
   Georg Washington, 114
   Johan, 107
   John, 114, 125
   John H., 241, 261
   Laura Rice, 261
   Mary, 241
   Mr., 297
   Peter, 125
WILILAMS, Emely Jane, 172
WILKE, Heinrich Christoph, 98
WILKENING, Annie A., 232
WILKENNING, Annie, 245, 247
   Catherine Loretta, 247
   Christian G., 270
   Christian John Miller, 245
   John, 247
   John H., 245
WILKERSON, James, 240
WILKIN, Johanna, 81
WILKINS, Anna, 170
WILKS, Hanna, 149
WILLER, Justus, 140

WILLIAM, Jane, 155
WILLIAMS, Anna Augusta, 186
   Antoinetta H., 172
   Capt., 282
   Charles Courtney, 177
   Charles Henry, 213
   Eduard, 192
   Elizabeth, 192
   Emily, 299
   Ino. V., 213
   Isabella, 51
   James Tyson, 278
   John, 186
   Martha L., 238
   Mary, 213
   Mr., 177
   Mrs., 302
   Reese, 145
   Sophia, 186
   Susanna, 177
WILLIART, Elisabeth, 99
WILLIS, Elizabeth N., 231
   William L., 168
WILLMANS, Henrich, 19
WILLS, Arthur Edmund, 252
   George W., 233, 252
   Mary Margaret, 203
   Sarah Ann, 252
WILMS, Anna Elisabeth, 45, 79
   Anna Mathilda, 79
   Carl Friedrich, 45
   Henrich Arnold, 45, 79
   Mr., 289
WILMSEN, Anna Elisabeth, 90, 102
   Elisabeth, 90, 284
   Heinrich Arnold, 90, 102, 284
   Heinrich Wilhelm, 102

WILSON, Agustus
  Schnebly, 184
 Anna Martha, 310
 Charles, 169
 Charles A., 212, 225
 Charles Alfred, 212
 Edward John, 180
 Elvira, 180
 G. B., 184
 George, 164
 George N., 238
 Greenbury, 307
 Harry, 233
 Henrich, 85
 Isabella, 225
 James S., 180
 John T., 242
 Joseph, 151
 L., 184
 Laura Mary Scheer, 275
 Louesa, 180
 Louisa, 267
 Lydia, 151
 Marie, 38
 Mary Ann, 212, 225
 Mary Jane, 166
 Sarah, 55
 Theodore Jarrett, 180
 V. C., 256
 William H., 166
WILT, Jacob, 138
WILY, Mary, 51
WINAND, Charles, 246
 Charles Moore, 246
 Elizabeth, 246
WINCHELHAUSEN,
  Henriette, 205
 Jacob, 205
 Susan Placke Henriette, 205
WINCKERT, Maria, 91

WINCKLE, Carolina
  Mathilda, 193
 George, 193
 Maria, 193
WINDOWS, Jane R. B., 159
WINGFIELD, Julius, 235
WINGMORE, Thomas, 309
WINGROVE, A. E., 227
 Ann Elizabeth, 248
 Annie, 248, 275
 Catherine Gertrude, 247
 Clara B., 246, 248, 249
 Clara Bell, 274
 Clara Florence, 227
 David S., 231, 246, 248, 249
 Edith Blanche, 248, 267
 Elizabeth, 267
 Elmer Reuben, 255
 Emma Agnus, 249
 Emma L., 229
 Eva Virginia Valient, 250
 Helen Rossiter, 248
 James C., 267
 James Clarence, 248
 Margaret Ruth, 246
 Mary, 255
 Mary E., 227, 247, 248, 250, 252, 253
 Mary Elizabeth, 247
 Maud Irene, 252
 Mrs., 255
 Thomas David, 253
 Thomas R., 227, 247, 248, 250, 252, 253, 255
WINKELHAUSEN,
  Eliza Ann, 129
 Henrietta, 129
 Jacob, 129
WINKELMANN, Anna
  Margaret, 271

 Anna S., 260, 261
 Flora Adahl, 261
 Florence M., 261
 Margaret Sybilla, 260
 William H., 260, 261
WINKERT, Elisabeth, 40, 279
WINKLEMANN, Charles H., 259
 Florence Christina, 259
 Margaret Florence, 259
 William H., 239
WINN, John W., 164
WINTERICH, Charles, 201
WIPPERD, David, 152
WIPPERT, David, 152
WIRKINGE, Elisabeth, 84
 Heinrich, 84
 Jacob, 84
WIRTENBERGER, Barbara, 6
 Johannes, 6
 Ludwig, 6, 17
WISE, Eduart, 104
 Elenja Ellen, 216
 Ino., 216
 John J., 164
 Maria, 104
 Mary, 165
 Sarah, 216
 Sarah C., 164
 Sophia, 104
 Susanna, 104
WISEBACH, Johann, 55
WISON, Mr., 142
WISOTZKY, Friederich, 139
WITT, Francis, 222
WITTAKER, Joseph M., 228
WITTE, Annie M., 253, 257, 258

Dora, 258
Frederick C., 253
Frederick Caspar, 258
Frederick Casper, 234, 257
Louisa Caroline Johanna, 253
Margaretta, 257
WITTERFIELD, Margaret, 145
WITTLE, Richard, 51
WOLF, Andreas, 60, 288, 289
Anna Margaretha, 49
Barbara, 12
Catharina, 90
Catherina, 139
Catherine, 302
Cathrina, 12, 14
Diederich, 83
Elisabeth, 49, 57, 91, 109
Elizabeth, 139
Frances A., 161
Georg Daniel, 284
Henrich, 12, 75
Jacob, 109, 294
Joh. Jacob, 11
Johan Heinrich, 117
Johan Jacob, 109
John, 275
Margareth, 12
Maria, 102
Michael, 11, 16, 126
Mr., 284
Philip, 289
Rosina, 14
Salome, 5, 11, 16
Tobias, 14, 51, 292
WOLF(IN), Cathrina, 14
WOLFE, Henry, 153
Thomas Jefferson, 157

WOLFERZ, Johann Abraham, 57
WOLFF, George, 165
Johannes, 5
Michael, 3, 5
Salome, 3, 5
Wilhelm, 3
WOLLMAN, Frederick W., 241
George, 243
WONDERLY, C. P., 219
Elenora Cummings, 176
Elenora P., 176
Elizabeth Virginia, 176
John Virginnus, 176
William S., 155, 176, 219
WONN, Catharine Celia, 224
Laura, 247
Mary, 229
Olevia, 247
Sarah, 224, 277
WONNEBERG, Elisabeth, 56
WOOD, Annie R., 238
James Edward, 241, 262
John C., 241
Marian Gladys, 262
Robert Washigton, 262
Susanna, 155
Wilmer P., 147
WOODALL, Newton Barrett, 242
WOODCOCK, Jesse, 157
WOODDEN, Ann E., 163
WOODEN, Kezia, 165
WOODTRAVER, Christian, 33, 68
Franz, 33, 68
Louise, 33, 68
Maria Louise, 33
WOODWORTH, Susanna, 113

WOODY, May C., 242
WOOL, Friederich, 10
Hanna, 10
Independens, 10
WORDEL, Georg, 83
Johan Jefferson, 83
Margaretha, 83
WORKING, Elisabeth, 90
Fredrick, 200
Getila, 200
Heinrich, 90
Mary Elizabeth, 200
WORLEY, Alexander E., 162
Henry, 145
WORLI, Catharina, 103
Elisabeth, 103
Johan, 103
WORMAN, Margaret, 237
WORMER, Georg, 52
WORSTER, Willis, 231
WORTH, Mary, 147
WORTHINGTON, Helen Elizabeth, 255
Howard H., 235, 255, 259, 262
Howard Schminck, 259
Lester George, 262
Rosa, 255, 259, 262
WOSS, ---, 75
Catharina, 9, 10
Jacob, 9
Johannes, 9, 10
WOSTMANN, ---, 75
Catharina, 9
Elisabeth, 9
Johannes, 9
WRIGHT, Alice Hunter, 271
Camilla M., 238
Frank C., 242
Maria, 109

Index

Thomas F., 156
William J., 243
WUAAD, Katharina, 42
WUCKE, Anna Catharina, 108
Wilhelm, 108
WUD, ---, 78
Eilsabeth, 8
Elisabetha, 6
Jacob, 6, 8
Maria, 6
Ursula, 8
WUELKEN, Fredrick Ernst, 152
WUNDERLICH, Jacob, 193
Mary, 193
William, 193
WUNNEBERG, Adelheit Elisabeth, 42
WUNNENBERG, Adelheid Elisabeth, 48, 49
WURST, Alma A., 251
Alma Augusta, 253, 256
Augusta Henrietta, 253
Elsie Frederica, 251
Florence Estelle, 256
Howard E., 274
Howard Elmer, 253
Martin, 251, 253, 256
WURTENBERGER, Barbara, 9
Jacob, 9
Ludwig, 9
WYALL, Edwin J., 243
WYANT, Anna Maria, 25
Elisabeth, 25, 144
Peter, 25, 57
WYANTS, Maria Clara, 62
WYATT, Emma Jane, 240
WYGANT, Elisabeth, 119
Heinrich, 119

WYLIE, Mary E., 231

-Y-
YAGER, Amelia D. C., 167
YAKEL, Mae Angelia, 243
YANNAWAY, Magdalena, 140
YAUS, Catharina, 115
Jakob, 115
YEAKLE, Alice M., 262
Herbert Elmer, 262
Louisa C., 261
Mary Elizabeth, 301
Samuel W., 242, 262
William H., 272
YEARLY, Nathaniel, 153
YEATMAN, Annie M., 240
YEATS, James, 172
Lucy, 52
YEISLEY, Elizabeth, 208
Emma Augusta, 208
Jacob, 208, 301
YELT, Jacob, 154
YENT, George Francis, 192
YEO, Alexander, 151
YIESLEY, Elizabeth L., 176, 218
George Conrad, 176
Jacob, 176, 218
Mary Elisabeth, 218
YIESLY, Anne Kate, 215
Elizabeth, 215
Jacob, 215
YINGLING, Leon C., 239, 259, 277
Mary E., 259
Sarah Violetta, 259
YOCHEIMER, Adolph, 226

John, 226
Sophia, 226
YOCHHEIM, Adolf, 227
Adolf Michael, 227
Sophia, 227
YOICE, Nancy, 49, 57
YONER, Harriot, 145
YONSON, Alice May, 259
Charles, 238, 252, 259
Emma May, 259
YORK, Israel, 153
YOST, William, 149
YOUNG, Bessie May, 253
Carrie E., 253, 255
Elmer, 261
Frances A., 163
Fredeick Sidney, 223
George, 275
Henry F., 235
Ida V., 258, 259
Ida Virginia, 260, 261, 262
James E., 223
John, 238, 258, 259, 260, 261, 262
John H. B., 229
Lillian May, 262
Maggie, 270
Margaret, 261
Mary E., 223
Mary P., 275
Mary Parker, 259
Michael, 223
Nellie, 255
Virginia, 172
William C., 241
William Christian, 261
William F., 234, 253, 255
YOUNGER, Casper W., 166
YOUS, Maria Elisabeth, 118
Mr., 124

William, 124
Wilson, 118
YOUSTON, Johan, 141

-Z-
ZABEL, Anna Mary E., 242
ZACHARIOS, Cath. Zinn, 275
ZADI, Johan Jost, 140
ZAHN, Magdalena, 42
ZAHNER, Catharina, 100
　Catharina, 140
　Elisabeth, 43
　Jacob, 77
　Johan, 292
　Johannes, 43
ZAHNERT, Barbara, 71
　Elisabeth, 65
　Henrich, 35
　Joh., 71
　Joh. George, 30
　Johannes, 35
　Mr., 30, 65
ZAHNIN, Catharina, 40
ZALOCK, Elisabet, 53
ZALODE, Elisabet, 53
ZANST, Johan, 96
　Johan Heinrich, 96
　Maria, 96
ZAPF, Daniel, 29
　Jacob, 29
　Johann, 29
　Magdalena, 29
　Wilhelm, 29
ZAPP, Annie, 257
　Annie Margaret, 234, 257
　George W., 257
　Mary C., 257
ZEIGLER, Mary E., 241
ZEISER, Elisabeth, 6
ZEIT, Henrich, 24

Jacob, 24
Nancy, 24
ZELL, Amelia Elizabeth, 195
　Andre Jackson, 195
　Anna, 37
　Anna Catharina, 35
　Anna Marg., 67
　Barbara, 32
　Bernhard, 37
　Bernhardt, 67
　Catharina, 32, 67
　Christian, 32, 35, 67
　Elizabeth, 195
　Henrich, 35
　John, 195
　Mary Jane, 195
　Sarah Ann, 195
ZELLE, Anna, 281
　Elisabeth, 48
ZELLER, Anna Maria, 92
　Carl Friderich, 68
　Doctor, 68
　Johan, 92
　Johannes, 68, 92
　Maria, 92
　Susanna, 92
ZELLERS, Johanna, 288
　Mr., 288
ZELLICH, Anna Maria, 80
　Johan Jacob, 96
　Johann, 80
　Susanna, 80
ZELTZER, Johan Ludewig, 107
　Miss, 107
ZESCH, Anna Maria, 40
　Hieronimus, 40
　Juliane, 40
ZETSMAN, Mrs., 251

ZETZMAN, Augustus Theodore, 277
　Mrs., 255
ZIEGLER, George W., 179
　Jacob, 99
　Johannes, 3
　Louisa, 245
　Mary Ellen, 247
　Mary Helen, 179
　Mattie S., 247, 273
　Samuel F., 247, 275
　Samuel L., 245
ZIESCH, George, 26
　Lille, 26
　Maria Magdalena, 26
ZIESH, George, 27
　Maria Cath., 27
ZILL, Christoph, 60
ZIMMERMAN, Anna Maria, 16
　Jacob, 16
　John William Lester, 259
　Josephine, 171
　Sarah Elizabeth, 259
　William, 259
　William S., 149
ZIMMERMANN, Andreas, 4
　Anna Maria, 34
　Barbara, 3, 4
　Johannes, 3
　Mathias, 3, 4
ZINCK, Charles H., 237
ZINGLING, Christian, 94, 139, 284
　Johanna, 94
ZINK, Annie J., 237
ZINKHAN, Alman B., 256
　Arthur Morris, 256
　James Garfield, 268
　Louis Bishop, 268

438 Index

Louis F., 256
ZINKHAU, Alman B., 256
  Arthur Morris, 256
  Ella B., 251
  Louis F., 251, 256
  Paul Hudson, 251
ZINKHAUN, Ella B., 251
  Louis F., 251
  Paul Hudson, 251
ZINSGONER, Peter, 293
ZINSMAIER, Philip, 283
ZINSSER, Eda V., 240
ZINSZONER, Peter, 293
ZINZERER, Maria, 106
ZISBY, Margaret Ann, 152
ZOBLEMAN, George, 304
ZODE, Caspar, 104, 289
  Christina, 289
  Johan Jost, 133
  Johann, 106
  Marg. Cath., 104
  Margaretha, 123
  Margaretha Catharina, 104
ZODI, Barbara, 88
  Caspar, 88
  Christina, 88
ZODR, Barbara, 81
  Caspar, 81
  Elisabeth, 81
ZOELLE, Anna, 43, 280
  Bernhard, 43, 280
  Jacob, 43, 280
  Johanna, 280
  Susanna, 43
ZOHORK, Anna Maria, 25
  Elisabeth, 25
  George, 25
ZOIN, Sarah, 55

ZOLL, Johannes, 285
ZOLLE, Susanna, 77
ZOLLER, Anna Maria, 92
  Carl Friederich, 94
  Carl Friedrich, 279
  Carl Heinrich, 44
  Christian Georg Eduart, 94
  Elisabeth, 9
  Elmer, 236
  Ernst Heinrich, 292
  Johan, 92
  Johann Andreas, 44
  Johanna Maria, 44
  Johannes, 92
  Karl Friederich, 32
  Ludwig, 279
  Maria, 32, 92, 94, 141, 279
  Susanna, 92
ZOLLERS, Karl Friederich, 35
  Maria, 35
  Sophia Catharina, 35
ZOLLIG, Anna Maria, 281
  Johann, 281
ZOLROK, Anna Maria, 25
  Elisabeth, 25
  George, 25
ZOMWALD, ---, 78
  Philip, 51
ZOWRIE, Caroline, 152
ZUD, ---, 78
  Jacob, 6
  Ursula, 6
ZUDE, Johan Jost, 133
ZUECHLAG, Andrew, 234
ZUELLICH, Gottfried, 40
  Johannes, 40
  Wilhelmine, 40

ZUGLER, Barbara, 86
  Leonard, 86
  Louisa, 86
ZUGLERIN, Barbara, 86
ZULAUF, Amelia C., 248
  Grace Edna, 248
  William N., 231, 248
ZUMPSTEIN, Franklin H., 233
ZUMSTEIN, Franklin H., 253, 256
  Franklin White, 253
  Frederick Allen, 256
  Sadie, 253
  Sarah J., 256
ZUMWALD, ---, 78
  Anna Barbara, 13
  Elisabeth, 14
  Gottfried, 13
  Joh. Michael, 14
  Margareth, 13
  Willy, 14
ZUND, Anna, 6
  Johannes, 6
ZWISLER, Adelheid Ludovica Maria, 106
  Anna, 31
  Christina, 106
  Christina Catharina, 95
  Jacob, 95
  James, 106
  Mrs., 71
ZWISSLER, Albert Louis, 283
  Mr., 94, 283

www.ingramcontent.com/pod-product-compliance
Lightning Source LLC
Chambersburg PA
CBHW050326230426
43663CB00010B/1750